Hands-On Software Engineering with Golang

Move beyond basic programming to design and build reliable software with clean code

Achilleas Anagnostopoulos

BIRMINGHAM - MUMBAI

Hands-On Software Engineering with Golang

Copyright © 2020 Packt Publishing

Commissioning Editor: Richa Tripathi
Acquisition Editor: Karan Gupta
Content Development Editor: Tiksha Sarang
Senior Editor: Storm Mann
Technical Editor: Pradeep Sahu
Copy Editor: Safis Editing
Project Coordinator: Francy Puthiry
Proofreader: Safis Editing
Indexer: Tejal Daruwale Soni
Production Designer: Arvindkumar Gupta

First published: January 2020

Production reference: 1230120

Published by Packt Publishing Ltd.
Livery Place
35 Livery Street
Birmingham
B3 2PB, UK.

ISBN 978-1-83855-449-1

www.packt.com

In memory of my mother, Rhea.

Subscribe to our online digital library for full access to over 7,000 books and videos, as well as industry leading tools to help you plan your personal development and advance your career. For more information, please visit our website.

Why subscribe?

- Spend less time learning and more time coding with practical eBooks and Videos from over 4,000 industry professionals

- Improve your learning with Skill Plans built especially for you

- Get a free eBook or video every month

- Fully searchable for easy access to vital information

- Copy and paste, print, and bookmark content

Did you know that Packt offers eBook versions of every book published, with PDF and ePub files available? You can upgrade to the eBook version at www.packt.com and as a print book customer, you are entitled to a discount on the eBook copy. Get in touch with us at customercare@packtpub.com for more details.

At www.packt.com, you can also read a collection of free technical articles, sign up for a range of free newsletters, and receive exclusive discounts and offers on Packt books and eBooks.

Contributors

About the author

Achilleas Anagnostopoulos has been writing code in a multitude of programming languages since the mid 90s. His main interest lies in building scalable, microservice-based distributed systems where components are interconnected via gRPC or message queues. Achilleas has over 4 years of experience building production-grade systems using Go and occasionally enjoys pushing the language to its limits through his experimental gopher-os project: a 64-bit kernel written entirely in Go. He is currently a member of the Juju team at Canonical, contributing to one of the largest open source Go code bases in existence.

I would like to thank my wife, Olga, and my daughter, Nefeli, for their understanding and support while I was putting in long hours to get this book completed on time.

What's more, I would also like to extend a massive thanks to my father, Panagiotis, for taking the time to read through the book and offer insightful suggestions on improving not only my writing style but also the content of the chapters themselves.

Finally, I would like to thank the editorial team at Packt for their input and assistance in getting the book ready for printing.

About the reviewer

Eduard Bondarenko is a long-time software developer. He prefers concise and expressive code with comments and has tried many programming languages, such as Ruby, Go, Java, and JavaScript.

Eduard has reviewed a couple of programming books and has enjoyed their broad topics and how interesting they are. Besides programming, he likes to spend time with the family, play soccer, and travel.

I want to thank my family for supporting me during my work on the book and also the author of this book for an interesting read.

Packt is searching for authors like you

If you're interested in becoming an author for Packt, please visit `authors.packtpub.com` and apply today. We have worked with thousands of developers and tech professionals, just like you, to help them share their insight with the global tech community. You can make a general application, apply for a specific hot topic that we are recruiting an author for, or submit your own idea.

Table of Contents

Preface

Over the last few years, Go has gradually turned into one of the industry's favorite languages for building scalable and distributed systems. The language's opinionated design and built-in concurrency features make it relatively easy for engineers to author code that efficiently utilizes all available CPU cores.

This book distills the industry's best practices for writing lean Go code that is easy to test and maintain and explores their practical implementation by creating a multi-tier application from scratch called 'Links 'R' Us.' You will be guided through all the steps involved in designing, implementing, testing, deploying, and scaling the application. You'll start with a monolithic architecture and iteratively transform the project into a **Service-Oriented Architecture (SOA)** that supports efficient out-of-core processing of large link graphs. You will learn about various advanced and cutting-edge software engineering techniques such as building extensible data-processing pipelines, designing APIs using gRPC, and running distributed graph processing algorithms at scale. Finally, you will learn how to compile and package your Go services using Docker and automate their deployment to a Kubernetes cluster.

By the end of this book, you will start to think like a professional developer/engineer who can put theory into practice by writing lean and efficient Go code.

Who this book is for

This book is for developers and software engineers interested in effectively using Go to design and build scalable distributed systems. This book will also be useful for amateur-to-intermediate level developers who aspire to become professional software engineers.

What this book covers

Chapter 1, *A Bird's-Eye View of Software Engineering*, explains the difference between software engineering and programming and outlines the different types of engineering roles that you may encounter in small, medium, and large organizations. What's more, the chapter summarizes the basic software design life cycle models that every **software engineer (SWE)** should be aware of.

Chapter 2, *Best Practices for Writing Clean and Maintainable Go Code*, explains how the SOLID design principles can be applied to Go projects and provides useful tips for organizing your Go code in packages and writing code that is easy to maintain and test.

Chapter 3, *Dependency Management*, highlights the importance of versioning Go packages and discusses tools and strategies for vendoring your project dependencies.

Chapter 4, *The Art of Testing*, advocates the use of primitives such as stubs, mocks, spies, and fake objects for writing comprehensive unit tests for your code. Furthermore, the chapter enumerates the pros and cons of different types of tests (for example, black- versus white-box, integration versus functional) and concludes with an interesting discussion on advanced testing techniques such as smoke testing and chaos testing.

Chapter 5, *The Links 'R' Us project*, introduces the hands-on project that we will be building from scratch in the following chapters.

Chapter 6, *Building a Persistence Layer*, focuses on the design and implementation of the data access layer for two of the Links 'R' Us project components: the link graph and the text indexer.

Chapter 7, *Data-Processing Pipelines*, explores the basic principles behind data-processing pipelines and implements a framework for constructing generic, concurrent-safe, and reusable pipelines using Go primitives such as channels, contexts, and go-routines. The framework is then used to develop the crawler component for the Links 'R' Us project.

Chapter 8, *Graph-Based Data Processing*, explains the theory behind the **Bulk Synchronous Parallel (BSP)** model of computation and implements, from scratch, a framework for executing parallel algorithms against graphs. As a proof of concept, we will be using this framework to investigate parallel versions of popular graph-based algorithms (namely, shortest path and graph coloring) with our efforts culminating in the complete implementation of the PageRank algorithm, a critical component of the Links 'R' Us project.

Chapter 9, *Communicating with the Outside World*, outlines the key differences between RESTful and gRPC-based APIs with respect to subjects such as routing, security, and versioning. In this chapter, we will also define gRPC APIs for making the link graph and text indexer data stores for the Links 'R' Us project accessible over the network.

Chapter 10, *Building, Packaging, and Deploying Software*, enumerates the best practices for dockerizing your Go applications and optimizing their size. In addition, the chapter explores the anatomy of a Kubernetes cluster and enumerates the essential list of Kubernetes resources that we can use. As a proof of concept, we will be creating a monolithic version of the Links 'R' Us project and will deploy it to a Kubernetes cluster that you will spin up on your local machine.

Chapter 11, *Splitting Monoliths into Microservices*, explains the SOA pattern and discusses some common anti-patterns that you should be aware of and pitfalls that you want to avoid when switching from a monolithic design to microservices. To put the ideas from this chapter to the test, we will be breaking down the monolithic version of the Links 'R' Us project into microservices and deploying them to Kubernetes.

Chapter 12, *Building Distributed Graph-Processing Systems*, combines the knowledge from the previous chapters to create a distributed version of the graph-based data processing framework, which can be used for massive graphs that do not fit in memory (out-of-core processing).

Chapter 13, *Metrics Collection and Visualization*, enumerates the most popular solutions for collecting and indexing metrics from applications with a focus on Prometheus. After discussing approaches to instrumenting your Go code to capture and export Prometheus metrics, we will delve into the use of tools such as Grafana for metrics visualization, and Alert manager for setting up alerts based on the aggregated values of collected metrics.

Chapter 14, *Epilogue*, provides suggestions for furthering your understanding of the material by extending the hands-on project that we have built throughout the chapters of the book.

To get the most out of this book

To get the most out of this book and experiment with the accompanying code, you need to have a fairly good understanding of programming in Go as well as sufficient experience working with the various tools that comprise the Go ecosystem.

In addition, the book assumes that you have a solid grasp of basic networking theory.

Finally, some of the more technical chapters in the book utilize technologies such as Docker and Kubernetes. While a priori knowledge of these technologies is *not strictly required*, any prior experience using these (or equivalent) systems will certainly prove beneficial in better understanding the topics discussed in those chapters.

Download the example code files

You can download the example code files for this book from your account at www.packt.com. If you purchased this book elsewhere, you can visit www.packtpub.com/support and register to have the files emailed directly to you.

You can download the code files by following these steps:

1. Log in or register at www.packt.com.
2. Select the **Support** tab.
3. Click on **Code Downloads**.
4. Enter the name of the book in the **Search** box and follow the onscreen instructions.

Once the file is downloaded, please make sure that you unzip or extract the folder using the latest version of:

- WinRAR/7-Zip for Windows
- Zipeg/iZip/UnRarX for Mac
- 7-Zip/PeaZip for Linux

The code bundle for the book is also hosted on GitHub at https://github.com/PacktPublishing/Hands-On-Software-Engineering-with-Golang. In case there's an update to the code, it will be updated on the existing GitHub repository.

We also have other code bundles from our rich catalog of books and videos available at https://github.com/PacktPublishing/. Check them out!

Code in Action

To see the Code in Action please visit the following link: http://bit.ly/37QWeR2.

Download the color images

We also provide a PDF file that has color images of the screenshots/diagrams used in this book. You can download it here: https://static.packt-cdn.com/downloads/9781838554491_ColorImages.pdf.

Conventions used

There are a number of text conventions used throughout this book.

CodeInText: Indicates code words in text, database table names, folder names, filenames, file extensions, pathnames, dummy URLs, user input, and Twitter handles. Here is an example: "In the following code, you can see the definition of a generic Sword type for our upcoming game."

A block of code is set as follows:

```
type Sword struct {
  name string // Important tip for RPG players: always name your swords!
}
// Damage returns the damage dealt by this sword.
func (Sword) Damage() int {
  return 2
}
```

When we wish to draw your attention to a particular part of a code block, the relevant lines or items are set in bold:

```
type Sword struct {
  name string // Important tip for RPG players: always name your swords!
}
// Damage returns the damage dealt by this sword.
func (Sword) Damage() int {
  return 2
}
```

Bold: Indicates a new term, an important word, or words that you see onscreen. For example, words in menus or dialog boxes appear in the text like this. Here is an example: "The following excerpt is part of a system that collects and publishes performance metrics to a **key-value** store."

 Warnings or important notes appear like this.

 Tips and tricks appear like this.

Get in touch

Feedback from our readers is always welcome.

General feedback: If you have questions about any aspect of this book, mention the book title in the subject of your message and email us at customercare@packtpub.com.

Errata: Although we have taken every care to ensure the accuracy of our content, mistakes do happen. If you have found a mistake in this book, we would be grateful if you would report this to us. Please visit www.packtpub.com/support/errata, selecting your book, clicking on the Errata Submission Form link, and entering the details.

Piracy: If you come across any illegal copies of our works in any form on the Internet, we would be grateful if you would provide us with the location address or website name. Please contact us at copyright@packt.com with a link to the material.

If you are interested in becoming an author: If there is a topic that you have expertise in and you are interested in either writing or contributing to a book, please visit authors.packtpub.com.

Reviews

Please leave a review. Once you have read and used this book, why not leave a review on the site that you purchased it from? Potential readers can then see and use your unbiased opinion to make purchase decisions, we at Packt can understand what you think about our products, and our authors can see your feedback on their book. Thank you!

For more information about Packt, please visit packt.com.

1
Section 1: Software Engineering and the Software Development Life Cycle

The objective of part one is to familiarize you with the concept of software engineering, the stages of the software development life cycle, and the various roles of software engineers.

This section comprises the following chapter:

- Chapter 1, *A Bird's-Eye View of Software Engineering*

1
A Bird's-Eye View of Software Engineering

"Hiring people to write code to sell is not the same as hiring people to design and build durable, usable, dependable software."

- Larry Constantine [6]

Through the various stages of my career, I have met several people that knew how to code; people whose skill level ranged from beginner to, what some would refer to as, guru. All those people had different backgrounds and worked for both start-ups and large organizations. For some, coding was seen as a natural progression from their CS studies, while others turned to coding as part of a career change decision.

Regardless of all these differences, all of them had one thing in common: when asked to describe their current role, *all* of them used the term **software engineer**. It is quite a common practice for job candidates to use this term in their CVs as the means to set themselves apart from a globally distributed pool of software developers. A quick random sampling of job specs published online reveals that a lot of companies – and especially high-profile start-ups – also seem to subscribe to this way of thinking, as evidenced by their search for professionals to fill software engineering roles. In reality, as we will see in this chapter, the term software engineer is more of an umbrella term that covers a wide gamut of bespoke roles, each one combining different levels of software development expertise with specialized skills pertaining to topics such as system design, testing, build tools, and operations management.

So, what is software engineering and how does it differ from programming? What set of skills should a software engineer possess and which models, methodologies, and frameworks are at their disposal for facilitating the delivery of complex pieces of software? These are some of the questions that will be answered in this chapter.

This chapter covers the following topics:

- A definition of software engineering
- The types of software engineering roles that you may encounter in contemporary organizations
- An overview of popular software development models and which one to select based on the project type and requirements

What is software engineering?

Before we dive deeper into this chapter, we need to establish an understanding of some of the basic terms and concepts around software engineering. For starters, how do we define software engineering and in what ways does it differ from software development and programming in general? To begin answering this question, we will start by examining the formal definition of software engineering, as published in *IEEE's Standard Glossary of Software Engineering Terminology* [7]:

> *"Software engineering is defined as the application of a systematic, disciplined, quantifiable approach to the development, operation, and maintenance of software."*

The main takeaway from this definition is that authoring code is just one of the many facets of software engineering. At the end of the day, any capable programmer can take a well-defined specification and convert it into a fully functioning program without thinking twice about the need to produce clean and maintainable code. A disciplined software engineer, on the other hand, would follow a more systematic approach by applying common design patterns to ensure that the produced piece software is extensible, easier to test, and well documented in case another engineer or engineering team assumes ownership of it in the future.

Besides the obvious requirement for authoring high-quality code, the software engineer is also responsible for thinking about other aspects of the systems that will be built. Some questions that the software engineer must be able to answer include the following:

- What are the business use cases that the software needs to support?
- What components comprise the system and how do they interact with each other?
- Which technologies will be used to implement the various system components?

- How will the software be tested to ensure that its behavior matches the customer's expectations?
- How does load affect the system's performance and what is the plan for scaling the system?

To be able to answer these questions, the software engineer needs a special set of skills that, as you are probably aware, go beyond programming. These extra responsibilities and required skills are the main factors that differentiate a software engineer from a software developer.

Types of software engineering roles

As we discussed in the previous section, software engineering is an inherently complex, multi-stage process. In an attempt to manage this complexity, organizations around the world have invested a lot of time and effort over the years to break the process down into a set of well-defined stages and train their engineering staff to efficiently deal with each stage.

Some software engineers strive to work across all the stages of the **Software Development Life Cycle (SDLC)**, while others have opted to specialize in and master a particular stage of the SDLC. This gave rise to a variety of software engineering roles, each one with a different set of responsibilities and a required set of skills. Let's take a brief look at the most common software engineering roles that you may encounter when working with both small- and large-sized organizations.

The role of the software engineer (SWE)

The **software engineer (SWE)** is the most common role that you are bound to interact with in any organization, regardless of its size. Software engineers play a pivotal role not only in designing and building new pieces of software, but also in operating and maintaining existing and legacy systems.

Depending on their experience level and technical expertise, SWEs are classified into three categories:

- **Junior engineer**: A junior engineer is someone who has recently started their software development career and lacks the necessary experience to build and deploy production-grade software. Companies are usually keen on hiring junior engineers as it allows them to keep their hiring costs low. Furthermore, companies often pair promising junior engineers with senior engineers in an attempt to grow them into mid-level engineers and retain them for longer.
- **Mid-level engineer**: A typical mid-level engineer is someone who has at least three years of software development experience. Mid-level engineers are expected to have a solid grasp of the various aspects of the software development life cycle and are the ones who can exert a significant impact on the amount of code that's produced for a particular project. To this end, they not only contribute code, but also review and offer feedback to the code that's contributed by other team members.
- **Senior engineer**: This class of engineer is well-versed in a wide array of disparate technologies; their breadth of knowledge makes them ideal for assembling and managing software engineering teams, as well as serving as mentors and coaches for less senior engineers. From their years of experience, senior engineers acquire a deep understanding of a particular business domain. This trait allows them to serve as a liaison between their teams and the other, technical or non-technical, business stakeholders.

Another way to classify software engineers is by examining the main focus of their work:

- **Frontend engineers** work exclusively on software that customers interact with. Examples of frontend work include the UI for a desktop application, a single-page web application for a **software as a service (SaaS)** offering, and a mobile application running on a phone or other smart device.
- **Backend engineers** specialize in building the parts of a system that implement the actual business logic and deal with data modeling, validation, storage, and retrieval.
- **Full stack engineers** are developers who have a good understanding of both frontend and backend technologies and no particular preference of doing frontend or backend work. This class of developers is more versatile as they can easily move between teams, depending on the project requirements.

The role of the software development engineer in test (SDET)

The **software development engineer in test** (**SDET**) is a role whose origins can be traced back to Microsoft's engineering teams. In a nutshell, SDETs are individuals who, just like their SWE counterparts, take part in software development, but their primary focus lies in software testing and performance.

An SDET's primary responsibility is to ensure that the development team produces high-quality software that is free from defects. A prerequisite for achieving this goal is to be cognizant of the different types of approaches to testing software, including, but not limited to, unit testing, integration testing, white/black-box testing, end-to-end/acceptance testing, and chaos testing. We will be discussing all of these testing approaches in more detail in the following chapters.

The main tool that SDETs use to meet their goals is testing automation. Development teams can iterate much faster when a **Continuous Integration** (**CI**) pipeline is in place to automatically test their changes across different devices and CPU architectures. Besides setting up the infrastructure for the CI pipeline and integrating it with the source code repository system that the team uses, SDETs are often tasked with authoring and maintaining a separate set of tests. These tests fall into the following two categories:

- **Acceptance tests**: A set of scripted end-to-end tests to ensure that the complete system adheres to all the customer's business requirements before a new version is given the green light for a release.
- **Performance regression tests**: Another set of quality control tests that monitor a series of performance metrics across builds and alert you when a metric exceeds a particular threshold. These types of tests prove to be a great asset in the case where a **service-level agreement** (**SLA**) has been signed that makes seemingly innocuous changes to the code (for example, switching to a different data structure implementation) that may trigger a breach of the SLA, even though all the unit tests pass.

Finally, SDETs collaborate with support teams to transform incoming support tickets into bug reports that the development team can work on. The combination of software development and debugging skills, in conjunction with the SDET's familiarity with the system under development, makes them uniquely capable of tracking down the location of bugs in production code and coming up with example cases (for example, a particular data input or a sequence of actions) that allow developers to reproduce the exact set of conditions that trigger each bug.

The role of the site reliability engineer (SRE)

The role of the **site reliability engineer (SRE)** came into the spotlight in 2016 when Google published a book on the subject of **Site Reliability Engineering** [4]. This book outlined the best practices and strategies that are used internally by Google to run their production systems and has since led to the wide adoption of the role by the majority of companies operating in the SaaS space.

The term was initially coined sometime around 2003 by Ben Treynor, the founder of Google's site reliability team. A site reliability engineer is a software engineer with a strong technical background who also focuses on the operations side of deploying and running production-grade services.

According to the original role definition, SREs spend approximately 50% of their time developing software and the other 50% dealing with ops-related aspects such as the following:

- Working on support tickets or responding to alerts
- Being on-call
- Running manual tasks (for example, upgrading systems or running disaster recovery scenarios)

It is in the best interests of SREs to increase the stability and reliability of the services they operate. After all, no one enjoys being paged at 2 a.m. when a service melts down due to a sudden spike in the volume of incoming requests. The end goal is always to produce services that are highly available and self-healing; services that can automatically recover from a variety of faults without the need for human intervention.

The basic mantra of SREs is to eliminate potential sources of human errors by automating repeated tasks. One example of this philosophy is the use of a **Continuous Deployment (CD)** pipeline to minimize the amount of time that's required to deploy software changes to production. The benefits of this type of automation become apparent when a critical issue affecting production is identified and a fix must be deployed as soon as possible.

Ultimately, software is designed and built by humans so bugs will undoubtedly creep in. Rather than relying on a rigorous verification process to prevent defects from being deployed to production, SREs operate under the premise that we live in a non-perfect world: systems do crash and buggy software will, at some point, get deployed to production. To detect defective software deployments and mitigate their effects on end users, SREs set up monitoring systems that keep track of various health-related metrics for each deployed service and can trigger automatic rollbacks if a deployment causes an increase in a service's error rate.

The role of the release engineer (RE)

In a world where complex, monolithic systems are broken down into multiple microservices and continuous delivery has become the new norm, debugging older software releases that are still deployed out in the wild becomes a major pain point for software engineers.

To understand why this can be a pain point, let's take a look at a small example: you arrive at work on a sunny Monday morning only to find out that one of your major customers has filed a bug against the microservice-based software your team is responsible for. To make things even worse, that particular customer is running a **long-term support** (LTS) release of the software, which means that some, if not all, of the microservices that the run on the customer's machines are based on code that is at least a couple of hundred commits behind the current state of development. So, how can you actually come up with a bug reproducer and check whether the bug has already been fixed upstream?

This is where the concept of **reproducible builds** comes into play. By reproducible builds, we mean that *at any point in time* we should be able to compile a particular version of all the system components where the resulting artifacts match, *bit by bit*, the ones that have been deployed by the customer.

A **release engineer** (RE) is effectively a software engineer who collaborates with all the engineering teams to define and document all the required steps and processes for building and releasing code to production. A prerequisite for a release engineer is having deep knowledge of all the tools and processes that are required for compiling, versioning, testing, and packaging software. Typical tasks for REs include the following:

- Authoring makefiles
- Implementing workflows for containerizing software artifacts (for example, as Docker or .rkt images)
- Ensuring all teams use exactly the same build tool (compilers, linkers, and so on) versions and flags
- Ensuring that builds are both **repeatable** and **hermetic**: changes to external dependencies (for example, third-party libraries) between builds of the *same software version* should have no effect on the artifacts that are produced by each build

The role of the system architect

The last role that we will be discussing in this section, and one that you will only probably encounter when working on bigger projects or collaborating with large organizations, is the system architect. While software engineering teams focus on building the various components of the system, the architect is the one person who sees the big picture: what components comprise the system, how each component must be implemented, and how all the components fit and interact with each other.

In smaller companies, the role of the architect is usually fulfilled by one of the senior engineers. In larger companies, the architect is a distinct role that's filled by someone with both a solid technical background and strong analytical and communication skills.

Apart from coming up with a high-level, component-based design for the system, the architect is also responsible for making decisions regarding the technologies that will be used during development and setting the standards that all the development teams must adhere to.

Even though architects have a technical background, they rarely get to write any code. As a matter of fact, architects tend to spend a big chunk of their time in meetings with the various internal or external stakeholders, authoring design documents or providing technical direction to the software engineering teams.

A list of software development models that all engineers should know

The software engineering definition from the previous section alludes to the fact that software engineering is a complicated, multi-stage process. In an attempt to provide a formal description of these stages, academia has put forward the concept of the SDLC.

 The SDLC is a systematic process for building high-quality software that matches the expectations of the end user or customer while ensuring that the project's cost stays within a reasonable bound.

Over the years, there has been an abundance of alternative model proposals for facilitating software development. The following diagram is a timeline illustrating the years when some of the most popular SDLC models were introduced:

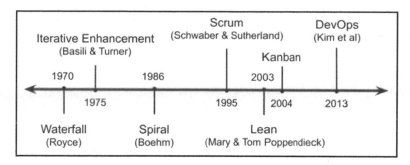

Figure 1: A timeline for the software development models that will be presented in this chapter

In the upcoming sections, we will explore each of the preceding models in more detail.

Waterfall

The waterfall model is probably the most widely known model out there for implementing the SDLC. It was introduced by Winston Royce in 1970 [11] and defines a series of steps that must be *sequentially* completed in a particular order. Each stage produces a certain output, for example, a document or some artifact, that is, in turn, consumed by the step that follows.

The following diagram outlines the basic steps that were introduced by the waterfall model:

- **Requirement collection**: During this stage, the customer's requirements are captured and analyzed and a requirements document is produced.
- **Design**: Based on the requirement's document contents, analysts will plan the system's architecture. This step is usually split into two sub-steps: the logical system design, which models the system as a set of high-level components, and the physical system design, where the appropriate technologies and hardware components are selected.
- **Implementation**: The implementation stage is where the design documents from the previous step get transformed by software engineers into actual code.

- **Verification**: The verification stage follows the implementation stage and ensures that the piece of software that got implemented actually satisfies the set of customer requirements that were collected during the requirements gathering step.
- **Maintenance**: The final stage in the waterfall model is when the developed software is deployed and operated by the customer:

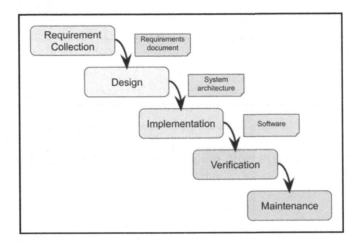

Figure 2: The steps defined by the waterfall model

One thing to keep in mind is that the waterfall model operates under the assumption that *all* customer requirements can be collected early on, especially before the project implementation stage begins. Having the full set of requirements available as a set of use cases makes it easier to get a more accurate estimate of the amount of time that's required for delivering the project and the development costs involved. A corollary to this is that software engineers are provided with all the expected use cases and system interactions in advance, thus making testing and verifying the system much simpler.

The waterfall model comes with a set of caveats that make it less favorable to use when building software systems. One potential caveat is that the model describes each stage in an abstract, high-level way and does not provide a detailed view into the processes that comprise each step or even tackle cross-cutting processes (for example, project management or quality control) that you would normally expect to execute in parallel through the various steps of the model.

While this model does work for small- to medium-scale projects, it tends, at least in my view, not to be as efficient for projects such as the ones commissioned by large organizations and/or government bodies. To begin with, the model assumes that analysts are always able to elicit the *correct* set of requirements from customers. This is not always the case as, oftentimes, customers are not able to accurately describe their requirements or tend to identify additional requirements just before the project is delivered. In addition to this, the sequential nature of this model means that a significant amount of time may elapse between gathering the initial requirements and the actual implementation. During this time – what some would refer to as an *eternity* in software engineering terms – the customer's requirements may shift. Changes in requirements necessitate additional development effort and this directly translates into increased costs for the deliverable.

Iterative enhancement

The iterative enhancement model that's depicted in the following diagram was proposed in 1975 by Basili and Victor [2] in an attempt to improve on some of the caveats of the waterfall model. By recognizing that requirements may potentially change for long-running projects, the model advocates executing a set of evolution cycles or iterations, with each one being allocated a fixed amount of time out of the project's time budget:

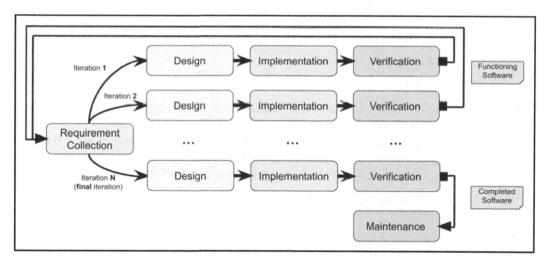

Figure 3: The steps of the interactive enhancement model

Instead of starting with the full set of specifications, each cycle focuses on building some parts of the final deliverable and refining the set of requirements from the cycle that precedes it. This allows the development team to make full use of any information available at that particular point in time and ensure that any requirement changes can be detected early on and acted upon.

One important rule when applying the iterative model is that the output of each cycle must be a *usable piece of software*. The last iteration is the most important as its output yields the final software deliverable. As we will see in the upcoming sections, the iterative model has exerted quite a bit of influence in the evolution of most of the contemporary software development models.

Spiral

The spiral development model was introduced by Barry Boehm in 1986 [5] as an approach to minimize risk when developing large-scale projects associated with significant development costs.

In the context of software engineering, **risks** are defined as any kind of situation or sequence of events that can cause a project to fail to meet its goals. Examples of various degrees of failure include the following:

- Missing the delivery deadline
- Exceeding the project budget
- Delivering software on time, depending on the hardware that isn't available yet

As illustrated in the following diagram, the spiral model combines the ideas and concepts from the waterfall and iterative models with a risk assessment and analysis process. As Boehm points out, a very common mistake that people who are unfamiliar with the model tend to make when seeing this diagram for the first time is to assume that the spiral model is just a sequence of incremental waterfall steps that have to be followed in a particular order for each cycle. To dispel this misconception, Boehms provided the following definition for the spiral model:

> *"The spiral development model is a risk-driven process model generator that takes a cyclic approach to progressively expand the project scope while at the same time decreasing the degree of risk."*

Under this definition, risk is the primary factor that helps project stakeholders answer the following questions:

- What steps should we follow next?
- How long should we keep following those steps before we need to reevaluate risk?

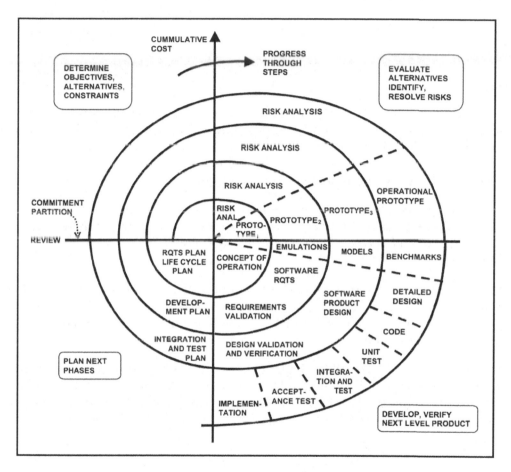

Figure 4: The original spiral model, as published by Boehm in 1986

At the beginning of each cycle, all the potential sources of risk are identified and mitigation plans are proposed to address any risk concerns. These set of risks are then ordered in terms of importance, for example, the impact on the project and the likelihood of occurring, and used as input by the stakeholders when planning the steps for the next spiral cycle.

Another common misconception about the spiral model is that the development direction is one-way and can only spiral *outward*, that is, no backtracking to a previous spiral cycle is allowed. This is generally not the case: stakeholders always try to make informed decisions based on the information that's available to them at a particular point in time. As the project's development progresses, circumstances may change: new requirements may be introduced or additional pieces of previously unknown information may become available. In light of the new information that's available to them, stakeholders may opt to reevaluate prior decisions and, in some cases, roll back development to a previous spiral iteration.

Agile

When we talk about agile development, we usually refer to a broader family of software development models that were initially proposed during the early 90s. Agile is a sort of umbrella term that encompasses not only a set of frameworks but also a fairly long list of best practices for software development. If we had to come up with a more specific definition for agile, we would probably define it as follows:

> *"Agile development advocates building software in an incremental fashion by iterating in multiple, albeit relatively, short cycles. Making use of self-organizing and cross-functional teams, it evolves project requirements and solutions by fostering intra-team collaboration."*

The popularity of agile development and agile frameworks, in particular, skyrocketed with the publication of the *Manifesto for Agile Software Development* in 2001 [3]. At the time of writing this book, agile development practices have become the *de facto* standard for the software industry, especially in the field of start-up companies.

In the upcoming sections, we will be digging a bit deeper into some of the most popular models and frameworks in the agile family. While doing a deep dive on each model is outside the scope of this book, a set of additional resources will be provided at the end of this chapter if you are interested in learning more about the following models.

Lean

Lean software development is one of the earliest members of the agile family of software development models. It was introduced by Mary and Tom Poppendieck in 2003 [10]. Its roots go back to the lean manufacturing techniques that were introduced by Toyota's production system in the 70s. When applied to software development, the model advocates seven key principles.

Eliminate waste

This is one of the key philosophies of the lean development model. Anything that does not directly add value to the final deliverable is considered as a *blocker* and must be removed.

Typical cases of things that are characterized as waste by this model are as follows:

- Introduction of non-essential, that is, nice-to-have features when development is underway.
- Overly complicated decision-making processes that force development teams to remain idle while waiting for a feature to be signed off – in other words: *bureaucracy!*
- Unnecessary communication between the various project stakeholders and the development teams. This disrupts the focus of the development team and hinders their development velocity.

Create knowledge

The development team should never assume that the customers' requirements are static. Instead, the assumption should always be that they are dynamic and can change over time Therefore, it is imperative for the development team to come up with appropriate strategies to ensure that their view of the world is always aligned with the customer's.

One way to achieve this is by borrowing and implementing some facets of other models, such as the iterative model we discussed in the previous section, or by tweaking their workflows accordingly so that deliverables are always built in an incremental fashion and always with an up-to-date version of the customer's requirements.

Externally acquired knowledge is, of course, only half of the equation; the development teams themselves are also another source of knowledge. As teams collaborate to deliver a piece of software, they discover that certain approaches and practices work better together than others. In particular, some approaches accelerate the team's development velocity, while others hinder it. Due to this, it is important for teams to capture this bit of tacit knowledge, internalize it, and make it available to other teams in the future. One way to achieve this is by making another team for the teams to sync up, reflect on their workflows, and discuss any potential issues.

Defer commitment

As with all the models in the agile family, the lean model is devoid of any attempt to force project stakeholders into making all the required decisions at the beginning of the project. The reasoning behind this is quite simple: people are more likely to be convinced that change is needed when they have not already committed to a particular set of actions.

The lean model actively encourages stakeholders to defer all the important and potentially irreversible decisions until a later stage in the project's development.

Build in quality

One of the primary reasons for project delays is undoubtedly the accumulation of defects. Defects have a definite impact on the development team's velocity as members often need to pause their current work to chase down and fix potentially field-critical bugs that were introduced by a previous development iteration.

The lean model prompts engineering teams to aggressively focus on following agile practices such as **test-** or **behavior-driven development (TDD/BDD)** in an attempt to produce lean, well-tested code with fewer defects. The benefits of this recommendation have also been corroborated by research that's been performed by Turhan and others [13].

Deliver fast

Every engineering team out there would probably agree that they would like nothing more than delivering the piece of software they are currently working on as fast as possible to the hands of the customer or the end user. The most common factors that prevent teams from delivering software fast are as follows:

- Over-analyzing the business requirements
- Over-engineering the solution to fit those requirements
- Overloading the development team

Congruent to the philosophy of lean development, teams must iterate quickly, that is, they must build a solution as simple as possible, present it to the target customer as early as possible, and collect useful feedback that's used to incrementally improve the solution in subsequent iterations.

Respect and empower people

Lean development endeavors to improve the development teams' working environment by filtering out unneeded sources of distraction that increase the cognitive load on engineers and can eventually lead to burnouts.

What's more, by discouraging micro-management and encouraging teams to self-organize, team members can feel more motivated and empowered. The Poppendiecks believe that engaged and empowered people can be more productive; ergo, they can bring more value to the team and, by extension, to the company that they are a part of.

See and optimize the whole

In *Lean Software Development: An Agile Toolkit*, Mary and Tom Poppendieck use a stream-based analogy to describe the software development process. By this definition, each stage of the development process can be treated as a potential generator of value (a *value stream*) for the business. The Poppendiecks claim that in order to maximize the value that flows through the various stages of development, organizations must treat the development process as a sequence of inter-linked activities and optimize them as a *whole*.

This is one of the most common pitfalls that organizations fall into when attempting to apply lean thinking concepts. You have probably heard of the old adage *miss the forest for the trees*. Many organizations, under the influence of other lean model principles such as quick delivery, focus all their efforts on optimizing a particular aspect of their development process. To the casual external observer, this approach seems to pay off in the short term. In the long term, however, the team is vulnerable to the negative side effects of *sub-optimization*.

To understand how sub-optimization can affect the team's performance in the long run, let's examine a hypothetical scenario: in an attempt to iterate faster, the development team takes a few shortcuts, that is, they push out less than stellar code or code that is not thoroughly tested. While the code does work, and the customer's requirements are being met, it also increases the complexity of the code base with the unavoidable side effect that more defects start creeping into the code that is delivered to the customer. Now, the development team is under even more pressure to fix the bugs that got introduced while maintaining their previous development velocity at the same time. As you can probably deduce, by this point, the development team is stuck in a vicious circle, and certainly one that is not easy to escape from.

On the other side of the spectrum, a popular and successful example of applying the concepts of whole system optimization in the way that's intended by the lean development model is Spotify's *squad-based* framework. Spotify squads are lean, cross-functional, multi-disciplined, and self-organizing teams that bring together all the people who are needed to take a feature through all the stages of development, from its inception to final product delivery.

Scrum

Scrum is hands-down the most widely known framework of the agile family and the go-to solution for many companies, especially the ones working on new products or the ones that actively seek to optimize their software development process. In fact, Scrum has become so popular that, nowadays, several organizations are offering Scrum certification courses. It was co-created by Ken Schwaber and Jeff Sutherland and initially presented to ACM's object-oriented programming, systems, languages, and applications conference in 1995.

As a process framework, Scrum is meant to be applied by cross-functional teams working on large projects that can be split into smaller chunks of work, where each chunk normally takes between two to four weeks – also known as a *sprint* in Scrum terminology – to complete.

Contrary to the other software development models we've discussed so far, Scrum does not explicitly advocate a particular design process or methodology. Instead, it promotes an empirical, feedback loop type of approach: initially, the team comes up with an idea on how to proceed based on the information available at the time. The proposed idea is then put to the test for the next sprint cycle and feedback is collected. The team then reflects on that feedback, refines the approach further, and applies it to the following sprint.

As more and more sprint cycles go by, the team learns to self-organize so that it becomes more efficient at tackling the task at hand. By improving the quality of communication between the team members while at the same time reducing distractions, teams often observe a boost in the team's output, also known as *team velocity* in agile terminology.

One important thing to keep in mind is that while this chapter examines Scrum from the perspective of a software engineer, the Scrum process and principles can also be applied when working on other types of projects that do not involve software development. For instance, Scrum can also be used to run marketing campaigns, hire personnel, or even tackle construction projects.

Scrum roles

When applying the Scrum framework to a software development team, each member can be mapped to one of the following three roles:

- The **Product Owner (PO)**
- The Development Team Member
- The **Scrum Master (SM)**

The official Scrum guide [12], which is freely available to download online in over 30 languages, defines the PO as the key stakeholder in a project, that is, the person who maximizes the product's value resulting from the work of the development team.

The primary responsibility of the PO is to manage the project backlog. The backlog is just a formal way of referring to the list of tasks that need to be completed for a particular project and includes new features, enhancements, or bug fixes for upcoming development cycles.

The PO must always make sure that all the backlog entries are described in a clear, consistent, and unambiguous way. Furthermore, the backlog's contents is never assumed to be static but should always be assumed to be dynamic: new tasks may be introduced while existing tasks may be removed to facilitate changes to the project requirements while development is underway. This adds an extra responsibility to the role of the PO: they need to be able to respond to such changes and reprioritize the backlog accordingly.

The development team comprises a set of individuals who implement the tasks that have been selected from the backlog. According to the basic tenets of Scrum, the team should be as follows:

- It should be cross-functional, bringing people together from different disciplines and varying skill sets
- It should not pay attention to the job titles of its members and focus on the work that's performed instead
- It should be aligned toward a single goal: completing the set of tasks that the team committed to at the beginning of each sprint

The last but equally important Scrum role is that of the SM. The SM supports both the PO and the development team members by ensuring that everyone has a clear understanding of not only the team goals but also the various Scrum processes. The SM is also responsible for organizing and running the appropriate Scrum events (ceremonies) as and when required.

Essential Scrum events

Scrum prescribes a sequence of events that are specially designed to aid teams in becoming more agile and boosting their performance. Let's take a brief look at the list of essential Scrum events for the purpose of software development.

The first Scrum event that we will be examining is the *planning session*. During planning, the team examines the items from the backlog and commits to a set of tasks that the team will be working on during the next sprint.

As you probably expect, the team needs to periodically sync up so that all the team members are on the same page with respect to the tasks that other team members are currently working on. This is facilitated by the daily *stand-up*, a *time-boxed* session that usually takes no longer than 30 minutes. Each team member speaks in turn and briefly answers the following questions:

- What was I working on yesterday?
- What will I be working on today?
- Are there any blockers for completing a particular task?

Blockers, if left unresolved, could jeopardize the team's goal for the sprint. Therefore, it is of paramount importance to detect blockers as early as possible and engage the team members to figure out ways to work around or address them.

At the end of a sprint, the team usually holds a *retrospective* session where team members *openly* discuss the things that went right, as well as the things that went wrong, during the sprint. For each problem that's encountered, the team attempts to identify its root cause and propose a series of actions to remedy it. The selected actions are applied during the next sprint cycle and their effect is re-evaluated in the next retrospective.

Kanban

Kanban, whose name loosely translates from Japanese as *a visual signal* or *a billboard*, is yet another very popular type of agile framework that has been reportedly in use at Microsoft since 2004. One of the iconic features of the Kanban model is, of course, the *Kanban board*, a concept outlined by David Anderson's 2010 book [1] that introduces the idea behind this particular model.

The Kanban board allows team members to visualize the set of items that teams are working on, along with their current state. The board is comprised of a series of vertically oriented *work lane*s or columns. Each lane has its own *label* and a *list* of items or tasks attached to it. As items or tasks are being worked on, they *transition* between the various columns of the board until they eventually arrive at a column that signals their completion. Completed items are then typically removed from the board and *archived* for future reference.

The standard lane configuration for software development consists of at least the following set of lanes:

- **Backlog**: A set of tasks to be worked on by the team in the near future
- **Doing**: The tasks in progress
- **In review**: Work that has been put up for review by other team members
- **Done**: Items that have been completed

It is only logical that each team will customize the lane configuration to fit their particular development workflow. For example, some teams may include an *in test* column to keep track of items undergoing QA checks by another team, a *deployed* column to track items that have been deployed to production, and even a *blocked* column to specify tasks that cannot proceed without the team taking some type of action.

I am sure that most of you will probably already be familiar with the *physical* implementation of a Kanban board: a dedicated spot on the office wall filled with colorful post-it notes. While local teams tend to enjoy having the board on a wall as it makes it quite easy to see what everyone is working on or to identify blockers just by walking by the board, this approach obviously cannot support partially or fully remote teams. For those use cases, several companies are offering the online, digital equivalent of a Kanban board that can be used instead.

DevOps

DevOps is the last software development model that we will be examining in this chapter. Nowadays, more and more organizations endeavor to scale out their systems by transitioning from monolithic to **service-oriented architectures** (SoA). The basic premise behind the DevOps model is that each engineering team owns the services they build. This is achieved by fusing development with operations, that is, the aspects involved in deploying, scaling, and monitoring services once they get deployed to production.

The DevOps model evolved in parallel with the other agile models and was heavily influenced by the principles put forward by the lean development model. While there is no recommended approach to implementing DevOps (one of the reasons why Google came up with SRE in the first place), DevOps advocates tend to gravitate toward two different models:

- **Culture, Automation, Measurement, and Sharing (CAMS)**
- The three ways model

The CAMS model

CAMS was originally invented by Damon Edwards and John Willis. Let's explore each one of these terms in a bit more detail.

As with other agile models, corporate **culture** is an integral part of DevOps methodology. To this end, Edwards and Willis recommend that engineering teams extend the use of practices such as Scrum and Kanban to manage both development and operations. Culture-wise, an extremely important piece of advice that Edwards and Willis offered is that each company must internally evolve its own culture and set of values that suit its unique set of needs instead of simply copying them over from other organizations because they just seem to be working in a particular context. The latter could lead to what is known as the **Cargo Cult** effect, which eventually creates a toxic work environment that can cause issues with employee retainment.

The second tenet of the CAMS model is *automation*. As we discussed in a previous section, automation is all about eliminating potential human sources of errors when executing tedious, repetitive tasks. In the context of DevOps, this is usually accomplished by doing the following:

- Deploying a CI/CD system to ensure that all the changes are thoroughly tested before they get pushed to production
- Treating infrastructure as code and managing it as such, that is, storing it in a **version control system** (**VCS**), having engineers review and audit infrastructure changes, and finally deploying them via tools such as Chef (`https://www.chef.io/`), puppet (`https://puppet.com/`), Ansible (`https://www.ansible.com/`), and Terraform (`https://www.terraform.io/`)

The letter **M** in CAMS stands for **measurement**. Being able to not only capture service operation metrics but also act on them offers two significant advantages to engineering teams. To begin with, the team can always be apprised of the health of the services they manage. When a service misbehaves, the metrics monitoring system will fire an alert and some of the team members will typically get paged. When this happens, having access to a rich set of metrics allows teams to quickly assess the situation and attempt to remedy any issue.

Of course, monitoring is not the only use case for measuring: services that are managed by DevOps teams are, in most cases, long-lived and therefore bound to evolve or expand over time; it stands to reason that teams will be expected to improve on and optimize the services they manage. High-level performance metrics help identify services with a high load that need to be scaled, while low-level performance metrics will indicate slow code paths that need to be optimized. In both cases, measuring can be used as a feedback loop to the development process to aid teams in deciding what to work on next.

The last letter in the CAMS model stands for **sharing**. The key ideas here are as follows:

- To promote visibility throughout the organization
- To encourage and facilitate knowledge sharing across teams

Visibility is quite important for all stakeholders. First of all, it allows all the members of the organization to be constantly aware of what other teams are currently working on. Secondly, it offers engineers a clear perspective of how each team's progress is contributing to the long-term strategic goals of the organization. One way to achieve this is by making the team's Kanban board accessible to other teams in the organization.

The model inventors encourage teams to be transparent about their internal processes. By allowing information to flow freely across teams, *information silos* can be prevented. For instance, senior teams will eventually evolve their own streamlined deployment process. By making this knowledge available to other, less senior, teams, they can directly exploit the learnings of more seasoned teams without having to reinvent the wheel. Apart from this, teams will typically use a set of internal dashboards to monitor the services they manage. There is a definite benefit in making these public to other teams, especially ones that serve as upstream consumers for those services.

At this point, it is important to note that, in many cases, transparency extends beyond the bounds of the company. Lots of companies are making a subset of their ops metrics available to their customers by setting up status pages, while others go even further and publish detailed postmortems on outages.

The three ways model

The three ways model is based on the ideas of Gene Kim, Kevin Behr, George Spafford [8], and other lean thinkers such as Michael Orzen [9]. The model distills the concept of DevOps into three primary principles, or *ways*:

- Systems thinking and workflow optimization
- Amplifying feedback loops
- Culture of continuous experimentation and learning

Systems thinking implies that the development team takes a holistic approach to software: in addition to tackling software development, teams are also responsible for operating/managing the systems that the software gets deployed to and establishing baselines for not only the target system's behavior but also for the expected behavior of other systems that depend on it:

Figure 5: Thinking of development as an end-to-end system where work flows from the business to the customer/end user

The preceding diagram represents this approach as a unidirectional sequence of steps that the engineering team executes to deliver a working feature to the end user or customer in a way that does not cause any disruption to existing services. At this stage, the team's main focus is to optimize the end-to-end delivery process by identifying and removing any bottlenecks that hinder the flow of work between the various steps.

Under the first principle, teams attempt to reduce the number of defects that flow downstream. Nevertheless, defects do occasionally slip through. This is where the second principle comes into play. It introduces *feedback loops* that enable information to flow backward, as shown in the following diagram, that is, from right to left. By themselves, however, feedback loops are not enough; they must also serve as amplification points to ensure that the team members are forced to act on incoming information in a *timely* fashion. For example, an incoming alert (*feedback loop*) will trigger a person from the team who is on call to get paged (*amplification*) so as to resolve an issue that affects production:

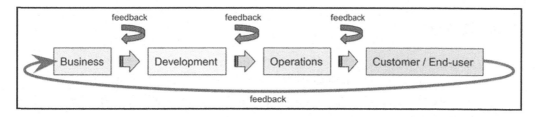

Figure 6: Utilizing feedback loops to allow information to flow backward

The final principle, and the one that most agile models are imbued with, has to do with fostering a company *culture* that allows people to pursue experiments and improvement ideas that may or may not pan out in the end as long as they share what they've learned with their colleagues. The same mindset also applies when dealing with incidents that have adverse effects on production systems. For instance, by holding blameless postmortems, the team members can outline the root causes of an outage in a way that doesn't put pressure on the peers whose actions caused the outage and, at the same time, disseminate the set of steps and knowledge that were acquired by resolving the issue.

Summary

Through the course of this chapter, we briefly discussed the different types of roles that you may encounter when working with companies of various sizes, as well as the special set of skills that each role depends on.

We started by examining a broad list of popular models, methodologies, and frameworks for delivering software, ranging from the traditional models that advocate a top-bottom approach (waterfall, iterative enhancement) to agile models that are better suited for the fast-paced and constantly changing environment that contemporary organizations operate in.

By reaching the end of this chapter, you should have acquainted yourself with the pros and cons of each model and the situations where each model should be applied. I sincerely hope that this knowledge will prove useful the next time you need to decide on which software development model to use for your next project.

Last but not least, we should always keep in mind that the cornerstone of the software engineering process is the actual *production of high-quality software*! In the next chapter, we will put on our engineering hat and discuss approaches for writing clean, organized, and easy-to-maintain code using Go.

Questions

1. What is the definition of software engineering?
2. What are some of the questions that every SWE should be able to answer?
3. Compare the role of an SWE and an SRE. What are the key differences between the two roles?
4. Name some of the deficiencies of the waterfall model. Explain how the iterative enhancement model attempts to address those deficiencies.
5. What are the most common sources of waste according to the lean development model?
6. Provide an example where focusing all the optimization efforts on a single step of the development process can have a negative effect on the efficiency of the end-to-end process.
7. What are the key responsibilities of the PO and the SM in the Scrum framework?
8. What is the role of retrospectives in Scrum? What topics should the team be discussing and what should be the expected outcome of each retrospective session?
9. Why are automation and measuring important when following the DevOps model?
10. You are working for ACME Gaming System, a company with the vision to disrupt the already *mature* and *highly competitive* gaming console market. To this end, the company has partnered with Advanced GPU Devices, a well-known graphics chip manufacturer, to prototype a new GPU design that *should* allow the upcoming gaming console to blow competitor consoles out of the water. Your task, as the project's lead engineer, is to design and build the software that will power the new console. Which software development model would you choose? Explain the reasoning behind your decision.

Further reading

1. Anderson, David: *Kanban: Successful Evolutionary Change in Your Technology Business*: Blue Hole Press, 2010 — ISBN 0984521402 (https://www.worldcat.org/title/kanban-successful-evolutionary-change-in-your-technology-business/oclc/693773272).
2. Basili, R.; Turner, J.: *Iterative Enhancement: A Practical Technique for Software Development*. In: *IEEE Transactions on Software Engineering* Vol. 1 (1975), pp. 390–396.

3. Beck, Kent; Beedle, Mike; Bennekum, Arie van; Cockburn, Alistair; Cunningham, Ward; Fowler, Martin; Grenning, James; Highsmith, Jim; et al.: *Manifesto for Agile Software Development*.

4. Beyer, Betsy; Jones, Chris; Petoff, Jennifer; Murphy, Niall Richard: *Site Reliability Engineering: How Google Runs Production Systems*. (https://landing.google.com/sre/sre-book/toc/index.html) (https://www.worldcat.org/title/site-reliability-engineering/oclc/1112558638).

5. Boehm, B: *A Spiral Model of Software Development and Enhancement*. In: *SIGSOFT Softw. Eng. Notes* Vol. 11. New York, NY, USA, ACM (1986), Nr. 4, pp. 14–24.

6. Constantine, L.: *Beyond Chaos: The Expert Edge in Managing Software Development*: Addison-Wesley Professional, 2001 — ISBN 9780201719604 (https://www.worldcat.org/title/beyond-chaos-the-expert-edge-in-managing-software-development/oclc/46713128).

7. IEEE: IEEE Standard Glossary of Software Engineering Terminology: IEEE; IEEE, 1990.

8. Kim, G.; Behr, K.; Spafford, G.: *The Phoenix Project: A Novel about IT, DevOps, and Helping Your Business Win*: IT Revolution Press, 2018 — ISBN 9781942788294 (https://www.worldcat.org/title/phoenix-project-a-novel-about-it-devops-and-helping-your-business-win/oclc/1035062278).

9. Orzen, M. A.; Paider, T. A.: *The Lean IT Field Guide: A Roadmap for Your Transformation*: Taylor and Francis, 2015 — ISBN 9781498730389 (https://www.worldcat.org/title/lean-it-field-guide/oclc/1019734287).

10. Poppendieck, Mary; Poppendieck, Tom: *Lean Software Development: An Agile Toolkit*. Boston, MA, USA: Addison-Wesley Longman Publishing Co., Inc., 2003 — ISBN 0321150783 (https://www.worldcat.org/title/lean-software-development-an-agile-toolkit/oclc/868260760).

11. Royce, W.: *Managing the development of large software systems: concepts and techniques*. In: *Proc. IEEE WESTCON, Los Angeles* (1970), pp. 1–9. — Reprinted in *Proceedings* of the Ninth International Conference on Software Engineering, March 1987, pp. 328–338.

12. Schwaber, Ken; Sutherland, Jeff: *The Scrum Guide* (2014).

13. Turhan, Burak; Layman, Lucak; Diep, Madeline; Shull, Forrst; Erdogmus, Hakan: *How Effective is Test-Driven Development?* In: Wilson, G.; Orham, A. (publisher): *Making software: what really works, and why we believe it*: ISBN 978-0596808327 (https://www.worldcat.org/title/making-software-what-really-works-and-why-we-believe-it/oclc/836148043), S. 207–219.

2

Section 2: Best Practices for Maintainable and Testable Go Code

The objective of part two is to bring you up to speed with industry best practices for producing clean, testable code that simplifies maintenance and prevents the accumulation of technical debt.

This section comprises the following chapters:

- Chapter 2, *Best Practices for Writing Clean and Maintainable Go Code*
- Chapter 3, *Dependency Management*
- Chapter 4, *The Art of Testing*

2
Best Practices for Writing Clean and Maintainable Go Code

"Any fool can write code that a computer can understand. Good programmers write code that humans can understand."

- *Martin Fowler* [8]

Writing clean code that is easy to test and maintain is much harder than it seems at first glance. Fortunately, Go, as a programming language, is quite opinionated and comes with its own set of best practices.

If you take a look at some of the available material for learning Go (for example, Effective Go [6]) or watch some talks by prominent members of the core Go team such as Rob Pike, it becomes evident that software engineers are gently *nudged* toward applying those principles when working on their own Go projects. From my perspective and experience, these best practices tend to have a measurable positive effect on the code quality metrics associated with a code base and at the same time aid in minimizing the accumulation of technical debt.

In this chapter, we will cover the following topics:

- Understanding the SOLID principles of object-oriented design through the eyes of a Go engineer
- Organizing source code at the package level
- Helpful tips and tools for writing lean and easy-to-maintain code in Go

The SOLID principles of object-oriented design

The **SOLID** principles are essentially a set of rules for helping you write clean and maintainable object-oriented code. Let's go over what the initials stand for:

- **Single responsibility**
- **Open/closed**
- **Liskov substitution**
- **Interface segregation**
- **Dependency inversion**

But hold on a minute! Is Go an object-oriented language or is it a functional programming language with some syntactic sugar tacked on top?

 Contrary to other, traditional object-oriented programming languages, such as C++ or Java, Go has no built-in support for classes. However, it *does* support the concepts of *interfaces* and *structs*. Structs allow you to define objects as a collection of fields and associated methods. Even though objects and interfaces can be *composed* together, there is, *by design*, no support for classic object-oriented inheritance.

With these observations in mind, we should be referring to Go as an *object-based* programming language and, as such, the following principles are still valid. Let's take a look at each principle in more detail from the perspective of a Go software engineer.

Single responsibility

The **single responsibility principle (SRP)** was described by Robert Martin [23], a seasoned software engineer who offers, under the nickname of *Uncle Bob*, advice about best practices for software development. The SRP states the following:

> *"In any well-designed system, objects should only have a single responsibility."*

In a nutshell, object implementations should focus on doing one thing well, and in an efficient way. To understand how this principle works, let's examine a piece of code that *violates* it. In the following imaginary scenario, we are working for the ACME drone company where we are using Go to build a drone-based goods delivery system.

The following code excerpt illustrates one of our initial attempts at defining a set of methods for the `Drone` type:

```
// NavigateTo applies any required changes to the drone's speed
// vector so that its eventual position matches dst.
func (d *Drone) NavigateTo(dst Vec3) error { //... }

// Position returns the current drone position vector.
func (d *Drone) Position() Vec3 { //... }

// Position returns the current drone speed vector.
func (d *Drone) Speed() Vec3 { //... }

// DetectTargets captures an image of the drone's field of view (FoV) using
// the on-board camera and feeds it to a pre-trained SSD MobileNet V1
neural
// network to detect and classify interesting nearby targets. For more info
// on this model see:
//
https://github.com/tensorflow/models/tree/master/research/object_detection
func (d *Drone) DetectTargets() ([]*Target, error) { //... }
```

The preceding code violates the SRP by conflating two separate responsibilities:

- Navigating the drone
- Detecting targets in close proximity to the drone

As the case may be, this is a valid, working solution. However, the extra coupling that is introduced makes the implementation harder to maintain and extend. For instance, what if we want to evaluate different neural network models for object-recognition purposes? What if we want to use the same object recognition code for different `Drone` types?

So, how can we apply the SRP to improve our design? To begin with, while operating under the assumption that all drones come with an on-board camera, we can expose a method on the `Drone` object to capture and return an image using the camera. At this point, you may be thinking: wait, isn't image capturing a *different* responsibility than navigation? The answer is: it's all a matter of perspective! Describing and assigning responsibilities to objects is an art in itself, and quite a subjective one. Conversely, we could counter-argue that navigation needs access to various sources of sensor data, and the camera is one of them. In that sense, the proposed refactoring is *not* violating the SRP.

In a second refactoring step, we can extract the target detection code into a separate, standalone object that would allow us to move on with the object-recognition model evaluation without having to modify any of the code in the Drone type. The second iteration of the implementation might look something like this:

```
// NavigateTo applies any required changes to the drone's speed vector
// so that its eventual position matches dst.
func (d *Drone) NavigateTo(dst Vec3) error { //... }

// Position returns the current drone position vector.
func (d *Drone) Position() Vec3 { //... }

// Position returns the current drone speed vector.
func (d *Drone) Speed() Vec3 { //... }

// CaptureImage records and returns an image of the drone's field of
// view using the on-board drone camera.
func (d *Drone) CaptureImage() (*image.RGBA, error) { //... }
```

In a separate file (possibly in a different package too), we would define the MobileNet type, which contains the implementation for our target detector:

```
// MobileNet performs target detection for drones using the
// SSD MobileNet V1 NN.
// For more info on this model see:
//
https://github.com/tensorflow/models/tree/master/research/object_detection
type MobileNet {
    // various attributes...
}

// DetectTargets captures an image of the drone's field of view and feeds
// it to a neural network to detect and classify interesting nearby
// targets.
func (mn *MobileNet) DetectTargets(d *drone.Drone) ([]*Target, error){
    //...
}
```

Success! We have split our original implementation into two separate objects, with each one having a single responsibility.

Open/closed principle

The **open/closed** principle was coined by Bertrand Meyer [24], who stated the following:

"A software module should be open for extension but closed for modification."

Almost all Go programs import and use types from a host of other packages, some being part of the Go standard library whereas other packages are provided by third parties. Any software engineer that imports a package into their code base should always safely assume that all the types that are exported by said package adhere to a contract that is guaranteed to be immutable. In other words, a package should not be able to modify the behavior of the types that are exported by *other* packages. While some programming languages allow this type of modification (via a technique colloquially referred to as *monkey patching*), the Go designers put safety mechanisms in place to ensure that this type of modification is strictly forbidden. Otherwise, Go programs would be able to violate the **closed** principle with unforeseen consequences for code that's deployed to production.

At this point, you may be wondering: does the closed principle also apply to code confined *within* the scope of a package? Additionally, how does Go implement the **open** principle? By Meyer's definition, we should be able to use object-oriented principles such as inheritance or composition to extend existing code with additional functionality without having to modify the original code units. As we discussed at the beginning of the chapter, Go does not support inheritance; that leaves *composition* as the only viable approach for extending existing code.

Let's examine how these principles are intertwined through a simple example. After a brief stint in drone design, we decided to switch industries and focus on building role-playing games instead. In the following code, you can see the definition of a generic Sword type for our upcoming game:

```go
type Sword struct {
    name string // Important tip for RPG players: always name your swords!
}
// Damage returns the damage dealt by this sword.
func (Sword) Damage() int {
    return 2
}

// String implements fmt.Stringer for the Sword type.
func (s Sword) String() string {
    return fmt.Sprintf(
        "%s is a sword that can deal %d points of damage to opponents",
        s.name, s.Damage(),
    )
}
```

One of our design requirements states that we need to support magic items, for example, an enchanted sword. Since our enchanted sword is merely a generic sword that deals a different amount of damage, we will apply the **open** principle and use *composition* to create a new type that embeds the Sword type and overrides the implementation of the Damage method:

```go
type EnchantedSword struct {
    // Embed the Sword type
    Sword
}

// Damage returns the damage dealt by the enchanted sword.
func (EnchantedSword) Damage() int {
    return 42
}
```

However, our implementation could not be complete without writing a few table-driven tests! The first test function that we will be creating is called TestSwordDamage and its purpose, as you can probably guess by its name, is to check whether calling Damage on the types we've defined so far produces the expected result. Here is how we would go about defining our expectations in a table-driven manner:

```go
specs := []struct {
    sword interface {
        Damage() int
    }
    exp int
}{
    {
        sword: Sword{name: "Silver Saber"},
        exp:    2,
    },
    {
        sword: EnchantedSword{Sword{name: "Dragon's Greatsword"}},
        exp:    42,
    },
}
```

The implementation of TestSwordDamage just iterates over the defined expectations and verifies that each one is met:

```go
func TestSwordDamage(t *testing.T) {
    specs := ... // see above code snippet for the spec definitions

    for specIndex, spec := range specs {
        if got := spec.sword.Damage(); got != spec.exp {
            t.Errorf("[spec %d] expected to get damage %d; got %d",
```

```
        specIndex, spec.exp, got)
            }
        }
    }
```

Our second test comes with its own list of expectations. This time, the goal is to make sure that the output of the `String` methods for the types we defined previously produces the correct output:

```
specs := []struct {
    sword fmt.Stringer
    exp   string
}{
    {
        sword: Sword{name: "Silver Saber"},
        exp:   "Silver Saber is a sword that can deal 2 points of damage to
opponents",
    },
    {
        sword: EnchantedSword{Sword{name: "Dragon's Greatsword"}},
        exp:   "Dragon's Greatsword is a sword that can deal 42 points of
         damage to opponents",
    },
}
```

Here is the implementation of `TestSwordToString`, which looks more or less the same as `TestSwordDamage`; no surprises here:

```
func TestSwordToString(t *testing.T) {
    specs := ... // see above code snippet for the spec definitions

    for specIndex, spec := range specs {
        if got := spec.sword.String(); got != spec.exp {
            t.Errorf("[spec %d] expected to get\n%q\ngot:\n%q",
                specIndex, spec.exp, got)
        }
    }
}
```

Now, we can run `go test`. However, one of our tests fails:

```
$ go test -v
=== RUN    TestSwordDamage
--- PASS: TestSwordDamage (0.00s)
=== RUN    TestSwordToString
--- FAIL: TestSwordToString (0.00s)
        sword_test.go:55: [spec 1] expected to get
                "Dragon's Greatsword is a sword that can deal 42 points of
```

```
        damage to opponents"
got:
"Dragon's Greatsword is a sword that can deal 2 points of
        damage to opponents"
```

So, what caused the second test to fail? To uncover the reason behind the failed test, we need to dig a bit deeper into how Go methods work under the hood. Go methods are nothing more than syntactic sugar for invoking a *function* with an object instance as an argument (also known as a receiver). In the preceding code snippet, String is always invoked with a Sword receiver and as a result, the call to the Damage method *always* gets dispatched to the implementation that's been defined by Sword type.

This is a prime example of the **closed** principle in action: Sword is *not aware of* any type that may embed it and its set of methods *cannot be altered* by objects it is embedded into. It is important to point out that while the EnchantedSword type cannot modify the implementation of the methods that have been defined on the embedded Sword instance, it can still *access* and *mutate* any fields defined by it (including private ones if both types are defined in the same package).

Liskov substitution

The third principle from SOLID that we will be exploring is the **Liskov substitution principle (LSP)**. It was introduced by Barbara Liskov in 1987 while delivering a keynote session at the **Object-Oriented Programming Systems, Languages, and Applications (OOPSLA)** conference [22]. The formal definition of LSP is as follows:

> *If, for each object, O1 of type S there is an object O2 of type T such that for all programs P defined in terms of T, the behavior of P is unchanged when O1 is substituted for O2, then S is a subtype of T.*

In layman's terms, two types are *substitutable* if their exhibited behavior follows exactly the same contract, thereby making it *impossible* for *callers* to distinguish between them. Thinking in pure OO terms, this is probably the textbook use case for abstract and concrete classes. As we mentioned in a previous section, Go does not support the concept of classes or inheritance but instead relies on *interfaces* as the means for facilitating type substitutions.

One interesting peculiarity of Go, at least for people coming from a Java or C++ background, is that Go interfaces are *implicit*. Each Go type defines an implicit interface consisting of all the methods it implements. This design decision allows the Go compiler to perform a *compile-time* variant of **duck typing** (the formal term for this is **structural typing**) when deciding whether an object instance can be passed as a substitute to a function or method that expects a particular interface as its argument.

The term duck typing has its roots in an old adage referred to as the *duck test*:

"If it looks like a duck and it quacks like a duck, then it is a duck."

Essentially, when given an object and an interface, the object can be used in place of the interface *if* its method set contains methods whose name and signature match the ones defined by the interface. Not having to explicitly indicate which interfaces a type implements is quite a handy feature. It helps us decouple the definition of an object (which may be an external or third-party package) from the place where the interface is defined and/or used.

In the following code snippet, we're defining the Adder interface and a simple function called PrintSum that uses any type that satisfies this interface to add two numbers together:

```go
package main

import "fmt"

// Adder is implemented by objects that can add two integers together.
type Adder interface {
    Add(int, int) int
}

func PrintSum(a, b int, adder Adder) {
    fmt.Printf("%d + %d = %d", a, b, adder.Add(a, b))
}
```

The adder package includes the Int type, which satisfies the Adder interface, and another type called Double, which doesn't; even though it defines a function called Add, you will notice that the argument *types* are different:

```go
package adder

// Int adds two integer values.
type Int struct{}

// Add returns the sum a+b.
func (Int) Add(a, b int) int { return a + b }

// Double adds two double values.
type Double struct{}

// Add returns the sum a+b.
func (Double) Add(a, b float64) float64 { return a + b }
```

The following code snippet illustrates how compile-time interface substitution checks work. We can safely pass Int instances to PrintSum as Int implicitly satisfies the Adder interface. However, attempting to pass an instance of Double to PrintSum will trigger a compile-time error:

```
package main

import "github.com/foo/adder"

func main() {
    PrintSum(1, 2, adder.Int{}) // prints: "1 + 2 = 3"

    // This line will trigger a compile-time error:
    //  cannot use adder.Double literal (type adder.Double) as type Adder
    //  in argument to PrintSum: adder.Double does not implement Adder
    //  (wrong type for Add method)
    //       have Add(float64, float64) float64
    //       want Add(int, int) int
    PrintSum(1, 2, adder.Double{})
}
```

In the cases where the type of the object to be substituted is not known at compile time, the compiler will automatically generate code to perform the check at runtime:

```
var placeholder interface{}

// Cast to io.Reader works; os.Stdin implements io.Reader
placeholder = os.Stdin
_ = placeholder.(io.Reader)

// Cast to io.Reader triggers a run-time panic:
// "panic: interface conversion: string is not io.Reader: missing method
Read"
placeholder = "cast check"
_ = placeholder.(io.Reader)

// Cast to io.Reader fails and isReader is set to false
placeholder = "cast check"
if _, isReader := placeholder.(io.Reader); !isReader {
    fmt.Printf("%T does not implement io.Reader\n", placeholder)
}
```

When you aren't sure whether a type instance or an `interface{}` can be cast to another type or interface at runtime, it is often good practice to use the dual return value variant of the cast operator (the *last* case in the preceding code sample) to avoid potential panics while your program is executing.

Interface segregation

Similar to the SRP, the **interface segregation principle (ISP)** was also coined by Robert Martin. According to this principle, clients should not be forced to depend upon the interfaces that they do not use.

This principle is quite important as it forms the basis for applying the other principles we've discussed so far. Going back to our previous RPG example, let's assume that we have augmented our `Sword` object with a few more interesting methods:

```
// Sharpen increases the damage dealt by this sword using a whetstone.
func (Sword) Sharpen() {
    //...
}

// MakeBlunt decreases the damage dealt by this sword due to constant use.
func (Sword) MakeBlunt(){
    //...
}

// Drop places the sword on the ground allowing others to pick it up.
func (Sword) Drop(){
    //...
}
```

So, how are we going to use weapons in our game? Obviously, we need to introduce some *monsters* for the player to attack! This is what the signature of an `Attack` function could potentially look like:

```
// Attack deals damage to a monster using a sword.
func Attack(m *Monster, s *Sword) {
    //...
}
```

However, there are a few issues with the preceding definition.

The *implicit* (see the previous section) Sword interface is quite *open*, that is, it includes a bunch of other methods that our Attack implementation has no need for. In fact, the software engineer implementing Attack may be tempted to include additional *business logic* rules that rely on the availability of those methods:

- Make the sword blunt after a number of attacks
- Cause the player to drop the sword if the monster uses some special armor

Going down this path would lead to a violation of the SRP and potentially make unit testing of the code harder. In addition, the proposed definition of Attack induces a strong coupling with objects that either are of the Sword type or are other types that *embed* it.

These two observations fully justify the existence of a famous Go proverb that was originally attributed to Rob Pike:

"The bigger the interface, the weaker the abstraction."

While Go implicit interfaces (see the previous section) would allow us to pass *any* type that embeds Sword (perhaps an EnchantedSword from our previous example), our requirements will undoubtedly state that Attack must be able to work with other types of weapons, for example, projectiles or magic spells.

On the other hand, Attack expects a Monster instance as its first argument. It stands to reason that the player should be able to use weapons to deal damage to non-monster entities, for example, to break down a bolted door or to cut the rope suspending the chandelier from the ceiling. Moreover, ideally, we would want to reuse the same implementation when monsters attack the player.

These are all great use cases for applying the ISP. Let's assume that our Attack implementation only needs the following:

- To figure out the amount of damage that's caused by a weapon
- Some mechanism to apply the damage to a particular *target*

With the preceding observations, we could change the signature of Attack to accept two explicit interfaces as arguments:

```
// DamageReceiver is implemented by objects that can receive weapon damage.
type DamageReceiver interface {
    ApplyDamage(int)
}
```

```go
// Damager is implemented by objects that can be used as weapons.
type Damager interface {
    Damage(int)
}

// Attack deals weapon damage to target.
func Attack(target DamageReceiver, weapon Damager) {
    //...
}
```

With this rather simple change, we kill two birds with one stone. Firstly, our code is more abstract and it's much easier to test its behavior by providing our own test types that implement the required interfaces. Secondly, our interfaces are, quite literally, the smallest possible; this fact not only makes the SRP application possible but it also alludes to a simpler implementation. As evidenced by a quick scan of the Go standard library, single-method interfaces (for example, `Reader` and `Writer` interfaces in the `io` package) are a rather prevailing idiom between the Go authors.

Dependency inversion

Yet another principle identified by Robert Martin is the **dependency inversion principle (DIP)**. It is, slightly verbosely, defined as follows:

> *"High-level modules should not depend on low-level modules. Both should depend on abstractions. Abstractions should not depend on details. Details should depend on abstractions."*

The DIP essentially summarizes all the other principles we've discussed so far. If you have been applying the rest of the SOLID principles to your code base, you will find that it already adheres to the preceding definition!

The introduction and use of interfaces aids in decoupling high-level and low-level modules. The open/closed principle ensures that interfaces themselves are immutable but does not preclude us from coming up with any number of alternative implementations (the *details* bit in the preceding definition) that satisfy an implicit or explicit interface. At the same time, the LSP guarantees that we can rely on the established abstractions while also having the flexibility to swap the underlying implementation at compile time or even runtime without worrying about breaking our applications.

Applying the SOLID principles

If you decide to apply these principles to your own projects, you will achieve greater flexibility in the way you design, connect to, and test software components, with the added benefit of requiring less time to extend the code base in the future.

However, one thing to keep in mind is that there is *no such thing as a free lunch*. What you gain in flexibility, you lose in the increased size of your code base; this could adversely affect the complexity metrics associated with the project.

In my view, this trade-off is not necessarily a bad thing. By following the best practices around testing your code (a subject that will be explored in detail in upcoming chapters), you can tame any potential increase in code complexity. At the same time, encountering difficulties while writing tests is often a good sign that your code is probably violating one or more of the SOLID principles and needs refactoring.

Finally, I would like to stress that even though we analyzed the SOLID principles through the eyes of a Go engineer, the principles themselves have a much wider scope and can also be applied to system design in general. For instance, in a microservice-based deployment, you should be aiming to build and deploy services with a single purpose (SRP) that communicate through clearly defined contracts and boundaries (ISP).

Organizing code into packages

As we saw in the previous section, the application of the SOLID principles works as a guide for splitting our code base into smaller packages where each package implements a specific bit of functionality and its interfaces serve as the glue for wiring packages together when building larger systems.

In this section, we will be examining the idiomatic Go way for naming packages, as well as some common potential pitfalls you may encounter while authoring code that relies on a complex package dependency graph.

Naming conventions for Go packages

Let's say you come across a package named `server`. Is that a good name, as per the preceding suggestion? Well, *obviously*, we can guess that it's some *kind* of server, but what kind is that? Is it an HTTP server, for instance, a TCP-based server implementing a text-based wire protocol, or maybe a UDP-based server for an online game? Some of you may argue that the package might export a type or function that alludes to the package's purpose (for example, `NewHTTPServer`). That certainly disambiguates things, but it also introduces a bit of repetition: in this particular case, the *server* literal is present in both the package name and a function exposed by it. As we will see in the *Improving code quality metrics with the help of linters* section, this practice is considered an anti-pattern and may cause linter warnings.

 Go package names should be short and concise and provide a clear indication of their purpose to the *intended* users of the package.

By browsing the code of the Go standard library, we can find quite a few characteristic examples of this clear package-naming philosophy:

- The `net` package provides mechanisms for creating various types of network listeners (tcp, udp, Unix domain sockets, and more).
- The `net/http` package provides, among other things, an HTTP server implementation: the `http.Server` type name is pretty unambiguous with respect to its use.

While package names should be kept short, you should avoid coming up with package names that can potentially clash with variable names that are commonly used by the code importing the package. Otherwise, package users would have to import the package using an *alias* (that is, import *blah* path-to-package). In such cases, it is usually better to abbreviate the package name (if possible). Typical examples from the Go standard library include the `fmt` and `bufio` packages. More specifically, the `bufio` package is named as such to avoid name clashes with `buf`, a variable name you are very likely to encounter when dealing with a piece of code that uses buffers.

Finally, in contrast to other programming languages whose standard libraries usually come with utility libraries or packages with generic-sounding names such as *common* or *util*, Go is quite opinionated *against* this practice. This is actually justified from the SOLID principles' point of view as those packages are more likely to be violating the SRP versus aptly named packages whose name enforces a logical boundary for their contents. To add to this, as the number of published Go packages grows over time, searching for and locating packages with generic-sounding names will become more and more difficult.

Circular dependencies

For a Go program to be well formed, its import graph must be acyclic; in other words, it must not contain any loops. Any violation of this predicate will cause the Go compiler to emit an error. As the systems you are building grow in complexity, so does the probability of eventually hitting the dreaded *import cycle detected* error.

Usually, import cycles are an indication of a fault in the design of a software solution. Fortunately, in many cases, we can refactor our code and work around most import cycles. Let's take a closer look at some common cases where circular dependencies occur and some strategies for dealing with them.

Breaking circular dependencies via implicit interfaces

In the following imaginary scenario, we are working for a start-up company that is building the software that's responsible for controlling fully automated warehouses. Autonomous robots equipped with gripping arms and lasers (what could possibly go wrong?) are busy moving around the warehouse floor locating and picking up order items from the shelves and placing them in cardboard boxes that are then shipped to the customers.

This is a tentative definition for a warehouse `Robot`:

```
package warehouse

import "context"

// Robot navigates the warehouse floor and fetches items for packing.
type Robot struct {
    // various fields
}

// AcquireRobot blocks until a Robot becomes available or until the
// context expires.
func AcquireRobot(ctx context.Context) *Robot { //...   }
```

```
// Pack instructs the robot to pick up an item from its shelf and place
// it into a box that will be shipped to the customer.
func (r *Robot) Pack(item *entity.Item, to *entity.Box) error { //...  }
```

In the preceding code snippet, the Item and Box types live in an external package called entity. All goes well until one day when someone attempts to introduce a new helper method to the Box type, which, unfortunately, introduces an import cycle:

```
package entity

// Box contains a list of items that are shipped to the customer.
type Box struct {
    // various fields
}

// Pack qty items of type i into the box.
func (b *Box) Pack(i *Item, qty int) error {
    robot := warehouse.Acquire() // compile error: import cycle detected
    // ...
}
```

Technically speaking, this is a bad design decision: boxes and items should not really be aware of the robot's existence. However, for the sake of this argument, we will ignore this design flaw and try to work around this problem using Go's support for implicit interfaces. The first step would be to define a Packer interface within the entity package. Secondly, we would need to provide an abstraction for obtaining an instance of Packer, as shown in the following code snippet:

```
package entity

import "context"

// Packer is implemented by objects that can pack an Item into a Box.
type Packer interface {
    Pack(*Item, *Box) error
}

// AcquirePacker returns a Packer instance.
var AcquirePacker func(context.Context) Packer
```

With these two mechanisms in place, the helper method can work *without* the need to import the warehouse package:

```
// Pack qty items of type i into the box.
func (b *Box) Pack(i *Item, qty int) error {
    p := AcquirePacker(context.Background())
    for j := 0; j < qty; j++ {
```

```
        if err := p.Pack(i, b); err != nil {
            return err
        }
    }
    return nil
}
```

The last bit of the puzzle that we need to address is how we are going to initialize `AcquirePacker` without importing the `warehouse` package. The only way we can do that is via a *third* package that imports the `warehouse` and `entity` packages:

```
package main

import "github.com/achilleasa/logistics/entity"
import "github.com/achilleasa/logistics/warehouse"

func wireComponents() {
    entity.AcquirePacker = func(ctx context.Context) entity.Packer {
        return warehouse.AcquireRobot(ctx)
    }
}
```

In the preceding code snippet, the `wireComponents` function ensures that the `warehouse` and `entity` packages are wired together without triggering any circular dependency errors.

Sometimes, code repetition is not a bad idea!

You have probably heard of the **don't repeat yourself** (DRY) principle before. The main idea behind DRY is to avoid code repetition by aiming to write reusable code that can be included where required. But is DRY *always* a good idea?

Go packages serve as a nice abstraction for organizing code into modular, reusable units. But, generally speaking, a good practice for writing Go programs is to try to keep your import dependency graph shallow and wide; this sounds counter-intuitive considering it's probably the exact opposite of what the DRY principle advocates: *include instead of repeat*.

When the dependency graph becomes deeper, circular dependencies become more likely, this time due to *transitive* dependencies, that is, dependencies of packages that your code imports. In the following example, we have three packages: x, y, and z.

Package *y* defines a helper function called `IsPrime`, which, as you can probably guess by its name, returns a Boolean indicating whether its input is a prime number or not. The same package imports and uses some types from package *z*:

```
package y

import "z"

func IsPrime(v uint64) bool {
    // ...
}

// Other functions referencing types exported from package z
```

Package *z* imports some types from package *x*:

```
package z

import "x"

// functions referencing types exported from package x
```

So far, so good. A few days go by and then we decide to add a new helper function to package *x* called `IsValid`. The function needs to perform a primality test and, since package *y* already provides `IsPrime`, we decide to follow the DRY approach and import *y* into our code, causing a circular dependency:

```
package x

import "y" // circular dependency. x imports y, y imports z and z imports x

func IsValid(v uint64) bool {
    return v != 0 && y.IsPrime(v)
}
```

In cases like this, and assuming the code we need from the included package is small enough, we can just duplicate it (along with its tests) and avoid the extra import that triggers a circular dependency. As a popular Go proverb goes:

> *"A little copying is better than a little dependency."*

Tips and tools for writing lean and easy-to-maintain Go code

In the upcoming sections, we will be covering some techniques, tools, and best practices that can assist you in writing more concise and clean code that is easier to test and at the same time help you get some praise from your colleagues and code reviewers.

Most of the topics that we will be discussing are specific to Go, but some of the principles can be generalized and applied to other programming languages and software engineering in general.

Optimizing function implementations for readability

During my early university days, my CS professors would be adamant about keeping function blocks short and concise. Their advice went along the lines of the following:

> *"If a function implementation does not fit on a single screen, then it must be split up into smaller functions."*

Keep in mind that these guidelines have their roots in an era when by *screen*, people were referring to the amount of code that could fit in an 80×25 character terminal! Fast forward to today where things have changed: software engineers have access to high-resolution monitors, editors, and bespoke IDEs that come preloaded a wide gamut of sophisticated analysis and refactoring tools. Still, the same bit of advice is just as important for writing code that is easy for *others* to review, extend, and maintain.

In the *Single responsibility* section, we discussed the merits of the SRP. Unsurprisingly, the same principle also applies to function blocks and is something to keep at the back of your mind when coding.

By decomposing a complex function into smaller functions, the code becomes easier to read and reason about. This may not seem important at first, but think about a case where you don't touch the code for a couple of months and then need to dive back into it while trying to track down a bug. As a bonus, the isolated bits of logic also become easier to test, especially if you are following the practice of writing table-driven tests.

Naturally, it follows that the same approach can be applied to existing code. If you find yourself navigating through a lengthy function that contains deeply nested `if/else` blocks, repeated blocks of code, or its implementation tackles several seemingly unrelated concerns, it would be a great opportunity to apply some drive-by refactoring and extract any potential self-contained blocks of logic into separate functions.

Additionally, when creating new functions or splitting existing functions into smaller ones, a good idea is to arrange the functions so that they appear in call order within the file they are defined in, that is, if `A()` calls `B()` and `C()`, then both `B()` and `C()` must appear below, but not necessarily immediately after, `A()`. This makes it much easier for other engineers (or people just curious to understand how something works) to skim through existing code.

Each rule comes with exceptions and this rule is no different. Unless the compiler is very good at inlining functions, splitting the business logic across functions sometimes takes a toll on performance. Although the performance hit is, in many cases, insignificant, when the end goal is to produce high-performance code that contains tight inner loops or code that is expected to be called with high frequency, it may be a good idea to keep the implementation neatly tucked within a single function to avoid the extra Go runtime overhead that's incurred when making function calls (for example, pushing arguments to the stack, checking that the stack is large enough for the callee, and popping things off the stack when the function call returns).

 There is always a trade-off between code readability and performance. When dealing with complex systems, readability is oftentimes preferred, but at the end of the day, it's up to you and your team to figure out which mix of readability versus performance works best for your particular use case.

Variable naming conventions

There is an ongoing debate regarding the ideal length for variables and type names in Go programs. On one hand, there are the proponents of the belief that all variables should have clear and self-descriptive names. This is a fairly common philosophy for people who have spent some time authoring code in the Java ecosystem. On the other side of the fence, we have the *minimalists*, that is, people who advocate for shorter identifier names, arguing that longer identifiers are too verbose.

The Go language authors certainly seem to be members of the latter camp. Case in point, here is the definition of two of the most popular Go interfaces: `io.Reader` and `io.Writer`:

```go
type Reader interface {
    Read(p []byte) (n int, err error)
}

type Writer interface {
    Write(p []byte) (n int, err error)
}
```

The same short identifier pattern is widely used throughout the Go standard library code base. My take on this is that using *shorter* but still *descriptive* variable names is a good thing as long as other engineers that will be called to work on the code base in the future can easily understand their purpose within the scope that each variable is being used in.

The most common example of this approach is naming index variables for nested loops where, typically, a single-letter variable such as `i`, `j`, and so on is used. In the following code snippet, however, the index variables are used to access an element of the multi-dimensional slice `s`:

```go
for i := 0; i < len(s); i++ {
    for j := 0; j < len(s[i]); j++ {
        value := s[i][j]
        // ...
    }
}
```

If someone who's not familiar with this part of the code is tasked with reviewing a pull request containing the preceding loop, they may find themselves struggling to figure out what `s` is and what each index level represents! Since the shortened variable names provide almost no information regarding their true purpose, to answer these questions, the reviewer would have to jump around the code base looking for clues: look up the type for `s`, then go to its definition, and so on and so forth. Now, contrast the preceding code block with the following one, which performs exactly the same function but uses *slightly longer* variable names. In my opinion, the second approach has higher information content while at the same time avoids being too verbose:

```go
for dateIdx := 0; dateIdx < len(tickers); dateIdx++ {
    for stockIdx := 0; stockIdx < len(tickers[dateIdx]); stockIdx++ {
        value := tickers[dateIdx][stockIdx]
        // ...
    }
}
```

At the end of the day, each engineer has their own preferred variable naming approach and philosophy. When deciding on which approach to adopt, try to take a few minutes to consider how your variable naming choices affect other engineers that collaborate with you on shared code bases.

Using Go interfaces effectively

"Accept interfaces, return structs."

- Jack Lindamood

The key point behind organizing code into packages is to make it reusable and available to external consumers in a frictionless way by providing a clean, well-documented API surface that consumers can build on. When authoring functions or methods that accept concrete types as arguments, we place an artificial constraint on the usefulness of our implementation: it only works with instances of a particular type.

While this may not always be an issue, in some cases, requiring a concrete type instance can potentially make testing non-trivial and slow, especially if the construction of such an instance is a costly operation. The following excerpt is part of a system that collects and publishes performance metrics to a **key-value (KV)** store.

The KV store implementation looks like this:

```
package kv

// Store implements a key-value store which stores data to disk.
type Store struct { // ...  }

func Open(path string) (*Store, error) { // Open path, load and verify
data, replay pending transactions etc.  }

// Put persists (key, value) to the store.
func (s *Store) Put(key string, value interface{}) error { // ...  }

// Get looks up the value associated with key.
func (s *Store) Get(key string) (interface{}, error) { // ...  }

// Close waits for any pending transactions to complete and then
// cleanly shuts down the KV store.
func (s *Store) Close() error { // ...  }
```

Within the `metrics` package, we can find the definition of the `ReportMetrics` function. It receives a `kv.Store` instance as an argument and persists the collected metrics to it:

```
package metrics

// ReportMetrics writes the collected metrics to a KV store instance.
func (c *Collector) ReportMetrics(s *kv.Store) error {
    // for each metric call s.Put(k, v)
}

// Observe records a value for a particular metric.
func (c *Collector) Observe(metric string, value interface{}) {
    // ...
}
```

Based on the previous discussion around SOLID principles, you should have already identified an issue with this code: *it only works with a specific KV store implementation!* What if we want to publish the metrics to a network socket, write them to a CSV file, or perhaps log them to the console?

There is, however, yet another issue with this bit of code: testing it requires quite a bit of effort. To understand why, let's put ourselves in the shoes of a consumer of this package. As part of our integration test suite, we want to make sure that all the collected metrics are actually written to the KV store instance.

First, our test code would have to create an instance of the KV store. Since the `Open` method requires a file and we could be running multiple tests concurrently, we would need to create a temporary unique file and pass it as an argument to `Open`. Of course, we shouldn't leave temporary files hanging around after our test run completes, so we need to make sure our test will clean up after itself:

```
// Generate a random file for the KV store
tmpfile, err := ioutil.TempFile("", "metrics")
if err != nil {
    t.Fatal(err)
}
defer func() { _ = os.Remove(tmpfile.Name()) }() // clean up when we are
                                                  // done
_ = tmpfile.Close()

// Create KV store
s, err := kv.Open(tmpfile.Name())
if err != nil {
    t.Fatal(err)
}
defer func() { _ = s.Close() }()
```

That brings us to the meat of the test: creating a metrics collector, populating it with a bunch of measurements, reporting the captured metrics to the KV store, and verifying that everything has been written to the store properly:

```
c := metrics.NewCollector()
for i := 0; i < 100; i++ {
    c.Observe(fmt.Sprintf("metric_%d", i), i)
}

if err = c.ReportMetrics(s); err != nil {
    t.Fatal(err)
}

// Ensure that all metrics have been written to the store
// ...
}
```

This test is pretty straightforward but it requires quite a bit of boilerplate code for setting it up. Additionally, kv.Open seems like it is quite an expensive call to make; imagine the overhead involved if our test suite was comprised of hundreds of tests where each one required a *real* kv.Store instance. If, on the other hand, ReportMetrics received an interface as an argument, we could pass an in-memory mock while testing and also retain the flexibility to report the metrics to any destination that satisfies that particular interface. Therefore, we can improve the preceding code by introducing an interface:

```
package metrics

// Sink is implemented by objects that metrics can be reported to.
type Sink interface {
    Put(k string, v interface{}) error
}

// ReportMetrics writes the collected metrics to a Sink.
func (c *Collector) ReportMetrics(s Sink) error {
    // for each metric call s.Put(k, v)
}
```

This small change makes testing a breeze! We can test the kv.Store code in isolation and switch to an in-memory store to run all our unit tests:

```
func TestReportMetrics(t *testing.T) {
    // Use in-memory store defined inside the test package
    s := new(inMemStore)

    // Create collector and populate some metrics
    c := metrics.NewCollector()
    for i := 0; i < 100; i++ {
```

```
        c.Observe(fmt.Sprintf("metric_%d", i), i)
    }

    if err = c.ReportMetrics(s); err != nil {
        t.Fatal(err)
    }

    // Ensure that all metrics have been written to the store...
}
```

The other piece of advice from Lindamood states that we should always try to return concrete types rather than interfaces. This advice actually makes sense: as a package consumer, if I am calling a function that creates a type, `Foo`, I am probably interested in calling one or more methods that are specific to that type. If the `NewFoo` function returns an interface, the client code would have to manually cast it to `Foo` so that it can invoke the `Foo`-specific methods; this would defeat the purpose of returning an interface in the first place.

It is also important to point out that, in the majority of cases, the implementation will create an instance of a concrete type; the main reason why we would opt to return an interface to begin with is to ensure that our concrete type always satisfies a particular interface. In essence, we are adding a compile-time check to our code! However, there are simpler ways to introduce such compile-time checks and still retain the ability for constructors to return concrete instances:

```
package metrics

import "fmt"

// Compile-time checks for ensuring a type implements a particular
// interface.
var (
    // Works but allocates a dummy Foo instance on the heap.
    _ fmt.Stringer = &Foo{}

    // Preferred way that does not allocate anything on the heap.
    _ fmt.Stringer = (*Foo)(nil)
)

type Foo struct { }

func (*Foo) String() string { return "Foo" }
```

The preceding code snippet outlines two fairly common approaches to achieve this compile-time check by defining a pair of global variables that use the reserved *blank identifier* as a hint to the compiler that they are not actually used.

Zero values are your friends

One great feature that Go offers is that each type is automatically assigned its zero value when it gets instantiated. Some interesting examples from Go and its standard library are as follows:

- Go channels; nil channels indefinitely block go-routines attempting to read off them
- The zero value for a Go slice; this is an empty slice that things can be appended to
- The `sync.Mutex` type, whose zero value indicates that the mutex is unlocked
- The `bytes.Buffer` type, whose zero value indicates an empty buffer

By relying on zero values when designing new types, we can provide implementations that work out of the box without the need to explicitly invoke a constructor or any other initializer method. The following code snippet defines a simple, thread-safe map:

```
package main

import (
    "fmt"
    "sync"
)

// SyncMap implements a thread-safe map. The zero SyncMap value is ready
// to use.
type SyncMap struct {
    mu   sync.RWMutex
    data map[string]interface{}
}
```

The actual Go map that will be used to store the `SyncMap` data will be lazily allocated when we attempt to add an item to the map. Acquiring a *writer* mutex before working with the underlying map ensures that both the initialization of the map and the insertion of items happen in an atomic fashion:

```
// Put inserts a key-value pair into the map.
func (sm *SyncMap) Put(key string, value interface{}) {
    sm.mu.Lock()
    defer sm.mu.Unlock()

    if sm.data == nil {
        sm.data = make(map[string]interface{})
    }
```

```
        sm.data[key] = value
    }
```

The lookup implementation is pretty straightforward. One noticeable difference compared to the implementation of `Put` is that `Get` acquires a *reader* mutex before performing lookups. The use of a reader/writer mutex provides concurrent access to multiple readers while only allowing a single writer to mutate the map's contents:

```
    // Get returns the value associate by key and a boolean value indicating
    // whether key is present in the map.
    func (sm *SyncMap) Get(key string) (interface{}, bool) {
        sm.mu.RLock()
        defer sm.mu.RUnlock()

        if sm.data == nil {
            return nil, false
        }

        return sm.data[key]
    }
```

Contrary to the built-in Go map type, which requires explicit initialization via a call to `make`, the zero value of a `SyncMap` can be safely used as is:

```
    func main() {
        var sm SyncMap // we are using the zero value of the map
        sm.Put("foo", "bar")
        fmt.Println(sm.Get("foo")) // Prints: bar true
    }
```

What's more, we can *embed* the preceding `SyncMap` implementation into other types that follow the same zero value pattern to provide complex types that require no initialization:

```
    type Foo struct {
        bar Bar
    }

    type Bar struct {
        sm SyncMap
    }


    func main() {
        var foo Foo // still using a zero value
        foo.bar.sm.Put("answer", 42) // storing into the embedded map also
                                     // works.
    }
```

In the preceding code snippet, the `SyncMap` instance is ready to use and can be accessed directly through an instance of `Foo` without having to type any additional code to set it up.

Using tools to analyze and manipulate Go programs

Go programs are inherently easy to parse. In fact, the Go library provides built-in packages that can parse Go programs into **abstract syntax trees (ASTs)**, which can be traversed, modified, and transformed back into Go code. Let's go through a simple example to show you how easy it is to work with these packages.

First, we need a helper function to convert a Go program into an AST representation. The following `parse` function does exactly that:

```go
import (
    "fmt"
    "go/ast"
    "go/parser"
    "go/token"
)

// parse a Go program into an AST representation.
func parse(program string) (*token.FileSet, *ast.File, error) {
    fs := token.NewFileSet()
    tree, err := parser.ParseFile(fs, "example.go", program, 0)
    if err != nil {
        return nil, nil, err
    }
    return fs, tree, nil
}
```

The `ast` package provides a couple of helpers that implement the visitor pattern and invokes a user-defined callback for each node in the AST. For this particular example, we will define a function called `inspectVariables` that visits every node in the AST, looking for nodes that correspond to identifiers (package, constant, type, variable, function, or label). For each discovered identifier, the function will check its `Kind` attribute and print out its name if the identifier represents a variable:

```go
// inspectVariables visits each AST node and prints any encountered Go
variable.
func inspectVariables(fs *token.FileSet, tree *ast.File) {
    ast.Inspect(tree, func(n ast.Node) bool {
        ident, ok := n.(*ast.Ident)
```

```
        if !ok || ident.Obj == nil || ident.Obj.Kind != ast.Var {
            return true
        }

        fmt.Printf("%s:\tvariable %q\n", fs.Position(n.Pos()), ident)
        return true
    })
}
```

To complete our example, we need to provide a `main` function that will parse a simple program and call `inspectVariables` on the resulting AST:

```
func main() {
    fs, tree, err := parse(`
        package foo

        var global = "foo"

        func main(){ x := 42 }
    `)

    if err != nil {
        fmt.Printf("ERROR: %v\n", err)
        return
    }

    inspectVariables(fs, tree)
}
```

Running the preceding program produces the following output:

```
$ go run print_vars.go
example.go:4:7: variable "global"
example.go:6:16: variable "x"
```

The Go ecosystem contains a plethora of tools that build on top of this parsing infrastructure and provide analysis, code modification, and generation services to software engineers. In the upcoming sections, we will examine a short list of such tools that can make your software development life easier.

Taking care of formatting and imports (gofmt, goimports)

Tabs or spaces? Should opening braces be preceded by line breaks? All engineers eventually face this dilemma when the time comes to choose a particular code formatting style for a new project or a project they've just inherited.

Source code formatting styles have always been the subject of long, often heated, arguments between team members. Contrary to other programming languages, Go is, by design, strongly opinionated toward a specific formatting style and ships with tools that help enforce that particular style. This design decision makes sense as Go was initially created with the goal of being used by the thousands of engineers employed by Google. At this massive development scale, uniformity in the authored code is not just a nicety – it's actually vital for ensuring that code can be handed off between development teams.

The `gofmt` tool [11] is available as part of the standard Go distribution. You provide it with the paths to one or more files and it can perform the following tasks:

- Format code according to the recommended standard
- Simplify code (`gofmt -s example.go`)
- Perform simple rewrites (`gofmt -r 'a[b:len(a)] -> a[len(a):b]' example.go`)

By default, `gofmt` will output the formatted programs to the standard output. However, users may pass the `-w` flag to force `gofmt` to write its output back to the source file that it just processed.

The `goimports` tool [12] is a drop-in replacement for `gofmt` that can be installed by running `go get golang.org/x/tools/cmd/goimports`. In addition to providing code-formatting facilities that match the output of `gofmt`, `goimports` also manages Go import lines: it can fill in missing imports and remove the ones that aren't referenced by the processed file. What's more, `goimports` also ensures that packages are sorted alphabetically and grouped together, depending on whether they belong to the standard library or are third-party packages.

The following is an example of a Go program that exhibits a couple of issues: missing imports, unused imports, extraneous whitespace, and incorrect indentation:

```
package main

import (
    "net" // Mixed stdlib and third-party packages
```

```
        "github.com/achilleasa/kv"
        "fmt" // Unused package
    )

    type Server struct {
        ctx     context.Context // missing referenced import
        socket net.Conn
    store *kv.Store // Incorrectly indented field definition
    }


    func foo(){} // Redundant line-breaks above foo()
```

The typical use case for these tools is to execute them as post-save hooks from your favorite editor or IDE. If we run `goimports` on the preceding code snippet, we will get a neatly formatted output:

```
    package main

    import (
        "context"
        "net"

        "github.com/achilleasa/kv"
    )

    type Server struct {
        ctx     context.Context
        socket net.Conn
        store *kv.Store
    }

    func foo() {}
```

As you can see, the import statements have been cleaned up and sorted, the missing packages have been imported, and unused packages have been removed. Adding to this, the code is now properly indented and all the extraneous whitespace has been removed.

Refactoring code across packages (gorename, gomvpkg, fix)

Oftentimes, you may come across a variable within a function that has a strange or non-descriptive name that you are quite keen on renaming. Performing such a rename operation is quite simple; just select the function block and run a find-and-replace operation. Simple as pie!

But what if you want to rename a public struct field or a function that is exported from your package? This is definitely not a trivial task as you need to track down all the references to the thing being renamed (the list may also include other packages) and update them to use the new name. This type of rename operation takes us into the realm of code refactoring; fortunately, there is a tool at our disposal for automating this tedious task: `gorename` [16]. It can be installed by running `go get golang.org/x/tools/cmd/gorename`.

One interesting feature of `gorename`, besides the fact that it works across packages, is that it is *type-aware*. Since it relies on parsing the program before it applies any rename operation, it is intelligent enough to tell the difference between a function called `Foo` and a struct field with the same name. Furthermore, it includes an extra layer of safety in that it will only apply rename operations as long as the end result is a piece of code that can compile without errors.

Sometimes, you may find yourself needing to rename a Go package or even move it to a different location either within the same project or across projects. The `gomvpkg` tool [15] can assist in that matter while also taking care of tracking down packages that depend on the renamed/moved package and updating their import statements to point to the new package location. It can be installed by running `go get golang.org/x/tools/cmd/gomvpkg`. Moving a package is as simple as running the following command:

```
# Rename foo to bar and update all imports for packages depending on foo.
$ gomvpkg -from foo -to bar
```

The Go standard library has changed a lot over the years since the release of the first stable Go version back in 2011. New APIs were introduced while other APIs were deprecated and eventually removed. In some cases, existing APIs are modified, often in a non-backward-compatible way, whereas in other cases, external or experimental packages eventually got accepted for inclusion in the standard library.

A relevant example is the `context` package. Prior to Go 1.7, this package was available at `golang.org/x/net/context` and quite a few Go programs were actively using it. But with the release of Go 1.7, that package became a part of the standard library and moved to a standalone `context` package. As soon as engineers switched to the new import path for the context package, their code would instantly become incompatible with code still using the old import path. Therefore, someone would have to undertake the task of reviewing the existing code base and rewriting existing imports to point to the new location for the context package!

The Go designers foresaw such issues and created a rule-based tool to detect code that relies on old, deprecated APIs or packages, and automatically rewrite it to use newer APIs. The tool, aptly named `fix` (https://golang.org/cmd/fix/), ships with each new Go release and can be invoked each time you switch to a newer Go version by running `go tool fix $path`. It is important to point out that all applied fixes are *idempotent*; therefore, it is safe to run the tool multiple times without the risk of your code base becoming corrupted.

Improving code quality metrics with the help of linters

Linters are specialized static analysis tools that parse Go files and attempt to detect, flag, and report cases where the following occurs:

- The code does not adhere to the standard formatting style guide; for example, it contains extraneous whitespace, is incorrectly indented, or contains comments with spelling typos
- The program contains possible logic bugs; for example, a variable declaration *shadowing* a previous variable declaration with the same name, calling functions such as `fmt.Printf` with an incorrect argument count or with arguments whose types do not match the format string, assigning values to variables but not actually using them, not checking errors returned by function calls, and so on
- The code may contain security vulnerabilities; for example, it contains hardcoded security credentials or points to where an SQL injection might be possible using insecure random number sources or cryptographically broken hash primitives (DES, RC4, MD5, or SHA1)
- The code exhibits high complexity (for example, deeply nested `if/else` blocks) or contains unnecessary type conversions, unused local or global variables, or code paths that are never invoked

The following table summarizes the most popular Go linters that you can invoke to check your programs and improve the quality metrics of the code that you author:

Category	Linter	Description
Logic bugs	`bodyclose` [2]	Check if `http.Response` bodies are always closed.
Logic bugs	`errcheck` [7]	Identify cases where returned errors are not being checked.
Logic bugs	`gosumcheck` [19]	Ensure that all possible cases of a type switch are handled properly.

Logic bugs	`go vet` (https://golang.org/cmd/vet/) [20]	Report suspicious constructs, for example, calling `fmt.Printf` with the wrong arguments.
Logic bugs	`ineffassign` [21]	Detect variable assignments that are not being used.
Code smell	`deadcode` (https://github.com/tsenart/deadcode) [4]	Report unused blocks of code.
Code smell	`dupl` (https://github.com/mibk/dupl) [5]	Report potentially duplicated blocks of code.
Code smell	`goconst` (https://github.com/jgautheron/goconst) [9]	Flag repeated strings that can be replaced with constants.
Code smell	`structcheck` (https://gitlab.com/opennota/check) [30]	Identify unused struct fields.
Code smell	`unconvert` (https://github.com/mdempsky/unconvert) [31]	Detect unnecessary type conversions.
Code smell	`unparam` (https://github.com/mvdan/unparam) [33]	Detect unused function parameters.
Code smell	`varcheck` [34]	Detect unused variables and constants.
Performance	`aligncheck` [1]	Identify inefficiently packed structs that take up more space due to padding.
Performance	`copyfighter` (https://github.com/jmhodges/copyfighter) [3]	Reports functions that pass large structs by value; this pattern triggers memory allocations and increases pressure on the garbage collector.
Performance	`prealloc` [26]	Identify slice declarations that could be preallocated.
Complexity	`gocyclo` [10]	Calculate cyclomatic complexities of Go functions.
Complexity	`gosimple` [18]	Report code that can be potentially simplified.
Complexity	`splint` [29]	Identify functions that are too long or receive too many arguments.
Security	`gosec` (https://github.com/securego/gosec) [17]	Scan source code for potential security issues.
Security	`safesql` (https://github.com/stripe/safesql) [28]	Check for potential SQL injection points.
Style	`gofmt -s` (https://golang.org/cmd/gofmt/) [11]	Ensure that a file is formatted according to `gofmt` rules.
Style	`golint` (https://github.com/golang/lint) [14]	Report stylistic deviations from the recommendations outlined in Effective Go [6].
Style	`misspell` (https://github.com/client9/misspell) [25]	Use a dictionary to identify spelling mistakes in comments.

Style	unindent (https://github.com/mvdan/unindent) [32]	Identify code that isn't indented correctly.

Using the preceding linters in your projects comes with a few caveats that you need to be aware of. First of all, each linter uses its own output format to report detected issues. The lack of a standardized way to report issues becomes a problem when you attempt to integrate the linters with your preferred editor or IDE workflows (for example, jump to the code location where an issue was detected). Secondly, each linter is oblivious to the existence of other linters. Consequently, *each* linter needs to reparse all the packages when it runs. This is usually not an issue when you're dealing with small code bases, but it becomes annoying when you're working with larger projects, as an end-to-end run of all the linters can take up to a few minutes to complete.

To address the preceding issues, you can use a **meta-linter** (also known as a **linter output aggregator**) tool such as `golangci-lint` [13] (a drop-in replacement for the now-deprecated gometalinter) or revive [27]. These tools are designed to execute a configurable list of linters in parallel, normalize their output, eliminate duplicate warnings, or even suppress warnings based on regular expressions (quite a handy feature when your project includes files that are autogenerated by other tools). What's more, they also seamlessly integrate with the majority of editors that are used by engineers working on Go programs. An easy way to invoke these meta-linter tools is to add a target to your project's *makefile*:

```
lint:
    golangci-lint run \
      --no-config --issues-exit-code=0 --deadline=30m \
      --disable-all --enable=deadcode  --enable=gocyclo --enable=golint \
      --enable=varcheck --enable=structcheck --enable=errcheck \
      --enable=dupl --enable=ineffassign \
      --enable=unconvert --enable=goconst --enable=gosec
```

Having a makefile rule for linting makes it easy to run the linters as part of your regular CI pipeline and block pull requests from being merged until the lint errors are addressed. At the same time, it offers you the flexibility of running the linters locally while you are working on the code base.

It is quite common for engineers to forgo running the linters before creating a pull request, thereby requiring additional commits just to address lint errors. You can avoid such situations by exploiting the fact that most version control systems (Git is one example) support some kind of pre-commit or pre-push hook and have your VCS run the linters automatically for you.

Summary

In the first section of this chapter, *The SOLID principles of object-oriented design,* we performed a deep dive into each of the SOLID principles and how they can be applied toward writing clean Go code:

- **SRP**: Group structs and functions based on their purpose and organize them into packages with clear logical boundaries.
- **Open/Closed principle**: Use composition and embedding of simple types to construct more complex types that still retain the same implicit interface as the types they consist of.
- **LSP**: Avoid unnecessary coupling by using interfaces rather than concrete types to define the contract between packages.
- **ISP**: Make sure your function or method signatures only depend on the behaviors they need and nothing more; use the smallest possible interface to describe function/method arguments and avoid coupling to the implementation details of concrete types.
- **DIP**: Use the appropriate level of abstraction when designing your code to decouple high-level and low-level modules while at the same time ensuring that the implementation details rely on the abstractions and not the other way round.

Halfway through this chapter, we touched on the subject of organizing code into packages, identified common package naming pitfalls that you should avoid, and discussed the concept of import cycles, including their causes. Then, we outlined strategies for mitigating the issue of circular dependencies.

Finally, we discussed useful tips and tools that you can use to facilitate writing clean code that is easy to reason about and for your software engineering colleagues to review and maintain.

As your Go projects grow in size, you will undoubtedly notice a bump in the number of package import statements throughout the code base. This is quite normal and, frankly, expected if you are applying the SOLID principles when creating packages. However, the increased number of imports, especially if they are authored by third parties that you do not control, also necessitate some kind of process to ensure that your programs can still compile as expected, even if an external dependency changes. This is the main topic of the next chapter.

Questions

1. What do the SOLID acronym initials stand for?

2. Why does the following piece of code violate the SRP? How would you refactor it to make sure it doesn't violate it?

```go
import (
    "crypto/ecdsa"
)

type Document struct { //... }

// Append adds a line to the end of the document.
func (d *Document) Append(line string) { //...  }

// Content returns the document contents as a string.
func (d *Document) Content() string { //... }

// Sign calculates a hash for the document contents, signs it with the
// provided private key and returns back the result.
func (d *Document) Sign(pk *ecdsa.PrivateKey) (string, error) {
//... }
```

3. What is the main concept behind the ISP? Discuss how would you apply it to improve the following function signature:

```go
// write a set of lines to a file.
func write(lines []string, f *os.File) error {
    //...
}
```

4. Explain why *util* is considered to be a less-than-ideal name for a Go package.

5. Why are import cycles an issue for Go programs?

6. Name some of the advantages of using the zero value when designing new Go types.

Further reading

1. `aligncheck`: Identify inefficiently packed structs. URL: `https://gitlab.com/opennota/check`.

2. `bodyclose`: A static analysis tool that checks whether `res.Body` is correctly closed. URL: `https://github.com/timakin/bodyclose`.

3. `copyfighter`: Statically analyze Go code and report functions while passing large structs by value. URL: `https://github.com/jmhodges/copyfighter`.

4. `deadcode`: Report unused blocks of code. URL: `https://github.com/tsenart/deadcode`.

5. `dupl`: Report potentially duplicated blocks of code. URL: `https://github.com/mibk/dupl`.

6. Effective Go: Tips for writing clear, idiomatic Go code.

7. `errcheck`: Ensure that returned errors are checked. URL: `https://github.com/kisielk/errcheck`.

8. Fowler, Martin: *Refactoring: Improving the Design of Existing Code.* Boston, MA, USA: Addison-Wesley, 1999 — ISBN 0-201-48567-2 (`https://www.worldcat.org/title/refactoring-improving-the-design-of-existing-code/oclc/863697997`).

9. `goconst`: Flag repeated strings that can be replaced with constants. URL: `https://github.com/jgautheron/goconst`.

10. `gocyclo`: Calculate cyclomatic complexity of code. URL: `https://github.com/alecthomas/gocyclo`.

11. `gofmt`: Format Go programs or check that they are properly formatted. URL: `https://golang.org/cmd/gofmt/`.

12. `goimports`: Update Go import lines by adding missing ones and removing unreferenced ones. URL: `https://godoc.org/golang.org/x/tools/cmd/goimports`.

13. `golangci-lint`: Linter runner. URL: `https://github.com/golangci/golangci-lint`.

14. `golint`: Report style issues in Go programs. URL: `https://github.com/golang/lint`.

15. `gomvpkg`: Move Go packages and update import declarations. URL: `https://godoc.org/golang.org/x/tools/cmd/gomvpkg`.

16. `gorename`: Perform precise type-safe renaming of identifiers in Go source code. URL: `https://godoc.org/golang.org/x/tools/cmd/gorename`.

17. `gosec`: Scan source code for potential security issues. URL: `https://github.com/securego/gosec`.

18. `gosimple`: Report code that can be potentially simplified. URL: `https://github.com/dominikh/go-tools/tree/master/cmd/gosimple`.

19. `gosumcheck`: Ensure that all possible types in a type switch are properly handled. URL: `https://github.com/haya14busa/gosum`.

20. `go vet`: Examine Go source code and report suspicious constructs, such as `printf` calls whose arguments do not align with the format string or shadowed variables. URL: `https://golang.org/cmd/vet/`.

21. `ineffassign`: Detect variable assignments that are not being used. URL: `https://github.com/gordonklaus/ineffassign`.

22. Liskov, Barbara: Keynote Address – Data Abstraction and Hierarchy. In: *Addendum to the Proceedings on Object-oriented Programming Systems, Languages and Applications (Addendum)*, OOPSLA '87. New York, NY, USA : ACM, 1987 — ISBN 0-89791-266-7 (`https://www.worldcat.org/title/oopsla-87-addendum-to-the-proceedings-object-oriented-programming-systems-languages-and-applications-october-4-8-1987-orlando-florida/oclc/220450625`), S. 17–34.

23. Martin, Robert C.: *Clean Architecture: A Craftsman's Guide to Software Structure and Design*, Robert C. Martin Series. Boston, MA: Prentice Hall, 2017 — ISBN 978-0-13-449416-6 (`https://www.worldcat.org/title/clean-architecture-a-craftsmans-guide-to-software-structure-and-design-first-edition/oclc/1105785924`).

24. Meyer, Bertrand: *Object-Oriented Software Construction*. 1st. Aufl. Upper Saddle River, NJ, USA: Prentice-Hall, Inc., 1988 — ISBN 0136290493 (`https://www.worldcat.org/title/object-oriented-software-construction/oclc/1134860513`).

25. `misspell`: Check source code for spelling mistakes. URL: `https://github.com/client9/misspell`.

26. `prealloc`: Identify slice declarations that could be pre-allocated. URL: `https://github.com/alexkohler/prealloc`.

27. `revive`: A stricter, configurable, extensible, and beautiful drop-in replacement for golint. URL: `https://github.com/mgechev/revive`.

28. `safesql`: Checks code for potential SQL injection points. URL: `https://github.com/stripe/safesql`.

29. `splint`: Identify functions that are too long or receive too many arguments. URL: `https://github.com/stathat/splint`.

30. `structcheck`: Identify unused struct fields. URL: `https://gitlab.com/opennota/check`.

31. `unconvert`: Detect unnecessary type conversions. URL: `https://github.com/mdempsky/unconvert`.

32. `unindent`: Identify code that is incorrectly indented. URL: `https://github.com/mvdan/unindent`.

33. `unparam`: Detect unused function parameters. URL: `https://github.com/mvdan/unparam`.

34. `varcheck`: Detect unused variables and constants. URL: `https://github.com/opennota/check`.

Dependency Management

3

"If at first you don't succeed, call it version 1.0."

- Pat Rice

Being strong believers in the SOLID principles we discussed in the previous chapter, several prominent figures in the Go community strongly advise software engineers to organize their code into self-contained and reusable packages.

When our code imports an external package, its dependency graph is augmented not only with the imported package but also with its set of transitive dependencies—that is, any other packages (and *their* dependencies) required by the packages that we import. As our projects grow larger in size, it becomes necessary to efficiently manage the versions of all our dependencies to ensure that changes in upstream transitive dependencies do not cause unexpected side effects (crashes, changes in behavior, and so on) to our own programs.

In this chapter, we will focus on the following topics:

- The importance of versioning for software
- Ways to apply semantic versioning for Go packages
- Strategies for managing the source code for multiversioned packages and tools that allow you to import a particular package version from your code
- The pros and cons of dependency vendoring and how it can be used to facilitate repeatable builds
- The most popular approaches and tools for vendoring Go packages

What's all the fuss about software versioning?

The idea of versioning is ingrained into everything around us. People all over the world are accustomed to using various forms of versioning on a daily basis. Note that I am not just talking about software here. The vast majority of physical products that you are using are associated with some sort of versioning scheme. Uses of versioning range from your computer's CPU to your mobile phone, and from the revision of the algorithm book on your bookshelf to your favorite superhero (or alternatively light-saber-wielding rebel) movie.

When we move to the realm of software, the concept of versioning becomes even more important. Nowadays, as more and more software engineers ascribe to the *release fast* mantra, having a sane versioning system in place makes it possible to do the following:

- Validate that a particular piece of software can be used as a safe drop-in replacement for an older piece of software that we are using as part of our production systems. This is especially important from a security standpoint, as *all* software, unless formally verified, may contain potential security bugs that can be discovered at any point in time—even weeks or years after it has been deployed to production. It is therefore of paramount importance for us to be able to mitigate such issues by upgrading to a newer release as soon as bug fixes become available.
- Pin down each dependency of our applications to a particular package version. This is a key prerequisite for setting up CI pipelines to implement the concept of repeatable builds. Having access to repeatable builds makes it possible to recompile, at any time, an exact copy of the software that a customer runs in production and use it as a reference when investigating bug reports.

In the following sections, we will delve into the details behind *semantic versioning*, a very popular approach for not only managing the version of your software packages but also for notifying the users that depend on them of upcoming and potentially breaking changes.

Semantic versioning

Semantic versioning [11] is a widely popular system for describing software versions in a way that makes it quite straightforward for the intended software users to figure out which versions are safe to upgrade to and which versions contain breaking API changes and therefore require development effort and time when upgrading.

Semantic versions are formatted as follows:
MAJOR.MINOR.PATCH

 Depending on the use case, additional suffixes may be optionally appended to indicate a prerelease (for example, alpha, beta, or RC (or release candidate)) or to convey other build-related information (for example, the Git SHA for the branch that is used to build a release or perhaps a timestamp for when the build artifacts were generated).

When working with Go packages, the three-component approach employed by semantic versioning makes it easy for package authors to let users of the package know what *type* of changes each release contains. For example, the PATCH field is incremented whenever a *backward-compatible bug fix* is applied to the code. Conversely, the MINOR field is incremented when *new functionality* gets added to a package, but, most importantly, only when this new functionality is added in a manner that ensures that the new version *remains backward compatible* with older package versions. Of course, as packages evolve over time, it is inevitable that at some point some breaking changes will have to be introduced. For instance, an existing function signature may need to be changed to support additional use cases. For those kinds of scenarios, the MAJOR component of the version string will need to be incremented.

Comparing semantic versions

If we are given two semantic versions, a.b.c and x.y.z, how can we tell which one is more recent? To compare two semantic versions, we need to compare each one of their individual components from left to right. Here is a short piece of code demonstrating how we can compare two semantic versions:

```go
// SemVer contains the major, minor, patch components of a semantic version
// string.
type SemVer [3]int

// GreaterThan returns true if the receiver version is greater than other.
func (sv SemVer) GreaterThan(other SemVer) bool {
    for i, v := range sv {
        if v != other[i] {
            return v > other[i]
        }
    }

    return false
}
```

Comparing or sorting semantic versions is quite an easy task for humans to perform, but nevertheless, as is evident in the preceding code snippet, it requires additional effort when performed by machines.

You have probably encountered this problem first hand if you have ever worked on makefile rules that check for the presence of a minimum version of a particular library or if you have ever attempted to sort a list of folders that follow this versioning scheme using the standard command-line tools. This is considered a caveat of semantic versioning compared to alternative versioning schemes that are either based on monotonically increasing build numbers or build dates in the YYYMMDD format.

Applying semantic versioning to Go packages

The semantic versioning definition that we discussed in the previous section left a few questions unanswered. To begin with, what should be the *initial* version number for a new package? What is more, as an external user of the package, how would we know when the package API has been stable enough for us to use it safely in our code?

There is no better way to answer these questions than with the help of a small example. Let's consider the following code snippet from an as *yet unreleased* package that deals with weather predictions:

```go
package weather

// Prediction describes a weather prediction.
type Prediction uint8

// The supported weather prediction types.
const (
    Sunny Prediction = iota
    Rain
    Overcast
    Snow
    Unknown
)

// predictAtCoords returns a weather prediction for the specified GPS
// coordinates.
func predictAtCoords(lat, long float64) (Prediction, error) { // ... }
```

Since we are talking about a brand new package, we need to decide on an *initial* version string. Given that the package is not exposing any public interface, we can start with *0.1.0* as our initial version number. The *0* value for the major version component serves as a warning to potential users of the package that it is still work in progress and the package implementation may frequently change in potentially breaking ways. In other words: *use the package at your own risk.*

After a few iterations and extensive refactoring of the package code (each time bumping the *minor* version of the package), we eventually reach version *0.9.0*. At this point, we decide that the package is safe to use *internally* on our production systems. To this end, we need to expose a *public API* so that our existing Go packages can interface with the new package. This is facilitated by a simple rename operation—change `predictAtCoords` to `PredictAtCoords` (and of course update all relevant unit tests), as shown in the following code block:

```
// PredictAtCoords returns a weather prediction for the specified GPS
coordinates.
func PredictAtCoords(lat, long float64) (Prediction, error) {
    // ...
}
```

Following a successful rollout to production, we should feel comfortable enough to make this package publicly available so other people can import and use it. The package is released as version *1.0.0* and it turns out to be a big hit in the weather-forecasting community!

That is, until one day, when a user of the package opens a GitHub issue with a bug: *passing a certain combination of lat/long parameters causes* `PredictAtCoords` *to panic.* We revisit the code, create a reproducer for the bug, and after a bit of digging around, we discover the root cause for the bug: the lack of proper checks allows a division by zero to occur. The fix is quite simple and does not alter the functionality of the package in any way, so we bump the *patch* version of the package and release *1.0.1*.

As more and more people start depending on our released package, we start receiving requests to add new features, for instance: to predict the weather for a location identified by a *plus code* [10]. To implement this new feature, we introduce a new public function to the package:

```
// PredictAtPlusCode the weather at the location specified by a plus code.
func PredictAtPlusCode(code string) (Prediction, error) {
    // ...
}
```

This change introduces new functionality to the package, but the package itself is still backward compatible with older versions. Therefore, we now need to bump the *minor* version component and release version *1.1.1* of the package. Similarly, we add functions for predicting the weather for a city or a specific address. After each addition, we make sure to bump the *minor* version of our package.

So far, so good. However, after a careful inspection of the code in our latest package version, we notice that the current implementation involves quite a bit of repetition—the public API consists of a set of functions that perform more or less the same task: predict the weather at a *location*. The only difference is that each function expects the location to be encoded in a particular way (that is, as GPS coordinates, a plus code, or an address).

In an attempt to simplify the package API and apply the **interface segregation principle (ISP)**, as we discussed in Chapter 2, *Best Practices for Writing Clean and Maintainable Go Code*, we decide to introduce a series of *breaking* API changes. To begin with, we define the `Locator` interface, which provides a necessary abstraction for converting locations into a set of GPS coordinates. Secondly, we replace the various `PredictAtXYZ` functions from the package with a new function called `Predict` that receives a `Locator` instance as its argument:

```
package weather

// Locator is implemented by objects that can represent a location as a
// pair of GPS coordinates.
type Locator interface {
    Coords() (float64, float64, error)
}

// Predict the weather at the specified location.
func Predict(loc Locator) (Prediction, error) {
    coords, err := loc.Coords()
    if err != nil {
        return Unknown, err
    }
    // ...
}
```

By refactoring `Predict`, as shown in the preceding code, we can now extract the various types that can be used to represent locations into their own standalone package, aptly called `location`:

```
package location

// GPSCoords holds a lat/long coordinate pair.
type GPSCoords [2]float64
```

```
// PlusCode encodes a location using a plus code.
type PlusCode string

// Address encapsulates the components of an address.
type Address struct {
    Street   string
    City     string
    PostCode string
    Country  string
}
```

Thanks to the magic of implicit interfaces, all we need to do to use these new types with the Predict function is to add methods that satisfy the Locator interface from the weather package:

```
func (g GPSCoords) Coords() (float64, float64, error) {
    return g[0], g[1], nil
}

func (pc PlusCode) Coords() (float64, float64, error) {
    // Decode plus code to gps coordinates...
}

func (a Address) Coords() (float64, float64, error) {
    // Use an external geocoding service to convert the address into a set
    // of GPS coordinates...
}
```

This change definitely improves the quality of the weather package, but at the cost of breaking backward compatibility. To indicate this to the users of the package, we bump the *major* version component and publish version *2.0.0* of the package.

By adopting semantic versioning for our packages, we not only allow package users to select which API version they want to work with, but also offer them the flexibility to upgrade to a newer package version at their own pace without any risk of breaking existing production systems.

Managing the source code for multiple package versions

One thing that may have struck you as odd about the previous section is the fact that while I keep going on about the *publishing* version x.y.z of the weather package, the section content itself is devoid of any information regarding the actual *process* involved in publishing a package.

At this point, you might also be asking yourself the question, *if we have released multiple major versions of a package, how do we manage the source code for each released version?* After all, as the package authors, we can opt to maintain and support several major or major/minor combinations of package versions in parallel and each version can potentially follow its own release cycle. For example, we can work on extending the API for the *2.x.x* line while still continuing to fix bugs or apply security patches to the *1.x.x* line. And how are the end users expected to import a particular version of a Go package?

To answer all these questions, we need to explore a few alternative approaches to versioning Go packages in depth.

Single repository with versioned folders

Using a single repository with versioned folders requires us to maintain the source code for all supported versions within a *single* repository. The simplest way to achieve this is to create a folder for each version at the root of the repository and copy all the version-specific files and subpackages inside.

Let's revisit the weather package example from the previous section. Let's assume that we use Git as our VCS and that we host our package on GitHub under the weather-as-a-service account in a repository called weather. The following flowchart illustrates how the folder layout would look using this approach:

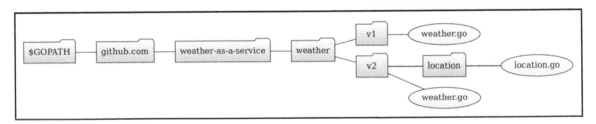

Figure 1: Managing multiple versions of a package in a single repository

It is important to point out that even though the `weather.go` files are located under the `v1` and `v2` folders, *both* of them declare a package named `weather`. This trick allows users of the package to explicitly select which package version they want to import and refer to its contents using the `weather` selector, as illustrated in the following code block:

```
import (
    "fmt"

    "github.com/weather-as-a-service/weather/v2"
    "github.com/weather-as-a-service/weather/v2/location"
)

func makePrediction() error{
    loc := location.PlusCode("9C3XGV00+")
    pred, err := weather.Predict(loc)
    if err != nil {
        return err
    }
    fmt.Printf("The weather prediction for London is: %v", pred)
}
```

This approach has a few benefits, both for package authors and for the intended end users of the package:

- The use of a single repository for all versions makes maintenance easier, as package authors can work on each version of the package in isolation.
- The repository always contains the latest release for each package version. The end users of the package can use a single command to get/update *all* versions of the package (for example, `go get -u github.com/weather-as-a-service/weather`).
- As the end user of the package, you have the option (although it is probably something you should probably avoid) to import and use *different* versions of the same package from within the same code base.

On the other hand, there are some caveats associated with this approach:

- Code duplication! Each versioned folder includes a full copy of the package implementation, which may also include one or more subpackages. This could prove to be a challenge for the package authors, especially if a security issue is identified whose fix requires patching the same code in different folders.
- As an end user of the package, how would you know whether a particular package utilizes this particular versioning scheme, or which versions are available to use? To answer these questions you would most likely need to visit the repository page on GitHub and examine the folder structure.

Single repository – multiple branches

A much better approach would be to still use a single repository but maintain a *different branch* (in Git terminology) for each major package version, extra feature, or development branches for ongoing work. If we were to apply this approach to the case of the weather package that we discussed before, our repository would normally contain the following branches:

- `v1`: This is the branch where the released *1.x.y* line of the weather package is located.
- `v2`: Another branch for the *2.x.y* release of the weather package.
- `develop`: Code in development branches is generally considered to be work in progress, and therefore unstable for use. Eventually, once the code stabilizes, it will be merged back into one or more of the stable release branches.

Similar to the versioned folder approach, the multibranch approach also ensures that the tip or head of each release branch contains the *latest* release version for a package; however, it is sometimes useful to be able to refer to an older semantic version of the package. A typical use case for this is repeatable builds, where we always want to compile against a specific version of the package and not the latest, albeit stable, version from a particular package line.

To satisfy the preceding requirement, we can exploit the VCS's capability to *tag* each release so we can easily locate it in the future without having to scan the commit history. I am using Git as an example here as it is my preferred VCS, but concepts such as tagging generalize to other VCS as well (tags in SVN, labels in Perforce, and so on).

This leads us to yet another question: if each version has its own branch, how do we import it from our code? If we are talking about a public package that is hosted on GitHub, the answer is that we need to use a redirect service such, as `gopkg.in` [7].

The gopkg.in service functions as a proxy for redirecting Go tools to the sources that correspond to a *specific* version of a Go package. The service achieves this by exposing a series of *versioned* URLs that, when accessed by go get, automatically resolve to a particular branch or tag within the repository where the package is hosted.

This convention not only yields cleaner and shorter package URLs, but more importantly, it also ensures that dependent packages can cleanly compile using the latest minor version of the packages they depend on, even if new major versions of those packages get released.

What's more, when the same URLs are accessed via a web browser, users are presented with a neat landing page that provides additional information regarding the purpose of the package and the commands needed to fetch or import it. The same page also contains links to the package sources and documentation.

For example, when you visit a gopkg.in URL for a particular package with your browser for the popular logging package called logrus, you will see a page that looks similar to the following screenshot. The left side of the page displays the import command that we need to use for the selected version of the package. The panel on the right side of the page states the available package versions (in this example: **v1** and **v0**) and the actual branch or tag that they resolve to:

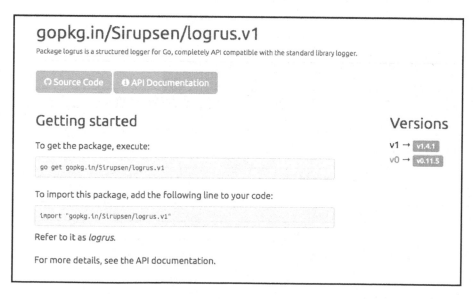

Figure 2: The gopkg.in page for the popular logrus package

Let's go back to the weather example from the previous section and update the imports to use `gopkg.in` URLs:

```
import (
    "fmt"

    "gopkg.in/weather-as-a-service/weather.v2"
    "gopkg.in/weather-as-a-service/weather.v2/location"
)
```

If we run `go get -u ...` within the folder where the preceding example lives, it will always pull the *latest v2* version of the weather package. You may be wondering how `gopkg.in` knows which one is the latest version and where that version lives. In order to correctly resolve a version request, `gopkg.in` first parses the list of available branches and tags for the project. Depending on the version selector suffix (the `.v2`, in this example), `gopkg.in` will always attempt to return the highest matching version of the package whose *major* version component matches the requested selector. This implies that the service is not only capable of working with the other versioning schemes we briefly mentioned before (for example, monotonically increasing build or version numbers, timestamps, and so on), but that it is also smart enough to parse and compare semantic versions of packages.

For example, let's assume that the weather package repository contains the following mix of tags and branches:

Name	Type	Notes
v1.0.10	Tag	
v1.1.9	Tag	
v1	Branch	Contents match v1.1.0 tag
v2.0	Tag	
v3~dev	Branch	Development branch for the upcoming v3

This is how `gopkg.in` would resolve the preceding imports depending on the value of the version selector suffix:

Selector	Resolves to
v1	v.1.1.9 (Tag)
v2	v2.0 (Tag)
v3	v3~dev (Branch)

To make a project compatible with the `gopkg.in` service, you need to make sure that either your branches or your tags match the expected patterns that `gopkg.in` looks for: `vx`, `vx.y`, `vx.y.z`, and so on. As the majority of the software engineering teams are quite opinionated when it comes to selecting a development flow (for example, Git flow versus GitHub flow) or branch naming conventions, my personal recommendation would be to stick to using tags for labeling package versions using the format that `gopkg.in` expects.

Vendoring – the good, the bad, and the ugly

The fact that services such as `gopkg.in` always redirect the `go get` tool to the *latest* available major version for a given version selector is, technically speaking, a show-stopper for engineering teams that endeavor to set up a development pipeline that guarantees repeatable builds. The typical CI pipeline will always pull both compile and test dependencies via a command such as `go get -t -u ...` prior to building the final output artifact. As a result, even if your code has not changed between builds, your service or application binary may be different because of changes in the dependencies that get pulled in.

However, what if I told you that there *is* actually a way to retain the benefits of lazy package resolution *and* at the same time have the flexibility to *pin down* package versions for each build? The mechanism that will assist us in this matter is called **vendoring**.

In the context of Go programming, we refer to vendoring as the *process* where **immutable** snapshots (also known as **vendored dependencies**) for all nodes in the import graph of a Go application get created. The vendored dependencies are used instead of the original imported packages whenever a Go application is compiled.

As we will see in the following sections, there are a few different approaches to creating dependency snapshots:

- Fork the repository that contains each imported dependency and update the import statements in the code base to point to the forked resources.
- Create a manifest that includes the current (that is, at the time a snapshot is made) commit identifiers (for example, Git SHAs) for each imported package and its transitive dependencies. The manifest, a small, human-readable YAML- or JSON-based file is generally committed to the VCS and used to fetch the appropriate versions of each dependency prior to invoking the compiler.

- Cache the imported dependencies locally (typically in a folder called `vendor`) and commit them together with the project files to the VCS. Contrary to the preceding approaches, local caching enables us to check out our project and immediately compile it without having to fetch any dependencies first.

Before we dive a bit deeper into each one of these approaches, let's take a few minutes to discuss the pros and cons of dependency vendoring.

Benefits of vendoring dependencies

First and foremost, the key promise of vendoring is nothing other than the capability to run reproducible builds. Many customers, especially larger corporations, tend to stick to stable or LTS releases for the software they deploy and forego upgrading their systems unless it's absolutely necessary. Being able to check out the exact software version that a customer uses and generate a bit-for-bit identical binary for use in a test environment is an invaluable tool for any field engineer attempting to diagnose and reproduce bugs that the customers are facing.

Another benefit of vendoring is that it serves as a safety net in case an upstream dependency suddenly disappears from the place where it is hosted (for example, a GitHub or GitLab repository), thereby breaking builds for software that depends on it. If you are thinking that this is a highly unlikely scenario, let me take you back to 2016 and share an interesting engineering horror story from the world of Node.js!

You may have heard of the now-infamous *left-pad* package. In case you haven't, it is just a single-function package that, as you can probably figure out by its name, provides a function to pad a string up to a specific length with a specific character. Nothing really scary so far... except that this small package was a direct dependency of over 500 packages, which in turn were transient dependencies of several other packages, and so on. Everything went fine until one day, the left-pad package maintainer received a cease-and-desist letter for one of his other packages and decided, as a form of protest, to take down *all* of his packages, including left-pad.

Now, picture the chaos that ensued as peoples' CI builds started breaking one after the other. But engineering teams that had been judiciously vendoring their dependencies were not affected by this issue at all.

Is vendoring always a good idea?

The previous section went into great effort to extol the virtues of vendoring. But is vendoring the panacea for all dependency management problems? This section attempts to dig a bit deeper into some of the caveats associated with vendoring.

One common problem across engineering teams is that in spite of the fact that engineers are keen on vendoring their dependencies, they often *forget* to periodically refresh them. As I argued in a previous section, all code can contain potential security bugs. It is therefore likely that some security bugs (perhaps from a transitive dependency of an imported package) will eventually end up in production.

Security-related or not, when bugs are reported to the package maintainers, a fix is usually promptly released and the package version is incremented accordingly (that is, if a package is using semantic versioning). As large-scale projects tend to import a large volume of packages, it is not feasible to monitor each imported package's repository for security fixes. Even if this was possible, we couldn't realistically do this for their transitive dependencies. As a result, production code can remain unpatched for a long time even though the affected upstream packages have already been patched.

Strategies and tools for vendoring dependencies

Initially, Go had no support for vendoring packages. This made sense at the time, as Google, the primary user of Go, would host all of their package dependencies in a single repository (commonly referred to as a mono-repo).

However, as the Go community began growing and more and more companies began porting their code bases to Go, dependency management became an issue. With the release of Go 1.5, the Go team added experimental support for *vendoring folders*. Users could enable this feature by defining an environment variable named GO15VENDOREXPERIMENT.

When this feature is enabled, each time the Go compiler attempts to resolve an import, it will *first* check whether the imported package exists inside the vendor folder and use it if found; otherwise, it will proceed, as usual, to scan each entry in the $GOPATH looking for the package.

As soon as this functionality became available, multiple third parties spearheaded initiatives to produce tools that took advantage of it. The brief, but not exhaustive, list of now deprecated tools for dealing with dependencies includes godep [5], govendor [9], glide [3], and gvt [4].

Nowadays, tooling around vendoring is much more streamlined. The following sections explore the recommended approaches to vendoring Go packages at the time of writing:

- The *dep* tool
- *Go modules*
- Manual forking of dependencies

The dep tool

The Go team—being well aware that having several competing tools for managing dependencies could result in the fragmentation of the Go ecosystem and encumber the growth of the Go community—decided to assemble a committee and produce an official specification document detailing the way to move forward regarding Go package dependency management. The dep tool [2] is the first tool that conforms to the published specification. It began its life some time around 2017 as an *official experiment* that was made available to users who upgraded to Go 1.9.

The dep tool provides precompiled binaries for various operating systems; however, it is probably easier to build it from the source by running go get -u github.com/golang/dep/cmd/dep. The first time that you want to use the dep tool for one of your projects, you need to run dep init within the root folder of the project to initialize the dep tool's state. Unless your import graph is shallow and small in size, this step will take a bit of time, as dep does the following:

- Identifies all imported packages, their transitive dependencies, and whether or not they also use dep.
- Selects the highest possible version for each node in the dependency graph.
- Downloads the selected packages to the vendor folder that lives in the project's root folder. Dep will additionally cache the downloaded packages locally at $GOPATH/pkg/dep/sources to speed up dependency lookups for other projects that might also be using dep.

If *none* of the dependencies uses dep, then the selected version is simply the *current* version of each dependency as it appears in $GOPATH. Things get a bit more interesting when some (or all) of the imported dependencies also use dep. In that case, dep treats the versions requested by each dep-enabled package as constraints that are then fed into the constraint solver engine that is bundled with the dep tool.

Constraint solver engines, such as the one used by the dep tool, transform the list of input constraints into a Boolean **satisfiability problem (SAT)** and then attempt to identify a solution, if one exists. SAT problems are typically represented as complex Boolean expressions; the solver's job is to find the right combination of values for the expression variables so that the expression evaluates to TRUE.

For example, given the expression ((A and B) or C) and not D, here is a subset of the total solutions that a SAT could suggest:

Solution	A	B	C	D
1	TRUE	TRUE	FALSE	FALSE
2	FALSE	FALSE	TRUE	FALSE
3	TRUE	FALSE	TRUE	FALSE

SAT solving is one of the first problems that have been proven to be NP-complete [11]. Over the course of the years, several algorithms have been proposed that can scale to larger SAT problems and yield solutions in a reasonable amount of time. The particular SAT solver implementation used by the dep tool is based on a variant of the **conflict-driven clause learning (CDCL)** algorithm [12] that has been tweaked to work for the Go package management use case. If all this has piqued your interest, you can take a look at its implementation, which is in the github.com/golang/dep/gps package.

The output of the dep constraints solver is the *highest possible supported* version across *all* dependencies. The dep tool creates two text-based files in the project's root folder that the user *must* commit to their VCS: Gopkg.toml and Gopkg.lock. To speed up CI builds, users may also *optionally* commit the populated vendor folder to version control. Alternatively, assuming that both Gopkg.toml and Gopkg.lock are available, a prebuild hook can populate the vendor folder on the fly by running dep ensure -vendor-only.

The Gopkg.toml file

The `Gopkg.toml` file serves as a manifest for controlling the dep tool's behavior. The `dep init` invocation will analyze the import graph of the project and produce a `Gopkg.toml` file with an initial set of constraints. From that point on, whenever a constraint needs to be updated (usually to bump the minimum supported version), users need to *manually* modify the generated `Gopkg.toml` file.

So what does the content of a `Gopkg.toml` file look like? `Gopkg.toml` files are composed of a list of blocks or stanzas. Each stanza contains one of the dep-supported rule types. The most frequently used rule types are as follows:

- **Constraints**, which specify the range of compatible dependency versions
- **Overrides**, which can force a particular package version when the dep tool cannot automatically find a version that satisfies the aggregated set of constraints specified by multiple `Gopkg.toml` files

For the full list of supported rule types that the dep tool recognizes, you can refer to the `Gopkg.toml` format specification document [8]. The following example defines a constraint that instructs go dep to fetch the package sources from the `master` branch of the package's GitHub repository:

```
[[constraint]]
  name = "github.com/sirupsen/logrus"
  branch = "master"
```

Alternatively, instead of `branch`, a constraint rule can include one of the following two keywords: `revision` or `version`.

The `revision` keyword allows a package dependency to be pinned down to a particular commit identifier (for example, a Git SHA). It exists for compatibility purposes, and dep users are strongly encouraged to avoid using it unless there is no better way to describe a version.

On the other hand, the version keyword is much more versatile in that it allows us to target a specific VCS tag or semantic version range. The following table lists the operators that dep understands when processing version-based constraints. If the version string *does not* contain an operator, the dep tool will work as if the caret (^) operator was used. For example, dep would interpret version 1.2.5 as if the following constraint had been specified instead: >= 1.2.5 and < 1.3.

Operator	Description	Example	Constraint interpretation
=	Equals	"=1.2.4"	Select version 1.2.4
!=	Not equal	"!=0.1"	Exclude version 0.1
>	Greater than	">1.2"	Versions newer than 1.3.0
<	Less than	"<2.0"	Versions older than 2.0.0
-	Literal range	"1.2-1.4"	Versions >= 1.2 and <= 1.4
~	Minor range	"~1.2.5"	Versions >= 1.2.5 and < 1.3
^	Major range	"~1.2.5"	Versions >= 1.2.5 and < ?

One other quite helpful keyword that you may encounter when working with Gopkg.toml files is the source keyword. The default behavior of the dep tool is to fetch package sources from the repository whose name matches the package name specified by the constraint.

There are some cases, however, where we may want to pull the package from a different location. One scenario where this can happen is if we have forked the imported package, pushed some experimental changes, and want to try them out in a code base that imports the original package. To demonstrate this, let's edit the Gopkg.toml file from the preceding example and have it pull the master branch from github.com/achilleasa/logrus instead of github.com/sirupsen/logrus:

```
[[constraint]]
  name = "github.com/sirupsen/logrus"
  branch = "master"

  # Pull the package sources from this alternative repository
  source = "github.com/achilleasa/logrus"
```

As we mentioned at the beginning of the section, the Gopkg.toml file is only a manifest that users can change at will. For the changes to actually take effect, we need to run dep ensure to do the following:

- Scan the code for any new dependencies
- Invoke the constraints solver to calculate the required version for each dependency

- Figure out which of the packages in the `vendor` folder are stale and update them
- Update the `Gopkg.lock` file

The Gopkg.lock file

The second file that gets generated by the dep tool when running either `dep init` or `dep ensure` is called `Gopkg.lock`. As you can probably tell by its extension, it is something that is not meant to be modified by end users.

The `Gopkg.lock` file stores a textual representation of the dep tool's constraint solver output. More specifically, it includes the complete list of dependencies, both direct and transient, that are required for compiling the project source code. Each dependency is pinned down to the particular commit identifier (for example, a Git SHA) that, according to the solver, satisfies all constraints that were supplied to it by the dep tool.

By committing the `Gopkg.lock` file to the VCS, the dep support in Go 1.9+ guarantees that we can produce repeatable builds, provided, of course, that all referenced dependencies remain available.

Go modules – the way forward

One limitation of the dep tool is that it does not let us use multiple major versions of a package in our projects, as each path to an imported package must be unique. The following diagram illustrates a simple scenario where packages **A** and **B** depend on the same version of package **C**:

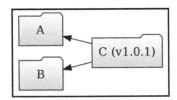

Figure 3: Two packages importing the same version of the C package

Let's say now that we want to test drive *v2.0.0*, the new major version of the **C** package. The point here is to *gradually update* the packages importing **C** to import the new major version in order to assess that everything works as expected. So we update the `Gopkg.toml` file in **B** to reference the new major version of **C**. Our dependency tree now looks as follows:

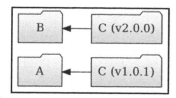

Figure 4: Each package imports a different version of the C package

This change causes no problems for packages **A** and **B** as their import graphs are disjointed; each package references a different version of **C**. Then, we decide to introduce a new package, say **D**, into the picture, which imports *both* **A** and **B** (as shown in the following figure). Now we have a problem! As both packages cannot use the *same* import path, the Go compiler will now bail out with an error when we try to build **D**:

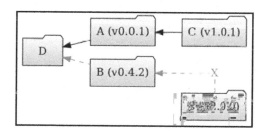

Figure 5: Package D imports both A and B, which depend on different major versions of C. This causes a conflict and prevents us from building D

The only way to make the preceding use case work with the dep tool is to change the constraints (`Copkg.toml`) file for *all* packages (**A** and **B** in this case) to depend on *v2.0.0* of package **C**. It goes without saying that this is not a solution that can scale to projects that import a large number of packages. With that in mind, the Go team led an initiative to come up with an official vendoring solution that could support scenarios such as the preceding one.

Go modules were introduced as an experimental feature in Go 1.11 that users could enable via the GO111MODULE environment variable (for example, export GO111MODULE=on). At the time of writing, the current Go version is 1.12.5, and Go modules are expected to be finalized just in time for the release of Go 1.13. The major difference of Go modules compared to the dep tool are as follows:

- Go modules fully integrate with the various commands, such as go get, go build, and go test.
- While the dep tool selects the *highest* common version for a package, Go modules select the *minimum* viable version.

- Go modules support multiversioned dependencies.
- Go modules do away with the `vendor` folder, which is used by the dep tool. For backward-compatibility purposes, Go modules come with an extra command to populate the `vendor` folder: `go mod vendor`.

The following simple example uses the popular `go-yaml` package to read a YAML stream from the standard input and output it as a Go map:

```
package main

import (
    "fmt"
    "os"

    "github.com/go-yaml/yaml"
)

func main() {
    var data map[string]interface{}
    if err := yaml.NewDecoder(os.Stdin).Decode(&data); err == nil {
        fmt.Printf("%v\n", data)
    }
}
```

To begin using Go modules, we first need to declare a new Go module by running `go mod init parser` in the folder where the preceding example is located. This will generate a file called `go.mod`. Its initial contents look pretty boring:

```
module parser

go 1.12
```

The real magic happens when we try to run a command such as `go build`:

```
$ go build
go: finding github.com/go-yaml/yaml v2.1.0+incompatible
go: downloading github.com/go-yaml/yaml v2.1.0+incompatible
go: extracting github.com/go-yaml/yaml v2.1.0+incompatible
```

As you can see, Go realized that we needed to fetch a new dependency, so it tried to work out the *current* version of the `go-yaml` package and resolved it to *v2.1.0*. It then proceeded to download the package and cache it locally under `$GOPATH/pkg/mod`.

If you list the contents of the project's folder, you will notice a new file called `go.sum`. This file stores the cryptographic hashes of the dependencies that have been downloaded and serves as a safeguard for ensuring that the contents of the packages have not been modified between builds (that is, a package maintainer force-pushed some changes, overwriting the previous version); a very useful feature when aiming for repeatable builds.

The `go.mod` and `go.sum` files serve the same purpose as the `Gopkg.toml` and `Gopkg.lock` files used by the dep tool, and they also need to be committed to your version control system.

Whenever a new dependency gets added, a line is appended to the `go.mod` file. In this case, the added line reads `require github.com/go-yaml/yaml v2.1.0+incompatible`. Each `require` line in the `go.mod` file defines the *minimum* supported version for a particular dependency. So, from our module's perspective, `v2.1.0` of the `go-yaml/yaml` package is the *minimum* version requirement for building the module. Even if a newer version is available, Go will *always* use this particular version unless we run one of the following commands:

- `go get -u`: To upgrade to the most recent minor or patch release
- `go get -u=patch`: To upgrade to the most recent patch release
- `go get package-name@version`: To force the specified version for the package

Now that we have a basic understanding of how Go modules work, let's revisit our initial use case: how can we use two different major versions of the same package inside our code base? As I mentioned before, Go import paths must be unique; that's something that is set in stone and cannot be overridden.

The `+incompatible` suffix in the `require` line indicates that while this package defines a valid semantic version, it hasn't actively opted in to using Go modules by defining its own `go.mod` file. If, however, a new version appeared in the future (say, v4) that did provide a `go.mod` file, Go modules would allow us to import it via a mechanism referred to as *semantic import versioning*. To put it in layman's terms, semantic import paths are just regular import paths that also carry an additional *version suffix*. The suffix addition creates a unique path for the package and effectively allows us to import and use multiple versions of the package even within the same file:

```
import (
    "github.com/go-yaml/yaml" // V2.1.0
    v4 "github.com/go-yaml/yaml/v4" // The V4 version of the package.
)
```

That concludes our short tour of Go modules. A deep dive into all operations and patterns supported by the Go modules extension is outside of the scope of this book; however, if you are interested in learning more about using Go modules, you can find a great amount of information by browsing the relevant articles on the Golang blog [6].

Fork packages

With the dep tool and Go modules at our disposal, why would we ever need to manually fork any of the packages we depend on? Before we answer this question, let me first elaborate on how this process works.

Firstly, we need to fork the dependency we are interested in. If the package sources are available on a platform such as GitHub, GitLab, or BitBucket, then forking the package is as simple as visiting the repository page and clicking a button (see the following screenshot); otherwise, we would need to rely on the functionality provided by our preferred VCS to persist a copy of the dependency to a location under our control:

Figure 6: Forking a package repository on a platform such as GitHub, GitLab, or BitBucket is as simple as clicking a button

After forking the repo, we would need to scan through the code base and replace the imports for the original package to point to our forked version. Of course, a much better alternative would be to use the dep tool's provided escape hatch for overriding the source for a package dependency. In the latter case, we wouldn't need to modify any of the import statements in our code.

That brings us back to the original question: why fork in the first place? When working for companies that process sensitive data, such as the ones that operate in the fintech or healthcare domains, it is quite common to have an in-house security team that must audit each imported dependency for potential security flaws before the engineering teams are allowed to use it in their code.

Performing a full security audit on a package is quite a lengthy process; it stands to reason that auditing each package from scratch each time a new release becomes available is neither feasible nor cost-effective. As a result, security teams seek to amortize the initial audit cost by forking packages, performing a full audit, and then vet and cherry-pick any upstream changes.

Summary

In this chapter, we discussed the reasons that necessitate the use of versioning for not only the packages that our code imports, but also the code itself that we, as software engineers, author. We then defined the concept of semantic versioning and the circumstances where each component of a semantic version needs to be incremented.

The meat of the chapter dealt with the concepts of vendoring as the primary mechanism for ensuring repeatable builds for our projects. After elaborating on the pros and cons of vendoring as a process, we examined the current state of vendoring in the Go ecosystem and provided a brief tour of the state-of-the-art tools (*dep* and *Go modules*) that engineers should use to manage their package dependencies.

Of course, as our code base evolves and the version requirements for our imports change over time, it is likely that, at some point, a newer version of one of the packages we depend on will break our code. Obviously, we want to be able to catch such regressions as early as possible. One way to achieve this, and the central theme of the next chapter, is to have a solid testing infrastructure in place.

Questions

1. Why is software versioning important?
2. What does a semantic version look like and when are its individual components incremented?
3. Which component of a package's semantic version would you increment in the following cases?
    1. A new API is introduced.
    2. An existing API is modified and a new, *required* parameter is added to it.
    3. A fix for a security bug is committed.
4. Name some alternative versioning schemes that we could use besides semantic versioning.
5. What are the pros and cons of vendoring?
6. Name some of the differences between the dep tool and Go modules.

Further reading

1. Cook, Stephen A., 'The Complexity of Theorem-proving Procedures', *Proceedings of the Third Annual ACM Symposium on Theory of Computing*, STOC '71. New York, NY, USA, ACM, 1971, S. 151–8

2. dep: a dependency management tool for Go: `https://github.com/golang/dep`

3. glide: `https://github.com/Masterminds/glide`

4. gvt: `https://github.com/FiloSottile/gvt`

5. godep: `https://github.com/tools/godep`

6. Golang blog: using Go modules: `https://blog.golang.org/using-go-modules`

7. `Gopkg.in`: stable APIs for the Go language: `https://labix.org/gopkg.in`

8. `Gopkg.toml` format specification: `https://golang.github.io/dep/docs/Gopkg.toml.html`

9. govendor: `https://github.com/kardianos/govendor`

10. Plus codes: short codes for locations, for places that don't have their own street address: `https://plus.codes/`

11. Semantic versioning 2.0.0: `https://semver.org/`

12. Silva, João P. Marques; Lynce, Inês; Malik, Sharad, Biere, A.; Heule, M. ; Maaren, H. van; Walsh, T. (Hrsg.), 'Conflict-Driven Clause Learning SAT Solvers', *Handbook of Satisfiability, Frontiers in Artificial Intelligence and Applications*, Bd. 185 : IOS Press, 2009, ISBN 978-1-58603-929-5 (`https://www.worldcat.org/title/handbook-of-satisfiability/oclc/840409693`), S. 131–53

The Art of Testing

4

"*Program testing can be used to show the presence of bugs, but never to show their absence!*"

- Edsger Dijkstra

Software systems are destined to grow and evolve over time. Open or closed source software projects have one thing in common: their *complexity* seems to follow an upward curve as the number of engineers working on the code base increases. To this end, having a comprehensive set of tests for the code base is of paramount importance. This chapter performs a deep dive into the different types of testing that can be applied to Go projects.

The following topics will be covered in this chapter:

- Identifying the differences between high-level primitives such as stubs, mocks, spies, and fake objects that you can use while writing unit tests as substitutes for objects that are used inside the code under test
- Comparing black-box and white-box testing: what's the difference and why both are needed for writing comprehensive test suites
- Differences between integration and functional (end-to-end) testing
- Advanced test concepts: smoke tests, and one of my personal favorites – chaos tests!
- Tips and tricks for writing clean tests in Go and pitfalls that you need to avoid

Technical requirements

The full code for the topics discussed within this chapter have been published to this book's GitHub repository under the `Chapter04` folder.

You can access this book's GitHub repository by going to `https://github.com/PacktPublishing/Hands-On-Software-Engineering-with-Golang`.

To get you up and running as quickly as possible, each example project includes a makefile that defines the following set of targets:

Makefile target	Description
deps	Install any required dependencies
test	Run all the tests and report coverage
lint	Check for lint errors

As with all the chapters in this book, you will need a fairly recent version of Go, which you can download at `https://golang.org/dl/`.

Unit testing

By definition, a unit is the smallest possible bit of code that we can test. In the context of Go programming, this would typically be a *single function*. However, according to the SOLID design principles that we explored in the previous chapters, each *Go package* could also be construed as an independent unit and tested as such.

 The term *unit testing* refers to the process of testing each *unit* of an application in *isolation* to verify that its behavior conforms to a particular set of specifications.

In this section, we will dive into the different methodologies of unit testing at our disposal (black- versus white-box testing). We will also examine strategies for making our code easier to unit test and cover the built-in Go testing packages, as well as third-party packages, that are designed to make writing tests more streamlined.

Mocks, stubs, fakes, and spies – commonalities and differences

Before digging deeper into the concepts behind unit testing, we need to discuss and disambiguate some of the terms that we will be using in the upcoming sections. While these terms have been out there for years, software engineers tend to occasionally conflate them when writing tests. A great example of such confusion becomes evident when you hear engineers use the terms *mock* and *stub* interchangeably.

To establish some common ground for a fruitful discussion and to clear any confusion around this terminology, let's examine the definition of each term, as outlined by Gerard Meszaros [5] in his *XUnit Test Patterns: Refactoring Test Code* book on test patterns.

Stubs and spies!

A **stub** is the simplest test pattern that we can use in our tests. Stubs typically implement a particular interface and don't contain any real logic; they just provide fixed answers to calls that are performed through the course of a test.

Let's dissect a short code example that illustrates how we can effectively use the concept of stubs for our tests. The Chapter04/captcha package implements the verification logic behind a CAPTCHA test.

CAPTCHA is a fairly straightforward way to determine whether a system is interacting with a human user or another program. This is achieved by displaying a random, often noisy, image containing a distorted sequence of letters and numbers and then prompting the user to type the text content of the image.

As a big fan of the SOLID principles, I opted to define two interfaces, `Challenger` and `Prompter`, to abstract the CAPTCHA image generation and the user-prompting implementation. After all, there is a plethora of different approaches out there for generating CAPTCHA images: we could pick a random image from a fixed set of images, generate them using a neural network, or perhaps even call out to a third-party image generation service. The same could be said about the way we actually prompt our users for an answer. This is how the two interfaces are defined:

```
// Challenger is implemented by objects that can generate CAPTCHA image
// challenges.
type Challenger interface {
    Challenge() (img image.Image, imgText string)
}

// Prompter is implemented by objects that display a CAPTCHA image to the
// user, ask them to type their contents and return back their response.
type Prompter interface {
    Prompt(img image.Image) string
}
```

At the end of the day, the actual business logic doesn't really care how the CAPTCHA images or the users' answers were obtained. All we need to do is fetch a challenge, prompt the user, and then perform a simple string comparison operation, as follows:

```
func ChallengeUser(c Challenger, p Prompter) bool {
    img, expAnswer := c.Challenge()
    userAnswer := p.Prompt(img)

    if subtle.ConstantTimeEq(int32(len(expAnswer)), int32(len(userAnswer)))
      == 0 {
        return false
    }

    return subtle.ConstantTimeCompare([]byte(userAnswer),
[]byte(expAnswer)) == 1
}
```

One interesting, at least in my opinion, aspect of the preceding code is that it uses constant-time string comparisons instead of using the built-in equality operator for comparing the expected answer and the user's response.

Constant-time comparison checks are a common pattern in security-related code as it prevents information leaks, which can be exploited by adversaries to perform a timing side-channel attack. When executing a timing attack, the attacker provides variable-length inputs to a system and then employs statistical analysis to collect additional information about the system's implementation based on the time it takes to execute a particular action.

Imagine if, in the preceding CAPTCHA scenario we had used a simple string comparison that essentially compares each character and returns false on the *first mismatch*. Here's how an attacker could slowly brute-force the answer via a timing attack:

- Start by providing answers following the $a pattern and measuring the time it takes to get a response. The $ symbol is a placeholder for all possible alphanumeric characters. In essence, we try combinations such as aa, ba, and so on.
- Once we have identified an operation that takes *longer than the rest*, we can assume that that particular value of $ (say, 4) is the expected first character of the CAPTCHA answer! The reason this takes longer is that the string comparison code matched the first character and then tried matching the next character instead of immediately returning it, like it would if there was a mismatch.
- Continue the same process of providing answers but this time using the 4$a pattern and keep extending the pattern until the expected CAPTCHA answer can be recovered.

In order to test the `ChallengeUser` function, we need to create a stub for each of its arguments. This would provide us with complete control over the inputs to the comparison business logic. Here's what the stubs might look like:

```
type stubChallenger string

func (c stubChallenger) Challenge() (image.Image, string) {
    return image.NewRGBA(image.Rect(0, 0, 100, 100)), string(c)
}
type stubPrompter string

func (p stubPrompter) Prompt(_ image.Image) string {
    return string(p)
}
```

Pretty simple, right? As you can see, the stubs are devoid of any logic; they just return a canned answer. With the two stubs in place, we can write two test functions that exercise the match/non-match code paths:

```
func TestChallengeUserSuccess(t *testing.T) {
    got := captcha.ChallengeUser(stubChallenger("42"), stubPrompter("42"))
    if got != true {
        t.Fatal("expected ChallengeUser to return true")
    }
}

func TestChallengeUserFail(t *testing.T) {
    got := captcha.ChallengeUser(stubChallenger("lorem ipsum"),
stubPrompter("42"))
    if got != false {
        t.Fatal("expected ChallengeUser to return false")
    }
}
```

Now that we have a general understanding of how stubs work, let's look at another useful test pattern: spies! A **spy** is nothing more than a stub that keeps a detailed log of all the methods that are invoked on it. For each method invocation, the spy records the arguments that were provided by the caller and makes them available for inspection by the test code.

Surely, when it comes to Go, the most popular spy implementation is the venerable `ResponseRecorder` type, which is provided by the `net/http/httptest` package. `ResponseRecorder` implements the `http.ResponseWriter` interface and can be used for testing HTTP request handling code without the need to spin up an actual HTTP server. However, HTTP server testing is not that interesting; let's take a look at a slightly more engaging example.

The `Chapter04/chat` package contains a simple chatroom implementation that is perfect for applying the spy test pattern. The following is the definition of the `Room` type and its constructor:

```
// Publisher is implemented by objects that can send a message to a user.
type Publisher interface {
    Publish(userID, message string) error
}

type Room struct {
    pub   Publisher
    mu    sync.RWMutex
    users []string
}

// NewRoom creates a new chat_root instance that used pub to broadcast
```

```
// messages.
func NewRoom(pub Publisher) *Room {
    return &Room{pub: pub}
}
```

As you can see, Room contains a Publisher instance that gets initialized by the value that's passed to the NewRoom constructor. The other interesting public methods that are exposed by the Room type (not shown here but available in this book's GitHub repo) are AddUser and Broadcast. The first method adds new users to the room, while the latter can be used to broadcast a particular message to all the users currently in the room.

Before we write our actual testing code, let's create a spy instance that implements the Publisher interface and records any published messages:

```
type entry struct {
    user     string
    message  string
}

type spyPublisher struct {
    published []entry
}

func (p *spyPublisher) Publish(user, message string) error {
    p.published = append(p.published, entry{user: user, message: message})
    return nil
}
```

In the preceding spy implementation, each time the Publish method is invoked, the stub will append a {user, message} tuple to the published slice. With our spy ready to be used, writing the actual test is a piece of cake:

```
func TestChatRoomBroadcast(t *testing.T) {
    pub := new(spyPublisher)
    room := chat.NewRoom(pub)
    room.AddUser("bob")
    room.AddUser("alice")
    _ = room.Broadcast("hi")
    exp := []entry{
        {user: "bob", message: "hi"},
        {user: "alice", message: "hi"},
    }
    if got := pub.published; !reflect.DeepEqual(got, exp) {
        t.Fatalf("expected the following messages:\n%#+v\ngot:\n%#+v", exp,
got)
    }
}
```

This test scenario involves creating a new room, adding some users to it, and broadcasting a message to everyone who has joined the room. The test runner's task is to verify that the call to `Broadcast` did in fact broadcast the message to all the users. We can achieve this by examining the list of messages that have been recorded by our injected spy.

Mocks

You can think of **mocks** as stubs on steroids! Contrary to the fixed behavior exhibited by stubs, mocks allow us to specify, in a *declarative* way, not only the list of calls that the mock is expected to receive but also their order and expected argument values. In addition, mocks allow us to specify different return values for each method invocation, depending on the argument tuple provided by the method caller.

All things considered, mocks are a very powerful primitive at our disposal for writing advanced tests. However, building mocks from scratch for every single object we want to substitute as part of our tests is quite a tedious task. This is why it's often better to use an external tool and code generation to automate the creation of the mocks that are needed for our tests.

Introducing gomock

In this section, we will be introducing `gomock` [4], a very popular mocking framework for Go that leverages reflection and code generation to automatically create mocks based on Go interface definitions.

The framework and its supporting tools can be installed by running the following commands:

```
$ go get github.com/golang/mock/gomock
$ go install github.com/golang/mock/mockgen
```

The `mockgen` tool is responsible for analyzing either individual Go files or entire packages and generating mocks for all (or specific) interfaces that are defined within them. It supports two modes of operation:

- **Source code scanning**: We pass a Gi file to `mockgen`, which is then parsed in order to detect interface definitions.
- **Reflection-assisted mode**: We pass a package and a list of interfaces to `mockgen`. The tool uses the Go reflection package to analyze the structure of each interface.

gomock provides a simple and concise API for specifying the expected behavior of mock instances that are created via the mockgen tool. To access this API, you need to create a new instance of the mock and invoke its oddly-cased EXPECT method. EXPECT returns a special object (a *recorder*, in gomock terminology) that provides the means for us to declare the behavior of the method calls that are performed against the mock.

To register a new expectation, we need to do the following:

1. Declare the name of the method that we expect to be called, along with its arguments.
2. Specify the return value (or values) that the mock should return to the caller when it invokes the method with the specified set of arguments.
3. Optionally, we need to specify the number of times that the caller is expected to invoke the method.

To further streamline the creation of tests, mockgen populates the returned recorder instances with methods whose names match the interfaces that we are trying to mock. All we need to do is invoke those methods on the recorder object and specify the arguments that the mock expects to receive from the caller as a variadic list of interface{} values. When defining the expected set of arguments, you basically have two options:

- Specify a value whose *type* matches the one from the method signature (for example, foo if the argument is of the string type). gomock will only match a call to an expectation if the input argument, *value*, is *strictly equal* to the value that's specified as part of the expectation.
- Provide a value that implements the gomock.Matcher interface. In this case, gomock will delegate the comparison to the matcher itself. This powerful feature gives us the flexibility to model any custom test predicate that we can think of. gomock already defines a few handy built-in matchers that we can use in our tests: Any, AssignableToTypeOf, Nil, and Not.

After specifying the expected method call and its arguments, gomock will return an expectation object that provides auxiliary methods so that we can configure the expected behavior further. For instance, we can use the expectation object's Return method to define the set of values to be returned to the caller once the expectation is matched. It is also important to note that unless we *explicitly* specify the expected number of calls to the mocked method, gomock will assume that the method can only be invoked *once* and will trigger a test failure if the method is not invoked at all or is invoked multiple times. If you require more fine-grained control over the number of expected invocations, the returned expectation object provides the following set of helper methods: Times, MinTimes, and MaxTimes.

In the next two sections, we will analyze an example project and go through all the individual steps for writing a complete, mock-based unit test for it.

Exploring the details of the project we want to write tests for

For the purpose of demonstrating the creation and use of mocks in our code, we will be working with the example code from the Chapter04/dependency package. This package defines a Collector type whose purpose is to assemble a set of direct and indirect (transitive) dependencies for a given project ID. To make things a bit more interesting, let's assume that each dependency can belong to one of the following two categories:

- A resource that we need to include (for example, an image file) or reserve (for example, a block of memory or an amount of disk space)
- Another project with its *own set of dependencies*

To obtain the list of *direct* dependencies and their respective types, the Collector dependency will be performing a series of calls to an external service. To ensure that the implementation lends itself to easier testing, we will not be working with a concrete client instance for the external service. Instead, we will define an interface with the set of required methods for accessing the service and have our test code inject a mock that satisfies that interface. Consider the following definition for the API interface:

```
type API interface {
    // ListDependencies returns the list of direct dependency IDs for a
    // particular project ID or an error if a non-project ID argument is
    // provided.
    ListDependencies(projectID string) ([]string, error)

    // DependencyType returns the type of a particular dependency.
    DependencyType(dependencyID string) (DepType, error)
}
```

To create a new Collector instance, we need to invoke the NewCollector constructor (not shown) and provide an API instance as an argument. Then, the *unique* set of dependencies for a particular project ID can be obtained via a call to the AllDependencies method. It's a pretty short method whose full implementation is as follows:

```
func (c *Collector) AllDependencies(projectID string) ([]string, error) {
    ctx := newDepContext(projectID)
    for ctx.HasUncheckedDeps() {
        projectID = ctx.NextUncheckedDep()
        projectDeps, err := c.api.ListDependencies(projectID)
        if err != nil {
```

```
                return nil, xerrors.Errorf("unable to list dependencies for
project %q: %w", projectID, err)
            }
            if err = c.scanProjectDependencies(ctx, projectDeps); err != nil {
                return nil, err
            }
        }
    }
    return ctx.depList, nil
}
```

The preceding block of code is nothing more than a **breadth-first search** (**BFS**) algorithm in disguise! The `ctx` variable stores an auxiliary structure that contains the following:

- *A queue* whose entries correspond to the set of dependencies (resources or projects) that we haven't visited yet. As we visit the nodes of the project dependency graph, any newly discovered dependencies will be appended to the tail of the queue so that they can be visited in a future search loop iteration.
- The unique set of discovered dependency IDs that are returned to the caller once all the entries in the queue have been processed.

To seed the search, initially, we populate the queue with the `projectID` value that was passed in as an argument to the method. With each loop iteration, we dequeue an unchecked dependency ID and invoke the `ListDependencies` API call to get a list of all its direct dependencies. The obtained list of dependency IDs is then passed as input to the `scanProjectDependencies` method, whose role is to examine the dependency list and update the contents of the `ctx` variable. The method's implementation is pretty straightforward:

```
func (c *Collector) scanProjectDependencies(ctx *depCtx, depList []string)
error {
    for _, depID := range depList {
        if ctx.AlreadyChecked(depID) {
            continue
        }
        ctx.AddToDepList(depID)
        depType, err := c.api.DependencyType(depID)
        if err != nil {
            return xerrors.Errorf("unable to get dependency type for id %q:
%w", depID, err)
        }
        if depType == DepTypeProject {
            ctx.AddToUncheckedList(depID)
        }
    }
    return nil
}
```

While iterating the dependency list, the implementation automatically skips any dependency that has already been visited. On the other hand, new dependency IDs are appended to the set of unique dependencies that have been tracked by the `ctx` variable via a call to the `AddToDepList` method.

As we mentioned previously, if the dependency corresponds to another project, we need to *recursively* visit its own dependencies and add them to our set as *transitive* dependencies. The `DependencyType` method from the `API` interface provides us with the means for querying the type of a dependency by its ID. If the dependency does in fact point to a *project*, we append it to the tail of the unvisited dependencies queue via a call to the `AddToUncheckedList` method. The last step guarantees that the dependency will eventually be processed by the search loop inside the `AllDependencies` method.

Leveraging gomock to write a unit test for our application

Now that we are aware of the implementation details of our example project, we can go ahead and write a simple, mock-based unit test for it. Before we begin, we need to create a mock for the `API` interface. This can be achieved by invoking the `mockgen` tool with the following options:

```
$ mockgen \
    -destination mock/dependency.go \
    github.com/PacktPublishing/Hands-On-Software-Engineering-with-
Golang/Chapter04/dependency \
    API
```

The preceding command does the following:

- Creates a `mock` folder in the `dependency` package
- Generates a file called `dependency.go` with the appropriate code for mocking the `API` interface and places it in the `mock` folder

To save you the trouble of having to manually type in the preceding command, the `Makefile` in the `Chapter04/dependency` folder includes a predefined target for rebuilding the mocks that were used in this example. All you need to do is switch to the folder with the example code in it and run `make mocks`.

So far, so good. How can we use the mock in our tests though? The first thing we need to do is create a gomock *controller* and associate it with the testing.T instance that gets passed to our test function by the Go standard library. The controller instance defines a Finish method that our code *must always run before returning from the test* (for example, via a *defer* statement). This method checks the expectations that were registered on each mock object and automatically fails the test if they were not met. Here's what the preamble of our test function would look like:

```
// Create a controller to manage all our mock objects and make sure
// that all expectations were met before completing the test
ctrl := gomock.NewController(t)
defer ctrl.Finish()

// Obtain a mock instance that implements API and associate it with the
controller.
api := mock_dependency.NewMockAPI(ctrl)
```

The purpose of this particular unit test is to verify that a call to the AllDependencies method with a specific input yields an expected list of dependency IDs. As we saw in the previous section, the implementation of the AllDependencies method uses an externally provided API instance to retrieve information about each dependency. Given that our test will inject a mocked API instance into the Collector dependency, our test code must declare the expected set of calls to the mock. Consider the following block of code:

```
gomock.InOrder(
    api.EXPECT().
        ListDependencies("proj0").Return([]string{"proj1", "res1"}, nil),
    api.EXPECT().
        DependencyType("proj1").Return(dependency.DepTypeProject, nil),
    api.EXPECT().
        DependencyType("res1").Return(dependency.DepTypeResource, nil),
    api.EXPECT().
        ListDependencies("proj1").Return([]string{"res1", "res2"}, nil),
    api.EXPECT().
        DependencyType("res2").Return(dependency.DepTypeResource, nil),
)
```

Under normal circumstances, gomock would just check that the method call expectations are met, *regardless of the order that they were invoked in*. However, if a test relies on a sequence of method calls being performed in a particular order, it can specify this to gomock by invoking the gomock.InOrder helper function with an ordered list of expectations as arguments. This particular pattern can be seen in the preceding code snippet.

With the mock expectations in place, we can complete our unit by introducing the necessary logic to wire everything together, invoke the `AllDependencies` method with the input (`proj0`) that our mock expects, and validate that the returned output matches a predefined value (`"proj1"`, `"res1"`, `"res2"`):

```
collector := dependency.NewCollector(api)
depList, err := collector.AllDependencies("proj0")
if err != nil {
    t.Fatal(err)
}

if exp := []string{"proj1", "res1", "res2"}; !reflect.DeepEqual(depList,
exp) {
    t.Fatalf("expected dependency list to be:\n%v\ngot:\n%v", exp, depList)
}
```

This concludes our short example about using `gomock` to accelerate the authoring of mock-based tests. As a fun learning activity, you can experiment with changing the expected output for the preceding test so that the test fails. Then, you can work backward and try to figure out how to tweak the mock expectations to make the test pass again.

Fake objects

In a similar fashion to the other test patterns that we have discussed so far, **fake objects** also adhere to a specific interface, which allows us to inject them into the subject under test. The main difference is that fake objects do, in fact, contain a *fully working* implementation whose behavior matches the objects that they are meant to substitute.

 So, what's the catch? Fake object implementations are typically optimized for running tests and, as such, they are not meant to be used in production. For example, we could provide an in-memory key-value store implementation for our tests, but our production deployments would require something with better availability guarantees.

To achieve a better understanding of how fake objects work, let's take a look at the contents of the `Chapter04/compute` package. This package exports a function called `SumOfSquares`, which operates on a slice of 32-bit floating-point values. The function squares each element of the slice, adds the results together, and returns their sum. Note that we are using a single function purely for demonstration purposes; in a real-world scenario, we would compose this function with other similar functions to form a compute graph that our implementation would then proceed to evaluate.

To purposefully add a bit of extra complexity to this particular scenario, let's assume that the input slices that are passed to this function typically contain a *very large number of values*. It is still possible, of course, to use the CPU to calculate the result. Unfortunately, the production service that depends on this functionality has a pretty strict time budget, so using the CPU is not an option. To this end, we have decided to implement a vectorized solution by offloading the work to a GPU.

The `Device` interface describes the set of operations that can be offloaded to the GPU:

```go
type Device interface {
    Square([]float32) []float32
    Sum([]float32) float32
}
```

Given an object instance that implements `Device`, we can define the `SumOfSquares` function as follows:

```go
func SumOfSquares(c Device, in []float32) float32 {
    sq := c.Square(in)
    return c.Sum(sq)
}
```

Nothing too complicated here... Alas, it wasn't until we started working on our tests that we realized that while the compute nodes where we normally run our production code do provide beefy GPUs, the same could not be said for *each one* of the machines that's used locally by our engineers or the CI environment that runs our tests each time we create a new pull request.

Obviously, even though our real workload deals with lengthy inputs, there is no strict requirement to do the same within our tests; as we will see in the following sections, this is a job for an end-to-end test. Therefore, we can fall back to a CPU implementation if a GPU is not available when our tests are running. This is an excellent example of where a fake object could help us out. So, let's start by defining a `Device` implementation that uses the CPU for all its calculations:

```go
type cpuComputeDevice struct{}

func (d cpuComputeDevice) Square(in []float32) []float32 {
    for i := 0; i < len(in); i++ {
        in[i] *= in[i]
    }
    return in
}

func (d cpuComputeDevice) Sum(in []float32) (sum float32) {
    for _, v := range in {
```

```
        sum += v
    }
    return sum
}
```

Our test code can then switch between the GPU- or the CPU-based implementation on the fly, perhaps by inspecting the value of an environment variable or some command-line flag that gets passed as an argument to the test:

```go
func TestSumOfSquares(t *testing.T) {
    var dev compute.Device
    if os.Getenv("USE_GPU") != "" {
        t.Log("using GPU device")
        dev = gpu.NewDevice()
    } else {
        t.Log("using CPU device")
        dev = cpuComputeDevice{}
    }
    // Generate deterministic sample data and return the expected sum
    in, expSum := genTestData(1024)
    if gotSum := compute.SumOfSquares(dev, in); gotSum != expSum {
        t.Fatalf("expected SumOfSquares to return %f; got %f", expSum,
gotSum)
    }
}
```

With the help of a fake object, we can always run our tests while still offering this ability to engineers who do have local access to GPUs to run the tests using the GPU-based implementation. Success!

Black-box versus white-box testing for Go packages – an example

Black- and white-box testing are two different approaches to authoring unit tests. Each approach has its own set of merits and goals. Consequently, we shouldn't treat them as competing approaches but rather as one complementing the other. So, what is the major difference between these two types of tests?

Black-box testing works under the assumption that the underlying implementation details of the package that we test, also known as the **subject under test** (**SUT**), are totally opaque (hence the name black-box) to us, the tester. As a result, we can only test the **public interface** or behavior of a particular package and make sure it adheres to its advertised contract.

On the other hand, white-box testing assumes that we have *prior* knowledge of the implementation details of a particular package. This allows the tester to either craft each test so that it exercises a particular code path within the package or to directly test the package's internal implementation.

To understand the difference between these two approaches, let's take a look at a short example. The `Chapter04/retail` package implements a *facade* called `PriceCalculator`.

A facade is a software design pattern that abstracts the complexity of one or more software components behind a simple interface.
In the context of microservice based design, the facade pattern allows us to transparently compose or aggregate data across multiple, specialized microservices while providing a simple API for the facade clients to access it.

In this particular scenario, the facade receives a UUID representing an item and a date representing the period we are interested in as input. Then, it communicates with two backend microservices to retrieve information about the item's price and the VAT rate that was applied on that particular date. Finally, it returns the VAT-inclusive price for the item to the facade's client.

The services behind the facade

Before we dive deeper into the inner workings of the price calculator, let's spend a bit of time examining how the two microservice dependencies work; after all, we will need this information to write our tests.

The `price` microservice provides a REST endpoint for retrieving an item's published price on a particular date. The service responds with a JSON payload that looks like this:

```
{
    "price": 10.0,
    "currency": "GBP"
}
```

The second microservice in this example is called `vat` and is also RESTful. It exposes an endpoint for retrieving the VAT rate that was applicable on a particular date. The service responds with a JSON payload as follows:

```
{
    "vat_rate": 0.29
}
```

As you can see, the returned JSON payload is quite simple and it would be trivial for our test code to mock it.

Writing black-box tests

For the purpose of writing our black-box tests, we will start by examining the *public* interface of the `retail` package. A quick browse of the `retail.go` file reveals a `NewPriceCalculator` function that receives the URLs to the `price` and `vat` services as arguments and returns a `PriceCalculator` instance. The calculator instance can be used to obtain an item's VAT-inclusive price by invoking the `PriceForItem` method and passing the item's UUID as an argument. On the other hand, if we are interested in obtaining a VAT-inclusive item price for a particular date in the past, we can invoke the `PriceForItemAtDate` method, which also accepts a time period argument.

The black-box tests will live *in a separate package* with the name `retail_test`. The `$PACKAGE_test` naming convention is, more or less, the standard way for doing black-box testing as the name itself alludes to the package being tested while at the same time preventing our test code from accessing the internals of the package under test.

One caveat of black-box testing is that we need to mock/stub any external objects and/or services that the tested code depends on. In this particular case, we need to provide stubs for the `price` and `vat` services. Fortunately, the `net/http/httptest` package, which ships with the Go standard library provides a convenient helper for spinning up a local HTTPS server using random, unused ports. Since we need to spin up two servers for our tests, let's create a small helper function to do exactly that:

```
func spinUpTestServer(t *testing.T, res map[string]interface{})
*httptest.Server {
    encResponse, err := json.Marshal(res)
    if err != nil {
        t.Fatal(err)
    }

    return httptest.NewServer(http.HandlerFunc(func(w http.ResponseWriter,
req *http.Request) {
```

```
        w.Header().Set("Content-Type", "application/json")
        if _, wErr := w.Write(encResponse); wErr != nil {
            t.Fatal(wErr)
        }
    }))
}
```

Nothing too complicated here; the spinUpTestServer function receives a map with the expected response's content and returns a server (which our test code needs to explicitly close) that always responds with the response payload formatted in JSON. With this helper function in place, setting up the stubs for our services becomes really easy:

```
// t is a testing.T instance
priceSvc := spinUpTestServer(t, map[string]interface{}{
    "price": 10.0,
})
defer priceSvc.Close()

vatSvc := spinUpTestServer(t, map[string]interface{}{
    "vat_rate": 0.29,
})
defer vatSvc.Close()
```

So, all we need to do now is call the NewPriceCalculator constructor and pass the addresses of the two fake servers. Hold on a minute! If those servers always listen on a random port, how do we know which addresses to pass to the constructor? One particularly convenient feature of the Server implementation that's provided by the httptest package is that it exposes the endpoint where the server is listening for incoming connections via a public attribute called URL. Here's what the rest of our black-box test would look like:

```
pc := retail.NewPriceCalculator(priceSvc.URL, vatSvc.URL)
got, err := pc.PriceForItem("1b6f8e0f-bbda-4f4e-ade5-aa1abcc99586")
if err != nil {
    t.Fatal(err)
}

if exp := 12.9; got != exp {
    t.Fatalf("expected calculated retail price to be %f; got %f", exp, got)
}
```

As we mentioned previously, the preceding code snippet lives in a different package, so our tests must import the package under test and access its public contents using the retail selector.

We could add a few more tests, for example, to validate the `PriceForItem` behavior when one or both of the services return an error, but that's as far as we can test using black-box testing alone! Let's run our test and see what sort of coverage we can get:

```
$ make test
[go test] running tests and collecting coverage metrics
=== RUN   TestPriceForItem
--- PASS: TestPriceForItem (0.01s)
PASS
coverage: 75.0% of statements
ok      github.com/PacktPublishing/Hands-On-Software-Engineering-with-Golang/ch04/retail      1.024s  coverage: 75.0% of statements
```

Figure 1: Running just the black-box tests

Not bad at all! However, if we need to boost our test coverage metrics further, we'll need to invest some time and come up with some white-box tests.

Boosting code coverage via white-box tests

One major difference compared to the tests we wrote in the previous section is that the new set of tests will live in the *same* package as the package we are testing. To differentiate from the black-box tests that we authored previously and hint to other engineers perusing the test code that these are internal tests, we will place the new tests in a file named `retail_internal_test.go`.

Now, it's time to pull the curtain back and examine the implementation details of the `retail` package! The public API of the package is always a good place to begin our exploratory work. An effective strategy would be to identify each exported function and then (mentally) follow its call-graph to locate other candidate functions/methods that we can exercise via our white-box tests. In the unlikely case that the package does not export any functions, we can shift our attention to other exported symbols, such as structs or interfaces. For instance, here is the definition of the `PriceCalculator` struct from the `retail` package:

```
type PriceCalculator struct {
    priceSvc svcCaller
    vatSvc   svcCaller
}
```

As we can see, the struct contains two private fields of the `svcCaller` type whose names clearly indicate they are somehow linked to the two services that the facade needs to call out to. If we keep browsing through the code, we will discover that `svcCaller` is actually an interface:

```
type svcCaller interface {
    Call(req map[string]interface{}) (io.ReadCloser, error)
}
```

The `Call` method receives a map of request parameters and returns a response stream as an `io.ReadCloser`. From the perspective of a test writer, the use of such an abstraction should make us quite happy since it provides us with an easy avenue for mocking the actual calls to the two services!

As we saw in the previous section, the public API exposed by the `PriceCalculator` type is composed of two methods:

- `PriceForItem`, which returns the price of an item at this point in time
- `PriceForItemAtDate`, which returns the price of an item at a particular point in time

Since the `PriceForItem` method is a simple wrapper that calls `PriceForItemAtDate` with the current date/time as an argument, we will focus our analysis on the latter. The implementation of `PriceForItemAtDate` is presented as follows:

```
func (pc *PriceCalculator) PriceForItemAtDate(itemUUID string, date
time.Time) (float64, error) {
    priceRes := struct {
        Price float64 `json:"price"`
    }{}
    vatRes := struct {
        Rate float64 `json:"vat_rate"`
    }{}
    req := map[string]interface{}{"item": itemUUID, "period": date}
    if err := pc.callService(pc.priceSvc, req, &priceRes); err != nil {
        return 0, xerrors.Errorf("unable to retrieve item price: %w", err)
    }
    req = map[string]interface{}{"period": date}
    if err := pc.callService(pc.vatSvc, req, &vatRes); err != nil {
        return 0, xerrors.Errorf("unable to retrieve vat percent: %w", err)
    }
    return vatInclusivePrice(priceRes.Price, vatRes.Rate), nil
}
```

The preceding code block makes use of a helper called `callService` to send out a request to the `price` and `vat` services and unpack their responses into the `priceRes` and `vatRes` variables. To gain a clearer understanding of what happens under the hood, let's take a quick peek into the implementation of `callService`:

```
func (pc *PriceCalculator) callService(svc svcCaller, req
map[string]interface{}, res interface{}) error {
    svcRes, err := svc.Call(req)
    if err != nil {
        return xerrors.Errorf("call to remote service failed: %w", err)
    }
    defer drainAndClose(svcRes)

    if err = json.NewDecoder(svcRes).Decode(res); err != nil {
        return xerrors.Errorf("unable to decode remote service response:
%w", err)
    }
    return nil
}
```

The `callService` method implementation is pretty straightforward. All it does is invoke the `Call` method on the provided `svcCaller` instance, treats the returned output as a JSON stream, and attempts to unmarshal it into the `res` argument that's provided by the caller.

Now, let's go back to the implementation of the `PriceForItemAtDate` method. Assuming that no error occurred while contacting the remote services, their individual responses are passed as arguments to the `vatInclusivePrice` helper function.

As you can probably tell by its name, it implements the business logic of applying VAT rates to prices. Keeping the business logic separate from the code that is responsible for talking to other services is not only a good indicator of a well-thought-out design but it also makes our test-writing job easier. Let's add a small table-driven test to validate the business logic:

```
func TestVatInclusivePrice(t *testing.T) {
    specs := []struct {
        price   float64
        vatRate float64
        exp     float64
    }{
        {42.0, 0.1, 46.2},
        {10.0, 0, 10.0},
    }
    for specIndex, spec := range specs {
        if got := vatInclusivePrice(spec.price, spec.vatRate); got !=
```

```
    spec.exp {
            t.Errorf("[spec %d] expected to get: %f; got: %f", specIndex,
    spec.exp, got)
        }
    }
}
```

With that test in place, the next thing we want to test is `PriceForItem`. To do that, we need to somehow control access to the external services. Although we will be using stubs for simplicity, we could also use any of the other test patterns that we discussed in the previous section. Here is a stub that implements the same approach as the test server from our black-box tests but without the need to actually spin up a server!

```
type stubSvcCaller map[string]interface{}

func (c stubSvcCaller) Call(map[string]interface{}) (io.ReadCloser, error)
{
    data, err := json.Marshal(c)
    if err != nil {
        return nil, err
    }

    return ioutil.NopCloser(bytes.NewReader(data)), nil
}
```

Using the preceding stub definition, let's add a test for the `PriceForItem` method's happy path:

```
func TestPriceForItem(t *testing.T) {
    pc := &PriceCalculator{
        priceSvc: stubSvcCaller{ "price": 42.0, },
        vatSvc: stubSvcCaller{ "vat_rate": 0.10, },
    }

    got, err := pc.PriceForItem("foo")
    if err != nil {
        t.Fatal(err)
    }

    if exp := 46.2; got != exp {
        t.Fatalf("expected calculated retail price to be %f; got %f", exp,
got)
    }
}
```

Of course, our tests wouldn't really be complete without explicitly testing what happens when a required dependency fails! For this, we need yet another stub, which always returns an error:

```
type stubErrCaller struct {
    err error
}

func (c stubErrCaller) Call(map[string]interface{}) (io.ReadCloser, error)
{
    return nil, c.err
}
```

With this stub implementation, we can test how the `PriceCalculator` method behaves when particular *classes of errors* occur. For example, here is a test that simulates a 404 response from the `vat` service to indicate to the caller that no VAT rate data is available for the specified time period:

```
func TestVatSvcErrorHandling(t *testing.T) {
    pc := &PriceCalculator{
        priceSvc: stubSvcCaller{ "price": 42.0, },
        vatSvc: stubErrCaller{
            err: errors.New("unexpected response status code: 404"),
        },
    }

    expErr := "unable to retrieve vat percent: call to remote service
failed: unexpected response status code: 404"
    _, err := pc.PriceForItem("foo")
    if err == nil || err.Error() != expErr {
        t.Fatalf("expected to get error:\n %s\ngot:\n %v", expErr, err)
    }
}
```

Let's run the black- and white-box tests together to check how the total coverage has changed now that we've introduced the new tests:

```
● ● ●                                    4. bash (bash)
$ make test
[go test] running tests and collecting coverage metrics
=== RUN    TestPriceForItem
--- PASS: TestPriceForItem (0.00s)
=== RUN    TestVatSvcErrorHandling
--- PASS: TestVatSvcErrorHandling (0.00s)
=== RUN    TestVatInclusivePrice
--- PASS: TestVatInclusivePrice (0.00s)
=== RUN    TestPriceForItem
--- PASS: TestPriceForItem (0.01s)
PASS
coverage: 81.2% of statements
ok        github.com/PacktPublishing/Hands-On-Software-Engineering-with-Golang/ch04/retail        1.026s  coverage: 81.2% of statements
```

Figure 2: Running both black- and white-box tests

While the ratio of white-box and black-box tests in the Go standard library's sources seems to strongly favor white-box testing, this should not be construed as a hint that you shouldn't be writing black-box tests! Black-box tests certainly have their place and are very useful when you're attempting to replicate the exact set of conditions and inputs that trigger the particular bug that you are trying to track down. What's more, as we will see in the upcoming sections, black-box tests can often serve as templates for constructing another class of tests, commonly referred to as *integration tests*.

Table-driven tests versus subtests

In this section, we will be comparing two slightly different approaches when it comes to grouping and executing multiple test cases together. These two approaches, namely table-driven tests and subtests, can easily be implemented using the basic primitives provided by Go's built-in `testing` package. For each approach, we will discuss the pros and cons and eventually outline a strategy to fuse the two approaches together so that we can get the best of both worlds.

Table-driven tests

Table-driven tests are a quite compact and rather terse way to efficiently test the behavior of a particular piece of code in a host of different scenarios. The format of a typical table-driven test consists of two distinct parts: the test case definitions and the test-runner code.

To demonstrate this, let's examine a possible implementation of the infamous
`FizzBuzz` test: given a number, *N*, the `FizzBuzz` implementation is expected to
return `Fizz` if the number is evenly divisible by 3, `Buzz` if the number is evenly divisible by
5, `FizzBuzz` if the number is evenly divisible by *both* 3 and 5, or the number itself in all
other cases. Here is a listing from the `Chapter04/table-driven/fizzbuzz.go` file,
which contains the implementation we will be working with:

```go
func Evaluate(n int) string {
    if n != 0 {
        switch {
        case n%3 == 0 && n%5 == 0:
            return "FizzBuzz"
        case n%3 == 0:
            return "Fizz"
        case n%5 == 0:
            return "Buzz"
        }
    }
    return fmt.Sprint(n)
}
```

In the majority of cases, test scenarios will only be accessed by a single test function. With
that in mind, a good strategy would be to encapsulate the scenario list inside the test
function with the help of a pretty nifty Go feature: anonymous structs. Here is how you
would go about defining the struct that contains the scenarios and a scenario list using a
single block of code:

```go
specs := []struct {
    descr string
    input int
    exp    string
}{
    {descr: "evenly divisible by 3", input: 9, exp: "Fizz"},
    {descr: "evenly divisible by 5", input: 25, exp: "Buzz"},
    {descr: "evenly divisible by 3 and 5", input: 15, exp: "FizzBuzz"},
    // The following case is intentionally wrong to trigger a test failure!
    {descr: "example of incorrect expectation", input: 0, exp: "FizzBuzz"},
    {descr: "edge case", input: 0, exp: "0"},
}
```

In the preceding code snippet, you may have noticed that I included a description for each test case. This is more of a personal preference, but in my opinion, it makes the test code more pleasant to the eyes and, more importantly, helps us easily locate the specs for failing test cases as opposed to visually scanning the entire list looking for the Nth scenario that corresponds to a failed test. Granted, either approach would be efficient for the *preceding* example where every test case is neatly laid out in a single line, but think how much more difficult things would be if each spec block contained nested objects and thus each spec was defined using a variable number of lines.

Once we have written down our specs, making sure that we have also included any *edge* cases that we can think of, it is time to run the test. This is actually the easy part! All we need to do is iterate the list of specs, invoke the subject under test with the input(s) provided by each spec, and verify that the outputs conform to the expected values:

```
for specIndex, spec := range specs {
    if got := fizzbuzz.Evaluate(spec.input); got != spec.exp {
        t.Errorf("[spec %d: %s] expected to get %q; got %q", specIndex,
spec.descr, spec.exp, got)
    }
}
```

One important aspect of the preceding test-runner implementation is that even when a test case fails, we don't *immediately* abort the test by invoking any of the `t.Fail`/`FailNow` or `t.Fatal`/`f` helpers, but rather exhaust our list of test cases. This is intentional as it allows us to see an overview of all the failing cases in one go. If we were to run the preceding code, we would get the following output:

```
● ○ ●                                    4. bash (bash)
$ make test
[go test] running tests and collecting coverage metrics
=== RUN    TestFizzBuzzTableDriven
--- FAIL: TestFizzBuzzTableDriven (0.00s)
    fizzbuzz_test.go:26: [spec 3: example of incorrect expectation] expected to get "FizzBuzz"; got "0"
FAIL
coverage: 100.0% of statements
FAIL    github.com/PacktPublishing/Hands-On Software Engineering-with-Golang/ch04/table-driven   0.013s
make: *** [test] Error 1
```

Figure 3: Example of a failing case in a table-driven test

One unfortunate caveat of this approach is that we cannot request for the `go test` command to explicitly target a specific test case. We can always ask `go test` to only run a *specific test function* in isolation (for example, `go test -run TestFizzBuzzTableDriven`), but not to *only* run the failing test case number 3 within that test function; we need to sequentially test all the cases every single time! Being able to target specific test cases would be a time-saver if our test-runner code was complex and each test case took quite a bit of time to execute.

Subtests

With the release of Go 1.7, the built-in *testing* package gained support for running subtests. Subtests are nothing more than a hierarchy of test functions that are executed sequentially. This hierarchical structuring of the test code is akin to the notion of a test suite that you may have been exposed to in other programming languages.

So, how does it work? The `testing.T` type has been augmented with a new method called `Run` that has the following signature:

```
Run(description string, func(t *testing.T))
```

This new method provides a new mechanism for spawning subtests that will run in isolation while still retaining the ability to use the parent test function to perform any required setup and teardown steps.

As you might expect, since each subtest function receives its own `testing.T` instance argument, it can, in turn, spawn additional subtests that are nested underneath it. Here's what a typical test would look like when following this approach:

```
func TestXYZ(t *testing.T){
    // Run suite setup code...

    t.Run("test1", func(t *testing.T){
        // test1 code
    })
    t.Run("test2", func(t *testing.T){
        // test2 code
    })

    // Run suite tear-down code...
}
```

What's more, each subtest gets its own unique name, which is generated by concatenating the names of all its ancestor test functions and the description string that gets passed to the invocation of Run. This makes it easy to target any subtest in a particular hierarchy tree by specifying its name to the -run argument when invoking go test. For example, in the preceding code snippet, we can target test2 by running go test -run TestXYZ/test2.

One disadvantage of subtests compared to their test-driven brethren is that they are defined in a much more verbose way. This could prove to be a bit of a challenge if we need to define a large number of test scenarios.

The best of both worlds

At the end of the day, nothing precludes us from combining these two approaches into a hybrid approach that gives us the best of both worlds: the terseness of table-driven tests and the selective targeting of subtests.

To achieve this, we need to define our table-driven specs, just like we did before. Following that, we iterate the spec list and spawn a subtest for each test case. Here's how we could adapt our FizzBuzz tests so that they follow this pattern:

```go
func TestFizzBuzzTableDrivenSubtests(t *testing.T) {
    specs := []struct {
        descr, exp string
        input      int
    }{
        {descr: "evenly divisible by 3", input: 9, exp: "Fizz"},
        {descr: "evenly divisible by 3 and 5", input: 15, exp: "FizzBuzz"},
        {descr: "edge case", input: 0, exp: "0"},
    }
    for specIndex, spec := range specs {
        t.Run(spec.descr, func(t *testing.T) {
            if got := fizzbuzz.Evaluate(spec.input); got != spec.exp {
                t.Errorf("[spec %d: %s] expected to get %q; got %q",
specIndex, spec.descr, spec.exp, got)
            }
        })
    }
}
```

Let's say we wanted to only run the second test case. We can easily achieve this by passing its fully qualified name as the value of the -run flag when running go test:

```
go test -run TestFizzBuzzTableDrivenSubtests/evenly_divisible_by_3_and_5
```

Using third-party testing frameworks

One great thing about testing Go code is that the language itself comes with batteries included: it ships with a built-in, albeit minimalistic, framework for authoring and running tests.

From a purist's perspective, that's all that you need to be up and running! The built-in `testing` package provides all the required mechanisms for running, skipping, or failing tests. All the software engineer needs to do is set up the required test dependencies and write the appropriate predicates for each test. One caveat of using the `testing` package is that it does not provide any of the more sophisticated test primitives, such as assertions or mocks, that you may be used to if you've come from a Java, Ruby, or Python background. Of course, nothing prevents you from implementing these yourself!

Alternatively, if importing additional test dependencies is something you don't object to, you can make use of one of the several readily available third-party packages that provide all these missing features. Since a full, detailed listing of all third-party test packages is outside of the scope of this book, we will focus our attention on one of the most popular test framework packages out there: `gocheck`.

The `gocheck` package [3] can be installed by running `go get gopkg.in/check.v1`. It builds on top of the standard Go `testing` package and provides support for organizing tests into test suites. Each suite is defined using a regular Go struct that you can also exploit so that it stores any additional bits of information that might be needed by your tests.

In order to run each test suite as part of your tests, you need to register it with `gocheck` and hook `gocheck` to the Go testing package. The following is a short example of how to do that:

```
import (
    "testing"

    "gopkg.in/check.v1"
)

type MySuite struct{}

// Register suite with go check
var _ = check.Suite(new(MySuite))

// Hook up gocheck into the "go test" runner.
func Test(t *testing.T) { check.TestingT(t) }
```

As you would expect of any framework that supports test suites, gocheck allows you to optionally specify setup and teardown methods for both the suite and each test by defining any of the following methods on the suite type:

- SetUpSuite(c *check.C)
- SetUpTest(c *check.C)
- TearDownTest(c *check.C)
- TearDownSuite(c *check.C)

Likewise, any suite method matching the TestXYZ(c *check.C) pattern will be treated as a test and executed when the suit runs. The check.C type gives you access to some useful methods, such as the following:

- Log/Logf: Prints a message to the test log
- MkDir: Creates a temporary folder that is automatically removed after the *suite* finishes running
- Succeed/SucceedNow/Fail/FailNow/Fatal/Fatalf: Controls the outcome of a running test
- Assert: Fails the test if the specified predicate condition isn't met

By *default*, gocheck buffers all its output and only emits it when a test fails. While this helps cut down the noise and speeds up the execution of chatty tests, you might prefer to see all the output. Fortunately, gocheck supports two levels of verbosity that can be controlled via command-line flags that are passed to the go test invocation.

To force gocheck to output its buffered debug log for all tests, regardless of their pass/fail status, you can run go test with the -check.v argument. The fact that gocheck prefers to buffer all the logging output is less than ideal when you're trying to figure out why one of your tests hangs. For such situations, you can dial up the verbosity and disable buffering by running gocheck with the -check.vv argument. Finally, if you wish to run a particular test from a test suite (akin to go test -run XYZ), you can run gocheck with -check.f XYZ, where XYZ is a regular expression matching the names of the test(s) you wish to run.

While we mentioned that the `check.C` object provides an `Assert` method, we haven't really gone into any detail on how it works or how the assertion predicates are defined. The signature of `Assert` is as follows:

```
Assert(obtained interface{}, checker Checker, args ...interface{})
```

The following table contains a list of useful `Checker` implementations provided by `gocheck` that you can use to write your test assertions.

Checker	Description	Example
Equals	Check for equality	c.Assert(res, check.Equals, 42)
DeepEquals	Check interfaces, slices, and others for equality	c.Assert(res, check.DeepEquals, []string{"hello", "world"})
IsNil	Check if the value is nil	c.Assert(err, check.IsNil)
HasLen	Check the length of the slice/map/channel/strings	c.Assert(list, check.HasLen, 2)
Matches	Check that the string matches the regex	c.Assert(val, check.Matches, ".*hi.*")
ErrorMatches	Check that the error message matches the regex	c.Assert(err, check.Matches, ".*not found")
FitsTypeOf	Check that the argument is assigned to a variable with the given type	c.Assert(impl, check.FitsTypeOf, os.Error(nil)
Not	Invert the check result	c.Assert(val, check.Not(check.Equals)), 42)

Of course, if your tests require more sophisticated predicates than the ones built into `gocheck`, you can always roll your own by implementing the `Checker` interface.

This concludes our tour of `gocheck`. If you are interested in using it in your projects, I would definitely recommend visiting the package home [3] and reading its excellent documentation. If you already use `gocheck` but want to explore other popular testing frameworks for Go, I would suggest taking a look at the `stretchr/testify` package [7], which offers similar functionality (test suites, assertions, and so on) to `gocheck` but also includes support for more advanced test primitives such as mocks.

Integration versus functional testing

In this section, we will attempt to dispel any confusion between the definitions of two very important and useful types of testing: **integration** tests and **functional** tests.

Integration tests

Integration tests pick up from where unit testing left off. Whereas unit testing ensures that each individual unit of a system works correctly in isolation, integration testing ensures that different units (or services, in a microservice architecture) interoperate correctly.

Let's consider a hypothetical scenario where we are building an e-shop application. Following the SOLID design principles, we have split our backend implementation into a bunch of microservices. Each microservice comes with its own set of unit tests and, by design, exposes an API that adheres to a contract agreed on by *all* engineering teams. For the purpose of this demonstration, and to keep things simple, we want to focus our efforts on authoring an integration test for the following two microservices:

- The **product** microservice performs the following functions:
    - It exposes a mechanism for manipulating and querying product metadata; for example, to add or remove products, return information about item prices, descriptions, and so on
    - It provides a notification mechanism for metadata changes that other services can subscribe to

- The **basket** microservice stores the list of items that have been selected by the customer. When a new item is inserted into a customer's basket, the basket service queries the product service for the item metadata and updates the price summary for the basket. At the same time, it subscribes to the product service change stream and updates the basket's contents if the product metadata is updated.

One important implementation aspect to be aware of is that each microservice uses its own dedicated data store. Keep in mind though that this approach does not necessarily mean that the data stores are physically separated. Perhaps we are using a single database server and each microservice gets its own database on that server.

The integration test for these two services would live in a separate Go test file, perhaps with an _integration_test.go suffix so that we can immediately tell its purpose just by looking at the filename. The setup phase of the tests expects that the DB instance(s) that are required by the services have already been externally prepared. As we will see later in this chapter, a simple way to provide DB connection settings to our tests is via the use of environment variables. The tests would proceed to spin up the services that we want to test and then run the following integration scenarios:

- Invoke the product service API to insert a new product into the catalog. Then, it would use the basket service API to add the product to a customer basket and verify that the DB that's used by the basket service contains an entry with the correct product metadata.
- Add a product to a customer basket. Then, it would use the product service API to mutate the item description and verify that the relevant basket DB entry is updated correctly.

One caveat of integration tests is that we need to maintain strict isolation between individual tests. Consequently, before running each test scenario, we must ensure that the internal state of each service is reset properly. Typically, this means that we need to flush the database that's used by each service and perhaps also restart the services in case they also maintain any additional in-memory state.

Evidently, the effort that's required to set up, wire together, and prime the various components that are needed for each integration test makes writing such tests quite a tedious process. Not to diminish the significance of integration testing, it is my belief that engineers can make better use of their time by writing a large number of unit tests and just a handful of integration tests.

Functional tests

Functional or end-to-end tests take system testing to a whole new level. The primary purpose of functional testing is to ensure that the *complete* system is working as expected. To this end, functional tests are designed to model complex interaction scenarios that involve multiple system components. A very common use case for functional tests is to verify end-to-end correctness by simulating a user's journey through the system.

For instance, a functional test for an online music streaming service would act as a new user who would subscribe to the service, search for a particular song, add it to their playlist, and perhaps submit a rating for the song once it's done playing.

It is important to clarify that all the preceding interactions are meant to occur via the web browser. This is a clear-cut case where we need to resort to a *scriptable* browser automation framework such as Selenium [6] in order to accurately model all the required button clicks that we expect a real user to perform while using the system.

While you could probably find a package that provides Go bindings for Selenium, the truth of the matter is that Go is not the best tool for writing functional tests. Contrary to unit and integration tests, which live within Go files, functional tests are normally written in languages such as Python, JavaScript, or Ruby. Another important distinction is that, due to their increased complexity, functional tests take a *significantly* longer time to run.

While it's not uncommon for software engineers working on a particular feature to also provide functional test suites, in the majority of cases, the task of authoring functional tests is one of the primary responsibilities of the **quality assurance (QA)** team. As a matter of fact, functional tests are the front and center part of the pre-release workflow that's followed by QA engineers before they can give the green light for a new release.

Functional tests don't usually target production systems; you wouldn't want to fill up your production DB with dummy user accounts, right? Instead, functional tests target **staging environments**, which are isolated and often downsized sandboxes that mirror the setup of the actual production environment. This includes all the services and resources (databases, message queues, and so on) that are needed for the system to operate. One exception is that access to external third-party services such as payment gateways or email providers is typically mocked unless a particular functional test requests otherwise.

Functional tests part deux – testing in production!

That's not to say that you cannot actually run your functional tests in a live production environment! Surely whether that's a good or bad idea is a debatable point, but if you do decide to go down that route, there are a few patterns that you can apply to achieve this in a *safe* and *controlled* way.

To get the ball rolling, you can begin by revising your DB schemas so that they include a field that indicates whether each row contains real data or is part of a test run. Each service could then silently ignore any test records when it handles live traffic.

If you are working with a microservice architecture, you can engineer your services so that they do not talk to other services directly but rather to do so via a local proxy that is deployed in tandem with each service as a *sidecar* process. This pattern is known as the *ambassador* pattern and opens up the possibility of implementing a wide range of really cool tricks, as we will see later in this chapter.

Since all the proxies are initially configured to talk to the already deployed services, nothing prevents us from deploying a newer version of a particular service and have it run side-by-side with the existing version. Since no traffic can reach the newly deployed service, it is common to use the term **dark launch** to refer to this kind of deployment.

Once the new versions of the services that we need to test against have been successfully deployed, each functional test can reconfigure the local proxies to divert *test* traffic (identified perhaps by an HTTP header or an other type of tag) to the newly deployed services. This can be seen in the following diagram:

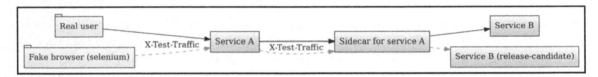

Figure 4: Using the ambassador pattern to test in production

This neat trick allows us to run our tests in production without interfering with live traffic. As you can tell, live testing requires substantially more preparation effort compared to testing in a sandbox. This is probably one of the reasons why QA teams seem to prefer using staging environments instead.

In my view, if your system is built in such a way that you can easily introduce one of these patterns to facilitate live testing, you should definitely go for it. After all, there is only so much data that you can collect when running in an isolated environment whose load and traffic profiles don't really align with the ones of your production systems.

Smoke tests

Smoke tests or build acceptance tests constitute a special family of tests that are traditionally used as early sanity checks by QA teams.

The use of the word *smoke* alludes to the old adage that *wherever there is smoke, there is also fire*. These checks are explicitly designed to identify early warning signals that something is wrong. It goes without saying that any issue uncovered by a smoke test is treated by the QA team as a show-stopper; if smoke tests fail, no further testing is performed. The QA team reports its findings to the development team and waits for a revised release candidate to be submitted for testing.

Once the smoke tests successfully pass, the QA team proceeds to run their suite of functional tests before giving the green light for release. The following diagram summarizes the process of running smoke tests for QA purposes:

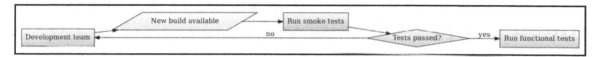

Figure 5: Running smoke tests as part of the QA process

When it comes to execution, smoke tests are the exact antithesis of functional tests. While functional tests are allowed to execute for long periods of time, smoke tests must execute as quickly as possible. As a result, smoke tests are crafted so as to exercise specific, albeit limited, flows in the user-facing parts of a system that are deemed critical for the system's operation. For example, smoke tests for a social network application would verify the following:

- A user can login with a valid username and password
- Clicking the **like** button on a post increases the like counter for that post
- Deleting a contact removes them from the user's friends list
- Clicking the **logout** button signs the user out of the service

The responsibility for authoring, evolving, and maintaining smoke tests usually falls on the shoulders of the QA team. Consequently, it makes sense for the QA team to maintain smoke tests in a separate, dedicated repository that they own and control. An interesting question here is whether the QA team will opt to execute the smoke tests manually or invest the time and effort that's required to automate the process. The logical, albeit slightly cliché, answer is: it depends...

At the end of the day, the decision boils down to the size of the QA team, the individual preferences of the team's members, and the test infrastructure that's available and is at the team's disposal. Needless to say, automated smoke tests are, hands down, the recommended option since the QA team can efficiently verify a plethora of scenarios in a small amount of time. On the other hand, if the build release frequency is low, you could argue that doing manual smoke tests has a smaller cost and makes better use of the QA team's time and resources.

Chaos testing – breaking your systems in fun and interesting ways!

Let me begin this section with a question! How confident are you about the quality of your current software stack? If your answer happens to be something along the lines of, *I don't really know until I make it fail*, then we are in total agreement! If not, let me introduce you to the concept of **chaos testing**.

Chaos testing is a term that was initially coined by the engineering team at Netflix. The key point behind chaos testing is to evaluate your system's behavior when various components exhibit different types of failure. So, what kinds of failure are we talking about here? Here are a few interesting examples, ordered by their relative severity (low to high):

- A service fails to reach another service it depends on
- Calls between services exhibit high latency/jitter
- Network links experience packet loss
- A database node fails
- We lose a critical piece of storage
- Our cloud provider suffers an outage in an entire availability zone

Netflix engineers point out that we shouldn't be afraid of failure but rather embrace it and learn as much as we can about it. All these learnings can be applied to fine-tune the design of our systems so that they become incrementally more and more robust and resilient against failure.

Some of these types of failure have a low likelihood of occurring. Nevertheless, it's better if we are prepared to mitigate them when they actually *do* occur. After all, from a system stability perspective, it's always preferred to operate in a preventive fashion rather than trying to react (often under lots of pressure) when an outage occurs.

You might be wondering: *but, if some failures are statistically unlikely to occur, how can we trigger them in the first place?* The only way to do this is to engineer our systems in such a way that failure can be injected on demand. In the *Functional tests part deux – testing in production!* section, we talked about the ambassador pattern, which can help us achieve exactly that.

The ambassador pattern decouples service discovery and communication from the actual service implementation. This is achieved with the help of a sidecar process that gets deployed with each service and acts as a proxy.

The sidecar proxy service can be used for other purposes, such as conditionally routing traffic based on tags or headers, acting as a circuit breaker, bifurcating traffic to perform A/B testing, logging requests, enforcing security rules, or to *inject artificial failures into the system.*

From a chaos engineering perspective, the sidecar proxy is an easy avenue for introducing failures. Let's look at some examples of how we can exploit the proxy to inject failure into the system:

- Instruct the proxy to delay outgoing requests or wait before returning upstream responses to the service that initiated the request. This is an effective way to model latency. If we opt not to use fixed intervals but to randomize them, we can inject jitter into intra-service communication.
- Configure the proxy to drop outgoing requests with probability P. This emulates a degraded network connection.
- Configure the proxy for a single service to drop all outgoing traffic to another service. At the same time, all the other service proxies are set up to forward traffic as usual. This emulates a network partition.

That's not all. We can take chaos testing even further if we are running our systems on a cloud provider that provides us with an API that we can use to break even more things! For instance, we could use such an API to randomly start killing nodes or to take down one or all of our load balancers and check whether our system can automatically recover by itself. With chaos testing, the only limit is your own imagination!

Tips and tricks for writing tests

In this section, I will be going through some interesting ideas that can help super-charge your daily test workflow. What's more, we will also be exploring some neat tricks that you can use to isolate tests, mock calls to system binaries, and control time within your tests.

Using environment variables to set up or skip tests

In a project of any size, you are eventually bound to come across a series of tests that depend on external resources that are created or configured in an ad hoc fashion.

A typical example of such a use case would be a test suite that talks to a database. As the engineers working locally on the code base, we would probably spin up a local database instance with a more or less predictable endpoint and use that for testing. However, when running under CI, we might be required to use an already provisioned database instance on some cloud provider or, more often than not, the CI setup phase may need to start a database in a Docker container, a process that would yield a non-predictable endpoint to be connected to.

To support scenarios such as these, we must avoid hardcoding the location of resource endpoints to our tests and *defer* their discovery and configuration until the time when the test runs. To this end, one solution would be to use a set of environment variables to supply this information to our tests. Here is a simple test example from the Chapter04/db package that illustrates how this can be achieved:

```
func TestDBConnection(t *testing.T) {
    host, port, dbName, user, pass := os.Getenv("DB_HOST"),
os.Getenv("DB_PORT"),
        os.Getenv("DB_NAME"), os.Getenv("DB_USER"), os.Getenv("DB_PASS")

    db, err := sql.Open("postgres", makeDSN(user, pass, dbName, host,
port))
    if err != nil {
        t.Fatal(err)
    }
    _ = db.Close()
    t.Log("Connection to DB succeeded")
}
```

The preceding example makes testing a breeze, regardless of whether we run the tests locally or in a CI environment. But what if our tests require a specialized DB that is not that easy to spin up locally? Maybe we need a DB that operates in a clustered configuration or one whose memory requirements exceed the memory that's available on our development machine. Wouldn't it be great if we could just *skip* that test when running locally?

It turns out that this is also quite easy to achieve with exactly the same mechanism that we used for configuring our DB endpoint. To be more precise, the *absence* of the required configuration settings could serve as a hint to the test that it needs to be skipped. In the preceding example, we can achieve this by adding a simple `if` block after fetching the environment values for the DB configuration:

```
if host == "" {
    t.Skip("Skipping test as DB connection info is not present")
}
```

Excellent! Now, if we don't export the DB_HOST environment variable before running our tests, this particular test will be skipped.

Speeding up testing for local development

In this section, we will be covering a couple of approaches to accelerating testing when working locally. Just to clarify, I am assuming that you already have a proper CI infrastructure in place; no matter what shortcuts we will be taking here, the CI will always run all the tests.

The first item on our agenda is slow versus fast tests. For the sake of argument, say that we find ourselves in a situation where we are writing a fully-fledged, pure CPU ray tracer implementation in Go. To ensure correctness and avoid regressions while we are tweaking our implementation, we have introduced a test suite that renders a sequence of example scenes and compares the ray tracer output to a series of prerendered reference images.

Since this is a pure CPU implementation and our tests render at full-HD resolution, running each test would take, as you can imagine, quite a bit of time. This is not an issue when running on the CI but can definitely be an impediment when working locally.

To make matters worse, `go test` will try to run all the tests, even if one of them fails. Additionally, it will automatically fail tests that take a long time (over 10 minutes) to run. Fortunately, the `go test` command supports some really useful flags that we can use to rectify these issues.

To begin with, we can notify long-running tests that they should try to shorten their runtime by passing the `-short` flag to the `go test` invocation. This flag gets exposed by the `testing` package via the `Short` helper function, which returns `true` when the `-short` flag is defined. So, how can we use this flag to make our ray tracer tests run faster?

One approach would be to simply skip tests that are known to take a really long time to run. A much better alternative would be to detect the presence of the `-short` flag and *dial down* the output resolution of the ray tracer, say, to something such as a quarter of the original resolution. This change would still allow us to verify the rendering output when testing locally while at the same time would constrain the total runtime of our tests to an acceptable level.

Coming back to the issue of `go test` running all the tests, even if one of them fails, we can actually instruct `go test` to immediately abort if it detects a failing test by passing the `-failfast` command-line flag. Moreover, we can tune the maximum, per-test execution time with the help of the `-timeout` flag. It accepts any string that can be parsed by the `time.Duration` type (for example, *1h*), but if your tests take an unpredictable amount of time to run, you could also pass a timeout value of *0* to disable timeouts.

Excluding classes of tests via build flags

So far, we have discussed white- and black-box tests, integration, and end-to-end tests. By including tests from all these categories in our projects, we can rest assured that the code base will behave as expected in a multitude of different scenarios.

Now, imagine we are working on a particular feature and we *only* want to run the unit tests. Alternatively, we may *only* need to run the integration tests to ensure that our changes do not introduce regression to other packages. How can we do that?

The rather simplistic approach would be to maintain separate folders for each test category, but that would veer away from what is considered to be idiomatic Go. Another alternative would be to add the category name as a prefix or suffix to our tests and run `go test` with the `-run` flag (or with the `-check.f` flag if we are using a third-party package such as `gocheck` [3]) to only run the tests whose names match a particular regular expression. It stands to reason that while this approach will work, it's quite error-prone; for larger code bases, we would need to compose elaborate regular expressions that might not match all the tests that we need to run.

A smarter solution would be to take advantage of Go's support for conditional compilation and repurpose it to serve our needs. This is a great time to explain what conditional compilation is all about and, most importantly, how it works under the hood.

When a package is being built, the `go build` command scans the comments inside each Go file, looking for special keywords that can be interpreted as compiler directives. **Build tags** are one example of such an annotation. They are used by `go build` to decide whether a particular Go file in a package should be passed to the Go compiler. The general syntax for a build tag is as follows:

```
// +build tag1 ... tagN

package some_package
```

To be correctly recognized by `go build`, all the build tags must appear as a comment at the *top* of a Go file. While you are allowed to define multiple build tags, it is very important that the *last* build tag is separated with a blank (non-comment) line from the package name declaration. Otherwise, `go build` will just assume that the build tag is part of a package-level comment and simply ignore it. Software engineers that are new to the concept of Go build tags occasionally fall into this trap, so if you find yourself scratching your head, wondering why build tags are not being picked up, the lack of a blank line after the build tag is the most likely suspect.

Let's take a closer look at the intricacies of the tag syntax and elaborate on the rules that are applied by `go build` to interpret the list of tags following the +build keyword:

- Tags separated by *whitespace* are evaluated as a list of OR conditions.
- Tags separated by a *comma* are evaluated as a list of AND conditions.
- Tags beginning with ! are treated as NOT conditions.
- If multiple +build lines are defined, they are joined together as an AND condition.

The `go build` command recognizes several predefined tags for the target operating system (for example, `linux`, `windows`, `darwin`), CPU architecture (for example, `amd64`, `386`, `arm64`), and even the version of the Go compiler (for example, `go1.10` to specify Go 1.10 onward). The following table shows a few examples that use tags to model complex build constraints.

Build Target Scenario	Build tag
Only when the target is Linux	linux
Linux or macOS	linux darwin
x64 targets but only with Go compiler >= 1.10	amd64,go1.10
32-bit Linux OR 64-bit all platforms *except* OS X	linux,386 amd64,!darwin

By now, you should have a better understanding of how build tags work. But how does all this information apply to our particular use case? First of all, let me highlight the fact that test files are also regular Go files and, as such, they are also scanned for the presence of build tags! Secondly, we are not limited to the built-in tags – we can also define our own custom tags and pass them to `go build` *or* `go test` via the `-tags` command-line flag.

You can probably see where I am going with this… We can start by defining a build tag for each family of tests, for example, `integration_tests`, `unit_tests`, and `e2e_tests`. Additionally, we will define an `all_tests` tag since we need to retain the capability to run all the tests together. Finally, we will edit our test files and add the following build tag annotations:

- `+build unit_tests all_tests` to the files containing the unit tests
- `+build integration_tests all_tests` to the files containing the integration tests
- `+build e2e_tests all_tests` to the files containing the end-to-end tests

If you wish to experiment with the preceding example, you can check out the contents of the `Chapter04/buildtags` package.

This is not the output you are looking for – mocking calls to external binaries

Have you ever struggled when trying to test code that calls out to an external process and then uses the output as part of the implemented business logic? In some cases, it might be possible to use some of the tricks we have discussed so far to decorate our code with hooks that tests can use to mock the executed command's output. Unfortunately, sometimes this will not be possible. For instance, the code under test could import a third-party package that is actually the one that's responsible for executing some external command.

The `Chapter04/pinger` package exports a function called `RoundtripTime`. Its job is to calculate the round-trip time for reaching a remote host. Under the hood, it calls out to the `ping` command and parses its output. This is how it is implemented:

```
func RoundtripTime(host string) (time.Duration, error) {
    var argList = []string{host}
    if runtime.GOOS == "windows" {
        argList = append(argList, "-n", "1", "-l", "32")
    } else {
        argList = append(argList, "-c", "1", "-s", "32")
    }
```

```
out, err := exec.Command("ping", argList...).Output()
if err != nil {
    return 0, xerrors.Errorf("command execution failed: %w", err)
}
return extractRTT(string(out))
}
```

Since the `ping` command flag names are slightly different between Unix-like systems and Windows, the code relies on OS sniffing to select the appropriate set of flags so that `ping` will send out a single request with a 32-byte payload. The `extractRTT` helper function just applies a regular expression to extract the timing information and convert it into a `time.Duration` value.

For the purpose of this demonstration, let's assume that we are operating a video streaming service and our business logic (which lives in another Go package) uses the `RoundtripTime` results to redirect our customers to the edge server that is closest to them. We have been tasked with writing an *end-to-end* test for the service so, unfortunately, we are not allowed to mock any of the calls to the `RoundtripTime` function; our test actually needs to invoke the `ping` command!

If you ever find yourself in a similar situation, let me suggest a nice trick that you can use to mock calls to external processes. I came across the concept that I am about to describe when I first joined Canonical to work on the juju code base. In hindsight, the idea is pretty straightforward. The implementation, however, is not something immediately obvious and requires some platform-specific tweaks, so kudos to the engineers that came up with it.

This approach exploits the fact that when you try to execute a binary (for example, using the `Command` function from the `os/exec` package), the operating system will look for the binary in the current working directory and if that fails, it will sequentially scan each entry in the system's `PATH` environment variable, trying to locate it. To our advantage, both Unix-like systems and Windows follow the same logic. Another interesting observation is that when you ask Windows to execute a command named `foo`, it will search for an executable called `foo.exe` *or* a batch file called `foo.bat`.

To mock an external process, we need to provide two pieces of information: the expected process output and an appropriate status code; an exit status code of *zero* would indicate that the process completed successfully. Therefore, if we could somehow create an *executable* shell script that prints out the expected output before exiting with a particular status code and prepend its path to the *front* of the system's `PATH` variable, we could trick the operating system into executing our script instead of the real binary!

At this point, we are entering the realm of OS-specific code. This practice will probably be frowned upon by some engineers, with the argument that Go programs are *usually* supposed to be portable across operating systems and CPU architectures. In this case, however, we just need to deal with two operating system families so we can probably get away with it. Let's take a look at the templates for the Unix and Windows shell scripts that our test code will be injecting. Here is the one for Unix:

```
#!/bin/bash
cat <<!!!EOF!!! | perl -pe 'chomp if eof'
%s
!!!EOF!!!
exit %d
```

The script uses the here document syntax [1] to output the text between the two !!!EOF!!! labels in verbatim. Since here documents include an extra, trailing line-feed character, we pipe the output to a Perl one-liner to strip it off. The %s placeholder will be replaced with the text (which can span several lines) that we want our command to output. Finally, the %d placeholder will be replaced with the exit code that the command will return.

The Windows version is much simpler since here documents are not supported by the built-in shell interpreter (cmd.exe). Due to this, I have opted to write the output to a file and just have the shell script print it to the standard output. Here's what this looks like:

```
@echo off
type %s
exit /B %d
```

In this case, the %s placeholder will be replaced with the path to the external file containing the output for the mocked command and, as before, the %d placeholder will be replaced with the exit code for the command.

In our test file, we will define a helper function called mockCmdOutput. Due to space constraints, I will not be including the full listing of the function here but rather a short synopsis of how it works (for the full implementation, you can check out the Chapter04/pinger sources). In a nutshell, mockCmdOutput does the following:

- Creates a temporary folder that will be automatically removed after the test completes
- Selects the appropriate shell script template, depending on the operating system

- Writes the shell script to the temporary folder and changes its permissions so that it becomes executable (important for Unix-like systems)
- Prepends the temporary folder to the beginning of the PATH environment variable for the currently running process (go test)

Since mockCmdOutput modifies the system path, we *must* ensure that it gets reset to its original value *before* each of our tests runs. We can easily achieve this by grouping our tests into a gocheck test suite and providing a test setup function to save the original PATH value and a test teardown function to restore it from the saved value. With all the plumbing in place, here is how we can write a test function that mocks the output of ping:

```
func (s *PingerSuite) TestFakePing(c *check.C) {
    mock := "32 bytes from 127.0.0.1: icmp_seq=0 ttl=32 time=42000 ms"
    mockCmdOutput(c, "ping", mock, 0)

    got, err := pinger.RoundtripTime("127.0.0.1")
    c.Assert(err, check.IsNil)
    c.Assert(got, check.Equals, 42*time.Second)
}
```

To make sure that the command was mocked correctly, we set up our test to do a round-trip measurement to localhost (typically taking 1 ms or less) and mock the ping command to return a ridiculously high number (42 seconds). Try running the test on OS X, Linux, or Windows; you will always get consistent results.

Testing timeouts is easy when you have all the time in the world!

I am pretty sure that, at some point, you have written some code that relies on the time-keeping functions provided by the standard library's time package. Perhaps it's some code that periodically polls a remote endpoint – a great case for using time.NewTicker – or maybe you are using time.After to implement a timeout mechanism inside a go-routine that waits for an event to occur. In a slightly different scenario, using time.NewTimer to provide your server code with ample time to drain all its connections before shutting down would also be a stellar idea.

However, testing code that uses any of these patterns is not a trivial thing. For example, let's say that you are trying to test a piece of code that blocks until an event is received or a specific amount of time elapses without receiving an event. In the latter case, it would return some sort of timeout error to the caller. To verify that the timeout logic works as expected and to avoid locking up the test runner if the blocking code never returns, the typical approach would be to spin up a go-routine that runs the blocking code and then signals (for example, over a channel) when the expected error is returned. The test function that starts the go-routine would then use a `select` block to wait for either a success signal from the go-routine or for a fixed amount of time to elapse, after which it would automatically fail the test.

If we were to apply this approach, how long should such a test wait for before giving up? If the max wait time for the blocking piece of code is known in advance (for example, defined as a *constant*), then things are relatively easy; our test needs to wait for at least that amount of time, *plus* some extra time to account for speed discrepancies when running tests in different environments (for example, locally versus on the CI). Failure to account for these discrepancies can lead to flaky tests – tests that *randomly* fail, making your CI system vehemently complain.

Things are much easier if the timeout is configurable or at least specified as a *global variable* that our tests can patch while they are executing. What if, however, the test time is specified as a constant, but its value is in the order of a couple of seconds. Clearly, having several tests that run for that amount of time literally doing *nothing but waiting* is counter-productive.

Similarly, in some cases, timeouts might be calculated via some formula that includes a random component. That would make the timeout much harder to predict in a deterministic way without resorting to hacks such as setting the random number generator's seed to a specific value. Of course, in this scenario, our tests would just break if another engineer even slightly tweaked the formula that's used to calculate the timeouts.

The `Chapter04/dialer` package is an interesting case for further examination as it exhibits both issues that I've described here: long wait times that are calculated via a formula! This package provides a dialing wrapper that overlays an exponential backoff retry mechanism on top of a network dialing function (for example, `net.Dial`).

To create a new retrying dialer, we need to call the `NewRetryingDialer` constructor:

```
func NewRetryingDialer(ctx context.Context, dialFunc DialFunc, maxAttempts
int) *RetryingDialer {
    if maxAttempts > 31 {
        panic("maxAttempts cannot exceed 31")
    }

    return &RetryingDialer{
        ctx:         ctx,
        dialFunc:    dialFunc,
        maxAttempts: maxAttempts,
    }
}
```

The caller provides a `context.Context` instance, which can be used to abort pending dial attempts if, for instance, the application receives a signal to shut down. Now, let's move on to the meat of the dialer implementation – the `Dial` call:

```
func (d *RetryingDialer) Dial(network, address string) (conn net.Conn, err
error) {
    for attempt := 1; attempt <= d.maxAttempts; attempt++ {
        if conn, err = d.dialFunc(network, address); err == nil {
            return conn, nil
        }

        log.Printf("dial %q: attempt %d failed; retrying after %s",
address, attempt, expBackoff(attempt))
        select {
        case <-time.After(expBackoff(attempt)): // Try again
        case <-d.ctx.Done():
            return nil, d.ctx.Err()
        }
    }
    return nil, ErrMaxRetriesExceeded
}
```

This is a pretty straightforward implementation: each time a dial attempt fails, we invoke the `expBackoff` helper to calculate the wait time for the next attempt. Then, we block until the wait time elapses or the context gets cancelled. Finally, if we happen to exceed the maximum configured number of retry attempts, the code will automatically bail out and return an error to the caller. How about writing a short test to verify that the preceding code handles timeouts as expected? This is what it would look like:

```
func TestRetryingDialerWithRealClock(t *testing.T) {
    log.SetFlags(0)
```

```
    // Dial a random local port that nothing is listening on.
    d := dialer.NewRetryingDialer(context.Background(), net.Dial, 20)
    _, err := d.Dial("tcp", "127.0.0.1:65000")
    if err !=  {
        t.Fatal(err)
    }
}
```

Running the preceding test yields the following output:

```
● ● ●                                    4. bash (bash)
[go test] running tests and collecting coverage metrics
=== RUN   TestRetryingDialerWithRealClock
dial "127.0.0.1:65000": attempt 1 failed; retrying after 414ms
dial "127.0.0.1:65000": attempt 2 failed; retrying after 829ms
dial "127.0.0.1:65000": attempt 3 failed; retrying after 953ms
dial "127.0.0.1:65000": attempt 4 failed; retrying after 790ms
dial "127.0.0.1:65000": attempt 5 failed; retrying after 280ms
dial "127.0.0.1:65000": attempt 6 failed; retrying after 212ms
dial "127.0.0.1:65000": attempt 7 failed; retrying after 830ms
dial "127.0.0.1:65000": attempt 8 failed; retrying after 1.027s
dial "127.0.0.1:65000": attempt 9 failed; retrying after 1.992s
dial "127.0.0.1:65000": attempt 10 failed; retrying after 2.838s
--- PASS: TestRetryingDialerWithRealClock (8.07s)
PASS
coverage: 73.3% of statements
ok      github.com/PacktPublishing/Hands-On-Software-Engineering-with-Golang/ch04/dialer       9.087s  coverage: 73.3% of statements
```

Figure 6: Testing the retrying dialer with a real clock

Success! The test passed. But hold on a minute; look at the test's runtime! *9 seconds*!!! Surely we can do better than this. Wouldn't it be great if we could somehow mock time in Go as we do when writing tests for other programming languages? It turns out that it is indeed possible with the help of packages such as `jonboulle/clockwork` [2] and `juju/clock` [8]. We will be using the latter package for our testing purposes as it also supports mock timers.

The `juju/clock` package exposes a `Clock` interface whose method signatures match the functions that are exported by the built-in `time` package. What's more, it provides a real clock implementation (`juju.WallClock`) that we should be injecting into production code, as well as a fake clock implementation that we can manipulate within our tests.

If we can inject a `clock.Clock` instance into the `RetryingDialer` struct, we can use it as a replacement for the `time.After` call in the retry code. That's easy: just modify the dialer constructor argument list so that it includes a clock instance.

Now, let's create a copy of the previous test but this time inject a fake clock into the dialer. To control the time, we will spin up a go-routine to keep advancing the clock by a fixed amount of time until the test completes. For brevity, the following listing only includes the code for controlling the clock; other than that, the rest of the test's setup and its expectations are exactly the same as before:

```
doneCh := make(chan struct{})
defer close(doneCh)
clk := testclock.NewClock(time.Now())
go func() {
    for {
        select {
        case <-doneCh: // test completed; exit go-routine
            return
        default:
            clk.Advance(1 * time.Minute)
        }
    }
}()
```

As expected, our new test also passes successfully. However, compared to the previous test run, the new test ran in a fraction of the time – just **0.010s**:

```
                                                    4. bash (bash)
$ go test -v -run TestRetryingDialerWithFakeClock
=== RUN   TestRetryingDialerWithFakeClock
dial "127.0.0.1:65000": attempt 1 failed; retrying after 414ms
dial "127.0.0.1:65000": attempt 2 failed; retrying after 829ms
dial "127.0.0.1:65000": attempt 3 failed; retrying after 953ms
dial "127.0.0.1:65000": attempt 4 failed; retrying after 790ms
dial "127.0.0.1:65000": attempt 5 failed; retrying after 280ms
dial "127.0.0.1:65000": attempt 6 failed; retrying after 212ms
dial "127.0.0.1:65000": attempt 7 failed; retrying after 830ms
dial "127.0.0.1:65000": attempt 8 failed; retrying after 1.027s
dial "127.0.0.1:65000": attempt 9 failed; retrying after 1.992s
dial "127.0.0.1:65000": attempt 10 failed; retrying after 2.838s
--- PASS: TestRetryingDialerWithFakeClock (0.00s)
PASS
ok      github.com/PacktPublishing/Hands-On-Software-Engineering-with-Golang/ch04/dialer      0.010s
```

Figure 7: Testing the retrying dialer with a fake clock

Personally speaking, fake clocks are one of my favorite test primitives. If you are not using fake clocks in your tests, I would strongly recommend that you at least experiment with them. I am sure that you will also reach the conclusion that fake clocks are a great tool for writing well-behaved tests for any piece of code that deals with some aspect of time. Moreover, increasing the stability of your test suites is a fair trade-off for the small bit of refactoring that's required to introduce clocks into your existing code base.

Summary

As the old proverb goes: you cannot build a house without good foundations. The same principle also applies to software engineering. Having a solid test infrastructure in place goes a long way to allowing engineers to work on new features while being confident that their changes will not break the existing code.

Through the course of this chapter, we performed a deep dive into the different types of testing that you need to be aware of when working on medium- to large-scale systems. To begin with, we discussed the concept of unit testing, the essential *must-have* type of test for all projects, regardless of size, whose primary role is to ensure that individual units of code work as expected in isolation. Then, we tackled more complex patterns, such as integration and functional testing, which verify that units and, by extension, the complete system work harmoniously together. The last part of this chapter was dedicated to exploring advanced test concepts such as smoke tests and chaos testing and concluded with a list of practical tips and tricks for writing tests in a more efficient manner.

Now, it's time for you to put on your software engineering hat and put all of the knowledge you have acquired so far to good use. To this end, over the course of the following chapters, we will be speccing out and building, from scratch, a complete end-to-end system using Go. This system will serve as a sandbox for the practical exploration of each of the concepts we will introduce throughout the rest of this book.

Questions

1. What is the difference between a stub and a mock?
2. Explain how fake objects work and describe an example scenario where you would opt to use a fake object instead of a mock.
3. What are the main components of a table-driven test?
4. What is the difference between a unit test and an integration test?
5. What is the difference between an integration test and a functional test?
6. Describe the *ambassador* pattern and how it can be exploited to safely run tests in production.

Further reading

1. **Bash manual**: here documents: `https://www.gnu.org/savannah-checkouts/gnu/bash/manual/bash.html#Here-Documents`.
2. `clockwork`: A fake clock for golang: `https://github.com/jonboulle/clockwork`.
3. `gocheck`: Rich testing for the Go language: `http://labix.org/gocheck`.
4. `gomock`: A mocking framework for the Go programming language: `https://github.com/golang/mock`.
5. Meszaros, Gerard: *XUnit Test Patterns: Refactoring Test Code*. Upper Saddle River, NJ, USA : Prentice Hall PTR, 2006 – ISBN 0131495054 (`https://www.worldcat.org/title/xunit-test-patterns-refactoring-test-code/oclc/935197390`).
6. **Selenium**: Browser automation: `https://www.seleniumhq.org`.
7. `testify`: A toolkit with common assertions and mocks that plays nicely with the standard library: `https://github.com/stretchr/testify`.
8. `juju/clock`: Clock definition and a testing clock: `https://github.com/juju/clock`.

3
Section 3: Designing and Building a Multi-Tier System from Scratch

The purpose of part three is to guide you through the various stages of designing, building, and deploying a complex system using Go.

This sections comprises the following chapters:

- Chapter 5, *The Links 'R' Us Project*
- Chapter 6, *Building a Persistence Layer*
- Chapter 7, *Data-Processing Pipelines*
- Chapter 8, *Graph-Based Data Processing*
- Chapter 9, *Communicating with the Outside World*
- Chapter 10, *Building, Packaging, and Deploying Software*

5
The Links 'R' Us Project

"The hardest part of the software task is arriving at a complete and consistent specification, and much of the essence of building a program is in fact the debugging of the specification."

- Frederick P. Brooks [3]

In this chapter, we will be discussing Links 'R' Us, a Go project that we will be building from scratch throughout the remaining chapters in this book. This project has been specifically designed to combine everything you have learned so far with some of the more technical topics that we will be touching on in the following chapters: databases, pipelines, graph processing, gRPC, instrumentation, and monitoring.

The following topics will be covered in this chapter:

- A brief overview of the system that we will be building and its primary function
- Selecting an appropriate SDLC model for the project
- Functional and non-functional requirements analysis
- Component-based modeling of the Links 'R' Us service
- Choosing an appropriate architecture (monolith versus microservices) for the project

System overview – what are we going to be building?

Throughout the next chapters, we will be assembling, piece by piece, our very own *search-engine*. As with all projects, we need to come up with a cool-sounding name for it. Let me introduce you to *Links 'R' Us!*

So, what are the core functionalities of the Links 'R' Us project? The primary, and kind of obvious, functionality is being able to search for content. However, before we can make our search engine available to the public, we first need to seed it with content. To this end, we need to provide the means for users to submit URLs to our search engine. The search engine would then crawl those links, index their content, and add any newly encountered links to its database for further crawling.

Is this all we need for launching Links 'R' Us? The short answer is no! While user searches would return results containing the keywords from the users' search queries, we would lack the capability to *order* them in a meaningful way, especially if the results range in the thousands.

Consequently, we need to introduce some sort of a link or content quality metric to our system and order the returned results by it. Instead of re-inventing the wheel, we will be stepping on the shoulders of search-engine *giants* (that would be Google) and implementing a battle-tested algorithm called `PageRank`.

The `PageRank` algorithm was introduced by a nowadays very popular and heavily cited paper titled *The PageRank Citation Ranking: Bringing Order to the Web*. The original paper was authored back in 1998 by Larry Page, Sergey Brin, Rajeev Motwani, and Terry Winograd [9] and, over the years, has served as the basis for the search-engine implementation at Google.

Given a graph containing links between web-pages, the `PageRank` algorithm assigns an importance score to each link in the graph taking into account the number of links that lead to it and their relative importance scores.

While `PageRank` was initially introduced as a tool for organizing web content, its generalized form applies to any type of link graph. For the last few years, there has been on-going research into applying `PageRank` ideas in a multitude of fields ranging from biochemistry [5] to traffic optimization [10].

We will be exploring the `PageRank` algorithm in more detail in `Chapter 8`, *Graph-Based Data Processing*, and `Chapter 12`, *Building Distributed Graph-Processing Systems*, as part of a larger discussion centered around the various approaches we can employ to facilitate processing of large graphs on a single node or across a cluster of nodes (out-of-core graph processing).

Selecting an SDLC model for our project

Before delving into the details of the Links 'R' Us project, we need to consider the SDLC models we discussed in `Chapter 1`, *A Bird's-Eye View of Software Engineering*, and select one that makes more sense for this type of project. The choice of a suitable model is of paramount importance: it will serve as our guide for capturing the requirements for the project, defining the components and the interface contracts between them, and appropriately dividing the work to be done in logical chunks that can be built and tested independently of each other.

In this section, we will outline the main reasoning behind the selection of an Agile framework for our project and elaborate on a set of interesting approaches for speeding up our development velocity using a technique known as *elephant carpaccio*.

Iterating faster using an Agile framework

To begin with, for all intents and purposes, Links 'R' Us is a typical example of a green-field type of project. Since there are no pressing deadlines for delivering the project, we should definitely take our time to explore the pros and cons of any alternative technologies at our disposal for implementing the various components of the system.

For instance, when it comes to indexing and searching the documents that our system will be crawling, there are several competing products/services that we need to evaluate before deciding on which one to use. Furthermore, if we decide to containerize our project using a tool such as Docker, there are several orchestration frameworks (for example, Kubernetes [6], Apache Mesos [2], or Docker Swarm [11]) available for deploying our services to our staging and production environments.

As far as the software development pace is concerned, we are going to be *gradually* and *incrementally* building the various components of Links 'R' Us for the next few chapters. Given that we are working on what is essentially a user-facing product, it is imperative to work in small iterations so that we can get the prototype versions out to user focus groups as early as possible. This will enable us to collect valuable feedback that will aid us in fine-tuning and polishing our product as development goes on.

For all of the preceding reasons, I think it would be prudent to adopt an Agile approach to developing Links 'R' Us. My personal preference would be to use Scrum. As we don't really have an actual development team to back the project's development, concepts such as stand-ups, planning, and retrospective sessions do not apply to our particular case. Instead, we need to compromise and adopt some of the ideas behind Scrum in our own Agile workflow.

To this end, in the requirements analysis section, we will focus on creating user stories. Once that process is complete, we will use those stories as input to infer the set of high-level components that we need to build, as well as the ways they are expected to interact with each other. Finally, when the time comes to implement each user story, we will assume the role of the *product owner* and break each story down into a set of cards which we will then arrange in a Kanban board.

But before we start working on user stories, I would like to introduce a quite useful and helpful technique that can help you to iterate even faster with your own projects: *elephant carpaccio*.

Elephant carpaccio – how to iterate even faster!

This peculiarly-named technique owes its existence to an exercise invented by Dr. Alistair Cockburn. The purpose of this exercise is to help people (engineers and non-engineers alike) to practice and learn how they can split complex story cards (the elephant) into very *thin vertical slices* that teams can oftentimes tackle in parallel.

It may strike you as odd but the slice size that I have found most helpful in projects that I have been involved with in the past is nothing more than a *single day's worth of work*. The rationale of the one-day split is to ship (behind a feature flag) small parts of the total work every single day, an approach that is congruent with the *ship fast* motto advocated by Agile development.

Suffice it to say, splitting cards into one-day slices is certainly not a trivial task. It does take a bit of practice and patience to condition your brain so it switches its focus from long-running tasks to breaking down and optimizing workloads for much shorter periods of time. On the flip side, this approach allows engineering teams to identify and resolve potential blockers as early as possible; it goes without saying that we would obviously prefer to detect blockers near the beginning of the sprint rather than the middle, or, even worse, close to the end of the sprint cycle!

Another advantage of this technique, at least from the perspective of Go engineers, is that it makes us think more carefully about the best way to organize our code base to ensure that, by the end of each day, we always have a piece of software that can be cleanly compiled and deployed. This constraint forces us into developing the good habit of thinking about code in terms of interfaces as per the tenets of the SOLID design principles we explored in Chapter 2, *Best Practices for Writing Clean and Maintainable Go Code*.

Requirements analysis

To perform a detailed requirements analysis for the Links 'R' Us project, we need to essentially come up with answers for two key questions: *what* do we need to build and *how well* would our proposed design fare against a set of goals?

To answer the *what* question, we need to list all of the core functionalities that our system is expected to implement as well as describe how the various actors will interact with it. This forms the **Functional Requirements (FRs)** for our analysis.

To answer the latter question, we have to state the **Non-Functional Requirements (NFRs)** for our solution. Typically, the list of non-functional requirements includes items such as **Service-Level Objectives (SLOs)** and capacity and scalability requirements, as well as security-related considerations for our project.

Functional requirements

As we have already decided on utilizing an Agile model for implementing our project, the next logical step for defining our functional list of requirements is to establish *user stories*.

> The concept of user stories pertains to the need of expressing software requirements from the perspective of an actor that interacts with the system. In many types of projects, actors are typically considered to be the end users of the system. However, in the general case, *other systems* (for example, a backend service) may also assume the role of an actor.

Each user story begins with a *succinct* requirement specification. It is important to note that the specification itself must *always* be expressed from the viewpoint of the actor that will be impacted by it. Furthermore, when creating user stories, we should always strive to capture the *business value*, also referred to as the *true reason*, behind each requirement. What's more, one of the core values of Agile development is the so-called *definition of done*. When authoring stories, we need to include a list of *acceptance criteria* that will be used as a verification tool to ensure that each story goal has been successfully met.

For defining the functional requirements for Links 'R' Us, we will be utilizing the following, rather standardized, Agile template:

As an [actor],
I need to be able to [short requirement],
so as to [reason/business value].

The acceptance criteria for this user story are as follows:
[list of criteria]

One final thing that I would like to point out is that, while each story will record a *need* for a particular feature, all of them will be completely devoid of any sort of implementation detail. This is quite intentional, and congruent with the recommended practices when working with any Agile framework. As we discussed in Chapter 1, *A Bird's-Eye View of Software Engineering*, our goal is to defer any technical implementation decisions up to the last possible moment. If we were to decide up-front about how we are going to implement each user story, we would be placing unnecessary constraints on our development process, hence limiting our flexibility and the amount of work we can achieve given a particular time budget.

Let's now apply the preceding template to capture the set of functional requirements for the Links 'R' Us project as a list of user stories that will be individually tackled throughout the following chapters.

User story – link submission

As an end user,
I need to be able to submit new links to Links 'R' Us,
so as to update the link graph and make their contents searchable.

The acceptance criteria for this user story are as follows:

- A frontend or API endpoint is provided for facilitating the link submission journey for the end users.
- Submitted links have the following criteria:
    - Must be added to the graph
    - Must be crawled by the system and added to their index
- Already submitted links should be accepted by the backend but not inserted twice to the graph.

User story – search

As an `end user`,
I need to be able to `submit full-text search queries`,
so as to `to retrieve a list of relevant matching results from the content indexed by Links 'R' Us.`

The acceptance criteria for this user story are as follows:

- A frontend or API endpoint is provided for the users to submit a full-text query.
- If the query matches multiple items, they are returned as a list that the end user can paginate through.
- Each entry in the result list must contain the following items: title or link description, the link to the content, and a timestamp indicating when the link was last crawled. *If feasible*, the link may also contain a relevance score expressed as a percentage.
- When the query does not match any item, an appropriate response should be returned to the end user.

User story – crawl link graph

As the `crawler backend system`,
I need to be able to `obtain a list of sanitized links from the link graph,`
so as to `fetch and index their contents while at the same time expanding the link graph with newly discovered links.`

The acceptance criteria for this user story are as follows:

- The crawler can query the link graph and receive a list of stale links that need to be crawled.
- Links received by the crawler are retrieved from the remote hosts unless the remote server provides an `ETag` or `Last Modified` header that the crawler has already seen before.
- Retrieved content is scanned for links and the link graph gets updated.
- Retrieved content is indexed and added to the search corpus.

User story – calculate PageRank scores

As the `PageRank calculator backend system,`
I need to be able to `access the link graph,`
so as to `calculate and persist the PageRank score for each link.`

The acceptance criteria for this user story are as follows:

- The PageRank calculator can obtain an immutable snapshot of the entire link graph.
- A PageRank score is assigned to every link in the graph.
- The search corpus entries are annotated with the updated PageRank scores.

User story – monitor Links 'R' Us health

As a `member of the Links 'R' Us Site Reliability Engineering (SRE) team,`
I need to be able to `monitor the health of all Links 'R' Us services,`
so as to `detect and address issues that cause degraded service performance.`

The acceptance criteria for this user story are as follows:

- All Links 'R' Us services should periodically submit health- and performance-related metrics to a centralized metrics collection system.
- A monitoring dashboard is created for each service.
- A high-level monitoring dashboard tracks the overall system health.
- Metric-based alerts are defined and linked to a paging service. Each alert comes with its own *playbook* with a set of steps that need to be performed by a member of the SRE team that is on-call.

Non-functional requirements

In this section, we will go through a list of non-functional requirements for the Links 'R' Us project. Please keep in mind that this list is not exhaustive. Since this is not a real-world project, I opted to describe only a small subset of the possible non-functional requirements that make sense from the viewpoint of the components that we will be building in the following chapters.

Service-level objectives

From a **Site Reliability Engineering (SRE)** perspective, we need to come up with a list of SLOs that will be used as a gauge for the Links 'R' Us project's performance. Ideally, we should be defining individual SLOs for each one of our services. That may not be immediately possible at the design stage but, at the very least, we need to come up with a realistic SLO for the user-facing components of our system.

SLOs consist of three parts: a description of the thing that we are measuring, the expected service level expressed as a percentage, and the period where the measurement takes place. The following table lists some initial and fairly standard SLOs for Links 'R' Us:

Metric	Expectation	Measurement Period	Notes
Links 'R' Us availability	99% uptime	Yearly	Tolerates up to 3d 15h 39m of downtime per year
Index service availability	99.9% uptime	Yearly	Tolerates up to 8h 45m of downtime per year
PageRank calculator service availability	70% uptime	Yearly	Not a user-facing component of our system; the service can endure longer periods of downtime
Search response time	30% of requests answered in 0.5s	Monthly	
Search response time	70% of requests answered in 1.2s	Monthly	
Search response time	99% of requests answered in 2.0s	Monthly	
CPU utilization for the PageRank calculator service	90%	Weekly	We shouldn't be paying for idle computing nodes
SRE team incident response time	90% of tickets resolved within 8h	Monthly	

Keep in mind that, at this stage, we don't really have any prior data available; we are more or less using *guesstimates* for the service levels that we are targeting. We will be revisiting and updating the SLOs to better reflect reality once the complete system gets deployed to production and our SRE team acquires a better understanding of the system's idiosyncrasies.

As a quick heads-up, `Chapter 13`, *Metrics Collection and Visualization*, of this book exclusively focuses on the SRE aspects involved in operating production services. In that chapter, we will be elaborating on popular tools that we can use to capture, visualize, and alert on our service-level-related metrics.

Security considerations

As we all know, when it comes to online services, *security* is characterized, above all, as a factor that can make or break a particular product. To this end, we need to discuss some potential security issues that may arise when building a project such as Links 'R' Us and devise strategies for dealing with them.

Our analysis operates under the premise that *you should never trust the client*, in this case, the user interacting with Links 'R' Us. Should our project become successful, it will inadvertently attract the attention of malicious actors that will, at some point, try to locate and exploit security holes in our system.

One of the use cases that I presented earlier involves the user submitting a URL that the service will eventually crawl and add to its search index. You may be wondering what could possibly go wrong with a service that just crawls user-submitted URLs? Here are a few interesting examples.

Most cloud providers run an internal metadata service that each computing node can query to obtain information about itself. This service is typically accessed via a *link-local* address such as `169.254.169.254` and nodes can perform simple HTTP GET requests to retrieve the information they are interested in.

Link-local addresses are a special block of addresses reserved by the **Internet Engineering Task Force (IETF)**. The range of IPv4 addresses within that block is described in CIDR notation as `169.254.0.0/16` (65,536 unique addresses). Similarly, the following address block has been reserved for use with IPv6: `fe80::/10`.

These addresses are special in that they are only valid within a particular network segment and they are not route-able beyond that; that is, routers will refuse to forward them to other networks. Link-local addresses are therefore safe to use internally.

Let's assume that we have deployed the Links 'R' Us project to Amazon EC2. The documentation page [1] for the EC2 metadata service references quite a few link-local endpoints that a malicious adversary could use. Here are two of the more interesting ones from an attacker's perspective:

- `http://169.254.169.254/latest/meta-data/iam/info` returns information about the roles associated with the compute node that the call originates from.
- `http://169.254.169.254/latest/meta-data/iam/security-credential s/<role-name>` returns a set of temporary security credentials associated with a particular role.

In a potential attack scenario, the malicious user submits the first URL to the crawler. If the crawler simply fetches the link and adds the response to the search index, the attacker can perform a targeted search and obtain the *name* of a security role associated with the nodes where the crawling service is deployed. Using that information, the attacker would then submit the second URL to the crawler, hoping to get lucky and retrieve a list of valid credentials by waiting once more for the link to be indexed and then performing a second targeted search query. This way, the adversary could gain unauthorized access to another service that the project is using *internally* (for example, a storage service such as S3).

In case you are wondering, both Google Cloud and Microsoft Azure mitigate this information leak loophole by requiring a special HTTP header to be present when a compute node contacts their metadata services. However, this doesn't mean that we shouldn't be excluding *other* IP ranges from our crawl operations. For starters, we should always exclude *private network* addresses. After all, some of the services that we might opt to use (Elasticsearch comes to mind) could expose potentially unauthenticated RESTful APIs that can be reached by the compute nodes running the crawler code. Evidently, we don't want information from our backend services to appear in our search index! The following table lists some of the special IPv4 ranges that we should definitely avoid crawling:

IP block (CIDR notation)	Description
10.0.0.0/8	Private network
172.16.0.0/12	Private network
192.168.0.0/16	Private network
169.254.0.0/16	Link-local addresses
127.0.0.1	Loop-back IP address
0.0.0.0/8	All IP addresses on the local machine
255.255.255.255/32	The broadcast address for the current network

The list from the preceding table is not complete. In fact, you would need to exclude a few more IP blocks such as the ones reserved for carrier-grade traffic, multicast, and test networks. What's more, we should also exclude the equivalent IPv6 ranges if our cloud provider's network stack supports IPv6. If you are interested in learning more about this topic, you can find a comprehensive IPv4 black-list at the GitHub repository for the MASSCAN project [8].

One final thing that you may or may not be aware of is that many URL crawling libraries support schemes other than `http/https`. One example of those schemes is `file`, which, unless disabled, might allow an attacker to trick the crawler into reading and indexing the contents of a local file (for example, `/etc/passwd`) from the node the crawler is executing on.

If you haven't used the file protocol scheme before, try typing the following address into your favorite web-browser: `file:///`.

Being good netizens

While our end-goal is to be able to crawl and index the entire internet, the truth of the matter is that the links that we are retrieving and indexing point to content that belongs to someone else. It can so happen that those third parties object to us indexing *some* or *all* links to the domains under their control.

Fortunately, there is a standardized way for web-masters to notify crawlers not only about which links they can crawl and which we are not allowed to but also to dictate an acceptable crawl speed to not incur a high load on the remote host. This is all achieved by authoring a `robots.txt` file and placing it at the root of each domain. The file contains a set of directives like the following:

- **User-Agent**: The name of the crawler (user agent string) which the following instructions apply to
- **Disallow**: A regular expression that excludes any matching URL from being crawled
- **Crawl-Delay**: The number of seconds for the crawler to wait before crawling subsequent links from this domain
- **Sitemap**: A link to an XML file which defines all links within a domain and provides metadata such as a *last-update* timestamp that crawlers can use to optimize their link access patterns

To be good netizens, we need to ensure that our crawler implementation respects the contents of any `robots.txt` file that it encounters. Last but not least, our parser should be able to properly handle the various status codes returned by remote hosts and dial down its crawl speed if it detects an issue with the remote host or the remote host decides to throttle us.

System component modeling

As the first step in mapping the project's architecture, we will begin by creating a UML component diagram. The main goal here is to identify and describe the structural connections between the various *components* that comprise our system.

A component is defined as an encapsulated standalone unit that constitutes an integral part of a system or a sub-system. Components communicate with each other by exposing and consuming one or several interfaces.

One key point of component-based design is that components should always be considered as abstract, logical entities that expose a particular behavior. This design approach is closely aligned with the SOLID principles and offers us the flexibility to freely change or even swap component implementations at any point throughout the project's development.

The following diagram breaks down the Links 'R' Us project into high-level components and visually illustrates the interfaces exposed and consumed by each one of them:

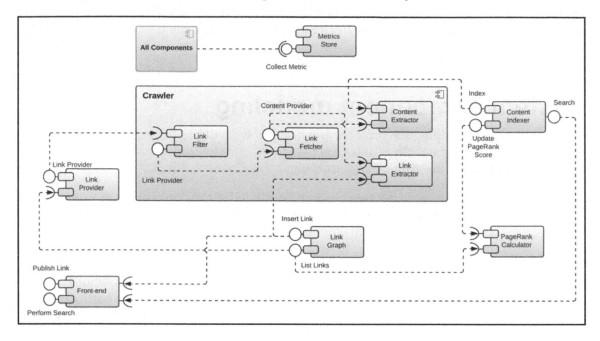

Figure 1: The UML component diagram for the Links 'R' Us project

In case you are not familiar with the symbols used by this type of diagram, here is a quick explanation of what each symbol represents:

- Boxes with two port-like symbols on the side represent components.
- Components can also be nested within other components. In that case, each sub-component is encapsulated within a box that represents its parent component. In the preceding diagram, **Link Filter** is a sub-component of **Crawler**.
- A full circle represents an *interface* **implemented** by a particular component. For instance, **Search** is one of the interfaces implemented by the **Content Indexer** component.
- A half-circle indicates that a component *requires* a particular interface. For example, the **Link Extractor** component requires the **Insert Link** interface implemented by the **Link Graph** component.

Now that we have mapped out a high-level view of the system components required for constructing our project, we need to spend some time and examine each one in a bit more detail.

The crawler

The crawler component is effectively the heart of the search engine. It operates on a set of links that are either seeded into the system or discovered while crawling a previous set of links. As you can see in the preceding component model diagram, the crawler itself is in fact a package that encapsulates several other sub-components that operate in a pipeline-like kind of configuration. Let's examine the role of each one of those sub-components in a bit more detail.

The link filter

A naive crawler implementation would attempt to retrieve any links that are provided as input to it. But as we all know, the web is home to all sorts of content ranging from text or HTML documents to images, music, videos, and a wide variety of other types of binary data (for example, archives, ISOs, executables, and so on).

You would probably agree that attempting to download items that cannot be processed by the search engine would not only be a waste of resources but it would also incur additional running costs to the operator of the Links 'R' Us service: us! Consequently, excluding such content from the crawler would be a beneficial cost reduction strategy.

This is where the *link filter* component comes into play. Before we try to fetch a remote link, the link filter will first attempt to identify the content at the other side and drop any links that do not seem to point to content that we can process.

The link fetcher

All links that survive the link filter are consumed by the *link fetcher* component. As its name implies, this component is responsible for establishing an HTTP connection to each link target and retrieving any content returned by the server at the other end.

The fetcher meticulously processes the HTTP status code and any HTTP headers returned by remote servers. If the returned status code indicates that the content has been moved to a different location (that is, 301 or 302), the fetcher will automatically follow redirects until it reaches the content's final destination. It stands to reason that we would not want our fetcher to get stuck in an infinite redirect loop trying to crawl an incorrectly configured (or malicious) remote host. To this end, the crawler will need to maintain a redirect hop counter and abort the crawl attempt when it exceeds a particular value.

Another important HTTP header that the fetcher pays close attention to is the `Content-Type` header. This header is populated by the remote server and identifies the type (also known as MIME type) of data returned by the server. If the remote server replies with an unsupported content type header (for example, indicating an image or a JavaScript file), the fetcher should automatically drop the link and prevent it from reaching the next stages of the crawl pipeline, the **content extractor** and the **content indexer**.

The content extractor

The **content extractor** attempts to identify and extract all text from a document downloaded from a remote server. For instance, if the link is pointed to a plaintext document, then the extractor would emit the document content as is. On the other hand, if the link pointed to an HTML document, the extractor would strip off any HTML elements and emit the text-only portion of the document.

The emitted content is sent off to the **content indexer** component so it can be tokenized and update the Links 'R' Us full-text search index.

The link extractor

The last crawler component that we will be examining is the **link extractor**. It scans retrieved HTML documents and attempts to identify and extract all links present inside.

Link extraction is unfortunately not a trivial task. While it's true that the majority of links can be extracted via a bunch of regular expressions, there are a few edge-cases that require additional logic from our end, as in the following examples:

- Relative links need to be converted into absolute links.
- If the document `<head>` section includes the `<base href="xxx">` tag, we need to parse it and use its content to rewrite relative links.
- We might encounter links that *do not* specify a protocol. These special links begin with `//` and are commonly used when referencing content from a CDN or in HTTPS pages that include static resources from non-HTTPS sources (for example, images in a cart checkout page). When a web-browser encounters such links, it will automatically use the protocol from the current URL to fetch those links.

The link extractor will transmit all newly discovered links to the *link graph* component so that existing graph connections can be updated and new ones created.

The content indexer

The **content indexer** is yet another very important component for the Links 'R' Us project. This component performs two distinct functions.

To begin with, the component maintains a full-text index for all documents retrieved by the crawler. Any new or updated document that is emitted by the **content extractor** component is propagated to the **content indexer** so that the index can be updated.

It stands to reason that having an index with no means of searching greatly diminishes its usefulness. To this end, the content indexer exposes mechanisms that allow other components to perform full-text searches against the index and to order the results according to retrieval date and/or PageRank score.

The link provider

The **link provider** component periodically scrubs the link graph and collects a list of candidate links for a new crawl pass. Candidate links include the following:

- Recently discovered links that haven't been crawled yet
- Links for which recent crawl attempts failed (for example, the crawler received a 404/NOT-FOUND response from the remote server)
- Links that the crawler successfully processed in the past but need to be re-visited in case the content they point to has changed

Given that the WWW is comprised of a mind-boggling number of pages (approximately 6.16 billion as of January 2020), it makes sense to assume that, as our discovered graph of links grows over time, we will eventually reach a point where the set of links we need to crawl will exceed the available memory capacity of our compute nodes! This is why the link provider component employs a *streaming* approach: while the link scrubbing process is executing, any selected link candidate will be immediately passed along to the *crawler* component for further processing.

The link graph

The **link graph** is responsible for keeping track not only of all links that the crawler has discovered so far but also of how they are connected. It exposes interfaces for other components to add or remove links from the graph and, of course, query the graph.

Several other system components depend on the interfaces exposed by the link graph component:

- The *link provider* queries the link graph to decide which links should be crawled next.
- The *link extractor* sub-component of the crawler adds newly discovered links to the graph.
- The *PageRank calculator* components require access to the entire graph's connectivity information so that it can calculate the PageRank score of each link.

Note that I am not talking about a *single* interface but I am using the plural form: *interfaces*. This is deliberate as the link graph component is a prime candidate for implementing the **Command Query Responsibility Segregation (CQRS)** pattern.

> The CQRS pattern belongs to the family of architectural patterns. The key idea behind CQRS is to separate the write and read models exposed by a particular component so they can be optimized in isolation. **Commands** refer to operations that mutate the state of the model, whereas *queries* retrieve and return the current model state.

> This separation allows us to execute different business logic paths for reads and writes, and, in effect, enables us to implement complex access patterns. For example, writes could be a synchronous process whereas reads might be asynchronous and provide a limited view over the data.
>
> As another example, the component could utilize separate data stores for writes and reads. Writes would eventually trickle into the read store but perhaps the read store data could also be augmented with external data obtained from other downstream components.

The PageRank calculator

The **PageRank** calculator implements an asynchronous, periodic process for re-evaluating the PageRank scores for each link in the Links 'R' Us graph.

Before starting a new calculation pass, the PageRank component will first use the interfaces exposed by the link graph component to obtain a snapshot of the current state of the graph. This includes both the graph vertices (links destinations) and the edges (links) connecting them.

Once the PageRank values for each link have been calculated, the PageRank component will contact the text indexer component and annotate each indexed document with its updated PageRank score. This is an asynchronous process and does not otherwise interfere with any searches performed by the Links 'R' Us users.

The metrics store

Given that the Links 'R' Us project consists of multiple components, it would make sense for us to deploy monitoring infrastructure so that we can keep track of the health of each component. This way, we can identify components that exhibit elevated error rates or experience high load and need to be scaled up.

This is the primary role of the **metrics store** component. As you can see in the component diagram, all components in our design transmit metrics to the metrics collector and therefore depend on it. Of course, this is not a *hard* dependency: our system design should assume that the metrics collector could go offline at any given moment and make sure that none of the other components are affected should this occur in production.

The frontend

The purpose of the **frontend** component is to render a simple, static HTML-based user interface that will facilitate the users' interaction with the project. More specifically, the design of the frontend component will enable users to perform the following set of functions:

- Directly submit new URLs for indexing.
- Type a keyword or phrase-based search query.
- Paginate the search results for a particular query.

It is important to note that, in our current design, the frontend component serves as the entry-point for making our project accessible by the outside world! Given that *none* of the other project components can be directly accessed by the end users, we could argue that the frontend also doubles as an *API gateway*, where each incoming API request is mapped to *one or more* calls to the internal system components. Besides the obvious security benefits of isolating our internal components from the rest of the world, the API gateway pattern provides the following set of additional benefits:

- If some of the internal calls need to be asynchronous, the gateway can execute them in parallel and wait for them to complete before aggregating their responses and returning them to the user in a synchronous manner.
- It enables us to decouple the way that our internal components communicate with each other from the mechanism that the outside world uses to interface with our system. This means that we can expose a RESTful API to the outside world while still retaining the flexibility to select the most suitable transport for each internal component (for example, REST, gRPC, or perhaps a message queue).

Monolith or microservices? The ultimate question

Before commencing development of the Links 'R' Us service, we need to decide whether our system components will be developed as parts of a big, monolithic service or whether we will just bite the bullet and implement a service-oriented architecture right from the start.

While the concept of using microservices does indeed seem enticing from the outside, it comes with a lot of operational overhead. Besides the mental effort required for building and wiring all components together, we would additionally need to worry about questions like the following:

- How does each service get deployed? Are we doing rolling deployments? What about dark or test releases? How easy is it to roll back to a previous deployment when something goes wrong?
- Are we going to use a container orchestration layer such as Kubernetes [6]? How does traffic get routed between services? Do we need to use a service mesh such as Istio [4] or Linkerd [7]?

- How can we monitor the health of our services? Furthermore, how can we collect the logs from all our services?
- How are we going to handle service downtime? Do we need to implement circuit-breakers to prevent a problematic service from breaking upstream services that depend on it?

Sure, we are all aware of the shortcomings of monolithic designs but, on the other hand, we don't have any available data to justify the extra cost of splitting components into microservices from the start of the project.

Weighing the pros and cons of each approach, it looks like the best course of action is to follow a hybrid approach! We will initially develop our components using a monolithic design. However, and this is the twist, each component will define an interface that other components will use to communicate with it.

To connect components without introducing any coupling between their concrete implementations, we will be making use of the *proxy* design pattern. Initially, we will be providing dummy proxy implementations that facilitate inter-component communication within the *same process*. This is, of course, functionally equivalent to directly wiring components together as we would normally do in a monolithic design.

As our system grows and evolves, we will eventually reach a point where we need to extract one or more components into standalone services. Using the preceding pattern, all we need to do is update our proxies to use the appropriate transport (for example, REST, gRPC, and message queues) for connecting components together without having to modify any of the existing component implementations.

Summary

This concludes the presentation of the Links 'R' Us project. I hope that, by this point, you have acquired a general understanding of what we are going to be building over the next few chapters. If you find yourself wondering about the technical implementation details associated with some of the project components, that's perfectly normal. The main purpose of this chapter was to introduce a high-level overview of the project. We will analyze the construction of each one of these components in *extensive* detail in the pages that follow!

To make the concepts and code for the following chapters easier to follow, we will be splitting each chapter into two core parts:

- In the first half of each chapter, we will be performing a deep dive into a particular technical topic, for example, a survey of popular types of databases (relational, NoSQL, and so on), how you can create pipelines in Go, how you can run graph operations at scale, what gRPC is and how you can use it, and so on.
- In the second half of the chapter, we will be taking the concepts from the first half and applying them toward building one or more components of the Links 'R' Us project.

In the next chapter, we will focus our attention on building one of the key components for the Links 'R' Us project: a fully-functioning data persistence layer for storing the links discovered by the crawler and indexing the contents of each web page retrieved by the crawler.

Questions

1. What is the difference between a functional and a non-functional requirement?
2. Describe the main components of a user story.
3. What things could possibly go wrong in the Links 'R' Us scenario if we blindly crawl any link that a user submits to the system?
4. Name the key components of an SLO.
5. What is the purpose of a UML component diagram?

Further reading

1. Amazon Elastic Compute Cloud: *Instance Metadata and User Data*: https://docs.aws.amazon.com/AWSEC2/latest/UserGuide/ec2-instance-metadata.html
2. Apache Mesos: Program against your data center like it's a single pool of resources: https://mesos.apache.org
3. Brooks, Frederick P., Jr.: *The Mythical Man-Month (Anniversary Ed.)*. Boston, MA, USA: Addison-Wesley Longman Publishing Co., Inc., 1995 — https://www.worldcat.org/title/mythical-man-month/oclc/961280727
4. Istio: *Connect, secure, control, and observe services*: https://istio.io
5. Ivn, Gbor and Grolmusz, Vince: *When the Web Meets the Cell: Using Personalized PageRank for Analyzing Protein Interaction Networks.*

6. Kubernetes: *Production-Grade Container Orchestration*: https://kubernetes.io

7. Linkerd: *Ultralight service mesh for Kubernetes and beyond*: https://linkerd.io

8. MASSCAN: Mass IP port scanner; reserved IP exclusion list: https://github.com/robertdavidgraham/masscan/blob/master/data/exclude.conf

9. Page, L.; Brin, S.; Motwani, R.; and Winograd, T.: *The PageRank Citation Ranking: Bringing Order to the Web*. In: Proceedings of the 7th International World Wide Web Conference. Brisbane, Australia, 1998, S. 161–172

10. Pop, Florin ; Dobre, Ciprian: *An Efficient PageRank Approach for Urban Traffic Optimization*.

11. Swarm: *a Docker-native clustering system*: https://github.com/docker/swarm

Building a Persistence Layer

6

"Database schemas are notoriously volatile, extremely concrete, and highly depended on. This is one reason why the interface between OO applications and databases is so difficult to manage, and why schema updates are generally painful."

- Robert C. Martin [14]

In this chapter, we will focus our attention on designing and implementing the data access layers for two of the Links 'R' Us components: the link graph and the text indexer. More specifically, in the pages that follow, we will do the following:

- Discuss and compare the different types of database technologies
- Identify and understand the main reasons that necessitate the creation of a data access layer as an abstraction over the underlying database layer
- Analyze the entities, relations, and query requirements for the link graph component, define a Go interface for the data layer, and build two alternative data layer implementations from scratch: a simple, in-memory store that we can use for testing purposes and a production-ready store backed by CockroachDB
- Come up with a document model for indexing and searching web page contents and implement both an in-memory indexer (based on the popular bleve Go package) as well as a horizontally scalable variant based on Elasticsearch
- Outline strategies for creating test suites that can be shared and reused across different data layer implementations

Technical requirements

The full code for the topics that will be discussed in this chapter have been published in this book's GitHub repository under the `Chapter06` folder.

You can access this book's GitHub repository at `https://github.com/` `PacktPublishing/Hands-On-Software-Engineering-with-Golang`.

To get you up and running as quickly as possible, each example project includes a makefile that defines the following set of targets:

Makefile target	Description
deps	Install any required dependencies.
test	Run all tests and report coverage.
lint	Check for lint errors.

As with all the other chapters in this book, you will need a fairly recent version of Go, which you can download from `https://golang.org/dl`.

Running tests that require CockroachDB

To run the link graph tests that use CockroachDB as a backend, you will need to download a recent version of CockroachDB (v19.1.2 or newer) from `https://www.cockroachlabs.com/get-cockroachdb`.

After downloading and unpacking the CockroachDB archive, you can spin up a CockroachDB instance for your tests by changing to the folder where the archive was extracted and run the following set of commands:

```
cockroach start --insecure --advertise-addr 127.0.0.1:26257.
cockroach sql --insecure -e 'CREATE DATABASE linkgraph;'
```

The link graph tests for the CockroachDB backend examine the contents of the CDB_DSN environment variable by looking for a valid **data source name** (**DSN**) for accessing the CockroachDB instance. If the environment variable is empty or not defined, all the CockroachDB tests will be automatically skipped.

Assuming you followed the preceding instructions to start a local CockroachDB instance, you can execute the following command to define a suitable DSN prior to running the CockroachDB test suite:

```
export
CDB_DSN='postgresql://root@localhost:26257/linkgraph?sslmode=disable'
```

Finally, it is important to note that all the tests operate under the assumption that the database schema has been set up in advance. If you have just created the database, you can apply the required set of DB migrations by switching to your local checked-out copy of this book's source code repository and running `make run-cdb-migrations`.

Running tests that require Elasticsearch

To run the link graph tests that use Elasticsearch as a backend, you will need to download a recent version of Elasticsearch (v7.2.0 or newer) from `https://www.elastic.co/downloads/elasticsearch`.

After downloading and unpacking the Elasticsearch archive, you can change to the location of the extracted files and start a local Elasticsearch instance (with a sane list of default configuration options) by running the following command:

```
bin/elasticsearch
```

The Elasticsearch tests obtain the list of Elasticsearch cluster endpoints to connect to by examining the contents of the `ES_NODES` environment variable. Assuming that you have started a local Elasticsearch instance by following the instructions above, you can define `ES_NODES` as follows:

```
export ES_NODES='http://localhost:9200'
```

As we will see in the following sections, the Elasticsearch indexer will be designed in a way that will allow the store to automatically define the schema for the indexed documents once it successfully establishes a connection to the Elasticsearch cluster. Consequently, there is no need for a separate migration step prior to running the Elasticsearch test suite.

Exploring a taxonomy of database systems

In the following sections, we will be presenting a list of the most popular DB technologies and analyze the pros and cons of each one. Based on our analysis, we will select the most appropriate type of database for implementing the link graph and the text indexer components of Links 'R' Us.

Key-value stores

The first type of database technology that we will be examining is a key-value store. As the name implies, a key-value store database persists data as a collection of key-value pairs, where keys serve as unique identifiers for accessing stored data within a particular collection. By this definition, key-value stores are functionally equivalent to a hashmap data structure. Popular key-value store implementations include memcached [15], AWS DynamoDB [8], LevelDB [13], and SSD-optimized RocksDB [20].

The basic set of operations supported by key-value stores are *insertions*, *deletions*, and *lookups*. However, some popular key-value store implementations also provide support for *range queries*, which allow clients to iterate an *ordered* list of key-value pairs between two particular keys. As far as keys and values are concerned, the majority of key-value store implementations do not enforce any constraints on their contents. This means that any kind of data (for example, strings, integers, or even binary blobs) can be used as a key.

The data access patterns that are used by key-value stores make data partitioning across multiple nodes much easier compared to other database technologies. This property allows key-value stores to scale horizontally so as to accommodate increased traffic demand.

Let's examine some common use cases where key-value stores are generally considered to be a great fit:

- Caches! We can use a key-value store as a general-purpose cache for all sorts of things. We could, for instance, cache web pages for a CDN service or store the results of frequently used database queries to reduce the response time for a web application.
- A distributed store for session data: Imagine for a moment that we operate a high-traffic website. To handle the traffic, we would normally spin up a bunch of backend servers and place them behind a load balancer. Unless our load balancer had built-in support for sticky sessions (always sending requests from the same user to the same backend server), each request would be handled by a different backend server. This could cause issues with stateful applications as they require access to the session data associated with each user. If we tagged each user request with a unique per-user ID, we could use that as a key and retrieve the session data from a key-value store.
- A storage layer for a database system. The properties of key-value stores make them a very attractive low-level primitive for implementing more sophisticated types of databases. For example, relational databases such as CockroachDB [5] and NoSQL databases such as Apache Cassandra [2] are prime examples of systems built on top of key-value stores.

The main caveat of key-value stores is that we cannot efficiently search *within* the stored data without introducing some kind of auxiliary data structure to facilitate the role of an index.

Relational databases

The idea of relational databases was introduced by E. F. Codd in 1970 [6]. The main unit of data organization in a relational database is referred to as a **table**. Each table is associated with a **schema** that defines the names and data types for each table **column**.

Within a table, each data record is represented by a **row** that is, in turn, identified by a **primary key**, a tuple of column values that must be *unique* among all the table rows. Table columns may also reference records that exist in other tables. This type of column is typically referred to as a **foreign key**.

The standardized way to access and query relational databases is via the use of an *English-like* **structured query language (SQL)**, which is actually a subset of various domain-specific languages:

- A data *definition* language, which includes commands for managing the database schema; for example, creating, altering, or dropping tables, indexes, and constraints
- A data *manipulation* language, which supports a versatile set of commands for inserting, deleting, and, of course, querying the database contents
- A data *control* language, which provides a streamlined way to control the level of access that individual users have to the database
- A *transaction control* language, which allows database users to start, commit, or abort database transactions

One of the most important features of relational databases is the concept of transactions. A transaction can be thought of as a wrapper around a sequence of SQL statements that ensures that either *all* of them will be applied or *none* of them will be applied. To ensure that transactions work reliably in the presence of errors or faults (for example, loss of power or network connectivity) *and* that their outcomes are always deterministic when multiple transactions execute concurrently, relational databases must be compliant with a set of properties that are commonly referred to with the acronym ACID. Let's go over what **ACID** stands for:

- **Atomicity**: Transactions are applied completely or not at all.

- **Consistency**: The contents of a transaction is not allowed to bring the database into an invalid state. This means that the database system must validate each of the statements included in a transaction against the constraints (for example, primary, foreign, or unique keys) that have been defined on the tables that are about to be modified.
- **Isolation**: Each transaction must execute in total isolation from other transactions. If multiple transactions are executing concurrently, the end result should be equivalent to running each transaction one after the other.
- **Durability**: Once a transaction has been committed, it will remain committed, even if the database system is restarted or the nodes it runs on experience loss of power.

In terms of performance, relational databases such as PostgreSQL [18] and MySQL [17] are generally easy to scale vertically. Switching to a beefier CPU and/or adding more memory to your database server is more or less a standard operating procedure for increasing the **queries per second (QPS)** or **transactions per second (TPS)** that the DB can handle. On the other hand, scaling relational databases horizontally is much harder and typically depends on the type of workload you have.

For *write-heavy* workloads, we usually resort to techniques such as data sharding. Data sharding allows us to split (partition) the contents of one or more tables into multiple database nodes. This partitioning is achieved by means of a per-row **shard key**, which dictates which node is responsible for storing each row of the table. One caveat of this approach is that it introduces additional complexity at query time. While writes are quite efficient, reads are not trivial as the database might need to query *each* individual node and then aggregate the results together in order to answer even a simple query such as SELECT COUNT(*) FROM X.

On the other hand, if our workloads are *read-heavy*, horizontal scaling is usually achieved by spinning up *read-replicas*, which mirror updates to one or more *primary* nodes. Writes are always routed to the primary nodes while reads are handled by the read-replicas (ideally) or even by the primaries if the read-replicas cannot be reached.

While relational databases are a great fit for transactional workloads and complex queries, they are not the best tool for querying hierarchical data with arbitrary nesting or for modeling graph-like structures. Moreover, as the volume of stored data exceeds a particular threshold, queries take increasingly longer to run. Eventually, a point is reached where reporting queries that used to execute in real-time can only be processed as offline batch jobs. As a result, companies with high-volume data processing needs have been gradually shifting their focus toward NoSQL databases.

NoSQL databases

NoSQL databases have met a sharp rise in popularity over the last couple of years. Their key value propositions are as follows:

- They are well suited for crunching massive volumes of data.
- By design, NoSQL database systems can effortlessly scale both vertically and horizontally. As a matter of fact, most NoSQL database systems promise a linear increase in performance as more nodes are added to the database cluster.
- More advanced NoSQL solutions can scale even across data centers and include support for automatically routing client requests to the nearest data center.

However, as we all know, there is no such thing as a free lunch. To achieve this performance boost, NoSQL databases have to sacrifice something! Being distributed systems, NoSQL databases must adhere to the rules of the *CAP theorem*.

The CAP theorem was proposed by Eric Brewer in 2000 [4] and is one of the fundamental theorems that governs the operation of distributed systems. It states that networked shared data systems can only guarantee up to *two* of the following properties:

- **Consistency**: Each node in the system has the same view of the stored data. This implies that each read operation on a piece of data will always return the value of the last performed write.
- **Availability**: The system can still process read and write requests in a reasonable amount of time, even if some of the nodes are not online.
- **Partition tolerance**: If a network split occurs, some of the cluster nodes will become isolated and therefore unable to exchange messages with the remaining nodes in the cluster. However, the system should remain operational and the cluster should be able to reach a consistent state when the partitioned nodes rejoin the cluster.

As shown in the following diagram, if we were to pair together two of the three fundamental properties of the CAP theorem, we can obtain a couple of interesting distributed system configurations:

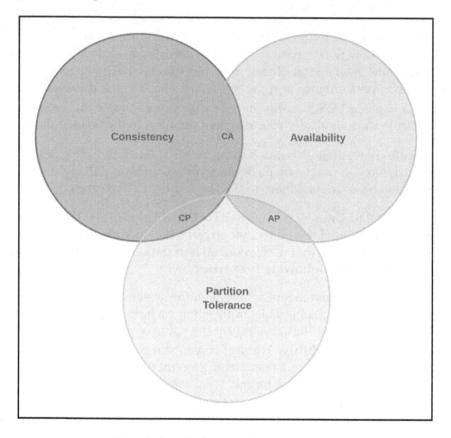

Figure 1: The intersection of the three properties of the CAP theorem

Let's briefly analyze the behavior as to how each of these configurations reacts in the presence of errors:

- **Consistency – Partition (CP) tolerance**: Distributed systems in this category typically use a voting protocol to ensure that the majority of nodes agree that they have the most recent version of the stored data; in other words, they reach a *quorum*. This allows the system to recover from network partitioning events. However, if not enough nodes are available to reach quorum, the system will return an error to clients as data consistency is preferred over availability.

- **Availability – Partition (AP) tolerance**: This class of distributed systems favors availability over consistency. Even in the case of a network partition, an AP system will try to process read requests, although *stale* data may be returned to the clients.
- **Consistency – Availability (CA)**: In practice, *all* distributed systems are, to some extent, affected by network partitions. Therefore, a pure CA type of system is not really feasible unless, of course, we are talking about a single-node system. We could probably classify a single-node deployment of a traditional relational database as a CA system.

At the end of the day, the choice of an appropriate NoSQL solution largely depends on your particular use case. What happens, though, if the use case requires all three of these properties? Are we simply out of luck?

Fortunately, over the years, several NoSQL solutions (for example, Cassandra [2]) have evolved support for what is now referred to as **tunable consistency**. Tunable consistency allows clients to specify their desired level of consistency on a *per-query* basis. For example, when creating a new user account, we would typically opt for strong consistency semantics. On the other hand, when querying the number of views of a popular video, we could dial down the desired level of consistency and settle for an approximate, eventually-consistent, value.

Document databases

Document databases are specialized NoSQL databases that store, index, and query complex and possibly deeply nested *document-like* objects. All documents are stored within a *collection*, which is the equivalent of a table in a relational database. The key differentiation that makes document databases unique is that they do not enforce a particular schema (that is, they are schema-less) but rather *infer* the schema from the stored data. This design decision allows us to store *different* types of documents in the *same* collection. What's more, both the schema and contents of each individual document can evolve over time with no visible impact on the database's query performance.

Contrary to relational databases, which have standardized on SQL, document databases typically implement their own **domain-specific language** (DSL) for querying data. However, they also provide advanced primitives (for example, support for map-reduce) for calculating complex aggregations across multiple documents in a collection. This makes document databases a great fit for generating **business intelligence** (BI) and other types of analytics reports.

The list of document database systems is quite long, so I will just be listing some of the more popular (in my view) implementations: MongoDB [16], CouchDB [3], and Elasticsearch [9].

Understanding the need for a data layer abstraction

Before we delve deeper into modeling the data layer for the link graph and text indexer components, we need to spend some time discussing the reasoning behind the introduction of a data layer abstraction.

First and foremost, the primary purpose of the data layer is to decouple our code from the underlying data store implementation. By programming against a well-defined and data store-agnostic interface, we ensure that our code remains clean, modular, and totally oblivious to the nuances of accessing each data store.

An extra benefit of this approach is that it offers us the flexibility to A/B test different data store technologies before we decide which one to use for our production systems. What's more, even if our original decision proves to be less than stellar in the long term (for example, service traffic exceeds the store's capability to scale vertically/horizontally), we can easily switch to a different system. This can be achieved by wiring in a new data store adapter implementation without the need to modify any of the higher levels of our services' implementation.

The final advantage of having such an abstraction layer has to do with *testing*. By providing individual Go packages for each data store that we are interested in supporting, we can not only encapsulate the store-specific logic but can also write comprehensive test suites to test each store's behavior in total isolation from the rest of the code base. Once we are confident that the implementation behaves as expected, we can use any of the testing mechanisms (for example, mocks, stubs, and fake objects) that we outlined in Chapter 4, *The Art of Testing*, to test other high-level components that require access to a data store without actually having to provision a real data store instance.

Initially, this might not seem to be a big benefit. However, for larger Go projects that spawn multiple packages, the cost of setting up, populating with fixtures, and finally cleaning a database *between tests* can be quite high. Compared to using an in-memory data store implementation, tests against a real database not only take more time to run but may also prove to be quite flaky.

One common problem that you may have encountered in the past is potential DB access races for tests that belong to *different packages* but try to access and/or populate the *same* database instance concurrently. As a result, some of the DB-related tests may start randomly failing in a non-deterministic manner. And of course, by virtue of Murphy's law, such problems rarely crop up when testing locally, but rather have the tendency to manifest themselves when the continuous integration system runs the tests for the pull request you just submitted for review!

It is pretty easy to end up in such a messy situation if multiple packages from your code base have a strong coupling to the underlying database due to the fact that the go test command will, *by default*, run tests that belong to different packages *concurrently*. As a temporary workaround, you could force go test to serialize the execution of *all* the tests by providing the -parallel 1 command-line flag. However, that option would severely increase the total execution time for your test suites and would be overkill for larger projects. Encapsulating the tests that require a real DB store instance into a single package and using mocks everywhere else is a clean and elegant solution for mitigating such problems.

Designing the data layer for the link graph component

In the following sections, we will perform an extended analysis of the data models that are required for the operation of the link graph component. We will kick off our analysis by creating an **Entity-Relationship** (ER) diagram for the entities that compose the data access layer. Then, we will define an interface that fully describes the set of operations that the data access layer must support.

Finally, we will design and build two alternative data access layer implementations (in-memory and CockroachDB-backed) that both satisfy the aforementioned interface. To ensure that both implementations behave in exactly the same manner, we will also create a comprehensive, store-agnostic test suite and arrange for our test code to invoke it for each individual store implementation.

All the code that we will be discussing in the following sections can be found in the Chapter06/linkgraph folder in this book's GitHub repository.

Creating an ER diagram for the link graph store

The following diagram presents the ER diagram for the link graph data access layer. Given that the crawler retrieves web page links and discovers connections between websites, it makes sense for us to use a graph-based representation for our system modeling. As you can see, the ER diagram is comprised of two models: **Link** and **Edge**:

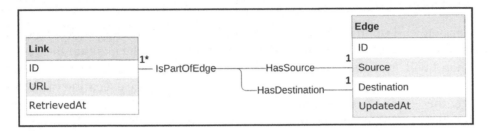

Figure 2: The ER diagram for the link graph component

Link model instances represent the set of web pages that have been processed or discovered by the crawler component. Its attribute set consists of an ID value for uniquely identifying each link, the URL associated with it, and a timestamp value indicating when it was last retrieved by the crawler. The preceding list constitutes the *bare minimum* set of attributes that are required for modeling the link graph for the Links 'R' Us project. In a real-world implementation, we would probably want to augment our link model with additional metadata, such as the following:

- The MIME type for the URL content (as indicated by the remote server) and its length in bytes.
- The HTTP status code of the last crawl attempt. This is quite useful for retrying failed attempts or for dropping dead links from our graph.
- A preferred (per-domain or per-link) time window for performing future crawl requests. As web crawlers tend to induce significant traffic spikes when fetching links from remote servers, this information can be used by our crawler to schedule its update cycle at off-peak times and thus minimize its impact on remote servers.

Each web page in the graph may contain *zero or more* outgoing links to other web pages. An Edge model instance represents a **uni-directional** connection between two links in the graph. As shown in the preceding diagram, the attribute set for the Edge model includes a unique ID for the edge itself, as well as the IDs of both the source and destination links. This modeling approach can also support **bi-directional** links (also known as backlinks) between web pages, with the minor caveat that they would need to be represented as two separate edge entries.

Moreover, the edge attribute set also contains a timestamp value that tracks the last time that the edge was visited by the crawler. A common challenge with graphs such as the WWW, whose structure changes at a very fast rate, is figuring out how to efficiently detect edge-related changes: new edges may appear and others may disappear at any point in time. Handling edge additions is a trivial task; all we need to do is **upsert** (insert or update if the entry already exists) an Edge model instance for every outgoing edge that's detected by the crawler. Handling edge *deletions, on the other hand,* is slightly more complicated.

The approach that we will be adopting for the crawler component will leverage the last update timestamp as the means of detecting whether an existing edge is *stale* and needs to be removed. Each time the crawler processes a link from the graph, it will perform the following actions:

1. Upsert a Link model entry for each outgoing link.
2. Upsert an Edge model for each unique outgoing link, where we have the following:
   - The `origin` is always set to the link that is currently being processed.
   - The `destination` is each detected outgoing link.
   - The `updatedAt` timestamp is the current system time.

By following these steps, any links with the same (`source, destination`) tuple will have their UpdatedAt field refreshed while stale, old links will retain their previous UpdatedAt value. If we arrange for the crawler to record the exact time when it started crawling a particular page, we can simply delete all the edges whose *source* is the link that was just crawled and whose UpdatedAt value is older than the recorded timestamp.

Listing the required set of operations for the data access layer

Following the SOLID design principles we discussed in the previous chapters, we will start designing the link graph data access layer by listing the operations (responsibilities, in SOLID terminology) that it needs to perform and then formally describe them by means of a Go interface.

For our particular use case, the link graph access layer must support the following set of operations:

1. Insert a link into the graph or update an existing link when the crawler discovers that its content has changed.

2. Look up a link by its ID.
3. Iterate *all the links* present in the graph. This is the primary service that the link graph component must provide to the other components (for example, the crawler and `PageRank` calculator) that comprise the Links 'R' Us project.
4. Insert an edge into the graph or refresh the `UpdatedAt` value of an existing edge.
5. Iterate the list of edges in the graph. This functionality is required by the `PageRank` calculator component.
6. Delete stale links that originated from a particular link and were not updated during the last crawler pass.

Defining a Go interface for the link graph

To satisfy the list of operations from the previous section, we shall define the `Graph` interface as follows:

```go
type Graph interface {
    UpsertLink(link *Link) error
    FindLink(id uuid.UUID) (*Link, error)

    UpsertEdge(edge *Edge) error
    RemoveStaleEdges(fromID uuid.UUID, updatedBefore time.Time) error

    Links(fromID, toID uuid.UUID, retrievedBefore time.Time) (LinkIterator, error)
    Edges(fromID, toID uuid.UUID, updatedBefore time.Time) (EdgeIterator, error)
}
```

The first two methods allow us to upsert a `Link` model and retrieve it from the backing store if we are aware of its ID. In the following code, you can see the definition of the `Link` type, whose fields match the ones from the ER diagram:

```go
type Link struct {
    ID          uuid.UUID
    URL         string
    RetrievedAt time.Time
}
```

Each link is assigned a unique ID (a V4 UUID, to be precise) and contains two fields: the URL for accessing the web page and a timestamp field that keeps track of the last time that the link's content was retrieved by the crawler.

The next two methods from the `Graph` interface allow us to manipulate the edges of the graph. Let's begin by examining the definition of the `Edge` type:

```
type Edge struct {
    ID        uuid.UUID
    Src       uuid.UUID
    Dst       uuid.UUID
    UpdatedAt time.Time
}
```

Similar to links, edges are also assigned their own unique ID (also a V4 UUID). In addition, the `Edge` model tracks the following:

- The ID of both the source and destination links that form the edge
- The timestamp when it was last updated

Partitioning links and edges for processing the graph in parallel

As you have probably noticed by their signatures, the `Links` and `Edges` methods are designed to return an *iterator* so that they can access a filtered subset of the graph's vertices and edges. More specifically, they do the following:

- The `Links` method returns a set of links whose ID belongs to the `[fromID, toID)` range *and* their last retrieval time before the provided timestamp.
- The `Edges` method returns the set of edges whose *origin vertex IDs* belong to the `[fromID, toID)` range and their last update time is before the provided timestamp.

At this point, we need to spend some time and elaborate on the reasoning behind the design of these methods. We could argue that, at some point, the link graph will grow large enough so that in order to process it in an efficient manner, we will eventually have to split it into chunks and process each chunk in parallel. To this end, our design must anticipate this need and include a mechanism for grouping links and edges into partitions based on their individual IDs. Given a `[fromID, toID)` range, all graph implementations will use the following logic to select which link and edge model instances to return via the iterator:

- Return links whose ID is within the `[fromID, toID)` range.
- Return edges for which the *origin link's ID* is within the `[fromID, toID)` range. In other words, edges always belong to the same partition as their origin links.

It is important to note that while the preceding method signatures accept a UUID range as their input, the implementation of a suitable partitioning scheme for calculating the UUID ranges themselves will be the *responsibility of the caller*. The `Links` and `Edges` methods will happily accept any UUID range that's provided by the caller as long as it is valid.

In `Chapter 10`, *Building, Packaging, and Deploying Software*, we will explore the use of the `math/big` package to facilitate the carving of the UUID space into non-overlapping regions that can then be fed into the aforementioned store methods.

Iterating Links and Edges

Since there is no upper bound in the number of links or edges that can be potentially returned by calls to the `Links` and `Edges` methods, we will be implementing the *iterator* design pattern and lazily fetch Link and Edge models on demand.
The `LinkIterator` and `EdgeIterator` types, which are returned by these methods, are interfaces themselves. This is intentional as their internal implementation details will obviously depend on the database technology that we select for the link graph persistence layer. Here is how they are defined:

```
// LinkIterator is implemented by objects that can iterate the graph links.
type LinkIterator interface {
    Iterator

    // Link returns the currently fetched link object.
    Link() *Link
}

// EdgeIterator is implemented by objects that can iterate the graph edges.
type EdgeIterator interface {
    Iterator

    // Edge returns the currently fetched edge objects.
    Edge() *Edge
}
```

Both of the preceding interfaces define a *getter* method for retrieving the `Link` or `Edge` instance that the iterator is currently pointing at. The common logic between the two iterators has been extracted into a separate interface called `Iterator`, which both of the interfaces embed. The definition of the `Iterator` interface is as follows:

```
type Iterator interface {
    // Next advances the iterator. If no more items are available or an
    // error occurs, calls to Next() return false.
    Next() bool
```

```
    // Error returns the last error encountered by the iterator.
    Error() error

    // Close releases any resources associated with an iterator.
    Close() error
}
```

To iterate a list of edges or links, we must obtain an iterator from the graph and run our business logic within a `for` loop:

```
// 'linkIt' is a link iterator
for linkIt.Next(){
    link := linkIt.Link()
    // Do something with link...
}

if err := linkIt.Error(); err != nil {
    // Handle error...
}
```

Calls to `linkIt.Next()` will return false when the following occurs:

- We have iterated all the available links
- An error occurs (for example, we lost connection to the database)

As a result, we don't need to check whether an error occurred inside the loop – we only need to check *once* after exiting the for loop. This pattern yields cleaner-looking code and is actually used in various places within the Go standard library, such as the `Scanner` type from the `bufio` package.

Verifying graph implementations using a shared test suite

As we mentioned in the previous sections, we will be building both an in-memory and a database-backed implementation of the `Graph` interface. To this end, we need to come up with a set of comprehensive tests to ensure that both implementations behave in exactly the same manner.

One way to achieve this is to write the tests for the first implementation and then duplicate them for each additional implementation that we may introduce in the future. However, this approach doesn't really scale well: what if we modify the `Graph` interface in the future? We would need to track down and update a whole bunch of tests that might be scattered across different packages.

A much better, and cleaner, approach would be to come up with a shared, implementation-agnostic test suite and then just wire it to each underlying graph implementation. I opted for this approach as it reduces the amount of maintenance that's required, while at the same time allowing us to run *exactly the same set of tests* against all implementations: a fairly efficient way of detecting regressions when we change one of our implementations.

But if the test suite is shared, where should it live so that we can include it in all implementation-specific test suites? The answer is to encapsulate the suite into its own dedicated testing package that our regular test code can import and use where it's needed.

The `SuiteBase` definition lives in the `Chapter06/linkgraph/graph/graphtest` package and depends on the `gocheck` [11] framework, which we introduced in `Chapter 4`, *The Art of Testing*. The suite includes the following groups of tests:

- **Link/Edge upsert tests**: These tests are designed to verify that we can insert new edges/links into the graph and that they are assigned a valid, unique ID.
- **Concurrent link/edge iterator support**: These tests ensure that no data races occur when the code concurrently accesses the graph's contents via multiple iterator instances.
- **Partitioned iterator tests**: These tests verify that if we split our graph into N partitions and assign an iterator to each partition, each iterator will receive a unique set of links/edges (that is, no item will be listed in more than one partition) and that all the iterators will process the full set of links/edges present in the graph. Additionally, the edge iterator tests ensure that each edge appears in the same partition as its source link.
- **Link lookup tests**: A simple set of tests that verify the graph implementation's behavior when looking up existing or unknown link IDs.
- **Stale edge removal tests**: A set of tests that verify that we can successfully delete stale edges from the graph using an *updated-before-X* predicate.

To create a test suite for a *new* graph implementation, all we have to do is to define a new test suite that does the following:

- Embeds `SuiteBase`
- Provides a suite setup helper that creates the appropriate graph instance and invokes the `SetGraph` method that's exposed by `SuiteBase` so that we can wire it to the base test suite before running any of the preceding tests

Implementing an in-memory graph store

The in-memory graph implementation will serve as a gentle introduction to writing a complete graph store implementation. By virtue of maintaining the graph in memory, this implementation is simple, self-contained, and safe for concurrent access. This makes it an ideal candidate for writing unit tests that require access to the link graph component.

Let's take a look at its implementation, starting with the definition of the InMemoryGraph type:

```
type edgeList []uuid.UUID

type InMemoryGraph struct {
    mu sync.RWMutex

    links map[uuid.UUID]*graph.Link
    edges map[uuid.UUID]*graph.Edge

    linkURLIndex map[string]*graph.Link
    linkEdgeMap  map[uuid.UUID]edgeList
}
```

The InMemoryGraph struct defines two maps (links and edges) that maintain the set of Link and Edge models that have been inserted into the graph. To accelerate ID-based lookups, both maps use the model IDs as their key.

Going back to our ER diagram, we can see that link URLs are also expected to be unique. To this end, the in-memory graph also maintains an auxiliary map (linkURLIndex) where keys are the URLs that are added to the graph and values are pointers to link models. We will go through the details of how this particular map is used when we examine the implementation of the UpsertLink method in the next section.

Another type of query that we should be able to answer *efficiently* in order to implement the Edges and RemoveStaleEdges methods is: *find the list of edges that originate from a particular link*. This is achieved by defining yet another auxiliary map called linkEdgeMap. This map associates link IDs with a slice of edge IDs that correspond to the edges *originating* from it.

Finally, to ensure that our implementation is safe for concurrent access, the struct definition includes a sync.RWMutex field. In contrast to the regular sync.Mutex, which provides single reader/writer semantics, sync.RWMutex supports *multiple concurrent readers* and thus provides much better throughput guarantees for *read-heavy* workloads.

Upserting links

Let's begin our tour of the in-memory graph implementation by taking a look at how the UpsertLink method is implemented. Since an upsert operation will always modify the graph, the method will acquire a *write* lock so that we can apply any modifications in an atomic fashion. The method contains two distinct code paths.

If the link to be upserted does not specify an ID, we treat it as an insert attempt *unless* we have *already* added another link with the same URL. In the latter case, we silently convert the insert into an *update* operation while making sure that we always retain the most recent RetrievedAt timestamp:

```
if link.ID == uuid.Nil {
    link.ID = existing.ID
    origTs := existing.RetrievedAt
    *existing = *link
    if origTs.After(existing.RetrievedAt) {
        existing.RetrievedAt = origTs
    }
    return nil
}

// Omitted: insert new link into the graph (see next block of code)...
```

Once we verify that we need to create a new entry for the link, we must assign a unique ID to it before we can insert it into the graph. This is achieved by means of a small for loop where we keep generating new UUID values until we obtain one that is unique. Since we are using V4 (random) UUIDs for our implementation, we are more or less guaranteed to obtain a unique value on our first attempt. The presence of the for loop guarantees that our code behaves correctly, even in the highly unlikely case of UUID collisions:

```
// Insert new link into the graph
// Assign new ID and insert link
for {
    link.ID = uuid.New()
    if s.links[link.ID] == nil {
        break
    }
}

lCopy := new(graph.Link)
*lCopy = *link
s.linkURLIndex[lCopy.URL] = lCopy
s.links[lCopy.ID] = lCopy
return nil
```

Once we have generated an ID for the link, we can make a *copy* of link that's provided by the caller to ensure that no code outside of our implementation can modify the graph data. Then, we insert the link into the appropriate map structures.

Upserting edges

The edge upsert logic in `UpsertEdge` has a lot of things in common with the `UpsertLink` implementation we examined in the previous section. The first thing we need to do is acquire the write lock and verify that the source and destination links for the edge actually exist:

```
s.mu.Lock()
defer s.mu.Unlock()

_, srcExists := s.links[edge.Src]
_, dstExists := s.links[edge.Dst]
if !srcExists || !dstExists {
    return xerrors.Errorf("upsert edge: %w", graph.ErrUnknownEdgeLinks)
}
```

Next, we scan the set of edges that originate from the specified source link and check whether we can find an *existing* edge to the same destination. If that happens to be the case, we simply update the entry's `UpdatedAt` field and copy its contents back to the provided `edge` pointer. This ensures that the `entry` value that's provided by the caller has both its `ID` and `UpdatedAt` synced with the values contained in the store:

```
// Scan edge list from source
for _, edgeID := range s.linkEdgeMap[edge.Src] {
    existingEdge := s.edges[edgeID]
    if existingEdge.Src == edge.Src && existingEdge.Dst == edge.Dst {
        existingEdge.UpdatedAt = time.Now()
        *edge = *existingEdge
        return nil
    }
}
```

If the preceding loop does not produce a match, we create and insert a new edge to the store. As you can see in the following code snippet, we follow the same methodology that we did for link insertions. First, we allocate a new, unique ID for the edge and populate its `UpdatedAt` value. Then, we create a *copy* of the provided `Edge` object and insert it into the store's `edges` map:

```
for {
    edge.ID = uuid.New()
```

```go
        if s.edges[edge.ID] == nil {
            break
        }
    }

    edge.UpdatedAt = time.Now()
    eCopy := new(graph.Edge)
    *eCopy = *edge
    s.edges[eCopy.ID] = eCopy

    // Append the edge ID to the list of edges originating from the edge's
    source link.
    s.linkEdgeMap[edge.Src] = append(s.linkEdgeMap[edge.Src], eCopy.ID)
    return nil
```

Finally, before returning, there is a last bit of book-keeping that we need to perform: we need to add the new link to the edge list that originates from the specified source link. To this end, we index the `linkEdgeMap` using the source link ID as a key and append the ID of the newly inserted edge to the appropriate edge list.

Looking up links

Looking up links is a fairly trivial operation. All we need to do is acquire a *read* lock, look up the link by its ID, and do either of the following things:

- Return the link back to the caller
- Return an error if no link with the provided ID was found

The link lookup logic is outlined in the following code snippet:

```go
func (s *InMemoryGraph) FindLink(id uuid.UUID) (*graph.Link, error) {
    s.mu.RLock()
    defer s.mu.RUnlock()

    link := s.links[id]
    if link == nil {
        return nil, xerrors.Errorf("find link: %w", graph.ErrNotFound)
    }

    lCopy := new(graph.Link)
    *lCopy = *link
    return lCopy, nil
}
```

Since we want to ensure that no external code can modify the graph's contents without invoking the `UpsertLink` method, the `FindLink` implementation always returns a *copy* of the link that is stored in the graph.

Iterating links/edges

To obtain an iterator for the graph links or edges, users need to invoke the `Links` or `Edges` methods. Let's take a look at how the `Links` method is implemented:

```
func (s *InMemoryGraph) Links(fromID, toID uuid.UUID, retrievedBefore
time.Time) (graph.LinkIterator, error) {
    from, to := fromID.String(), toID.String()

    s.mu.RLock()
    var list []*graph.Link
    for linkID, link := range s.links {
        if id := linkID.String(); id >= from && id < to &&
link.RetrievedAt.Before(retrievedBefore) {
            list = append(list, link)
        }
    }
    s.mu.RUnlock()

    return &linkIterator{s: s, links: list}, nil
}
```

In the preceding implementation, we obtain a *read* lock and then proceed to iterate all the links in the graph, searching for the ones that belong to the [fromID, toID) partition range *and* whose `RetrievedAt` value is less than the specified `retrievedBefore` value. Any links that satisfy this predicate are appended to the `list` variable.

To figure out whether a link ID belongs to the specified partition range, we convert it into a string and then rely on string comparisons to verify that it is either equal to `fromID` or falls between the two ends of the partition range. Obviously, performing string conversions and comparisons is not as efficient as directly comparing the underlying byte representation of the UUID values. However, since this particular implementation is meant to be used just for debugging purposes, we can focus on keeping the code simple rather than worrying about its performance.

Once we have finished iterating all the links, we create a new `linkIterator` instance and return it to the user. Now, let's examine how the iterator is implemented, starting with its type definition:

```
type linkIterator struct {
    s *InMemoryGraph

    links    []*graph.Link
    curIndex int
}
```

As you can see, the iterator stores a pointer to the in-memory graph, a list of `Link` models to iterate, and an index for keeping track of the iterator's offset within the list.

The implementation of the iterator's `Next` method is quite trivial:

```
func (i *edgeIterator) Next() bool {
    if i.curIndex >= len(i.links) {
        return false
    }
    i.curIndex++
    return true
}
```

Unless we have already reached the end of the list of links, we advance `curIndex` and return true to indicate that more data is available for retrieval via a call to the `Link` method, whose implementation is listed as follows:

```
func (i *linkIterator) Link() *graph.Link {
    i.s.mu.RLock()
    link := new(graph.Link)
    *link = *i.links[i.curIndex-1]
    i.s.mu.RUnlock()
    return link
}
```

Keep in mind that the `Link` model instances associated with this iterator are maintained by the in-memory graph and may potentially be *shared* with other iterator instances. As a result, while one go-routine may consuming links from the iterator, another go-routine may be modifying their contents. To avoid data races, whenever the user invokes the iterator's `Link` method, we obtain a *read* lock on the link graph. While holding the lock, we can safely fetch the next link and make a copy, which is then returned to the caller.

Finally, let's take a look at the implementation of the `Edges` method. The logic is quite similar to `Links`, but with a minor difference in the way we populate the list of edges that belong to the requested partition:

```go
func (s *InMemoryGraph) Edges(fromID, toID uuid.UUID, updatedBefore
time.Time) (graph.EdgeIterator, error) {
    from, to := fromID.String(), toID.String()
    s.mu.RLock()
    var list []*graph.Edge
    for linkID := range s.links {
        if id := linkID.String(); id < from || id >= to {
            continue
        }
        for _, edgeID := range s.linkEdgeMap[linkID] {
            if edge := s.edges[edgeID];
edge.UpdatedAt.Before(updatedBefore) {
                list = append(list, edge)
            }
        }
    }
    s.mu.RUnlock()
    return &edgeIterator{s: s, edges: list}, nil
}
```

As we mentioned in the *Partitioning links and edges for processing the graph in parallel* section, each edge belongs to the same partition as the link it originates from. Therefore, in the preceding implementation, we begin by iterating the set of links in the graph and skip the ones that do not belong to the partition we need. Once we have located a link belonging to the requested partition range, we iterate the list of edges that originate from it (via the `linkEdgeMap` field) and append any edges that satisfy the *updated-before-X* predicate to the `list` variable.

The content of the `list` variable is then used to create a new `edgeIterator` instance, which is then returned to the caller. The `edgeIterator` is implemented in more or less the same way as the `linkIterator`, so we will attempt to save some space by not including its full implementation here. You can easily look it up by visiting this book's GitHub repository.

Removing stale edges

The last bit of functionality that we need to explore is the `RemoveStaleEdges` method. The caller invokes it with the ID of a link (the origin) and an `updatedBefore` value:

```
func (s *InMemoryGraph) RemoveStaleEdges(fromID uuid.UUID, updatedBefore
time.Time) error {
    s.mu.Lock()
    defer s.mu.Unlock()

    var newEdgeList edgeList
    for _, edgeID := range s.linkEdgeMap[fromID] {
        edge := s.edges[edgeID]
        if edge.UpdatedAt.Before(updatedBefore) {
            delete(s.edges, edgeID)
            continue
        }
        newEdgeList = append(newEdgeList, edgeID)
    }
    s.linkEdgeMap[fromID] = newEdgeList
    return nil
}
```

As with other operations that mutate the graph's contents, we need to acquire a *write* lock. Then, we iterate the list of edges that originate from the specified source link and ignore the ones whose `UpdatedAt` value is less than the specified `updatedBefore` argument. Any edge that survives the culling is added to a `newEdgeList`, which becomes the new list of outgoing edges for the specified source link.

Setting up a test suite for the graph implementation

Before we conclude our tour of the in-memory graph implementation, we need to spend some time authoring a test suite that will execute the shared verification suite against the store implementation we just created. This can be achieved with only a handful of lines, as follows:

```
var _ = gc.Suite(new(InMemoryGraphTestSuite))

type InMemoryGraphTestSuite struct {
    graphtest.SuiteBase
}

func (s *InMemoryGraphTestSuite) SetUpTest(c *gc.C) {
    s.SetGraph(NewInMemoryGraph())
}
```

```
// Register our test-suite with go test.
func Test(t *testing.T) { gc.TestingT(t) }
```

Since we are working with a pure, in-memory implementation, we can cheat and recreate the graph before running each test by providing a `SetUpTest` method that the `gocheck` framework will automatically invoke for us when running the test suite.

Scaling across with a CockroachDB-backed graph implementation

While the in-memory graph implementation is definitely a great asset for running our unit tests or even for spinning up small instances of the Links 'R' Us system for demonstration or end-to-end testing purposes, it's not really something that we would actually want to use in a production-grade system.

First and foremost, the data in the in-memory store will not persist across service restarts. Even if we could somehow address this limitation (for example, by creating periodic snapshots of the graph to disk), the best we can do is scale our graph up: for example, we can run the link graph service on a machine with a faster CPU and/or more memory. But that's about it; as we anticipate the graph size eventually outgrowing the storage capacity of a single node, we need to come up with a more efficient solution that can scale across multiple machines.

To this end, the following sections will explore a second graph implementation that utilizes a database system that can support our scaling requirements. While there are undoubtedly quite a few DBMS out there that can satisfy our needs, I have decided to base the graph implementation on CockroachDB [5] for the following set of reasons:

- It can easily scale horizontally just by increasing the number of nodes available to the cluster. CockroachDB clusters can automatically rebalance and heal themselves when nodes appear or go down. This property makes it ideal for our use case!
- CockroachDB is fully ACID-compliant and supports distributed SQL transactions.
- The SQL flavor supported by CockroachDB is compatible with the PostgreSQL syntax, which many of you should already be familiar with.
- CockroachDB implements the PostgreSQL wire protocol; this means that we do not require a specialized driver package to connect to the database but can simply use the battle-tested pure-Go Postgres [19] package to connect to the database.

Dealing with DB migrations

When creating a dependency on a DBMS, we need to introduce an external mechanism to assist us in managing the schema for the tables that we will be running queries against.

Following the recommended industry best practices, changes to our database schema need to be made in small, incremental steps that can be applied when deploying a new version of our software to production, or reverted if we decide to roll back a deployment due to the discovery of a bug.

For this particular project, we will be managing our database schema with the help of the `gomigrate` tool [7]. This tool can work with most popular database systems (including CockroachDB) and provides a handy command-line tool that we can use to apply or revert DB schema changes. `gomigrate` expects database migrations to be specified as two separate files: one containing the SQL commands to apply the migration (the *up* path) and another to revert the migration (the *down* path). The standard format for migration file names uses the following pattern:

```
timestamp-description-{up/down}.sql
```

The addition of a timestamp component ensures that `gomigrate` always picks up and applies the changes in the correct order.

To execute any required migrations, we need to invoke the `gomigrate` CLI tool and provide it with the following bits of information:

- A data source **name** (**DSN**) URL for the target database.
- The path to the location of the migration files. The tool not only supports local paths but it can also pull migrations from GitHub, GitLab, AWS S3, and Google Cloud Storage.
- A migration *direction* command. This is typically `up` to apply the migrations or `down` to revert them.

You may be wondering: how does `gomigrate` ensure that migrations are only executed once? The answer is: by maintaining state! So, where is that state stored then? The first time you run the `gomigrate` tool against a database, it will create two additional tables that are used by the tool to keep track of which migrations it has applied so far. This makes the tool safe to run multiple times (for example, each time we deploy a new version of our software to production).

All the required migrations for the link graph project live in
the `Chapter06/linkgraph/store/cdb/migrations` folder. What's more, the top-level
makefile includes a `run-cdb-migrations` target that will install (if missing) the
`gomigrate` tool and automatically run any *pending* migrations. In fact, this command is
leveraged by the CI system linked to this book's GitHub repository to bootstrap a test
database before running the CockroachDB tests.

An overview of the DB schema for the CockroachDB implementation

Setting up the tables we need for the CockroachDB graph implementation is a fairly
straightforward process. The following is a combined list of the SQL statements that will be
applied when we run the included DB migrations:

```
CREATE TABLE IF NOT EXISTS links (
    id UUID PRIMARY KEY DEFAULT gen_random_uuid(),
    url STRING UNIQUE,
    retrieved_at TIMESTAMP
);

CREATE TABLE IF NOT EXISTS edges (
    id UUID PRIMARY KEY DEFAULT gen_random_uuid(),
    src UUID NOT NULL REFERENCES links(id) ON DELETE CASCADE,
    dst UUID NOT NULL REFERENCES links(id) ON DELETE CASCADE,
    updated_at TIMESTAMP,
    CONSTRAINT edge_links UNIQUE(src,dst)
);
```

You probably noticed that, while building the in-memory graph implementation, we had to
manually enforce some constraints. For example, we had to check the following:

- The link and edge IDs are unique
- The URLs are unique
- The source and destination link IDs for edges point to existing links
- The `(source, destination)` tuple for edges is unique

For the CockroachDB implementation, we can simply delegate those checks to the DB itself by introducing uniqueness and foreign-key constraints when defining the table schemas. A small caveat of this approach is that when a SQL statement execution attempt returns an error, we need to inspect its contents to detect whether a constraint validation occurred. If that happens to be the case, we can return a more meaningful, typed error such as `graph.ErrUnknownEdgeLinks` to the caller matching the behavior of the in-memory implementation.

Upserting links

To upsert a link to the CockroachDB store, we will use an upsert-like SQL query that leverages the database's support for specifying an action to be applied when a conflict occurs:

```
INSERT INTO links (url, retrieved_at) VALUES ($1, $2)
ON CONFLICT (url) DO UPDATE SET retrieved_at=GREATEST(links.retrieved_at,
$2)
RETURNING id, retrieved_at
```

Basically, if we try to insert a link that has the same `url` as an existing link, the preceding conflict resolution action will ensure that we simply update the `retrieved_at` column to the maximum of the original value and the one specified by the caller. Regardless of whether a conflict occurs or not, the query will always return the row's `id` (existing or assigned by the DB) and the value for the `retrieved_at` column. The relevant `UpsertLink` method implementation is as follows:

```
func (c *CockroachDBGraph) UpsertLink(link *graph.Link) error {
    row := c.db.QueryRow(upsertLinkQuery, link.URL, link.RetrievedAt.UTC())
    if err := row.Scan(&link.ID, &link.RetrievedAt); err != nil {
        return xerrors.Errorf("upsert link: %w", err)
    }

    link.RetrievedAt = link.RetrievedAt.UTC()
    return nil
}
```

This method binds the fields from the provided model, which are bound to the `upsertLinkQuery`, and proceeds to execute it. Then, it scans the `id` and `retrieved_at` values that are returned by the query into the appropriate model fields.

Upserting edges

To upsert an edge, we will be using the following query:

```
INSERT INTO edges (src, dst, updated_at) VALUES ($1, $2, NOW())
ON CONFLICT (src,dst) DO UPDATE SET updated_at=NOW()
RETURNING id, updated_at
```

As you can see, the query includes a conflict resolution step for the case where we try to insert an edge with the same (src, dst) tuple. If that happens, we simply change the updated_at column value to the current timestamp.

Unsurprisingly, the code to upsert an edge to the CockroachDB store looks quite similar to the link upsert code:

```
func (c *CockroachDBGraph) UpsertEdge(edge *graph.Edge) error {
    row := c.db.QueryRow(upsertEdgeQuery, edge.Src, edge.Dst)
    if err := row.Scan(&edge.ID, &edge.UpdatedAt); err != nil {
        if isForeignKeyViolationError(err) {
            err = graph.ErrUnknownEdgeLinks
        }
        return xerrors.Errorf("upsert edge: %w", err)
    }

    edge.UpdatedAt = edge.UpdatedAt.UTC()
    return nil
}
```

Once again, we bind the relevant fields to a query that we proceed to execute and update the provided edge model with the id and updated_at fields that were returned by the query.

The preceding code comes with a small twist! When we defined the schema for the edges table, we also specified a *foreign-key* constraint for the src and dst fields. Therefore, if we try to upsert an edge with an unknown source and/or destination ID, we will get an error. To check whether the error was actually caused by a foreign-key violation, we can use the following helper:

```
func isForeignKeyViolationError(err error) bool {
    pqErr, valid := err.(*pq.Error)
    if !valid {
        return false
    }
    return pqErr.Code.Name() == "foreign_key_violation"
}
```

To match the behavior of the in-memory store implementation, if the error points to a foreign-key violation, we return the more user-friendly `graph.ErrUnknownEdgeLinks` error.

Looking up links

To look up a link by its ID, we will be using the following standard SQL selection query:

```
SELECT url, retrieved_at FROM links WHERE id=$1"
```

The implementation of the `FindLink` method is as follows:

```
func (c *CockroachDBGraph) FindLink(id uuid.UUID) (*graph.Link, error) {
    row := c.db.QueryRow(findLinkQuery, id)
    link := &graph.Link{ID: id}
    if err := row.Scan(&link.URL, &link.RetrievedAt); err != nil {
        if err == sql.ErrNoRows {
            return nil, xerrors.Errorf("find link: %w", graph.ErrNotFound)
        }
        return nil, xerrors.Errorf("find link: %w", err)
    }
    link.RetrievedAt = link.RetrievedAt.UTC()
    return link, nil
}
```

After executing the query, we create a new `Link` model instance and populate it with the returned link fields. If the selection query does not match any link, the SQL driver will return a `sql.ErrNoRows` error. The preceding code checks for this error and returns a user-friendly `graph.ErrNotFound` error to the caller.

Iterating links/edges

To select the links that correspond to a particular partition and whose retrieved timestamp is older than the provided value, we will use the following query:

```
SELECT id, url, retrieved_at FROM links WHERE id >= $1 AND id < $2 AND
retrieved_at < $3
```

The implementation of the `Links` method is shown in the following listing:

```
func (c *CockroachDBGraph) Links(fromID, toID uuid.UUID, accessedBefore
time.Time) (graph.LinkIterator, error) {
    rows, err := c.db.Query(linksInPartitionQuery, fromID, toID,
accessedBefore.UTC())
    if err != nil {
        return nil, xerrors.Errorf("links: %w", err)
    }

    return &linkIterator{rows: rows}, nil
}
```

As you can see, the method executes the query with the specified arguments and returns a `linkIterator` to consume the returned result set. The link CockroachDB iterator implementation is nothing more than a wrapper on top of the `sql.Rows` value that's returned by the SQL query. This is what the `Next` method's implementation looks like:

```
func (i *linkIterator) Next() bool {
    if i.lastErr != nil || !i.rows.Next() {
        return false
    }

    l := new(graph.Link)
    i.lastErr = i.rows.Scan(&l.ID, &l.URL, &l.RetrievedAt)
    if i.lastErr != nil {
        return false
    }
    l.RetrievedAt = l.RetrievedAt.UTC()

    i.latchedLink = l
    return true
}
```

The `Edges` method uses the following query, which yields exactly the same set of results as the in-memory implementation:

```
SELECT id, src, dst, updated_at FROM edges WHERE src >= $1 AND src < $2 AND
updated_at < $3"
```

Here's what the implementation of Edges looks like:

```
func (c *CockroachDBGraph) Edges(fromID, toID uuid.UUID, updatedBefore
time.Time) (graph.EdgeIterator, error) {
    rows, err := c.db.Query(edgesInPartitionQuery, fromID, toID,
updatedBefore.UTC())
    if err != nil {
        return nil, xerrors.Errorf("edges: %w", err)
    }

    return &edgeIterator{rows: rows}, nil
}
```

The implementation of the edgeIterator is quite similar to the linkIterator, so we will conserve some space and omit it. You can take a look at the complete iterator implementations by examining the source code in the iterator.go file, which can be found within the Chapter06/linkgraph/store/cdb package of this book's GitHub repository.

Removing stale edges

The last piece of functionality that we will be examining is the RemoveStaleEdges method, which uses the following query to delete edges that have not been updated after a particular point in time:

```
DELETE FROM edges WHERE src=$1 AND updated_at < $2
```

Let's take a look at the RemoveStaleEdges method implementation:

```
func (c *CockroachDBGraph) RemoveStaleEdges(fromID uuid.UUID, updatedBefore
time.Time) error {
    _, err := c.db.Exec(removeStaleEdgesQuery, fromID, updatedBefore.UTC())
    if err != nil {
        return xerrors.Errorf("remove stale edges: %w", err)
    }

    return nil
}
```

There' nothing out of the ordinary here; the code in the preceding snippet simply binds the arguments to the delete query and executes it.

Setting up a test suite for the CockroachDB implementation

To create and wire the test suite for the CockroachDB implementation, we will follow exactly the same steps that we did for the in-memory implementation. The first step is to define a test suite that embeds the shared `graphtest.SuiteBase` type and register it with `go test`:

```
var _ = gc.Suite(new(CockroachDBGraphTestSuite))

type CockroachDBGraphTestSuite struct {
    graphtest.SuiteBase
    db *sql.DB
}

// Register our test-suite with go test.
func Test(t *testing.T) { gc.TestingT(t) }
```

Then, we need to provide a setup method for the test suite that will create a new CockroachDB graph instance and wire it to the base suite. Following the testing paradigm we discussed in *Chapter 4, The Art of Testing*, our test suite relies on the presence of an environment variable that should contain the DSN for connecting to the CockroachDB instance. If the environment variable is not defined, the entire test suite will be automatically skipped:

```
func (s *CockroachDBGraphTestSuite) SetUpSuite(c *gc.C) {
    dsn := os.Getenv("CDB_DSN")
    if dsn == "" {
        c.Skip("Missing CDB_DSN envvar; skipping cockroachdb-backed graph
test suite")
    }

    g, err := NewCockroachDBGraph(dsn)
    c.Assert(err, gc.IsNil)
    s.SetGraph(g)

    // keep track of the sql.DB instance so we can execute SQL statements
    // to reset the DB between tests!
    s.db = g.db
}
```

To ensure that all the tests work exactly as expected, one of our requirements is that each test in the suite is provided with a clean DB instance. To this end, we need to define a *per-test* setup method that empties all the database tables:

```
func (s *CockroachDBGraphTestSuite) SetUpTest(c *gc.C) { s.flushDB(c) }

func (s *CockroachDBGraphTestSuite) flushDB(c *gc.C) {
    _, err := s.db.Exec("DELETE FROM links")
    c.Assert(err, gc.IsNil)
    _, err = s.db.Exec("DELETE FROM edges")
    c.Assert(err, gc.IsNil)
}
```

Finally, we need to provide a teardown method for the test suite. Once the test suite has finished executing, we truncate the DB tables once more and release the DB connection:

```
func (s *CockroachDBGraphTestSuite) TearDownSuite(c *gc.C) {
    if s.db != nil {
        s.flushDB(c)
        c.Assert(s.db.Close(), gc.IsNil)
    }
}
```

Note that flushing the database's contents during teardown is not mandatory. In my opinion, it's good practice to always do so just in case some other set of tests from a different package use the same DB instance but expect it to be initially empty.

Designing the data layer for the text indexer component

In the following sections, we will perform an in-depth analysis of the text indexer component. We will identify the set of operations that the text indexer component must be able to support and formally encode them as a Go interface named Indexer.

In a similar fashion to the link graph analysis, we will be constructing two concrete implementations of the Indexer interface: an in-memory implementation based on the popular bleve [1] package and a horizontally-scalable implementation using Elasticsearch [9].

A model for indexed documents

As the first step in our analysis of the indexer component, we will start by describing the document model that the `Indexer` implementations will index and search:

```go
type Document struct {
    LinkID uuid.UUID

    URL string

    Title string
    Content string

    IndexedAt time.Time
    PageRank float64
}
```

All the documents must include a non-empty attribute called `LinkID`. This attribute is a UUID value that connects a document with a link that's obtained from the link graph. In addition to the link ID, each document also stores the URL of the indexed document and allows us to not only display it as part of the search results but to also implement more advanced search patterns in future (for example, constraint searches to a particular domain).

The `Title` and `Content` attributes correspond to the value of the `<title>` element if the link points to an HTML page, whereas the `Content` attribute stores the block of text that was extracted by the crawler when processing the link. Both of these attributes will be indexed and made available for searching.

The `IndexedAt` attribute contains a timestamp that indicates when a particular document was last indexed, while the `PageRank` attribute keeps track of the `PageRank` score that will be assigned to each document by the `PageRank` calculator component. Since `PageRank` scores can be construed as a quality metric for each link, the text indexer implementations will attempt to optimize the returned result sets by sorting search matches *both* by their relevance to the input query and by their `PageRank` scores.

Listing the set of operations that the text indexer needs to support

For the text indexer component use case, we need to be able to perform the following set of operations:

1. Add a document to the index or reindex an existing document when its content changes. This operation will normally be invoked by the crawler component.
2. Perform a lookup for a document by its ID.
3. Perform a full-text query and obtain an *iterable* list of results. The frontend component for our project will invoke this operation when the user clicks the search button and consume the returned iterator to present a paginated list of results to the end user.
4. Update the `PageRank` score for a particular document. This operation will be invoked by the `PageRank` calculator component when the `PageRank` score for a particular link needs to be updated.

Defining the Indexer interface

Similar to the approach we followed when we modeled the link graph component, we shall encapsulate the preceding list of operations into a Go interface called `Indexer`:

```
type Indexer interface {
    Index(doc *Document) error
    FindByID(linkID uuid.UUID) (*Document, error)
    Search(query Query) (Iterator, error)
    UpdateScore(linkID uuid.UUID, score float64) error
}
```

The `Search` method expects a `Query` type instead of a simple string value as its input argument. This is by design; it offers us the flexibility to expand the indexer's query capabilities further down the road to support richer query semantics without having to modify the signature of the `Search` method. Here is the definition of the `Query` type:

```
type Query struct {
    Type       QueryType
    Expression string
    Offset     uint64
}

type QueryType uint8
```

```
const (
    QueryTypeMatch QueryType = iota
    QueryTypePhrase
)
```

The `Expression` field stores the search query that's entered by the end user. However, its interpretation by the indexer component can vary, depending on the value of the `Type` attribute. As proof of concept, we will only implement two of the most common types of searches:

- Searching for a list of keywords *in any order*
- Searching for an *exact* phrase match

In the future, we can opt to add support for other types of queries such as *boolean-, date-, or domain-based* queries.

After executing a search query, the text indexer will return an `Iterator` interface instance that provides a simple API for consuming the search results. This is the definition of the `Iterator` interface:

```
type Iterator interface {
    // Close the iterator and release any allocated resources.
    Close() error

    // Next loads the next document matching the search query.
    // It returns false if no more documents are available.
    Next() bool

    // Error returns the last error encountered by the iterator.
    Error() error

    // Document returns the current document from the result set.
    Document() *Document

    // TotalCount returns the approximate number of search results.
    TotalCount() uint64
}
```

After obtaining an iterator instance, we can consume each search result using a simple `for` loop:

```
// 'docIt' is a search iterator
for docIt.Next() {
    doc := docIt.Document()
    // Do something with doc...
}
```

```
if err := docIt.Error(); err != nil {
    // Handle error...
}
```

Calls to `docIt.Next()` will return false either when we have iterated all the results or an error has occurred. In a similar fashion to the link graph iterators we examined in the previous sections, we only need to check *once* for the presence of errors after exiting the iteration loop.

Verifying indexer implementations using a shared test suite

In the next few pages, we will be constructing two completely different Indexer implementations. In a similar fashion to the link graph component, we will again devise a shared test suite that will help us verify that both implementations behave in exactly the same way.

The `SuiteBase` definition for our shared indexer tests can be found in the `Chapter06/textindexer/index/indextest` package and depends on the `gocheck` [11] framework that we introduced in `Chapter 4`, *The Art of Testing*. The suite defines tests for the following groups of index operations:

- **Document indexing tests**: These tests are designed to verify that the indexer component successfully processes valid documents and rejects any document that does not define the required set of document attributes (for example, it includes an empty link ID).
- **Document lookup tests**: These tests validate that we can look up a previously indexed document via its link ID and that the returned document model is identical to the document that was passed and indexed.
- **Keyword search tests**: A series of tests designed to verify that keyword searches yield the correct set of documents.
- **Exact phrase search tests**: Yet another series of tests that verifies that exact phrase searches yield the correct set of documents.
- `PageRank` **score update tests**: These tests exercise the `PageRank` score update code path and verify that changes to the score values for indexed documents are reflected in the order of returned search results.

To create a test suite for an actual indexer implementation, all we have to do is the following:

- Define a new test suite that embeds `SuiteBase`
- Provide a suite setup helper that creates the appropriate indexer instance and then invokes the `SetIndexer` method exposed by `SuiteBase` to wire the indexer to the base test suite

An in-memory Indexer implementation using bleve

Our first attempt at implementing an in-memory indexer will be based on a popular full-text search package for Go called bleve [1]. While bleve is primarily designed to store its index on disk, it also supports an in-memory index. This makes it an excellent candidate for running unit tests in isolation or for demonstration purposes if we don't want to spin up a much more resource intensive option such as Elasticsearch.

The full source for the bleve based Indexer implementation is available in the `Chapter06/textindexer/store/memory` package in this book's GitHub repository. The definition of the `InMemoryBleveIndexer` type is pretty straightforward:

```
type InMemoryBleveIndexer struct {
    mu   sync.RWMutex
    docs map[string]*index.Document

    idx bleve.Index
}
```

The `idx` field stores a reference to the bleve index. To speed up indexing, we don't pass the full `Document` model to bleve and instead make use of a more lightweight representation that only contains the three fields we need for performing searches: the title, content, and `PageRank` score.

An obvious caveat of this approach is that since bleve stores a partial view of the document data, we cannot recreate the original document from the result list returned by bleve after executing a search query. To solve this problem, the in-memory indexer maintains a map where keys are the document link IDs and values are *immutable* copies of the documents that are processed by the indexer. When processing a result list, the returned document IDs are used to index the map and to recover the original document. To ensure that the in-memory indexer is safe for concurrent use, access to the map is guarded with a read/write mutex.

Indexing documents

The implementation of the `Index` method for the in-memory indexer is outlined as follows:

```go
func (i *InMemoryBleveIndexer) Index(doc *index.Document) error {
    if doc.LinkID == uuid.Nil {
        return xerrors.Errorf("index: %w", index.ErrMissingLinkID)
    }
    doc.IndexedAt = time.Now()
    dcopy := copyDoc(doc)
    key := dcopy.LinkID.String()
    i.mu.Lock()
    if orig, exists := i.docs[key]; exists {
        dcopy.PageRank = orig.PageRank
    }
    if err := i.idx.Index(key, makeBleveDoc(dcopy)); err != nil {
        return xerrors.Errorf("index: %w", err)
    }
    i.docs[key] = dcopy
    i.mu.Unlock()
    return nil
}
```

To guarantee that the only way to mutate an already-indexed document is via a reindex operation, the indexer is designed to work with immutable copies of the documents that are passed as arguments to the `Index` method. The `copyDoc` helper creates a copy of the original document that we can safely store in the internal document map.

To add a new document to the index or to reindex an existing document, we need to provide bleve with two parameters: a *string-based* document ID and the document to be indexed. The `makeBleveDoc` helper returns a partial, lightweight view of the original document that, as we mentioned in the previous section, only contains the fields we want to use as part of our search queries.

When updating an existing document, we don't want the index operation to mutate the `PageRank` score that has already been assigned to the document as this would interfere with how the search results are ordered. To this end, if a document already exists, we need to patch the lightweight document that we pass to bleve so that it reflects the correct `PageRank` value.

Looking up documents and updating their PageRank score

If we know a document's link ID, we can invoke the `FindByID` method to look up the indexed document. The implementation is pretty straightforward; we just acquire a read lock and lookup for the specified ID in the internal map maintained by the indexer. If a matching entry exists, we create a copy and return it to the caller:

```
func (i *InMemoryBleveIndexer) FindByID(linkID uuid.UUID) (*index.Document,
error) {
    return i.findByID(linkID.String())
}

func (i *InMemoryBleveIndexer) findByID(linkID string) (*index.Document,
error) {
    i.mu.RLock()
    defer i.mu.RUnlock()

    if d, found := i.docs[linkID]; found {
        return copyDoc(d), nil
    }

    return nil, xerrors.Errorf("find by ID: %w", index.ErrNotFound)
}
```

You may be wondering why the `FindByID` implementation converts the input UUID into a string and delegates the actual document look up to the unexported `findByID` method. In the previous section, we saw that when we request bleve to index a document, we need to provide a string-based ID for the document. Bleve will return that ID to us when the document is matched by a search query. As will become evident in the following section, by providing a `findByID` method that accepts the linkID as a string, we can *reuse* the document lookup code when iterating search results.

To update the `PageRank` score for an existing document, clients invoke the `UpdateScore` method, which expects a document's link ID and the updated `PageRank` score:

```
func (i *InMemoryBleveIndexer) UpdateScore(linkID uuid.UUID, score float64)
error {
    i.mu.Lock()
    defer i.mu.Unlock()
    key := linkID.String()
    doc, found := i.docs[key]
    if !found {
        doc = &index.Document{LinkID: linkID}
```

```
        i.docs[key] = doc
    }

    doc.PageRank = score
    if err := i.idx.Index(key, makeBleveDoc(doc)); err != nil {
        return xerrors.Errorf("update score: %w", err)
    }
    return nil
}
```

Updating *any* searchable document attribute requires a reindex operation. Consequently, the UpdateScore implementation will acquire a *write* lock and look up the document in the internal document map. If the document is found, its PageRank score will be updated *in-place* and the document will be passed to bleve for indexing.

Searching the index

The clients of the in-memory indexer submit search queries by invoking the Search method. The implementation of this method is as follows:

```
func (i *InMemoryBleveIndexer) Search(q index.Query) (index.Iterator,
error) {
    var bq query.Query
    switch q.Type {
    case index.QueryTypePhrase:
        bq = bleve.NewMatchPhraseQuery(q.Expression)
    default:
        bq = bleve.NewMatchQuery(q.Expression)
    }

    searchReq := bleve.NewSearchRequest(bq)
    searchReq.SortBy([]string{"-PageRank", "-_score"})
    searchReq.Size = batchSize
    searchReq.From = q.Offset
    rs, err := i.idx.Search(searchReq)
    if err != nil {
        return nil, xerrors.Errorf("search: %w", err)
    }
    return &bleveIterator{idx: i, searchReq: searchReq, rs: rs, cumIdx:
q.Offset}, nil
}
```

The first thing that our implementation needs to do is check what type of query the caller asked us to perform and then invoke the appropriate bleve helper to construct a query from the caller-provided expression.

Next, the generated query is transformed into a new search request where we also ask bleve to order the results by `PageRank` and relevance in descending order. Bleve search results are always paginated. Consequently, in addition to any sorting preferences, we must also specify the number of results per page that we want bleve to return (the batch size). The search request object also allows us to control the offset in the result list by specifying a value for its `From` field.

The next step is to submit the search request to bleve and check for the presence of errors. If everything goes according to plan and no error is returned, the implementation creates a new iterator instance that the caller can use to consume the matched documents.

Iterating the list of search results

The `bleveIterator` type implements the `indexer.Iterator` interface and is defined as follows:

```
type bleveIterator struct {
    idx        *InMemoryBleveIndexer
    searchReq  *bleve.SearchRequest

    cumIdx uint64
    rsIdx  int
    rs     *bleve.SearchResult

    latchedDoc *index.Document
    lastErr    error
}
```

The iterator implementation keeps track of two pointers:

- A pointer to the in-memory indexer instance, which allows the iterator to access the stored documents when the iterator is advanced
- A pointer to the executed search request, which the iterator uses to trigger new bleve searches once the current page of results has been consumed

To track the position in the paginated search result list, the iterator also maintains two counters:

- A cumulative counter (`cumIdx`) that tracks the absolute position in the *global* result list
- A counter (`rsIdx`) that tracks the position in the *current* page of results

The `bleve.SearchResult` objects returned by bleve queries provide information about both the total number of matched results and the number of documents in the current result page. The iterator's `Next` method makes use of this information to decide whether the iterator can be advanced.

When the iterator's `Next` method is invoked, the implementation performs a quick check to see if an error has occurred or we have already iterated the full set of results. If that is the case, `Next` will return `false` to indicate that no more items are available. The latter check is facilitated by comparing the total result count reported by bleve to the `cumIdx` value that the iterator tracks within its internal state:

```
if it.lastErr != nil || it.rs == nil || it.cumIdx >= it.rs.Total {
    return false
}
```

Our next course of action is to check whether we have exhausted the current page of results. This is facilitated by comparing the number of documents in the current result page to the value of the `rsIdx` counter. If all the documents in the *current* result page have been consumed and *no* additional result pages are available, the method returns `false` to indicate this to the caller.

Otherwise, the implementation automatically fetches the next pages of results by doing the following:

1. Updating the stored search request so that the result offset points to the beginning of the *next* page
2. Executing a new bleve search request to obtain the next page of results
3. Resetting the `rsIdx` counter so that we can process the first result of the newly retrieved page

The preceding steps are outlined in the following code snippet:

```
if it.rsIdx >= it.rs.Hits.Len() {
    it.searchReq.From += it.searchReq.Size
    if it.rs, it.lastErr = it.idx.idx.Search(it.searchReq); it.lastErr !=
nil {
        return false
    }
    it.rsIdx = 0
}

nextID := it.rs.Hits[it.rsIdx].ID
if it.latchedDoc, it.lastErr = it.idx.findByID(nextID); it.lastErr != nil {
    return false
}
```

```
it.cumIdx++
it.rsIdx++
return true
```

To latch the next document from the result set, we extract its ID from the bleve result and look up the full document by invoking the `findByID` method on the in-memory index. As we saw in the previous section, the document lookup code always returns a *copy* of the indexed document that we can safely cache within the iterator. Lastly, both position-tracking counters are incremented and a `true` value is returned to the caller to indicate that the iterator has been successfully advanced and that the next document can be retrieved via a call to the iterator's `Document` method.

Setting up a test suite for the in-memory indexer

The test suite for the in-memory indexer implementation embeds the shared test suite we outlined in the *Verifying indexer implementations using a shared test suite* section. Since the suite depends on the `gocheck` framework, we need to add some extra code to register the suite with the `go test` framework:

```
var _ = gc.Suite(new(InMemoryBleveTestSuite))

type InMemoryBleveTestSuite struct {
    indextest.SuiteBase
    idx *InMemoryBleveIndexer
}

// Register our test-suite with go test.
func Test(t *testing.T) { gc.TestingT(t) }
```

To ensure that each test uses a clean index instance, the suite provides a per-test setup method that recreates the index before running each test:

```
func (s *InMemoryBleveTestSuite) SetUpTest(c *gc.C) {
    idx, err := NewInMemoryBleveIndexer()
    c.Assert(err, gc.IsNil)
    s.SetIndexer(idx)
    // Keep track of the concrete indexer implementation so we can clean up
    // when tearing down the test
    s.idx = idx
}
func (s *InMemoryBleveTestSuite) TearDownTest(c *gc.C) {
c.Assert(s.idx.Close(), gc.IsNil) }
```

Since bleve index instances are held in memory, we also need to define a per-test teardown method to ensure that the index is closed and that any acquired resources are freed after each test completes.

Scaling across an Elasticsearch indexer implementation

A caveat of the in-memory bleve-based indexer implementation is that we are more or less limited to running our index on a single node. This not only introduces a single point of failure to our overall system design but it also places a hard limit on the amount of search traffic that our service can handle.

We could definitely argue that we could try to scale our implementation horizontally. At the time of writing, bleve does not provide any built-in mechanism for running in distributed mode; we would need to roll out a custom solution from scratch. One approach would be to create a multi-master setup. The idea here would be to spin up multiple instances of our index service and place them behind a *gateway service* that allows clients to access the index via an API. When clients provide a document for indexing, the gateway will ask *all* the index instances to process the document and will only return to the caller when all the instances have successfully indexed the document. On the other hand, the gateway can delegate incoming search requests to any random index instance in the pool. Given that searching is a read-intensive type of workload, the preceding approach would *probably* work nicely. I say probably because there are quite a few things that could possibly go wrong with such an implementation.

Building distributed systems is hard; figuring out how they behave when faults occur is even harder. We would definitely be better off using an off-the-self solution that has been battle-tested in large-scale production systems; preferably one whose failure modes (discovered via a framework such as Jepsen [12]) are known and well understood. To this end, we will be basing our second indexer implementation on Elasticsearch [9]. Here are some of the benefits of using Elasticsearch:

- We can run Elasticsearch on our own infrastructure or use one of the commercially available managed Elasticsearch SaaS offerings.
- Elasticsearch has built-in support for clustering and can scale horizontally.
- It exposes a REST API and clients are available for most popular programming languages. The client list includes an official Go client [21] that we will be using for our indexer implementation.

Creating a new Elasticsearch indexer instance

To create a new Elasticsearch search indexer, clients need to invoke the NewElasticSearchIndexer constructor and provide a list of elastic search nodes to connect to. Our implementation will use the official Go client for Elasticsearch, which is provided by the go-elastic package [21]:

```go
func NewElasticSearchIndexer(esNodes []string) (*ElasticSearchIndexer,
error) {
    cfg := elasticsearch.Config{
        Addresses: esNodes,
    }
    es, err := elasticsearch.NewClient(cfg)
    if err != nil {
        return nil, err
    }
    if err = ensureIndex(es); err != nil {
        return nil, err
    }

    return &ElasticSearchIndexer{
        es: es,
    }, nil
}
```

After creating a new go-elastic client, the constructor invokes the ensureIndex helper, which checks whether the Elasticsearch index (the equivalent of a table, in DB terminology) that we will be using for storing our documents already exists. If not, the helper will automatically create it for us using the following set of field mappings (table schema, in DB terminology):

```json
{
  "mappings" : {
    "properties": {
      "LinkID": {"type": "keyword"},
      "URL": {"type": "keyword"},
      "Content": {"type": "text"},
      "Title": {"type": "text"},
      "IndexedAt": {"type": "date"},
      "PageRank": {"type": "double"}
    }
  }
}
```

Providing field mappings is not strictly required by Elasticsearch! In fact, the indexing engine is quite capable of inferring the types of each document field simply by analyzing their contents. However, if we explicitly provide the field mapping on our end, we not only force Elasticsearch to use a *specific indexer implementation* for each field type but we can also individually configure and fine-tune the behavior of each field indexer.

The preceding JSON document defines the following set of mappings:

- The `LinkID` and `URL` fields specify a `keyword` field type. This type instructs Elasticsearch to index them as a blob of text and is suited for queries such as `find the document whose LinkID is X`.
- The `Content` and `Title` fields specify a `text` field type. Elasticsearch will use a special indexer that allows us to perform full-text searches against these fields.
- The `IndexedAt` and `PageRank` fields are parsed and stored as date and double values.

Indexing and looking up documents

To upsert a document to the index, we need to submit an update operation to the Elasticsearch cluster. The update request's contents is populated using the following block of code:

```
esDoc := makeEsDoc(doc)
update := map[string]interface{}{
    "doc":           esDoc,
    "doc_as_upsert": true,
}
```

The `makeEsDoc` helper converts the input `indexer.Document` instance into a representation that Elasticsearch can process. It is important to note that the mapped document does not include a `PageRank` score value, even if that is present in the original docs. This is intentional as we only allow `PageRank` scores to be mutated via a call to `UpdateScore`. The `doc_as_upsert` flag serves as a hint to Elasticsearch that it should create the document if it does not exist, that is, it should treat the update request as an upsert operation.

After populating the update document, we just need to serialize it into JSON, execute a *synchronous* update, and check for any reported errors:

```
var buf bytes.Buffer
err := json.NewEncoder(&buf).Encode(doc)
if err != nil {
    return xerrors.Errorf("index: %w", err)
}

res, err := i.es.Update(indexName, esDoc.LinkID, &buf,
i.es.Update.WithRefresh("true"))
if err != nil {
    return xerrors.Errorf("index: %w", err)
}

var updateRes esUpdateRes
if err = unmarshalResponse(res, &updateRes); err != nil {
    return xerrors.Errorf("index: %w", err)
}
```

When performing any API call to Elasticsearch using the go-elastic client, errors can be reported in two different ways:

- The client returns an error and a `nil` response value. This can happen, for instance, if the DNS resolution for the Elasticsearch nodes fails or if the client can't connect to any of the provided node addresses.
- Elasticsearch sends a JSON response that contains a structured error as its payload.

To deal with the latter case, we can use the handy `unmarshalResponse` helper, which checks for the presence of errors in the response and returns them as regular Go error values.

What about document lookups? This operation is modeled as a search query where we try to match a single document with a specific link ID value. Like any other request to the Elasticsearch cluster, search queries are specified as JSON documents that are sent to the cluster via an HTTP POST request. The `FindByID` implementation creates the search query inline by defining a nested block of `map[string]interface{}` items which are then serialized via a JSON encoder instance:

```
var buf bytes.Buffer
query := map[string]interface{}{
    "query": map[string]interface{}{
        "match": map[string]interface{}{
            "LinkID": linkID.String(),
        },
```

```
        },
        "from": 0,
        "size": 1,
    }
    if err := json.NewEncoder(&buf).Encode(query); err != nil {
        return nil, xerrors.Errorf("find by ID: %w", err)
    }
```

At this point, I would like to point out that I only opted to use an inline, *type-less* approach to define the search query for simplicity. Ideally, instead of using maps, you would define nested structs for each portion of the query. Besides the obvious benefits of working with typed values, one other important benefit of working with structs is that we can switch to a much more efficient JSON encoder implementation that doesn't require the use of *reflection*. One such example is easyjson [10], which utilizes code generation to create efficient JSON encoder/decoders and promises a 4x-5x increase in speed over the JSON encoder implementation that ships with the Go standard library.

After our query has been successfully serialized to JSON, we invoke the runSearch helper, which submits the query to Elasticsearch. The helper will then unserialize the obtained response into a nested struct while at the same time checking for the presence of errors:

```
    searchRes, err := runSearch(i.es, query)
    if err != nil {
        return nil, xerrors.Errorf("find by ID: %w", err)
    }

    if len(searchRes.Hits.HitList) != 1 {
        return nil, xerrors.Errorf("find by ID: %w", index.ErrNotFound)
    }

    doc := mapEsDoc(&searchRes.Hits.HitList[0].DocSource)
```

If everything goes according to plan, we will receive a single result. The obtained result is then passed to the mapEsDoc helper, which converts it back into a Document model instance, as follows:

```
func mapEsDoc(d *esDoc) *index.Document {
    return &index.Document{
        LinkID:    uuid.MustParse(d.LinkID),
        URL:       d.URL,
        Title:     d.Title,
        Content:   d.Content,
        IndexedAt: d.IndexedAt.UTC(),
        PageRank:  d.PageRank,
    }
}
```

As you can see in the preceding snippet, the majority of the fields are just copied over to the document with the exception of the `LinkID` field, which must be parsed from a string representation into a UUID value first. The converted document is then returned to the caller of the `FindByID` method.

Performing paginated searches

As you might expect from a product whose primary job is searching within documents, Elasticsearch supports a plethora of different query types, ranging from keyword-based searches to complex geospatial or time-based queries. Unfortunately, the syntax for specifying queries varies slightly, depending on the type of query that we wish to perform.

It turns out that, for our particular use case, we can get away with using the same query syntax for both keyword- and phrase-based queries. All we need to do is convert the `QueryType` provided by the caller into an Elasticsearch-specific value that we can plug into a predefined search template. To achieve this, the indexer implementation makes use of the *switch* block to convert the incoming query type into a value that Elasticsearch can recognize and interpret:

```
var qtype string
switch q.Type {
case index.QueryTypePhrase:
    qtype = "phrase"
default:
    qtype = "best_fields"
}
```

We can then proceed to assemble our search query in the (quite verbose) format that's expected by Elasticsearch using a series of nested `map[string]interface{}` values, as follows:

```
query := map[string]interface{}{
    "query": map[string]interface{}{
        "function_score": map[string]interface{}{
            "query": map[string]interface{}{
                "multi_match": map[string]interface{}{
                    "type":   qtype,
                    "query":  q.Expression,
                    "fields": []string{"Title", "Content"},
                },
            },
            "script_score": map[string]interface{}{
                "script": map[string]interface{}{
                    "source": "_score + doc['PageRank'].value",
```

```
                },
              },
          },
      },
      "from": q.Offset,
      "size": batchSize,
  }
```

To handle pagination of the matched results, the query specifies both the page offset and the page size via the `from` and `size` query fields.

The preceding query template demonstrates another very useful Elasticsearch feature: **score boosting**. By default, Elasticsearch sorts the returned documents in terms of their *relevance* to the submitted query. For some kinds of queries, the default built-in relevance score calculation algorithm may not yield a meaningful value for sorting (for example, all the documents contain the search keywords and are assigned the same relevance score). To this end, Elasticsearch provides helpers for manipulating or even completely overriding the relevance scores of matched documents.

Our particular query template specifies a custom script that calculates the effective relevance score by **aggregating** the matched document's PageRank score and the query relevance score calculated by Elasticsearch (exposed via the `_score` field). This little trick ensures that documents with a higher `PageRank` score always sort higher in the set of results.

Just as we did for the `FindByID` implementation, we once again invoke the `runSearch` helper to submit a search request to Elasticsearch and unserialize the first page of returned results. If the operation succeeds, a new `esIterator` instance is created and returned to the caller so that the results of the search query can be consumed:

```
searchRes, err := runSearch(i.es, query)
if err != nil {
    return nil, xerrors.Errorf("search: %w", err)
}

return &esIterator{es: i.es, searchReq: query, rs: searchRes, cumIdx:
q.Offset}, nil
```

In a similar fashion to its in-memory sibling, the `esIterator` implementation maintains its own set of global and per-page counters for keeping track of its position within the result set returned by Elasticsearch. Each time the iterator's `Next` method is invoked, the iterator checks if an error has occurred or whether all the search results have been consumed. If this happens to be the case, then the call to `Next` returns `false` to notify the caller that no more results are available.

If the iterator hasn't exhausted the current page of results yet, it does the following:

- Both internal position-tracking counters are incremented
- The next available result is converted into a `Document` model via a call to the `mapEsDoc` helper (see the previous section) and latched inside the iterator object
- A `true` value is returned to the caller to indicate that the next result is available for retrieval via a call to the iterator's `Document` method

Otherwise, if the end of the current page of results has been reached and more results are available, the iterator adjusts the offset field of the last search query and sends out a new search request to obtain the next page of results.

In the interest of brevity, we will not be listing the source code for the `esIterator` implementation here since it is almost identical to the in-memory indexer implementation that we've already examined. You can take a look at the fully documented source code for the iterator by opening the `iterator.go` file in this `Chapter06/textindexer/store/es` package, which is available in this book's GitHub repository.

Updating the PageRank score for a document

To update the `PageRank` score for an existing document, we need to construct an update request payload that the go-elastic client will submit to the Elasticsearch cluster via an HTTP POST request. The update payload includes a map with the fields names and values that need to be updated.

To facilitate document updates, the go-elastic client exposes an `Update` method that expects the following set of arguments:

- The name of the index that contains the document to be updated
- The ID of the document to be updated
- The document update payload encoded as JSON

The following code snippet illustrates how the update request is assembled and passed to the `Update` method:

```
var buf bytes.Buffer
update := map[string]interface{}{
    "doc": map[string]interface{}{
        "LinkID":   linkID.String(),
        "PageRank": score,
```

```
        },
        "doc_as_upsert": true,
    }
    if err := json.NewEncoder(&buf).Encode(update); err != nil {
        return xerrors.Errorf("update score: %w", err)
    }
```

If the caller of the `UpdateScore` method provides a document link ID that does not exist, we want to be able to create a placeholder document containing just the `LinkID` and `PageRank` scores. This is facilitated by including the `doc_as_upsert` flag to our update payload.

Setting up a test suite for the Elasticsearch indexer

The Elasticsearch-backed indexer implementation defines its own go-check test suite that embeds the shared indexer test suite and provides setup and teardown methods that are specific to the Elasticsearch implementation.

Each the tests in the suite use the same `ElasticSearchIndexer` instance that is initialized once with the following suite setup method:

```
func (s *ElasticSearchTestSuite) SetUpSuite(c *gc.C) {
    nodeList := os.Getenv("ES_NODES")
    if nodeList == "" {
        c.Skip("Missing ES_NODES envvar; skipping elasticsearch-backed
index test suite")
    }

    idx, err := NewElasticSearchIndexer(strings.Split(nodeList, ","))
    c.Assert(err, gc.IsNil).
    s.SetIndexer(idx)
    // Keep track of the concrete indexer implementation so we can access
    // its internals when setting up the test
    s.idx = idx
}
```

Given the fact that Elasticsearch is quite a resource-intensive application, it stands to reason that you might not be running it locally on your dev machine. In anticipation of this, the suite setup code will check for the presence of the `ES_NODES` environment variable, which contains a comma-delimited list of Elasticsearch nodes to connect to. If the variable is not defined, then the entire test suite will be automatically skipped.

To guarantee that the tests don't interfere with each other, it is important to provide each test with a blank Elasticsearch index. To this end, before each test runs, a per-test setup method drops the Elasticsearch index and, by extension, any documents that were added to the index by the previous test runs:

```
func (s *ElasticSearchTestSuite) SetUpTest(c *gc.C) {
    if s.idx.es != nil {
        _, err := s.idx.es.Indices.Delete([]string{indexName})
        c.Assert(err, gc.IsNil)
    }
}
```

The remainder of the test suite code is responsible for registering the suite with the go-check framework and adding the appropriate hooks so that the suite can run when `go test` is invoked.

Summary

In this chapter, we started laying the groundwork for the Links 'R' Us system by defining a data layer abstraction for the link graph and the text indexer components. Furthermore, as proof that our abstraction layer does indeed make it easy to swap the underlying implementation, we provided two compatible and fully testable implementations for each of the components.

In the next chapter, we will discuss strategies and patterns for building efficient data processing pipelines using Go and implement the web scraping component of the Links 'R' Us project.

Questions

1. What are the key differences between a relational database and a NoSQL database? Provide an example use case where a relational database would be a better fit than a NoSQL database and vice versa.
2. How would you scale a relational database system for a read-heavy and a write-heavy workload?
3. What is the CAP theorem and is it important when choosing which NoSQL implementation to use?

4. Why is it important to provide an abstraction layer between our business logic and the underlying database?
5. How would you go about adding a new method to the `Indexer` interface we discussed in the last part of this chapter?

Further reading

1. A modern text indexing library for Go. Available at: `https://github.com/blevesearch/bleve`.
2. Apache Cassandra: Manage massive amounts of data, fast, without losing sleep. Available at: `http://cassandra.apache.org`.
3. Apache CouchDB. Available at: `https://couchdb.apache.org`.
4. Brewer, Eric A.: *Towards Robust Distributed Systems.* In: Symposium on **Principles of Distributed Computing (PODC)**, 2000.
5. CockroachDB: Ultra-resilient SQL for global business. Available at: `https://www.cockroachlabs.com`.
6. Codd, E. F.: *A Relational Model of Data for Large Shared Data Banks.* In: Commun. ACM Bd. 13. New York, NY, USA, ACM (1970), Nr. 6, S. 377–387.
7. Database migrations. CLI and Golang library. Available at: `https://github.com/golang-migrate/migrate`.
8. DynamoDB: Fast and flexible NoSQL database service for any scale. Available at: `https://aws.amazon.com/dynamodb`.
9. Elasticsearch: Open Source Search and Analytics. Available at: `https://www.elastic.co/`.
10. Fast JSON serializer for golang. Available at: `https://github.com/mailru/easyjson`.
11. gocheck: rich testing for the Go language. Available at: `http://labix.org/gocheck`.
12. Jepsen: Breaking distributed systems so you don't have to. Available at: `https://github.com/jepsen-io/jepsen`.
13. LevelDB: A fast key-value storage library written at Google that provides an ordered mapping from string keys to string values. Available at: `https://github.com/google/leveldb`.
14. Martin, Robert C.: Clean Architecture: *A Craftsman's Guide to Software Structure and Design,* Robert C. Martin Series. Boston, MA : Prentice Hall, 2017 — ISBN `978-0-13-449416-6`.

15. memcached: A distributed memory object caching system. Available at: `https://memcached.org`.

16. MongoDB: The most popular database for modern apps. Available at: `https://www.mongodb.com`.

17. MySQL: The world's most popular open source database. Available at: `https://www.mysql.com`.

18. PostgreSQL: The world's most advanced open source relational database. Available at: `https://www.postgresql.org`.

19. Pure Go Postgres driver for database/SQL. Available at: `https://github.com/lib/pq`.

20. RocksDB: An embeddable persistent key-value store for fast storage. Available at: `https://rocksdb.org`.

21. The official Go client for Elasticsearch. Available at: `https://github.com/elastic/go-elasticsearch`.

Data-Processing Pipelines

"Inside every well-written large program is a well-written small program."

- Tony Hoare

Pipelines are a fairly standard and widely used way to segregate the processing of data into multiple stages. In this chapter, we will be exploring the basic principles behind data-processing pipelines and present a blueprint for implementing generic, concurrent-safe, and reusable pipelines using Go primitives, such as channels, contexts, and go-routines.

In this chapter, you will learn about the following:

- Designing a generic processing pipeline from scratch using Go primitives
- Approaches to modeling pipeline payloads in a generic way
- Strategies for dealing with errors that can occur while a pipeline is executing
- Pros and cons of synchronous and asynchronous pipeline design
- Applying pipeline design concepts to building the Links 'R' Us crawler component

Technical requirements

The full code for the topics discussed in this chapter has been published to this book's GitHub repository under the Chapter07 folder.

 You can access the GitHub repository that contains the code and all required resources for each of this book's chapters by going to https://github.com/PacktPublishing/Hands-On-Software-Engineering-with-Golang.

To get you up and running as quickly as possible, each example project includes a makefile that defines the following set of targets:

Makefile target	Description
deps	Install any required dependencies
test	Run all tests and report coverage
lint	Check for lint errors

As with all other book chapters, you will need a fairly recent version of Go, which you can download at https://golang.org/dl.

Building a generic data-processing pipeline in Go

The following figure illustrates the high-level design of the pipeline that we will be building throughout the first half of this chapter:

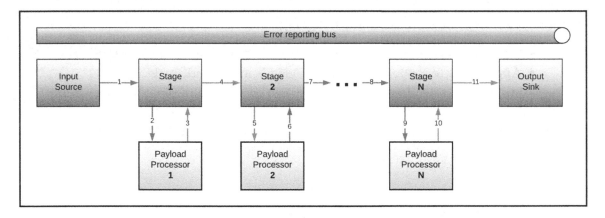

Figure 1: A generic, multistage pipeline

Keep in mind that this is definitely not the only, or necessarily the best, way to go about implementing a data-processing pipeline. Pipelines are inherently application specific, so there is not really a one-size-fits-all guide for constructing efficient pipelines.

Having said that, the proposed design is applicable to a wide variety of use cases, including, but not limited to, the crawler component for the Links 'R' Us project. Let's examine the preceding figure in a bit more detail and identify the basic components that the pipeline comprises:

- The **input source**: Inputs essentially function as data-sources that pump data into the pipeline. From this point onwards, we will be referring to this set of data with the term **payload**. Under the hood, inputs facilitate the role of an **adapter**, reading data typically available in an external system, such as a database or message queue, and converting it into a format that can be consumed by the pipeline.

- One or more processing **stages**: Each stage of the pipeline receives a payload as its input, applies a processing function to it, and passes the result to the stage that follows.

- The **output sink**: After stepping through each of the pipeline's stages, payloads eventually reach the output sink. In a similar fashion to input sources, sinks also work as **adapters**, only this time the conversion works in reverse! Payloads are converted into a format that can be consumed by an external system.

- An **error bus**: The error bus provides a convenient abstraction that allows the pipeline components to report any errors that occur while the pipeline is executing.

The full source code and tests for the pipeline are available at the book's GitHub repository under the `Chapter07/pipeline` folder.

Design goals for the pipeline package

Let's quickly enumerate some of the design goals for the `pipeline` package that we will be building. The key principles that will serve as guides for the design decisions that we will be making are: simplicity, extensibility, and genericness.

First and foremost, our design should be able to adapt to different types of payloads. Keep in mind that payload formats are, in the majority of cases, dictated by the end user of the pipeline package. Consequently, the pipeline internals should not make any assumptions about the internal implementation details of payloads that traverse the various pipeline stages.

Secondly, the main role of a data-processing pipeline is to facilitate the flow of payloads between a source and a sink. In a similar manner to payloads, the endpoints of a pipeline are also provided by the end user. As a result, the pipeline package needs to define the appropriate abstractions and interfaces for allowing the end users to register their own source and sink implementations.

Moreover, the pipeline package should go beyond just allowing the end users to specify a processing function for each stage. Users should also be able to choose, on a per-stage basis, the strategy used by the pipeline for delivering payloads to processing functions. It stands to reason that the package should come with *batteries included*–that is, provide built-in implementations for the most common payload delivery strategies; however, the user should be given the flexibility to define their own custom strategies if the built-in ones are not sufficient for their particular use cases.

Finally, our implementation must expose simple and straightforward APIs for creating, assembling, and executing complex pipelines. Furthermore, the API dealing with the pipeline execution should not only provide users with the means to cancel long-running pipelines, but it should also provide a mechanism for capturing and reporting any errors that might occur while the pipeline is busy processing payloads.

Modeling pipeline payloads

The first and most crucial question we need to answer before we begin working on the pipeline package implementation is *how can we describe pipeline payloads in a generic way using Go?*

The kind of obvious answer to this question is to define payloads as empty interface values (an `interface{}` in Go terminology). The key argument in favor of this approach is that the pipeline internals shouldn't really care about payloads per se; all the pipeline needs to do is shuttle payloads between the various pipeline stages.

The interpretation of the payload contents (for example, by casting the input to a known type) should be the sole responsibility of the processing functions that execute at each stage. Given that the processing functions are specified by the end user of the pipeline, this approach would probably be a good fit for our particular requirements.

However, as Rob Pike quite eloquently puts it in one of his famous Go proverbs, `interface{}` *says nothing*. There is quite a bit of truth in that statement. The empty interface conveys no useful information about the underlying type. As a matter of fact, if we were to follow the empty interface approach, we would be effectively disabling the Go compiler's ability to do static type checking of some parts of our code base!

On one hand, the use of empty interfaces is generally considered an antipattern by the Go community and is therefore a practice we would ideally want to avoid. On the other hand, Go has no support for generics, which makes it much more difficult to write code that can work with objects whose type is not known in advance. So, instead of trying to find a silver bullet solution to this problem, let's try to compromise: how about we try to enforce a set of common operations that all payload types must support and create a `Payload` interface to describe them? That would give us an extra layer of type-safety while still making it possible for pipeline processor functions to cast incoming payloads to the type they expect. Here is a possible definition for the `Payload` interface:

```
// Payload is implemented by values that can be sent through a pipeline.
type Payload interface {
    Clone() Payload
    MarkAsProcessed()
}
```

As you can see, we expect that, regardless of the way that a payload is defined, it must be able to perform at least two simple (and quite common) operations:

- **Perform a deep-copy of itself**: As we will see in one of the following sections, this operation will be required for avoiding data races when multiple processors are operating on the same payload concurrently.
- **Mark itself as processed**: Payloads are considered to be processed when they either reach the end of the pipeline (the sink) or if they are discarded at an intermediate pipeline stage. Having such a method invoked on payloads when they exit the pipeline is quite useful for scenarios where we are interested in collecting per-payload metrics (total processing time, time spent in the queue before entering the pipeline, and so on).

Multistage processing

The key concept behind pipelining is to break down a complex processing task into a series of smaller steps or **stages** that can be executed *independently* of each other and in a *predefined order*. Multistage processing, as an idea, also seems to resonate quite well with the single-responsibility principle that we discussed in `Chapter 2`, *Best Practices for Writing Clean and Maintainable Go Code*.

When assembling a multistage pipeline, the end user is expected to provide a set of functions, or **processors**, that will be applied to incoming payloads as they flow through each stage of the pipeline. I will be referring to these functions with the notation F_i, where i corresponds to a stage number.

Under normal circumstances, the output of each stage will be used as input by the stage that follows—that is $Output_i = F_i(\ Output_{i-1}\ )$. Yet, one could definitely picture scenarios where we would actually like to discard a payload and prevent it from reaching any of the following pipeline stages.

For example, let's say we are building a pipeline to read and aggregate data from a CSV file. Unfortunately, the file contains some rows with garbage data that we must exclude from our calculations. To deal with cases like this, we can add a **filter stage** to the pipeline that inspects the contents of each row and drops the ones containing malformed data.

With the preceding cases in mind, we can describe a stage `Processor` interface as follows:

```
type Processor interface {
    // Process operates on the input payload and returns back a new payload
    // to be forwarded to the next pipeline stage. Processors may also opt
    // to prevent the payload from reaching the rest of the pipeline by
    // returning a nil payload value instead.
    Process(context.Context, Payload) (Payload, error)
}
```

There is a small issue with the preceding definition that makes it a bit cumbersome to use in practice. Since we are talking about an interface, it needs to be implemented by a type such as a Go struct; however, one could argue that in many cases, all we really need is to be able to use a simple function, or a **closure** as our processor.

Given that we are designing a *generic* pipeline package, our aim should be to make its API as convenient as possible for the end users. To this end, we will also define an auxiliary type called `ProcessorFunc` that serves the role of a function *adapter*:

```
type ProcessorFunc func(context.Context, Payload) (Payload, error)

// Process calls f(ctx, p).
func (f ProcessorFunc) Process(ctx context.Context, p Payload) (Payload,
error) {
    return f(ctx, p)
}
```

If we have a function with the appropriate signature, we can cast it to a `ProcessorFunc` and automatically obtain a type that implements the `Processor` interface! If this trick seems vaguely familiar to you, chances are that you have already used it before if you have written any code that imports the `http` package and registers HTTP handlers. The `HandlerFunc` type from the `http` package uses exactly the same idea to convert user-defined functions into valid HTTP `Handler` instances.

Stageless pipelines – is that even possible?

Should a pipeline definition include a minimum number of stages for it to be considered as valid? More specifically, should we be allowed to define a pipeline with *zero* stages? In my view, stages should be considered as an optional part of a pipeline definition. Remember that for a pipeline to function, it requires, at minimum, an input source and an output sink.

If we were to directly connect the input to the output and execute the pipeline, we would get the same result as if we had executed a pipeline with just a single stage whose `Processor` is an *identity* function—that is, a function that always outputs the value passed to it as input. We could easily define such a function using the `ProcessorFunc` helper from the previous section:

```
identityFn := ProcessorFunc( func(_ context.Context, p Payload) (Payload,
error) {  return p, nil },)
```

Is there a practical real-world use for this kind of pipeline? The answer is yes! Such a pipeline facilitates the role of an adapter for linking together two, potentially incompatible, systems and transferring data between them. For example, we could use this approach for reading events off a message queue and persisting them into a noSQL database for further processing.

Strategies for handling errors

As a pipeline executes, each one of the components that comprise it may potentially encounter errors. Consequently, prior to implementing the internals of our pipeline package, we need to devise a strategy for detecting, collecting, and handling errors.

In the following sections, we will be exploring some alternative strategies for dealing with errors.

Accumulating and returning all errors

One of the simplest strategies at our disposal involves the introduction of a mechanism for collecting and accumulating *all* errors emitted by any of the pipeline components while the pipeline is executing. Once the pipeline detects an error, it automatically discards the payload that triggered the error, but appends the captured error to a list of collected errors. The pipeline resumes its execution with the next payload till all payloads have been processed.

After the pipeline execution completes, any collected errors are returned back to the user. At this point, we have the option to either return a slice of Go error values or use a helper package, such as `hashicorp/go-multierror` [6], which allows us to aggregate a list of Go error values into a container value that implements the `error` interface.

A great candidate for this type of error handling is pipelines where the processors implement best-effort semantics. For example, if we were building a pipeline to pump out events in a fire-and-forget manner, we wouldn't want the pipeline to stop if one of the events could not be published.

Using a dead-letter queue

In some scenarios, the user of the pipeline package might be interested in obtaining a list of all the payloads that could not be processed by the pipeline because of the presence of errors.

The following points apply, depending on the application requirements:

- Detailed information about each error and the content of each failed payload can be logged out for further analysis
- Failed payloads can be persisted to an external system (for example, via a messaging queue) so that they can be manually inspected and corrected (when feasible) by human operators
- We could start a new pipeline run to process the payloads that failed during the previous run

The concept of storing failed items for future processing is quite prevalent in event-driven architectures, and is typically referred to as the **dead-letter queue**.

Terminating the pipeline's execution if an error occurs

One important caveat of the previous strategies is that they cannot be applied to *long-running* pipelines. Even if an error occurs, we will not find out about it until the pipeline completes. This could take hours, days, or even forever if the pipeline's input never runs out of data. An example of the latter case would be a pipeline whose input is connected to a message queue and blocks while waiting for new messages to arrive.

To deal with such scenarios, we could *immediately* terminate the pipeline's execution when an error occurs and return the error back to the user. As a matter of fact, this is the error-handling strategy that we will be using in our pipeline implementation.

At first glance, you could argue that this approach is quite limiting compared to the other strategies we have discussed so far; however, if we dig a bit deeper, we will discover that this approach is better suited for a greater number of use cases, as it is versatile enough to emulate the behavior of the other two error-handling strategies.

To gain a better understanding of how this can be achieved, we first need to talk a bit about the nature of errors that might occur while a pipeline is executing. Depending on whether errors are fatal, we can classify them into two categories:

- **Nontransient errors**: Such errors are considered to be fatal and applications cannot really recover from them. An example of a nontransient error would be running out of disk space while writing to a file.
- **Transient errors**: Applications can, and should, always attempt to recover from such errors, although this may not always be possible. This is usually achieved by means of some sort of retry mechanism. For instance, if the application loses its connection to a remote server, it can attempt to reconnect using an exponential back-off strategy. If a maximum number of retries is reached, then this becomes a nontransient error.

The following is a simple example illustrating how a user can apply the decorator design pattern to wrap a `Processor` function and implement a retry mechanism that can distinguish between transient and nontransient errors:

```
func retryingProcessor(proc Processor, isTransient func(error) bool,
maxRetries int) Processor {
    return ProcessorFunc(func(ctx context.Context, p Payload) (Payload,
error) {
        var out Payload
        var err error
        for i := 0; i < maxRetries; i++ {
            if out, err = proc.Process(ctx, p); err != nil &&
!isTransient(err) {
                return nil, err
            }
        }
        return nil, err
    })
}
```

The `retryingProcessor` function wraps an existing `Processor` to provide support for automatic retries in the presence of errors. Each time an error occurs, the function consults the `isTransient` helper function to decide whether the obtained error is transient and whether another attempt at processing the payload can be performed. Nontransient errors are considered to be nonrecoverable, and in such cases, the function will return the error to cause the pipeline to terminate. Finally, if the maximum number of retries is exceeded, the function treats the error as nontransient and bails out.

Synchronous versus asynchronous pipelines

A critical decision that will influence the way we implement the core of the pipeline is whether it will operate in a synchronous or an asynchronous fashion. Let's take a quick look at these two modes of operation and discuss the pros and cons of each one.

Synchronous pipelines

A synchronous pipeline essentially processes one payload at a time. We could implement such a pipeline by creating a `for` loop that does the following:

- Dequeues the next payload from the input source or exits the loop if no more payloads are available
- Iterates the list of pipeline stages and invokes the `Processor` instance for each stage
- Enqueues the resulting payload to the output source

Synchronous pipelines are great for workloads where payloads must always be processed in **first-in-first-out** (**FIFO**) fashion, a quite common case for event-driven architectures which, most of the time, operate under the assumption that events are always processed in a specific order.

As an example, let's say that we are trying to construct an **ETL** (short for **extract, transform, and load**) pipeline for consuming an event-stream from an order-processing system, enriching some of the incoming events with additional information by querying an external system and finally transforming the enriched events into a format suitable for persisting into a relational database. The pipeline for this use-case can be assembled using the following two stages:

- The first stage inspects the event type and enriches it with the appropriate information by querying an external service
- The second stage converts each enriched event into a sequence of SQL queries for updating one or more database tables

By design, our processing code expects that an `AccountCreated` event must always precede an `OrderPlaced` event, which includes a reference (a UUID) to the account of the customer who placed the order. If the events were to be processed in the wrong order, the system might find itself trying to process `OrderPlaced` events before the customer records in the database have been created. While it is certainly possible to code around this limitation, it would make the processing code much more complicated and harder to debug when something goes wrong. A synchronous pipeline would enforce in-order processing semantics and make this a nonissue.

So what's the catch when using synchronous pipelines? The main issue associated with synchronous pipelines is *low throughput*. If our pipeline consists of N stages and each stage takes *1 time unit* to complete, our pipeline would require N *time-units* to process and emit *each* payload. By extension, each time a stage is processing a payload, the remaining $N-1$ stages are *idling*.

Asynchronous pipelines

In an asynchronous pipeline design, once a stage processes an incoming payload and emits it to the next stage, it can immediately begin processing the next available payload without having to wait for the currently processed payload to exit the pipeline, as would be the case in a synchronous pipeline design. This approach ensures that all stages are continuously kept busy processing payloads instead of idling.

It is important to note that asynchronous pipelines typically require some form of concurrency. A common pattern is to run each stage in a separate goroutine. Of course, this introduces additional complexity to the mix as we need to do the following:

- Manage the lifecycle of each goroutine
- Make use of concurrency primitives, such as locks, to avoid data races

Nevertheless, asynchronous pipelines have much better throughput characteristics compared to synchronous pipelines. This is the main reason why the pipeline package that we will be building in this chapter will feature an asynchronous pipeline implementation... with a small twist! Even though all pipeline components (input, output, and stages) will be running *asynchronously*, end users will be interacting with the pipeline using a *synchronous* API.

A quick survey of the most popular Go **software development kits (SDKs)** out there will reveal a general consensus toward exposing synchronous APIs. From the perspective of the API consumer, synchronous APIs are definitely easier to consume as the end user does not need to worry about managing resources, such as Go channels, or writing complex `select` statements to coordinate reads and/or writes between channels. Contrast this approach with having an asynchronous API, where the end user would have to deal with an input, output, and error channel every time they wanted to execute a pipeline run!

As mentioned previously, the pipeline internals will be executing asynchronously. The typical way to accomplish this in Go would be to start a goroutine for each pipeline component and link the individual goroutines together by means of Go channels. The pipeline implementation will be responsible for fully managing the lifecycle of any goroutine it spins up, in a way that is totally transparent to the end user of the pipeline package.

 When working with goroutines, we must always be conscious about their individual lifecycles. A sound piece of advice is to never start a goroutine unless you know when it will exit and which conditions need to be satisfied for it to exit.

Failure to heed this bit of advice can introduce goroutine leaks in long-running applications that typically require quite a bit of time and effort to track down.

Exposing a synchronous API for the pipeline package has yet another benefit that we haven't yet mentioned. It is pretty trivial for the end users of the pipeline package to wrap the synchronous API in a goroutine and make it asynchronous. The goroutine would simply invoke the blocking code and use a channel to signal the application code when the pipeline execution has completed.

Implementing a stage worker for executing payload processors

One of the goals of the pipeline package is to allow the end users to specify a per-stage strategy for dispatching incoming payloads to the registered processor functions. In order to be able to support different dispatch strategies in a clean and extensible way, we are going to be introducing yet another abstraction, the `StageRunner` interface:

```
type StageRunner interface {
    Run(context.Context, StageParams)
}
```

Concrete `StageRunner` implementations provide a `Run` method that implements the payload processing loop for a single stage of the pipeline. A typical processing loop consists of the following steps:

1. Receive the next payload from the previous stage or the input source, if this happens to be the first stage of the pipeline. If the upstream data source signals that it has run out of data, or the externally provided `context.Context` is cancelled, then the `Run` method should automatically return.

2. Dispatch the payload to a user-defined processor function for the stage. As we will see in the following sections, the implementation of this step depends on the dispatch strategy that is being used by the `StageRunner` implementation.

3. If the error processor returns an *error*, enqueue the error to the shared error bus and return.

4. Push successfully processed payloads to the next pipeline stage, or the output sink, if this is the last stage of the pipeline.

The preceding steps make it quite clear that `Run` is a blocking call. The pipeline implementation will start a goroutine for each stage of the pipeline, invoke the `Run` method of each registered `StageRunner` instance, and wait for it to return. Since we are working with goroutines, the appropriate mechanism for interconnecting them is to use Go channels. As both the goroutine and channel lifecycles are managed by the pipeline internals, we need a way to configure each `StageRunner` with the set of channels it will be working with. This information is provided to the `Run` method via its second argument. Here is the definition of the `StageParams` interface:

```
type StageParams interface {
    StageIndex() int

    Input() <-chan Payload
    Output() chan<- Payload
```

```
    Error() chan<- error
}
```

The `Input` method returns a *read-only* channel that the worker will be watching for incoming payloads. The channel will be *closed* to indicate that no more data is available for processing. The `Output` method returns a *write-only* channel where the `StageRunner` should publish the input payload after it has been successfully processed. On the other hand, should an error occur while processing an incoming payload, the `Error` channel returns a *write-only* channel where the error can be published. Finally, the `StageIndex` method returns the position of the stage in the pipeline that can be optionally used by `StageRunner` implementations to annotate errors.

In the following sections, we will be taking a closer look at the implementation of three very common payload dispatch strategies that we will be bundling with the pipeline package: FIFO, fixed/dynamic worker pools, and broadcasting.

FIFO

As the name implies, when a stage operates in FIFO mode, it processes payloads sequentially, thereby maintaining their order. By creating a pipeline where *all* stages use FIFO dispatching, we can enforce synchronous-like semantics for data processing, but still retain the high throughput benefits associated with an asynchronous pipeline.

The `fifo` type is private within the `pipeline` package, but it can be instantiated via a call to the `FIFO` function, which is outlined as follows:

```
type fifo struct {
    proc Processor
}

// FIFO returns a StageRunner that processes incoming payloads in a
// first-in first-out fashion. Each input is passed to the specified
// processor and its output is emitted to the next stage.
func FIFO(proc Processor) StageRunner {
    return fifo{proc: proc}
}
```

Let's now take a look at the Run method implementation for the `fifo` type:

```
func (r fifo) Run(ctx context.Context, params StageParams) {
    for {
        select {
        case <-ctx.Done():
            return // Asked to cleanly shut down
        case payloadIn, ok := <-params.Input():
            if !ok {
                return // No more data available.
            }
            // Process payload, handle errors etc.
            // (see following listing)
        }
    }
}
```

As you can see, Run is, by design, a blocking call; it runs an infinite for-loop with a single select statement. Within the `select` block, the code does the following:

- Monitors the provided context for cancellation and exits the main loop when the context gets cancelled (for example, if the user cancelled it or its timeout expired).
- Attempts to retrieve the next payload from the input channel. If the input channel closes, the code exits the main loop.

Once a new input payload has been received, the FIFO runner executes the following block of code:

```
payloadOut, err := r.proc.Process(ctx, payloadIn)
if err != nil {
    wrappedErr := xerrors.Errorf("pipeline stage %d: %w",
params.StageIndex(), err)
    maybeEmitError(wrappedErr, params.Error())
    return
}
if payloadOut == nil {
    payloadIn.MarkAsProcessed()
    continue
}

select {
case params.Output() <- payloadOut:
case <-ctx.Done():
    return  // Asked to cleanly shut down
}
```

The input payload is first passed to the user-defined `Processor` instance. If the processor returns an error, the code annotates it with the current stage number and attempts to enqueue it to the provided error channel by invoking the `maybeEmitError` helper before exiting the worker:

```
// maybeEmitError attempts to queue err to a buffered error channel. If the
// channel is full, the error is dropped.
func maybeEmitError(err error, errCh chan<- error) {
    select {
    case errCh <- err: // error emitted.
    default: // error channel is full with other errors.
    }
}
```

If the payload is processed without an error, then we need to check whether the processor returned a valid payload that we need to forward or a *nil* payload to indicate that the input payload should be discarded. Prior to discarding a payload, the code invokes its `MarkAsProcessed` method before commencing a new iteration of the main loop.

On the other hand, if the processor returns a valid payload, we attempt to enqueue it to the output channel with the help of a `select` statement that blocks until either the payload is written to the output channel or the context gets cancelled. In the latter case, the worker terminates and the payload is dropped to the floor.

Fixed and dynamic worker pools

Oftentimes, processor functions can take quite a bit of time to return. This could be either because the actual payload processing involves CPU-intensive calculations or simply because the function is waiting for an I/O operation to complete (for example, the processor function performed an HTTP request to a remote server and is waiting for a response).

If all stages were linked using the FIFO dispatch strategy, then slowly executing processors could cause the pipeline to stall. If *out-of-order* processing of payloads is not an issue, we can make much better use of the available system resources by introducing worker pools into the mix. Worker pools is a pattern that can significantly improve the throughput of a pipeline by enabling stages in order to process multiple payloads in *parallel*.

The first worker pool pattern that we will be implementing is a **fixed** worker pool. This type of pool spins up a preconfigured number of workers and distributes incoming payloads among them. Each one of the pool workers implements the same loop as the FIFO StageRunner. As the following code shows, our implementation actively exploits this observation and avoids duplicating the main loop code by creating a FIFO instance for each worker in the pool:

```
type fixedWorkerPool struct {
    fifos []StageRunner
}

func FixedWorkerPool(proc Processor, numWorkers int) StageRunner {
    if numWorkers <= 0 {
        panic("FixedWorkerPool: numWorkers must be > 0")
    }
    fifos := make([]StageRunner, numWorkers)
    for i := 0; i < numWorkers; i++ {
        fifos[i] = FIFO(proc)
    }

    return &fixedWorkerPool{fifos: fifos}
}
```

The Run method shown in the following code spins up the individual pool workers, executes their Run method, and uses a sync.WaitGroup to prevent it from returning until all the spawned worker goroutines terminate:

```
func (p *fixedWorkerPool) Run(ctx context.Context, params StageParams) {
    var wg sync.WaitGroup

    // Spin up each worker in the pool and wait for them to exit
    for i := 0; i < len(p.fifos); i++ {
        wg.Add(1)
        go func(fifoIndex int) {
            p.fifos[fifoIndex].Run(ctx, params)
            wg.Done()
        }(i)
    }

    wg.Wait()
}
```

In terms of wiring, things are pretty simple here. All we need to do is pass the incoming parameters, as-is, to each one of the FIFO instances. The effect of this wiring is as follows:

- All FIFOs are set up to read incoming payloads from the *same* input channel, which is connected to the previous pipeline stage (or input source). This approach effectively acts as a load balancer for distributing payloads to idle FIFOs.
- All FIFOs output processed payloads to the *same* output channel, which is linked to the next pipeline stage (or output sink).

Fixed worker pools are quite easy to set up, but come with a caveat: the number of workers must be specified *in advance*! In some cases, coming up with a good value for the number of workers is really easy. For instance, if we know that the processor will be performing CPU-intensive calculations, we can ensure that our pipeline fully utilizes all available CPU cores by setting the number of workers equal to the result of the `runtime.NumCPU()` call. Sometimes, coming up with a good estimate for the number of workers is not that easy. A potential solution would be to switch to a *dynamic* worker pool.

The key difference between a static and a dynamic worker pool is that with the latter, the number of workers is not fixed but varies over time. This fundamental difference allows us to make better use of available resources by allowing the dynamic pool to automatically scale the number of workers up or down to adapt to variances in the throughput from the previous stages.

It goes without saying that we should always enforce an upper limit for the number of workers that can be spawned by the dynamic pool. Without such a limit in place, the number of goroutines spawned by the pipeline might grow out of control and cause the program to either grind to a halt or, even worse, to crash! To avoid this problem, the dynamic worker pool implementation presented in the following code uses a primitive known as a **token pool**:

```
type dynamicWorkerPool struct {
    proc      Processor
    tokenPool chan struct{}
}

func DynamicWorkerPool(proc Processor, maxWorkers int) StageRunner {
    if maxWorkers <= 0 {
        panic("DynamicWorkerPool: maxWorkers must be > 0")
    }
    tokenPool := make(chan struct{}, maxWorkers)
    for i := 0; i < maxWorkers; i++ {
        tokenPool <- struct{}{}
    }
```

```
        return &dynamicWorkerPool{proc: proc, tokenPool: tokenPool}
}
```

A token pool is modeled as a buffered `chan struct{}`, which is prepopulated with a number of tokens equal to the maximum number of concurrent workers that we wish to allow. Let's see how this primitive can be used to as a concurrency-control mechanism by breaking down the dynamic pool's `Run` method implementation into logical blocks:

```
func (p *dynamicWorkerPool) Run(ctx context.Context, params StageParams) {
stop:
    for {
        select {
        case <-ctx.Done():
            break stop // Asked to cleanly shut down
        case payloadIn, ok := <-params.Input():
            if !ok { break stop }
            // Process payload... (see listings below)
        }
    }

    for i := 0; i < cap(p.tokenPool); i++ { // wait for all workers to exit
        <-p.tokenPool
    }
}
```

Similarly to the FIFO implementation, the dynamic pool executes an infinite for-loop containing a `select` statement; however, the code that deals with payload processing is quite different in this implementation. Instead of calling the payload processor code directly, we will just spin up a goroutine to take care of that task for us in the background, while the main loop attempts to process the next incoming payload.

Before a new worker can be started, we must first fetch a token from the pool. This is achieved via the following block of code that blocks until a token can be read off the channel or the provided context gets cancelled:

```
var token struct{}
select {
case token = <-p.tokenPool:
case <-ctx.Done():
    break stop
}
```

The preceding block of code serves as a choke point for limiting the number of concurrent workers. Once all tokens in the pool are exhausted, attempts to read off the channel will be blocked until a token is returned to the pool. So how do tokens get returned to the pool? To answer this question, we need to take a look at what happens *after* we successfully read a token from the pool:

```go
go func(payloadIn Payload, token struct{}) {
    defer func() { p.tokenPool <- token }()
    payloadOut, err := p.proc.Process(ctx, payloadIn)
    if err != nil {
        wrappedErr := xerrors.Errorf("pipeline stage %d: %w",
params.StageIndex(), err)
        maybeEmitError(wrappedErr, params.Error())
        return
    }
    if payloadOut == nil {
        payloadIn.MarkAsProcessed()
        return // Discard payload
    }
    select {
    case params.Output() <- payloadOut:
    case <-ctx.Done():
    }
}(payloadIn, token)
```

This block of code is more or less the same as the FIFO implementation, with two small differences:

- It executes inside a goroutine.
- It includes a defer statement to ensure that the token is returned to the pool once the goroutine completes. This is important as it makes the token available for reuse.

The last bit of code that we need to discuss is the for-loop at the end of the Run method. To guarantee that the dynamic pool does not leak any goroutines, we need to make sure that any goroutines that were spawned while the method was running have terminated before Run can return. Instead of using a sync.WaitGroup, we can achieve the same effect by simply draining the token pool. As we already know, workers can only run while holding a token; once the for-loop has extracted all tokens from the pool, we can safely return knowing that all workers have completed their work and their goroutines have been terminated.

1-to-*N* broadcasting

The 1-to-*N* broadcasting pattern allows us to support use cases where each incoming payload must to be processed in parallel by *N* different processors, each one of which implements FIFO-like semantics.

The following code is the definition of the `broadcast` type and the `Broadcast` helper function that serves as its constructor:

```
type broadcast struct {
    fifos []StageRunner
}

func Broadcast(procs ...Processor) StageRunner {
    if len(procs) == 0 {
        panic("Broadcast: at least one processor must be specified")
    }
    fifos := make([]StageRunner, len(procs))
    for i, p := range procs {
        fifos[i] = FIFO(p)
    }

    return &broadcast{fifos: fifos}
}
```

As you can see, the variadic `Broadcast` function receives a list of `Processor` instances as arguments and creates a FIFO instance for each one. These FIFO instances are stored inside the returned `broadcast` instance and used within its `Run` method implementation, which we will be dissecting as follows:

```
var wg sync.WaitGroup
var inCh = make([]chan Payload, len(b.fifos))
for i := 0; i < len(b.fifos); i++ {
    wg.Add(1)
    inCh[i] = make(chan Payload)
    go func(fifoIndex int) {
        fifoParams := &workerParams{
            stage: params.StageIndex(),
            inCh:  inCh[fifoIndex],
            outCh: params.Output(),
            errCh: params.Error(),
        }
        b.fifos[fifoIndex].Run(ctx, fifoParams)
        wg.Done()
    }(i)
}
```

Similar to the fixed worker pool implementation that we examined in the previous section, the first thing that we do inside Run is to spawn up a goroutine for each FIFO StageRunner instance. A sync.WaitGroup allows us to wait for all workers to exit before Run can return.

To avoid data races, the implementation for the broadcasting stage must intercept each incoming payload, *clone* it, and deliver a copy to each one of the generated FIFO processors. Consequently, the generated FIFO processor instances cannot be directly wired to the input channel for the stage, but must instead be configured with a dedicated input channel for reading . To this end, the preceding block of code generates a new workerParams value (an internal type to the pipeline package that implements the StageParams interface) for each FIFO instance and supplies it as an argument to its Run method. Note that while each FIFO instance is configured with a separate input channel, they all share the same output and error channels.

The next part of the Run method's implementation is the, by now familiar, main loop where we wait for the next incoming payload to appear:

```
done:
    for {
        // Read incoming payloads and pass them to each FIFO
        select {
        case <-ctx.Done():
            break done
        case payload, ok := <-params.Input():
            if !ok {
                break done
            }
            // Clone payload and dispatch to each FIFO worker...
            // (see following listing)
        }
    }
```

Once a new payload is received, the implementation writes a copy of the payload to the input channel for each FIFO instance, but the first one receives the original incoming payload:

```
for i := len(b.fifos) - 1; i >= 0; i-- {
    var fifoPayload = payload
    if i != 0 {
        fifoPayload = payload.Clone()
    }
    select {
    case <-ctx.Done():
        break done
```

```
    case inCh[i] <- fifoPayload:
        // payload sent to i_th FIFO
    }
}
```

After publishing the payload to all FIFO instances, a new iteration of the main loop begins. The main loop keeps executing until either the input channel closes or the context gets cancelled. After exiting the main loop, the following sentinel block of code gets executed before `Run` returns:

```
// Close input channels and wait for all FIFOs to exit
for _, ch := range inCh {
    close(ch)
}
wg.Wait()
```

In the preceding code snippet, we signal each one of the FIFO workers to shut down by closing their dedicated input channels. We then invoke the `Wait` method of the `WaitGroup` to wait for all FIFO workers to terminate.

Implementing the input source worker

In order to begin a new pipeline run, users are expected to provide an input source that generates the application-specific payloads that drive the pipeline. All user-defined input sources must implement the `Source` interface, whose definition is as follows:

```
type Source interface {
    Next(context.Context) bool
    Payload() Payload
    Error() error
}
```

The `Source` interface contains the standard set of methods that you would expect for any data source that supports iteration:

- `Next` attempts to advance the iterator. It returns `false` if either no more data is available or an error occurred.
- `Payload` returns the a new `Payload` instance after a successful call to the iterator's `Next` method.
- `Error` returns the last error encountered by the input.

To facilitate the asynchronous polling of the input source, the pipeline package will run the following `sourceWorker` function inside a goroutine. Its primary task is to iterate the data source and publish each incoming payload to the specified channel:

```
func sourceWorker(ctx context.Context, source Source, outCh chan<- Payload,
errCh chan<- error) {
    for source.Next(ctx) {
        payload := source.Payload()
        select {
        case outCh <- payload:
        case <-ctx.Done():
            return // Asked to shutdown
        }
    }

    // Check for errors
    if err := source.Error(); err != nil {
        wrappedErr := xerrors.Errorf("pipeline source: %w", err)
        maybeEmitError(wrappedErr, errCh)
    }
}
```

The `sourceWorker` function keeps running until a call to the source's `Next` method returns `false`. Before returning, the worker implementation will check for any errors reported by the input source and publish them to the provided error channel.

Implementing the output sink worker

Of course, our pipeline would not be complete without an output sink! After all, payloads that travel through the pipeline do not disappear into thin air once they clear the pipeline; they must end up somewhere. So, together with an input source, users are expected to provide an output sink that implements the `Sink` interface:

```
type Sink interface {
    // Consume processes a Payload instance that has been emitted out of
    // a Pipeline instance.
    Consume(context.Context, Payload) error
}
```

In order to deliver processed payloads to the sink, the pipeline package will spawn a new goroutine and execute the `sinkWorker` function, whose implementation is as follows:

```
func sinkWorker(ctx context.Context, sink Sink, inCh <-chan Payload, errCh
chan<- error) {
    for {
```

```
select {
case payload, ok := <-inCh:
    if !ok { return }
    if err := sink.Consume(ctx, payload); err != nil {
        wrappedErr := xerrors.Errorf("pipeline sink: %w", err)
        maybeEmitError(wrappedErr, errCh)
        return
    }
    payload.MarkAsProcessed()
case <-ctx.Done():
    return // Asked to shutdown
}
    }
}
```

The `sinkWorker` loop reads payloads from the provided input channel and attempts to publish them to the provided `Sink` instance. If the `sink` implementation reports an error while consuming the payload, the `sinkWorker` function will publish it to the provided error channel before returning.

Putting it all together – the pipeline API

After thoroughly describing the ins and outs of each individual pipeline component, it is finally time to bring everything together and implement an API that the end users of the pipeline package will depend on for assembling and executing their pipelines.

A new pipeline instance can be created by invoking the variadic `New` function from the `pipeline` package. As you can see in the following code listing, the construction function expects a list of `StageRunner` instances as arguments where each element of the list corresponds to a stage of the pipeline:

```
type Pipeline struct {
    stages []StageRunner
}

// New returns a new pipeline instance where input payloads will traverse
// each one of the specified stages.
func New(stages ...StageRunner) *Pipeline {
    return &Pipeline{
        stages: stages,
    }
}
```

Users can either opt to use the `StageRunner` implementations that we outlined in the previous sections (FIFO, `FixedWorkerPool`, `DynamicWorkerPool`, or `Broadcast`) and that are provided by the `pipeline` package or, alternatively, provide their own application-specific variants that satisfy the single-method `StageRunner` interface.

After constructing a new pipeline instance and creating a compatible input source/output sink, users can execute the pipeline by invoking the `Process` method on the pipeline instance that is obtained:

```
func (p *Pipeline) Process(ctx context.Context, source Source, sink Sink)
error {
    // ...
}
```

The first argument to `Process` is a context instance that can be cancelled by the user to force the pipeline to terminate. Calls to the `Process` method will be blocked until one of the following conditions is met:

- The context is cancelled.
- The source runs out of data and all payloads have been processed or discarded.
- An error occurs in any of the pipeline components or the user-defined processor functions. In the latter case, an error will be returned back to the caller.

Let's take a look at the implementation details of the `Process` method:

```
var wg sync.WaitGroup
pCtx, ctxCancelFn := context.WithCancel(ctx)

// Allocate channels for wiring together the source, the pipeline stages
// and the output sink.
stageCh := make([]chan Payload, len(p.stages)+1)
errCh := make(chan error, len(p.stages)+2)
for i := 0; i < len(stageCh); i++ {
    stageCh[i] = make(chan Payload)
}
```

First of all, we create a new context (`pCtx`) that wraps the user-defined context, but also allows us to manually cancel it. The wrapped context will be passed to all pipeline components, allowing us to easily tear down the entire pipeline if we detect any error.

After setting up our context, we proceed to allocate and initialize the channels that we need to interconnect the various workers that we are about to spin up. If we have a total of *N* stages, then we need *N*+1 channels to connect everything together (including the source and sink workers). For instance, if *no* stages were specified when the pipeline was created, then we would still need one channel to connect the source to the sink.

The error channel functions as a *shared error bus*. In the preceding code snippet, you can see that we are creating a *buffered* error channel with *N*+2 slots. This provides enough space to hold a potential error for each one of the pipeline components (*N* stages and the source/sink workers).

In the following block of code, we start a goroutine whose body invokes the Run method of the StageRunner instance associated with each stage of the pipeline:

```
// Start a worker for each stage
for i := 0; i < len(p.stages); i++ {
    wg.Add(1)
    go func(stageIndex int) {
        p.stages[stageIndex].Run(pCtx, &workerParams{
            stage: stageIndex,
            inCh: stageCh[stageIndex],
            outCh: stageCh[stageIndex+1],
            errCh: errCh,
        })
        close(stageCh[stageIndex+1])
        wg.Done()
    }(i)
}
```

As you probably noticed, the output channel of the *n*th worker is used as the input channel for worker *n*+1. Once the Run method for the *n*th worker returns, it closes its output channel to signal to the next stage of the pipeline that no more data is available.

After starting the stage workers, we need to spawn two additional workers: one for the input source and one for the output sink:

```
wg.Add(2)
go func() {
    sourceWorker(pCtx, source, stageCh[0], errCh)
    close(stageCh[0])
    wg.Done()
}()
go func() {
    sinkWorker(pCtx, sink, stageCh[len(stageCh)-1], errCh)
    wg.Done()
}()
```

So far, our pipeline implementation has spawned quite a few goroutines. By this point, you may be wondering: how can we be sure that *all* of these goroutines will actually terminate?

Once the source worker runs out of data, the call to `sourceWorker` returns and we proceed to close the `stageCh[0]` channel. This triggers an avalanche effect that causes each stage worker to cleanly terminate. When the *i*th worker detects that its input channel has been closed, it assumes that no more data is available and closes its own output channel (which also happens to be the *i+1* worker's input) before terminating. The *last* output channel is connected to the sink worker. Consequently, the sink worker will also terminate once the last stage worker closes its output.

This brings us to the final part of the `Process` method's implementation:

```
go func() {
    wg.Wait()
    close(errCh)
    ctxCancelFn()
}()

// Collect any emitted errors and wrap them in a multi-error.
var err error
for pErr := range errCh {
    err = multierror.Append(err, pErr)
    ctxCancelFn()
}
return err
```

As you can see in the preceding snippet, we spawn one final worker that serves the role of a **monitor**: it waits for all other workers to complete before closing the shared error channel and cancelling the wrapped context.

While all workers are happily running, the `Process` method is using the `range` keyword to iterate the contents of the error channel. If any error gets published to the shared error channel, it will be appended to the `err` value with the help of the `hashicorp/multierror` package [6] and the wrapped context will be cancelled to trigger a shutdown of the entire pipeline.

On the other hand, if no error occurs, the preceding for-loop will block indefinitely until the channel is closed by the monitor worker. Since the error channel will only be closed once all other pipeline workers have terminated, the same range loop prevents the call to `Process` from returning until the pipeline execution completes, with or without an error.

Building a crawler pipeline for the Links 'R' Us project

In the following sections, we will be putting the generic pipeline package that we built to the test by using it to construct the crawler pipeline for the Links 'R' Us project!

Following the single-responsibility principle, we will break down the crawl task into a sequence of smaller subtasks and assemble the pipeline illustrated in the following figure. The decomposition into smaller subtasks also comes with the benefit that each stage processor can be tested in total isolation without the need to create a pipeline instance:

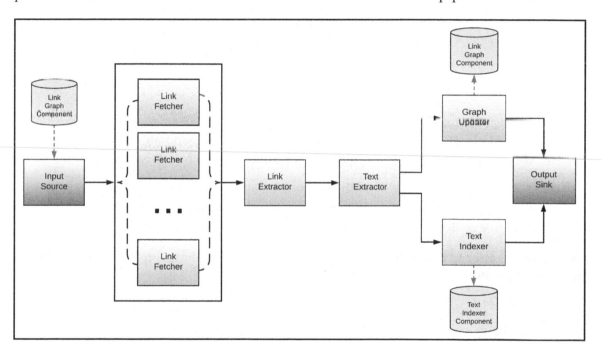

Figure 2: The stages of the crawler pipeline that we will be constructing

The full code for the crawler and its tests can be found in the `Chapter07/crawler` package, which you can find at the book's GitHub repository.

Defining the payload for the crawler

First things first, we need to define the payload that will be shared between the processors for each stage of the pipeline:

```
type crawlerPayload struct {
    LinkID      uuid.UUID
    URL         string
    RetrievedAt time.Time

    RawContent bytes.Buffer

    // NoFollowLinks are still added to the graph but no outgoing edges
    // will be created from this link to them.
    NoFollowLinks []string

    Links       []string
    Title       string
    TextContent string
}
```

The first three fields, `LinkID`, `URL`, and `RetrievedAt`, will be populated by the input source. The remaining fields will be populated by the various crawler stages:

- `RawContent` is populated by the link fetcher
- `NoFollowLinks` and `Links` are populated by the link extractor
- `Title` and `TextContent` are populated by the text extractor

Of course, in order to be able to use this payload definition with the pipeline package, it needs to implement the `pipeline.Payload` interface:

```
type Payload interface {
    Clone() Payload
    MarkAsProcessed()
}
```

Before we go about implementing these two methods on our payload type, let's take a small break and spend some time learning about the memory-allocation patterns for our application-specific pipeline. Given that our plan is to have the crawler executing as a long-running process and tentatively process a high volume of links, we need to consider whether memory allocations will have an impact on the crawler's performance.

While the pipeline is executing, the input source will allocate a new payload for each new link entering the pipeline. In addition, as we saw in *Figure 2*, one extra copy will be made at the fork point where the payload is sent to the graph updater and text indexer stages. Payloads can either be discarded early on (for example, the link fetcher can filter links using a list of blacklisted file extensions) or eventually make their way to the output sink.

Consequently, we will be generating a large number of small objects that at some point need to be garbage-collected by the Go runtime. Performing a large number of allocations in a relatively short amount of time increases the pressure on the Go **garbage collector** (**GC**) and triggers more frequent GC pauses that affect the latency characteristics of our pipeline.

The best way to verify our theory is to capture a memory-allocation profile for a running crawler pipeline using the `runtime/pprof` package [3] and analyze it using the `pprof` tool. Using `pprof` [8] is outside of the scope of this book, so this step is left as an exercise for the curious reader.

Now that we have a better understanding of the expected allocation patterns for our crawler, the next question is: what can we do about it? Fortunately for us, the `sync` package in the Go standard library includes the `Pool` type [4], which is designed for exactly this use case!

The `Pool` type attempts to relieve the pressure on the garbage collector by amortizing the cost of allocating objects across multiple clients. This is achieved by maintaining a cache of allocated, but not used, instances. When a client requests a new object from the pool, they can either receive a cached instance or a newly allocated instance if the pool is empty. Once clients are done using the object they obtained, they must return it to the pool so it can be reused by other clients. Note that any objects *within* the pool that are not in use by clients are fair game for the garbage collector and can be reclaimed at any time.

Here is the definition of the pool that we will be using for recycling payload instances:

```
var (
    payloadPool = sync.Pool{
        New: func() interface{} {
            return new(crawlerPayload)
        },
    }
)
```

The New method will be automatically invoked by the underlying pool implementation to service incoming client requests when it has run out of cached items. As the zero value of the Payload type is already a valid payload, all we need to do is allocate and return a new Payload instance. Let's see how we can use the pool that we just defined to implement the Clone method for the payload:

```go
func (p *crawlerPayload) Clone() pipeline.Payload {
    newP := payloadPool.Get().(*Payload)
    newP.LinkID = p.LinkID
    newP.URL = p.URL
    newP.RetrievedAt = p.RetrievedAt
    newP.NoFollowLinks = append([]string(nil), p.NoFollowLinks...)
    newP.Links = append([]string(nil), p.Links...)
    newP.Title = p.Title
    newP.TextContent = p.TextContent

    _, err := io.Copy(&newP.RawContent, &p.RawContent)
    if err != nil {
        panic(fmt.Sprintf("[BUG] error cloning payload raw content: %v",
err))
    }
    return newP
}
```

As you can see, a new payload instance is allocated from the pool and all fields from the original payload are copied over before it is returned to the caller. Finally, let's take a look at the MarkAsProcessed method implementation:

```go
func (p *crawlerPayload) MarkAsProcessed() {
    p.URL = p.URL[:0]
    p.RawContent.Reset()
    p.NoFollowLinks = p.NoFollowLinks[:0]
    p.Links = p.Links[:0]
    p.Title = p.Title[:0]
    p.TextContent = p.TextContent[:0]
    payloadPool.Put(p)
}
```

When MarkAsProcessed is invoked, we need to clear the payload contents before returning it to the pool so it can be safely used by the next client that retrieves it.

One other thing to note is that we also employ a small optimization trick to reduce the total number of allocations that are performed while our pipeline is executing. We set the length of both of the slices and the byte buffer to zero without modifying their original capacities. The next time that a recycled payload is sent through the pipeline, any attempt to write to the byte buffer or append to one of the payload slices will reuse the already allocated space and only trigger a new memory allocation if additional space is required.

Implementing a source and a sink for the crawler

A prerequisite for executing the crawler pipeline is to provide an input source that conforms to the `pipeline.Source` interface and an output sink that implements `pipeline.Sink`. We have discussed both these interfaces in the previous sections, but I am copying their definitions as follows for reference:

```
type Source interface {
    Next(context.Context) bool
    Payload() Payload
    Error() error
}
```

```
type Sink interface {
    Consume(context.Context, Payload) error
}
```

In `Chapter 6`, *Building a Persistence Layer*, we put together the interface of the link graph component and came up with two alternative, concrete implementations. One of the methods of the `graph.Graph` interface that is of particular interest at this point is `Links`. The `Links` method returns a `graph.LinkIterator`, which allows us to traverse the list of links within a section (partition) of the graph or even the graph in its entirety. As a quick refresher, here is the list of methods included in the `graph.LinkIterator` interface:

```
type LinkIterator interface {
    Next() bool
    Error() error
    Close() error
    Link() *Link
}
```

As you can see, the `LinkIterator` and the `Source` interfaces are quite similar to each other. As it turns out, we can apply the decorator design pattern (as shown in the following code) to wrap a `graph.LinkIterator` and turn it into an input source that is compatible with our pipeline!

```go
type linkSource struct {
    linkIt graph.LinkIterator
}

func (ls *linkSource) Error() error                  { return ls.linkIt.Error()
}
func (ls *linkSource) Next(context.Context) bool { return ls.linkIt.Next()
}
func (ls *linkSource) Payload() pipeline.Payload {
    link := ls.linkIt.Link()
    p := payloadPool.Get().(*crawlerPayload)
    p.LinkID = link.ID
    p.URL = link.URL
    p.RetrievedAt = link.RetrievedAt
    return p
}
```

The `Error` and `Next` methods are simply proxies to the underlying iterator object. The `Payload` method fetches a `Payload` instance from the pool and populates its fields from the `graph.Link` instance that was obtained via the iterator.

Things are much simpler as far as the output sink is concerned. After each payload goes through the link updater and text indexer stages, we have no further use for it! As a result, all we need to do is to provide a sink implementation that functions as a black hole:

```go
type nopSink struct{}

func (nopSink) Consume(context.Context, pipeline.Payload) error {
    return nil
}
```

The `Consume` method simply ignores payloads and always returns a `nil` error. Once the call to `Consume` returns, the pipeline worker automatically invokes the `MarkAsProcessed` method on the payload, which, as we saw in the previous section, ensures that the payload gets returned to the pool so it can be reused in the future.

Fetching the contents of graph links

The link fetcher serves as the first stage of the crawler pipeline. It operates on `Payload` values emitted by the input source and attempts to retrieve the contents of each link by sending out HTTP GET requests. The retrieved link web page contents are stored within the payload's `RawContent` field and made available to the following stages of the pipeline.

Let's now take a look at the definition of the `linkFetcher` type and its associated methods:

```go
type linkFetcher struct {
    urlGetter URLGetter
    netDetector PrivateNetworkDetector
}

func newLinkFetcher(urlGetter URLGetter, netDetector
PrivateNetworkDetector) *linkFetcher {
    return &linkFetcher{
        urlGetter: urlGetter,
        netDetector: netDetector,
    }
}

func (lf *linkFetcher) Process(ctx context.Context, p pipeline.Payload)
(pipeline.Payload, error) {
    //...
}
```

While the Go standard library comes with the `http` package that we could directly use to fetch the link contents, it is often a good practice to allow the intended users of the code to plug in their preferred implementation for performing HTTP calls. As the link fetcher is only concerned about making GET requests, we will apply the interface segregation principle and define a `URLGetter` interface:

```go
// URLGetter is implemented by objects that can perform HTTP GET requests.
type URLGetter interface {
    Get(url string) (*http.Response, error)
}
```

This approach brings a few important benefits to the table. To begin with, it allows us to test the link fetcher code without the need to spin up a dedicated test server. While it is quite common to use the `httptest.NewServer` method to create servers for testing, arranging for the test server to return the right payload and/or status code for each individual test requires extra effort.

Moreover, having a test server available doesn't really help in scenarios where we expect the Get call to return an error and a nil http.Response. This could be quite useful for evaluating how our code behaves in the presence of DNS lookup failures or TLS validation errors. By introducing this interface-based abstraction, we can use a package such as gomock [5] to generate a compatible mock for our tests, as we illustrated in Chapter 4, *The Art of Testing.*

Besides testing, this approach makes our implementation much more versatile! The end users of the crawler are now given the flexibility to either pass http.DefaultClient if they prefer to use a sane default, or to provide their own customized http.Client implementation, which can additionally deal with retries, proxies, and so on.

In Chapter 5, *The Links 'R' Us Project,* we discussed a list of potential security issues associated with automatically crawling links that are obtained through third-party resources that are outside of our control. The key takeaway from that discussion was that our crawler should never attempt to fetch links that belong to private network addresses, as that could lead in sensitive data ending up in our search index! To this end, the newLinkFetcher function also expects an argument that implements the PrivateNetworkDetector interface:

```
// PrivateNetworkDetector is implemented by objects that can detect whether a
// host resolves to a private network address.
type PrivateNetworkDetector interface {
    IsPrivate(host string) (bool, error)
}
```

The Chapter07/crawler/privnet package contains a simple private network detector implementation that first resolves hosts into an IP address and then checks whether the IP address belongs to any of the private network ranges defined by RFC1918 [7].

Now that we have covered all of the important details surrounding the creation of a new linkFetcher instance, let's take a look at its internals. As expected by any component that we want to include in our pipeline, linkFetcher adheres to the pipeline.Processor interface. Let's break down the Process method into smaller chunks so we can analyze it further:

```
payload := p.(*crawlerPayload)

if exclusionRegex.MatchString(payload.URL) {
    return nil, nil // Skip URLs that point to files that cannot contain
                    // html content.
}
```

```
if isPrivate, err := lf.isPrivate(payload.URL); err != nil || isPrivate {
    return nil, nil // Never crawl links in private networks
}

res, err := lf.urlGetter.Get(payload.URL)
if err != nil {
    return nil, nil
}
```

The first step is to cast the incoming `pipeline.Payload` value into the concrete `*crawlerPayload` instance that the input source injected into the pipeline. Next, we check the URL against a case-insensitive regular expression (its definition will be shown in the following section) designed to match file extensions that are known to contain binary data (for example, images) or text content (for example, loadable scripts, JSON data, and so on) that the crawler should ignore. If a match is found, the link fetcher instructs the pipeline to discard the payload by returning the values `nil, nil`. The second and final precheck ensures that the crawler always ignores URLs that resolve to private network addresses. Finally, we invoke the provided `URLGetter` to retrieve the contents of the link.

Let's now see what happens after the call to the `URLGetter` returns:

```
_, err = io.Copy(&payload.RawContent, res.Body)
_ = res.Body.Close()
if err != nil {
    return nil, err
}
if res.StatusCode < 200 || res.StatusCode > 299 {
    return nil, nil
}
if contentType := res.Header.Get("Content-Type");
!strings.Contains(contentType, "html") {
    return nil, nil
}

return payload, nil
```

For GET requests that complete without an error, we copy the response body into the payload's `RawContent` field and then close the body to avoid memory leaks. Before allowing the payload to continue to the next pipeline stage, we perform two additional sanity checks:

- The response status code should be in the 2xx range. If not, we discard the payload rather than returning an error as the latter would cause the pipeline to terminate. Not processing a link is not a big issue; the crawler will be running periodically, so the crawler will revisit problematic links in the future.
- The `Content-Type` header should indicate that the response contains an HTML document; otherwise, there is no point in further processing the response, so we can simply discard it.

Extracting outgoing links from retrieved webpages

The task of the link extractor is to scan the body of each retrieved HTML document and extract the unique set of links contained within it. Each **uniform resource locator** (URL) in a web page can be classified into one of the following categories:

- **URL with a network path reference** [1]: This type of link is quite easy to identify as it *does not* include a URL scheme (for example, `<img src="//banner.png"/>`). When the web browser (or crawler, in our case) needs to access the link, it will substitute the protocol used to access the web page that contained it. Consequently, if the parent page was accessed via HTTPS, then the browser will also request the banner image over HTTPS.
- **Absolute links**: These links are fully qualified and are typically used to point at resources that are hosted on different domains.
- **Relative links**: As the name implies, these links are resolved relative to the current page URL. It is also important to note that web pages can opt to override the URL used for resolving relative links by specifying a `<base href="XXX">` tag in their `<head>` section.

By design, the link graph component only stores fully qualified links. Therefore, one of the key responsibilities of the link extractor is to resolve all relative links into absolute URLs. This is achieved via the `resolveURL` helper function, which is shown as follows:

```
func resolveURL(relTo *url.URL, target string) *url.URL {
    tLen := len(target)
    if tLen == 0 {
```

```
        return nil
    } else if tLen >= 1 && target[0] == '/' {
        if tLen >= 2 && target[1] == '/' {
            target = relTo.Scheme + ":" + target
        }
    }
    if targetURL, err := url.Parse(target); err == nil {
        return relTo.ResolveReference(targetURL)
    }

    return nil
}
```

The `resolveURL` function is invoked using a parsed `url.URL` and a target path to resolve relative to it. Resolving relative paths is not a trivial process because of the number of rules specified in RFC 3986 [1]. Fortunately, the `URL` type provides the handy `ResolveReference` method that takes care of all the complexity for us. Before passing the target to the `ResolveReference` method, the code performs an extra check to detect network path references. If the target begins with a `//` prefix, the implementation will rewrite the target link by prepending the scheme from the provided `relTo` value.

Before we examine the link extractor's implementation, we need to define a few useful regular expressions that we will be using in the code:

```
var (
    exclusionRegex =
regexp.MustCompile(`(?i)\.(?:jpg|jpeg|png|gif|ico|css|js)$`)
    baseHrefRegex =
regexp.MustCompile(`(?i)<base.*?href\s*?=\s*?"(.*?)\s^?"`)
    findLinkRegex =
regexp.MustCompile(`(?i)<a.*?href\s*?=\s*?"\s*?(.*?)\s*?".*?>`)
    nofollowRegex = regexp.MustCompile(`(?i)rel\s*?=\s*?"?nofollow"?`)
)
```

We will be using the preceding case-insensitive regular expressions to do the following:

- Skip extracted links that point to non-HTML content. Note that this particular regular expression instance is shared between this stage and the link fetcher stage.
- Locate the `<base href="XXX">` tag and capture the value in the `href` attribute.

- Extract links from the HTML contents. The second regular expression is designed to locate the `<a href="XXX">` elements and capture the value in the `href` attribute.
- Identify links that should be inserted into the graph but should not be considered when calculating the `PageRank` score for the page that links to them. Web masters can indicate such links by adding a `rel` attribute with the `nofollow` value to the `<a>` tag. For instance, forum operators can add `nofollow` tags to links in posted messages to prevent users from artificially increasing the `PageRank` scores to their websites by cross-posting links to multiple forums.

The following listing shows the definition of the `linkExtractor` type. Similar to the `linkFetcher` type, the `linkExtractor` also requires a `PrivateNetworkDetector` instance for further filtering extracted links:

```
type linkExtractor struct {
    netDetector PrivateNetworkDetector
}

func newLinkExtractor(netDetector PrivateNetworkDetector) *linkExtractor {
    return &linkExtractor{
        netDetector: netDetector,
    }
}
```

The business logic of the link extractor is encapsulated inside its `Process` method. As the implementation is a bit lengthy, we will once again split it into smaller chunks and discuss each chunk separately. Consider the following code block:

```
payload := p.(*crawlerPayload)
relTo, err := url.Parse(payload.URL)
if err != nil {
    return nil, err
}

// Search page content for a <base> tag and resolve it to an abs URL.
content := payload.RawContent.String()
if baseMatch := baseHrefRegex.FindStringSubmatch(content); len(baseMatch) == 2 {
    if base := resolveURL(relTo, ensureHasTrailingSlash(baseMatch[1]));
base != nil {
        relTo = base
    }
}
```

In order to be able to resolve any relative link we might encounter, we need a fully qualified link to use as a base. By default, that would be the incoming link URL that the code parses into a `url.URL` value. As we mentioned previously, if the page includes a valid `<base href="XXX">` tag, we must resolve relative links using *that* instead.

To detect the presence of a `<base>` tag, we execute the `baseHrefRegex` regular expression against the page content. If we obtain a valid match, `baseMatch`[1] will contain the value of the tag's `href` attribute. The captured value is then passed to the `resolveURL` helper and the resolved URL (if valid) is used to override the `relTo` variable.

The following block of code outlines the link extraction and deduplication steps:

```
seenMap := make(map[string]struct{})
for _, match := range findLinkRegex.FindAllStringSubmatch(content, -1) {
    link := resolveURL(relTo, match[1])
    if link == nil || !le.retainLink(relTo.Hostname(), link) {
        continue
    }

    link.Fragment = "" // Truncate anchors
    linkStr := link.String()
    if _, seen := seenMap[linkStr]; seen ||
exclusionRegex.MatchString(linkStr) {
        continue // skip already seen links and links that do not contain
HTML
    }
    seenMap[linkStr] = struct{}{}
    if nofollowRegex.MatchString(match[0]) {
        payload.NoFollowLinks = append(payload.NoFollowLinks, linkStr)
    } else {
        payload.Links = append(payload.Links, linkStr)
    }
}
```

The `FindAllStringSubmatch` method returns a list of successive matches for a particular regular expression. The second argument to `FindAllStringSubmatch` controls the maximum number of matches to be returned. Therefore, by passing −1 as an argument, we effectively ask the regular expression engine to return *all* `<a>` matches. We then iterate each matched link and resolve it into an absolute URL. The captured `<a>` tag contents and the resolved link are passed to the `retainLink` predicate, which returns `false` if the link must be skipped.

The final step of the processing loop entails the deduplication of links within the page. To achieve, this we will be using a map where link URLs are used as keys. Prior to checking the map for duplicate entries, we make sure to trim off the fragment part (also known as an HTML **anchor**) of each link; after all, from the perspective of our crawler, both `http://example.com/index.html#foo` and `http://example.com/index.html` reference the same link. For each link that survives the `is-duplicate` check, we scan its `<a>` tag for the presence of a `rel="nofollow"` attribute. Depending on the outcome of the check, the link is appended either to the `NoFollowLinks` or the `Links` slice of the payload instance and is made available to the following stages of the pipeline.

The last part of code that we need to explore is the `retainLink` method implementation:

```
func (le *linkExtractor) retainLink(srcHost string, link *url.URL) bool {
    if link == nil {
        return false // Skip links that could not be resolved
    }
    if link.Scheme != "http" && link.Scheme != "https" {
        return false // Skip links with non http(s) schemes
    }
    if link.Hostname() == srcHost {
            return true // No need to check for private network
    }
    if isPrivate, err := le.netDetector.IsPrivate(link.Host); err != nil ||
isPrivate {
        return false // Skip links that resolve to private networks
    }
    return true
}
```

As you can see from the preceding code, we perform two types of checks beforehand to decide whether a link should be retained or skipped:

- Links with a scheme other than HTTP or HTTPS should be skipped. Allowing other scheme types is a potential security risk! A malicious user could submit a web page containing links using `file://` URLs, which could possibly trick the crawler into reading (and indexing) files from the local filesystem.
- We have already enumerated the security implications of allowing crawlers to access resources located at private network addresses. Therefore, any links pointing to private networks are automatically skipped.

Extracting the title and text from retrieved web pages

The next stage of the pipeline is responsible for extracting an index-friendly, text-only version of the web page contents and its title. The easiest way to achieve this is by stripping off any HTML tag in the page body and replacing consecutive whitespace characters with a single space.

A fairly straightforward approach would be to come up with a bunch of regular expressions for matching and then removing HTML tags. Unfortunately, the fact that HTML syntax is quite forgiving (that is, you can open a tag and never close it) makes HTML documents notoriously hard to properly clean up just with the help of regular expressions. Truth be told, to cover all possible edge cases, we need to use a parser that understands the structure of HTML documents.

Instead of reinventing the wheel, we will rely on the bluemonday [2] Go package for our HTML sanitization needs. The package exposes a set of configurable filtering policies that can be applied to HTML documents. For our particular use case, we will be using a strict policy (obtained via a call to the `bluemonday.StrictPolicy` helper) that effectively removes all HTML tags from the input document.

A small caveat is that bluemonday policies maintain their own internal state and are therefore not safe to use concurrently. Consequently, to avoid allocating a new policy each time we need to process a payload, we will be using a `sync.Pool` instance to recycle bluemonday policy instances. The pool will be initialized when a new `textExtractor` instance is created, as follows:

```
type textExtractor struct {
    policyPool sync.Pool
}

func newTextExtractor() *textExtractor {
    return &textExtractor{
        policyPool: sync.Pool{
            New: func() interface{} {
                return bluemonday.StrictPolicy()
            },
        },
    }
}
```

Let's take a closer look at the text extractor's `Process` method implementation:

```go
func (te *textExtractor) Process(ctx context.Context, p pipeline.Payload)
(pipeline.Payload, error) {
    payload := p.(*crawlerPayload)
    policy := te.policyPool.Get().(*bluemonday.Policy)

    if titleMatch :=
titleRegex.FindStringSubmatch(payload.RawContent.String()); len(titleMatch)
== 2 {
        payload.Title =
strings.TrimSpace(html.UnescapeString(repeatedSpaceRegex.ReplaceAllString(
            policy.Sanitize(titleMatch[1]), " ",
        )))
    }
    payload.TextContent =
strings.TrimSpace(html.UnescapeString(repeatedSpaceRegex.ReplaceAllString(
        policy.SanitizeReader(&payload.RawContent).String(), " ",
    )))

    te.policyPool.Put(policy)
    return payload, nil
}
```

After obtaining a new bluemonday policy from the pool, we execute a regular expression to detect whether the HTML document contains a `<title>` tag. If a match is found, its content is sanitized and saved into the `Title` attribute of the payload. The same policy is also applied against the web page contents, but this time, the sanitized result is stored in the `TextContent` attribute of the payload.

Inserting discovered outgoing links to the graph

The next crawler pipeline stage that we will be examining is the graph updater. Its main purpose is to insert newly discovered links into the link graph and create edges connecting them to the web page they were retrieved from. Let's take a look at the definition of the `graphUpdater` type and its constructor:

```go
type graphUpdater struct {
    updater Graph
}
func newGraphUpdater(updater Graph) *graphUpdater {
    return &graphUpdater{
        updater: updater,
    }
}
```

The constructor expects an argument of the `Graph` type, which is nothing more than an interface describing the methods needed for the graph updater to communicate with a link graph component:

```
type Graph interface {
    UpsertLink(link *graph.Link) error
    UpsertEdge(edge *graph.Edge) error
    RemoveStaleEdges(fromID uuid.UUID, updatedBefore time.Time) error
}
```

The astute reader will probably notice that the preceding interface definition includes a subset of the methods from the similarly named interface in the `graph` package. This is a prime example of applying the interface-segregation principle to distill an existing, more open interface into the minimum possible interface that our code requires for it to function. Next, we will take a look at the implementation of the graph updater's `Process` method:

```
payload := p.(*crawlerPayload)

src := &graph.Link{
    ID:          payload.LinkID,
    URL:         payload.URL,
    RetrievedAt: time.Now(),
}
if err := u.updater.UpsertLink(src); err != nil {
    return nil, err
}
```

Before we iterate the list of discovered links, we first attempt to upsert the origin link from the payload to the graph by creating a new `graph.Link` object and invoking the graph's `UpsertLink` method. The origin link already exists in the graph, so all that the preceding upsert call does is update the timestamp for the `RetrievedAt` field.

The next step entails the addition of any discovered links with a no-follow `rel` attribute to the graph:

```
for _, dstLink := range payload.NoFollowLinks {
    dst := &graph.Link{URL: dstLink}
    if err := u.updater.UpsertLink(dst); err != nil {
        return nil, err
    }
}
```

After processing all no-follow links, the graph updater iterates the slice of regular links and adds each one into the link graph together with a directed edge from the origin link to each outgoing link:

```
removeEdgesOlderThan := time.Now()
for _, dstLink := range payload.Links {
    dst := &graph.Link{URL: dstLink}

    if err := u.updater.UpsertLink(dst); err != nil {
        return nil, err
    }

    if err := u.updater.UpsertEdge(&graph.Edge{Src: src.ID, Dst: dst.ID});
err != nil {
        return nil, err
    }
}
```

All edges created or updated during this pass will be assigned an `UpdatedAt` value that is greater than or equal to the `removeEdgesOlderThan` value that we capture before entering the loop. We can then use the following block of code to remove any existing edges that were not touched by the preceding loop:

```
if err := u.updater.RemoveStaleEdges(src.ID, removeEdgesOlderThan); err !=
nil {
    return nil, err
}
```

To understand how the preceding process works, let's walk through a simple example. Assume that at time t_0, the crawler processed a web page located at `https://example.com`. At that particular point in time, the page contained outgoing links to `http://foo.com` and `https://bar.com`. After the crawler completed its first pass, the link graph would contain the following set of edge entries:

Source	Destination	UpdatedAt
https://example.com	http://foo.com	t_0
https://example.com	https://bar.com	t_0

Next, the crawler makes a new pass, this time at time t_1 (where $t_1 > t_0$); however, the contents for the page located at `https://example.com` have now changed: the link to `http://foo.com` is now **gone** and the page authors introduced a new link to `https://baz.com`.

After we have updated the edge list and before we prune any stale edges, the edge entries in the link graph would look as follows:

Source	Destination	UpdatedAt
`https://example.com`	`http://foo.com`	t_0
`https://example.com`	`https://bar.com`	t_1
`https://example.com`	`https://baz.com`	t_1

The prune step deletes all edges originating from *https://example.com* that were last updated before t_1. As a result, once the crawler completes its second pass, the final set of edge entries will look as follows:

Source	Destination	UpdatedAt
`https://example.com`	`bar.com`	t_1
`https://example.com`	`baz.com`	t_1

Indexing the contents of retrieved web pages

The last component in our pipeline is the text indexer. As the name implies, the text indexer is responsible for keeping the search index up to date by reindexing the content of each crawled web page.

In a similar fashion to the graph updater stage, we apply the single-responsibility principle and define the `Indexer` interface that gets passed to the text indexer component via its constructor:

```
// Indexer is implemented by objects that can index the contents of
webpages retrieved by the crawler pipeline.
type Indexer interface {
    Index(doc *index.Document) error
}

type textIndexer struct {
    indexer Indexer
}

func newTextIndexer(indexer Indexer) *textIndexer {
    return &textIndexer{
        indexer: indexer,
    }
}
```

The following code listing outlines the `Process` method implementation for the `textIndexer` type:

```go
func (i *textIndexer) Process(ctx context.Context, p pipeline.Payload)
(pipeline.Payload, error) {
    payload := p.(*crawlerPayload)
    doc := &index.Document{
        LinkID:    payload.LinkID,
        URL:       payload.URL,
        Title:     payload.Title,
        Content:   payload.TextContent,
        IndexedAt: time.Now(),
    }
    if err := i.indexer.Index(doc); err != nil {
        return nil, err
    }

    return p, nil
}
```

Nothing out of the ordinary in the preceding code snippet: we create new `index.Document` instance and populate it with the title and content values provided by the text extractor stage of the pipeline. The document is then inserted into the search index by invoking the `Index` method on the externally provided `Indexer` instance.

Assembling and running the pipeline

Congratulations for making it this far! We have finally implemented all individual components that are required for constructing a pipeline for our crawler service. All that's left is to add a little bit of glue code to assemble the individual crawler stages into a pipeline and provide a simple API for running a full crawler pass. All this glue logic is encapsulated inside the `Crawler` type whose definition and constructor details are listed as follows:

```go
type Crawler struct {
    p *pipeline.Pipeline
}

// NewCrawler returns a new crawler instance.
func NewCrawler(cfg Config) *Crawler {
    return &Crawler{
        p: assembleCrawlerPipeline(cfg),
    }
}
```

The `Config` type holds all required configuration options for creating a new crawler pipeline:

```
// Config encapsulates the configuration options for creating a new
Crawler.
type Config struct {
    PrivateNetworkDetector PrivateNetworkDetector
    URLGetter URLGetter
    Graph Graph
    Indexer Indexer

    FetchWorkers int
}
```

The caller of the crawler's constructor is expected to provide the following configuration options:

- An object that implements the `PrivateNetworkDetector` interface, which will be used by the link fetcher and link extractor components to filter out links that resolve to private network addresses
- An object that implements the `URLGetter` interface (for example, `http.DefaultClient`), which the link fetcher will use to perform HTTP GET requests
- An object that implements the `Graph` interface (for example, any of the link graph implementations from the previous chapter), which the graph updater component will use to upsert discovered links into the link graph
- An object that implements the `Indexer` interface (for example, any of the indexer implementations from the previous chapter), which the text indexer component will use to keep the search index in sync
- The size of the worker pool for executing the link fetcher stage of the pipeline

The constructor code calls out to the `assembleCrawlerPipeline` helper function, which is responsible for instantiating each stage of the pipeline with the appropriate configuration options and calling out to `pipeline.New` to create a new pipeline instance :

```
func assembleCrawlerPipeline(cfg Config) *pipeline.Pipeline {
    return pipeline.New(
        pipeline.FixedWorkerPool(
            newLinkFetcher(cfg.URLGetter, cfg.PrivateNetworkDetector),
            cfg.FetchWorkers,
        ),
        pipeline.FIFO(newLinkExtractor(cfg.PrivateNetworkDetector)),
        pipeline.FIFO(newTextExtractor()),
        pipeline.Broadcast(
```

```
                        newGraphUpdater(cfg.Graph),
                        newTextIndexer(cfg.Indexer),
                ),
        )
}
```

As illustrated in *Figure 2*, the first stage of the crawler pipeline uses a fixed-size worker pool that executes the link-fetcher processor. The output from this stage is piped into two sequentially connected FIFO stages that execute the link-extractor and text-extractor processors. Finally, the output of those FIFO stages is copied and broadcast to the graph updater and text indexer components in parallel.

The last piece of the puzzle is the `Crawl` method implementation, which constitutes the API for using the crawler from other packages:

```
func (c *Crawler) Crawl(ctx context.Context, linkIt graph.LinkIterator)
(int, error) {
    sink := new(countingSink)
    err := c.p.Process(ctx, &linkSource{linkIt: linkIt}, sink)
    return sink.getCount(), err
}
```

The method accepts a context value, which can be cancelled at any time by the caller to force the crawler pipeline to terminate, as well as an iterator, which provides the set of links to be crawled by the pipeline. It returns the total number of links that made it to the pipeline sink.

On a side-note, the fact that `Crawl` creates new source and sink instances on each invocation, combined with the observation that none of the crawler stages maintains any internal state, makes `Crawl` safe to invoke concurrently!

Summary

In this chapter, we built from scratch our very own generic, extensible pipeline package using nothing more than the basic Go primitives. We have analyzed and implemented different strategies (FIFO, fixed/dynamic worker pools, and broadcasting) for processing data throughout the various stages of our pipeline. In the last part of the chapter, we applied everything that we have learned so far to implement a multistage crawler pipeline for the Links 'R' Us Project.

In summary, pipelines provide an elegant solution for breaking down complex data processing tasks into smaller and easier-to-test steps that can be executed in parallel to make better use of the compute resources available at your disposal. In the next chapter, we are going to take a look at a different paradigm for processing data that is organized as a graph.

Questions

1. Why is it considered an antipattern to use `interface{}` values as arguments to functions and methods?
2. You are trying to design and build a complex data-processing pipeline that requires copious amounts of computing power (for example, face recognition, audio transcription, or similar). However, when you try to run it on your local machine, you realize that the resource requirements for some of the stages exceed the ones that are currently available locally. Describe how you could modify your current pipeline setup so that you could still run the pipeline on your machine, but arrange for some parts of the pipeline to execute on a remote server that you control.
3. Describe how you would apply the decorator pattern to log errors returned by the processor functions that you have attached to a pipeline.
4. What are the key differences between a synchronous and an asynchronous pipeline implementation?
5. Explain how dead-letter queues work and why you might want to use one in your application.
6. What is the difference between a fixed-size worker pool and a dynamic pool?
7. Describe how you would modify the Links 'R' Us crawler payload so that you can track the time each payload spent inside the pipeline.

Further reading

1. Berners-Lee, T. ; Fielding, R. ; Masinter, L., RFC 3986, Uniform Resource Identifier (URI): Generic Syntax.
2. bluemonday: a fast golang HTML sanitizer (inspired by the OWASP Java HTML Sanitizer) to scrub user generated content of XSS: `https://github.com/microcosm-cc/bluemonday`

3. Documentation for the Go pprof package: `https://golang.org/pkg/runtime/pprof`

4. Documentation for the Pool type in the sync package: `https://golang.org/pkg/sync/#Pool`

5. gomock: a mocking framework for the Go programming language: `https://github.com/golang/mock`

6. go-multierror: a Go (golang) package for representing a list of errors as a single error: `https://github.com/hashicorp/go-multierror`

7. Moskowitz, Robert ; Karrenberg, Daniel ; Rekhter, Yakov ; Lear, Eliot ; Groot, Geert Jan de: Address Allocation for Private Internets.

8. The Go blog: profiling Go programs: `https://blog.golang.org/profiling-go-programs`

Graph-Based Data Processing

8

"Big data is at the foundation of all of the megatrends that are happening today, from social to mobile to the cloud to gaming."

- Chris Lynch

Ask any highly successful company out there and they will all unequivocally agree that data is a precious commodity. Companies use data to not only make informed short-term decisions that affect their day to day operations but also as a guide for shaping their strategy in the long term. In fact, in some industries (such as advertising), data *is* the product!

Nowadays, with the advent of cheap storage solutions, the collection of data has increased exponentially in comparison to the last few years. Furthermore, the rate of increase in storage requirements is expected to keep following an exponential curve well into the future.

While there are quite a few solutions for processing structured data (such as systems supporting map-reduce operations), they fall short when the data to be processed is organized as a *graph*. Running specialized algorithms against massive graphs is a fairly common use case for companies in the field of logistics or companies that operate social networks.

In this chapter, we will be focusing our attention on systems that process graphs at scale. More specifically, the following topics will be covered:

- Understanding the **Bulk Synchronous Parallel** (BSP) model for distributing computation across multiple nodes
- Applying the BSP model principles to create our very own graph processing system in Go

- Using the graph system as a platform for solving graph-based problems such as shortest path and graph coloring
- Implementing an iterative version of the PageRank algorithm for the Links 'R' Us project

Technical requirements

The full code for the topics that will be discussed in this chapter has been published in this book's GitHub repository under the `Chapter08` folder.

 You can access this book's GitHub repository by visiting the following URL: `https://github.com/PacktPublishing/Hands-On-Software-Engineering-with-Golang`.

To get you up and running as quickly as possible, each example project includes a Makefile that defines the following set of targets:

Makefile target	Description
`deps`	Install any required dependencies
`test`	Run all tests and report coverage
`lint`	Check for lint errors

As with all other chapters in this book, you will need a fairly recent version of Go, which you can download at `https://golang.org/dl`.

Exploring the Bulk Synchronous Parallel model

How can we efficiently run a graph algorithm against a massive graph? To be able to answer this question, we need to clarify what we mean by the word *massive*. Is a graph with 1 million nodes considered to be massive? How about 10 million, 100 million, or even 1 billion nodes? The real question we should be asking ourselves is whether the graph can actually *fit in memory*. If the answer is yes, then we can simply buy (or rent from a cloud provider) a server with a beefy CPU, max out the amount of installed memory, and execute our graph-processing code on a single node.

On the other hand, things get much more interesting when the answer to the preceding question is *no*... Congratulations; you can now claim that you work with big data! In such cases, traditional compute models are evidently inadequate; we need to start exploring alternative applications that are explicitly designed for out of core processing.

The BSP model is one of the most popular models for building systems that can process massive datasets by distributing calculations to a cluster of processing nodes. It was proposed in 1990 by Leslie Valiant [10] as a novel and elegant approach for bridging together parallel hardware and software.

At the heart of the BSP model lies the **BSP computer**. The BSP computer, which can be seen in the following diagram, is an abstract computer model made up of a collection of, potentially heterogeneous, processors that are interconnected via a computer network:

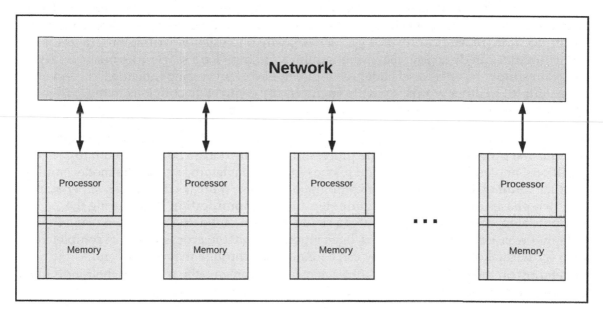

Figure 1: The components that comprise the BSP computer model

The BSP model itself is not particularly concerned with the network implementation details. In fact, the network is treated as a black box; the model can support any type of network as long as the network provides a mechanism for routing messages between processors.

Processors can not only access their own local memory, but they can also use the network link to exchange data with other processors. To this end, the BSP computer is effectively a *distributed memory* computer that can perform computations in parallel. However, this functionality comes with a catch! While access to local memory is fast, accessing a remote processor's memory is significantly slower as it involves an exchange of messages over the network link. Therefore, the BSP computer can be also characterized as a **non-uniform memory access (NUMA)** architecture.

So, what kinds of programs can we run on a BSP computer? Algorithms or data processing operations that can be expressed as a *sequence of iteration steps* are generally a good fit for the BSP model. The BSP model uses the term *super-step* to refer to the execution of a single iteration of a user-defined program.

One thing that differentiates the BSP model from other concurrent programming models is that BSP achieves parallelism through the use of a technique referred to as **Single Program Multiple Data (SPMD)**. Software engineers who are interested in writing programs for the BSP computer can do so as if they were writing a program for a single-core machine. The program simply receives a set of data as input, applies a processing function to it, and emits some output. In other words, software engineers are completely oblivious to the existence of individual processors and the network that connects them.

Before commencing the execution of the user's program, the BSP computer transparently uploads the program to every single processor, splits the data to be processed into a set of partitions, and assigns each partition to one of the available processors. The model employs a rather cunning strategy to reduce computation latency: it breaks down each super-step into two phases or substeps: a **compute** step and a **communication** step. During the compute step, each processor executes a single iteration of the user's program using the data that was assigned to the processor as input. Once *all* the processors have completed their individual computations, they can communicate through the network and – depending on the use case – compare, exchange, or aggregate the results of their individual computations.

Given that each processor can perform computation work in parallel and independently from other processors, the BSP model makes use of **blocking barriers** to synchronize processors. The following diagram summarizes the way in which the BSP computer model executes programs as a sequence of super-steps that are isolated from each other via write barriers:

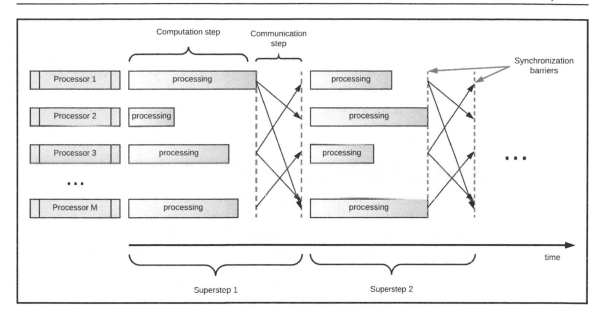

Figure 2: The BSP computer model executes programs as a sequence of super-steps that are isolated from each other via write barriers

In Go parlance, a blocking barrier is equivalent to a `sync.WaitGroup`; the BSP computer waits for all the processors to reach the barrier before assigning them the next chunk of work.

In the last couple of years, interest in models such as BSP has spiked. This can largely be attributed to Google, which (excluding state-funded three-letter agencies) is the undisputed worldwide leader in big data processing. Google engineers incorporated several of the BSP model concepts into Pregel, an in-house solution for out-of-core graph processing. In 2010, Google published a paper [7] detailing the design decisions and architecture behind Pregel. This publication paved the way for creating open source equivalents such as Stanford's GPS [4] and Apache Giraph [1]. The latter is currently used at Facebook to analyze the social graph that's formed by the network's users and their connections.

Building a graph processing system in Go

There is no better way to gain a deeper understanding of the BSP model principles than to build, from scratch, our very own scalable Pregel-like graph processing system in Go.

Here are a few of the design requirements for the system we will be building:

- Graphs will be represented as a collection of vertices and directed edges. Each vertex will be assigned a unique ID. In addition, both vertices and edges can optionally store a user-defined value.
- At every super-step, the system executes a user-defined compute function for *every* vertex in the graph.
- Compute functions are allowed to inspect and modify the internal state of the vertex they are invoked on. They can also iterate the list of outgoing edges and exchange messages with other vertices.
- Any outgoing messages that are produced during a super-step will be buffered and delivered to their intended recipients in the *following* super-step.
- The system must be able to support both single- and multi-node (distributed) graph topologies. In a multi-node topology, each node is responsible for managing a subset of the graph vertices and their outgoing edges. While operating in a multi-node configuration, the system should provide a mechanism for relaying vertex messages between nodes (for example, over a network link).

In the following sections, we will analyze each of these requirements in more detail and elaborate on how they can be implemented in Go. You can find the fully documented source code and test suites for the graph processing system from this chapter in the `Chapter08/bspgraph` folder in this book's GitHub repository.

Queueing and delivering messages

One of the core ideas of the BSP model is that graph components communicate with each other by exchanging messages. The fact that each vertex in the graph can potentially receive multiple messages mandates the introduction of some sort of abstraction for storing or queuing incoming messages until they are ready to be processed by the intended recipient.

In the three sections that follow, we will kick off our design discussion by defining the required interfaces for modeling messages and queues. Then, we will take a stab at implementing a simple, concurrent-safe in-memory queue.

The Message interface

It logically follows that the contents of messages that are exchanged between vertices heavily depend on the application or graph algorithm that we are trying to execute. Consequently, to avoid passing plain `interface{}` values around, we need to come up with a plausible interface for describing messages in a generic way. The `Message` interface, which lives in the `Chapter08/bspgraph/message` package, is an attempt at doing exactly that:

```
type Message interface {
    // Type returns the type of this Message.
    Type() string
}
```

At this point, you are probably dubious about the usefulness of having a `Type` method on this interface. Can this really be any better than simply using an `interface{}`?

If you recall our discussion of the BSP computer model, processors communicate with each other over network links. Before a message can be transmitted over the network, the sender must serialize it into a byte stream. On the receiving end, the byte stream is unserialized back into a message and delivered to the intended recipient.

The `Type` method is quite handy for supporting use cases where the sender and the receiver can exchange *different* types of messages over the same channel (for example, a TCP socket). At serialization time, the sender queries the type of the message and attaches this information as additional metadata to the serialized payload. The receiver can then decode the metadata and unserialize the payload's byte stream back to the appropriate type of message.

Queues and message iterators

Queues serve as buffers for storing incoming messages and making them available for consumption by compute functions. Users of the graph processing system can either make use of the built-in in-memory queue (see the next section) or inject their application-specific queue implementation as long as it adheres to the `Queue` interface, whose definition is listed as follows:

```
type Queue interface {
    // Cleanly shutdown the queue.
    Close() error

    // Enqueue inserts a message to the end of the queue.
    Enqueue(msg Message) error
```

```
    // PendingMessages returns true if the queue contains any messages.
    PendingMessages() bool

    // Flush drops all pending messages from the queue.
    DiscardMessages() error

    // Messages returns an iterator for accessing the queued messages.
    Messages() Iterator
}
```

The methods on the `Queue` interface are pretty standard for any type of queue system. A call to `PendingMessages` reveals whether the queue is currently empty, while a call to `DiscardMessages` can be used to flush any stored messages. The `Enqueue` method can be used to append a new `Message` to the queue, while the `Messages` method returns an `Iterator` for accessing the list of already enqueued messages. Since iterator implementations are typically coupled to the underlying queue system, `Iterator` is also defined as an interface:

```
type Iterator interface {
    // Next advances the iterator so that the next message can be retrieved
    // via a call to Message(). If no more messages are available or an
    // error occurs, Next() returns false.
    Next() bool

    // Message returns the message currently pointed to by the iterator.
    Message() Message

    // Error returns the last error that the iterator encountered.
    Error() error
}
```

This interface follows exactly the same iterator pattern that you should be familiar with from the previous chapters. Calling `Next` advances the iterator and returns a Boolean value to indicate whether more messages are available. After a successful call to `Next`, the current message can be retrieved by calling `Message`.

Implementing an in-memory, thread-safe queue

For the majority of applications, using an in-memory queue implementation such as the one presented here should suffice. Implementing support for other types of queue systems (for example, Kafka, nats-streaming, or even plain files) is left as an exercise for you.

Let's start by defining the `inMemoryQueue` type and its constructor:

```
type inMemoryQueue struct {
    mu   sync.Mutex
    msgs []Message

    latchedMsg Message
}

func NewInMemoryQueue() Queue {
    return new(inMemoryQueue)
}
```

As you can see, the in-memory queue is nothing more than a slice of `Message` instances – a slot for storing the message that's being currently pointed to by an iterator and a `sync.Mutex` for serializing access to the list of messages.

Next, we will take a look at the implementation of `Enqueue` and `PendingMessages`:

```
func (q *inMemoryQueue) Enqueue(msg Message) error {
    q.mu.Lock()
    q.msgs = append(q.msgs, msg)
    q.mu.Unlock()
    return nil
}

func (q *inMemoryQueue) PendingMessages() bool {
    q.mu.Lock()
    pending := len(q.msgs) != 0
    q.mu.Unlock()
    return pending
}
```

To enqueue a new message, we acquire the lock and then append the messages to the list. In a similar fashion, checking for pending messages is facilitated by obtaining the lock and checking whether the message list is empty.

The last set of functions that we need to implement so that the type satisfies the `Queue` interface are as follows:

```
func (q *inMemoryQueue) DiscardMessages() error {
    q.mu.Lock()
    q.msgs = q.msgs[:0]
    q.mu.Unlock()
    return nil
}
```

```
func (*inMemoryQueue) Close() error { return nil }

func (q *inMemoryQueue) Messages() Iterator { return q }
```

As you can see in the preceding code block, the implementation of the `DiscardMessages` method uses a nifty trick: the message list is purged via a slice operation that *retains* the already allocated slice capacity but resets its length to zero. This allows us to reduce the number of memory allocations that need to be performed and, by extension, reduce the pressure on the Go garbage collector.

Furthermore, the `Messages` method body is quite interesting in itself as the returned value implies that the `inMemoryQueue` type must *also* implement the `Iterator` interface! The following code shows the implementation of the relevant methods for satisfying the `Iterator` interface:

```
func (q *inMemoryQueue) Next() bool {
    q.mu.Lock()
    qLen := len(q.msgs)
    if qLen == 0 {
        q.mu.Unlock()
        return false
    }
    q.latchedMsg = q.msgs[qLen-1] // Dequeue message from the tail of the
queue.
    q.msgs = q.msgs[:qLen-1]
    q.mu.Unlock()
    return true
}

func (q *inMemoryQueue) Message() Message {
    q.mu.Lock()
    msg := q.latchedMsg
    q.mu.Unlock()
    return msg
}
```

While most queue implementations use FIFO semantics, as you can easily tell by the `Message` method's implementation, the in-memory queue follows **last-in first-out (LIFO)** semantics. This is intentional; if we were to dequeue from the head of the list (for example, `q.msgs = q.msgs[1:]`), its capacity would decrease and we wouldn't be able to reuse the already allocated memory to append new messages in the future.

As the graph system that we are building is not required to provide any guarantee about the order of incoming messages, our in-memory queue implementation can be used as-is without any issue. Now that we have a solution for storing messages, we can go ahead and define the necessary structures that will represent the vertices and edges of our graph.

Modeling the vertices and edges of graphs

As we mentioned when we discussed the requirements for the graph processing system, we need to come up with a model for describing the vertices and edges that comprise a graph. Moreover, we need to provide an API that we can use to insert new vertices and edges into the graph.

Defining the Vertex and Edge types

The Vertex type encapsulates the state of each vertex that is part of a Graph instance:

```
type Vertex struct {
    id       string
    value    interface{}
    active   bool
    msgQueue [2]message.Queue
    edges    []*Edge
}
```

An interesting tidbit about the Vertex type definition is that we actually need to maintain two message.Queue instances. Any messages produced by compute function invocations while executing a super-step must be buffered so that they can be delivered to the intended recipient in the *following* super-step. To this end, our implementation will employ a double-buffering scheme. We will use one queue to hold the messages for the current super-step and another queue to buffer the messages for the next super-step. At the end of each super-step, we will swap the queues around so that the output queue from the previous super-step becomes the input queue for the following super-step and vice versa. To avoid having to physically swap the queue pointers for every vertex in the graph, we will rely on modulo arithmetic to select the input and output queues based on the current super-step number:

- The queue at index super_step%2 holds the messages that should be consumed during the current super-step
- The queue at index (super_step+1)%2 buffers the messages for the next super-step

Moving on, we shouldn't allow users of the `bspgraph` package to directly mutate the internal state of vertices. Therefore, none of the `Vertex` fields are exported outside of the `bspgraph` package. Instead, we will define the following set of helper methods so that we can access and/or safely manipulate the state of a vertex instance:

```
func (v *Vertex) ID() string { return v.id }

func (v *Vertex) Value() interface{} { return v.value }

func (v *Vertex) SetValue(val interface{}) { v.value = val }

func (v *Vertex) Freeze() { v.active = false }

func (v *Vertex) Edges() []*Edge { return v.edges }
```

Each vertex is uniquely identified by a string-based ID that can be queried via a call to the `ID` method. In addition, vertices can optionally store a user-defined value that compute functions can read or write via the `Value` and `SetValue` methods.

What's more, a vertex can be in one of the following two states: *active* or *inactive* state. All the vertices are initially marked as *active*. To conserve compute resources, the graph framework will only invoke compute functions on active vertices. If the compute method implementation decides that a particular vertex has reached a terminal state and no further calculations are required, it can opt to explicitly mark the vertex as inactive via a call to its `Freeze` method. However, should an inactive vertex receive a new message during a super-step, the graph framework will automatically mark it as active at the next super-step.

Finally, the `Edges` method returns a slice of `Edge` objects that correspond to the outgoing, directed edges originating from a particular vertex. The following code shows the definition of the `Edge` type and its helper methods:

```
type Edge struct {
    value interface{}
    dstID string
}

func (e *Edge) DstID() string { return e.dstID }

func (e *Edge) Value() interface{} { return e.value }

func (e *Edge) SetValue(val interface{}) { e.value = val }
```

Similar to the `Vertex` type, edges can also store an optional user-defined value that can be read/written to via the `Value` and `SetValue` methods. Every edge has a destination vertex whose ID can be obtained via a call to the `DstID` method. As we will see in the *Sending and receiving messages* section, the vertex ID is the only piece of information that we need to be aware of in order to send a message to a particular vertex.

Inserting vertices and edges into the graph

The `Graph` type keeps track of all vertices that comprise the graph with the help of a map where keys are vertex IDs and values are `Vertex` instances. Besides the fact that the vertex map allows us to quickly lookup vertices by their ID – a very important feature for delivering incoming messages – it also provides an efficient mechanism (as opposed to using a slice) for *deleting* vertices if we ever wish to allow users to mutate the graph topology between super-steps.

New vertices can be inserted into the graph via the `AddVertex` method. It expects two arguments:

- A unique vertex ID
- An initial value (which may also be `nil`):

```
func (g *Graph) AddVertex(id string, initValue interface{}) {
    v := g.vertices[id]
    if v == nil {
        v = &Vertex{
            id: id,
            msgQueue: [2]message.Queue{
                g.queueFactory(),
                g.queueFactory(),
            },
            active: true,
        }
        g.vertices[id] = v
    }
    v.SetValue(initValue)
}
```

If a vertex with the same ID already exists, we simply override its stored initial value. Otherwise, a new `Vertex` instance must be allocated. The code populates its ID field, sets the vertex status to active, and invokes the configured (at graph construction time) queue factory to instantiate the two queues that we need in order to store incoming messages for the current and next super-steps. Finally, the new vertex instance is inserted into the map.

Similarly, the `AddEdge` method creates a new directed edge between two vertices:

```go
func (g *Graph) AddEdge(srcID, dstID string, initValue interface{}) error {
    srcVert := g.vertices[srcID]
    if srcVert == nil {
        return xerrors.Errorf("create edge from %q to %q: %w", srcID,
dstID, ErrUnknownEdgeSource)
    }

    srcVert.edges = append(srcVert.edges, &Edge{
        dstID: dstID,
        value: initValue,
    })
    return nil
}
```

As we mentioned in a *Defining the Vertex and Edge types* section, edges are *owned* by the vertices they originate from. Ergo, the `AddEdge` implementation must check whether the `srcID` can be resolved to an existing vertex. If the source vertex cannot be located, then an error is returned to the caller. Otherwise, a new edge is created and appended to the edge list of the source vertex.

Note that while we expect the source vertex for the edge to be known locally, the same assumption cannot be made for the destination vertex. For instance, if the graph was spread across two nodes, the source vertex could be managed by the first node while the destination vertex could be managed by the second node.

Sharing global graph state through data aggregation

Aggregators are a key component for implementing several graph-based algorithms that rely on sharing global state between vertices. They are concurrent-safe primitives that apply an aggregation operator to a set of values and make the result available to *all* the vertices at the next super-step.

Any kind of operator can be used to create an aggregator as long as it is commutative and associative. Aggregators are commonly used to implement counters, accumulators, or for keeping track of the minimum and/or maximum value of some quantity.

In the upcoming sections, we will do the following:

- Define a generic interface for aggregators
- Augment our Graph type with helper methods for registering and looking up Aggregator instances by name
- Build an example aggregator that accumulates float64 values

Defining the Aggregator interface

The Aggregator interface describes the set of methods that must be implemented by Go types so that they can be used with our graph processing framework for data aggregation purposes:

```go
type Aggregator interface {
    // Type returns the type of this aggregator.
    Type() string

    // Set the aggregator to the specified value.
    Set(val interface{})

    // Get the current aggregator value.
    Get() interface{}

    // Aggregate updates the aggregator's value based on the provided
    // value.
    Aggregate(val interface{})

    // Delta returns the change in the aggregator's value since the last
    // call to Delta.
    Delta() interface{}
}
```

One of my pet peeves is that the methods in the preceding interface definition use interface{} values. Unfortunately, this is one of the few cases where we cannot actually avoid the use of interface{} since the types of values that can be aggregated are implementation-specific.

Whenever we want to apply the aggregation operation to a new value, we can do so by invoking the Aggregate method. Furthermore, the current value can be retrieved via a call to the Get method. On the other hand, if we want to set the aggregator to a *specific* value (for example, reset a counter to zero), we can invoke the Set method. The Type method provides an identifier for the aggregator's type that can be used for serialization purposes (for example, if we want to take a snapshot of the graph's state).

The `Delta` method returns the *change* in the aggregator's value since the *last* time that either `Delta` or `Set` was called. This method is meant to be used in a distributed graph computation scenario (see `Chapter 12`, *Building Distributed Graph Processing Systems*) to reduce the values from individual local aggregators into a single global aggregated value.

To understand how the `Delta` method is used, let's picture a scenario where we deploy three nodes: a master and two workers. Our goal is to create a distributed counter whose value is synchronized with all the nodes prior to executing a new super-step. To achieve this, each node (including the master) defines a *local* aggregator instance that implements a simple counter. While executing a super-step, compute functions are only allowed access to the local counter of the worker they are executing on. The master node is not assigned any vertices. Instead, it is responsible for collecting the partial *deltas* from each worker, aggregating those into its own counter, and *broadcasting* the new total back to the workers. The workers then use the `Set` method to update their local counters to the new total.

Registering and looking up aggregators

To facilitate efficient name-based aggregator lookups, `Graph` instances store aggregators in a map where the aggregator name is used as a key. New aggregator instances can be linked to a `Graph` instance through the `RegisterAggregator` method:

```
func (g *Graph) RegisterAggregator(name string, aggr Aggregator) {
    g.aggregators[name] = aggr
}
```

Compute functions that need access to a particular aggregator can invoke the `Aggregator` method to look up a registered aggregator instance by name:

```
func (g *Graph) Aggregator(name string) Aggregator {
    return g.aggregators[name]
}
```

In an effort to make it easier for clients to create snapshots of the graph's state, we will also be providing the auxiliary `Aggregators` method, which just returns a copy of the map that contains the complete set of registered aggregator instances.

Implementing a lock-free accumulator for float64 values

In the `Chapter08/bspgraph/aggregator` package, you can find two concurrent-safe accumulator implementations that are designed to work with `int64` and `float64` values and can also double as distributed counters.

Instead of using a mutex to guarantee concurrent access, both accumulators are implemented using compare and swap instructions. The int64-based version is pretty straightforward and can easily be implemented with the help of the functions provided by the `sync/atomic` package. The float64-based version, which we will be dissecting here, is more challenging (and fun!) since the `sync/atomic` package offers no support for dealing with floating-point values. To work around this limitation, we will import the `unsafe` package and employ a few *creative value casting tricks* to roll our very own set of atomic functions that can work with `float64` values!

Let's begin by defining the `Float64Accumulator` type:

```
type Float64Accumulator struct {
    prevSum float64
    curSum  float64
}
```

The `Float64Accumulator` type keeps track of two `float64` values: the first one holds the current sum while the latter keeps track of the last value that was reported by a call to the `Delta` method.

Now, let's define the necessary set of methods for satisfying the `Accumulator` interface. The first method that we will be defining is `Get`:

```
func (a *Float64Accumulator) Get() interface{} {
    return loadFloat64(&a.curSum)
}

func loadFloat64(v *float64) float64 {
    return math.Float64frombits(
        atomic.LoadUint64((*uint64)(unsafe.Pointer(v))),
    )
}
```

Here, the `loadFloat64` helper function is where all the magic happens. The trick that we will be using is based on the observation that a `float64` value takes exactly the same space in memory (8 bytes) as a `uint64` value. With the help of the `unsafe` package, we can cast a *pointer* to the `float64` value we want to read into a `*uint64` value and use the `atomic.LoadUint64` function to read it atomically as a raw `uint64` value. Then, we can use the handy `Float64frombits` function from the built-in `math` package to *interpret* the raw `uint64` value as a `float64`.

Next, let's examine the implementation for `Aggregate`:

```
func (a *Float64Accumulator) Aggregate(v interface{}) {
    for v64 := v.(float64); ; {
        oldV := loadFloat64(&a.curSum)
        newV := oldV + v64
        if atomic.CompareAndSwapUint64(
            (*uint64)(unsafe.Pointer(&a.curSum)),
            math.Float64bits(oldV),
            math.Float64bits(newV),
        ) {
            return
        }
    }
}
```

As you can see in the preceding code snippet, we enter an infinite `for` loop where we fetch the current aggregator value, add the `float64` value that was passed to the method, and keep trying to execute a compare and swap operation until we succeed. Like we did previously, we exploit the observation that `float64` values take the same space in memory as an `uint64` and use `atomic.CompareAndSwapUint64` to perform the swap. This function expects `uint64` values as arguments, so this time, we leverage the `math.Float64bits` function to convert the `float64` values that we are working with into raw `uint64` values for the compare-and-swap operation.

We can apply exactly the same methodology to implement the `Delta` method, as follows:

```
func (a *Float64Accumulator) Delta() interface{} {
    for {
        curSum := loadFloat64(&a.curSum)
        prevSum := loadFloat64(&a.prevSum)
        if atomic.CompareAndSwapUint64(
            (*uint64)(unsafe.Pointer(&a.prevSum)),
            math.Float64bits(prevSum),
            math.Float64bits(curSum),
        ) {
            return curSum - prevSum
        }
    }
}
```

Once again, we enter an infinite for loop where we latch on to the current and previous values and then use a compare and swap operation to copy `curSum` to `prevSum`. Once the swap succeeds, we subtract the two latched values and return the result to the caller.

To complete the set of methods for implementing our accumulator, we also need to provide an implementation for `Set`, which, as you see in the following code listing, is slightly more complicated:

```
func (a *Float64Accumulator) Set(v interface{}) {
    for v64 := v.(float64); ; {
        oldCur := loadFloat64(&a.curSum)
        oldPrev := loadFloat64(&a.prevSum)
        swappedCur := atomic.CompareAndSwapUint64(
            (*uint64)(unsafe.Pointer(&a.curSum)),
            math.Float64bits(oldCur),
            math.Float64bits(v64),
        )
        swappedPrev := atomic.CompareAndSwapUint64(
            (*uint64)(unsafe.Pointer(&a.prevSum)),
            math.Float64bits(oldPrev),
            math.Float64bits(v64),
        )
        if swappedCur && swappedPrev {
            return
        }
    }
}
```

The extra complexity arises from the fact that we need to perform two sequential compare and swap operations, both of which must succeed before we can exit the `for` loop.

Sending and receiving messages

As we mentioned previously, vertices communicate with each other by exchanging messages. Sending the *same* message to all immediate neighbors of a particular vertex is an often recurring pattern in several graph algorithms. Let's define a convenience method for handling this fairly common use case:

```
func (g *Graph) BroadcastToNeighbors(v *Vertex, msg message.Message) error
{
    for _, e := range v.edges {
        if err := g.SendMessage(e.dstID, msg); err != nil {
            return err
        }
    }

    return nil
}
```

`BroadcastToNeighbors` simply iterates the list of edges for a particular vertex and attempts to send the message to each neighbor with the help of the `SendMessage` method. With the help of `SendMessage`, compute functions can send a message to any vertex in the graph, provided that its ID is known to them (for example, discovered through the use of a gossip protocol).

Let's take a look at the implementation for `SendMessage`:

```
func (g *Graph) SendMessage(dstID string, msg message.Message) error {
    dstVert := g.vertices[dstID]
    if dstVert != nil {
        queueIndex := (g.superstep + 1) % 2
        return dstVert.msgQueue[queueIndex].Enqueue(msg)
    }

    if g.relayer != nil {
        if err := g.relayer.Relay(dstID, msg); !xerrors.Is(err,
ErrDestinationIsLocal) {
            return err
        }
    }
    return xerrors.Errorf("message cannot be delivered to %q: %w", dstID,
ErrInvalidMessageDestination)
}
```

First things first, we need to look up the destination vertex in the graph's vertex map. If the lookup yields a valid `Vertex` instance, then we can enqueue the message so that it can be delivered to the vertex in the following super-step.

Things get a bit more interesting when the vertex lookup fails… A failed lookup can occur because of two reasons:

- We are running in distributed mode and the vertex is managed by a *remote* graph instance
- The vertex simply does not exist

To handle vertices that are potentially hosted remotely, the `Graph` type allows users of the `bspgraph` package to register a helper that can relay messages between remote graph instances. More specifically, these helpers:

- Are aware of the topology of a distributed graph (that is, the vertex ID ranges that are managed by each node in a cluster)
- Provide a mechanism for shuttling messages back and forth between the cluster nodes

User-defined relay helpers must implement the `Relayer` interface and can be registered with a graph instance through the `RegisterRelayer` method:

```go
type Relayer interface {
    // Relay a message to a vertex that is not known locally. Calls
    // to Relay must return ErrDestinationIsLocal if the provided dst value
    // is not a valid remote destination.
    Relay(dst string, msg message.Message) error
}

func (g *Graph) RegisterRelayer(relayer Relayer) {
    g.relayer = relayer
}
```

To make it easier for users to provide functions or closures as a suitable `Relayer` implementation, let's also go ahead and define the `RelayerFunc` adapter, which converts a function with the appropriate signature into a `Relayer`:

```go
type RelayerFunc func(string, message.Message) error

// Relay calls f(dst, msg).
func (f RelayerFunc) Relay(dst string, msg message.Message) error {
    return f(dst, msg)
}
```

If the destination vertex ID cannot be located by the graph and the user has registered a `Relayer` instance, `SendMessage` invokes its `Relay` method and checks the response for errors. If we get an error *other* than `ErrDestinationLocal`, we return the error as-is back to the caller.

If the relay helper detects that the destination vertex ID should, in fact, be managed by the local graph instance, it will fail with the typed `ErrDestinationIsLocal` error to indicate this. In such a case, we assume that the vertex ID is invalid and return the typed `ErrInvalidMessageDestination` error to the caller.

Implementing graph-based algorithms using compute functions

In order for a compute function to be used with the `bspgraph` package, it must adhere to the following signature:

```go
type ComputeFunc func(g *Graph, v *Vertex, msgIt message.Iterator) error
```

The first argument to the compute function is a pointer to the `Graph` instance itself. This allows compute functions to use the graph API to query the current super-step number, look up aggregators, and send messages to vertices. The second argument is a pointer to the `Vertex` instance that the compute function is operating on, while the third and final argument is a `message.Iterator` for consuming the messages that were sent to the vertex during the *previous* super-step.

It is important to note that the system operates under the assumption that compute functions can be safely executed concurrently. The only runtime guarantee that's provided by the system is that at each super-step, compute functions will be executed for each vertex *exactly once*. Consequently, compute function implementations can use any of the `Vertex` methods without having to worry about data races and synchronization issues. Given that vertices effectively *own* the edges originating from them, the same data access principles also apply to any `Edge` instances that are obtained by invoking the `Edges` method on a vertex.

Achieving vertical scaling by executing compute functions in parallel

Next, we will shift our focus to the mechanism that's used to execute compute functions. A rather simplistic approach would be to use a `for` loop construct to iterate the vertices in the graph and invoke the compute function for each vertex in a sequential fashion. While the approach would undoubtedly work as expected, it would be a rather inefficient use of the compute resources that are at our disposal. Running compute functions sequentially would only make use of a single CPU core; that would be quite a waste given that machines with up to 64 cores are readily available from the majority of cloud providers.

A much better alternative would be to fan out the execution of compute functions to a pool of workers. This way, compute functions can run in parallel and make full use of all the available CPU cores. The graph constructor initializes the pool of workers via a call to the `startWorkers` method, whose implementation is as follows:

```go
func (g *Graph) startWorkers(numWorkers int) {
    g.vertexCh = make(chan *Vertex)
    g.errCh = make(chan error, 1)
    g.stepCompletedCh = make(chan struct{})

    g.wg.Add(numWorkers)
    for i := 0; i < numWorkers; i++ {
        go g.stepWorker()
    }
}
```

The first thing that startWorkers does is create a set of channels that are needed to communicate with the workers in the pool. Let's briefly talk about each channel's purpose:

- vertexCh is a channel that is polled by workers to obtain the next vertex to be processed.
- errCh is a buffered channel where workers publish any errors that may occur while invoking compute functions. The graph processing system implementation will treat all errors as *fatal*. Therefore, we only need room to store a single error value. When a worker detects an error, it will attempt to enqueue it to errCh; if the channel is full, another fatal error has already been written to it, so the new error can safely be ignored.
- Since we are using a worker pool to execute compute functions in parallel, we need to introduce some sort of synchronization mechanism to detect when all the vertices have been processed. The stepCompletedCh channel allows workers to signal when the *last* enqueued vertex has been processed.

The remainder of the startWorkers method is pretty straightforward: we start a go-routine for each worker and use a sync.WaitGroup to keep track of their completion status.

The step method, as shown in the following code, is responsible for executing a single super-step. If the super-step completes without an error, step returns the number of vertices that were active during the super-step:

```
func (g *Graph) step() (activeInStep int, err error) {
    g.activeInStep, g.pendingInStep = 0, int64(len(g.vertices))
    if g.pendingInStep == 0 {
        return 0, nil // no work required
    }
    for _, v := range g.vertices {
        g.vertexCh <- v
    }
    <-g.stepCompletedCh

    select {
    case err = <-g.errCh: // dequeued
    default: // no error available
    }
    return int(g.activeInStep), err
}
```

The preceding block of code should be self-explanatory. First, we reset the `activeInStep` counter to zero and load the `pendingInStep` counter with the number of vertices in the graph. Then, the map that holds the set of the graph `Vertex` instances is iterated and each vertex value is written to `vertexCh` so that it can be picked up and processed by an idle worker.

Once all the vertices have been enqueued, `step` waits for all vertices to be processed by the worker pool by performing a blocking read on `stepCompletedCh`. Before returning, the code checks whether an error has been enqueued to the error channel. If that happens to be the case, the error is dequeued and returned to the caller.

Now, let's take a look at the `stepWorker` method's implementation:

```
for v := range g.vertexCh {
    buffer := g.superstep % 2
    if v.active || v.msgQueue[buffer].PendingMessages() {
        _ = atomic.AddInt64(&g.activeInStep, 1)
        v.active = true
        if err := g.computeFn(g, v, v.msgQueue[buffer].Messages()); err !=
nil {
            tryEmitError(g.errCh, xerrors.Errorf("running compute function
for vertex %q failed: %w", v.ID(), err))
        } else if err := v.msgQueue[buffer].DiscardMessages(); err != nil {
            tryEmitError(g.errCh, xerrors.Errorf("discarding unprocessed
messages for vertex %q failed: %w", v.ID(), err))
        }
    }
    if atomic.AddInt64(&g.pendingInStep, -1) == 0 {
        g.stepCompletedCh <- struct{}{}
    }
}
g.wg.Done()
```

The channel's `range` statement ensures that our worker will keep executing until the `vertexCh` is closed. After dequeuing the next vertex from `vertexCh`, the worker uses modulo arithmetic to select the message queue that contains the messages that should be consumed by the compute function during the current super-step.

Vertices are considered to be active if either their `active` flag is set or if their input message queue contains any undelivered messages. For any vertex deemed to be active, we set its `active` flag to `true` and atomically increment the `activeInStep` counter. As we will see in the following sections, several graph algorithms use the number of active vertices in a super-step as a predicate for deciding whether the algorithm has completed or not.

Next, we invoke the registered compute function and check for any errors. If an error occurs, we invoke the `tryEmitError` helper to enqueue the error to `errCh`:

```
func tryEmitError(errCh chan<- error, err error) {
    select {
    case errCh <- err: // queued error
    default: // channel already contains another error
    }
}
```

The last bit of housekeeping that we need to do within the `stepWorker` method is to call the queue's `DiscardMessages` method and flush any messages that were not consumed by the compute function that we executed in the previous step. This ensures that the queue is always empty and ready to store incoming messages for `superstep+2`.

Regardless of whether the vertex is active or not, the worker invokes the `atomic.AddInt64` function to *decrement* the `pendingInStep` counter and check whether it has reached zero. When that occurs, all the vertices for the current super-step have been processed and the worker writes an empty `struct{}` value to `stepCompletedCh` to unblock the `step` method and allow it to return.

Orchestrating the execution of super-steps

In the previous section, we performed a detailed analysis of the mechanism that's used by the `Graph` type to execute a single super-step. However, graph algorithms typically involve several super-steps. For the bspgraph package users to be able to run generic graph algorithms using the system we are building, they require more fine-grained control over the execution of a sequence of super-steps.

Before executing a super-step, we need to reset the value of one or more aggregators. Likewise, after a super-step completes, we might be interested in examining or modifying an aggregator's final value. Furthermore, each algorithm defines its own termination condition. For example, an algorithm might terminate when the following occurs:

- After a fixed number of steps
- When all vertices in the graph become inactive
- When the value of some aggregator exceeds a threshold

To cater to such requirements, we need to introduce a high-level API that provides an orchestration layer for governing the execution of a sequential list of super-steps. This API is provided by the `Executor` type, whose definition is as follows:

```
type Executor struct {
    g  *Graph
    cb ExecutorCallbacks
}
```

An `Executor` wraps a `Graph` instance and is parameterized with a set of user-defined `ExecutorCallbacks`:

```
type ExecutorCallbacks struct {
    PreStep func(ctx context.Context, g *Graph) error
    PostStep func(ctx context.Context, g *Graph, activeInStep int) error
    PostStepKeepRunning func(ctx context.Context, g *Graph, activeInStep
int) (bool, error)
}
```

The `PreStep` and `PostStep` callbacks are invoked – if defined – before and after the execution of a new super-step. If the `PostStepKeepRunning` callback is defined, it will be automatically invoked by the `Executor` after `PostStep`. The callback is responsible for checking whether the termination condition for the algorithm has been met and to return `false` when no further super-steps need to be executed.

The `NewExecutor` function serves as a constructor for creating new `Executor` instances:

```
func NewExecutor(g *Graph, cb ExecutorCallbacks) *Executor {
    patchEmptyCallbacks(&cb)
    g.superstep = 0
    return &Executor{
        g:         g,
        cb:        cb,
    }
}
```

To avoid nil pointer dereference errors when trying to invoke undefined callbacks, the constructor uses the following helper to patch missing callbacks with a dummy no-op stub:

```
func patchEmptyCallbacks(cb *ExecutorCallbacks) {
    if cb.PreStep == nil {
        cb.PreStep = func(context.Context, *Graph) error { return nil }
    }
    if cb.PostStep == nil {
        cb.PostStep = func(context.Context, *Graph, int) error { return nil
    }
    }
```

```
    if cb.PostStepKeepRunning == nil {
        cb.PostStepKeepRunning = func(context.Context, *Graph, int) (bool,
error) { return true, nil }
    }
}
```

The high-level interface that's exposed by the `Executor` consists of the following set of methods:

```
func (ex *Executor) Graph() *Graph { return ex.g }

func (ex *Executor) Superstep() int { return ex.g.Superstep() }

func (ex *Executor) RunSteps(ctx context.Context, numSteps int) error {
    return ex.run(ctx, numSteps)
}

func (ex *Executor) RunToCompletion(ctx context.Context) error {
    return ex.run(ctx, -1)
}
```

The `Graph` method provides access to the `Graph` instance that's linked to the `Executor`, while `Superstep` reports the *last* super-step that was executed. The `RunSteps` and `RunToCompletion` methods repeatedly execute super-steps until one of the following conditions is met:

- The context expires
- An error occurs
- The `PostStepKeepRunning` callback returns false
- The maximum number of `numSteps` has been executed (only for `RunSteps`)

Both of these functions are simply proxies for the `run` method, whose implementation is as follows:

```
func (ex *Executor) run(ctx context.Context, maxSteps int) error {
    var activeInStep int
    var err          error
    var keepRunning  bool
    var cb           = ex.cb
    for ; maxSteps != 0; ex.g.superstep, maxSteps = ex.g.superstep+1,
maxSteps-1 {
        if err = ensureContextNotExpired(ctx); err != nil {
            break
        } else if err = cb.PreStep(ctx, ex.g); err != nil {
            break
        } else if activeInStep, err = ex.g.step(); err != nil {
```

```
                    break
        } else if err = cb.PostStep(ctx, ex.g, activeInStep); err != nil {
            break
        } else if keepRunning, err = cb.PostStepKeepRunning(ctx, ex.g,
    activeInStep); !keepRunning || err != nil {
            break
        }
    }
    return err
}
```

The `run` method enters a `for` loop that keeps running until the caller-provided `maxSteps` value becomes equal to zero. At the end of each iteration, `maxSteps` is decremented while the graph's `superstep` counter is incremented. However, if the caller specifies a *negative* value for `maxSteps` when invoking `run`, then the preceding loop is functionally equivalent to an infinite loop.

The `Executor` begins a new iteration by checking whether the provided context has been canceled and then proceeds to invoke the `PreStep` callback. Then, it executes a new super-step by invoking the `step` method of the wrapped `Graph` instance. Following that, it invokes the `PostStep` and `PostStepKeepRunning` callbacks. If any of the callbacks or the `step` method returns an error, then we break out of the loop and return the error back to the caller.

Creating and managing Graph instances

Our graph processing system is nearly complete! To finalize our implementation, we need to define a constructor that will create new `Graph` instances and some auxiliary methods that will manage the graph's life cycle.

As we saw in the previous sections, there are quite a few knobs for configuring `Graph` instances. Passing each individual configuration option as an argument to the graph's constructor is considered to be an anti-pattern – not to mention that we would have to bump the major version of our package every time we want to add a new configuration option; changing a constructor's signature is the very definition of a breaking change!

A much better solution is to define a typed configuration object and pass that as an argument to the constructor:

```
type GraphConfig struct {
    QueueFactory message.QueueFactory
    ComputeFn ComputeFunc
    ComputeWorkers int
}
```

`QueueFactory` will be used by the `AddVertex` method to create the required message queue instances for each new vertex that is being added to the graph. The `ComputeFn` setting is used to specify the compute function that will be executed for each super-step. Finally, the `ComputeWorkers` option allows the end users of the package to fine-tune the size of the worker pool so that they can execute the provided compute function.

From the preceding list of configuration options, only `ComputeFn` is required. Let's create a validator helper to check a `GraphConfig` object and to populate missing fields with sane defaults:

```
func (g *GraphConfig) validate() error {
    var err error
    if g.QueueFactory == nil {
        g.QueueFactory = message.NewInMemoryQueue
    }
    if g.ComputeWorkers <= 0 {
        g.ComputeWorkers = 1
    }

    if g.ComputeFn == nil {
        err = multierror.Append(err, xerrors.New("compute function not
specified"))
    }

    return err
}
```

If a nil `QueueFactory` instance is provided by the caller, the validator code will use the in-memory implementation as a sane default. Furthermore, if an invalid number of compute workers is specified, the validator will fall back to using a single worker. Of course, doing so would effectively turn processing graph vertices for every super-step into a *sequential* operation. Nevertheless, this might prove to be a useful feature when the end users wish to debug misbehaving compute functions.

A new `Graph` instance can be created via the `NewGraph` constructor, which is as follows:

```
func NewGraph(cfg GraphConfig) (*Graph, error) {
    if err := cfg.validate(); err != nil {
        return nil, xerrors.Errorf("graph config validation failed: %w",
err)
    }

    g := &Graph{
        computeFn:     cfg.ComputeFn,
        queueFactory:  cfg.QueueFactory,
        aggregators:   make(map[string]Aggregator),
        vertices:      make(map[string]*Vertex),
    }
    g.startWorkers(cfg.ComputeWorkers)

    return g, nil
}
```

The first thing that the constructor needs to do is run a validation check on the provided configuration options. With a valid configuration at hand, the code creates the `Graph` instance, plugs in the provided configuration options, and allocates the maps that are needed to hold the graph's `Vertex` and `Aggregator` instances. The last thing that the constructor needs to do before returning the new `Graph` instance to the caller is initialize the worker pool via a call to `startWorkers`.

After creating a new `Graph` instance, users can proceed with populating the graph vertices and edges, register aggregators, and make use of an `Executor` to orchestrate the execution of a particular graph-based algorithm. However, after a completed run, users may want to reuse a `Graph` instance to run the exact same algorithm again but this time to use a different graph layout. Let's provide them with a `Reset` method to reset the graph's internal state:

```
func (g *Graph) Reset() error {
    g.superstep = 0
    for _, v := range g.vertices {
        for i := 0; i < 2; i++ {
            if err := v.msgQueue[i].Close(); err != nil {
                return xerrors.Errorf("closing message queue #%d for vertex
%v: %w", i, v.ID(), err)
            }
        }
    }
    g.vertices = make(map[string]*Vertex)
    g.aggregators = make(map[string]Aggregator)
    return nil
}
```

As you may recall, every vertex is associated with two message queue instances. The `message.Queue` interface defines a `Close` method that we must call to release any resources (for example, file handles, sockets, and so on) that are used by the underlying queue implementation. Lastly, to completely reset the graph's internal state, we can simply reset the graph's super-step counter to zero and recreate the maps that store the graph's vertices and aggregator instances.

Given that the worker pool consists of a bunch of long-running go-routines, we must also provide a mechanism for managing their life cycle and, more importantly, to shut them down when we are done with the graph. The last method that we will be defining on the `Graph` type is `Close`:

```
func (g *Graph) Close() error {
    close(g.vertexCh)
    g.wg.Wait()

    return g.Reset()
}
```

To force the worker pool to cleanly shut down and all its workers to exit, the `Close` method implementation closes `vertexCh`, which each worker polls for incoming vertex processing jobs. The code then blocks on a wait group until all the workers have exited. Before returning, we make a tail call to the `Reset` method to ensure that the per-vertex queue instances are properly closed.

This concludes the development of a framework that allows us to execute graph-based algorithms using the BSP computation model. Next, we will explore how we can leverage the framework to solve some real-world problems that involve graphs!

Solving interesting graph problems

In this section, we will be examining three very popular graph-based problems that are good fits for the graph processing system we have just finished building.

After describing each problem in detail and listing some of its potential real-world applications, we will continue our discussion by presenting a *sequential* algorithm that can be used to solve it. Following that, we will come up with an equivalent parallel version of the same algorithm and encode it as a compute function that can be used with the `bspgraph` package.

Searching graphs for the shortest path

If we look around, we are bound to encounter a plethora of quite challenging problems that essentially boil down to finding a path or set of paths within a graph that minimize a particular cost function. Pathfinding has a multitude of real-world use cases, ranging from building efficient computer networks to logistics and even games!

> The definition of a suitable cost function and its interpretation is typically application-specific.

> For instance, in the context of a map service, the cost associated with a graph edge could reflect the distance between two points or the time that's required to drive from one point to another due to traffic congestion. On the other hand, if we were talking about packet routing application, cost could represent the amount of money that the network operator would need to pay in order to use a peering connection with another provider.

For simplicity, the sole focus of this section will be about finding the shortest paths within a graph. It goes without saying that the principles and algorithms we will be discussing can be applied, as-is, to any *type* of cost function as long as *lower* cost value for a graph edge indicates a *better* path through the graph.

Depending on how we define the path origin and destination, we can classify shortest path queries into three general categories:

- **Point to point**: In a *point to point* search query, we are interested in locating the shortest path that connects *two points*. An interesting example of this type of search would be a real-time strategy game where the user selects a unit (the path origin) and subsequently clicks on the map location where they want the unit to move to (the path destination). The game engine searches for the shortest unobstructed path between the two points (typically by implementing an algorithm such as A* [5]) and navigates the unit along the path.
- **Point to multi-point**: A *point to multi-point* search query involves finding the shortest paths connecting a *single* graph vertex to *multiple* vertices. For example, a user of a map application might be interested in obtaining a list of coffee shops located within a particular radius from their current location sorted by distance. If we flip this query around, we can identify even more interesting use cases. For instance, a ride-hailing application is aware of both the users' and the drivers' locations. A multi-point to point query would allow the application to dispatch the nearest driver to a user's location and reduce the time-to-pickup. These types of queries can be efficiently answered using Dijkstra's algorithm, one of the most widely-known graph algorithms.

- **Multi-point to multi-point**: The third, and most complicated, pathfinding query category consists of *multi-point to multi-point* queries where we are effectively seeking the shortest path from each vertex to *all* the other vertices in the graph. Arguably, we could answer this kind of query by running Dijkstra's algorithm for each vertex in the graph at the cost of a much longer total runtime, especially if the graph contains a large number of vertices. A much better alternative performance-wise for answering such queries would be to use a dynamic programming algorithm such as Floyd-Warshall [3].

Let's take a stab at implementing Dijkstra's algorithm using the graph processing framework that we developed in the first half of this chapter. While the original version of Dijkstra's algorithm was meant to find the shortest path between two points, the variant that we will be working with is designed to locate the *shortest path tree*, that is, the shortest path from a point to all the other points in the graph.

The sequential Dijkstra algorithm

Before we adapt Dijkstra's algorithm so that it works with our graph processing system, we need to have a clear idea of how the original algorithm works. The following snippet outlines an implementation of the sequential version of Dijkstra's algorithm in pseudocode form:

```
function Dikstra(Graph):
  for each vertex v in Graph:
     min_cost_via[v] = infinity
     prev[v] = nil
  min_cost_via[src] = 0
  Q = set of all vertices in graph
  while Q is not empty:
    u = entry from Q with smallest min_cost_via[]
    remove u from Q

    for each neighbor v from u:
      cost_via_u = min_cost_via[u] + cost(u, v)
      if cost_via_u < min_cost_via[v]:
        min_cost_via[v] = cost_via_u
        prev[v] = u
```

The preceding implementation maintains two arrays, each one having a length equal to the number of vertices in the graph:

- The first array, `min_cost_via`, tracks the minimum cost (distance) for reaching the source vertex from the i_{th} vertex in the graph.
- The `prev` array keeps track of the previous vertex in the optimal path leading from the source vertex to the i_{th} vertex.

At initialization time, we set all the entries in the `prev` array to `nil`. Additionally, all the entries in the `min_cost_via` array are initialized to a large number with the exception of the entry for the source vertex, whose entry is set to `0`. If we were implementing this algorithm in Go and path costs were `uint64` values, we would set the initial value to `math.MaxUint64`.

Dijkstra's algorithm is bootstrapped by placing all the graph vertices in a set called `Q`. The algorithm then executes a number of iterations equal to the number of vertices in the graph. At each iteration, we select vertex `u` from `Q` which has the *lowest* `min_cost_via` value and remove it from the set.

Then, the algorithm examines each neighbor `v` of the selected vertex `u`. If a lower cost path from `v` to the source vertex can be constructed by passing through `u`, then we update the `min_cost_via` entry for `v` and make `u` the predecessor of the optimal path to `v`.

The algorithm completes when all the vertices in set `Q` have been processed. The shortest path from the source vertex to any other vertex in the graph can be reconstructed by starting at the destination vertex and following the `prev` array entries until we reach the source vertex.

What's more, we can slightly tweak the preceding algorithm to obtain the original variant that answers point to point queries. All we need to do is terminate the algorithm after processing the destination vertex for our query. Those of you who are familiar with, or have implemented, the A* algorithm in the past will definitely notice a lot of similarities between the two algorithms. In fact, Dijkstra's algorithm is a special case of the A* algorithm where no distance heuristic is used.

Leveraging a gossip protocol to run Dijkstra in parallel

Dijkstra's algorithm is fairly straightforward to implement and its runtime can be sped up considerably with the introduction of specialized data structures (for example, min-heap or Fibonacci heap) for selecting the next vertex for each iteration. Let's take a look at how we can leverage the graph processing system that we have built to execute Dijkstra's algorithm in parallel.

To break the sequential nature of the original algorithm, we will swap out the next vertex selection step and replace it with a *gossip protocol*. Whenever a vertex identifies a better path to it via another vertex, it will *broadcast* this information to all its neighbors by sending them a `PathCostMessage`. The neighbors would then process these messages during the *next* super-step, update their own min-distance estimates, and broadcast any better paths, if found, to their own neighbors. The key concept here is to trigger a wavefront of path updates throughout the graph that can be processed by each vertex in parallel.

The first thing we need to do is to define the types for the following:

- The message that's exchanged by the vertices
- Storing the state for each vertex

Consider the following piece of code:

```
type PathCostMessage struct {
    // The ID of the vertex this cost announcement originates from.
    FromID string

    // The cost of the path from this vertex to the source vertex via
    // FromID.
    Cost int
}

func (pc PathCostMessage) Type() string { return "cost" }

type pathState struct {
    minDist    int
    prevInPath string
}
```

The `pathState` struct encodes the same kind information as the `min_cost_via` and `prev` arrays from the sequential version of the algorithm. The only difference is that each vertex maintains its own `pathState` instance, which is stored as the vertex value.

Next, let's try to put together a compute function for the graph. As you may recall from the previous sections, compute functions receive the following input arguments: a pointer to the graph, the currently processed vertex, and an iterator for the messages that are sent to the vertex during the previous super-step. At super-step *0*, each vertex initializes its own internal state with the maximum possible distance value:

```
if g.Superstep() == 0 {
    v.SetValue(&pathState{ minDist: int(math.MaxInt64) })
}
```

Then, each vertex processes any path announcements from its neighbors and keeps track of the path announcement with the minimum cost:

```
minDist := int(math.MaxInt64)
if v.ID() == c.srcID { // min cost from source to source is always 0
    minDist = 0
}
var via string
for msgIt.Next() {
    m := msgIt.Message().(*PathCostMessage)
    if m.Cost < minDist {
        minDist = m.Cost
        via = m.FromID
    }
}
```

After all the messages have been processed, we compare the cost of the best path from all the announcements to the cost of the best path we've seen so far by this vertex. If the vertex is already aware of a better path with a lower cost, we don't really need to do anything. Otherwise, we update the local vertex state to reflect the new best path and send out a message to each of our neighbors:

```
st := v.Value().(*pathState)
if minDist < st.minDist {
    st.minDist = minDist
    st.prevInPath = via
    for _, e := range v.Edges() {
        costMsg := &PathCostMessage{
            FromID: v.ID(),
            Cost:   minDist + e.Value().(int),
        }
        if err := g.SendMessage(e.DstID(), costMsg); err != nil {
            return err
        }
    }
}
v.Freeze()
```

Each outgoing `PathCostMessage` includes the cost of reaching each neighbor through the current vertex and is calculated by adding the cost for the next hop (the value associated with the outgoing edge) to the new minimum cost for reaching the current vertex.

Regardless of whether the best path to a vertex was updated or not, we always invoke the `Freeze` method on each vertex and mark it as processed. This means that the vertex will not be reactivated in a future super-step unless it receives a message from its neighbors. Eventually, all the vertices will figure out the optimal path to the source vertex and stop broadcasting cost updates to their neighbors. When this happens, all the vertices will end up in a frozen state and the algorithm will terminate.

We could definitely argue that this particular approach requires much more effort compared to the traditional sequential version. However, contrary to the sequential version of the algorithm, the parallel version can run efficiently on massive graphs that can be potentially distributed across multiple compute nodes.

The full source code and tests for the shortest path calculator from this section can be found in this book's GitHub repository in the `Chapter08/shortestpath` folder.

Graph coloring

The next graph-based problem that we will be trying to solve using our graph processing system is **graph coloring**. The idea behind graph coloring is to assign a color to each vertex in the graph so that no adjacent vertices have the same color. The following diagram illustrates an example graph whose vertices have been colored with the optimal (minimum possible) number of colors:

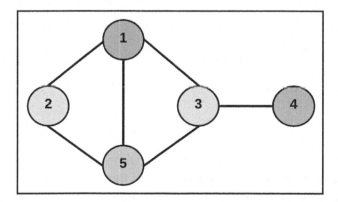

Figure 3: A graph with optimal coloring

Graph coloring has numerous real-world applications:

- It is frequently used by compilers to perform register allocation [2].
- Mobile operators use graph coloring as the means for solving the frequency assignment problem [9] where the goal is to assign frequencies from a limited frequency pool to a set of communication links so that there is no interference between links in the same vicinity.
- Many popular puzzle games such as Sudoku can be modeled as a graph and solved with the help of a graph coloring variant where the allowed set of colors is fixed (k-color graph coloring).

A sequential greedy algorithm for coloring undirected graphs

Calculating the optimal graph coloring is known to be NP-hard. Therefore, researchers have proposed greedy algorithms that produce good enough, but not necessarily optimal, solutions. The sequential greedy algorithm listed here works with undirected graphs and guarantees an upper bound of *d+1* colors where *d* is the maximum out-degree (number of outgoing edges) for all the vertices in the graph:

```
function assignColors(Graph):
  C holds the assigned color for each vertex
  for each vertex u in Graph:
    C[u] = 0

  for each vertex u in Graph:
    already_in_use is a map where keys indicate colors that are currently
in use
    for each neighbor v of u:
      already_in_use[ C[v] ] = true

    assigned_color = 1
    while already_in_use[ color ] is true:
      assigned_color = assigned_color + 1

    C[u] = assigned_color
```

The algorithm maintains an array called C that holds the assigned color for each vertex in the graph. During initialization, we set each entry of the C array to the value *0* to indicate that no color has been assigned to any of the graph vertices.

For each vertex u in the graph, the algorithm iterates its neighbor list and inserts the colors that have been already assigned to each neighbor into a map using the color value as a key. Next, the `assigned_color` variable is set to the lowest possible color value (in this case, *1*) and the `already_in_use` map is consulted to check whether that color is currently in use. If that happens to be the case, we increment the `assigned_color` variable and repeat the same steps until we finally land on a color value that is not in use. The unused color value is assigned to vertex u and the process continues until all the vertices have been colored.

An interesting fact about the preceding algorithm is that we can tweak it slightly to add support for handling pre-colored graphs. In this type of graph, a subset of the vertices have been already assigned a color value and the goal is to assign non-conflicting colors to the remaining vertices. All we need to do is the following:

- Set C[u] to the already assigned color instead of *0* during initialization
- When iterating the graph vertices, skip the ones that have already been colored

Exploiting parallelism for undirected graph coloring

Parallel graph coloring algorithms are based on the observation that if we split the graph into multiple *independent sets of vertices*, we can color those in parallel without introducing any conflict.

An independent set is defined as the collection or set of vertices where no two vertices share an edge.

To develop a parallelized version of the sequential greedy graph coloring algorithm from the previous section, we will be relying on a simple, yet effective algorithm proposed by Jones and Plassmann [6]. Before diving into the implementation details, let's take a few minutes to explain how the algorithm generates independent sets and how can we guarantee that our compute function will avoid data races while accessing the graph.

At initialization time, each vertex is assigned a random token. During each super-step, every vertex that hasn't been colored yet compares its own token value to the value of every *uncolored* neighbor. In the highly unlikely case that two neighboring vertices have been assigned the same random token, we can use the vertex ID as an extra comparison predicate to break the tie. The vertex with the highest token value gets to choose the next color using the same steps as the sequential algorithm while the neighboring vertices remain idle, waiting for their turn.

The concept of using tokens to enforce a coloring order guarantees that, at every super-step, we only color exactly one vertex from *each* independent set. At the same time, since connected vertices wait for their turn before they can pick a color, no data races can occur.

Just like we did with the shortest path implementation, we will begin by defining a type for holding the state of each vertex and a type that describes the messages that are exchanged between neighboring vertices:

```
type vertexState struct {
    token int
    color int
    usedColors map[int]bool
}

type VertexStateMessage struct {
    ID      string
    Token int
    Color int
}

func (m *VertexStateMessage) Type() string { return "vertexStateMessage" }
```

The `vertexState` struct keeps track of the token and colors that are assigned to the vertex. Furthermore, the `usedColors` map tracks colors that have already been assigned to the vertex neighbors. Vertices broadcast their state to each of their neighbors by exchanging `VertexStateMessage` instances. In addition to the token and color value, these messages also include a vertex ID. As we mentioned previously, the vertex ID is required for breaking ties while comparing token values.

Now, let's break down the compute function for this algorithm into small chunks and examine each chunk in more detail:

```
v.Freeze()
state := v.Value().(*vertexState)

if g.Superstep() == 0 {
    if state.color == 0 && len(v.Edges()) == 0 {
        state.color = 1
        return nil
    }
    state.token = random.Int()
    state.usedColors = make(map[int]bool)
    return g.BroadcastToNeighbors(v, state.asMessage(v.ID()))
}
```

First things first, each super-step iteration begins by marking *all* the vertices as inactive. This way, vertices will only be reactivated in subsequent super-steps when a neighbor gets to pick a color and broadcast its selection. Consequently, once the last remaining vertex has been colored, no further messages will be exchanged and all the vertices will be marked as inactive. This observation will serve as the termination condition for the algorithm.

Super-step *0* serves as an initialization step. During this step, we assign random tokens to all the vertices and have them *all* announce their initial state to their neighbors. If any of the vertices are pre-colored, their assigned colors will also be included in the broadcasted state update message. The `vertexState` type defines a handy helper method called `asMessage` which generates a `VertexStateMessage`, that can be sent to neighbors via the graph's `BroadcastToNeighbors` method:

```
func (s *vertexState) asMessage(id string) *VertexStateMessage {
    return &VertexStateMessage{
        ID:    id,
        Token: s.token,
        Color: s.color,
    }
}
```

Of course, the input graph may potentially include vertices with no neighbors. If these vertices have not been already pre-colored, we simply assign them the first available color, which in our particular implementation is color *1*.

The next block of code processes state announcements from the vertex neighbors. Before iterating each state message, each vertex sets its local `pickNextColor` variable to `true`. Then, the message list is iterated and the following occurs:

- If a neighbor has been assigned a color, we insert it into the `usedColors` map for the local vertex.
- If any of the neighbors has a higher token value or has the *same* token value but their ID string value is greater than the local vertex one, they have a higher priority for picking the next color. Therefore, the `pickNextColor` variable will be set to `false` for the local vertex.

Once all state announcements have been processed, we check the value of the `pickNextColor` variable. If the vertex is not allowed to pick the next color, it simply broadcasts its current state and waits for the next super-step, as follows:

```
pickNextColor := true
myID := v.ID()
for msgIt.Next() {
    m := msgIt.Message().(*vertexStateMessage)
```

```
        if m.Color != 0 {
            state.usedColors[m.Color] = true
        } else if state.token < m.Token || (state.token == m.Token && myID <
    m.ID) {
            pickNextColor = false
        }
    }

    if !pickNextColor {
        return g.BroadcastToNeighbors(v, state.asMessage(v.ID()))
    }
```

Otherwise, the vertex gets to select the next color to be assigned to it:

```
        for nextColor := 1; ; nextColor++ {
            if state.usedColors[nextColor] {
                continue
            }

            state.color = nextColor
            return g.BroadcastToNeighbors(v, state.asMessage(myID))
        }
```

Since some of the vertices in the graph might be pre-colored, our goal is to pick the *smallest* not used color for this vertex. To do this, we initialize a counter with the smallest allowed value and enter a loop: at each step, we check whether usedColors contains an entry for the nextColor value. If so, we increment the counter and try again. Otherwise, we assign nextColor to the vertex and broadcast our updated state to the neighbors.

In case you are having concerns about the space requirements for keeping track of the used colors on a per-vertex basis, we can actually do much better if we don't need to support potentially pre-colored graphs. If that happens to be the case, each vertex only needs to keep track of the *maximum* color value that's assigned to its neighbors. At color selection time, the vertex picks maxColor + 1 as its own color.

The full source code and tests for the graph coloring implementation from this section can be found in this book's GitHub repository in the Chapter08/color folder.

Calculating PageRank scores

Whenever someone hears the name Google, the first thing that would probably spring to mind is, of course, the widely popular search engine that made its appearance some time around 1997 and since then has consistently managed to eclipse all other competition in the search engine space.

The heart of Google's search engine technology is undoubtedly the patented PageRank algorithm, which was published in the 1999 paper by the Google co-founders, Larry Page and Sergey Brin [8]. Fortunately, the patent to the algorithm expired in June 2019; that's a great piece of news as it allows us to freely implement it for the Links 'R' Us project!

The PageRank algorithm treats all indexed web pages as a massive, directed graph. Each page is represented as a vertex in the graph, while outgoing links from each page are represented as directed edges. All the pages in the graph are assigned what is referred to as a *PageRank score*. PageRank scores express the importance (ranking) of every page compared to all the other pages in the graph. The key premise of this algorithm is that if we were to sort the results of a keyword-based search by both keyword match relevance and by their PageRank score, we would be able to increase the quality of the results that are returned to the user performing the search.

In the following sections, we will explore the formula for calculating PageRank scores and implement our very own PageRank calculator using the graph processing framework that we developed at the beginning of this chapter.

The model of the random surfer

To calculate the score for each vertex in the graph, the PageRank algorithm utilizes the model of the **random surfer**. Under this model, a user performs an initial search and lands on a page from the graph. From that point on, users randomly select one of the following two options:

- They can click any outgoing link from the current page and navigate to a new page. Users choose this option with a predefined probability that we will be referring to with the term **damping factor**.
- Alternatively, they can decide to run a new search query. This decision has the effect of *teleporting* the user to a random page in the graph.

The PageRank algorithm works under the assumption that the preceding steps are repeated in perpetuity. As a result, the model is equivalent to performing a random walk of the web page graph. PageRank score values reflect the *probability* that a surfer lands on a particular page. By this definition, we expect the following to occur:

- Each PageRank score should be a value in the *[0, 1]* range
- The sum of all assigned PageRank scores should be exactly equal to 1

An iterative approach to PageRank score calculation

To estimate the PageRank score for web page P from the graph, we need to take two factors into account:

- The number of links leading to P
- The quality of the pages linking to P, as indicated by their own individual PageRank scores

If we only took the number of links into account, we would allow malicious users to game the system and artificially boost the score of a particular target page by creating a large number of links pointing at it. One way that this could be achieved would be, for instance, by cross-posting the same link to online forums. On the other hand, if we were to use the PageRank scores of the source pages to *weight* the incoming link contributions to the target page, pages with just a few incoming links from reputable sources (for example, major news outlets) would get a much better score than pages with a greater number of links but from sources that are not as popular.

To figure out the score of a particular page, we need to be aware of the score of every page linking to it. To make matters even worse, pages might also link *back* to some or all pages that link to them. This sounds a bit like a chicken and egg problem! So, how does the calculation work? It turns out that we can actually calculate PageRank scores using an iterative algorithm that uses the following formula to calculate the PageRank score for page P:

$$PR(P, i) = \begin{cases} \frac{1}{N} & i = 0 \\ (1 - d) * \frac{1}{N} + d * \sum_{J \in LT(P)} \frac{PR(J, i-1)}{OutLinkCount(J)} & i > 0 \end{cases}$$

At step *0*, all the vertices in the graph are assigned an initial PageRank score of *1/N*, where N is the number of vertices in the graph. For the i_{th} step, we calculate the PageRank score by taking the weighted sum of two terms:

- The first term encodes the PageRank score contribution from a random page in the graph due to a teleport operation. According to the random surfer model, users can decide to stop clicking outgoing links from the page they are currently visiting and instead run a new query which lands them on page P. This is equivalent to creating a *one-off* connection to P. As a result, it transfers *1/N* units of PageRank to P.

- The second term encodes the score contributions for every page in the graph that has an outgoing link to *P*. In the preceding equation, *LT(P)* represents the set of pages that link to page *P*. For each page *J* in that set, we calculate the PageRank contribution to *P* by dividing its accumulated PageRank score from step *i-1* by the number of outgoing links. Essentially, at each step, each and every page *evenly distributes* its PageRank score to all outgoing links.

Since the two terms refer to mutually exclusive events that occur with specific probabilities, we need to weigh each term by its respective probability to make sure that all PageRank scores add up to 1.0. Given that users click outgoing links with a probability equal to the damping factor *d*, we need to multiply the first term by *1-d* and the second term by *d*.

Reaching convergence – when should we stop iterating?

By virtue of the fact that we are using an iterative formula to calculate PageRank scores, the more steps we execute, the more accurate results we will get. This raises an interesting question: how many steps do we need to execute so as to reach a desired level of accuracy for the calculated scores?

To answer this question, we must come up with a suitable metric that will allow us to measure how close we are to reaching convergence. For this purpose, we will be calculating the **sum of absolute differences (SAD)** for PageRank scores between two subsequent iterations using the following formula:

$$SAD(i) = \sum_{P \in G} |PR(P, i) - PR(P, i-1)|$$

The intuition behind this metric is that while the first few iterations will cause significant, in absolute terms, changes to the PageRank scores, as we get closer to convergence, the magnitude of each subsequent change will keep decreasing and become zero as the number of iterations reaches infinity. Obviously, for our particular use case, we need to execute a finite number of steps. Consequently, we have to decide on a suitable threshold value (for example, 10^{-3}) and keep iterating until the SAD score drops below the target threshold.

Web graphs in the real world – dealing with dead ends

The preceding formula for calculating PageRank scores assumes that all the pages link to at *least* one page. In real life, this is not always the case! Let's consider the graph shown in the following diagram. Here, all the vertices are connected to each other with the exception of vertex **D**, which has incoming links but no outgoing links. In other words, **D** is a dead end!

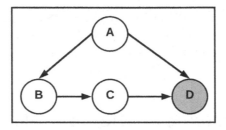

Figure 4: An example graph where vertex D is a dead end

Would the presence of dead ends in the input graph cause problems with our PageRank score calculations? So far, we know that at each iteration of the PageRank algorithm, pages evenly distribute their currently accumulated PageRank score across all outgoing links. In the case of a dead-end scenario like the one shown in the preceding diagram, vertex **D** would keep receiving the PageRank scores from every other vertex in the graph but *never* distribute its own accumulated score since it has no outgoing links. Therefore, **D** will end up with a relatively high PageRank score while all the other vertices will end up with significantly lower scores.

One strategy for mitigating this issue is to pre-process the graph, identify vertices that are dead ends, and exclude them from our PageRank calculations. However, dead-end elimination is far from a trivial task: the removal of an existing dead end might cause some of the vertices that used to link to it to transform into dead ends that also need to be removed and so on. As a result, implementing this solution and scaling it up to work with large graphs would be quite costly in terms of the required compute power.

A much better alternative, and the one that we will be using for our Go implementation, would be to treat dead ends as having an implicit connection to *all* the other vertices in the graph. This approach mitigates the problem of skewed scores by distributing the accumulated PageRank scores from each dead end back to all the vertices in the graph.

The naive approach for implementing this strategy using our graph processing system would be to have each dead-end node broadcast a message that would transfer a quantity equal to *PR/N* to every other vertex in the graph. Obviously, this idea would never scale for large graphs, so we need to come up with something better... What if, instead of following a push-based approach, we switched to a pull-based approach? In fact, this is actually a great use case for leveraging the graph processing system's support for aggregators! Rather than have each vertex with no outgoing links distribute its PageRank to every other vertex in the graph by means of message broadcasting, they can simply add their per-node contribution (the *PR/N* quantity) into an accumulator. We can then extend the PageRank formula with an extra term to take this *residual* PageRank into account when performing our calculations:

$$
PR(P, i) = \begin{cases} \frac{1}{N} & i = 0 \\ (1 - d) * \frac{1}{N} + d * [ResPR(i - 1) + \sum_{J \in LT(P)} \frac{PR(J, i-1)}{OutLinkCount(J)}] & i > 0 \end{cases}
$$

In the preceding formula, `ResPR(i)` returns the residual PageRank accumulated while executing the i_{th} step. Given that we treat dead ends as having outgoing links to every other node in the graph and that surfers click outgoing links with a probability equal to the damping factor *d*, we need to multiply the residual PageRank by the damping factor. This yields the preceding equation, which will form the basis for our PageRank score calculator.

Defining an API for the PageRank calculator

Now, let's discuss how we can implement a PageRank calculator on top of the functionality provided by the graph processing framework we have built. The full source code and tests for the PageRank calculator can be found in this book's GitHub repository in the `Chapter08/pagerank` folder.

The `Calculator` type is nothing more than a container for a `bspgraph.Graph` instance and a bunch of configuration options:

```
type Calculator struct {
    g   *bspgraph.Graph
    cfg Config

    executorFactory bspgraph.ExecutorFactory
}
```

The executorFactory points to the executor factory that will be used to create new Executor instances each time we want to execute the PageRank algorithm on a graph. By default, the Calculator constructor will use bspgraph.NewExecutor as the factory implementation, but users will be allowed to override it with a SetExecutorFactory helper method:

```
func (c *Calculator) SetExecutorFactory(factory bspgraph.ExecutorFactory) {
    c.executorFactory = factory
}
```

You might be curious why we allow the user to provide a custom factory for creating graph executors. The benefit of being able to specify a custom factory is that it permits us to intercept, inspect, and modify the ExecutorCallbacks object *before* it gets passed to the default factory. In Chapter 12, *Building Distributed Graph Processing Systems*, we will be leveraging this functionality to build a distributed version of the PageRank calculator. We will do all of this *without changing a single line of code* in the calculator implementation... Sounds impossible? Keep reading and all will be revealed in due course!

The following is the definition of the Config type, which encapsulates all the required configuration options for executing the PageRank algorithm:

```
type Config struct {
    // DampingFactor is the probability that a random surfer will click on
    // one of the outgoing links on the page they are currently visiting
    // instead of visiting (teleporting to) a random page in the graph.
    DampingFactor float64

    // The algorithm will keep executing until the aggregated SAD for all
    // vertices becomes less than MinSADForConvergence.
    MinSADForConvergence float64

    // The number of workers to spin up for computing PageRank scores.
    ComputeWorkers int
}
```

The validate method, which is defined on the Config type, checks the validity of each configuration parameter and populates empty parameters with a sane default value:

```
func (c *Config) validate() error {
    var err error
    if c.DampingFactor < 0 || c.DampingFactor > 1.0 {
        err = multierror.Append(err, xerrors.New("DampingFactor must be in
the range (0, 1]"))
    } else if c.DampingFactor == 0 {
        c.DampingFactor = 0.85
    }
```

```
    if c.MinSADForConvergence < 0 || c.MinSADForConvergence >= 1.0 {
        err = multierror.Append(err, xerrors.New("MinSADForConvergence must
be in the range (0, 1)"))
    } else if c.MinSADForConvergence == 0 {
        c.MinSADForConvergence = 0.001
    }
    if c.ComputeWorkers <= 0 {
        c.ComputeWorkers = 1
    }
    if c.ExecutorFactory == nil {
        c.ExecutorFactory = bspgraph.DefaultExecutor
    }
    return err
}
```

To create new `Calculator` instances, the clients populate a `Config` object that invokes the `NewCalculator` constructor:

```
func NewCalculator(cfg Config) (*Calculator, error) {
    if err := cfg.validate(); err != nil {
        return nil, xerrors.Errorf("PageRank calculator config validation
failed: %w", err)
    }

    g, err := bspgraph.NewGraph(bspgraph.GraphConfig{
        ComputeWorkers: cfg.ComputeWorkers,
        ComputeFn:      makeComputeFunc(cfg.DampingFactor),
    })
    if err != nil {
        return nil, err
    }

    return &Calculator{cfg: cfg, g: g, executorFactory:
bspgraph.NewExecutor}, nil
}
```

Before proceeding any further, the constructor has to validate the provided set of configuration options. After the configuration object has been successfully validated, the next step is to create a new `bspgraph.Graph` instance and store it in a newly allocated `Calculator` instance. To instantiate the graph, we need to provide a compute function that is parameterized by the provided `DampingFactor` value. This is achieved with the help of the `makeComputeFunc` helper, which closes over the `dampingFactor` argument and makes it accessible by the returned closure:

```
func makeComputeFunc(dampingFactor float64) bspgraph.ComputeFunc {
    return func(g *bspgraph.Graph, v *bspgraph.Vertex, msgIt
message.Iterator) error {
```

```
        // ....
    }
}
```

Since the underlying bspgraph.Graph instance is encapsulated in the Calculator type, we also need to provide a set of convenience methods so that we can add vertices or edges to the graph and access the raw bspgraph.Graph instance:

```go
func (c *Calculator) AddVertex(id string) {
    c.g.AddVertex(id, 0.0)
}

func (c *Calculator) AddEdge(src, dst string) error {
    // Don't allow self-links
    if src == dst {
        return nil
    }
    return c.g.AddEdge(src, dst, nil)
}

func (c *Calculator) Graph() *bspgraph.Graph {
    return c.g
}
```

Of course, once the PageRank algorithm converges, users should be able to query the PageRank scores that have been assigned to each vertex in the graph. This is facilitated via a call to the Scores method. The method implementation invokes a user-defined visitor function for each vertex in the graph with the vertex ID and assigned PageRank score as arguments:

```go
func (c *Calculator) Scores(visitFn func(id string, score float64) error)
error {
    for id, v := range c.g.Vertices() {
        if err := visitFn(id, v.Value().(float64)); err != nil {
            return err
        }
    }

    return nil
}
```

After creating a new `Calculator` instance and specifying the graph layout via calls to `AddVertex` and `AddEdge`, we are ready to execute the PageRank algorithm. To do so, we need to obtain a `bspgraph.Executor` instance by invoking the calculator's `Executor` method:

```
func (c *Calculator) Executor() bspgraph.Executor {
    c.registerAggregators()
    cb := bspgraph.ExecutorCallbacks{
        PreStep: func(_ context.Context, g *bspgraph.Graph) error {
            // Reset sum of abs differences and residual aggregators for
next step.
            g.Aggregator("SAD").Set(0.0)
            g.Aggregator(residualOutputAccumName(g.Superstep())).Set(0.0)
            return nil
        },
        PostStepKeepRunning: func(_ context.Context, g *bspgraph.Graph, _
int) (bool, error) {
            // Super-steps 0 and 1 are part of the algorithm
initialization; predicate should only be evaluated for super-steps >1
            sad := c.g.Aggregator("SAD").Get().(float64)
            return !(g.Superstep() > 1 && sad <
c.cfg.MinSADForConvergence), nil
        },
    }
    return c.executorFactory(c.g, cb)
}
```

The first task of the `Executor` method is to call the `registerAggregators` helper. This helper, whose implementation is outlined in the following code, is responsible for registering a set of aggregators that will be used by both the PageRank compute function and the executor callbacks that we will be defining next:

```
func (c *Calculator) registerAggregators() {
    c.g.RegisterAggregator("page_count", new(aggregator.IntAccumulator))
    c.g.RegisterAggregator("residual_0",
new(aggregator.Float64Accumulator))
    c.g.RegisterAggregator("residual_1",
new(aggregator.Float64Accumulator))
    c.g.RegisterAggregator("SAD", new(aggregator.Float64Accumulator))
}
```

Let's take a closer look at the role of each of these aggregators:

- `link_count` keeps track of the total number of vertices in the graph.
- `residual_0` and `residual_1` accumulate the residual PageRank quantities for even and odd super-steps. In case you are wondering, the reason why we need two accumulators is that, while calculating the PageRank scores for the i_{th} step, we need to add the residual PageRank from the *previous* step and at the same time accumulate the residual PageRank for the *next* step. While executing the i_{th} step, the compute function will read from the accumulator at index i%2 and write to the accumulator at index (i+1)%2.
- `SAD` is yet another accumulator that tracks the sum of absolute PageRank score differences between two sequential super-steps. The algorithm will keep executing while the accumulator's value is greater than the `MinSADForConvergence` configuration option.

The second responsibility of the `Executor` method is to define the appropriate set of callbacks for executing the PageRank algorithm and invoke the configured `ExecutorFactory` to obtain a new `bspgraph.Executor` instance, which is then returned to the caller.

The `PreStep` callback ensures that each of the required accumulators is set to a zero value prior to executing a new step. The handy `residualOutputAccName` helper function returns the name of the accumulator that will store the residual PageRank score to be used as input by the *next* super-step, as shown here:

```
func residualOutputAccName(superstep int) string {
    if superstep%2 == 0 {
        return "residual_0"
    }
    return "residual_1"
}
```

Once the executor successfully runs the compute function for each vertex in the graph, it invokes the `PreStepKeepRunning` callback, whose purpose is to decide whether a new super-step needs to be executed. The registered callback looks up the `SAD` aggregator's value, compares it to the configured threshold, and terminates the algorithm's execution once the value becomes less than the threshold.

Implementing a compute function to calculate PageRank scores

Now that we have completed our brief tour of the `Calculator` API, it's time to shift our focus to the most important part of the implementation: the *compute function*.

At the end of each super-step, vertices are expected to evenly distribute their PageRank score to their neighbors. Under our graph processing model, this task is facilitated by broadcasting a message. The `IncomingScoreMessage` type describes the payload for the exchanged messages:

```
type IncomingScoreMessage struct {
    Score float64
}

func (pr IncomingScoreMessage) Type() string { return "score" }
```

To bootstrap the calculator, we need to set the initial PageRank score for every vertex in the graph to the value *1/N*, where *N* is the number of vertices (pages) in the graph. An easy way to calculate *N* is to simply access the graph and count the number of vertices (for example, `len(g.Vertices())`). However, keep in mind that the end goal is to run the algorithm in a distributed fashion. In distributed mode, each worker node would only have access to a *subset* of the graph vertices. As a result, simply counting the vertices in the *local* graph instance would not produce a correct result.

On the other hand, aggregators provide an elegant solution to our vertex counting problem that works for both single- and multi-node scenarios. Super-step *0* serves as our initialization step: every compute function invocation increments the value of the `page_count` aggregator. At the end of the super-step, the counter will contain the total number of vertices in the graph:

```
superstep := g.Superstep()
pageCountAgg := g.Aggregator("page_count")

if superstep == 0 {
    pageCountAgg.Aggregate(1)
    return nil
}
```

For every other super-step, we apply the PageRank formula to estimate the new PageRank score for the current vertex:

```
pageCount := float64(pageCountAgg.Get().(int))
var newScore float64
switch superstep {
```

```
case 1:
    newScore = 1.0 / pageCount
default:
    // Process incoming messages and calculate new score.
    dampingFactor := c.cfg.DampingFactor
    newScore = (1.0 - dampingFactor) / pageCount
    for msgIt.Next() {
        score := msgIt.Message().(IncomingScoreMessage).Score
        newScore += dampingFactor * score
    }
    // Add accumulated residual page rank from any dead-ends encountered
during the previous step.
    resAggr := g.Aggregator(residualInputAccName(superstep))
    newScore += dampingFactor * resAggr.Get().(float64)
}
```

Before storing the new PageRank estimate for the current vertex, we calculate the absolute difference from the previous value and add it to the SAD aggregator, whose role is to track the *sum* of absolute score differences for the current super-step:

```
absDelta := math.Abs(v.Value().(float64) - newScore)
g.Aggregator("SAD").Aggregate(absDelta)

v.SetValue(newScore)
```

If the vertex has no neighbors (that is, it is a dead end), our model assumes that it is *implicitly* connected to every other node in the graph. To ensure that the PageRank score for the vertex is evenly distributed to every other vertex in the graph, we add a quantity equal to newScore/pageCount to the residual PageRank aggregator that will be used as input in the following super-step. Otherwise, we need to evenly distribute the calculated PageRank score to the existing vertex neighbors. To achieve this, we send out a series of IncomingScore messages that contribute a quantity equal to newScore/numOutLinks to every neighbor at the next super-step:

```
// Check if this is a dead-end
numOutLinks := float64(len(v.Edges()))
if numOutLinks == 0.0 {
    g.Aggregator(residualOutputAccName(superstep)).Aggregate(newScore /
pageCount)
    return nil
}

// Otherwise, evenly distribute this node's score to all its neighbors.
return g.BroadcastToNeighbors(v, IncomingScoreMessage{newScore /
numOutLinks})
```

That's basically it! The graph processing system we have developed made it quite easy to construct a fully functioning and vertically scalable PageRank calculator that can properly handle dead ends. All that remains is to hook it up to the link graph and text indexer components that we created in Chapter 6, *Building a Persistence Layer*, and we are in business!

Summary

We began this chapter by presenting the BSP model for building systems that can support out-of-core processing for massive datasets. Then, we applied the key principles of the BSP model so that we could create our own graph processing system that can execute user-defined compute functions for every vertex in the graph in parallel while taking advantage of all the available CPU cores.

In the second half of this chapter, we explored a variety of graph-related problems and came up with parallel algorithms that can be efficiently executed against graphs of any size. In the last part of this chapter, we described the theory behind Google's PageRank algorithm and outlined the formulas for calculating PageRank scores in an iterative way. We leveraged the graph processing system to build a fully fledged PageRank calculator that will form the basis for implementing the PageRank component for the Links 'R' Us project.

As we are getting closer and closer to completing the required components for our project, we need to plan ahead and design some APIs so that our components can exchange information between them. This is the main focus of the next chapter.

Further reading

1. Apache Giraph: An iterative graph processing system built for high scalability. URL. https://giraph.apache.org/.
2. Chaitin, G. J.: *Register Allocation & Spilling via Graph Coloring*. In: Proceedings of the 1982 SIGPLAN Symposium on Compiler Construction, SIGPLAN '82. New York, NY, USA : ACM, 1982 — ISBN 0-89791-074-5, S. 98–105.
3. Floyd, Robert W.: *Algorithm 97: Shortest Path*. In: Commun. ACM Bd. 5. New York, NY, USA, ACM (1962), Nr. 6, S. 345
4. GPS: A graph processing system. URL: http://infolab.stanford.edu/gps.

5. Hart, P. E. ; Nilsson, N. J. ; Raphael, B.: *A Formal Basis for the Heuristic Determination of Minimum Cost Paths*. In: IEEE Transactions on Systems Science and Cybernetics Bd. 4 (1968), Nr. 2, S. 100–107.

6. Jones, Mark T. ; Plassmann, Paul E.: *A Parallel Graph Coloring Heuristic*. In: SIAM J. Sci. Comput. Bd. 14. Philadelphia, PA, USA, Society for Industrial; Applied Mathematics (1993), Nr. 3, S. 654–669.

7. Malewicz, Grzegorz ; Austern, Matthew H. ; Bik, Aart J. C ; Dehnert, James C. ; Horn, Ilan ; Leiser, Naty ; Czajkowski, Grzegorz: Pregel: *A System for Large-scale Graph Processing*. In: Proceedings of the 2010 ACM SIGMOD International Conference on Management of Data, SIGMOD '10. New York, NY, USA : ACM, 2010 — ISBN 978-1-4503-0032-2, S. 135–146.

8. Page, Lawrence ; Brin, Sergey ; Motwani, Rajeev ; Winograd, Terry: *The PageRank Citation Ranking: Bringing Order to the Web.*(Technical Report Nr. 1999-66) : Stanford InfoLab; Stanford InfoLab, 1999. – Previous number = SIDL-WP-1999-0120.

9. Park, Taehoon ; Lee, Chae Y.: *Application of the graph coloring algorithm to the frequency assignment problem*. In: Journal of the Operations Research Society of Japan Bd. 39 (1996), Nr. 2, S. 258–265.

10. Valiant, Leslie G.: *A Bridging Model for Parallel Computation*. In: Commun. ACM Bd. 33. New York, NY, USA, ACM (1990), Nr. 8, S. 103–111.

Communicating with the Outside World

9

"An API that isn't comprehensible isn't usable."

- James Gosling

All software systems eventually need to exchange data with the outside world. In many cases, this is achieved via an API. This chapter provides a comparison between the REST and RPC patterns for building APIs and discusses some common API issues such as authentication, versioning, and security. The rest of this chapter explores the gRPC ecosystem in depth and concludes with a gRPC-based API implementation for the Links 'R' Us project.

The following topics will be covered in this chapter:

- Basic principles of RESTful APIs
- Strategies for securing APIs and pitfalls that you should avoid
- Approaches for API versioning
- gRPC as an alternative to building high-performance services
- Describing messages and RPC services using the protocol buffers definition language
- The different RPC modes (unary, client, server-streaming, and bi-directional streaming)
- Locking down gRPC APIs

Technical requirements

The full code for the topics discussed that will be within this chapter have been published to this book's GitHub repository in the `Chapter09` folder.

You can access this book's GitHub repository, which contains the code and all the required resources for each of this book's chapters, by pointing your web browser to the following URL: `https://github.com/PacktPublishing/Hands-On-Software-Engineering-with-Golang`.

To get you up and running as quickly as possible, each example project includes a Makefile that defines the following set of targets:

Makefile target	Description
deps	Install any required dependencies
test	Run all tests and report coverage
lint	Check for lint errors

As with all the other chapters in this book, you will need a fairly recent version of Go, which you can download at `https://golang.org/dl`.

Designing robust, secure, and backward-compatible REST APIs

Whenever an engineer hears the word API, **REST**, the acronym for **Representational State Transfer**, is undoubtedly one of the first words that springs to mind. Indeed, the vast majority of online services and applications that people use on a daily basis are using a REST API to communicate with the backend servers.

The proliferation of what we commonly refer to as RESTful APIs is indeed not coincidental. REST, as an architectural style for building applications for the web, offers quite a few enticing advantages over alternatives such as the **Simple Object Access Protocol (SOAP)**:

- **Ease of interaction**: A web browser or a command tool such as `curl` is all that is required to interact with REST endpoints
- The majority of programming languages ship with built-in support for performing HTTP requests
- It is quite easy to intercept HTTP requests (for example, via a proxy) and provided canned responses for testing purposes

- By virtue of the fact that RESTful APIs are built on top of HTTP, clients (for example, web browsers) can opt to cache large HTTP GET responses locally, query the remote server to figure out whether the cached data has become stale, and needs to be refreshed

REST APIs are built around the concept of accessing and mutating resources. A resource represents any piece of application data (for example, a product, user, order, collection of documents, and so on) that clients can operate on. A typical RESTful API exposes a set of endpoints that allow clients to **create**, **read**, **update**, and **delete** (**CRUD**) resources of a particular type. Each one of these actions maps to an HTTP verb, as follows:

- A new resource can be created via a POST request
- Existing resources can be retrieved via a GET request
- Resources can be fully or partially updated via a PUT or PATCH request
- A resource can be deleted via a DELETE request

While the REST architecture does not dictate the use of a particular data format for delivering data to clients, nowadays, JSON has become the de facto standard for implementing REST APIs. This can be largely attributed to the fact that it is lightweight, human-readable, and easy to compress. Having said that, you can still find several organizations out there (banks and payment processing gateways are a typical example) that provide RESTful APIs that expect and produce XML payloads.

Using human-readable paths for RESTful resources

One of the key ideas, and something that clients would typically expect when dealing with a RESTful API, is that each resource instance can be individually addressed via a **Uniform Resource Identifier** (**URI**). Since the format of URIs plays a significant role in conveying the API's resource model to the clients that will be consuming it, software engineers should always strive to come up with consistent URI naming schemes when designing new APIs or introducing new resource types to existing APIs.

The following opinionated set of conventions for naming resources can help you design APIs that are easier for end users to understand and work with:

- Resource names must always be nouns and never verbs or verb-like expressions. Verbs can be used as suffixes to indicate an action to be performed on a particular resource. For example, /basket/checkout triggers the checkout flow for the current user's basket.

- As an exception to the previously mentioned guideline, verbs related to CRUD operations should not be included as part of the resource URI; they can be inferred by the HTTP verb that's used when performing requests. In other words, instead of using a URI such as `/users/123/delete` to delete a user, clients should perform an HTTP **DELETE** request to `/users/123` instead.

- When referring to a specific resource instance by name, a singular noun must be used. For instance, `/user/account` returns the account details for the currently logged-on user. While it might be tempting to use the singular noun pattern to refer to a particular item within a collection (for example, `/user/123`), it is recommended to avoid this practice as it tends to create inconsistent paths for CRUD operations.

- A plural noun must be used when referring to a collection of resources or a specific resource instance within a collection. For example, `order/123/items` would return the list of items in order with ID `123`, while `/users/789` would return information about the user with ID `789`.

- Avoid appending trailing forward slashes (/) to the end of URIs. Doing so does not provide any additional information to clients and could lead to confusion; that is, is the URI complete or does it lack a portion of its path?

- RFC3986 [6] defines URIs as being case-sensitive. Therefore, for consistency purposes, it's good practice to stick to lowercase characters for URI paths. What's more, the use of hyphens (-) to separate long path segments can oftentimes result in paths that are much easier to read. Arguably, `/archived-resource` is much easier to read than `/archivedresource`.

The following table summarizes the combination of HTTP verbs and URI patterns for performing CRUD operations against a collection of products. The set of HTTP verbs and resource paths for working with a `products` resource are given as follows:

HTTP Verb	Path	Expects (JSON)	Returns (JSON)	HTTP Status	Description
POST	`/products`	A product entry	The new product entry including its ID	200 (success) or 201 (created)	Create a new product
GET	`/products`	Nothing	An array with product entries	200 (success)	Get a list of products
GET	`/products/:id`	Nothing	The product with the specified ID	200 (success) or 404 (not found)	Get product by ID
PUT	`/products/:id`	A product entry	The updated product entry	200 (success) or 404 (not found)	Update product by ID

| PATCH | `/products/:id` | A partial product entry | The updated product entry | 200 (success) or 404 (not found) | Update individual fields for a product by ID |
| DELETE | `/products/:id` | Nothing | Nothing | 200 (success) or 404 (not found) | Delete product by ID |

As you can probably surmise, the aforementioned patterns can also be applied to address resources that form hierarchies. For instance, to retrieve the set of permissions that have been assigned to the user with ID 123 within a security group with ID 789, `/security-groups/789/users/123/permissions` can be used as a path. In this example, the use of a forward slash to separate the security group and user resources implies the existence of a hierarchical relationship between them.

Controlling access to API endpoints

After defining the endpoints for referring to resources, the next logical step is to implement a mechanism for enforcing access control. For instance, while `/orders/123` and `orders/789` are both valid resource paths, they might belong to different users; obviously, we would expect that each user should only be able to access their own orders.

In a different scenario, a user might be able to list the users that belong to a particular security group by performing a GET request to `/security-groups/123/users`, but only an administrator would be allowed to add or remove users from that group (for example, by performing POST and DELETE requests to the same endpoint). A fairly common pattern for achieving this kind of granular access to resources is **Role-Based Access Control (RBAC)**.

To apply this pattern, we need to define a list of roles (for example, normal user, administrator, and so on) and associate each role with a set of access permissions. Each user of the system is assigned to one or more roles that the system consults when considering whether it should grant access to a particular resource or not.

Before we can go ahead and implement RBAC, we need to establish a mechanism for authenticating users prior to them attempting to access non-public API endpoints.

A lot of people tend to conflate the terms authentication and authorization when, in fact, they cannot be used interchangeably.

To avoid any confusion, let's spend a bit of time properly defining the two terms:

- **Authentication**: This proves that a particular entity (for example, a client making API requests) is who they claim to be by providing some form of credential. This is akin to displaying your passport when going through security at an airport.
- **Authorization**: This proves that an entity has a right to access a particular resource. For instance, a metro ticket grants you access to a train platform without you having to disclose your identity.

In the following two sections, we will be examining two popular approaches to handling authentication, namely, basic HTTP authentication over TLS and authorization to an external service provider via **OAuth2**.

Basic HTTP authentication

Basic HTTP authentication is probably the easiest and simplest way to implement an authentication layer for any API. Each client is provided either with a username and password tuple or with an API key. The latter approach is generally preferred as it allows application developers to generate multiple access keys that are tied to the same user account but can be independently managed, metered, and even revoked, should the need arise.

Whenever clients need to perform an authenticated API request, they have to encode their access credentials and attach them to the outgoing request by means of the standard HTTP authorization header. Clients construct the content of the header field in the following way:

1. Concatenate the username and password with a colon separator. So, if the username is `foo` and the password is `bar`, the concatenated result would be `foo:bar`. On the other hand, if the client is only provided with an API key, they need to use it as the username and concatenate it with a blank password. In other words, if the API key is `abcdefg`, then the concatenated result would be `abcdefg:`.
2. The concatenated credentials are then base64-encoded. For the username and password scenario we mentioned previously, the encoded output for `foo:bar` becomes `Zm9vOmJhcg==`.
3. The authorization method (basic) followed by a space character is prepended to the encoded credentials to yield the final header value, that is, `Authorization: Basic Zm9vOmJhcg==`.

The obvious caveat of this approach is that the client's credentials are transmitted in plaintext over the wire. Therefore, in order to avoid credential leaks, API requests need to be transmitted over a secure channel. In principle, this is achieved by establishing a TLS session between the client and the server.

Securing TLS connections from eavesdropping

It is also important to note that while TLS sessions do offer a secure channel for exchanging data, TLS encryption is not a panacea; it is still possible for a malicious adversary to intercept and decode TLS traffic by using a proxy to perform a **man-in-the-middle (MITM)** attack:

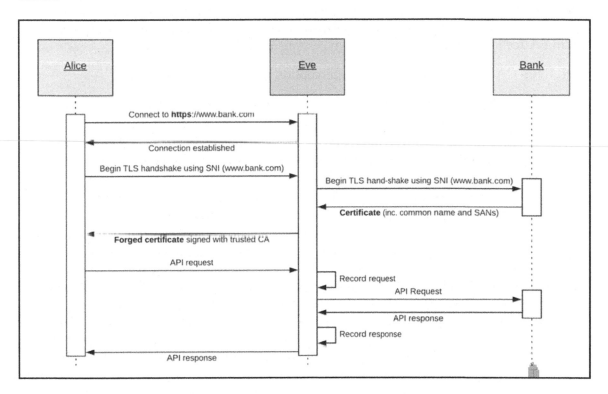

Figure 1: Using a MITM attack to intercept TLS traffic

The preceding diagram illustrates a scenario where **Alice** uses her bank's application on her mobile phone to query the balance in her bank account. **Eve** is a malicious actor trying to intercept the API calls between the application running on **Alice's** phone and the bank backend servers.

To achieve this, **Eve** needs to install a MITM proxy that will intercept and record outgoing connection requests from **Alice's** phone and either proxy them to the intended server or return fake responses. However, as we mentioned previously, the bank's server uses TLS-based encryption, so the bank application will not complete the TLS handshake steps unless the server provides a valid TLS certificate for the bank's domain.

In order for the MITM attack to succeed, the proxy server needs to be able to provide forged TLS certificates to Alice, which not only matches the bank's domain but is also signed by one of the globally trusted **Certificate Authorities (CAs)** that are preinstalled on **Alice's** phone.

Given that **Eve** does not have access to the private keys of any global CA, a prerequisite for forging certificates is for **Eve** to install a custom certificate authority on **Alice's** phone. This can be achieved either by exploiting a security hole via social engineering or simply by forcing **Alice** to do so if **Eve** happens to be a state actor.

With **Eve's** CA certificate in place, the interception process works as follows:

1. **Alice** tries to connect to a website, for example, `https://www.bank.com`.
2. **Eve** intercepts the request and establishes a TCP socket with **Alice**.
3. **Alice** initiates the TLS handshake. The handshake headers include a **Server Name Indication (SNI)** entry, which indicates the domain name it is trying to reach.
4. Eve opens a connection to the real `https://www.bank.com` server and initiates a TLS handshake, making sure to pass the same SNI entry as **Alice**.
5. The bank server responds with its TLS certificate that also includes information about the server **Common Name (CN)**, which in this case would normally be `www.bank.com` or `bank.com`. The certificate may also include a **Subject Alternative Name (SAN)** entry, which enumerates a list of additional domains that are also secured by the same certificate.
6. **Eve** forges a new TLS certificate that matches the information from the bank's TLS certificate and signs it with the private keys that correspond to the custom CA cert installed on **Alice's** phone. The forged certificate is returned to **Alice**.
7. **Alice** successfully verifies the forged TLS certificate, that is, it has the correct SNI and its parent certificate chain can be fully traced back to a trusted root CA. At this point, **Alice** completes the TLS handshake and sends out an API request to the bank API, which includes her access credentials.

8. **Alice's** request is encrypted with the forged TLS certificate. **Eve** decrypts the request and makes a record of it. Acting as a proxy, she opens a connection to the real bank server and sends **Alice's** request through.
9. **Eve** records the response from the bank server and sends it back to **Alice**.

Now that we are fully aware of the extent of damage that can be potentially caused by MITM attacks, what steps can we actually take to make our APIs more resistant to attacks like this? One approach to mitigating the issue of forged TLS certificates is to employ a technique known as public key pinning.

Each time we release a new client for our application, we embed the fingerprint of the public key that corresponds to the TLS certificate that's used to secure the API gateway. After completing the TLS handshake, the client calculates the public key fingerprint for the certificates that are presented by the server and compares it to the embedded value. If a mismatch is detected, the client immediately aborts the connection attempt and notifies the user that a potential MITM attack might be in progress.

Now, let's look at how we can implement public key pinning in our Go applications. The full source code for the following example is available in the Chapter09/pincert/dialer package of this book's GitHub repository.

Go's http.Transport type is a low-level primitive that is used by http.Client to perform HTTP and HTTPS requests. When creating a new http.Transport instance, we can override its DialTLS field with a custom function that will be invoked each time a new TLS connection needs to be established. This sounds like the perfect spot to implement the public key fingerprint verification logic.

The WithPinnedCertVerification helper, whose listing is shown in the following code, returns a dialer function that can be assigned to the DialTLS field of http.Transport:

```
func WithPinnedCertVerification(pkFingerprint []byte, tlsConfig
*tls.Config) TLSDialer {
    return func(network, addr string) (net.Conn, error) {
        conn, err := tls.Dial(network, addr, tlsConfig)
        if err != nil {
            return nil, err
        }
        if err := verifyPinnedCert(pkFingerprint,
conn.ConnectionState().PeerCertificates); err != nil { _ = conn.Close()
            return nil, err
        }
        return conn, nil
    }
}
```

The returned dialer attempts to establish a TLS connection by invoking the `tls.Dial` function with the caller-provider network, destination address, and `tls.Config` parameters as arguments. Note that the `tls.Dial` call will also automatically handle the validation of the TLS certificate chain that's presented by the remote server for us. After successfully establishing a TLS connection, the dialer delegates the verification of the pinned certificate to the `verifyPinnedCert` helper function, which is shown in the following code snippet:

```
func verifyPinnedCert(pkFingerprint []byte, peerCerts []*x509.Certificate)
error {
    for _, cert := range peerCerts {
        certDER, err := x509.MarshalPKIXPublicKey(cert.PublicKey)
        if err != nil {
            return xerrors.Errorf("unable to serialize certificate public
key: %w", err)
        }
        fingerprint := sha256.Sum256(certDER)

        // Matched cert PK fingerprint to the one provided.
        if bytes.Equal(fingerprint[:], pkFingerprint) {
            return nil
        }
    }
    return xerrors.Errorf("remote server presented a certificate which does
not match the provided fingerprint")
}
```

The `verifyPinnedCert` implementation iterates the list of X509 certificates presented by the remote server and calculates the SHA256 hash for each certificate's public key. Each calculated fingerprint is then compared to the pinned certificate's fingerprint. If a match is found, then `verifyPinnedCert` returns without an error and the TLS connection can be safely used to make API calls. On the other hand, an error will be returned if no match was found. In the latter case, the dialer will terminate the connection and propagate the error back to the caller.

Using this dialer to improve the security of your API clients is quite easy. All you need to do is create your own `http.Client` instance, as follows:

```
client := &http.Client{
    Transport: &http.Transport{
        DialTLS: dialer.WithPinnedCertVerification(
            fingerprint,
            new(tls.Config),
        ),
    },
}
```

You can now use this client instance to perform HTTPS requests to your backend servers, just like you would normally do, but with the added benefit that your code can now detect MITM attack attempts. A complete end-to-end example of using this dialer to perform public key pinning can be found in the `Chapter09/pincert` package of this book's GitHub repository.

Authenticating to external service providers using OAuth2

OAuth is an open standard for authorization that was initially proposed as an alternative to the basic authentication pattern that we examined in the previous section.

OAuth was designed to solve the following problem: let's assume that we have two services, A and B, which are typically unrelated to each other. As end users of service A, we wish to grant it access to some of our personal data that is hosted by service B. However, we want to avoid having to divulge our credentials so that we can access service B from service A.

Common use cases for using OAuth are as follows:

- Using a third-party service as a **single sign-on** (SSO) provider instead of creating individual accounts for each service we are interested in using. The login with X buttons that you commonly see when attempting to sign in to online services is a great example of this pattern. Furthermore, SSO providers often provide a dashboard where users can examine the list of services that they have granted access to and revoke their access at any point in time.
- Allowing a service to use another service's API on behalf of a particular user. For instance, a user can log in to a **Continuous Integration** (CI) service with their GitHub account and allow the CI service to use GitHub's API to query the user's repositories or to set up webhooks that will trigger CI runs when a pull request is created.

So, how does this work under the hood and how can we integrate the OAuth framework into our Go applications? For the remainder of this section, we will be focusing on the three-legged OAuth2 flow, which can facilitate data exchange between applications without sharing user credentials.

The three-legged OAuth2 flow involves the following four parties:

- **The Resource Owner**: This is the user who wants to give access to their data that's hosted by service B to service A without sharing their credentials.
- **The OAuth client**: In our scenario, service A wants to leverage an API offered by service B to obtain the user's data or to execute some action on behalf of the user.
- **The Resource Server**: In our scenario, service B hosts the user data that service A attempts to access.
- **The Authorization Server**: This is a part of service B and acts as the key component in this particular OAuth flow. It generates the appropriate set of access tokens that allow service A to access a specific subset of the user data hosted by service B.

The following diagram illustrates the three-legged OAuth2 flow:

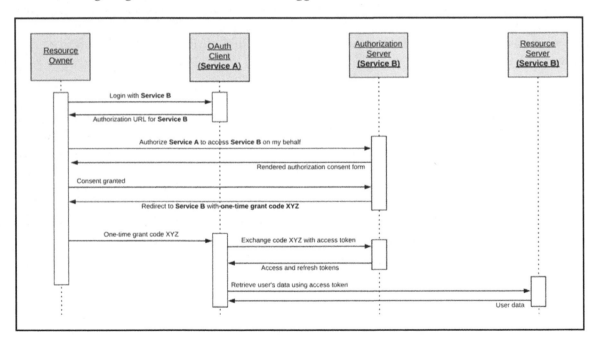

Figure 2: The steps in the three-legged OAuth2 flow

In order for service A to be able to trigger the three-legged OAuth2 flow, it needs to be registered with the authorization server for service B. Upon registering, service A will be assigned a unique client ID and client secret token. The client ID is a public token that allows the authorization server to identify the application that requires access. On the other hand, the client secret is private and is used to authenticate the OAuth client whenever it needs to contact the authorization server.

Let's examine what happens during the three-legged OAuth2 flow:

1. The user visits the website for service A and clicks the login with the B button.
2. The backend server for service A is configured with the API endpoints of the authorization server for service B. It returns an authorization URL to the user that embeds the following pieces of information:
    - The client ID token that is used by the authorization server to identify the service requesting access
    - A set of granular access permissions (grants) to be granted to service A
    - A URL hosted by service A, which the user will be redirected to by the authorization server once they consent to give access
    - A nonce value, which is to be used as a unique identifier for the authorization request
3. The user visits the authorization URL using their web browser.
4. The authorization server renders a consent page providing details (name, author, and so on) about the application that requires access to the user's data, as well as a description for the types of grants that can be requested.

An example of a consent page for authorizing access to a user's GitHub account can be seen in the following screenshot:

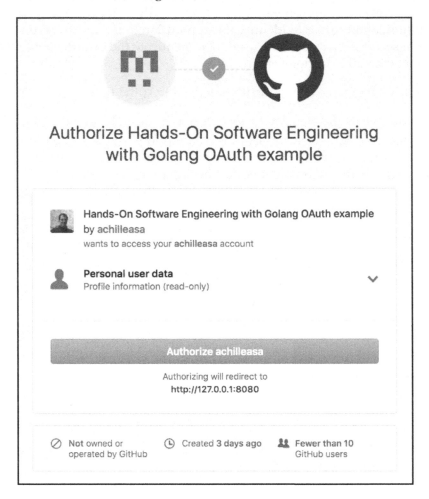

Figure 3: An example consent page for granting access to a user's GitHub account

5. Once the user reviews and authorizes the list of permissions that have been requested by service A and authorizes them, their web browser will be redirected to the URL included in the authorization request URL that was generated in *step 2*. The authorization server appends two additional values to that URL – the nonce value from the authorization request and an access code.

6. After receiving the access code and matching the incoming nonce value to the one included in the authorization request, the OAuth client contacts the server and attempts to exchange the obtained access co de with an access token.
7. The authorization server returns two tokens: a short-lived access token that can be used to access data on the resource server and a long-lived refresh token that the OAuth client can use to refresh expired access tokens.
8. The OAuth client contacts the resource server and obtains the required data using the access token.

In a similar fashion to the basic authentication mechanism we discussed previously, all outgoing requests to the resource server include an HTTP authorization header that the client populates with the obtained access token. The only difference is that instead of specifying a basic authorization method, this time, the client specifies bearer as the authorization method, that is, the transmitted header looks like Authorization: Bearer ACCESS_TOKEN.

Fortunately, most of the plumbing that's needed for implementing the three-legged OAuth flow in our applications is already provided by the golang.org/x/oauth2 package. All we need to do is implement the redirect handling logic we described in *step 5*. Let's begin by creating a new type called Flow to encapsulate the logic for our OAuth implementation. The type definition lives in the Chapter09/oauthflow/auth package and contains the following set of fields:

```
type Flow struct {
    cfg oauth2.Config

    mu sync.Mutex
    srvListener net.Listener
    pendingRequests map[string]chan Result
}
```

The cfg field holds a oauth2.Config value, which describes the OAuth provider's endpoints for:

- Authorizing requests
- Obtaining access tokens
- Refreshing access tokens when they expire

The srvListener field stores the net.Listener instance, which is where our implementation will listen for incoming OAuth redirects, while the pendingRequests map keeps track of all authorization attempts that are currently in flight. A sync.Mutex guards the access to both these variables and ensures that our implementation is safe for concurrent use.

To work with our package, users must create a new Flow instance by invoking the NewOAuthFlow constructor, whose implementation is shown in the following code snippet:

```
func NewOAuthFlow(cfg oauth2.Config, callbackListenAddr, redirectHost
string) (*Flow, error) {
    if callbackListenAddr == "" {
        callbackListenAddr = "127.0.0.1:8080"
    }
    l, err := net.Listen("tcp", callbackListenAddr)
    if err != nil {
        return nil, xerrors.Errorf("cannot create listener for handling
OAuth redirects: %w", err)
    }
    if redirectHost == "" {
        redirectHost = l.Addr().String()
    }

    cfg.RedirectURL = fmt.Sprintf("http://%s/oauth/redirect", redirectHost)
    f := &Flow{srvListener: l, cfg: cfg, pendingRequests:
make(map[string]chan Result)}

    mux := http.NewServeMux()
    mux.HandleFunc(redirectPath, f.handleAuthRedirect)
    go func() { _ = http.Serve(l, mux) }()
    return f, nil
}
```

The constructor expects three arguments:

- An oauth2.Config instance for the provider that the user wishes to authenticate against.
- A local address so that it can listen for incoming redirect requests. If not specified, the implementation will bind to the default address, 127.0.0.1:8080.
- A redirect URL that is sent to the remote server as part of the three-legged OAuth flow. If not specified, the implementation will use the address that the listener has bound to.

You might be wondering why users need to specify both the listen address and the redirect URL. When we are testing our application locally, these two values will always be the same. In fact, we can leave both parameters blank and our application will work just fine with the default values!

In this scenario, once we log in to the remote service, the OAuth server will redirect our browser to a loopback address that the browser can successfully connect to, given that it executes on the same machine as our OAuth redirect listener.

In a production deployment, our code would run on an isolated virtual machine hosted by a cloud provider. While our OAuth-handling code would still be listening to a loopback address, the users' browsers would only be able to connect to it through a load balancer with a public IP address. In such a case, the only way to make the three-legged OAuth flow work correctly is to provide a redirect URL whose DNS record resolves to the IP of the external load balancer.

Going back to the constructor implementation, the first thing that we need to do is bind a new net.Listener to the requested address and populate the value of the redirectHost parameter (if it's not been specified). Next, we overwrite the RedirectURL field of the user-provided OAuth configuration object with a URL that is generated by concatenating the value of the redirectHost parameter with a known static path (in this example, /oauth/redirect). Before returning the newly allocated Flow instance, the code spawns a go-routine and starts an HTTP server for processing incoming redirects from the remote authorization server.

After obtaining a new Flow instance, users can trigger a three-legged OAuth flow by invoking its Authenticate method, whose source is displayed in the following code snippet:

```
func (f *Flow) Authenticate() (string, <-chan Result, error) {
    nonce, err := genNonce(16)
    if err != nil {
        return "", nil, err
    }

    authURL := f.cfg.AuthCodeURL(nonce, oauth2.AccessTypeOffline)
    resCh := make(chan Result, 1)
    f.mu.Lock()
    f.pendingRequests[nonce] = resCh
    f.mu.Unlock()

    return authURL, resCh, nil
}
```

From the preceding code snippet, to distinguish between concurrent authentication requests, the `Authenticate` method generates a unique nonce value and associates it with every pending request. The generated nonce is then passed to the OAuth configuration's `AuthCodeURL` method to generate an authorization URL (pointing at the remote service) where the end user can log in using their web browser and consent to the grants that have been requested by our application.

The remaining steps of the OAuth flow happen asynchronously. To this end, the code allocates a buffered `Result` channel, appends it to the `pendingRequests` map while using the generated nonce as a key, and returns both the authorization URL and the result channel to the caller. The application must then redirect the end user's browser to the generated URL and block until a `Result` instance can be read off the returned channel.

The `Result` type encapsulates the result of an authorization attempt and is defined as follows:

```
type Result struct {
    authErr error
    authCode string
    cfg *oauth2.Config
}
```

Once the user completes the authorization process, the remote OAuth server will redirect their browser to the HTTP server that we launched in the `Flow` type's constructor. Next, we will examine the implementation of the `handleAuthRedirect` HTTP handler.

 In the following code snippets, the `r` variable refers to an `http.Request` instance, while the `w` variable refers to an `http.ResponseWriter` instance.

The first task of the HTTP handler is to parse and validate the parameters that were sent to us by the authorization server using the following block of code:

```
if err := r.ParseForm(); err != nil {
    w.WriteHeader(http.StatusBadRequest)
    return
}

nonce := r.FormValue("state")
code := r.FormValue("code")
```

The `ParseForm` method of the `http.Request` object is quite flexible in that it is able to decode parameters both from the URL (if this is a **GET** request) and the HTTP request body (if this is a **POST** request). If the call returns without an error, we use the handy `FormValue` method to extract the state parameter, which contains the nonce value that we embedded in our initial authorization request URL, and the code value, which contains the access code that was returned by the authorization server.

Next, the handler acquires the lock and indexes the `pendingRequests` map using the provided nonce value in an attempt to look up the result channel for the pending request. If no match is found, we print out a simple warning message that will be displayed to the user's browser and exit the handler. Otherwise, we remove the pending result channel from the map and publish a `Result` instance to it. The following block of code illustrates how the aforementioned steps are implemented:

```
f.mu.Lock()
resCh, exists := f.pendingRequests[nonce]
if !exists {
    f.mu.Unlock()
    _, _ = fmt.Fprint(w, unknownNonce)
    return
}
delete(f.pendingRequests, nonce)
f.mu.Unlock()

resCh <- Result{ authCode: code, cfg: &f.cfg }
close(resCh)

_, _ = fmt.Fprint(w, successMsg)
```

Once the HTTP handler writes the `Result` value to the channel, the application waiting on the channel unblocks and can invoke the result's `Client` method to obtain an `http.Client` instance so that it can make authenticated calls to the remote service. The returned `http.Client` instance is specially configured to automatically inject the obtained access token into all outgoing requests and transparently refresh it when it expires. The complete implementation for this method is outlined in the following code snippet:

```
func (ar *Result) Client(ctx context.Context) (*http.Client, error) {
    if ar.authErr != nil {
        return nil, ar.authErr
    }

    token, err := ar.cfg.Exchange(ctx, ar.authCode)
    if err != nil {
        return nil, xerrors.Errorf("unable to exchange authentication code
with OAuth token: %w", err)
```

```
    }

    return ar.cfg.Client(ctx, token), nil
}
```

As shown in the preceding code snippet, we complete the three-legged OAuth flow by exchanging the short-lived authentication code that's sent back to us by the authorization server with a long-lived access token. Finally, we pass the OAuth access token to the similarly-named Client method of the stored oauth2.Config value to create a token-aware http.Client instance, which is then returned to the caller.

To understand how all the pieces of the puzzle fit together, you can take a look at the Chapter09/oauthflow package in this book's GitHub repository. It contains a complete, end-to-end example of a simple CLI application that uses the code from this section to gain access to GitHub's API and to print out a user's login name.

Dealing with API versions

Once a public API for a particular service gets published and third parties begin using it, API developers need to be very careful to avoid introducing any changes that could cause third-party applications to stop working.

Imagine that we are building a payment processor similar to PayPal, Stripe, or Adyen. The core business value proposition of such a service is to provide a solid and easy-to-use API for handling payments. To this end, we expect hundreds or thousands of application instances (e-commerce sites, recurring subscription services, and so on) to be tightly coupled to our payment processor's public API.

Introducing new API endpoints would be a relatively trivial task; after all, none of the applications that depend on the service API will be using the new endpoints, so we can't really break something. On the other hand, changing existing or removing old API endpoints cannot be done without giving advance notice to all the users of our API.

The problem is compounded even further by the fact that each application integrator moves at a different pace; some may update their applications in a relatively short amount of time, while others may take months to come up with an update. Likewise, application integrators can also go out of business, leaving end users with no channel for receiving updates for already deployed application instances.

So, what if we were in complete control of both the server and the client? Would it be easier to introduce breaking changes if we were building, for instance, a mobile application and opted to use a proprietary API for communicating with the backend servers? The answer is still no! To figure out why this is the case, let's pretend that we are the operator that's responsible for running a ride-hailing application.

One strategy that we can use to our advantage is to ship our mobile application with a built-in force-update mechanism. When the application starts, it can contact our API servers and check whether an update must be installed before continuing. If that happens to be the case, the application can nag the user until they agree to update it. That would definitely work... unless, of course, our users were standing in the pouring rain on a Saturday night, desperately trying to get a taxi.

In such a scenario, displaying a "please upgrade the application to continue" message is definitely a sign of bad UX and would probably trigger many users to immediately switch to a competitor's application. In addition, some of our users might be owners of older phone models that cannot be upgraded to a newer version of our application because they either run on older hardware or because the phone manufacturer revoked the keys that are used to sign applications for OS versions that are not supported anymore.

In hindsight, the evolution of APIs is inevitable. Therefore, we need to come up with some kind of versioning mechanism for the RESTful APIs that would allow us to introduce breaking changes while at the same time still being able to handle requests from legacy API clients.

Including the API version as a route prefix

The most popular approach for implementing API versioning is for clients to include the requested API version as part of the requested API endpoint paths. For instance, /v1/account and /v2/account are versioned endpoints for retrieving the user's account details. However, the /account endpoint, when mounted under the v2 prefix, might return a completely different payload than the one mounted under the v1 prefix.

The choice of the version naming scheme is totally arbitrary and is up to the API designer to decide on. Common versioning schemes include the following:

- Numeric values; for example, v4
- API release dates; for example, 20200101
- Season names that coincide with new API releases; for example, spring2020

It is important to be aware that this particular versioning approach violates the principle that URIs should refer to unique resources. Clearly, in the previous example, `/v1/account` and `/v2/account` both refer to the same resource. What's more, a limitation of this approach is that we cannot version individual API endpoints.

Negotiating API versions via HTTP Accept headers

The version as part of the route approach works fine if we assume that the API server is always supporting the latest API version. In this scenario, the client can simply select the highest version that it can work with without any concern about the server hosting the API. What if this assumption does not hold?

Let's say that we are developing a chat server that users can download and deploy on their own infrastructure. Besides the chat server package, we also develop and maintain the official client for connecting to the chat server. The chat server exposes an API endpoint with a `/messages/:channel` path, which clients can invoke to obtain a list of messages for a particular channel.

In version 1 of the API, each returned message includes two fields: the name of the user who sent the message and the message itself. In version 2 of the API, the message payload is augmented with two additional fields, namely, a timestamp and a link to the user's avatar image.

Given that the version of the server that gets deployed is ultimately controlled by the end user, clients that connect to the server have no means of knowing which API version they can safely use. Granted, we could provide a dedicated API endpoint that clients could use to query the server version and then select the API version based on the server response. However, this approach is not really elegant and cannot really scale if we want to version specific endpoints but not the entire API.

Clearly, we need to introduce a sort of negotiation protocol that would allow the client and server to select the maximum common supported API version that is understood by both parties. As it turns out, the HTTP protocol already comes with such functionality baked in.

The client can use the HTTP Accept header to specify the API versions that it supports when it invokes the `/messages/:channel` endpoint. The contents of the Accept header must follow the media type specification format defined in RFC6838 [9]. For JSON-based APIs, the `application/vnd.apiVersion+json` template is typically used.

The vnd part indicates a vendor-specific media type. The apiVersion part is used to specify the supported version number, while the +json part indicates that the client expects a well-formed JSON document to be returned by the server. The media type syntax also allows clients to specify multiple media types as a comma-separated list. For the scenario we are currently discussing, a client that supports both API versions but prefers to use version 2 of the API would populate the header with the value application/vnd.v2+json, application/vnd.v1+json.

The server parses the header value, locates the highest supported API version, and routes the request to it or returns an error if none of the proposed client API versions are supported. When responding to the client with the payload, the server sets the value of the Content-Type header to indicate the API version that was actually used to process the request. The client parses this information and uses it to correctly unmarshal and handle the response payload.

Building RESTful APIs in Go

Nowadays, building RESTful APIs in Go is a fairly streamlined process. If you don't mind a little bit of elbow grease (for example, using regular expressions to manually extract parameters from request paths), you can build your very own HTTP router by leveraging the functionality offered by http.Mux, a component that ships with the Go standard library.

While building your own router from scratch would undoubtedly be a great learning experience, you should probably save quite a bit of time (and effort) and simply use one of the popular, battle-tested router packages such as gorilla-mux [5] or HttpRouter [3].

On the other hand, if fully-fledged web frameworks (combining a router, middleware, and perhaps an ORM into a single package) are your cup of tea, you will be positively surprised to find out that there are a plethora of packages to choose from! An indicative list of popular (based on the number of stars on GitHub) web framework packages would definitely include buffalo [1], revel [4], and gin-gonic [10].

All of these packages have one thing in common: they are all built on top of the net/http package. If you happen to be building APIs that can potentially receive a large (that is, more than one million requests per server) volume of concurrent requests, you may find that the net/http package actually becomes a bottleneck that caps your API's throughput.

If you ever find yourself in this predicament and don't mind programming against a slightly different API than the one offered by the net/http package, you should take a look at the fasthttp [8] package.

Building RPC-based APIs with the help of gRPC

gRPC [2] is a modern open source framework that was created by Google to assist the process of implementing APIs that are based on the **Remote Procedure Call (RPC)** paradigm. In contrast to the REST architecture, which is more suited for connecting web-based clients such as browsers to backend services, gRPC was proposed as a cross-platform and cross-language alternative for building low-latency and highly scalable distributed systems.

Do you know what the letter g in gRPC stands for? A lot of people naturally think that it stands for Google, a reasonable assumption given that gRPC was released by Google in the first place. Others believe that **gRPC** is a recursive acronym, that is, **gRPC Remote Procedure Calls**.

The fun fact is that both interpretations are wrong! According to the gRPC documentation on GitHub, the meaning of the letter g changes with every new gRPC release [11].

While the construction of high-performance APIs to link together microservices is the bread and butter of gRPC, as we will see in the following sections, it can also be used as a replacement for existing REST APIs.

Comparing gRPC to REST

While using REST as an architecture for building APIs provides several benefits, it also comes with a few caveats attached. Let's examine these caveats in more detail.

REST APIs are typically implemented on top of the HTTP/1.x protocol, which lacks proper support for managing and reusing connections. As a result, clients must establish a new TCP connection with the backend server and perform a complete TLS handshake every time they wish to invoke an API endpoint. This requirement not only incurs additional latency to API calls but also increases the load on backend servers (or load balancers, if you are doing TLS termination at the edge) since TLS handshaking comes with a non-insignificant computation cost.

In an attempt to mitigate this issue, HTTP/1.1 introduced the model of HTTP pipelining. In this connection-management mode, the client opens a single TCP socket to the server and sends a batch of successive requests through. The server processes the batch of requests and sends back a batch of responses that match the order of the requests sent in by the client. One limitation of this model is that it can only be applied to idempotent requests (HEAD, GET, PUT, and DELETE). Furthermore, it is susceptible to head-of-line blocking, that is, a request that takes a long time to execute will delay the processing of subsequent requests in the same batch.

On the other hand, gRPC is built on top of HTTP/2, which defines a new connection management model, that is, multiplexed streams. With this model, gRPC can support bi-directional streams that are interleaved and transmitted over a single TCP connection. This approach avoids the head-of-line blocking problem altogether and also allows the server to send push notifications back to the client.

The text-based nature of the HTTP/1.x protocol and the choice of JSON as the dominant serialization format for requests and responses makes RESTful APIs a bit too verbose to work with in use cases where the goal is to maximize throughput. While JSON payloads can definitely be compressed (for example, using gzip), we wouldn't be able to achieve the same efficiency as protocol buffers, the binary format that gRPC uses to compactly encode messages exchanged between the client and the server.

Finally, RESTful APIs do not mandate a particular structure for requests and response payloads. It's up to the client and server to correctly unmarshal JSON payloads and coerce the payload values to the correct type for the language they are written in. This approach could lead to errors or, even worse, data corruption.

For example, if the server tries to unmarshal a 64-bit integer into a 32-bit integer variable, the value might be truncated if the original value cannot be coerced into 32 bits. On the other hand, gRPC uses strongly-typed messages, which always unmarshal to the correct types, regardless of the programming language that's used by the client or the server.

Defining messages using protocol buffers

Protocol buffers are language- and platform-neutral mechanisms for serializing structured data in a very efficient manner. To achieve language neutrality, protocol buffers describe both messages and RPC services in a high-level **interface definition language** (**IDL**).

To start working with protocol buffers, we need to install the protoc compiler for our development environment. You can do this by compiling from source or by installing a pre-built binary release for your platform from `https://github.com/protocolbuffers/protobuf/releases`.

In addition, you will also need to install the Go output generator for the protoc compiler and the Go packages that are required for working with protocol buffers and the gRPC framework by executing the following commands:

```
go get -u google.golang.org/grpc
go get -u github.com/golang/protobuf/protoc-gen-go
```

Protocol buffer message definitions typically live in files with a `.proto` extension. They are processed by specialized tools that compile the definitions into language-specific types that we can use to build our applications. For Go, the protoc compiler is generally invoked as follows:

```
protoc --go_out=plugins=grpc:. -I. some-file.proto
```

The `--go_out` argument instructs the protoc compiler to enable the Go output generator. It expects a comma-delimited list of options that end with a colon character. In the aforementioned example, the option list includes a plugin option to enable the gRPC plugin. The argument after the colon character specifies the location for any file that's generated by the compiler. Here, we set it to the current working directory.

The `-I` argument can be used to specify additional include paths that the compiler scans when resolving include directives. In this example, we add the current working directory to the include path.

Finally, the last argument to the protoc compiler is the name of the `.proto` file to be compiled.

Defining messages

So, what does a protocol buffer message definition look like? Here is a short example:

```
syntax = "proto3";
package geocoding;

message Address {
  string query = 1;
  int32 page_number = 2;
  int32 result_per_page = 3;
}
```

In the preceding definition, the first line announces the version of the protocol buffer format that's going to be used for the rest of the file to the compiler. In this example, we are using version 3, which is the latest version and the one should be used for any new projects. The second line defines the name of the package, which will be used as a container for the generated protocol buffer definitions. As you can probably guess, the use of packages avoids conflicts between projects that define messages with the same names.

Message definitions begin with the `message` keyword, which is followed by the message name and a list of (field type, field name) tuples. Protocol buffer compilers recognize the following set of built-in types [7]:

.proto Type	Equivalent Go Type	Notes
double	float64	
float	float32	
int32	int32	Uses variable-length encoding
int64	int64	Uses variable-length encoding
uint32	uint32	Uses variable-length encoding
uint64	uint64	Uses variable-length encoding
sint32	int32	More efficient for storing negative integer values than int32
sint64	int64	More efficient for storing negative integer values than int64
fixed32	uint32	Always 4 bytes; more efficient for values > 228 than uint32
fixed64	uint64	Always 8 bytes; more efficient for values > 256 than uint64
sfixed32	int32	Always 4 bytes
sfixed64	int64	Always 8 bytes
bool	bool	
string	string	
bytes	[]byte	

As we mentioned in the previous sections, protocol buffers try to encode messages into a compact and space-efficient format. To this end, integers are generally serialized using variable-length encoding. Since this approach does not work that well for negative values, protocol buffers also define auxiliary types for (mostly) negative values (for example, `sint32` and `sint64`), which are encoded in a different and more space-efficient way.

Of course, we are not limited to just the built-in types. We can use already-defined message types as field types too! In fact, these definitions might even live in a separate `.proto` file that we include in the following way:

```
import "google/protobuf/timestamp.proto";

message Record {
  bytes data = 1;
  google.protobuf.Timestamp created_at = 2;
}
```

Another interesting feature of protocol buffers is enumerations, which allow us to define fields that can only be assigned a value from a fixed, predefined list of values. The following code expands the `Address` message definition so that it includes a type field to help us identify the address type:

```
message Address {
  string query = 1;
  int32 page_number = 2;
  int32 result_per_page = 3;
  AddressType type = 4; // We can only assign an address type value to this
  field.
}

enum AddressType {
  UNKNOWN = 0;
  HOME = 1;
  BUSINESS = 2;
}
```

The `enum` block defines the list of constants that can be assigned to the newly introduced type field. One important thing to keep in mind is that every enumeration list must include a constant that maps to the zero value as its first element. This serves as the default value for the field.

Versioning message definitions

Each field in a protocol buffer message is assigned a unique ID. The most common pattern is to assign IDs in an incremental fashion, starting from 1. When a field is serialized to the wire format, the serializer emits a small header that contains information about the field type, its size (for variable-sized fields), and its ID.

The receiver scans the header and checks whether a field with that ID is present in its local message definition. If so, the field value is unserialized from the stream to the appropriate field. Otherwise, the receiver uses the information in the header to skip over any fields it does not recognize.

This feature is extremely important as it forms the basis for versioning message definitions. Since message definitions evolve over time, new fields can be added or existing fields may be reordered without breaking existing consumers who are working with messages that have been compiled from older .proto files.

Representing collections

What's more, protocol buffers can also model two types of collections, namely, lists and maps. To create a list of items, all we need to do is add the repeated keyword as a prefix of the field's type. On the other hand, maps are defined with a special notation, that is, map<K, V>, where K and V represent the types for the map keys and values. The following snippet is an example of defining collections:

```
message User {
    string id = 1;
    string name = 2;
}

message Users {
    repeated User user_list = 1;
    map<string, User> user_by_id = 2;
}
```

When compiled to Go code, the fields for the Users message will be mapped to a []User type and a map[string]User type, respectively.

Modeling field unions

One frequent requirement for many kinds of applications is the ability to model unions. A union is a special kind of value that can have multiple representations, all of which point to the same location in memory. The use of shared memory implies that every time we write a value to a particular union field, any attempt to read one of the other union fields will result in garbled data.

The concept of unions extends quite nicely to protocol buffers. If you are working with messages that contain multiple fields where, at most, one field can be set at any given time, you can reduce the amount of required memory by grouping all these fields in a union.

A union definition begins with the `oneof` keyword, followed by the field name and a list of fields that comprise the union. The following snippet shows a simple example that demonstrates a very common API use case:

```
message CreateAccountResponse {
  string correlation_id = 1;
  oneof payload {
    Account account = 2;
    Error error = 3;
  }
}
```

In this example, all the responses have an associated correlation ID value. However, depending on the outcome of the API call invocation, the response payload will either contain an `Account` or an `Error`.

After compiling the aforementioned message definition, the protoc compiler will generate two special types, namely, `CreateAccountResponse_Account` and `CreateAccountResponse_Error`, that can be assigned to the `Payload` field of the `CreateAccountResponse` type:

```
type CreateAccountResponse_Account struct {
    Account *Account `protobuf:"bytes,1,opt,name=account,proto3,oneof"`
}

type CreateAccountResponse_Error struct {
    Error *Error `protobuf:"bytes,2,opt,name=error,proto3,oneof"`
}
```

To prevent other types from being assigned to the `Payload` field, the protoc compiler uses an interesting trick: it defines a private interface with an unexported dummy method and arranges it so that only the previous two type definitions implement it:

```
type isCreateAccountResponse_Payload interface {
    isCreateAccountResponse_Payload()
}

func (*CreateAccountResponse_Account) isCreateAccountResponse_Payload() {}
func (*CreateAccountResponse_Error) isCreateAccountResponse_Payload() {}
```

The protoc compiler specifies the interface mentioned in the preceding code snippet as the type of the `Payload` field, thus making it a compile-time error to assign any other type to the field. Moreover, to facilitate the retrieval of the union values, the compiler will also generate `GetAccount` and `GetError` helpers on the `CreateAccountResponse` type. These helpers peek into the `Payload` field's contents and either return the assigned value (`Account` or `Error`) or `nil` if no value of that type has been assigned to the union field.

The Any type

When building event-driven systems, a common pattern is to define a top-level message that acts as an envelope for different event payloads. Since new event types may be added (or removed) at any point in time, using a union is simply not going to suffice. Furthermore, the following are from the standpoint of event consumers:

- Consumers might ship with older `.proto` versions than the event producers do. It is quite possible for them to encounter an event payload that they don't really know how to decode.
- Some consumers may only be interested in processing a *subset* of the events. In such a scenario, consumers should only decode the messages they care about and skip over all other messages.

To cater for such cases, we can use the `Any` type to define our envelope message:

```
import "google/protobuf/any.proto";

message Envelope {
    string id = 1;
    google.protobuf.Any payload = 2;
}
```

The `Any` type, as the name implies, can store any protocol buffer message. Internally, this is achieved by storing a serialized version of the message, as well as a string identifier that describes the type of message stored within. The type identifier has the form of a URL and is constructed by concatenating `type.googleapis.com/` with the message name. The `ptypes` package (you can find it at www.github.com/golang/protobuf/ptypes) provides several useful helpers for dealing with `Any` messages.

The following code is an example of how we would populate an `Envelope` instance:

```
func wrapInEnvelope(id string, payload proto.Message) (*Envelope, error) {
    any, err := ptypes.MarshalAny(payload)
    if err != nil {
        return nil, err
```

```
    }

    return &Envelope{
        Id: id,
        Payload: any,
    }, nil
}
```

The `MarshalAny` helper takes any value that implements the `proto.Message` interface and serializes it into an `Any` message, which we then assign to the `Payload` field of the `Envelope` type.

On the consumer end, we can use the following block of code to process incoming envelopes:

```
func handleEnvelope(env *Envelope) error {
    if env.Payload == nil {
        return nil
    }

    switch env.Payload.GetTypeUrl() {
    case "type.googleapis.com/Record":
        var rec *Record
        if err := ptypes.UnmarshalAny(env.Payload, &rec); err != nil {
            return err
        }
        return handleRecord(rec)
    default:
        return ErrUnknownMessageType
    }
}
```

Essentially, the handler switches on the message type and uses the `UnmarshalAny` helper to unserialize and handle supported messages. On the other hand, if the message type is unknown or not one that the consumer is interested in, they can either skip it or return an error, which is what is happening in the preceding code.

After defining the set of messages that we want to use in our application using the protocol buffer definition language, the next logical step is to create RPCs that make use of them! In the following section, we will explore how we can enable the *grpc* plugin and have the protoc compiler automatically generate the required code stubs for our RPCs.

Implementing RPC services

The gRPC framework leverages the stream multiplexing capabilities of HTTP/2 so that it can handle both synchronous and asynchronous RPCs. The protoc compiler, when invoked with the *grpc* plugin enabled, will generate the following:

- Client and server **interfaces** for every RPC service definition in the compiled .proto file. For a service named Foo, the compiler will generate a FooServer and a FooClient interface. This is quite a useful feature as it allows us to inject mocked clients into our code at test time.
- Complete client implementation for each service that adheres to the generated client interface.
- A helper function to register our service implementation with a gRPC server instance. Once again, for a service called Foo, the compiler will generate a function with a signature similar to RegisterFooServer(*grpc.Server, FooServer).

The following short code snippet demonstrates how we can create a new gRPC server, register our implementation for the Foo service, and start serving incoming RPCs:

```
func serve(addr string, serverImpl FooServer) error {
    l, err := net.Listen("tcp", addr)
    if err != nil {
        return err
    }
    grpcServer := grpc.NewServer()
    RegisterFooServer(grpcServer, serverImpl)
    return grpcServer.Serve(l)
}
```

In the following four sections, we will examine the different types of RPC modes that are supported by the gRPC framework.

Unary RPCs

A unary RPC is equivalent to the request-response model that's used in traditional RESTful APIs. In the following example, we are defining a service with the name AccountService that exposes a CreateAccount method that receives CreateAccountRequest as input and returns a CreateAccountResponse to the caller:

```
message CreateAccountRequest {
    string user_name = 1;
    string password = 2;
```

```
      string email = 3;
   }

   message CreateAccountResponse {
      string account_id = 1;
   }

   service AccountService {
      rpc CreateAccount (CreateAccountRequest) returns (CreateAccountResponse);
   }
```

Defining the server handler is also quite similar to a regular RESTful API. Consider the following code:

```
   var _ AccountServiceServer = (*server)(nil)

   func (*server) CreateAccount(_ context.Context, req *CreateAccountRequest)
   (*CreateAccountResponse, error) {
      accountID, err := createAccount(req)
      if err != nil {
          return nil, err
      }

      return &CreateAccountResponse{AccountId: accountID}, nil
   }
```

To be able to register our server implementation with gRPC, we need to implement the AccountServiceServer interface. The server-side implementation in the listing (given in the preceding code snippet) receives a CreateAccountRequest message as an argument. It invokes the createAccount helper, which validates the request, creates the new account record, and returns its ID. Then, a new CreateAccountResponse instance is created and returned to the client.

On the client side, things are also quite simple. The following code shows that the accountAPI type simply offers a friendly API for abstracting the RPC call to the server:

```
   func (a *accountAPI) CreateAccount(account model.Account) (string, error) {
      req := makeCreateAccountRequest(account)
      res, err := a.accountCli.CreateAccount(context.Background(), req)
      if err != nil {
          return "", err
      }
      return res.AccountId, nil
   }
```

The method receives a model instance that describes the account to be created, converts it into `CreateAccountInstance`, and sends it to the server via the `AccountServiceClient` instance that was injected at construction time. Upon receiving a response, the client extracts the ID that was assigned to the new account and returns it to the caller.

Server-streaming RPCs

In a server-streaming RPC scenario, the client initiates an RPC on the server and receives a stream of responses. Clients block reading on the stream until new data becomes available or the server closes the stream. In the latter case, the client read request will return an `io.EOF` error to indicate that no more data is available.

In the following example, we are defining a service that streams price updates for a particular cryptocurrency:

```
message CryptoPriceRequest {
    string crypto_type = 1;
}

message CryptoPrice {
    double price = 1;
}

service PriceService {
    rpc StreamCryptoPrice (CryptoPriceRequest) returns (stream CryptoPrice);
}
```

The following code shows the server-side implementation for the `StreamCryptoPrice` RPC:

```
var _ PriceServiceServer = (*server)(nil)

func (*server) StreamCryptoPrice(req *CryptoPriceRequest, resSrv
PriceService_StreamCryptoPriceServer) error {
    for price := range priceStreamFor(req.CryptoType) {
        if err := resSrv.Send(&CryptoPrice{Price: price}); err != nil {
            return err
        }
    }
    return nil
}
```

The StreamCryptoPrice signature shown in the preceding code snippet is different than the unary RPC signature we examined in the previous section. Besides the incoming request, the handler also receives a helper type that the protoc compiler created for us to deal with the streaming aspects of this particular RPC call.

The server handler calls out to the priceStreamFor helper (implementation omitted) to obtain a channel where price updates for the requested currency type are posted. Once a new price has been received, the server code invokes the Send method on the provided stream helper to stream a new response to the client. Once the server handler returns (for example, when the price stream channel closes), gRPC will automatically shut down the stream and send an io.EOF error to the client, whose implementation is shown in the following code block:

```
func (a *priceAPI) ListPrices(cryptoType string) error {
    stream, err := a.priceCli.StreamCryptoPrice(context.Background(),
&CryptoPriceRequest{CryptoType: cryptoType})
    if err != nil {
        return err
    }

    for {
        res, err := stream.Recv()
        if err != nil {
            if err == io.EOF {
                return nil
            }
            return err
        }
        updateListing(cryptoType, res.Price)
    }
}
```

The client API wrapper uses the injected PriceServiceClient instance to initiate the RPC and obtain a stream where price updates can be read from. The client then enters an infinite for loop where it blocks on the stream's Recv method until a new price update (or an error) is received.

Client-streaming RPCs

Client-streaming RPCs are the opposite of server-streaming RPCs. In this case, it's the client that streams data to the server. Once the server has received *all* the data, it replies with a *single* response.

In the following example, we are defining a service that receives a stream of metric values from the client and responds with a set of aggregated statistics (count, min, max, and avg value) for the entire batch:

```
syntax = "proto3";

message Observation {
  double value = 1;
}

message StatsResponse {
  int32 count = 1;
  double min = 2;
  double max = 3;
  double avg = 4;
}

service StatsService {
  rpc CalculateStats (stream Observation) returns (StatsResponse);
}
```

The following block of code builds on top of the functionality offered by the RPC client for this service and exposes an API for calculating the statistics for a stream of values that are read off a caller-provided Go channel:

```
func (a *statsAPI) GetStats(valueCh <-chan float32) (*Stats, error) {
    stream, err := a.statsCli.CalculateStats(context.Background())
    if err != nil {
        return nil, err
    }
    for val := range valueCh {
        if err := stream.Send(&Observation{Value: val}); err != nil {
            return nil, err
        }
    }
    res, err := stream.CloseAndRecv()
    if err != nil {
        return nil, err
    }
    return makeStats(res), err
}
```

As shown in the preceding code snippet, the GetStats implementation initially makes a call to the underlying RPC client's CalculateStats method and obtains a (client-side) stream helper. With the help of a range loop, each value from the provided valueCh is wrapped into a new Observation message and transmitted to the server for processing. Once the client has sent all observed values to the server, it invokes the CloseAndRecv method, which performs two tasks:

- It notifies the server that no more data is available
- It blocks until the server returns a StatsResponse

Next, we will take a look at the server-side implementation for the aforementioned RPC:

```
var _ StatsServiceServer = (*server)(nil)

func (*server) CalculateStats(statsSrv StatsService_CalculateStatsServer)
error {
    var observations []*Observation
    for {
        stat, err := statsSrv.Recv()
        if err == nil {
            if err == io.EOF {
                return statsSrv.SendAndClose(calcStats(observations))
            }

            return err
        }
        observations = append(observations, stat)
    }
}
```

The server reads incoming Observation instances from the stream that's passed as an argument to CalculateStats and appends them to a slice. Once the server detects (via the presence of an io.EOF error) that the client has transmitted all data, it passes the collected observations slice to the calcStats helper, which calculates the statistics for the batch and returns them as a StatsResponse message that the server forwards to the client.

Bi-directional streaming RPCs

The last RPC mode that we will explore is bi-directional streaming. This mode combines client- and server-side streaming and provides us with two independent channels where the client and server can *asynchronously* publish and consume messages.

To understand how this mode works, let's examine the definition for an asynchronous Echo service:

```
message EchoMessage {
   string message = 1;
}

service EchoService {
   rpc Echo (stream EchoMessage) returns (stream EchoMessage);
}
```

The server-side logic for the echo service is not that interesting. As shown in the following code snippet, the server runs a for loop where it reads the next message from the client and echoes it back. The server's for loop keeps executing until the client terminates the RPC:

```
func (*server) Echo(echoSrv EchoService_EchoServer) error {
    for {
        msg, err := echoSrv.Recv()
        if err != nil {
            if err == io.EOF {
                return nil
            }
            return err
        }

        if err := echoSrv.Send(msg); err != nil {
            return err
        }
    }
}
```

Now, let's take a look at the client implementation, which turns out to be a bit more convoluted since we need to deal with two asynchronous streams. In a typical bi-directional RPC implementation, we would spin up a go-routine to handle each end of the streams. However, to keep this example as simple as possible, we will only use a go-routine to process echo responses from the server, as shown in the following code snippet:

```
func (a *echoAPI) Echo(msgCount int) error {
    stream, err := a.echoCLI.Echo(context.Background())
    if err != nil {
        return err
    }

    errCh := make(chan error, 1)
    go processEcho(stream, errCh)
    if err := sendEcho(stream, msgCount); err != nil {
```

```
        return err
    }
    for err := range errCh {
        return err
    }
    return nil
}
```

As shown in the preceding code snippet, the client invokes the Echo method on the echo service client and obtains a helper object (assigned to a variable called stream) to assist us with sending and receiving streaming data to and from the server. We then spin up a go-routine to execute processEcho, which is the function that's responsible for handling incoming echo responses. The function receives the stream object we obtained as an argument and a buffered error channel for reporting received errors.

The following code shows the implementation of processEcho:

```
func processEcho(stream EchoService_EchoClient, errCh chan<- error) {
    defer close(errCh)
    for {
        msg, err := stream.Recv()
        if err != nil {
            if err != io.EOF {
                errCh <- err
            }
            return
        }
        fmt.Printf("Received echo for: %q\n", msg)
    }
}
```

The receiving end is almost identical to the server-side implementation. We keep reading echo messages from the stream until we get an error. If the Recv method returns an error other than io.EOF, we write it to the error channel prior to returning it.

Note that, in the preceding code snippet, the error channel is *always closed* when the function returns. The Echo method exploits this behavior so that it blocks until processEcho returns and dequeues emitted errors by using a for loop to range on errCh.

While the `processEcho` function is running in the background, the code calls out to `sendEcho`, a *synchronous* function that sends out `msgCount` echo requests and then returns:

```go
func sendEcho(stream EchoService_EchoClient, msgCount int) error {
    for i := 0; i < msgCount; i++ {
        if err := stream.Send(&EchoMessage{Message: fmt.Sprint(i)}); err != nil {
            return err
        }
    }
    return stream.CloseSend()
}
```

So, how do we terminate this RPC? The call to the `CloseSend` method terminates the upstream channel to the server and causes the `Recv` method in the *server-side* code to return an `io.EOF` error. This triggers the server handler to exit and subsequently close its downstream channel to the client.

The `sendEcho` function returns to `Echo`, which then waits for `processEcho` to exit. As soon as the server terminates the downstream channel, the `Recv` call in `processEcho` will also return an `io.EOF` error and cause the `processEcho` go-routine to return. This last step unblocks the `Echo` call, which can now return to its caller.

Security considerations for gRPC APIs

The constructor for each of the RPC clients that the protoc compiler generated for you expects a `grpc.Connection` argument. This is intentional as a single remote server might expose multiple RPC services. Given that HTTP/2 supports request multiplexing, it makes sense to instantiate a single connection to the server and share it between the various RPC clients.

So, how can we obtain a `grpc.Connection` instance? The `grpc` package provides a convenience helper called `Dial`, which handles all the low-level details for establishing a connection to a gRPC server. The `Dial` function expects the address of the gRPC server we want to connect to and a variadic list of `grpc.DialOption` values.

At this point, it is important to note that the gRPC dialer assumes that the remote server will be secured with TLS and will fail to establish a connection if this happens not to be the case. We can definitely come up with scenarios where the use of TLS might not be required:

- We might be running a local gRPC server on our development machine
- We might spin up a gRPC server as part of a test
- All of our backend services might be running in a private subnet that can't be reached from the internet

To cater for such use cases, we can force gRPC to establish connections to non-TLS servers by providing the `grpc.WithInsecure()` dial option to the `Dial` function.

If you do opt for the recommended approach and use TLS everywhere, you will be pleasantly surprised to find that the methods for securing RESTful APIs that we discussed at the beginning of this chapter can also be applied to gRPC! The gRPC framework allows you to configure security at two different levels, namely, at the **connection** and at the **application** level.

At the connection level, gRPC allows us to manually configure the options for the TLS handshake with the help of the `grpc.WithTransportCredentials` dial option, which takes a `credentials.TransportCredentials` argument.
The `grpc/credentials` package contains helpers that produce `TransportCredentials` from certificates (if you wish to implement client authentication via provisioned TLS certificates) and `tls.Config` instances (for implementing server certificate pinning).

As far as application-level security is concerned, gRPC offers the `grpc.WithPerRPCCredentials` dial option. This option accepts a `credentials.PerRPCCredentials` instance and allows gRPC clients to automatically inject the provided set of credentials into every outgoing RPC.
The `grpc/credentials/oauth` package provides helpers for dealing with different authorization mechanisms. For instance, the `oauth.NewOauthAccess` function allows us to use an `oauth2.Token` instance that we have obtained via a three-legged OAuth2 flow with our RPCs.

On the other end, the server uses specialized middleware (gRPC refers to middleware with the term *request interceptors*) to access the credentials provided by clients and control access to RPC methods.

Decoupling Links 'R' Us components from the underlying data stores

Both the link-crawler component that we created in `Chapter 7`, *Data-Processing Pipelines*, and the PageRank calculator component that we built in `Chapter 8`, *Graph-Based Data Processing*, were designed to work with one of the data store implementations from `Chapter 6`, *Building a Persistence Layer*.

To this end, when configuring these components, we are expected to provide suitable concrete data store implementations that satisfy the `graph.Graph` and `index.Indexer` interfaces. If we were building a monolithic application, we would normally be performing this bit of initialization inside the `main` package, as follows:

1. Import the package with the data store drivers we want to use in our application (for example, the **CockroachDB** backed link-graph and the **Elasticsearch** backed text indexer).
2. Create new driver instances and configure them accordingly with a static or externally provided driver-specific set of settings (for example, the endpoints for the CockroachDB or Elasticsearch cluster).
3. Initialize the link-crawler and PageRank calculator components using the data store instances we just created. This works out of the box as all datastore implementations from `Chapter 6`, *Building a Persistence Layer*, satisfy the aforementioned interfaces and can be directly assigned to the configuration objects that are passed as arguments to the component constructors.

As we will see in the next chapter, we can make our application a bit more flexible by having our code import the packages for all the supported link-graph and text-indexer provider implementations and dynamically instantiate one of them at runtime after consulting the value of a command-line flag.

One of the issues with this approach is that it introduces a strong coupling to a particular data store implementation. What if our design requirements involve the creation of multiple applications that all need to use the same datastore providers?

To apply the aforementioned steps, we would need to duplicate the same initialization logic across all our applications. That would violate the **Don't Repeat Yourself (DRY)** principle and make our code base harder to maintain. Moreover, think about the amount of effort that would be required if we are asked to add support for a new data store implementation. We would essentially need to modify and recompile all our applications!

Given the list of problems related to having a strong coupling between applications and data stores, what options do we, as software engineers, have to reduce or ideally eliminate this coupling when designing new systems? An elegant solution would be to create a standalone proxy service that provides access to a particular data store implementation through a REST or (preferably) gRPC-based API. This pattern allows us to effectively switch to a different data store at any point in time without having to recompile any of our applications that consume the API.

In the last part of this chapter, we will apply what we have learned so far and build gRPC-based APIs so that we can access the link-graph and text-indexer components over the network. To keep things as consistent as possible, both the RPC names and the field list of the messages that are exchanged between the client and the server will *mimic* the signatures of the methods defined by the `graph.Graph` and `index.Indexer` interfaces.

In accordance with the instructions from the previous sections, we will be using the protocol buffer definition language to specify the RPCs for our APIs.

Defining RPCs for accessing a remote link-graph instance

The first API that we will be designing will grant our project's applications access to any concrete link-graph implementation that satisfies the `graph.Graph` interface over a network link. The following snippet outlines the protocol buffer definitions for the RPC endpoints that we will need:

```
syntax="proto3";
package proto;

import "google/protobuf/timestamp.proto";
import "google/protobuf/empty.proto";

service LinkGraph {
  rpc UpsertLink(Link) returns (Link);
  rpc UpsertEdge(Edge) returns (Edge);
  rpc RemoveStaleEdges(RemoveStaleEdgesQuery) returns
(google.protobuf.Empty);
  rpc Links(Range) returns (stream Link);
  rpc Edges(Range) returns (stream Edge);
}
```

The UpsertLink call inserts a new link to the graph or updates the details of an existing link. The call receives and returns a Link message, whose definition is shown in the following snippet:

```
message Link {
  bytes uuid = 1;
  string url = 2;
  google.protobuf.Timestamp retrieved_at = 3;
}
```

The Link message includes the following bits of information:

- The UUID of the link. Given that protocol buffers do not offer a native type for storing UUIDs (16-byte values), we will be representing them as a *byte slice*.
- The link's URL.
- The timestamp when the link was last retrieved by the crawler.

The UpsertEdge call inserts a new edge to the graph or updates the details of an existing edge. The call receives and returns an Edge message with the following definition:

```
message Edge {
  bytes uuid = 1;
  bytes src_uuid = 2;
  bytes dst_uuid = 3;
  google.protobuf.Timestamp updated_at = 4;
}
```

Each Edge message includes the following bits of information:

- The UUID of the edge
- The UUIDs of the source and destination vertices
- A timestamp indicating when the edge was last updated by the crawler

The next call on our list is RemoveStaleEdges. As you may recall from Chapter 7, *Data-Processing Pipelines*, this call is required by the web-crawler component to discard missing (stale) edges every time it retrieves the latest contents of a web page in the link-graph.

What's interesting about this particular RPC is that while it accepts a RemoveStaleEdgesQuery message as input, it doesn't really need to return a result to the caller. However, since gRPC mandates that all RPCs return some message to the caller, we will use google.protobuf.Empty (a placeholder type for an empty/void message) as the RPC's return type.

Let's take a quick look at the definition of the `RemoveStaleEdgesQuery` message:

```
message RemoveStaleEdgesQuery {
  bytes from_uuid = 1;
  google.protobuf.Timestamp updated_before = 2;
}
```

The last two methods on our RPC list are `Links` and `Edges`. Both calls expect the client to provide a `Range` message as input. This message allows clients to specify the set of arguments that the server will pass through to the similarly-named method of the underlying concrete link-graph implementation, namely, the UUID range for selecting the set of entities (links or edges) to return and a cutoff timestamp for filtering entities with a more recent last retrieved/updated value.

The following snippet outlines the definition of the `Range` message:

```
message Range {
  bytes from_uuid = 1;
  bytes to_uuid = 2;

  // Return results before this filter timestamp.
  google.protobuf.Timestamp filter = 3;
}
```

Up to this point, all the RPCs that we have examined are unary. However, the `Links` and `Edges` calls differ in that they are declared as *server-streaming* RPCs. The use of streaming allows clients to process the returned list of links and edges more efficiently.

In the next section, we will examine the RPC definitions for accessing the text-indexer.

Defining RPCs for accessing a text-indexer instance

The second API that we will be designing will grant our project's applications access to any concrete link-graph implementation that satisfies the `index.Indexer` interface over a network link. The following snippet outlines the protocol buffer definitions for the RPC endpoints that we will need:

```
syntax="proto3";
package proto;

import "google/protobuf/timestamp.proto";
import "google/protobuf/empty.proto";
```

```
service TextIndexer {
  rpc Index(Document) returns (Document);
  rpc UpdateScore(UpdateScoreRequest) returns (google.protobuf.Empty);
  rpc Search(Query) returns (stream QueryResult);
}
```

The `Index` method inserts a document into the search index or triggers a reindexing operation if the document already exists. As you can see by its method definition, the call expects and returns a `Document` message, which is shown in the following code snippet:

```
message Document {
  bytes link_id = 1;
  string url = 2;
  string title = 3;
  string content = 4;
  google.protobuf.Timestamp indexed_at = 5;
}
```

A successful call to `Index` will return the same `Document` that was passed as input. However, the document will also have the `indexed_at` field populated/updated by the remote server.

The next call that we will be examining is `UpdateScore`. This call will be used by the PageRank calculator component to set the PageRank score for a particular document. The call accepts an `UpdateScoreRequest` message and returns nothing (hence the use of the `google.protobuf.Empty` placeholder message):

```
message UpdateScoreRequest {
  bytes link_id = 1;
  double page_rank_score = 2;
}
```

The last, and more interesting, RPC method that we will be discussing is `Search`. Calls to `Search` accept a `Query` message as input and return a *stream* of `QueryResult` responses:

```
message Query {
  Type type = 1;
  string expression = 2;
  uint64 offset = 3;
  enum Type {
    MATCH = 0;
    PHRASE = 1;
  }
}

message QueryResult {
  oneof result {
```

```
        uint64 doc_count = 1;
        Document doc = 2;
    }
}
```

As you can see, the message definitions for `Query` and `QueryResult` are a bit more complicated. To begin with, the `Query` message defines a nested enumeration for specifying the type of query to be executed. By default, the query expression is treated as a regular keyword-based search (`MATCH` is the default value for the `type` field).

However, the caller can also request a phrase-based search by specifying `PHRASE` as the value of the `type` field. Furthermore, callers are also allowed to specify an offset and instruct the server to skip a number of results from the top of the returned result set. This mechanism can be used by clients to implement pagination.

The `QueryResult` message uses the **one-of** feature of protocol buffers. This message can either contain a `uint64` value that describes the total number of documents matched by the query or the next `Document` from the result set. Our server implementation will use the following simple protocol to stream results to the client:

- The *first* message in the result stream will *always* describe the total number of results for the search. If no documents matched the search query, the server will indicate this by setting the `doc_count` field to the value 0.
- Each subsequent message will push the `Document` that matches the client.

Creating high-level clients for accessing data stores over gRPC

The *protoc* compiler, given the RPC definitions from the previous two sections as input, will generate a client and the required server stubs for the data store proxy service.

From the perspective of the API server, each RPC method is nothing more than a wrapper for invoking the similarly-named method of the underlying concrete store implementation that we configured the server to use. More specifically, to implement the RPC method called **X**, we perform the following steps:

1. Convert the fields of the RPC's input message (where required) into the values expected by the wrapped method, X.
2. Invoke X while watching out for any errors.

3. Convert and pack the output of X into the appropriate return message for the RPC.
4. Return the generated response to the client.

As you can probably tell, our server implementation will mostly consist of boring boilerplate code that uses the recipe we just described as a template. To conserve some space, we will omit the implementation details from this book. However, you can take a look at the full source code for the two API servers by examining the `server.go` files in the `Chapter09/linksrus/linkgraphapi` and `Chapter09/linksrus/textindexerapi` packages, which can be found in this book's GitHub repository.

With the RPC server in place, our applications can establish a connection to it and use the gRPC client that the *protoc* compiler generated for us to access the link-graph and text-indexer components on the other end. An unfortunate caveat of our current implementation is that since the auto-generated gRPC clients do not implement the `graph.Graph` and `index.Indexer` interfaces, we cannot use them as drop-in replacements for configuring the crawler and PageRank calculator components.

Fortunately, there is an elegant way to work around this inconvenience! The package for each API will also need to define a *high-level* client that *wraps* the gRPC client that the protoc compiler generated for us and implements, depending on the API, either the `graph.Graph` interface or the `index.Indexer` interface.

Behind the scenes, the high-level client will transparently handle all interactions with the remote gRPC server. While this approach does require additional development effort, it makes the high-level client appear as yet another graph or indexer implementation that we can inject into the **Links 'R' Us components** without requiring any code changes. In Chapter 11, *Splitting Monoliths into Microservices,* we will be exploiting this trick to split the Links 'R' Us project into a set of microservices!

In a similar fashion to the server implementation, the high-level client also consists of quite a bit of repetitive boilerplate code, so in the interest of brevity, we will also omit its listing from this chapter. The full source code for the two high-level clients can be found in a file called `client.go`, which is in the same location as the server implementation.

Summary

In the first part of this chapter, we discussed the key principles behind RESTful APIs. We focused on effective strategies for handling hot topics such as security and versioning. Then, we analyzed the pros and cons of RESTful APIs compared to the RPC-base paradigm used by the gRPC framework and highlighted the key differences that make gRPC more suitable for building high-performance services.

Now that you're at the end of this chapter, you should be familiar with the protocol buffer definition language and know how to leverage the various features supported by the gRPC framework for building high-performance secure APIs based on the RPC pattern.

In the next chapter, we will find out how we can perform hermetic builds of our software, package it as a container image, and deploy it on a Kubernetes cluster.

Questions

1. Describe the CRUD endpoints for a user entity.
2. Explain how basic authentication over TLS can help us secure APIs.
3. Are TLS connections immune to eavesdropping?
4. Describe the steps in the three-legged OAuth2 flow.
5. What is the benefit of using protocol buffers compared to JSON for request/response payloads?
6. Describe the different RPC modes that are supported by gRPC.

Further reading

1. *A Go web development eco-system, designed to make your life easier;* refer to the following link for more information: `https://github.com/gobuffalo/buffalo`.
2. *A high performance, open-source universal RPC framework;* refer to the following link for more information: `https://www.grpc.io`.
3. *A high-performance HTTP request router that scales well;* refer to the following link for more information: `https://github.com/julienschmidt/httprouter`.
4. *A high productivity, full-stack web framework for the Go language;* refer to the following link for more information: `https://github.com/revel/revel`.

5. *A powerful HTTP router and URL matcher for building Go web servers;* refer to the following link for more information: `https://github.com/gorilla/mux`.

6. Berners-Lee, T.; Fielding, R.; Masinter, L.: RFC 3986, **Uniform Resource Identifier (URI)**: Generic Syntax.

7. *Developer guide for protocol buffer v3;* refer to the following link for more information: `https://developers.google.com/protocol-buffers/docs/proto3`.

8. *Fast HTTP package for Go. Tuned for high performance. Zero memory allocations in hot paths. Up to 10x faster than net/http;* refer to the following link for more information: `https://github.com/valyala/fasthttp`.

9. *Media Type Specifications and Registration Procedures;* refer to the following link for more information: `https://tools.ietf.org/html/rfc6838`.

10. *The fastest full-featured web framework for Go;* refer to the following link for more information:`https://github.com/gin-gonic/gin`.

11. *The meaning of the letter g in gRPC;* refer to the following link for more information: `https://github.com/grpc/grpc/blob/master/doc/g_stands_for.md`.

10
Building, Packaging, and Deploying Software

"Kubernetes is the Linux of distributed systems."

– Kelsey Hightower

This chapter will guide you through the steps involved in dockerizing Go programs and will iterate the best practices for building the smallest possible container image for your applications. Following this, this chapter will focus on Kubernetes.

We'll begin our tour of Kubernetes by comparing the different types of nodes that comprise a Kubernetes cluster and take a closer look at the function of the various services that make up Kubernetes' control plane. Moving forward, we will be describing a step-by-step walkthrough for setting up a Kubernetes cluster on your local development machine. The last part of this chapter is a practical application of everything you have learned so far. We will bring all the components that we created in the previous chapters together, join them with a fully functioning frontend, and create a monolithic version of Links 'R' Us that we will then deploy on Kubernetes.

The following topics will be covered in this chapter:

- Using intermediate build containers to compile static binaries for your Go applications
- Using the correct set of linker flags to ensure that Go binaries compile to the smallest possible size
- The anatomy of the components that comprise a Kubernetes cluster

- The different types of resource types supported by Kubernetes and their application
- Spinning up a Kubernetes cluster on your local workstation
- Building a monolithic version of the Links 'R' Us application using the components we developed in the previous chapters and deploying it on Kubernetes

Technical requirements

The full code for the topics that will be discussed in this chapter has been published to this book's GitHub repository under the Chapter10 folder.

 You can access this book's GitHub repository, which contains the code and all the required resources for the chapters in this book, by pointing your web browser to the following URL: https://github.com/ PacktPublishing/Hands-On-Software-Engineering-with-Golang.

To get you up and running as quickly as possible, each example project includes a Makefile that defines the following set of targets:

Makefile target	Description
deps	Install any required dependencies.
test	Run all tests and report coverage.
lint	Check for lint errors.

As with all the other chapters in this book, you will need a fairly recent version of Go, which you can download at https://golang.org/dl.

To run some of the code in this chapter, you will need to have a working Docker [5] installation on your machine. Furthermore, a subset of the examples have been designed to run on Kubernetes [8]. If you don't have access to a Kubernetes cluster for testing, you can simply follow the instructions laid out in the following sections to set up a small cluster on your laptop or workstation.

Building and packaging Go services using Docker

Over the last few years, more and more software engineers started using systems such as Docker to containerize their applications. Containers offer a simple and clean way to execute an application without having to worry about the underlying hardware or operating system. In other words, the same container image can run on your local development machine, a VM on the cloud, or even on a bare-metal server located in your company's data center.

Benefits of containerization

Other than portability, containerization offers a few more important benefits, both from a software engineering and DevOps perspective. To begin with, containers make it easy to deploy a new version of a piece of software and to effortlessly roll back the deployment if something goes wrong. Secondly, containerization introduces an extra layer of security; every application executes in complete isolation from not only other applications but also from the underlying host itself.

Whenever a new container image is being built (for example, as part of a continuous integration pipeline), the target application gets packaged with an *immutable* copy of all the required dependencies for running it. As a result, when an engineer runs a particular container, they are guaranteed to run exactly the same binary as their other colleagues, whereas compiling and running the application locally could produce different results, depending on what compiler version or system libraries were installed on the development machine.

To take this a step further, apart from containerizing our applications, we can also containerize the tools that are used to build them. This allows us to create **hermetic** builds and paves the way for supporting repeatable builds, whose benefits we have already enumerated in Chapter 3, *Dependency Management*.

 When executing a hermetic build, the emitted binary artifact is not affected by any of the software or system libraries that are installed on the build machine. Instead, the build process uses pinned compiler and dependency versions to ensure that compiling the same snapshot (for example, a specific git SHA) of the code base will always produce the same, bit-by-bit identical binary.

In the next section, we will delve into the process of building Docker containers for your Go applications and explore a set of best practices for producing containers that are optimized for size.

Best practices for dockerizing Go applications

Go comes with built-in support for producing standalone, static binaries, making it an ideal candidate for containerization! Let's take a look at the best practices for building Docker containers for your Go applications.

Since static Go binaries tend to be quite large, we must take extra steps to ensure that the containers we build do not include any of the build tools (for example, the Go compiler) that are used at build time. Unless you are using a really old version of Docker, your currently installed version will most likely support a feature known as *build containers*.

A build container includes all the tools that are needed for compiling our Go application: the Go compiler and the Go standard library, git, tools for compiling protocol buffer definitions, and so on. We will be using the build compiler as an *intermediate* container for compiling and linking our application. Then, we will create a *new* container, copy the compiled binary over, and discard the build container.

To understand how this process works, let's examine the Dockerfile for building the Links 'R' Us application that we will be building in the last part of this chapter. You can find the Dockerfile in the `Chapter10/linksrus` folder of this book's GitHub repository:

```
FROM golang:1.13 AS builder

WORKDIR $GOPATH/src/github.com/PacktPublishing/Hands-On-Software-
Engineering-with-Golang
COPY . .
RUN make deps

RUN GIT_SHA=$(git rev-parse --short HEAD) && \
    CGO_ENABLED=0 GOARCH=amd64 GOOS=linux \
    go build -a \
    -ldflags "-extldflags '-static' -w -s -X main.appSha=$GIT_SHA" \
    -o /go/bin/linksrus-monolith \
    github.com/PacktPublishing/Hands-On-Software-Engineering-with-
Golang/Chapter10/linksrus
```

The first line specifies the container that we will be using as the base for our build container. We can reference this container within the Dockerfile using the `builder` alias. The rest of the commands from the preceding Dockerfile perform the following operations:

- The source files for the application are copied from the host into the build container. Note that we copy the **entire** book repository into the container to ensure that the `make deps` command can resolve all package imports from this book's repository and not try to download them from GitHub.
- The `make deps` command is invoked to fetch any external package dependencies.
- Finally, the Go compiler is invoked to compile the application and place the resulting binary in a known location (in this case, `/go/bin/linksrus-monolith`).

Let's zoom in and explain what actually happens when the `go build` command is executed:

- The `GIT_SHA` environment variable is set to the short git SHA of the current commit. The `-X main.appSha=$GIT_SHA` linker flag overrides the value of the placeholder variable called `appSha` in the main package with the SHA value that we just calculated. We will be outputting the value of the `appSha` variable in the application logs to make it easy for operators to figure out which application version is currently deployed simply by tailing the logs.
- The `CGO_ENABLED=0` environment variable notifies the Go compiler that we won't be invoking any C code from our program and allows it to optimize away quite a bit of code from the final binary.
- The `-static` flag instructs the compiler to produce a static binary.
- Finally, the `-w` and `-s` flags instruct the Go linker to drop debug symbols (more specifically, the DWARF section and symbol information) from the final binary. This still allows you to get full stack traces in case of a panic but prevents you from attaching a debugger (for example, delve) to the binary. On the bright side, these flags will significantly reduce the total size of the final binary!

The next section of the Dockerfile contains the steps for building the final container:

```
FROM alpine:3.10
RUN apk update && apk add ca-certificates && rm -rf /var/cache/apk/*
COPY --from=builder /go/bin/linksrus-monolith /go/bin/linksrus-monolith

ENTRYPOINT ["/go/bin/linksrus-monolith"]
```

Since we know that the Links 'R' Us application will most probably be making TLS connections, we need to ensure that the final container image ships with the CA certificates for trusted authorities around the world. This is achieved by installing the `ca-certificates` package. To complete the build, we *copy* the compiled binary from the **build** container into the final container.

Selecting a suitable base container for your application

In the previous example, I chose to use *Alpine* as the base container for the application. So, why pick alpine over something more widely known, such as Ubuntu? The answer is size!

The Alpine Linux [1] container is one of the smallest base containers you can find out there. It ships with a small footprint libc implementation (musl) and uses busybox as its shell. As a result, the total size of the alpine container is only 5 M, thus making it ideal for hosting our Go static binaries. Furthermore, it includes its own package manager (apk), which lets you install additional packages such as the ca-certificates or network tools while the final container is being built.

What if we don't need this extra functionality, though? Is it possible to produce an application container that is even smaller? The answer is yes! We can use the special **scratch** container as our base container. As the name implies, the scratch container is literally empty... It has no root filesystem and only includes our application binary. However, it does come with a few caveats:

- It does not include any CA certificates, nor is there any way to install them besides copying them over from an intermediate build container. However, if your application or microservice will only communicate with services in a private subnet using non-TLS connections, this might not be a problem.
- The container does not include a shell. This makes it impossible to actually SSH into a running container for debugging purposes (for example, to check that DNS resolution works or to grep through log files).

 My recommendation is to always use a tiny container such as alpine or something similar instead of the scratch container.

At this point, you should be able to apply the best practices we outlined in the previous sections and create space-efficient container images for your own Go applications. So, what's next? The next step is, of course, to deploy and scale your applications. As you probably suspect, we won't be doing this manually! Instead, we will be leveraging an existing, industrial-grade solution for managing containers at scale: Kubernetes.

A gentle introduction to Kubernetes

Kubernetes [8] is an open source platform for managing containerized workloads that was built from the start with future extensibility in mind. It was originally released by Google back in 2014 and it encompasses both their insights and best practices for running large-scale, production-grade applications. Nowadays, it has eclipsed the managed container offerings of the most popular cloud providers and is en route to becoming the *de facto* standard for deploying applications on-premises and in the cloud.

Describing Kubernetes in detail is not within the scope of this book. Instead, the goal of the following sections is to provide you with a brief introduction to Kubernetes and distill some of its basic concepts into an easily digestible format that conveys enough information to allow you to spin up a test cluster and deploy the Links 'R' Us project to it.

Peeking under the hood

Okay, so we have already mentioned that Kubernetes will do the heavy lifting and manage different types of containerized workloads for you. But how does this work under the hood? The following diagram illustrates the basic components that comprise a Kubernetes cluster:

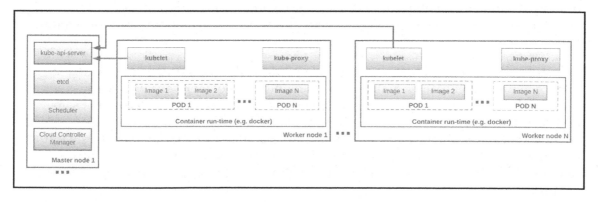

Figure 1: A high-level overview of a Kubernetes cluster

A Kubernetes cluster consists of two types of nodes: **masters** and **workers**. These can be either physical or virtual machines. The master nodes implement the control plane for your cluster, whereas the worker nodes pool their resources together (CPUs, memory, disk, or even GPUs) and execute the workloads that are assigned to them by the master.

Every master node runs the following processes:

- The **kube-api-server**. You can think of this as an API gateway for allowing worker nodes and cluster operators to access the control plane for the cluster.
- **etcd** implements a key-value store where the cluster's current state is persisted. It also provides a convenient API that allows clients to watch a particular key or set of keys and receive a notification when their values change.
- The **scheduler** monitors the cluster state for incoming workloads and makes sure that every workload is assigned to one of the available worker nodes. If the workload requirements cannot be met by any of the worker nodes, the scheduler might opt to **reschedule** an existing workload to a different worker so as to make room for the incoming workload.
- The **cloud controller manager** handles all the necessary interactions with the underlying cloud substrate that hosts the cluster. Examples of such interactions include provisioning *cloud-specific* services, such as storage or load balancers, and creating or manipulating resources such as routing tables and DNS records.

A production-grade Kubernetes cluster will typically be configured with multiple master nodes; the control plane manages the cluster state, so it is quite important for it to be *highly available*. In such a scenario, data will be automatically replicated across the master nodes and DNS-based load balancing will be used to access the kube-api-server gateway.

Now, let's take a look at the internals of a worker node. Given that Kubernetes manages containers, a key requirement is that each worker node provides a suitable container runtime. As you've probably guessed, the most commonly used runtime is Docker; however, Kubernetes will happily work with other types of container runtime interfaces, such as containerd [4] or rkt [12].

Each and every workload that is scheduled on a particular worker node is executed in isolation within its container runtime. The minimum unit of work in Kubernetes is referred to as a **pod**. Pods consist of one or *more* container images that are executed on the same worker instance. While single-container pods are the most typical, multi-container pods are also quite useful. For instance, we could deploy a pod that includes nginx and a sidecar container that monitors an external configuration source and regenerates the nginx configuration as needed. An application can be horizontally scaled by creating additional pod instances.

The worker nodes also run the following processes:

- The **kubelet** agent connects to the master's **api-server** and watches for workload assignments to the worker node it is running on. It ensures that the required containers are always up and running by automatically restarting them if they suddenly die.
- The **kube-proxy** works like a network proxy. It maintains a set of rules that control the routing of internal (cluster) or external traffic to the pods that are currently executing on the worker.

Summarizing the most common Kubernetes resource types

Operators interact with the Kubernetes cluster by creating, deleting, or otherwise manipulating different types of resources via a CRUD-like interface. Let's take a brief look at some of the most common Kubernetes resource types.

It is quite rare to come across an application that doesn't require any sort of configuration. While we could definitely hardcode the configuration settings when we create our pods, this is generally considered to be bad practice and frankly becomes a major source of frustration when we need to change a configuration setting (for example, the endpoint for a database) that is shared between multiple applications. To alleviate this problem, Kubernetes offers the *config map* resource. Config maps are collections of key-value pairs that can be injected into pods either as environment variables or mounted as plain text files. This approach allows us to manage configuration settings at a single location and avoid hardcoding them when creating pods for our applications. Kubernetes also provides the **secret** resource, which works in a similar fashion to a config map but is meant to be used for sharing sensitive information such as certificate keys and service credentials between pods.

A **namespace** resource works as a virtual container for logically grouping other Kubernetes resources and controlling access to them. This is a very handy feature if multiple teams are using the same cluster for their deployments. In such a scenario, each team is typically assigned full access to their own namespace so that they cannot interfere with the resources that are deployed by other teams unless they are granted explicit access.

Once a pod dies, any data stored within any of its containers will be lost. To support use cases where we want to persist data across pod restarts or we simply want to share the same set of data (for example, the pages served by a web server) across multiple pod instances, Kubernetes provides the **persistent volume (PV)** and **persistent volume claim (PVC)** resources. A persistent volume is nothing more than a piece of block storage that is made available to the cluster. Depending on the substrate, it can either be manually provisioned by the cluster administrators or dynamically allocated on-demand by the underlying substrate (for example, an EBS volume when running on AWS). On the other hand, a persistent volume claim represents an operator's request for a block of storage with a particular set of attributes (for example, size, IOPS, and spinning disk or SSD). The Kubernetes control plane attempts to match the available volumes with the operator-specified claims and mount the volumes to the pods that reference each claim.

To deploy a stateless application on Kubernetes, the recommended approach is to create a **deployment** resource. A deployment resource specifies a **template** for instantiating a single pod of the application and the desired number of replicas. Kubernetes continuously monitors the state of each deployment and attempts to synchronize the cluster state with the desired state by either creating new pods (using the template) or deleting existing pods when the number of active pods exceeds the requested number of replicas. Each pod in a deployment gets assigned a random hostname by Kubernetes and shares the *same PVC* with every other pod.

Many types of workloads, such as databases or message queues, require a stateful kind of deployment where pods are assigned stable and predictable hostnames and each individual pod gets its own PVC. What's more, these applications usually operate in a clustered configuration and expect nodes to be deployed, upgraded, and scaled in a particular sequence. In Kubernetes, this type of deployment is accomplished by creating a **StatefulSet**. Similar to a deployment resource, a StatefulSet also defines a pod template and a number of replicas. Each replica is assigned a hostname, which is constructed by concatenating the name of the StatefulSet and the index of each pod in the set (for example, web-0 and web-1).

Being able to scale the number of deployed pods up and down is a great feature to have but not that useful unless other resources in the cluster can connect to them! To this end, Kubernetes supports another type of resource, called a **service**. Services come in two flavors:

- A service can sit in front of a group of pods and act as a **load balancer**. In this scenario, the service is automatically assigned both an IP address and a DNS record to aid its discovery by clients. In case you are wondering, this functionality is implemented by the **kube-proxy** component that runs on each worker node.

- A **headless** service allows you to implement a custom service discovery mechanism. These services are not assigned a cluster IP address and they are totally ignored by kube-proxy. However, these services create DNS records for the service and resolve to the address of every single pod behind the service.

The last Kubernetes resource that we will be examining is **ingresses**. Depending on its configuration, an ingress exposes HTTP or HTTPS endpoints for routing traffic from outside the cluster to particular services within the cluster. The common set of features that are supported by the majority of ingress controller implementations include TLS termination, name-based virtual hosts, and URL rewriting for incoming requests.

This concludes our overview of the most common Kubernetes resource types. Keep in mind that this is only the tip of the iceberg! Kubernetes supports many other resource types (for example, cron jobs) and even provides APIs that allow operators to define their own custom resources. If you want to learn more about Kubernetes resources, I would strongly recommend browsing the quite extensive set of Kubernetes documentation that is available online [8].

Next, you will learn how to easily set up your very own Kubernetes cluster on your laptop or workstation.

Running a Kubernetes cluster on your laptop!

A few years ago, experimenting with Kubernetes was more or less restricted to engineers who were either granted access to a test or dev cluster or they had the resources and knowledge that was required to bootstrap and operate their own cluster on the cloud. Nowadays, things are much simpler... In fact, you can even spin up a fully operational Kubernetes cluster on your laptop in just a couple of minutes!

Let's take a look at some of the most popular, dev-friendly Kubernetes distributions that you can deploy on your development machine:

- K3S [7] is a tiny (it's literally a 50 M binary!) distribution that allows you to run Kubernetes on resource-constrained devices. It provides binaries for multiple architectures, including ARM64/ARMv7. This makes it a great candidate for running Kubernetes on Raspberry Pi.
- Microk8s [9] is a project by Canonical that promises zero-ops Kubernetes cluster setups. Getting a Kubernetes cluster up and running on Linux is as simple as running `snap install microk8s`. On other platforms, the recommended approach for installing microk8s is to use an application such as Multipass [11] to spin up a VM and run the aforementioned command inside it.

- Minikube [10] is yet another distribution, this time by the Kubernetes authors. It can work with different types of hypervisors (for example, VirtualBox, Hyperkit, Parallels, VMware Fusion, or Hyper-V) and can even be deployed on bare metal (Linux only).

To make it as easy as possible for you to set up your own Kubernetes cluster on your favorite OS and run the examples shown in the upcoming sections, we will be working exclusively with Minikube and use VirtualBox as our hypervisor.

Before we begin, make sure that you have downloaded and installed the following software:

- Docker [5].
- VirtualBox [13].
- The kubectl binary for your platform.
- The helm [6] binary for your platform. Helm is a package manager for Kubernetes and we will be using it to deploy the CockroachDB and Elasticsearch instances for the Links 'R' Us project.
- The latest Minikube version for your platform.

With all the preceding dependencies in place, we are ready to bootstrap our Kubernetes cluster using the following code:

```
minikube start --kubernetes-version=v1.15.3 \
               --memory=4g \
               --network-plugin=cni
```

This command will create a virtual machine with 4 GB of RAM and deploy Kubernetes 1.15.3 to it. It will also update the local configuration for kubectl so that it automatically connects to the cluster we have just provisioned. What's more, it will enable the **Container Networking Interface (CNI)** plugin for the cluster. In the next chapter, we will leverage this functionality to install a network security solution such as Calico [2] or Cilium [3] and define fine-grained network policies to lock down our cluster.

As our deployed services will be running inside Minikube's virtual machine, the only way to access them from the **host** machine is by provisioning an ingress resource. Luckily for us, Minikube provides a suitable ingress implementation as an add-on that we can activate by running `minikube addons enable ingress`. What's more, for our tests, we want to use a private Docker registry for pushing the Docker images that we will be building. Minikube ships with a private registry add-on that we can enable by running `minikube addons enable registry`.

However, by default, Minikube's private registry runs in insecure mode. When using insecure registries, we need to explicitly configure our local Docker daemon to allow connections to them; otherwise, we won't be able to push our images. The registry is exposed on port 5000 at the IP used by Minikube.

 You can find Minikube's IP address by running `minikube ip`.

On Linux, you can edit `/etc/docker/daemon.json`, merge in the following JSON block (replacing `$MINIKUBE_IP` with the IP we obtained with the `minikube ip` command), and then *restart the Docker daemon*, as follows:

```
{
  "insecure-registries" : [
    "$MINIKUBE_IP:5000"
  ]
}
```

On OS X and Windows, you can simply right-click on the Docker for desktop, select **preferences**, and then click on the **Daemon** tab to access the list of trusted insecure registries.

The last thing we need to do is install the required cluster resources so that we can use the helm package manager. We can do this by running `helm init`.

 To save you some time, I have encoded all the preceding steps into a Makefile, which you can find in the `Chapter10/k8s` folder of this book's GitHub repository.

To bootstrap the cluster, install all the required add-ons, and configure helm, you can simply type `make bootstrap-minikube`.

That's it! We have a fully functioning Kubernetes cluster at our disposal. Now, we are ready to build and deploy a monolithic version of the Links 'R' Us project.

Building and deploying a monolithic version of Links 'R' Us

This is the moment of truth! In the following sections, we will leverage everything we have learned in this chapter to assemble all the Links 'R' Us components that we developed in the previous chapters into a monolithic application that we will then proceed to deploy on Kubernetes.

Based on the user stories from `Chapter 5`, *The Links 'R' Us Project*, in order for our application to satisfy our design goals, it should provide the following services:

- A periodically running, multi-pass crawler for scanning the link graph, retrieving links for indexing, and augmenting the graph with newly discovered links to be crawled during a future pass
- Another periodically running service to recalculate and persist PageRank scores for the continuously expanding link graph
- A frontend for our end users to perform search queries and to submit website URLs for indexing

So far, we haven't really discussed the frontend. Don't worry; we will be building a fully fledged frontend for our application in one of the following sections.

As you've probably guessed, due to the number of components involved, the final application will undoubtedly include quite a bit of boilerplate code. Given that it is not feasible to include the full source code in this chapter, we will only focus on the most interesting parts. Nevertheless, you can find the documented source code for the entire application in the `Chapter10/linksrus` folder of this book's GitHub repository.

Distributing computation across application instances

In anticipation of the Links 'R' Us project becoming an overnight success and attracting a lot of traffic, especially after posting a link on sites such as Hacker News and Slashdot, we need to come up with a reasonable plan for scaling. Even though we are currently dealing with a monolithic application, we can always scale horizontally by spinning up additional instances. Moreover, as our link graph size grows, we will undoubtedly need additional compute resources for both our web crawlers and our PageRank calculator.

One of the key benefits of using a container orchestration platform such as Kubernetes is that we can effortlessly scale up (or down) any deployed application. As we saw at the beginning of this chapter, a `Service` resource connected to an `Ingress` can act as a load balancer and distribute *incoming* traffic to our application. This transparently takes care of our frontend scaling issues with no additional development effort on our end.

On the other hand, making sure that *each* application instance crawls a specific *subset* of the graph isn't straightforward as it requires application instances to coordinate with each other. This implies that we need to establish a communication channel between the individual instances. Or does it?

Carving the UUID space into non-overlapping partitions

In `Chapter 6`, *Building a Persistence Layer*, we mentioned that the caller of the `Links` and `Edges` methods that are exposed by the link-graph component is responsible for implementing a suitable partitioning scheme and providing the appropriate UUID ranges as arguments to these methods. So, how can we go about implementing such a partitioning scheme?

Our approach exploits the observation that the link (and edge) IDs are, in fact, V4 (random) UUIDs and are therefore expected to be more or less evenly distributed in the massive (2^{128}) UUID space. Let's assume that the total number of workers (that is, the number of partitions) available to us is N. For the time being, we will treat the number of workers as being fixed and a priority known. In the following section, we will learn how to leverage the Kubernetes infrastructure to automatically discover this information.

To figure out the range of UUIDs that the M_{th} worker (where $0 <= M < N$) needs to provide as arguments to the `Links` and `Edges` methods of the graph, we need to perform some calculations. First, we need to subdivide the 128-bit UUID space into N equally sized sections; in essence, each section will contain $C = 2^{128} / N$ UUIDs. Consequently, to calculate the M_{th} worker's UUID range, we can use the following formula:

$$Range(M) = \begin{cases} [\, C * M, C * (M+1)\,) & M < (N-1) \\ [\, C * M, maxUUID)\,) & M = (N-1) \end{cases}$$

$$\text{where } C = 2^{128}/N$$
$$N = \text{The number of workers}$$

If the number of workers (*N*) is *odd*, then we will not be able to divide the UUID space evenly; therefore, the **last** (N-1) section is treated in a special manner: it always extends to the **end** of the UUID space (the UUID value `ffffffff-ffff-ffff-ffff-ffffffffffff`). This ensures that we always cover the entire UUID space, regardless of whether *N* is odd or even!

The rationale behind this type of split is as follows:

- Most modern database systems tend to cache the primary key index in memory
- They contain special optimized code paths for performing *range scans* on primary key ranges

The combination of the preceding two properties makes this solution quite attractive for the read-heavy workloads that are performed by both the crawler and the PageRank calculator components. One small nuisance is that UUIDs are 128-bit values and Go does not provide scalar types for performing 128-bit arithmetic. Fortunately, the standard library provides the `math/big` package, which can perform arbitrary-precision arithmetic operations!

Let's go ahead and create a helper that will take care of all these calculations for us. The `Range` helper implementation will live in a file called `range.go`, which is part of the `Chapter10/linksrus/partition` package (see this book's GitHub repository). Its type definition is as follows:

```
type Range struct {
    start        uuid.UUID
    rangeSplits  []uuid.UUID
}
```

For our particular application, we will provide two constructors for creating ranges. The first constructor creates a `Range` that spans the full UUID space and splits it into `numPartitions`:

```
func NewFullRange(numPartitions int) (Range, error) {
    return NewRange(
        uuid.Nil,
        uuid.MustParse("ffffffff-ffff-ffff-ffff-ffffffffffff"),
        numPartitions,
    )
}
```

As you can see, the constructor delegates the creation of the range to the `NewRange` helper, whose implementation has been broken down into smaller snippets:

```
if bytes.Compare(start[:], end[:]) >= 0 {
    return Range{}, xerrors.Errorf("range start UUID must be less than the
end UUID")
} else if numPartitions <= 0 {
    return Range{}, xerrors.Errorf("number of partitions must be at least
equal to 1")
}

// Calculate the size of each partition as: ((end - start + 1) /
numPartitions)
tokenRange := big.NewInt(0)
partSize := big.NewInt(0)
partSize = partSize.Sub(big.NewInt(0).SetBytes(end[:]),
big.NewInt(0).SetBytes(start[:]))
partSize = partSize.Div(partSize.Add(partSize, big.NewInt(1)),
big.NewInt(int64(numPartitions)))
```

Before we proceed, the code verifies that the provided UUID range is valid by making sure that the start UUID is smaller than the end UUID. To achieve this, we use the handy `bytes.Compare` function, which compares two byte slices and returns a value greater than or equal to zero if the two byte slices are either equal or the first byte slice is greater than the second. One caveat here is that the UUID type is defined as `[16]byte`, whereas the `bytes.Compare` function expects byte slices. However, we can easily convert each UUID into a byte slice using the convenience operator, `[:]`.

After the preliminary argument validation, we create an empty `big.Integer` value and use the cumbersome API of the `math/big` package to load it with the result of the `(end - start) + 1` expression. Once the value has been loaded, we divide it by the number of partitions that the caller provided as an argument to the function. This yields the `C` value from the formula we saw in the previous section.

The following block of code uses a `for` loop to calculate and store the **end** UUID for each partition that is part of the range we are creating:

```
var to uuid.UUID
var err error
var ranges = make([]uuid.UUID, numPartitions)
for partition := 0; partition < numPartitions; partition++ {
    if partition == numPartitions-1 {
        to = end
    } else {
        tokenRange.Mul(partSize, big.NewInt(int64(partition+1)))
        if to, err = uuid.FromBytes(tokenRange.Bytes()); err != nil {
```

```
                return nil, xerrors.Errorf("partition range: %w", err)
            }
        }
        ranges[partition] = to
    }
    return &Range{start: start, rangeSplits: ranges}, nil
```

As we mentioned in the previous section, the end UUID for the last partition is always the maximum possible UUID value. For all the other partitions, we calculate the end by multiplying the size of each partition by the partition number, plus one. Once all the calculations have been completed, a new `Range` object is allocated and returned to the caller. In addition to the calculated end ranges, we also keep track of the start UUID for the range.

Now, to make the `Range` type easier to use from within the crawler service code, let's define two auxiliary methods:

```
func (r *Range) Extents() (uuid.UUID, uuid.UUID) {
    return r.start, r.rangeSplits[len(r.rangeSplits)-1]
}

func (r *Range) PartitionExtents(partition int) (uuid.UUID, uuid.UUID, error) {
    if partition < 0 || partition >= len(r.rangeSplits) {
        return uuid.Nil, uuid.Nil, xerrors.Errorf("invalid partition index")
    }
    if partition == 0 {
        return r.start, r.rangeSplits[0], nil
    }
    return r.rangeSplits[partition-1], r.rangeSplits[partition], nil
}
```

The `Extents` method returns the start (inclusive) and end (exclusive) UUID value for the *entire* range. On the other hand, the `PartitionExtents` function returns the start and end UUID values for a specific *partition* within the range.

Assigning a partition range to each pod

With the help of the Range type from the previous section, we now have the means to query the UUID range that's assigned to every single partition. For our particular use case, the number of partitions is equal to the number of pods that we launch. However, one crucial bit of information that we are lacking is the partition number that's assigned to each individual launched pod! Consequently, we now have two problems that we need to solve:

- What is the partition number of an individual pod?
- What is the total number of pods?

If we deploy our application as a StatefulSet with *N* replicas, every pod in the set will be assigned a hostname that follows the pattern SET_NAME-INDEX, where INDEX is a number from *0* to *N-1* that indicates the index of the pod in the set. All we need to do is read the pod's hostname from our application, parse the numeric suffix, and use that as the partition number.

One approach to answering the second question would be to query the Kubernetes server API. However, this requires additional effort to set up (for example, create service accounts, RBAC records) – not to mention that it effectively locks us into Kubernetes! Fortunately, there is an easier way...

If we were to create a **headless** service for our application, it would automatically generate a set of SRV records that we can query and obtain the host for each individual pod that belongs to the service. The following diagram shows the results of running an SRV query from within a pod in the Kubernetes cluster:

```
$ host -t SRV linksrus-headless
linksrus-headless.linksrus.svc.cluster.local has SRV record 0 25 8080 10-1-1-14.linksrus-headless.linksrus.svc.cluster.local.
linksrus-headless.linksrus.svc.cluster.local has SRV record 0 25 8080 10-1-1-17.linksrus-headless.linksrus.svc.cluster.local.
linksrus-headless.linksrus.svc.cluster.local has SRV record 0 25 8080 10-1-1-21.linksrus-headless.linksrus.svc.cluster.local.
linksrus-headless.linksrus.svc.cluster.local has SRV record 0 25 8080 10-1-1-22.linksrus-headless.linksrus.svc.cluster.local.
$
```

Figure 2: The linksrus-headless service is associated with four pods whose hostnames are visible on the right-hand side

Based on the information displayed in the preceding screenshot, we could write a helper for figuring out the partition number and the total number of partitions for a running application instance, as follows:

```
func (det FromSRVRecords) PartitionInfo() (int, int, error) {
    hostname, err := os.Hostname()
    if err != nil {
        return -1, -1, xerrors.Errorf("partition detector: unable to detect
host name: %w", err)
```

```
    }
    tokens := strings.Split(hostname, "-")
    partition, err := strconv.ParseInt(tokens[len(tokens)-1], 10, 32)
    if err != nil {
        return -1, -1, xerrors.Errorf("partition detector: unable to
extract partition number from host name suffix")
    }
    _, addrs, err := net.LookupSRV("", "", det.srvName)
    if err != nil {
        return -1, -1, ErrNoPartitionDataAvailableYet
    }
    return int(partition), len(addrs), nil
}
```

To get the hostname, we invoke the `Hostname` function provided by the `os` package. Then, we split on the dash separator, extract the right-most part of the hostname, and use `ParseInt` to convert it into a number.

Next, to get the SRV records, we use the `LookupSRV` function from the `net` package and pass the service name as the last argument. Then, we count the number of results to figure out the total number of pods in the set. One important thing to be aware of is that SRV record creation is not instantaneous! When the StatefulSet is initially deployed, it will take a bit of time for the SRV records to become available. To this end, if the SRV lookup does not yield any results, the code will return a typed error to let the caller know that they should try again later.

Building wrappers for the application services

So far, we intentionally designed the various Link 'R' Us components so that they are more or less decoupled from their input sources. For example, the crawler component from Chapter 7, *Data-Processing Pipelines*, expects an iterator that yields the set of links to be crawled, while the PageRank calculator component from Chapter 8, Graph-*Based Data Processing*, only provides convenience methods for creating the nodes and edges of the graph that are used by the PageRank algorithm.

To integrate these components into a larger application, we need to provide a thin layer that implements two key functions:

- It connects each component with a suitable link graph and the text indexer data store implementation from Chapter 6, *Building a Persistence Layer*
- It manages the *refresh cycle* for each component (for example, triggering a new crawler pass or recalculating PageRank scores)

Each service will be started from the main package of the Links 'R' Us application and execute independently of other services. If any of the services exit due to an error, we want our application to cleanly shut down, log the error, and exit with the appropriate status code. This necessitates the introduction of a supervisor mechanism that will manage the execution of each service. Before we get to that, let's start by defining an interface that each of our application services needs to implement:

```
type Service interface {
    Name() string
    Run(context.Context) error
}
```

No surprise there... The `Name` method returns the name of the service, which we can use for logging purposes. As you've probably guessed, the `Run` method implements the business logic for the service. Calls to `Run` are expected to block until either the provided context expires or an error occurs.

The crawler service

The business logic for the crawler service is quite straightforward. The service uses a timer to sleep until the next update interval is due and then executes the following steps:

1. First, it queries the most recent information about partition assignments. This includes the partition number for the pod and the total number of partitions (pod count).
2. Using the partition count information from the previous step, a new full `Range` is created and the extents (UUID range) for the currently assigned partition number are calculated.
3. Finally, the service obtains a link iterator for the calculated UUID range and uses it as a data source to drive the crawler component that we built in `Chapter` `7`, *Data-Processing Pipelines*.

The service constructor expects a configuration object that includes not only the required configuration options but also a set of interfaces that the service depends on. This approach allows us to test the service in total isolation by injecting mock objects that satisfy these interfaces. Here's what the `Config` type for the crawler service looks like:

```
type Config struct {
    GraphAPI GraphAPI
    IndexAPI IndexAPI
    PrivateNetworkDetector crawler_pipeline.PrivateNetworkDetector
    URLGetter crawler_pipeline.URLGetter
```

```
        PartitionDetector partition.Detector
        Clock clock.Clock
        Fand so onhWorkers int
        UpdateInterval time.Duration
        ReIndexThreshold time.Duration
        Logger *logrus.Entry
    }
```

You might be wondering why I chose to redefine the GraphAPI
and IndexAPI interfaces inside this package instead of simply importing and using the
original interfaces from the graph or index packages. This is, in fact, an application of the
interface segregation principle! The original interfaces contain more methods than what we
actually need for this service. For example, the following is the set of methods that the
crawler requires to access the link graph and indexing documents:

```
    type GraphAPI interface {
        UpsertLink(link *graph.Link) error
        UpsertEdge(edge *graph.Edge) error
        RemoveStaleEdges(fromID uuid.UUID, updatedBefore time.Time) error
        Links(fromID, toID uuid.UUID, retrievedBefore time.Time)
    (graph.LinkIterator, error)
    }

    type IndexAPI interface {
        Index(doc *index.Document) error
    }
```

A very handy side effect of using the smallest possible interface definitions for the graph
and index APIs is that these minimal interfaces also happen to be compatible with the
gRPC clients that we created in the previous chapter. We will be exploiting this observation
in the next chapter so that we can split our monolithic application into microservices! Now,
let's take a look at the rest of the configuration fields:

- PartitionDetector will be queried by the service to obtain its partition
  information. When running in Kubernetes, the detector will use the code from
  the previous section to discover the available partitions. Alternatively, a partition
  detector that always reports a single partition can be injected to allow us to run
  the application as a standalone binary on our development machine.
- Clock allows us to inject a fake clock instance for our tests. Just as we did in
  Chapter 4, *The Art of Testing*, we will be using the juju/clock package to mock
  time-related operations within our tests.
- Fand so onhWorkers controls the number of workers that are used by the
  crawler component to retrieve links.
- UpdateInterval specifies how often the crawler should perform a new pass.

- `ReIndexThreshold` is used as a filter when selecting the set of links to be crawled in the next crawler pass. A link will be considered for crawling when its *last retrieval time* is *older* than `time.Now() - ReIndexThreshold`.
- `Logger` specifies an optional logger instance to use for log messages. We will talk more about structured logging in the next chapter.

The PageRank calculator service

In a similar fashion to the crawler service, the PageRank service also wakes up periodically to recalculate the PageRank scores for every link in the graph. Under the hood, it uses the PageRank calculator component that we built in `Chapter 8`, *Graph-Based Data Processing*, to execute a complete pass of the PageRank algorithm. The service layer is responsible for populating the internal graph representation that's used by the calculator component, invoking it to calculate the updated PageRank scores, and updating the PageRank scores for every indexed document.

The service constructor also accepts a `Config` object that looks like this:

```
type Config struct {
    GraphAPI GraphAPI
    IndexAPI IndexAPI
    PartitionDetector partition.Detector
    Clock clock.Clock

    ComputeWorkers int
    UpdateInterval time.Duration
    Logger *logrus.Entry
}
```

The `pagerank` service package defines its own version of the `GraphAPI` and `IndexAPI` types. As shown in the following code, the method list for these interfaces is different from the one we used for the crawler service in the previous section:

```
type GraphAPI interface {
    Links(fromID, toID uuid.UUID, retrievedBefore time.Time)
(graph.LinkIterator, error)
    Edges(fromID, toID uuid.UUID, updatedBefore time.Time)
(graph.EdgeIterator, error)
}

type IndexAPI interface {
    UpdateScore(linkID uuid.UUID, score float64) error
}
```

The `ComputeWorkers` parameter is passed through to the PageRank calculator component and controls the number of workers that are used to execute the PageRank algorithm. On the other hand, the `UpdateInterval` parameter controls the score refresh frequency.

Unfortunately, it is not *currently* feasible to run the PageRank service in partitioned mode. As we saw in `Chapter 8`, *Graph-Based Data Processing*, the calculator implementation operates under the assumption that every node in the graph can send messages to *every* other node in the graph and that all the vertices have access to the shared global state (aggregators). For the time being, we will use the detected partition information as a constraint to execute the service on a **single** pod (more specifically, the one assigned to partition 0). No need to worry, though! In `Chapter 12`, *Building Distributed Graph-Processing Systems*, we will revisit this implementation and rectify all the aforementioned issues.

Serving a fully functioning frontend to users

Of course, our little project can't really be complete without a proper frontend for our users! To build one, we will leverage the Go standard library's support for HTML templates (the `text/template` and `html/template` packages) to design a fully functioning static website for Links 'R' Us. For simplicity, all the HTML templates will be embedded into our application as *strings* and parsed into `text.Template` when the application starts. In terms of functionality, our frontend must implement a number of features.

First, it must implement an index/landing page where the user can enter a search query. Queries can either be keyword- or phrase-based. The index page should also include a link that can navigate users to another page where they can submit a website for indexing. The following screenshot shows a rendering of the index page template:

Figure 3: The landing page for Links 'R' Us

Next, we need a page where webmasters can manually submit their websites for indexing. As we mentioned previously, the index/landing page will include a link to the site submission page. The following screenshot shows what the rendered site submission page for indexing will look like:

Figure 4: A form for manually submitting sites for indexing

The final, and obviously most important, page in our entire application is the search results page. As shown in the following screenshot, the results page renders a **paginated** list of websites matching the user's search query. The header of the page includes a search text box that displays the currently searched term and allows users to change their search terms without leaving the page:

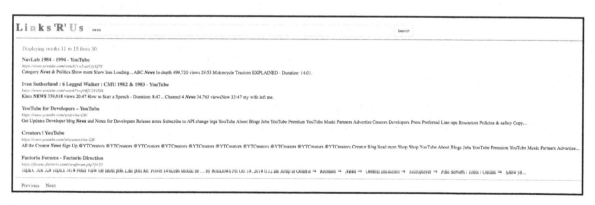

Figure 5: The paginated list of search results

The template for rendering the individual search result blocks, as portrayed in the preceding screenshot, consists of three sections:

- A link to the web page. The link text will either display the title of the matched page or the link to the page itself, depending on whether the crawler was able to extract its title.
- The URL to the matched web page in a smaller font.
- A summary of the page's contents where the matched keywords are highlighted.

Now that we have defined all the necessary templates for rendering the pages that compose the Links 'R' Us frontend, we need to register a series of HTTP routes to allow our end users to access our service.

Specifying the endpoints for the frontend application

The following table lists the HTTP request types and endpoints that our frontend service needs to handle in order to implement all the features we described previously:

Request Type	Path	Description
GET	/	Displays the index page
GET	/search?q=TERM	Displays the first page of results for TERM
GET	/search?q=TERM&offset=X	Displays the results for TERM, starting from a particular offset
GET	/submit/site	Displays the site submission form
POST	/submit/site	Handles a site submission
ANY	Any other path	Displays a 404 page

To make our life easier, we will be using `gorilla/mux` as our preferred router. Creating the router and registering the endpoint handlers is as simple as using the following code:

```
svc := &Service{
    router: mux.NewRouter(),
    cfg:    cfg,
}

svc.router.HandleFunc(indexEndpoint, svc.renderIndexPage).Methods("GET")
svc.router.HandleFunc(searchEndpoint,
svc.renderSearchResults).Methods("GET")
svc.router.HandleFunc(submitLinkEndpoint, svc.submitLink).Methods("GET",
"POST")
svc.router.NotFoundHandler = http.HandlerFunc(svc.render404Page)
```

To make the frontend service easier to test, the `Service` type stores a reference to the router. This way, we can use the `httptest` package primitives to perform HTTP requests directly at the mux without having to spin up any servers.

Performing searches and paginating results

Searching and paginating results is more or less a straightforward task for the frontend service. All our service needs to do is parse the search terms, offset from the request's query string, and invoke the `Query` method of the text indexer store that was passed as a configuration option when the service was instantiated.

Then, the service consumes the result iterator until it has either processed enough results to populate the results page or the iterator reaches the end of the result set. Consider the following code:

```
for resCount := 0; resultIt.Next() && resCount < svc.cfg.ResultsPerPage;
resCount++ {
    doc := resultIt.Document()
    matchedDocs = append(matchedDocs, matchedDoc{
        doc: doc,
        summary: highlighter.Highlight(
            template.HTMLEscapeString(
                summarizer.MatchSummary(doc.Content),
            ),
        ),
    })
}
```

The service creates a decorated model for each result that provides some convenience methods that will be called by the Go code blocks within the template. In addition, the `matchedDoc` type includes a `summary` field, which is populated with a short excerpt of the matched page's contents, with the search terms highlighted.

To highlight search terms in the text summary, the keyword highlighter will wrap each term in a <em> tag. However, this approach requires the result page template to render summaries as **raw HTML**. Consequently, we must be very careful not to allow any other HTML tags in our result summaries as this would make our application vulnerable to **cross-site scripting (XSS)** attacks. While the crawler component strips all the HTML tags from crawled pages, it doesn't hurt to be a little paranoid and escape any HTML characters from the generated summaries before passing them through to our keyword highlighter.

To be able to render the navigation header and footer, we need to provide the page template with information about the current pagination state. The following code shows how the `paginationDetails` type is populated with the required bits of information:

```
pagination := &paginationDetails{
    From:  int(offset + 1),
    To:    int(offset) + len(matchedDocs),
    Total: int(resultIt.TotalCount()),
}
if offset > 0 {
    pagination.PrevLink = fmt.Sprintf("%s?q=%s", searchEndpoint,
searchTerms)
    if prevOffset := int(offset) - svc.cfg.ResultsPerPage; prevOffset > 0 {
        pagination.PrevLink += fmt.Sprintf("&offset=%d", prevOffset)
    }
}
if nextPageOffset := int(offset) + len(matchedDocs); nextPageOffset <
pagination.Total {
    pagination.NextLink = fmt.Sprintf("%s?q=%s&offset=%d", searchEndpoint,
searchTerms, nextPageOffset)
}
```

A *previous* result page link will always be rendered when the current result offset is greater than 0. Unless we are moving back to the *first* result page, the link will always include an offset parameter. Similarly, the *next* result page link will be rendered as long as we haven't reached the end of the result set.

Generating convincing summaries for search results

Generating a descriptive short summary that conveys enough information to the user about the contents of a web page that matched their query is quite a hard problem to solve. As a matter of fact, automatic summarization is an active research field for natural language processing and machine learning.

Arguably, building such a system is outside the scope of this book. Instead, we will be implementing a much simpler algorithm that yields plausible summaries that should be good enough for our particular use case. Here is an outline of the algorithm's steps:

1. Split the matched page's content into sentences.
2. For each sentence, calculate the ratio of matched keywords to the total number of words. This will serve as our quality metric for selecting and prioritizing the set of sentences to be included in the summary.

3. Skip any sentences where the ratio is zero; that is, they don't contain any of the searched keywords. These sentences are not really useful for our summary.

4. Add the remaining sentences to a list where each entry is a tuple of `{ordinal, text, matchRatio}`. The ordinal value refers to the location of the sentence in the text.

5. Sort the list by *match ratio* in *descending* order.

6. Initialize a second list for the sentence fragments that will be used for the summary and a variable that keeps track of the remaining characters for the summary.

7. Iterate the sorted list; for each entry, do the following: If its length is *less* than the remaining summary characters, append the entry as is to the second list and subtract its length from the remaining characters, variable. If its length is *more* than the remaining summary character, truncate the sentence text to the remaining summary characters, append it to the second list, and *terminate* the iteration.

8. Sort the summary fragment list by *ordinal* in *ascending* order. This ensures that sentence fragments appear in the same order as the text.

9. Iterate the sorted fragment list and concatenate the entries as follows:
   - If the ordinal of the current sentence is one more than the previous sentence's ordinal, they should be joined with a single period, just like they were connected together in the original text.
   - Otherwise, the sentences should be joined with an ellipsis since they belong to different parts of the text.

The complete Go implementation of the preceding algorithm is too long to list here, but if you're curious, you can take a look at it by visiting this book's GitHub repository and browsing the contents of the `summarizer.go` file, which you can find under the `Chapter10/linksrus/service/frontend` folder.

Highlighting search keywords

Once we have generated a summary for a matched document, we need to identify and highlight all the search keywords that are present within it. For this task, we will create a helper type named `matchHighlighter` that constructs a set of regular expressions for matching each search keyword and wrap it with a special HTML tag that our frontend template renders using a highlighted style.

The frontend creates a single `matchHighlighter` instance for the entire set of results by invoking the `newMatchHighlighter` function, which is listed in the following code:

```
func newMatchHighlighter(searchTerms string) *matchHighlighter {
    var regexes []*regexp.Regexp
    for _, token := range strings.Fields(strings.Trim(searchTerms, `"`)) {
        re, err := regexp.Compile(
            fmt.Sprintf(`(?i)%s`, regexp.QuoteMeta(token)),
        )
        if err != nil {
            continue
        }
        regexes = append(regexes, re)
    }

    return &matchHighlighter{regexes: regexes}
}
```

The constructor receives the user's search terms as input and splits them into a list of words. Note that the search term will be enclosed in quotes if the user is searching for an exact phrase. Therefore, before passing the term string to `strings.Fields`, we need to trim any quotes at the beginning and end of the input string.

Then, for each individual term, we compile a *case-insensitive* regular expression, which will be used by the `Highlight` method. This is as follows:

```
func (h *matchHighlighter) Highlight(sentence string) string {
    for _, re := range h.regexes {
        sentence = re.ReplaceAllStringFunc(sentence, func(match string) string {
            return "<em>" + match + "</em>"
        })
    }
    return sentence
}
```

The `Highlight` method simply iterates the list of regular expressions and wraps each match in a <em> tag that our result page template can style using CSS rules.

Orchestrating the execution of individual services

So far, we have created three services for our monolith that all implement the Service interface. Now, we need to introduce a supervisor for coordinating their execution and making sure that they all cleanly terminate if any of them reports an error. Let's define a new type so that we can model a group of services and add a helper Run method to manage their execution life cycle:

```
type Group []Service

func (g Group) Run(ctx context.Context) error {...}
```

Now, let's break down the Run method's implementation into smaller chunks and go through each one:

```
if ctx == nil {
    ctx = context.Background()
}
runCtx, cancelFn := context.WithCancel(ctx)
defer cancelFn()
```

As you can see, first, we create a new cancelable context that wraps the one that was externally provided to us by the Run method caller. The wrapped context will be provided as an argument to the Run method of each individual service, thus ensuring that *all* the services can be canceled in one of two ways:

- By the caller if, for instance, the provided context is canceled or expires
- By the supervisor, if any of the services raise an error

Next, we will spin up a goroutine for each service in the group and execute its Run method, as follows:

```
var wg sync.WaitGroup
errCh := make(chan error, len(g))
wg.Add(len(g))
for _, s := range g {
    go func(s Service) {
        defer wg.Done()
        if err := s.Run(runCtx); err != nil {
            errCh <- xerrors.Errorf("%s: %w", s.Name(), err)
            cancelFn()
        }
    }(s)
}
```

If an error occurs, the goroutine will annotate it with the service name and write it to a buffered error channel before invoking the cancel function for the wrapped context. As a result, if any service fails, all the other services will be automatically instructed to shut down.

A `sync.WaitGroup` helps us keep track of the currently running goroutines. As we mentioned previously, we are working with long-running services whose `Run` method only returns if the context is canceled or an error occurs. In either case, the wrapped context will expire so that we can have our service runner wait for this event to occur and then call the wait group's `Wait` method to ensure that all the spawned goroutines have terminated before proceeding. The following code demonstrates how this is achieved:

```
<-runCtx.Done()
wg.Wait()
```

Before returning, we must check for the presence of errors. To this end, we close the error channel so that we can iterate it using a `range` statement. Closing the channel is safe since all the goroutines that could potentially write to it have already terminated. Consider the following code:

```
var err error
close(errCh)
for srvErr := range errCh {
    err = multierror.Append(err, srvErr)
}
return err
```

As shown in the preceding snippet, after closing the channel, the code dequeues and aggregates any reported errors and returns them to the caller. Note that a nil error value will be returned if no error has occurred.

Putting everything together

The main package serves as the entry point for our application. It exposes the configuration options for the various services as command-line flags and takes care of the following:

- Instantiating the appropriate data store implementations for the link graph (memory or CockroachDB) and text indexer (memory or Elasticsearch)
- Instantiating the various application services with the correct configuration options

The `runMain` method implements the main loop of the application:

```
func runMain(logger *logrus.Entry) error {
    svcGroup, err := setupServices(logger)
    if err != nil {
        return err
    }

    ctx, cancelFn := context.WithCancel(context.Background())
    defer cancelFn()
    return svcGroup.Run(ctx)
}
```

As shown in the preceding code, the first line instantiates all the required services and adds them to a `Group`. Then, a new cancelable context is created and is used to invoke the group's (blocking) `Run` method.

Terminating the application in a clean way

At this point, you are probably wondering: how does the application terminate? The answer is by receiving a signal from the operating system. The `signal` package in the Go standard library comes with a `Notify` function that allows an application to register for, and receive, notifications when the application receives a particular signal type. Common signal types include the following:

- `SIGINT`, which is normally sent to a foreground application when the user presses *Ctrl + C*.
- `SIGHUP`, which many applications (for example, HTTP servers) hook and use as a trigger to reload their configuration.
- `SIGKILL`, which is sent to an application before the operating system kills it. This particular signal cannot be caught.
- `SIGQUIT`, which is sent to a foreground application when the user presses *Ctrl+ _*. The Go runtime hooks this signal so that it can print the stacks for every running goroutine before terminating the application.

Since our application will be running as a Docker container, we are only interested in handling `SIGINT` (sent by Kubernetes when the pod is about to shut down) and `SIGHUP` (for debug purposes). Since the preceding code blocks on the group's `Run` method, we need to use a goroutine to watch for incoming signals:

```
go func() {
    sigCh := make(chan os.Signal, 1)
    signal.Notify(sigCh, syscall.SIGINT, syscall.SIGHUP)
```

```
        select {
        case s := <-sigCh:
            cancelFn()
        case <-ctx.Done():
        }
    }()
```

Upon receiving one of the specified signals, we immediately invoke the cancellation function for the context and return. This action will cause all the services in the group to cleanly shut down and for the `svcGroup.Run` call to return, thus allowing `runMain` to also return and for the application to terminate.

Dockerizing and starting a single instance of the monolith

The `Chapter10/linksrus` package comes with a Dockerfile that includes the necessary steps for building a dockerized version of the monolithic application that you can then run either locally or deploy to Kubernetes using the guide in the following section.

To create a Docker image for testing purposes, you can simply type `make dockerize` into the package directory. Alternatively, if you wish to build and push the generated images to a Docker registry, you can type `make dockerize-and-push`. The Makefile target assumes that you are running Minikube and have enabled the private registry add-on according to the instructions from the previous sections.

The tags for all the Docker images that are created by this Makefile will include the private registry URL as a prefix. For example, if the IP currently in use by Minikube is `192.168.99.100`, the generated image will be tagged as follows:

- `192.168.99.100/linksrus-monolith:latest`
- `192.168.99.100/linksrus-monolith:$GIT_SHA`

If you want to use a different private registry (for example, `localhost:32000`, if you're using microk8s), you can run `make PRIVATE_REGISTRY=localhost:32000 dockerize-and-push` instead.

On the other hand, if you want to push the images to the **public** Docker registry, you can invoke the command with an **empty** `PRIVATE_REGISTRY` environment variable with `make PRIVATE_REGISTRY= dockerize-and-push`.

To make it easier for those of you who don't want to spin up a Kubernetes cluster to test-drive the monolithic application, the application default command-line values will start the application in standalone mode:

- An in-memory store will be used for both the link graph and the text indexer
- A new crawler pass will be triggered every 5 minutes and a PageRank recalculation will occur every hour
- The frontend is exposed on port 8080

The receding default settings make it easy to start the application either locally by running a command such as `go run main.go` or inside a Docker container by running `docker run -it --rm -p 8080:8080 $(minikube ip):5000/linksrus monolith:latest`.

Deploying and scaling the monolith on Kubernetes

In the last part of this chapter, we will deploy the Links 'R' Us monolithic application on Kubernetes and put the partitioning logic to the test by scaling our deployment horizontally.

The following diagram illustrates what our final setup will look like. As you can see, we will be using Kubernetes namespaces to logically split the various components for our deployment:

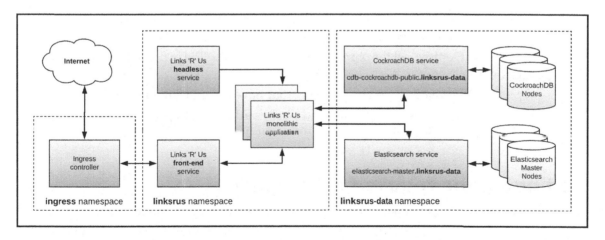

Figure 6: Deploying a monolithic version of Links 'R' Us on Kubernetes

From the preceding diagram, we can see that the `linksrus-data` namespace will host our data stores, which will be configured in highly available mode. The CockroachDB cluster consists of multiple nodes that are hidden behind a Kubernetes service resource called `cdb-cockroachdb-public`. Our application can access the DB cluster via the service's DNS entry, `cdb-cockroachdb-public.linksrus-data`. The Elasticsearch cluster follows exactly the same pattern; it also exposes a service that we can use to reach the master nodes by connecting to `elasticsearch-master.linksrus-data:9200`.

On the other hand, the `linksrus` namespace is where our application will be deployed as a StatefulSet consisting of four replicas. The choice of the number of replicas is arbitrary and can be easily adjusted upward or downward at any point in time by reconfiguring the StatefulSet.

To be able to query the SRV records for all the pods in the StatefulSet, we will create a **headless** Kubernetes service. This service makes it possible for us to use the partition discovery code that we described in *The crawler service* section. Before we can expose our frontend to the outside world, we need to create yet another Kubernetes service that will act as a load balancer for distributing incoming traffic to the pods in our StatefulSet.

The final ingredient in our deploy recipe is an Ingress resource, which will allow our end users to access the frontend service over the internet.

Every Kubernetes manifest that we will be working with in the following sections is available in the `Chapter10/k8s` folder of this book's GitHub repository. Inside the same folder, you can find a Makefile with the following handy targets:

- `bootstrap-minikube`: Bootstraps a Kubernetes cluster using Minikube and installs all the required add-ons for deploying Links 'R' Us
- `deploy`: Deploys all the components for the Links 'R' Us project, including the data stores
- `purge`: Removes all the components that have been installed via `make deploy`
- `dockerize-and-push`: Builds and pushes **all** the required container images for the Links 'R' Us project

Setting up the required namespaces

To create the required namespaces for the deployment, you need to switch to the `Chapter10/k8s` folder and apply the `01-namespaces.yaml` manifest by running the following command:

```
kubectl apply -f 01-namespaces.yaml
```

After applying the manifest, the new namespaces should show up when you run `kubectl get namespaces`. The following screenshot shows a list of the Kubernetes cluster namespaces:

```
● ● ●                          4. bash (bash)
$ kubectl get namespaces
NAME                 STATUS    AGE
container-registry   Active    4d8h
default              Active    4d8h
kube-node-lease      Active    4d8h
kube-public          Active    4d8h
kube-system          Active    4d8h
linksrus             Active    13m
linksrus-data        Active    13m
$ ▌
```

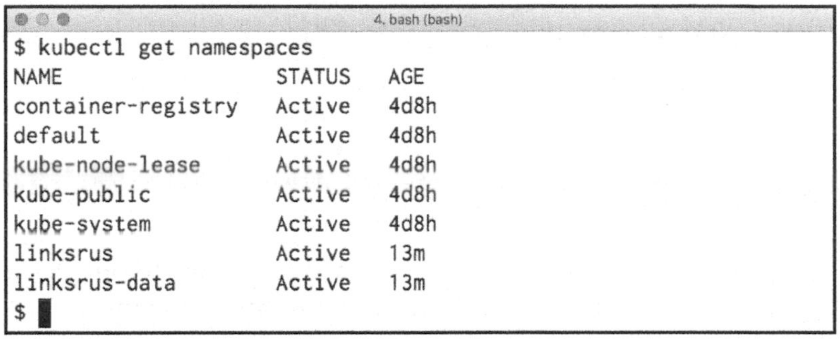

Figure 7: Listing the Kubernetes cluster namespaces

The following steps entail the deployment of our database services, followed by the deployment of the monolithic Links 'R' Us application.

Deploying CockroachDB and Elasticsearch using Helm

Setting up the CockroachDB and Elasticsearch cluster is quite tedious and involves applying quite a few manifests. Instead of doing this manually, we will actually cheat and deploy both data stores using the `helm` tool!

For CockroachDB, we can run the following command to deploy a three-node cluster:

```
helm install --namespace=linksrus-data --name cdb \
    --values chart-settings/cdb-settings.yaml \
    --set ImageTag=v19.1.5 \
    stable/cockroachdb
```

The `cdb-settings.yaml` file that's referenced by the preceding command contains overrides for the default chart values, which restrict the spawned database instance to using 512 M of RAM and 100 M of disk space.

The `helm` charts for Elasticsearch are currently maintained in an external repository that must be registered with `helm` before we can proceed with the installation. Similar to CockroachDB, a settings override file is also provided that restricts the Elasticsearch master nodes to using 512 M of RAM and 300 M of disk space. The following command will take care of the Elasticsearch deployment:

```
helm repo add elastic https://helm.elastic.co
helm install --namespace=linksrus-data --name es \
    --values chart-settings/es-settings.yaml \
    --set imageTag=7.4.0 \
    elastic/elasticsearch
```

After running all of the preceding commands, you should be able to type `kubectl -n linksrus-data get pods` and see an output similar to the following:

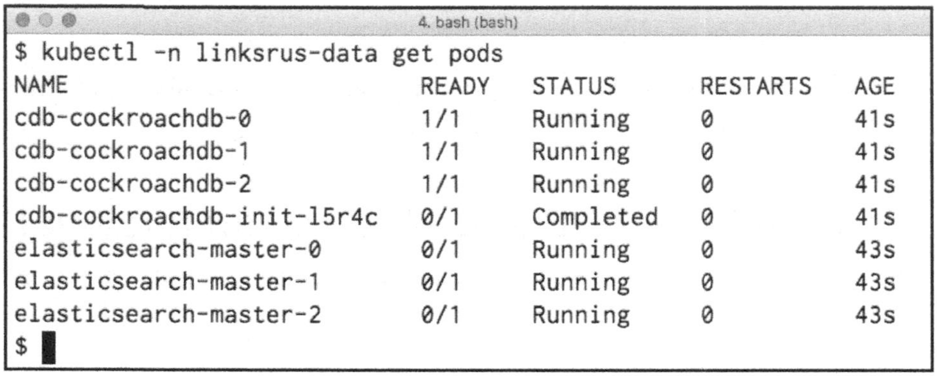

```
4. bash (bash)
$ kubectl -n linksrus-data get pods
NAME                        READY   STATUS      RESTARTS   AGE
cdb-cockroachdb-0           1/1     Running     0          41s
cdb-cockroachdb-1           1/1     Running     0          41s
cdb-cockroachdb-2           1/1     Running     0          41s
cdb-cockroachdb-init-15r4c  0/1     Completed   0          41s
elasticsearch-master-0      0/1     Running     0          43s
elasticsearch-master-1      0/1     Running     0          43s
elasticsearch-master-2      0/1     Running     0          43s
$
```

Figure 8: Listing the pods in the linksrus-data namespace

Once all the data store pods show up as *running*, we can deploy Links 'R' Us!

Deploying Links 'R' Us

Before we can create the Links 'R' Us StatefulSet, there is one more aspect that we need to take care of: the CockroachDB instance is not aware of the schema for the link graph. Nothing to worry about... We can remedy this issue by spawning a one-off container that will create the database for the link graph and apply the schema migrations from Chapter 6, *Building a Persistence Layer*.

You can find the source code and Dockerfile for this container in the `Chapter10/cdb-schema` folder. Assuming that you are currently using Minikube for your cluster, you can run the following command in the preceding folder to create the Docker image and push it to the private registry exposed by Minikube:

```
make dockerize-and-push
```

Moving back to the manifests inside the `Chapter10/k8s` folder, you can apply the `02-cdb-schema.yaml` manifest to create a one-off Kubernetes `Job` that waits for the DB cluster to become available, ensures that the link-graph database and schema are up to date, and then exits. Here's what the content of this YAML file looks like:

```yaml
apiVersion: batch/v1
kind: Job
metadata:
  name: cdb-ensure-schema
  namespace: linksrus-data
spec:
  template:
    spec:
      containers:
      - name: cdb-schema
        imagePullPolicy: Always
        image: localhost:5000/cdb-schema:latest
        args:
         - "linkgraph"
         - "cdb-cockroachdb-public.linksrus-data"
      restartPolicy: Never
```

Finally, we can deploy the remaining Links 'R' Us resources by applying the `03-linksrus-monolith.yaml` manifest. If you haven't done so already, make sure that you run `make dockerize-and-push` in the `Chapter10/linksrus` folder prior to applying the manifest to make sure that Kubernetes can find the referenced container images.

 The Makefile in the `k8s` folder also defines a `dockerize-and-push` target that can build and push **all** the required container images for running the Links 'R' Us demo from this section with a single command.

After a few seconds, you can type `kubectl -n linksrus get` `pods,statefulsets,services,ingresses` to get a list of all the resources we just deployed. The following screenshot shows the expected output of this command:

```
● ● ●                              4. bash (bash)
$ kubectl -n linksrus get pods,statefulsets,services,ingresses
NAME                                 READY   STATUS    RESTARTS   AGE
pod/linksrus-monolith-instance-0     1/1     Running   0          4m14s
pod/linksrus-monolith-instance-1     1/1     Running   0          2m11s
pod/linksrus-monolith-instance-2     1/1     Running   0          2m9s
pod/linksrus-monolith-instance-3     1/1     Running   0          2m7s

NAME                                            READY   AGE
statefulset.apps/linksrus-monolith-instance     4/4     4m14s

NAME                        TYPE        CLUSTER-IP       EXTERNAL-IP   PORT(S)   AGE
service/linksrus-frontend   ClusterIP   10.108.213.197   <none>        80/TCP    4m14s
service/linksrus-headless   ClusterIP   None             <none>        80/TCP    4m14s

NAME                                    HOSTS   ADDRESS     PORTS   AGE
ingress.extensions/linksrus-ingress     *       10.0.2.15   80      4m14s
$ ▮
```

Figure 9: Listing all the resources in the linksrus namespace

Success! Our monolithic application has been deployed and connected to the data stores in the `linksrus-data` namespace. You can access the frontend service by pointing your browser to the IP address of your ingress. In the preceding output, I was using Minikube inside a VM and therefore the displayed ingress address is not accessible from the host. However, you can easily find out the public IP that was used by Minikube by running `minikube ip` and pointing your browser to it.

You can tail the logs of each individual pod in the StatefulSet using the `kubectl -n linksrus logs linksrus-monolith-instance-X` `-f` command, where *X* is a pod number from the set.

Moreover, you can also tail the logs from *all* the pods in the set using the `kubectl -n linksrus logs -lapp=linksrus-monolith-instance -f` command.

Summary

In this chapter, we learned how to dockerize our Go applications in a way that yields container images with the smallest possible size. Then, we talked about the design philosophy and general architecture behind Kubernetes and elaborated on the different types of resources that you can create and manage on a Kubernetes cluster. In the last part of this chapter, we pieced together the first fully functioning version of the Links 'R' Us project and deployed it as a single monolithic application on Kubernetes.

In the next chapter, we will discuss the challenges and potential caveats involved when switching to a microservice architecture.

Questions

1. Name some benefits of containerization.
2. What is the difference between a master and a worker node in a Kubernetes cluster?
3. What is the difference between a regular service and a headless service?
4. What kind of Kubernetes resource would you use to share your OAuth2 client ID and secret with your frontend?
5. Explain the difference between a deployment and a StatefulSet.

Further reading

1. Alpine Linux: A security-oriented, lightweight Linux distribution based on musl libc and busybox. https://alpinelinux.org.
2. Calico: Secure networking for the cloud-native era. https://www.projectcalico.org.
3. Cilium: API-aware networking and security. https://cilium.io.
4. Containerd: An industry-standard container runtime with an emphasis on simplicity, robustness, and portability. https://containerd.io.
5. Docker: Enterprise container platform. https://www.docker.com.
6. Helm: The package manager for Kubernetes. https://helm.sh.
7. K3S: Lightweight Kubernetes. https://k3s.io/.

8. Kubernetes: Production-grade container orchestration. `https://www.kubernetes.io`.

9. Microk8s: Zero-ops Kubernetes for workstations and edge / IoT. `https://microk8s.io`.

10. Minikube: Local Kubernetes, focused on application development and education. `https://minikube.sigs.k8s.io`.

11. Multipass: Orchestrates virtual Ubuntu instances. `https://multipass.run/`.

12. rkt: A security-minded, standards-based container engine. `https://coreos.com/rkt`.

13. VirtualBox: A powerful x86 and AMD64/Intel64 virtualization product for enterprise as well as home use. `https://www.virtualbox.org`.

Section 4: Scaling Out to Handle a Growing Number of Users

This section of the book evaluates different approaches for horizontally scaling and monitoring distribution systems.

This section comprises the following chapters:

11
Splitting Monoliths into Microservices

"If the components do not compose cleanly (when migrating to microservices), then all you are doing is shifting the complexity from inside a component to the connections between components. This does not just move complexity around; it moves it to a place that's less explicit and harder to control."

– Martin Fowler and James Lewis

This chapter introduces the concept of **Service-Oriented Architecture (SOA)** and compares it with the traditional monolithic design pattern. This will help us discuss the various challenges of microservices such as logging, tracing, and service introspection, and provides advice for reducing the pain points from moving to an SOA.

Toward the end of this chapter, we will be breaking down the monolithic Links 'R' Us implementation from the previous chapter into several microservices and deploying them to Kubernetes.

The following topics will be covered in this chapter:

- When is a good time to switch from monolithic design to a microservice-based architecture?
- Common anti-patterns for microservice implementations and how to work around them
- Tracing requests through distributed systems
- Best practices for logging and pitfalls to avoid

- Introspection of live Go services
- Breaking down the Links 'R' Us monolith into microservices and deploying them to Kubernetes
- Locking down access to microservices using Kubernetes network policies

By leveraging the knowledge you will have obtained in this chapter, you will be able to horizontally scale your own projects so as to better handle spikes in incoming traffic.

Technical requirements

The full code for the topics that will be discussed in this chapter has been published to this book's GitHub repository under the `Chapter11` folder.

 You can access this book's GitHub repository, which contains the code and all the required resources for each chapter in this book, by pointing your web browser to the following URL: `https://github.com/PacktPublishing/Hands-On-Software-Engineering-with-Golang`.

To get you up and running as quickly as possible, each example project includes a Makefile that defines the following set of targets:

Makefile target	Description
deps	Installs any required dependencies
test	Runs all tests and report coverage
lint	Checks for lint errors

As with all the other chapters in this book, you will need a fairly recent version of Go, which you can download at `https://golang.org/dl/`.

To run some of the code examples in this chapter, you will need to have a working Docker [4] installation on your machine.

Furthermore, a subset of the examples are designed to run on Kubernetes. If you don't have access to a Kubernetes cluster for testing, you can simply follow the instructions laid out in the following sections to set up a small cluster on your laptop or workstation.

Monoliths versus service-oriented architectures

In the last couple of years, more and more organizations, especially in the start up scene, have been actively embracing the SOA paradigm either for building new systems or for modernizing existing legacy systems.

 SOA is an architectural approach to creating systems that have been built from autonomous services that may be written in different programming languages and communicate with each other over a network link.

In the following sections, we will examine this architectural pattern in more detail and highlight some best practices for migrating from a monolithic application to microservices. At the same time, we will explore some common anti-patterns that can impede the transition to a microservice-based architecture.

Is there something inherently wrong with monoliths?

Before you decide to take the plunge and convert your monolithic application into an SOA, you should take a small pause and ask yourself: is a microservice-based design the right model for my application *at this point in time*?

 Try not to be influenced by the hype surrounding microservices! Just because this kind of model works at a massive scale for companies such as Google, Netflix, or Twitter, it doesn't mean that it also will for your particular use case.

Monolithic system designs have been around for much longer and have proven themselves time and time again when it comes to supporting business-critical systems. As the saying goes: if it's good enough for banks and airlines, it's probably adequate for your next start up idea!

In many cases, the decision to transition to a microservice-based architecture is driven purely by necessity; scaling large, monolithic systems to deal with irregular spikes in traffic can prove to be quite costly and can oftentimes lead to underutilization of the resources available at our disposal. This is a great example where switching to microservices would most probably have both an observable and measurable effect.

On the other hand, if you are building a new product or a **minimum viable product** (**MVP**), it is always much easier to begin with a monolithic design and introduce the right abstractions from the start to facilitate an easier transition path to microservices, if and when that is required.

Lots of new start-ups get trapped in the mentality that microservices are the next best thing since sliced bread and forget about the hidden cost of such an architecture: increased complexity, which directly translates to increased demand for DevOps. As a result, engineering teams tend to spend a significant chunk of their development time debugging communication issues or setting up elaborate schemes for monitoring microservices instead of focusing their efforts on building and developing their core product.

Microservice anti-patterns and how to deal with them

Now, let's take a look at some anti-patterns that you might encounter when working with microservice-based projects and explore alternative ways of dealing with them.

Sharing a database is probably the biggest mistake that engineers new to the microservice pattern make when they attempt to split a monolith into microservices for the first time. As a rule of thumb, each microservice must be provisioned with its own, private data store (assuming it needs one) and expose an API so that other microservices can access it. This pattern provides us with the flexibility to select the most suitable technology (for example, NoSQL, relational) for the needs of each particular microservice.

Communication between microservices might fail for a variety of reasons (for example, a service crash, network partition, or lost packets). A correct microservice implementation should operate under the assumption that outbound calls can fail at any time. Instead of immediately bailing out with an error when things go wrong, microservices should always implement some sort of *retry logic*.

A corollary to the preceding statement is that when a connection to a remote microservice drops before receiving a reply, the client cannot be sure whether the remote server actually managed to process the request. Based on the preceding recommendation, the client will typically retry the call. Consequently, every microservice that exposes an API must be written in such a way so that requests are always *idempotent*.

Another common anti-pattern is to allow a service to become a *single point of failure* for the entire system. Imagine a scenario where you have three services that all depend on a piece of data that's been exposed by a fourth, downstream service. If the latter service is underprovisioned, a sudden request in traffic to the three upstream services might cause requests to the downstream service to time out. The upstream services would then retry their requests, increasing the load on the downstream service even further, up to the point where it becomes unresponsive or crashes. As a result, the upstream services now begin experiencing elevated error rates that affect calls that are made to them by other upstream services, and so on and so forth.

To avoid situations like this, microservices can implement the circuit breaker pattern: when the number of errors from a particular downstream service exceeds a particular threshold, the circuit breaker is tripped and all future requests automatically fail with an error. Periodically, the circuit breaker lets some requests go through and after a number of successful responses, the circuit breaker switches back to the open position, allowing all requests to go through.

By implementing this pattern into your microservices, we allow downstream services to recover from load spikes or crashes. Moreover, some services might be able to respond with cached data when downstream services are not available, thus ensuring that the system remains functional, even in the presence of problems.

As we have already explained, microservice-based architectures are inherently complex as they consist of a large number of moving parts. The biggest mistake that we can make is switching to this kind of architecture before laying down the necessary infrastructure for collecting the log output of each microservice and monitoring its health. Without this infrastructure in place, we are effectively flying blind. In the next section, we will explore a few different approaches to microservice instrumentation and monitoring.

Monitoring the state of your microservices

In the following sections, we will be analyzing an array of different approaches for monitoring the state of a microservice deployment:

- Request tracing
- Log collection and aggregation
- Introspection of live Go services with the help of `pprof`

Tracing requests through distributed systems

In a world where you might have distributed systems with hundreds or thousands of microservices running, request tracing is an invaluable tool for figuring out bottlenecks, understanding the dependencies between individual services, and figuring out the root cause of issues that affect production systems.

The idea behind tracing is to tag an incoming (usually external) request with a unique identifier and keep track of it as it propagates through the system, hopping from one microservice to the next until it eventually exits the system.

The concept of a distributed tracing system is definitely not new. In fact, systems such as Google's Dapper [17] and Twitter's Zipkin [16] have been around for almost a decade. So, why isn't everyone jumping on the wagon and implementing it for their code bases? The reason is simple: up until now, updating your entire code base to support request tracing used to be a daunting task.

Imagine a system where the components communicate with each other via different types of transports, that is, some microservices use REST, others use gRPC, and others perhaps exchange events over WebSockets. Ensuring that request IDs get injected into all outgoing requests and unmarshaled on the receiving end requires quite a bit of effort to implement across all microservices. What's more, if you were to go down this route, you would be expected to do a bit of research, select a tracing *vendor* to use, and finally integrate with their (typically proprietary) API, which would effectively lock you into their offering.

There's got to be a better way to implement request tracing!

The OpenTracing project

The OpenTracing [18] project was created to solve exactly the set of problems that we outlined in the previous section. It provides a standardized, vendor-neutral API that software engineers can use to instrument their code base to enable support for request tracing. Moreover, OpenTracing not only dictates the appropriate encoding for transferring trace contexts *across service boundaries*, but also provides APIs to facilitate the exchange of tracing context over REST and gRPC transports.

Before we continue, let's spend some time explaining a term that we will be using quite a lot in the following sections. A request trace is comprised of a sequence of **spans**. A span represents a timed unit of work that executes inside a microservice. In a typical scenario, a new span begins when the service receives a request and ends when the service returns a response.

Furthermore, spans can also be nested. If service *A* needs to contact downstream services *B* and *C* for additional data before it can send back a response, then the spans from *B* and *C* can be added as children of *A*'s span. Consequently, a request trace can be thought of as a *tree of spans* whose root is the service that received the initial request.

Stepping through a distributed tracing example

To understand how distributed tracing works, let's build a small demo application that simulates a system for collecting price quotes for a particular SKU from a variety of vendors. You can find the full source code for this demo in the `Chapter11/tracing` folder of this book's GitHub repository.

Our system will feature three types of services, all of which will be built on top of gRPC:

- The **provider** service returns price quotes for a single vendor. For our example scenario, we will be spinning up multiple provider instances to simulate different vendor systems.
- An **aggregator** service that sends incoming queries to a list of downstream services (providers or other aggregators) collects the responses and returns the aggregated results.
- An **API gateway** service, which will serve as the root of the captured request traces. In the real world, the API gateway would handle requests from a frontend application running on the users' browser.

Let's begin by listing the protocol buffer and RPC definitions for the services:

```
message QuotesRequest {
    string SKU = 1;
}

message QuotesResponse {
    repeated Quote quotes = 1;
}

message Quote {
    string vendor = 1;
    double price = 2;
}

service QuoteService {
    rpc GetQuote(QuotesRequest) returns (QuotesResponse);
}
```

As you can see, we define a single RPC named `GetQuote` that receives a `QuotesRequest` and returns a `QuotesResponse`. The response is simply a collection to `Quote` objects, with each one consisting of a `vendor` and a `price` field.

The provider service

The first and easiest service to implement is `Provider`. The following is the definition for the `Provider` type and its constructor:

```
type Provider struct {
    vendorID string
}

func NewProvider(vendorID string) *Provider {
    return &Provider{ vendorID: vendorID }
}
```

Next, we will implement the `GetQuote` method, as specified in the preceding protocol buffer definitions. To keep our example as simple as possible, we will provide a dummy implementation that returns a single quote with a random price value and the `vendorID` value that was passed as an argument to the `NewProvider` constructor:

```
func (p *Provider) GetQuote(ctx context.Context, req *proto.QuotesRequest)
(*proto.QuotesResponse, error) {
    return &proto.QuotesResponse{
        Quotes: []*proto.Quote{
            &proto.Quote{ Vendor: p.vendorID, Price:  100.0 *
rand.Float64() },
        },
    }, nil
}
```

To simulate a microservice architecture, our main file will start multiple instances of this service. Each service instance will create its own gRPC server and bind it to a random port. Let's implement this functionality for the `Provider` type:

```
func (p *Provider) Serve(ctx context.Context) (string, error) {
    return doServe(ctx, p, tracer.MustGetTracer(p.vendorID))
}
```

The `tracer` package encapsulates the required logic for creating tracer instances that satisfy the `opentracing.Tracer` interface. The obtained tracer will be used for each of the services that we will be creating so that it can collect and report spans. In the following sections, we will explore the implementation of this package when we select a suitable tracing provider for our example.

After obtaining a tracer, the `Serve` method calls out to `doServe`, whose task is to expose a gRPC server to a random available port and return its listen address. The `doServe` code, which is listed in the following code block, has been intentionally extracted since we will be using this to implement the aggregator service:

```
func doServe(ctx context.Context, srv proto.QuoteServiceServer, tracer
opentracing.Tracer) (string, error) {
    l, err := net.Listen("tcp", ":0")
    if err != nil {
        return "", err
    }
    tracerOpt :=
grpc.UnaryInterceptor(otgrpc.OpenTracingServerInterceptor(tracer))
    gsrv := grpc.NewServer(tracerOpt)
    proto.RegisterQuoteServiceServer(gsrv, srv)
    go func() {
        go func() { _ = gsrv.Serve(l) }()
        <-ctx.Done()
        gsrv.Stop()
        _ = l.Close()
    }()
    return l.Addr().String(), nil
}
```

The first lines in the preceding function ask the `net` package to listen to a random free port by passing `:0` as the listen address. The next line is where the real magic happens! The `grpc-opentracing` [10] package provides gRPC interceptors that decode tracing-related information from incoming gRPC requests and *embed* them into the request context that is passed to the RPC method implementations.

> A gRPC interceptor is a kind of middleware that wraps an RPC call and provides additional functionality. Depending on the type of call that is being wrapped, interceptors are classified as unary or streaming.
>
> Moreover, interceptors can be applied on the server- or client-side. On the server-side, interceptors are typically used to implement features such as authentication, logging, and metrics collection. Client-side interceptors can be used to implement patterns such as circuit breakers or retries.

Since our service only defines a unary RPC, we need to create a unary interceptor and pass it to the `grpc.NewServer` function. Then, we register the RPC implementation with the server and spin up a goroutine so that we can start serving requests until the provided context expires. While the goroutine is running, the function returns with the address of the server listener.

The aggregator service

The next service that we will be implementing is the `Aggregator` type. As shown in the following code snippet, it stores a vendor ID, a list of provider addresses to query, and a list of gRPC clients for those addresses:

```
type Aggregator struct {
    vendorID        string
    providerAddrs   []string
    clients         []proto.QuoteServiceClient
}

func NewAggregator(vendorID string, providerAddrs []string) *Aggregator {
    return &Aggregator{
        vendorID:       vendorID,
        providerAddrs:  providerAddrs,
    }
}
```

The gRPC clients are lazily created when the `Serve` method is invoked:

```
func (a *Aggregator) Serve(ctx context.Context) (string, error) {
    tracer := tracer.MustGetTracer(a.vendorID)
    tracerClientOpt :=
grpc.WithUnaryInterceptor(otgrpc.OpenTracingClientInterceptor(tracer))

    for _, addr := range a.providerAddrs {
        conn, err := grpc.Dial(addr, grpc.WithInsecure(), tracerClientOpt)
        if err != nil {
            return "", xerrors.Errorf("dialing provider at %s: %w", addr,
err)
        }
        a.clients = append(a.clients, proto.NewQuoteServiceClient(conn))
    }

    return doServe(ctx, a, tracer)
}
```

This time, we create a **client** unary interceptor and pass it as an option to each client connection that we dial. Then, we invoke the `doServe` helper that we examined in the previous section so that we can start our server. The use of interceptors for both the server **and** the client ensures that the trace context information that we receive from incoming requests gets **automatically** injected into any outgoing gRPC request without us having to do anything.

Finally, let's examine how the `GetQuote` method is implemented for the `Aggregator` type:

```
func (a *Aggregator) GetQuote(ctx context.Context, req
*proto.QuotesRequest) (*proto.QuotesResponse, error) {
    // Run requests in parallel and aggregate results
    aggRes := new(proto.QuotesResponse)
    for quotes := range a.sendRequests(ctx, req) {
        aggRes.Quotes = append(aggRes.Quotes, quotes...)
    }
    return aggRes, nil
}
```

This method is quite straightforward. All it does is allocate a new `QuotesResponse`, invoke the `sendRequests` helper, flatten the results into a list, and return it to the caller.
The `sendRequests` method queries the downstream providers in parallel and returns a channel where the quotes are posted:

```
func (a *Aggregator) sendRequests(ctx context.Context, req
*proto.QuotesRequest) <-chan []*proto.Quote {
    var wg sync.WaitGroup
    wg.Add(len(a.clients))
    resCh := make(chan []*proto.Quote, len(a.clients))
    for _, client := range a.clients {
        go func(client proto.QuoteServiceClient) {
            defer wg.Done()
            if res, err := client.GetQuote(ctx, req); err == nil {
                resCh <- res.Quotes
            }
        }(client)
    }
    go func() {
        wg.Wait()
        close(resCh)
    }()
    return resCh
}
```

Notice how the request context argument from `GetQuote` is passed along to the `client.GetQuote` calls. This is all we need to do to associate the span from this service with the spans of the downstream services. Easy, right?

The gateway

The gateway service is nothing more than a wrapper on top of a gRPC client. The interesting bit of its implementation is the CollectQuotes method, which is what our main package will invoke to *begin a new trace*:

```
func (gw *Gateway) CollectQuotes(ctx context.Context, SKU string)
(map[string]float64, error) {
    span, ctx := opentracing.StartSpanFromContext(ctx, "CollectQuotes")
    defer span.Finish()

    res, err := gw.client.GetQuote(ctx, &proto.QuotesRequest{SKU: SKU})
    if err != nil {
        return nil, err
    }

    quoteMap := make(map[string]float64, len(res.Quotes))
    for _, quote := range res.Quotes {
        quoteMap[quote.Vendor] = quote.Price
    }
    return quoteMap, nil
}
```

Here, we use StartSpanFromContext to create a new *named* span and embed its trace details into a new context that wraps the one that was provided as an argument to the method.

The rest of the code is pretty self-explanatory: we invoke the GetQuote method on the embedded client instance, collect the responses, and place them in a map that we then return to the caller.

Putting it all together

The main file prepares a microservice deployment environment via a call to the deployServices helper function. The idea here is to string together the services in such a manner so that tracing a request through the system will yield an interesting trace graph. Let's see how this is done.

First, the helper starts three Provider instances and keeps track of their addresses:

```
var err error
providerAddrs := make([]string, 3)
for i := 0; i < len(providerAddrs); i++ {
    provider := service.NewProvider(fmt.Sprintf("vendor-%d", i))
    if providerAddrs[i], err = provider.Serve(ctx); err != nil {
        return nil, err
```

```
        }
    }
```

Then, it starts an `Aggregator` instance and sets it up to connect to providers *1* and *2* from the preceding list:

```
aggr1 := service.NewAggregator("aggr-1", providerAddrs[1:])
aggr1Addr, err := aggr1.Serve(ctx)
if err != nil {
    return nil, err
}
```

Following that, it instantiates yet another `Aggregator` type and connects it to provider *0* and the aggregator we just created:

```
aggr0 := service.NewAggregator("aggr-0", []string{providerAddrs[0],
aggr1Addr})
aggr0Addr, err := aggr0.Serve(ctx)
if err != nil {
    return nil, err
}
```

Finally, a `Gateway` instance is created with the preceding aggregator as its target and returned to the caller:

```
return service.NewGateway("api-gateway", aggr0Addr)
```

The `Gateway` instance that's returned by the `deployServices` function is used by `runMain` to trigger the execution of a quote query that marks the beginning of a new request trace:

```
func runMain(ctx context.Context) error {
    gw, err := deployServices(ctx)
    if err != nil {
        return err
    }
    defer func() { _ = gw.Close() }()

    res, err := gw.CollectQuotes(ctx, "example")
    if err != nil {
        return err
    }
    fmt.Printf("Collected the following quotes:\n")
    for k, v := range res {
        fmt.Printf("  %q: %3.2f\n", k, v)
    }
    return nil
}
```

In the following section, we will be hooking up a tracer implementation to our code so that we can capture and visualize the request traces that our code generates.

Capturing and visualizing traces using Jaeger

In the previous sections, we saw how OpenTracing allows us to create and propagate span information across microservice boundaries. But, *how* and, more importantly, *where* is this information collected and processed? After all, having this information available without the means to slice and dice it greatly diminishes its value.

As we mentioned previously, one of the key design goals of the OpenTracing framework is to avoid vendor lock-in. To this end, when it comes to span collection and visualization, you can either select an open source solution such as Uber's Jaeger [11] or Elastic's APM [5], which you host yourself. Alternatively, you can use one of the several available **Software as a Service (SaaS)** solutions [19].

As far as our open tracing example is concerned, we will be using Jaeger [11] as our tracer implementation. Jaeger is simple to install and integrate with the code we have already written so far. It is written in Go and can also be used as a drop-in replacement for Zipkin [16]. A Jaeger deployment typically consists of two components:

- A local span collection agent is normally deployed as a sidecar container alongside your application. It collects spans that are published by the application over UDP, applies *configurable* probabilistic sampling so that it can select a subset of the spans to be sent upstream, and transmits them to the Jaeger collector service.

- The collector service aggregates the spans that are transmitted by the various Jaeger agent instances and persists them to a data store. Depending on the rate at which new spans are produced, collectors can be configured to work in either *direct-to-storage* mode, where they interface directly with the DB, or in *streaming* mode, where a Kafka instance is used as a buffer between the collectors and another process that ingests, indexes, and stores the data in the DB.

For our testing purposes, we will use the official all-in-one Docker image, which includes an agent and collector (backed by an in-memory store) instance, as well as the Jaeger UI. We can start the container using the following command:

```
docker run -d --name jaeger \
  -p 6831:6831/udp \
  -p 16686:16686 \
  jaegertracing/all-in-one:1.14
```

Port 6831 is where the Jaeger agent listens for spans that our instrumented services will publish over UDP. On the other hand, port 16686 exposes the Jaeger UI where we can browse, search, and visualize captured request traces.

As we mentioned in the previous sections, the `tracer` package will encapsulate the logic for instantiating new Jaeger tracer instances.

Let's take a look at the `GetTracer` function's implementation.
The `MustGetTracer` function that our services invoke calls `GetTracer` and panics in case of an error, as shown here:

```
func GetTracer(serviceName string) (opentracing.Tracer, error) {
    cfg, err := jaegercfg.FromEnv()
    if err != nil {
        return nil, err
    }
    cfg.ServiceName = serviceName
    cfg.Sampler = &jaegercfg.SamplerConfig{
        Type: jaeger.SamplerTypeConst,
        Param: 1, // Sample all traces generated by our demo
    }
    tracer, closer, err := cfg.NewTracer()
    if err == nil {
        // Omitted: keep track of closer so we can close all tracers when
exiting
        return tracer, nil
    }
    return err
}
```

The Go client for Jaeger provides several convenience helpers for creating new tracers. The approach we chose here was to instantiate a tracer from a configuration object that we can obtain via the `FromEnv` helper. `FromEnv` initializes a configuration object with a set of sane defaults and then examines the environment for the presence of Jaeger-specific variables that override the default values. For instance, JAEGER_AGENT_HOST and JAEGER_AGENT_PORT can be used to specify the address where the Jaeger agent is listening for incoming spans. By default, the agent is expected to listen at `localhost:6831`, which matches the port that was exposed by the Docker container we just launched.

Next, we need to configure a sampling strategy for the tracer. It stands to reason that if we were operating a deployment with very high throughput, we wouldn't necessarily want to trace every single request as that would generate an enormous amount of data that would need to be stored and indexed. To this end, Jaeger allows us to configure different sampling strategies, depending on our particular application requirements:

- A **constant** sampler always makes the same decision for each trace. This is the strategy we are using for our example to ensure that traces are always persisted each time we run our demo.
- A **probabilistic** sampler retains traces with a specific probability (for example, 10% of traces).
- The **rate-limiting** sampler ensures that traces are sampled at a particular rate (for example, 10 traces per second).

The following screenshot shows a detailed view of a captured trace that was generated by running the example application that we just built:

Figure 1: Visualizing a request trace in Jaeger's UI

The first row represents the *total* time spent in the api-gateway waiting for a response to the outgoing quote request. The rows beneath it contain the nested spans that correspond to other requests that were executing in parallel. Here is a brief overview of the events that occurred:

1. The gateway makes a request to **aggr-0** and blocks waiting for a response.
2. **aggr-0** makes two requests in parallel: one to **vendor-0** and one to **aggr-1**. Then, it blocks waiting for the downstream responses before returning a response to the gateway.
3. **aggr-1** makes two requests in parallel: one to **vendor-1** and one to **vendor-2**. It blocks waiting for the downstream responses before returning a response to **aggr-0**.

One other very cool feature of the Jaeger UI is that it can display the dependencies between services as a **directed acyclic graph (DAG)**. The following screenshot shows the DAG for our example microservice deployment, which matches the preceding event sequence:

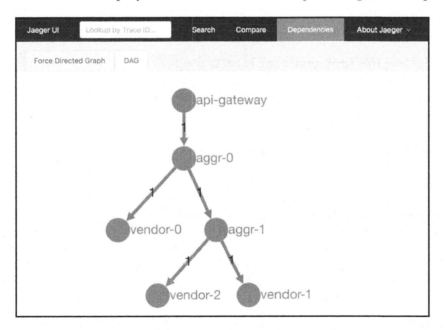

Figure 2: Visualizing the dependencies between services

In conclusion, request tracing is a great tool for gaining a deeper insight into the internals of modern, complex microservice-based systems. I would strongly recommend considering it for your next large-scale project.

Making logging your trusted ally

Time and time again, logging always proves to be an invaluable resource for investigating the root cause of a problem in contemporary computer software. However, in the context of a microservice-based architecture, where requests cross service boundaries, being able to collect, correlate, and search the log entries that are emitted by each individual service is of paramount importance.

In the following sections, we will focus on the best practices for writing succinct log entries that are easily searchable and highlight some common pitfalls that you definitely want to avoid. Furthermore, we will discuss solutions for collecting and shipping the logs from your Kubernetes pods (or dockerized services) to a central location where they can be indexed.

Logging best practices

The first item on our best practice checklist is **leveled logging**. When using leveled logging, there are two aspects you need to consider:

- **Selecting the appropriate log level to use for each message**: The majority of logging packages for Go applications support at least the *DEBUG*, *INFO*, and *ERROR* levels. However, your preferred logging solution might also support more granular log levels, such as *TRACE*, *DEBUG*, and *WARNING*.
- **Deciding which log levels to actually output**: For instance, perhaps you want your application to only output messages at the *INFO* and *ERROR* levels to reduce the volume of produced logs.

When debugging an application, it makes sense to also include *DEBUG* or *TRACE* messages in the logs so that you can get a better understanding of what's going on. It stands to reason that you shouldn't have to recompile and redeploy an application just to change its log level! To this end, it's good practice to implement some sort of hook to allow you to dynamically change the active log level of an application while it is executing. Here are a few suggestions you can try:

- Toggle between the configured log level and the *DEBUG* level when the application receives a particular signal (for example, SIGHUP). If your application reads the initial log level from a config file, you could use the same signal-based approach to force a reload of the config file.
- Expose an HTTP endpoint to change the log level.

- Store the per-application log level setting in a distributed key-value store such as etcd [6], which allows clients to watch a key for changes. If you are running multiple instances of your application, this is an effective way to change the log level for all the instances in a single step.

If you haven't already done so, you can step up your logging game simply by switching to **structured** logging. While the good old way of extracting timestamps and messages from logs using regular expressions certainly does work, updating your applications to output logs in a format that is easily parsed by the service that indexes them goes a long way toward increasing the volume of logs that can be ingested per unit of time. Consequently, application logs become searchable in real time or near real-time fashions, allowing you to diagnose problems much quicker. There are quite a few Go packages out there that implement structured loggers. If we had to single out some, our list would definitely include `sirupsen/logrus` [14], `uber-go/zap` [20], `rs/zerolog` [21], and `gokit/log` [9].

So, what does a structured log entry look like? The following screenshot demonstrates how the `sirupsen/logrus` package formats and prints the same set of logs using two of its built-in text formatters. The Terminal at the top uses a text-based formatter that is more suited for running applications on your development machine, while the Terminal at the bottom displays the same output as JSON. As you can see, each log entry consists, as a minimum, of a level, a timestamp, and a message. In addition, log entries can contain a variable number of key-value pairs:

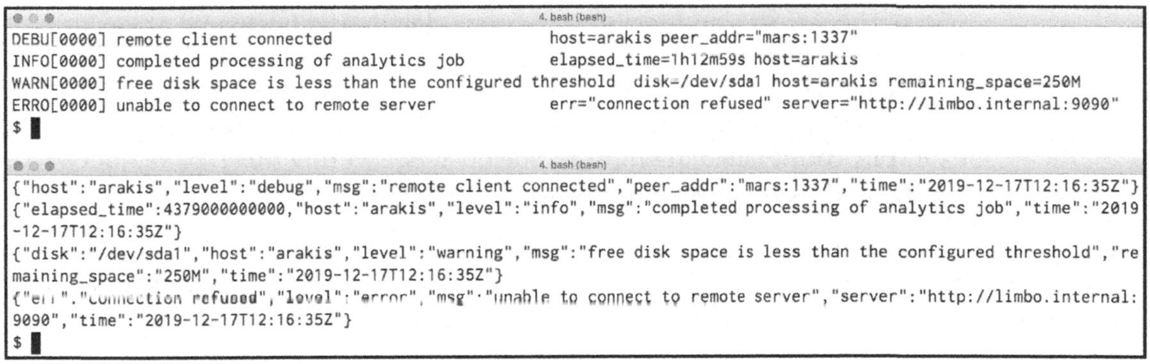

Figure 3: Example log output produced by logrus

When the log ingestion platform consumes such a log entry, it will also index the key-value pairs and make them available for searching. Consequently, you can compose highly targeted queries by slicing and dicing the log entries by multiple attributes (for example, a customer ID, service name, and data center location).

Always make sure that the *message* portion of your log entries never includes *variable* parts. To explain why not adhering to this advice could lead to problems, let's take a look at two equivalent error messages that are produced by a service whose task is to redirect users:

- `level=error message="cannot connect to server: dial tcp4: lookup invalid.host: no such host" service=redirector customer-id=42`
- `level=error message="cannot connect to server" err="dial tcp4: lookup invalid.host: no such host" host=invalid.host service=redirector customer-id=42`

The first message embeds the error that's returned by the Go dialer into the log message. Given that the *no such host* error will most probably change for each request, adding it to the log message introduces a variable component that makes searching harder. What if we want to find the logs for *all* failed connection attempts? The only way to do that would be to use a regular expression, which would be quite slow since the log search engine would need to perform a full table scan and apply the regular expression to each entry.

On the other hand, the second message uses a constant message for errors of a particular *class* and includes the error details and hostname as key-value pairs. Searching for this type of error is much easier: the log search engine can probably answer this type of query quickly and efficiently using an index. What's more, we can keep slicing the data further, for example, count failed attempts by the host. Answering this type of query for the first message would be nearly impossible!

We have already argued about the usefulness of structured logging. At this point, you might be wondering whether there's a list of fields that should always be included in your log messages. I would definitely recommend including at least the following bits of information:

- The application/service **name**. Having this value present allows you to answer one of the most common queries out there: "display the logs for application *foo*".
- The **hostname** where the application is executing. When your log storage is centralized, having this field available is quite handy if you need to figure out which machine (or container, if you're using Kubernetes) produced the log.

- The **SHA** of the git (or your preferred VCS) branch that's used to compile the binary for the application. If your organization is a fan of the *ship frequently* mantra, adding the SHA to your logs makes it easy to link an error to a particular snapshot of the code base.

Imagine that, against your better judgment, you decided to ignore the *never deploy on a Friday* rule and push a set of seemingly innocent changes to some of the microservices in production; after all, the code was thoroughly reviewed and all the tests passed. What could possibly go wrong, right? You come back to work on Monday and your mailbox is full of tickets that have been opened by the support team. According to the tickets, several users experienced issues adding products to their carts. To assist you with tracking down the problem, the support team has included both the affected user IDs and the approximate time when they were accessing the service in the tickets.

You fire up your log search tool, plug in the timestamp and user details, and receive a list of logs for the API gateway, which is the first microservice that users hit when they request something from their web browser. The gateway service makes several calls to downstream services that, unfortunately, *do not* have access to the user ID and therefore don't show up in the logs... Good luck tracking down the cause of the problem!

To avoid hairy situations like this, it's good practice to also include a **correlation ID** in your log entries. In this particular scenario, the API gateway would generate a unique correlation ID for incoming requests and inject it into requests to downstream services (which then include it in their own log entries), and so on and so forth. This approach is quite similar to request tracing, but instead of tracking spans and time-related request details, it allows us to correlate logs across service boundaries.

The devil is in the (logging) details

When using structured logging, it is very easy to get carried away and try to stuff as much information as possible into the key-value pairs. Unfortunately, this can often prove to be dangerous security-wise! Take a look at the following code snippet, which retrieves a user's data from a URL they have provided to us:

```
func fetchUserData(url *url.URL) (*user.Data, error) {
    tick := time.Now()
    res, err := http.Get(url.String())
    if err != nil {
        return nil, err
    }
    defer func() { _ = res.Body.Close() }()

    logrus.WithFields(logrus.Fields{
```

```
        "url":  url,
        "time": time.Since(tick).String(),
    }).Info("retrieved user data")

    // omitted: read and unmarshal user data
}
```

Whenever we succeed in fetching the data, we log an *INFO* message with the URL and the time it took to retrieve it. This code looks pretty innocent, right? Wrong! The following screenshot shows the log output from this function:

```
● ● ●                                    4. bash (tail)
$ tail -f log
time="2019-10-28T12:30:12Z" level=info msg="retrieved user data" fields.time=110ms url="https://foo:secret@userdata.com"
time="2019-10-28T12:30:12Z" level=info msg="retrieved user data" fields.time=251ms url="https://1234123:b4df00dc0ffee@example.com"
time="2019-10-28T12:30:12Z" level=info msg="retrieved user data" fields.time=121ms url="https://bar:csacj9qwrEd@somewhere.com"
```

Figure 4: Forgetting to properly sanitize log output can lead to credential leaks

Yikes! We just splatted the user's credentials all over our logs... We have to be very careful not to leak any credentials or any other bits of sensitive information (for example, credit card, bank account, or SSN numbers) to the logs. But how can we achieve this without having to audit every single log line in our code base? Most logging frameworks allow you to provide an `io.Writer` instance for receiving the logger output. You can leverage this capability to implement a filtering mechanism that uses a set of regular expressions to either mask or strip away sensitive information that adheres to specific patterns.

Another pitfall that you must be aware of is **synchronous** logging. The golden rule here is that logging should always be considered as an auxiliary function and should never interfere with the normal operation of your service. If you are using a synchronous logger and the output stream blocks (that is, it cannot keep up with the volume of generated logs), your service would also block and cause noticeable delays for upstream services depending on it. Whenever possible, try to use an **asynchronous** logger implementation – ideally, one that uses a leaky bucket abstraction to drop messages when it cannot keep up with the load.

Shipping and indexing logs inside Kubernetes

If you have been following the guidelines from the previous sections, your applications will now emit clean and succinct logs in a format that makes them suitable for ingestion by a log aggregation system. The only missing piece of the puzzle is how we can collect the individual logs from each application instance running on a Kubernetes cluster and ship them either to a self-hosted or SaaS log indexing solution.

Running a log collector on each Kubernetes node

This option uses a Kubernetes *DaemonSet* to install a log collection daemon on each node of the Kubernetes cluster. Besides being relatively easy to implement, the main benefit of this particular approach is that it is totally transparent to running applications.

> A DaemonSet is a special type of Kubernetes resource that ensures that all cluster nodes run a copy of a particular pod. Using daemon sets is a quite common pattern for the following reasons:
>
> - Running cluster storage daemons (for example, ceph or glusterd)
> - Collecting and shipping logs
> - Monitoring nodes and transmitting node-specific metrics (for example, load, memory, or disk space usage)

When a pod executes, Kubernetes will capture its standard output and error streams and redirect them to a pair of log files. When you run the `kubectl logs` command, the `kubelet` instance running on the worker node streams the logs by reading off those files.

The log collector pod that's shown in the following diagram digests the captured log files for each executing pod, transforms them (if necessary) into the format expected by the log indexing service, and optionally augments them with additional information such as the Kubernetes namespace and container hostname. Depending on the log ingesting solution in use, logs can be either directly uploaded for ingestion or written to a message queue such as Kafka:

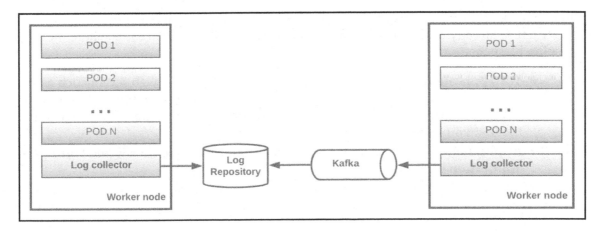

Figure 5: Running a log collector using a DaemonSet

The two most popular log collection daemons out there are Fluent Bit [8], which is written in C, and Logstash [15], which is written in Ruby. Quite often, logs will be shipped to an Elasticsearch cluster for indexing, and a frontend such as Kibana [12] will be used to browse and search the logs. You will hear this type of setup commonly referred to as an EFK or ELK stack, depending on which log collection daemon is being used.

Using a sidecar container to collect logs

The second option when it comes to collecting logs is to run a sidecar container for each application, as shown in the following diagram:

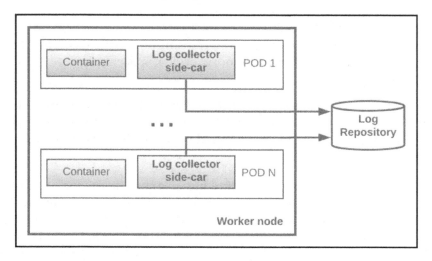

Figure 6: Running a log collector as a sidecar container

While this approach might feel a bit more cumbersome compared to using the infrastructure already built into Kubernetes, it can work quite nicely in cases where the following happens:

- The application writes to multiple log files. For example, a web server such as Apache or Nginx might be configured to write error logs to a different location than access logs. In such a case, you would add a sidecar container for each log file that you want to scrape.
- Applications use non-standard log formats that need to be transformed on a **per-application** basis.

Shipping logs directly from the application

The last log shipping strategy that we will be examining is to actually embed the log shipping logic into each application. As shown in the following diagram, the application is sending its logs directly to a log repository:

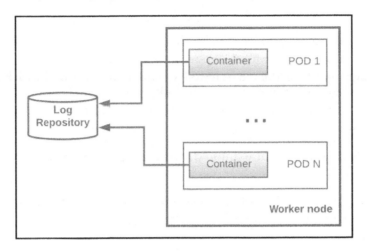

Figure 7: Shipping logs directly from within the application

An interesting use case for this strategy is to integrate with an external, third-party SaaS offering that requires applications to import and use a vendor-specific software development kit.

Introspecting live Go services

After a long journey transitioning from a monolithic application into one based on microservices, you have reached a point where all your new and shiny services are happily running in production. At this stage, you will probably start becoming more and more curious about their operation in the long run:

- How much memory are they using?
- How many goroutines are currently running?
- Are there any leaks (memory or goroutines) that can eventually force the service to crash?
- How often does the Go garbage collector run and how much time does each run actually take?

If you are using a container orchestration framework such as Kubernetes, crashing services are not normally a big concern; just bump the number of instances and Kubernetes will take care of restarting them when they crash. However, if the root cause of the crash is a memory leak or an unbounded explosion in the number of running goroutines, crashes will become more and more frequent as the traffic to your system increases. This pattern will inevitably lead to service disruption.

Fortunately, the Go runtime exposes a heap of information that we can use to answer these questions. All we need to do is extract, export, and aggregate this information. In `Chapter 13`, *Metrics Collection and Visualization*, where we will be discussing the SRE aspects of operating microservice architectures, we will explore metrics collection systems such as Prometheus, which let us not only collect this information but also act on it by creating alerts that can eventually turn into page calls for the SRE team.

In some cases, however, we might want to dig a bit deeper... Here are a few interesting examples:

- A service suddenly became unresponsive but the Go deadlock detector is not complaining about any deadlocks. The service still accepts requests but never sends out any reply and we need to find out why.
- Our metrics dashboard indicates that instance X of service Y is using quite a lot of heap memory. But how can we inspect the heap's contents and see what is taking up all that memory? Perhaps we are leaking file handles (for example, forgot to close the response body off from the HTTP calls we are making) or maintain unneeded references to objects that prevent the Go garbage collector from freeing them.
- A data ingestion service unexpectedly pegs the CPU, but only when running in production! So far, you have been unable to replicate this issue on your local development machine.

To debug issues such as the ones described in the first example, we can SSH into the container that the service executes in and send it a *SIGQUIT* signal. This will force the Go runtime to dump a stack trace for each running goroutine and exit. Then, we can examine the log stream and figure out where exactly the service got stuck.

If your Go application, which seemingly appears to be stuck, is running on the foreground, instead of looking for its pid so that you can send it a *SIGQUIT* signal, you can force it to dump the stack trace for every executing goroutine by pressing *CTRL+* .

Note that, behind the scenes, this key combination actually sends a *SIGQUIT* to the running process and will cause it to exit.

However, the obvious caveat of this trick is that our application or service will effectively crash. What's more, it doesn't really allow us to introspect its internal state, which is more or less required for dealing with situations such as the ones from the other examples.

Fortunately, Go allows us to embed the pprof package into our services and expose a frontend to it over HTTP. You might be worried that shipping what is effectively a sampling profiler with your code will undoubtedly make it run slower. In principle, this is not really the case as you can ask pprof to capture various kinds of profiles on demand, thus allowing it to stay out of the way until you need it. As the following code snippet shows, all you need to do is import the net/http/pprof package and launch an HTTP server:

```
import (
    "log"
    "net/http"
    _ "net/http/pprof" // import for side-effects
)

func exposeProfile() {
    go func() {
        log.Println(http.ListenAndServe("localhost:6060", nil))
    }()
}
```

The net/http/pprof function defines an init function, which registers various pprof-related route handlers to the default http.ServeMux. Therefore, the package is typically imported only for its side effects. After spinning up an HTTP server, you can simply point your web browser to http://localhost:6060/debug/pprof and access a minimalistic frontend for capturing pprof profiles and make them available for download so that they can be processed offline via the pprof tool.

The following screenshot is exposing a `pprof` frontend to introspect running applications:

```
/debug/pprof/

Types of profiles available:
Count Profile
4      allocs
0      block
0      cmdline
22     goroutine
4      heap
0      mutex
0      profile
17     threadcreate
0      trace
full goroutine stack dump

Profile Descriptions:

 • allocs:        A sampling of all past memory allocations
 • block:         Stack traces that led to blocking on synchronization primitives
 • cmdline:       The command line invocation of the current program
 • goroutine:     Stack traces of all current goroutines
 • heap:          A sampling of memory allocations of live objects. You can specify the gc GET parameter to run GC before taking the heap sample.
 • mutex:         Stack traces of holders of contended mutexes
 • profile:       CPU profile. You can specify the duration in the seconds GET parameter. After you get the profile file, use the go tool pprof command to investigate the profile.
 • threadcreate:  Stack traces that led to the creation of new OS threads
 • trace:         A trace of execution of the current program. You can specify the duration in the seconds GET parameter. After you get the trace file, use the go tool trace command to investigate the trace.
```

Figure 8: Exposing a pprof frontend to introspect running applications

As shown in the preceding screenshot, the `pprof` UI allows you to capture the following profile types on-demand:

- **allocs**: A sampling of all past memory allocations
- **block**: Stack traces that led to blocking on synchronization primitives
- **cmdline**: The command-line invocation of the current program
- **goroutine**: Stack traces of all current goroutines
- **heap**: A sample of the memory allocations of live objects
- **mutex**: Stack traces of holders of contended mutexes
- **profile**: CPU profile
- **threadcreate**: Stack traces that led to the creation of new OS threads
- **trace**: A trace of the execution of the current program

If your application/service already spins up its own HTTP server that can potentially be exposed to the outside world (for example, via a Kubernetes ingress), make sure you bind its routes to a **new mux** instance and expose the `pprof` routes using the **default mux** via a second HTTP server running on a different (internal) port.

This way, you don't run the risk of allowing unauthorized access to your introspection endpoints.

I would strongly recommend enabling `pprof` support for your production services using the approaches we discussed in this section. It only requires a little bit of effort on your end to set up but will prove to be a great asset if you ever need to debug a live application.

Building a microservice-based version of Links 'R' Us

In the last part of this chapter, we will take the monolithic Links 'R' Us application that we built and deployed in the previous chapter and apply *everything* we have learned so far to break it down into a bunch of microservices. The following diagram illustrates the expected state of our cluster after we've made all the necessary changes:

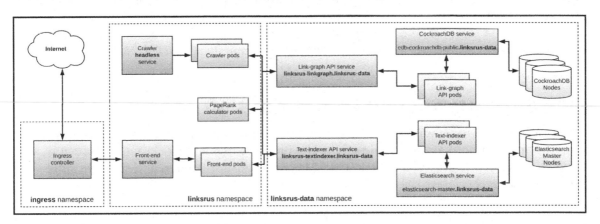

Figure 9: Breaking down the Links 'R' Us monolith into microservices

The Kubernetes manifest files that we will be using for the microservice-based version of Links 'R' Us are available under the `Chapter11/k8s` folder of this book's GitHub repository.

If you haven't already set up a Minikube cluster and whitelisted its private registry, you can either take a quick break and manually follow the step-by-step instructions from `Chapter 10`, *Building, Packaging, and Deploying Software*, or simply run `make bootstrap-minikube`, which will take care of everything for you. On the other hand, if you have already deployed the monolithic version of Links 'R' Us from the previous chapter, make sure to run `kubectl delete namespace linksrus` before proceeding. By deleting the **linksrus** namespace, Kubernetes will get rid of all pods, services, and ingresses for Links 'R' Us but leave the data stores (which live in the **linksrus-data** namespace) intact.

To deploy the various Links 'R' Us components that we will be defining in the following sections, you will need to build and push a handful of Docker images. To save you some time, the Makefile in the `Chapter11/k8s` folder provides two handy build targets to get you up and running as quickly as possible:

- `make dockerize-and-push` will build all required Docker images and push them to Minikube's private registry
- `make deploy` will ensure that all the necessary data stores have been provisioned and apply all the manifests for deploying the microservice-based version of Links 'R' Us in one go

Before we can start breaking down our monolith into microservices, there is one small task we need to take care of first: removing the coupling between our service and the underlying data stores. The next section explores how this can be achieved using the knowledge we acquired in `Chapter 9`, *Communicating with the Outside World*.

Decoupling access to the data stores

One fundamental issue with the monolithic implementation from the previous chapter is that our application was talking directly to the Elasticsearch and CockroachDB clusters. We have effectively introduced a tight coupling between the application and the data store implementations.

Now that it's time to create the microservice-based version of Links 'R' Us, we need to take a few steps to rectify this problem. To this end, the first two services that we will be creating as part of our refactoring work will serve as a kind of proxy for facilitating access to the underlying data stores. The **text-indexer** and **link-graph** services will be deployed in the **linksrus-data** namespace and allow other services to interact with the data stores through the gRPC-based APIs that we defined in `Chapter 9`, *Communicating with the Outside World*.

An important benefit of introducing an indirection layer between the services and the data stores is that we gain the ability to change the data store implementation *at any moment* without having to change, update, or otherwise reconfigure any of the other Links 'R' Us services.

In terms of service implementation, things are surprisingly simple. Each service binary receives the URI of the data store to connect to as an argument. Then, it creates a gRPC server on port 8080 and exposes the pprof debug endpoints on port 6060. All the boilerplate code fits nicely into a single main file, which you can find in the Chapter11/linksrus/linkgraph and Chapter11/linksrus/textindexer folders of this book's GitHub repository.

Breaking down the monolith into distinct services

In this section, we will extract the individual services from the Links 'R' Us monolith and build a standalone service binary for each one. This is also the point where you will probably realize that our clean, interface-based design that we have been preaching about since the beginning of this book finally begins to pay off.

As it turns out, we can take the service-specific code from Chapter 10, *Building, Packaging, and Deploying Software*, and use it as is with a few minor changes. For each service, we will create a main package that performs the following set of tasks:

- Creates a logger instance for each service
- Exposes the pprof debug endpoints on a configurable port
- Instantiates the gRPC clients for accessing the link-graph and text-indexer
- Populates the configuration object for each service with the appropriate settings
- Runs the service main loop and cleanly shuts down the application upon receiving a signal

All of this boilerplate code is more or less the same for each service, so we will omit it for brevity. However, if you want to, you can extract the common parts into a separate package and make the main.go files for each service a bit leaner.

The configuration of each service is one of the places where we will be deviating slightly compared to the monolithic implementation from the previous chapter. We want our services to be configured either via command-line flags or via environment variables. The latter offers us the flexibility to define all the configuration options in a shared Kubernetes ConfigMap and inject them into our service manifests. Since the built-in flags package does not support this kind of functionality, we will be switching to the urfave/cli [1] package for our flag parsing needs. This package supports an elegant way of defining typed flags, which also allows us to (optionally) specify the name of an environment variable that can be set to override each flag value:

```
app.Flags = []cli.Flag{
    cli.StringFlag{
```

```
        Name:    "link-graph-api",
        EnvVar: "LINK_GRAPH_API",
        Usage:   "The gRPC endpoint for connecting to the link graph",
    },
    cli.StringFlag{
        Name:    "text-indexer-api",
        EnvVar: "TEXT_INDEXER_API",
        Usage:   "The gRPC endpoint for connecting to the text indexer",
    },
    // omitted: additional flags
}
```

Each of our new services will need to access both the link-graph and the text-indexer data stores. Both of these stores are exposed over gRPC via the two services we described in the previous section. The following code snippet shows how to obtain a high-level (see Chapter 9, *Communicating with the Outside World*) client instance for each of the two services:

```
// Obtain high-level client for link graph.
dialCtx, cancelFn := context.WithTimeout(ctx, 5*time.Second)
defer cancelFn()
linkGraphConn, err := grpc.DialContext(dialCtx, linkGraphAPI,
grpc.WithInsecure(), grpc.WithBlock())
if err != nil {
    return nil, nil, xerrors.Errorf("could not connect to link graph API:
%w", err)
}
graphCli := linkgraphapi.NewLinkGraphClient(ctx,
linkgraphproto.NewLinkGraphClient(linkGraphConn))

// Obtain high-level client for text-indexer.
dialCtx, cancelFn := context.WithTimeout(ctx, 5*time.Second)
defer cancelFn()
indexerConn, err := grpc.DialContext(dialCtx, textIndexerAPI,
grpc.WithInsecure(), grpc.WithBlock())
if err != nil {
    return nil, nil, xerrors.Errorf("could not connect to text indexer API:
%w", err)
}
indexerCli := textindexerapi.NewTextIndexerClient(ctx,
textindexerproto.NewTextIndexerClient(indexerConn))
```

As you may recall, back in Chapter 9, *Communicating with the Outside World,* we meticulously designed the high-level clients so that they implement a subset of the graph.Graph and index.Indexer interfaces. This makes it possible to use the clients as a *drop-in replacement* for the concrete graph and indexer store implementations that are used in the monolithic Links 'R' Us version. This is a testament to the benefits of applying the SOLID design principles to make our code more modular and easier to interface with.

Deploying the microservices that comprise the Links 'R' Us project

Now that we have built standalone binaries for each of the new Links 'R' Us services, it's time to deploy them on Kubernetes! Let's take a quick look at the required Kubernetes resources for deploying each individual service.

Deploying the link-graph and text-indexer API services

For the link-graph and text-indexer API services, we will be using a Kubernetes deployment resource to spin up two replicas for each service in the **linksrus-data** namespace.

To allow clients from the **linksrus** namespace to access the API, we will be creating a Kubernetes service to load balance traffic to the pods that we will be spinning up.

Clients can then access the data stores by connecting their gRPC clients to the following endpoints:

- `linksrus-textindexer.linksrus-data:8080`
- `linksrus-linkgraph.linksrus-data:8080`

Deploying the web crawler

The crawler service deployment will use the same partition detection logic that the monolithic implementation from the previous chapter did. Consequently, we will be deploying two instances of the crawler service as a Kubernetes Stateful set, which guarantees that each pod will be assigned a predictable hostname that includes the pod's ordinal in the set.

In addition, we will be creating a **headless** Kubernetes service that will populate the SRV records for the crawler pods and allow the partition detection code to query the total number of available pods.

Deploying the PageRank service

The PageRank service is still subject to the same constraints and limitations that we discussed in the previous chapter. As a result, we will only run a *single* instance of the service by creating a Kubernetes deployment with the replica count set to *one*.

Deploying the frontend service

The last service that we will be deploying is the frontend. As with most other services in our cluster, we will create a Kubernetes deployment with the required number of replicas for the frontend.

Just as we did in the previous chapter, we will define a Kubernetes service to load balance traffic to the frontend pods and then expose it outside the cluster with the help of a Kubernetes ingress resource.

Locking down access to our Kubernetes cluster using network policies

As the number of microservices begins to increase, it is probably a good time to start thinking more actively about security. Do we really want each and every pod in our cluster to be able to access every other pod across all namespaces? Truth be told, for our current deployment, it is not that important. However, for larger projects, that's definitely a question that you need to answer.

Kubernetes offers a special type of resource called **NetworkPolicy** to assist us with the creation of fine-grained rules for governing access to namespaces and pods. A prerequisite to creating and enforcing network policies is for your cluster to run with the *cni* network plugin enabled and to use a network provider implementation that is compliant with the **Container Networking Interface (CNI)**. Examples of such providers include Calico [2], Cilium [3], and Flannel [7].

If you have bootstrapped a Minikube cluster using the `make bootstrap-minikube` target from the Makefile in either the `Chapter10/k8s` or the `Chapter11/k8s` folder, Calico has already been installed for you.

Alternatively, you can manually install Calico to your test cluster by running the following command:

```
kubectl apply -f \
https://docs.projectcalico.org/v3.10/manifests/calico.yaml
```

The installation might take a few moments. You can monitor the status of the deployment by running `kubectl -n kube-system get pods -lk8s-app=calico-node -w` and waiting for the pod status to show up as *running*.

What would be a good example of a network policy for our Links 'R' Us deployment? Since the various pods in the **linksrus** namespace are now expected to access the data stores over gRPC, it would be good practice to specify a network policy that would block access to any other pod in the **linksrus-data** namespace from other namespaces.

A really cool thing about Kubernetes network policies is that we can combine multiple policies to construct more elaborate policies. For our use case, we will start with a **DENY ALL** policy:

```
kind: NetworkPolicy
apiVersion: networking.k8s.io/v1
metadata:
  namespace: linksrus-data
  name: deny-from-other-namespaces
spec:
  podSelector:
    matchLabels:
  ingress:
  - from:
    - podSelector: {}
```

Each policy has two sections:

- The destination is where we specify the set of pods that we want to control access to. In this example, we are using a podSelector block with an empty matchLabels selector to match *all* pods in the namespace.
- The traffic origin, which is where we specify the set of pods that are subject to the policy when attempting to access a pod in the destination list.

So, the preceding policy can be interpreted as *deny access to any pod in the **linksrus-data** namespace from any pod in another namespace.* Moving on, we will define a second network policy that will explicitly whitelist the pods that we want to grant access to:

```
kind: NetworkPolicy
apiVersion: networking.k8s.io/v1
metadata:
  namespace: linksrus-data
  name: allow-access-to-data-apis
spec:
  podSelector:
    matchLabels:
      role: data-api
  ingress:
  - from:
    - namespaceSelector:
        matchLabels:
          role: linksrus-components
```

The pods for the two gRPC services have been tagged with a role: data-api label, which the preceding policy uses to explicitly target the pods we are interested in. On the other hand, the pods running in the **linksrus** namespace have been tagged with a role: linksrus-components label, which allows us to specify them as part of the ingress selector. This rule is interpreted as *allow access from **all** pods with a **linksrus-components** role to pods with a **data-api** role in the **linksrus-data** namespace.*

Let's apply these rules by running `kubectl apply -f 08-net-policy.yaml` and verify that they work as expected by connecting to the pods in both namespaces and running the *nc* command to check whether we are allowed to connect to the pods protected by the two network policies. The following screenshot shows us how to verify that our network policies work as expected:

```
# Try to access CockroachDB directly from the crawler pod
$ kubectl -n linksrus exec -it linksrus-crawler-instance-0 -- \
  nc -w 3 -v cdb-cockroachdb-public.linksrus-data 26257
nc: cdb-cockroachdb-public.linksrus-data (10.96.164.228:26257): Operation timed out

# Try to access the text-indexer API directly from the crawler pod
$ kubectl -n linksrus exec -it linksrus-crawler-instance-0 -- \
  nc -w 3 -v linksrus-textindexer.linksrus-data 8080
linksrus-textindexer.linksrus-data (10.108.46.253:8080) open

# Try to access the CockroachDB directly from the text-indexer pod
$ kubectl -n linksrus-data exec -it linksrus-textindexer-instance-d55584c45-1dt7p -- \
  nc -w 3 -v cdb-cockroachdb-public.linksrus-data 26257
cdb-cockroachdb-public.linksrus-data (10.96.164.228:26257) open
$
```

Figure 10: Verifying that our network policies work as expected

Success! As shown in the preceding screenshot, attempting to connect from one of the crawler pods in the **linksrus** namespace to the CockroachDB cluster times out, while attempts to connect to the text indexer API succeed. On the other hand, the connection attempt to CockroachDB succeeds when the same command is executed inside a pod running in the **linksrus-data** namespace.

Of course, this brief introduction to Kubernetes network policies barely scratches the surface. The Kubernetes documentation contains several other match rules that you can use to formulate the appropriate network policies for your particular use case. For those of you who are interested in exploring the different types of policies that you can implement further, I would strongly recommend taking a look at the *Kubernetes network policy recipes* [13] GitHub repository.

Summary

In this chapter, we focused on the process of splitting a monolithic application into a series of microservices. We identified some common anti-patterns for building microservices and elaborated on ways for working around them.

In the second part of this chapter, we examined some interesting approaches for tracing requests through distributed systems, as well as collecting, aggregating, and searching logs. In the last part of this chapter, we split the monolithic Links 'R' Us project from the previous chapter into a series of microservices and deployed them to our test Kubernetes cluster.

In the next chapter, we will discuss building fault-tolerant systems and build a distributed version of the PageRank calculator using the master/slave pattern.

Questions

1. Explain why using the microservices pattern for an MVP or **proof of concept (PoC)** project is often considered to be a bad idea.
2. Describe how the circuit breaker pattern works.
3. List some of the benefits of being able to trace requests as they travel through the system.
4. Why is it important to sanitize log output?
5. Briefly describe the three strategies for collecting logs from the pods running inside a Kubernetes cluster.

Further reading

1. A simple, fast, and fun package for building command-line apps in Go: `https://github.com/urfave/cli`
2. **Calico**: Secure networking for the cloud-native era: `https://www.projectcalico.org`
3. **Cilium**: API-aware networking and security: `https://cilium.io`
4. **Docker**: Enterprise container platform: `https://www.docker.com`

5. **Elastic APM**: Open source application performance monitoring: `https://www.elastic.co/products/apm`

6. **etcd**: A distributed, reliable key-value store for the most critical data of a distributed system: `https://etcd.io`

7. **Flannel**: A network fabric for containers, designed for Kubernetes: `https://github.com/coreos/flannel`

8. **Fluent Bit**: A cloud-native log forwarder: `https://fluentbit.io`

9. **gokit/log**: A minimal interface for structured logging in services: `https://github.com/go-kit/kit/tree/master/log`

10. **grpc-opentracing**: A package for enabling distributed tracing in gRPC clients via the OpenTracing project: `https://github.com/grpc-ecosystem/grpc-opentracing`

11. **Jaeger**: For open source, end-to-end distributed tracing: `https://jaegertracing.io`

12. **kibana**: Your window into the Elastic Stack `https://www.elastic.co/products/kibana`

13. **Kubernetes Network Policy Recipes**: `https://github.com/ahmetb/kubernetes-network-policy recipes`

14. **logrus**: Structured, pluggable logging for Go: `https://github.com/sirupsen/logrus`

15. **Logstash**: Centralize, transform, and stash your data: `https://www.elastic.co/products/logstash`

16. **OpenZipkin**: A distributed tracing system: `https://zipkin.io`

17. Sigelman, Benjamin H.; Barroso, Luiz André; Burrows, Mike; Stephenson, Pat; Plakal, Manoj; Beaver, Donald; Jaspan, Saul; Shanbhag, Chandan: *Dapper, a Large-Scale Distributed Systems Tracing Infrastructure*. Google, Inc., 2010.

18. **The OpenTracing project**: `https://opentracing.io`

19. **The OpenTracing project: Supported tracers**: `https://opentracing.io/docs/supported-tracers`

20. **zap**: Blazing fast, structured, leveled logging in Go: `https://github.com/uber-go/zap`

21. **zerolog**: Zero allocation JSON logger: `https://github.com/rs/zerolog`

Building Distributed Graph-Processing Systems

12

"A distributed system is one in which the failure of a computer you didn't even know existed can render your own computer unusable."

- Leslie Lamport

The master/worker pattern is a popular approach for building fault-tolerant, distributed systems. The first part of this chapter explores this pattern in depth with a focus on some of the more challenging aspects of distributed systems, such as node discovery and error handling.

In the second part of this chapter, we will apply the master/worker pattern to build, from scratch, a distributed graph-processing system that can handle massive graphs whose size exceeds the memory capacity of most modern compute nodes. Finally, in the last part of this chapter, we will apply everything learned so far to create a distributed version of the PageRank calculator service for the Links 'R' Us project.

The following topics will be covered in this chapter:

- The application of the master/worker model for distributed computation
- Strategies for discovering master and worker nodes
- Approaches for dealing with errors
- Using the master/worker model to execute the graph-based algorithms from Chapter 8, *Graph-Based Data Processing*, in a distributed fashion
- Creating the distributed version of the Links 'R' Us PageRank calculator service and deploying it to Kubernetes

Technical requirements

The full code for all topics discussed within this chapter has been published to this book's GitHub repository in the `Chapter12` folder.

You can access the GitHub repository that contains the code and all required resources for each one of this book's chapters by pointing your web browser at the following URL: `https://github.com/PacktPublishing/Hands-On-Software-Engineering-with-Golang`.

Each example project for this chapter includes a common Makefile that defines the following set of targets:

Makefile target	Description
deps	Install any required dependencies.
test	Run all tests and report coverage.
lint	Check for lint errors.

As with all other chapters from this book, you will need a fairly recent version of Go, which you can download at `https://golang.org/dl/`.

To run some of the code in this chapter, you will need to have a working Docker [2] installation on your machine. Furthermore, for the last part of this chapter, you will need access to a Kubernetes cluster. If you don't have access to a Kubernetes cluster for testing, you can simply follow the instructions laid out in the following sections to set up a small cluster on your laptop or workstation.

Introducing the master/worker model

The master/worker model is a commonly used pattern for building distributed systems that have been around for practically forever. When building a cluster using this model, nodes can be classified into two distinct groups, namely, masters and workers.

The key responsibility of worker nodes is to perform compute-intensive tasks such as the following:

- Video transcoding
- Training large-scale neural networks with millions of parameters
- Calculating **Online Analytical Processing (OLAP)** queries
- Running a **Continuous Integration (CI)** pipeline
- Executing map-reduce operations on massive datasets

On the other hand, master nodes are typically assigned the role of the coordinator. To this end, they are responsible for the following:

- Discovering and keeping track of available worker nodes
- Breaking down jobs into smaller tasks and distributing them to each connected worker
- Orchestrating the execution of a job and ensure that any errors are properly detected and handled

Ensuring that masters are highly available

In a system built using the master/worker model, losing one or more worker nodes due to crashes or network partitions is not a big issue. The master can detect this and work around the problem by re-distributing the workload to the remaining workers.

 A crucial piece of advice when designing distributed systems is to make sure that your system does not contain **Single Points of Failure (SPoFs)**.

On the other hand, the loss of the master node will most certainly take the entire system offline! Fortunately, there are a few different approaches at our disposal for making sure that master nodes are highly available, which we'll cover next.

The leader-follower configuration

The **leader-follower** configuration achieves high availability by introducing multiple master nodes to the cluster. The master nodes implement a leader-election algorithm and, after a few rounds of voting, they assign the role of the cluster leader to one of the master nodes.

From that point onward, the leader is responsible for coordinating the execution of any future jobs and each worker node is instructed to connect to it.

The non-leader master nodes (followers) utilize a heartbeat mechanism to continuously monitor the health status of the active leader. If the leader fails to acknowledge a specific number of sequential heartbeat requests, the other master nodes assume that the leader is dead and automatically hold a new election round for selecting a new leader for the cluster.

Meanwhile, the workers attempt to reconnect to the master and eventually establish a connection to the newly elected cluster leader.

The multi-master configuration

In a **multi-master** configuration, we still spin up multiple master node instances. However, as the name implies, there isn't really a designated leader for the cluster. In a multi-master cluster, we don't need to provide a mechanism for workers to figure out which node is the leader; they can freely connect to any of the master nodes.

While this type of configuration has much better throughput characteristics than the equivalent leader-follower configuration, it comes with an important caveat, that is, all master nodes must share the same view of the cluster's state *at all times*.

Consequently, masters are required to implement some kind of distributed consensus algorithm such as Paxos [3] or Raft [5] to ensure that mutations to the cluster's state are processed by all masters in the same order.

Strategies for discovering nodes

For the workers to be able to connect to the master, they first need to be aware of its existence! Depending on our particular use case, the following discovery strategies can be used:

- **Connecting to a bootstrap node**: This discovery strategy assumes that one of the master nodes (commonly referred to as the **bootstrap** node) is reachable at an IP address that is known beforehand. Both masters and workers attempt to establish an initial connection to the bootstrap node and obtain information about the other nodes of the cluster using a **gossip** protocol.
- **Using an external discovery service**: This strategy relies on the presence of an external discovery service that we can query to obtain information about all services running inside our cluster. Consul [1] is a very popular solution for implementing this particular pattern.
- **Locating nodes using DNS records**: If our system is deployed inside an environment that allows us to create and manipulate local DNS records (for example, Kubernetes), we can generate **A records** that point to the leader of the cluster. Workers can look up the leader via a simple DNS query.

Recovering from errors

Distributed systems are inherently complex. While executing a job in a master/worker setup, numerous things can go wrong, for instance, processes can run out of memory and crash or simply become non-responsive, network packets might be dropped, or network devices might fail and hence lead to network splits. When building distributed systems, we must not only anticipate the presence of errors but we should also devise strategies for dealing with them once they occur.

In this section, we will discuss the following approaches for recovering from errors in a master/worker system:

- **Restart on error**: This kind of strategy is better suited for workloads whose calculations are idempotent. Once a fatal error is detected, the master asks all workers to abort the current job and restart the workload from scratch.
- **Re-distribute the workload to healthy workers**: This strategy is quite effective for systems that can dynamically change the assigned workloads while a job is executing. If any of the workers goes offline, the master can re-distribute its assigned workload to the remaining workers.
- **Use a checkpoint mechanism**: This strategy is best suited for long-running workloads that involve non-idempotent calculations. While the job is executing, the master periodically asks the workers to create a *checkpoint*, a snapshot of their current internal state. If an error occurs, instead of restarting the job from scratch, the master asks the workers to restore their state from a particular checkpoint and resume the execution of the job.

Out-of-core distributed graph processing

Back in `Chapter 8`, *Graph-Based Data Processing*, we designed and built our very own system for implementing graph-based algorithms based on the **Bulk Synchronous Parallel (BSP)** model. Admittedly, our final implementation was heavily influenced by the ideas from the Google paper describing Pregel [4], a system that was originally built by Google engineers to tackle graph-based computation at scale.

While the `bspgraph` package from `Chapter 8`, *Graph-Based Data Processing*, can automatically distribute the graph computation load among a pool of workers, it is still limited to running on a single compute node. As our Links 'R' Us crawler augments our link index with more and more links, we will eventually reach a point where the PageRank computation will simply take too long. Updating the PageRank scores for the entire graphs might take a day or, worse, even days!

We can try to buy ourselves some time by **scaling up**, in other words, running our PageRank calculator service on the most powerful (CPU-wise) machine we can get our hands on from our cloud provider. That would give us some breathing room until the graph becomes too large to fit in memory! Once we reach this point, our only viable alternative is to **scale out**, or launch multiple compute nodes and assign a section of the, now massive, graph to each node.

In the following sections, we will be applying (quite literally!) everything that we have learned so far to build, from scratch, a distributed version of the `bspgraph` package, which will live in the `Chapter12/dbspgraph` folder, which you can browse at this book's GitHub repository.

As we did in the previous chapters, we will be once again applying the SOLID principles for our design to re-use as much code as possible. To this end, the new package will be nothing more than a sophisticated wrapper that transparently imbues any existing `bspgraph.Graph` instance with distributed computing superpowers!

This practically means that we can design and test our algorithms on a single machine using the `bspgraph` framework from Chapter 8, *Graph-Based Data Processing*, and once satisfied with their output, switch to `dsbpgraph` for out-of-core processing.

As we all are aware, building distributed systems is a difficult task. In an attempt to minimize the complexity of the system we will be creating and make the code easier to follow, we will be splitting the implementation into a bunch of smaller, independent components and dedicate a section to the implementation of each one. Don't worry though—by the end of this chapter, you will have a clear understanding of how all of the bits and bobs fit together!

Describing the system architecture, requirements, and limitations

The title of this chapter alludes to the type of architecture that we will be using for our distributed graph-processing framework; unsurprisingly, it will be based on the **master/worker** pattern.

To better understand the role of the master and the worker nodes in our design, we will first need to do a quick refresher on how the `bspgraph` package from Chapter 8, *Graph-Based Data Processing*, works. If you haven't already read Chapter 8, *Graph-Based Data Processing*, I would recommend doing so before continuing.

The `bspgraph` package executes graph algorithms using the **Bulk Synchronous Model** (**BSP**). To this end, the chosen algorithm is essentially executed in sequential steps (super-steps). During each super-step, the framework invokes, **in parallel**, a user-defined **compute function** for every vertex in the graph.

 The compute function can access both the **local** vertex state and **global** graph state (aggregator instances that model counters, min/max trackers, and so on). Vertices communicate with each other by exchanging messages. Any message published during a super-step is **queued** and delivered to the intended recipient in the **following** super-step. Finally, before commencing the execution of the next super-step, the framework waits for all compute functions to return and any in-flight messages to be queued for delivery. This reflects the *synchronous* behavior of the BSP model.

So, what would it take to implement the same process in a distributed manner? Let's see:

- First of all, both the master and the workers need to run exactly the same compute functions. That's pretty easy to do since we will first develop our algorithm using the `bspgraph` package and then use the `dbspgraph` package to execute it either on a master or worker node.
- Secondly, to enforce the synchronous aspects of the BSP model, we must introduce some kind of concurrency primitive to ensure that all workers execute the super-steps in **lock-step**. This primitive, which we will be referring to as a **step barrier**, will be implemented by the **master** node.

As you probably guessed, the master will not really do any computation work; it will rather play the role of the coordinator for the execution of the graph algorithm. More specifically, the master will be responsible for the following:

- Provide an endpoint for workers to connect to and wait for job assignments.
- Calculate and broadcast the partition assignments for each worker.
- Coordinate the execution of each super-step with the help of a barrier primitive.
- Keep track of the **global** state of the graph algorithm currently executing. This includes not only the current super-step but also global aggregator values. The master must collect the partial aggregator values from each worker, update its state, and broadcast the new global state to all workers.

- Relay messages between workers. The master is aware of the partition assignments for each worker and can route messages by consulting the destination ID.
- Monitor the state of each worker and broadcast a job abort request if an error occurs or any worker crashes.

On the other hand, the role of the worker is much simpler. Every worker connects to the master and waits for a job assignment. Once a new job is received, the worker initializes its local graph with the vertices and edges that correspond to the **Universal Unique Identifier (UUID)** range assigned to it. Then, in coordination with the master node (via the barrier), the worker executes the graph algorithm in lock-step with the other workers until the user-defined termination condition for the algorithm is met. Any outgoing message whose destination is not a local graph vertex will be automatically relayed via the master node.

To be able to properly partition the graph and relay messages between workers, our only prerequisite is that vertex IDs are always valid UUIDs. If the underlying graph representation uses a different type of ID (for example, an integer value), the end user will need to manually re-map them to UUIDs during the graph initialization step.

Modeling a state machine for executing graph computations

To execute a graph algorithm, the `bspgraph` package provides the `Executor` type, a convenience helper that orchestrates the execution of the individual super-steps and allows the end user to define a set of optional callbacks that the executor invokes, if defined, at the various computation stages. The set of optional callbacks includes the following:

- The `PRE_STEP` callback: This is invoked *before* executing a super-step. This hook enables the end user to perform any required algorithm-specific initialization steps before the following super-step. For instance, some algorithms might require resetting the value stored in one or more aggregators before each super-step.
- The `POST_STEP` callback: This is invoked *after* executing a super-step. A typical use case for this hook is to perform additional calculations and update the global aggregator values. For example, to calculate an average value, we could set up two aggregators, a counter and a summer, which are updated by the compute function invocations during the super-step. Then, in the `POST_STEP` callback, we can simply fetch their values, calculate the average, and record it in another aggregator.

- The `POST_STEP_KEEP_RUNNING` callback: This is invoked after `POST_STEP` and its role is to decide whether the algorithm has completed its execution or additional super-steps are required. Some typical examples of stop conditions are given as follows:
  - A particular super-step number is reached.
  - No more vertices are active (for example, the shortest path algorithm from `Chapter 8`, *Graph-Based Data Processing*).
  - An aggregator value reaches a threshold (for example, the PageRank calculator).

If we treat these callbacks as states in a state machine model, its state diagram will look as follows:

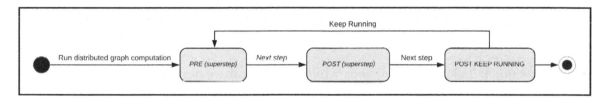

Figure 1: The state diagram for the bspgraph package

While the preceding model works quite nicely when we are running on a single node, it is not quite enough when the graph is executing in a distributed fashion. Why is that? Well, remember that in the distributed version, each worker operates on a *subset* of the graph. Consequently, at the end of the algorithm's execution, each worker will have access to a subset of the solution.

A state machine is a popular mathematical model of computation. The model defines a set of computation states, rules for transitioning from one state to another, and an abstract machine that performs a particular computation task.

At any point in time, the machine can only reside in **one** of the allowed states. Whenever the machine executes a computation step, the transition rules are consulted to select the next stage to transition to.

We can't really say that the algorithm has, in fact, completed *unless* the results from **all** workers have been successfully persisted! Therefore, for the distributed case, we need to extend our state diagram so that it looks as follows:

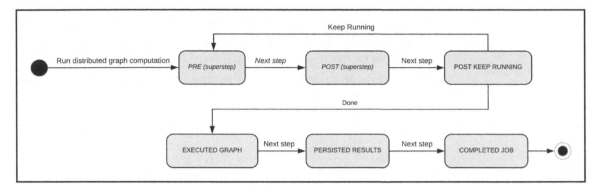

Figure 2: The state diagram for the dbspgraph package

Let's take a quick look at what happens while inside the three new states that we just introduced to the state machine:

- Once the POST_STEP_KEEP_RUNNING callback decides that the terminal condition for the graph algorithm execution has been met, we move to the EXECUTED_GRAPH step, where each worker attempts to persist its local calculation results.
- Workers reach the PERSISTED_RESULTS state once they have successfully persisted their local calculation results to the backing store.
- Finally, workers reach the JOB_COMPLETED state. When in this state, they are free to reset their internal state and wait for a new job.

Establishing a communication protocol between workers and masters

A key prerequisite for implementing any kind of distributed system is to introduce a protocol that will allow the various system components to communicate with each other. The same requirement also applies to the distributed graph processing system that we are building in this chapter.

As the workers and masters communicate with each other over network links, we will be applying the concepts learned in `Chapter 9`, *Communicating with the Outside World*, and use gRPC as our transport layer.

The message and RPC definitions from the following sections can be found in the `Chapter12/dbspgraph/api` folder in this book's GitHub repository.

Defining a job queue RPC service

We will be taking a slightly unorthodox approach and start by defining our one and only RPC first. The reason for this is that the selection of the RPC type (unary versus stream) will greatly influence the way we define the various payloads.

For example, if we opt to use a streaming RPC, we will need to define a kind of envelope message that can represent the different types of messages exchanged between the master and the workers. On the other hand, if we decide in favor of unary RPCs, we can presumably define multiple methods and avoid the need for envelope messages.

Without further ado, let's take a look at the RPC definition for our job queue:

```
service JobQueue {
  rpc JobStream(stream WorkerPayload) returns (stream MasterPayload);
}
```

As you can see, we will actually be using a *bi-directional streaming* RPC! This comes with a cost; we need to define two envelope messages, one for workers and one for the master. So, what was the deciding factor that drove us to the ostensibly more complicated solution of bi-directional streaming?

The answer has to do with the way that gRPC schedules messages for delivery. If you carefully examine the gRPC specification, you will notice that *only* streaming RPCs guarantees that messages will be delivered in the order in which they were published.

This fact is of paramount importance for our particular use case, that is, if we are not able to enforce in-order message delivery, a worker waiting on a barrier could potentially handle a message before exiting the barrier. As a result, the worker would not only behave in a non-deterministic way (good luck debugging that!), but the algorithm would also produce the wrong results.

Another benefit of the stream-based approach is that we can exploit the heartbeat mechanism that is inherently built into gRPC and efficiently detect whether a worker's connection to the master gets severed.

Establishing protocol buffer definitions for worker payloads

As we saw in the previous section, we need to define an envelope message for worker payloads:

```
message WorkerPayload {
 oneof payload {
 Step step = 1;
 RelayMessage relay_message = 2;
 }
}
```

With the help of the `oneof` type, we can emulate a message union. A `WorkerPayload` can contain either a `Step` message or a `RelayMessage` message. The `Step` message is more interesting, so we will examine its definition first:

```
message Step {
  Type type = 1;
  map<string, google.protobuf.Any> aggregator_values = 2;
  int64 activeInStep = 3;

  enum Type {
    INVALID = 0;
    PRE = 1;
    POST = 2;
    POST_KEEP_RUNNING = 3;
    EXECUTED_GRAPH = 4;
    PESISTED_RESULTS = 5;
    COMPLETED_JOB = 6;
  }
}
```

The `Step` message will be sent by the worker to enter the master's barrier for a particular execution step. The barrier type is indicated by the `type` field, which can take any of the nested `Type` values. These values correspond to the steps from the state diagram we saw before. Depending on the step type, the worker will transmit its **local** state to the master under the following situations:

- When entering the barrier for the POST step, the worker will fetch the **partial** local aggregator (in Chapter 8, *Graph-Based Data Processing*, we referred to them as **deltas**) values, marshal them into an `Any` message, and add them into a map where the keys correspond to the aggregator names.

- When entering the barrier for the POST_KEEP_RUNNING step, the worker will populate the activeInStep field with the number of **local** vertices that were active in the step.

The other type of message that a worker can send is RelayMessage. This message requests the master to relay a message to the worker that is responsible for handling its destination ID. The definition is quite simple and given as follows:

```
message RelayMessage {
  string destination = 1;
  google.protobuf.Any message = 2;
}
```

The destination field encodes the destination ID (a UUID) while the message field contains the actual message contents serialized as an Any value.

Establishing protocol buffer definitions for master payloads

Now, let's take a look at the protocol buffer definition for the payloads sent by the master to the individual workers:

```
message MasterPayload {
  oneof payload {
    JobDetails job_details = 1;
    Step step = 2;
    RelayMessage relay_message = 3;
  }
}
```

When a worker connects to the job queue, it blocks until the master assigns it a new job by sending out a JobDetails message:

```
message JobDetails {
  string job_id = 1;
  google.protobuf.Timestamp created_at = 2;
  // The [from, to) UUID range assigned to the worker. Note that from is
  // inclusive and to is exclusive.
  bytes partition_from_uuid = 3;
  bytes partition_to_uuid = 4;
}
```

The `job_id` field contains a unique ID for the job to be executed while `created_at` encodes the job creation timestamp. The `partition_from_uuid` and `partition_to_uuid` fields define the extents of the UUID range assigned to this worker by the master. Workers are expected to use this information to load the appropriate section of the graph in memory.

To enter a barrier for a particular step, workers send a `Step` message to the master. Once all workers reach the same barrier, the master will broadcast a notification to exit the barrier by sending back a `Step` message with the same step type.

However, when a `Step` message originates from the master node, the two state-related fields are used to push the new **global** state to each worker:

- When exiting the barrier for the `POST` step, the master will send back the new **global** aggregator values, which have been calculated by applying the deltas sent in by each worker. Workers are expected to overwrite their local aggregator values with the values received by the master.

- When exiting the barrier for the `POST_KEEP_RUNNING` step, the master will send back the **global** number of vertices that were active during the last step. Workers are expected to use this global value to test the stop condition for the algorithm.

Finally, if the master receives a relay request, it examines its destination to select the worker responsible for dealing with it and simply forwards the message over the gRPC stream.

Defining abstractions for working with bi-directional gRPC streams

As we saw in Chapter 9, *Communicating with the Outside World*, bi-directional gRPC streams are full-duplex; the receive and send channels operate independently of each other. However, reading from a gRPC stream is a blocking operation. Therefore, to process both sides of the stream, we need to spin up some goroutines.

Another important caveat of gRPC streams is that, while we can call `Recv` and `Send` from different goroutines, calling each of these methods concurrently from different goroutines is not safe and can lead to data loss! Therefore, we need a mechanism to *serialize* send and receive operations on the gRPC stream. The kind of obvious Go primitives for exactly this type of task are channels.

To make our life a bit easier and isolate the rest of our code from having to deal with the underlying gRPC streams, we will go ahead and introduce a set of abstractions to wrap the gRPC streams and provide a clean, channel-based interface for reading and writing from/to the stream.

Remote worker stream

remoteWorkerStream, the definition of which is shown in the following listing, is used by the master to wrap an incoming worker connection:

```
type remoteWorkerStream struct {
    stream proto.JobQueue_JobStreamServer
    recvMsgCh chan *proto.WorkerPayload
    sendMsgCh chan *proto.MasterPayload
    sendErrCh chan error

    mu sync.Mutex
    onDisconnectFn func()
    disconnected bool
}
```

As you can see in the preceding code, remoteWorkerStream defines three channels for interacting with the stream:

- recvMsgCh is used for receiving payloads sent in by the worker.
- sendMsgCh is used for sending payloads from the master to the worker.
- sendErrCh allows the master to disconnect the worker connection with or without an error code.

The code that interacts with a remote worker stream can use the following methods to obtain the appropriate channel instance for reads and writes as well as for closing the stream:

```
func (s *remoteWorkerStream) RecvFromWorkerChan() <- chan
*proto.WorkerPayload {
    return s.recvMsgCh
}

func (s *remoteWorkerStream) SendToWorkerChan() chan<- *proto.MasterPayload
{
    return s.sendMsgCh
}

func (s *remoteWorkerStream) Close(err error) {
```

```
        if err != nil {
            s.sendErrCh <- err
        }
        close(s.sendErrCh)
    }
```

The `remoteWorkerStream` struct also includes two fields (protected by a mutex) for tracking the connection status for the remote worker. While the master is coordinating the execution of a job, it must monitor the health of each individual worker and abort the job if any of the workers suddenly disconnects. To do so, the master can register a disconnect callback via the following method:

```
func (s *remoteWorkerStream) SetDisconnectCallback(cb func()) {
    s.mu.Lock()
    s.onDisconnectFn = cb
    if s.disconnected {
        s.onDisconnectFn()
    }
    s.mu.Unlock()
}
```

Since `SetDisconnectCallback` may be invoked *after* the worker stream has already disconnected, the stream uses the Boolean `disconnected` field to keep track of this event and automatically invokes the provided callback if it is required.

All we need to do to create a new `remoteWorkerStream` instance is to invoke its constructor and pass the gRPC stream as an argument. The constructor implementation (shown in the following) will initialize the various buffered channels required for working with the stream:

```
func newRemoteWorkerStream(stream proto.JobQueue_JobStreamServer)
*remoteWorkerStream {
    return &remoteWorkerStream{
        stream: stream,
        rcvMsgCh: make(chan *proto.WorkerPayload, 1),
        sendMsgCh: make(chan *proto.MasterPayload, 1),
        sendErrCh: make(chan error, 1),
    }
}
```

The `HandleSendRecv` method implements the required logic for working with the underlying stream. As you can see in the following snippet, it first creates a cancelable context, which is always canceled when the method returns. Then, it spins up a goroutine to asynchronously handle the receiving end of the stream. The method then enters an infinite `for` loop, where it processes the sending end of the stream until either the stream is gracefully closed or an error occurs:

```go
func (s *remoteWorkerStream) HandleSendRecv() error {
    ctx, cancelFn := context.WithCancel(context.Background())
    defer cancelFn()
    go s.handleRecv(ctx, cancelFn)
    for {
        select {
        case mPayload := <-s.sendMsgCh:
            if err := s.stream.Send(mPayload); err != nil {
                return err
            }
        case err, ok := <-s.sendErrCh:
            if !ok { // signalled to close without an error
                return nil
            }
            return status.Errorf(codes.Aborted, err.Error())
        case <-ctx.Done():
            return status.Errorf(codes.Aborted, errJobAborted.Error())
        }
    }
}
```

As far as the send implementation is concerned, the previous code uses a `select` block to wait for one of the following events:

- A payload is emitted via `sendMsgCh`. In this case, we attempt to send it through the stream and return any error to the caller.
- An error is emitted via `sendErrCh` or the channel is closed (see the `Close` method implementation a few lines up). If no error has occurred, the method returns with a `nil` error. Otherwise, we use the `grpc/status` package to tag the error with the gRPC specific `codes.Aborted` error code and return the error to the caller.
- Finally, if the context is canceled by the `handleRecv` goroutine, we exit with a typed `errJobAborted` error message.

Let's now take a closer look at the implementation of the `handleRecv` method:

```go
func (s *remoteWorkerStream) handleRecv(ctx context.Context, cancelFn
func()) {
    for {
        wPayload, err := s.stream.Recv()
        if err != nil {
            s.handleDisconnect()
            cancelFn()
            return
        }

        select {
        case s.recvMsgCh <- wPayload:
        case <-ctx.Done():
            return
        }
    }
}
```

Calling the stream's `Recv` method blocks until either a message becomes available or the remote connection is severed. If we receive an incoming message from the worker, a `select` block is used to either enqueue the message to the `recvMsgCh` or to exit the goroutine if the context is canceled (for example, `HandleSendRecv` exits due to an error).

On the other hand, if we do detect an error, we always assume that the client disconnected and invoke the `handleDisconnect` helper method before canceling the context and exiting the goroutine:

```go
func (s *remoteWorkerStream) handleDisconnect() {
    s.mu.Lock()
    if s.onDisconnectFn != nil {
        s.onDisconnectFn()
    }
    s.disconnected = true
    s.mu.Unlock()
}
```

The preceding implementation is pretty straightforward. The `mu` lock is acquired and a check is performed to see whether a disconnect callback has been specified. If that's the case, then the callback is invoked and then the `disconnected` flag is set to `true` to keep track of the disconnect event.

Remote master stream

Next, we will move to the worker side and examine the equivalent stream helper for handling a connection to the master node. The definition of the `remoteMasterStream` type is pretty much the same as `remoteWorkerStream`, given as follows:

```
type remoteMasterStream struct {
    stream proto.JobQueue_JobStreamClient
    recvMsgCh chan *proto.MasterPayload
    sendMsgCh chan *proto.WorkerPayload

    ctx context.Context
    cancelFn func()

    mu sync.Mutex
    onDisconnectFn func()
    disconnected bool
}
```

Once the worker connects to the master node and receives a job assignment, it will invoke the `newRemoteMasterStream` function to wrap the obtained stream connection with a `remoteMasterStream` instance:

```
func newRemoteMasterStream(stream proto.JobQueue_JobStreamClient)
*remoteMasterStream {
    ctx, cancelFn := context.WithCancel(context.Background())

    return &remoteMasterStream{
        ctx: ctx,
        cancelFn: cancelFn,
        stream: stream,
        recvMsgCh: make(chan *proto.MasterPayload, 1),
        sendMsgCh: make(chan *proto.WorkerPayload, 1),
    }
}
```

As you can see in the previous code snippet, the constructor creates a cancelable context and allocates a pair of channels to be used for interfacing with the stream.

Just as we did for the `remoteWorkerStream` implementation, we will define a pair of convenience methods for accessing these channels, as follows:

```
func (s *remoteMasterStream) RecvFromMasterChan() <-chan
*proto.MasterPayload {
    return s.recvMsgCh
}
```

```
func (s *remoteMasterStream) SendToMasterChan() chan<- *proto.WorkerPayload
{
    return s.sendMsgCh
}
```

The `HandleSendRecv` method is responsible for receiving incoming messages from the master and for transmitting outgoing messages from the worker.

As you can see in the following block of code, the implementation is more or less the same as the `remoteWorkerStream` implementation with two small differences. Can you spot them? Take a look:

```
func (s *remoteMasterStream) HandleSendRecv() error {
    defer func() {
        s.cancelFn()
        _ = s.stream.CloseSend()
    }()
    go s.handleRecv()
    for {
        select {
        case wPayload := <-s.sendMsgCh:
            if err := s.stream.Send(wPayload); err != nil &&
!xerrors.Is(err, io.EOF) {
                return err
            }
        case <-s.ctx.Done():
            return nil
        }
    }
}
```

The first difference has to do with the way we handle errors returned by the stream's `Send` method. If the worker closes the send stream while the preceding block of code is attempting to send a payload to the master, `Send` will return an `io.EOF` error to let us know that we cannot send any more messages through the stream. Since the worker is the one that controls the send stream, we treat `io.EOF` errors as *expected* and ignore them.

Secondly, as the worker is the initiator of the RPC, it is not allowed to terminate the send stream with a specific error code as we did in the case of the master stream implementation. Consequently, for this implementation, there is no need to maintain (and poll) a dedicated error channel.

On the other hand, the following receive side code is implemented in exactly the same way as remoteMasterStream:

```
func (s *remoteMasterStream) handleRecv() {
    for {
        mPayload, err := s.stream.Recv()
        if err != nil {
            s.handleDisconnect()
            s.cancelFn()
            return
        }
        select {
        case s.recvMsgCh <- mPayload:
        case <-s.ctx.Done():
            return
        }
    }
}
```

To actually shut down the stream and cause the HandleSendRecv method to exit, the worker can invoke the Close method of remoteMasterStream:

```
func (s *remoteMasterStream) Close() {
    s.cancelFn()
}
```

The Close method first cancels the context monitored by the select blocks in both the receive and send code. As we discussed a few lines preceding, the latter action will cause any pending Send calls to fail with an io.EOF error and allow the HandleSendRecv method to return. Furthermore, the cancelation of the context enables the handleRecv goroutine to also return, hence ensuring that our implementation is not leaking any goroutines.

Creating a distributed barrier for the graph execution steps

A barrier can be thought of as a rendezvous point for a set of processes. Once a process enters the barrier, it is prevented from making any progress until all other expected processes also enter the barrier.

In Go, we could model a barrier with the help of the `sync.WaitGroup` primitive, as follows:

```
func barrier(numWorkers int) {
    var wg sync.WaitGroup
    wg.Add(numWorkers)

    for i := 0; i < numWorkers; i++ {
        go func() {
            wg.Done()
            fmt.Printf("Entered the barrier; waiting for other goroutines
to join")
            wg.Wait()
            fmt.Printf("Exited the barrier")
        }()
    }

    wg.Wait()
}
```

To guarantee that each worker executes the various stages of the graph state machine in lock-step with the other workers, we must implement a similar barrier primitive. However, as far as our particular application is concerned, the goroutines that we are interested in synchronizing execute on different hosts. This obviously complicates things as we now need to come up with a distributed barrier implementation!

As we mentioned in the previous section, the master node will serve the role of the coordinator for the distributed barrier. To make the code easier to follow, in the following subsections, we will split our distributed barrier implementations into a worker-side and master-side implementation and examine them separately of each other.

Implementing a step barrier for individual workers

The `workerStepBarrier` type encapsulates the required logic for enabling a worker to enter the barrier for a particular graph execution step and to wait until the master notifies the worker that it can now exit the barrier.

The `workerStepBarrier` type is defined as follows:

```
type workerStepBarrier struct {
    ctx context.Context
    stream *remoteMasterStream
    waitCh map[proto.Step_Type]chan *proto.Step
}
```

To understand how these fields are initialized, let's take a look at the constructor for a new barrier instance:

```
func newWorkerStepBarrier(ctx context.Context, stream *remoteMasterStream)
*workerStepBarrier {
    waitCh := make(map[proto.Step_Type]chan *proto.Step)
    for stepType := range proto.Step_Type_name {
        if proto.Step_Type(stepType) == proto.Step_INVALID {
            continue
        }
        waitCh[proto.Step_Type(stepType)] = make(chan *proto.Step)
    }

    return &workerStepBarrier{
        ctx: ctx,
        stream: stream,
        waitCh: waitCh,
    }
}
```

As you can see, the constructor accepts a context and a `remoteMasterStream` instance as an argument. The context allows the barrier code to block until either a notification is received by the master or the context gets canceled (for example, because the worker is shutting down).

To allow the worker to block until a notification is received from the master, the constructor will allocate a separate channel for each type of step that we want to create a barrier for. When the protoc compiles our protocol buffer definitions into Go code, it will also provide us with the handy `Step_Type` map that normally is used to obtain the string-based representation of a step type (protocol buffers model `enum` types as `int32` values). The constructor exploits the presence of this map to automatically generate the required number of channels using a plain `for` loop block.

When the worker wants to enter the barrier for a particular step, it creates a new `Step` message with the local state that it wants to share with the master and invokes the blocking `Wait` method, which is shown as follows:

```
func (b *workerStepBarrier) Wait(step *proto.Step) (*proto.Step, error) {
    ch, exists := b.waitCh[step.Type]
    if !exists {
        return nil, xerrors.Errorf("unsupported step type %q",
proto.Step_Type_name[int32(step.Type)])
    }
    select {
    case b.stream.SendToMasterChan() <- &proto.WorkerPayload{Payload:
&proto.WorkerPayload_Step{Step: step}}:
```

```
        case <-b.ctx.Done():
            return nil, errJobAborted
        }

        select {
        case step = <-ch:
            return step, nil
        case <-b.ctx.Done():
            return nil, errJobAborted
        }
    }
```

The `Wait` method consists of two basic parts. After validating the step type, the implementation tries to push a new `WorkerPayload` into `remoteMasterStream` so it can be sent to the master via the gRPC stream.

Once the payload is successfully enqueued, the worker then waits on the appropriate channel for the specified step type and the master broadcasts a `Step` message to all workers to let them know that they can exit the barrier. Once that message is received, it is returned to the caller, which is then free to perform the required chunk of work for implementing this particular graph computation step.

By now, you are probably wondering who is responsible for publishing the master's broadcast step to the channel that the `Wait` method is trying to read from. To enforce a clear separation of concerns (and to make testing easier), the barrier implementation does not concern itself with the low-level details of reading the responses from the master. Instead, it provides a `Notify` method that another component (the job coordinator) will invoke once a step message is received by the master:

```
func (b *workerStepBarrier) Notify(step *proto.Step) error {
    ch, exists := b.waitCh[step.Type]
    if !exists {
        return xerrors.Errorf("unsupported step type %q",
proto.Step_Type_name[int32(step.Type)])
    }

    select {
    case ch <- step:
        return nil
    case <-b.ctx.Done():
        return errJobAborted
    }
}
```

The code in the `Notify` method's implementation examines the step type field and uses it to select the channel for publishing the `Step` response.

Now, let's move on to examine the equivalent step barrier implementation for the master side.

Implementing a step barrier for the master

Now, let's take a look at the other half of the barrier implementation logic that runs on the master node. The `masterStepBarrier` type, the definition of which is given as follows, is admittedly more interesting as it contains the actual barrier synchronization logic:

```
type masterStepBarrier struct {
    ctx context.Context
    numWorkers int
    waitCh map[proto.Step_Type]chan *proto.Step
    notifyCh map[proto.Step_Type]chan *proto.Step
}
```

One key difference is that the `masterStepBarrier` type defines two types of channels:

- **Wait channel**: It is a channel for which the barrier monitors for incoming `Step` messages from workers.
- **Notify channel**: It is a channel where remote worker streams will block waiting for a `Step` message to be broadcast by the master node.

As you can see by skimming through the constructor logic for creating the master barrier, we automatically create the required set of channels by iterating the `Step_Type` variable that the protoc generated for use when the protocol buffer definitions were compiled.

What's more, when creating a new barrier, the caller is expected to also provide the number of workers that are expected to join the barrier as an argument:

```
func newMasterStepBarrier(ctx context.Context, numWorkers int)
*masterStepBarrier {
    waitCh := make(map[proto.Step_Type]chan *proto.Step)
    notifyCh := make(map[proto.Step_Type]chan *proto.Step)
    for stepType := range proto.Step_Type_name {
        if proto.Step_Type(stepType) == proto.Step_INVALID {
            continue
        }
        waitCh[proto.Step_Type(stepType)] = make(chan *proto.Step)
        notifyCh[proto.Step_Type(stepType)] = make(chan *proto.Step)
    }
```

```
        return &masterStepBarrier{
            ctx: ctx,
            numWorkers: numWorkers,
            waitCh: waitCh,
            notifyCh: notifyCh,
        }
    }
```

In the previous section, we saw that, when the worker invokes the `Wait` method on `workerStepBarrier`, a `Step` message is published via `remoteMasterStream`. Now, we will examine what happens on the receiving end. Once the published `Step` message is received, the master invokes the `Wait` method on `masterStepBarrier`.

In principle, this is nothing more than a good old unary RPC implemented over a gRPC stream! Here is what happens inside the master's `Wait` method:

```
    func (b *masterStepBarrier) Wait(step *proto.Step) (*proto.Step, error) {
        waitCh, exists := b.waitCh[step.Type]
        if !exists {
            return nil, xerrors.Errorf("unsupported step type %q",
    proto.Step_Type_name[int32(step.Type)])
        }
        select {
        case waitCh <- step:
        case <-b.ctx.Done():
            return nil, errJobAborted
        }
        select {
        case step = <-b.notifyCh[step.Type]:
            return step, nil
        case <-b.ctx.Done():
            return nil, errJobAborted
        }
    }
```

The implementation first attempts to publish the incoming `Step` message to the *wait* channel responsible for handling the barrier for the step advertised by the `Step` message's `type` field. This bit of code will block until the master is ready to enter the same barrier (or the context expires due to the master shutting down).

Following a successful write to the *wait* channel, the code will then block a second time waiting for a notification from the master to be published to the appropriate *notify* channel for the step type. Once the `Step` response from the master is dequeued, `Wait` unblocks and returns the `Step` to the caller. The caller is then responsible for transmitting the `Step` message back to the worker, where it will be provided as an argument to the worker barrier's `Notify` method.

When the master node is ready to enter the barrier for a particular step, it invokes the blocking `WaitForWorkers` method providing the step type as an argument. This method, the implementation of which is shown as follows, is equivalent to the worker side's `Wait` method:

```
func (b *masterStepBarrier) WaitForWorkers(stepType proto.Step_Type)
([]*proto.Step, error) {
    waitCh, exists := b.waitCh[stepType]
    if !exists {
        return nil, xerrors.Errorf("unsupported step type %q",
proto.Step_Type_name[int32(stepType)])
    }

    collectedSteps := make([]*proto.Step, b.numWorkers)
    for i := 0; i < b.numWorkers; i++ {
        select {
        case step := <-waitCh:
            collectedSteps[i] = step
        case <-b.ctx.Done():
            return nil, errJobAborted
        }
    }
    return collectedSteps, nil
}
```

The purpose of the preceding method is to wait until the expected number of workers join the barrier for the particular step type (via the `Wait` method) and to collect the individual `Step` messages published by each worker. To this end, the code first initializes a slice with enough capacity to hold the incoming messages and performs `numWorkers` reads from the appropriate *wait* channel for the step.

Once all workers have joined the barrier, `WaitForWorkers` unblocks and returns the slice of `Step` messages to the caller. At this point, while all workers are still blocked, the master is now within what is referred to as a *critical section*, where it is free to implement any operation it requires in an **atomic** fashion. For instance, while inside the critical section for `POST_STEP`, the master will iterate the workers' step messages and apply the partial aggregator deltas from each worker into its own global aggregator state.

Then, once the master is ready to exit its critical section, it invokes the `NotifyWorkers` method with a `Step` message to be broadcast to the workers currently blocked on the barrier:

```
func (b *masterStepBarrier) NotifyWorkers(step *proto.Step) error {
    notifyCh, exists := b.notifyCh[step.Type]
    if !exists {
```

```
        return xerrors.Errorf("unsupported step type %q",
proto.Step_Type_name[int32(step.Type)])
    }

    for i := 0; i < b.numWorkers; i++ {
        select {
        case notifyCh <- step:
        case <-b.ctx.Done():
            return errJobAborted
        }
    }
    return nil
}
```

All `NotifyWorkers` needs to do is to push `numWorkers` copies of the master's `Step` message to the appropriate notification channel for the barrier step. Writing to the notification channel unblocks the callers of the `Wait` method and allows the step message to be propagated back to the worker.

Does all of this seem confusing to you? The following diagram visualizes all the barrier-related interactions between the master and the server and will hopefully allow you to connect the dots:

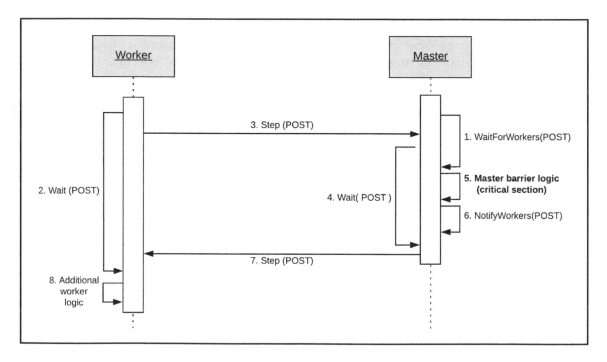

Figure 3: An end-to-end illustration of the barrier interactions between the master and the worker

Here is a brief summary of what's going on in the preceding diagram:

1. The master calls `WaitForWorkers` for the `POST` step and blocks.
2. The worker calls `Wait` for the `POST` step on its local barrier instance and blocks.
3. A `Step` message is published by through `remoteMasterStream`.
4. The piece of code on the master side that processes incoming worker messages receives the worker's `Step` message and invokes `Wait` on the master barrier and blocks.
5. As the required number of workers (one in this example) has joined the barrier, the master's `WaitForWorkers` call unblocks allowing the master to enter a critical section where the master executes its step-specific logic.
6. The master then invokes `NotifyWorkers` with a new `Step` message for the `POST` step.
7. The `Wait` method on the master side now unblocks and the `Step` message that the master just broadcast is sent back through the stream to the worker.
8. Upon receiving the `Step` response from the master, the worker's `Wait` method unblocks and the worker is now free to execute its own step-specific logic.

Creating custom executor factories for wrapping existing graph instances

In `Chapter 8`, *Graph-Based Data Processing*, we explored the use of the `bspgraph` package to implement a few popular graph-based algorithms such as Dijkstra's shortest path, graph coloring, and PageRank. To orchestrate the end-to-end execution of the aforementioned algorithms, we relied on the API provided by the package's `Executor` type. However, instead of having our algorithm implementations *directly* invoke the `Executor` types constructor, we allowed the end users to optionally specify a custom executor factory for obtaining an `Executor` instance.

Any Go function that satisfies the following signature can be effectively used in place of the default constructor for a new `Executor` constructor:

```
type ExecutorFactory func(*bspgraph.Graph, bspgraph.ExecutorCallbacks)
*bspgraph.Executor
```

The key benefit of this approach is that the executor factory is given full access to the *algorithm-specific* callbacks for the various stages of the computation. In this chapter, we will be exploiting this mechanism to intercept and decorate the user-defined callbacks with the necessary glue logic for interfacing with the barrier primitive that we built in the previous section. The patched callbacks will then be passed to the original Executor constructor and the result will be returned to the caller.

This little trick, while completely *transparent* to the original algorithm implementation, is all that we really need to ensure that all callbacks are executed in lock-step with all other workers.

The workers' executor factory

To create a suitable executor factory for workers, we can use the following helper function:

```
func newWorkerExecutorFactory(serializer Serializer, barrier
*workerStepBarrier) bspgraph.ExecutorFactory {
    f := &workerExecutorFactory{ serializer: serializer, barrier: barrier }
    return func(g *bspgraph.Graph, cb bspgraph.ExecutorCallbacks)
*bspgraph.Executor {
        f.origCallbacks = cb
        patchedCb := bspgraph.ExecutorCallbacks{
            PreStep: f.preStepCallback,
            PostStep: f.postStepCallback,
            PostStepKeepRunning: f.postStepKeepRunningCallback,
        }
        return bspgraph.NewExecutor(g, patchedCb)
    }
}
```

The newWorkerExecutorFactory function expects two arguments, namely a Serializer instance and an initialized workerStepBarrier object. The serializer instance is responsible for serializing and unserializing the aggregator values to and from the any.Any protocol buffer messages that workers exchange with the master when they enter or exit the various step barriers. In the following code, you can see the definition of the Serializer interface:

```
type Serializer interface {
    Serialize(interface{}) (*any.Any, error)
    Unserialize(*any.Any) (interface{}, error)
}
```

As you can see in the preceding code snippet, the `newWorkerExecutorFactory` function allocates a new `workerExecutorFactory` value and returns a closure that satisfies the `ExecutorFactory` signature. When the generated factory function is invoked, its implementation captures the original callbacks and invokes the real executor constructor with a set of patched callbacks.

Let's take a look at what happens inside each one of the patched callbacks, starting with the one responsible for handling the PRE step:

```go
func (f *workerExecutorFactory) preStepCallback(ctx context.Context, g
*bspgraph.Graph) error {
    if _, err := f.barrier.Wait(&proto.Step{Type: proto.Step_PRE}), err !=
nil {
        return err
    }

    if f.origCallbacks.PreStep != nil {
        return f.origCallbacks.PreStep(ctx, g)
    }
    return nil
}
```

As you can see, the callback immediately joins the barrier and, once instructed to exit, it invokes the original (if defined) PRE step callback. The following code shows the next callback on our list, invoked immediately after executing a graph super-step:

```go
func (f *workerExecutorFactory) postStepCallback(ctx context.Context, g
*bspgraph.Graph, activeInStep int) error {
    aggrDeltas, err := serializeAggregatorDeltas(g, f.serializer)
    if err != nil {
        return xerrors.Errorf("unable to serialize aggregator deltas")
    }
    stepUpdateMsg, err := f.barrier.Wait(&proto.Step{
        Type: proto.Step_POST,
        AggregatorValues: aggrDeltas,
    })
    if err != nil {
        return err
    } else if err = setAggregatorValues(g, stepUpdateMsg.AggregatorValues,
f.serializer); err != nil {
        return err
    } else if f.origCallbacks.PostStep != nil {
        return f.origCallbacks.PostStep(ctx, g, activeInStep)
    }
    return nil
}
```

We mentioned before that, during the POST step, workers must transmit their partial aggregator deltas to the master when they enter the POST step barrier. This is exactly what happens in the preceding previous snippet.

The serializeAggregatorDeltas helper function iterates the list of aggregators that are defined on the graph and uses the provided Serializer instance to convert them into map[string]*any.Any. The map with the serialized deltas is then attached to a Step message and sent to the master via the barrier's Wait method.

The master tallies the deltas from each worker and broadcasts back a new Step message that contains the updated set of global aggregator values. Once we receive the updated message, we invoke the setAggregatorValues helper, which unserializes the incoming map[string]*any.Any map entries and overwrites the aggregator values for the local graph instance. Before returning, the callback wrapper invokes the original user-defined POST step callback if one is actually defined.

The last callback wrapper implementation that we will inspect is the one invoked for the POST_KEEP_RUNNING step, given as follows:

```
func (f *workerExecutorFactory) postStepKeepRunningCallback(ctx
context.Context, g *bspgraph.Graph, activeInStep int) (bool, error) {
    stepUpdateMsg, err := f.barrier.Wait(&proto.Step{
        Type: proto.Step_POST_KEEP_RUNNING,
        ActiveInStep: int64(activeInStep),
    })
    if err != nil {
        return false, err
    }

    if f.origCallbacks.PostStepKeepRunning != nil {
        return f.origCallbacks.PostStepKeepRunning(ctx, g,
int(stepUpdateMsg.ActiveInStep))
    }
    return true, nil
}
```

As with every other callback wrapper implementation, the first thing we do is to enter the barrier for the current step type. Note that the outgoing Step message includes the **local** number of active vertices in this step. The response we get back from the master includes the **global** number of active vertices, which is the actual value that must be passed to the user-defined callback for this step.

The master's executor factory

The code for generating an executor factory for the master is quite similar; to avoid repeating the same code blocks again, we will only list the implementations for each one of the individual callback wrappers, starting with preStepCallback:

```go
func (f *masterExecutorFactory) preStepCallback(ctx context.Context, g
*bspgraph.Graph) error {
    if _, err := f.barrier.WaitForWorkers(proto.Step_PRE); err != nil {
        return err
    } else if err := f.barrier.NotifyWorkers(&proto.Step{Type:
proto.Step_PRE}), err != nil {
        return err
    }

    if f.origCallbacks.PreStep != nil {
        return f.origCallbacks.PreStep(ctx, g)
    }
    return nil
}
```

Compared to the worker-side implementation, the master behaves a bit differently. To begin with, the master waits until all workers enter the barrier. Then, with the help of the masterStepBarrier primitive, it broadcasts a notification message that unblocks the workers and allows both the master and the workers to execute the same user-defined callback for the step.

Let's now see what happens inside the callback override for the POST step:

```go
func (f *masterExecutorFactory) postStepCallback(ctx context.Context, g
*bspgraph.Graph, activeInStep int) error {
    workerSteps, err := f.barrier.WaitForWorkers(proto.Step_POST)
    if err != nil {
        return err
    }
    for _, workerStep := range workerSteps {
        if err = mergeWorkerAggregatorDeltas(g,
workerStep.AggregatorValues, f.serializer); err != nil {
            return xerrors.Errorf("unable to merge aggregator deltas into
global state: %w", err)
        }
    }
    globalAggrValues, err := serializeAggregatorValues(g, f.serializer,
false)
    if err != nil {
        return xerrors.Errorf("unable to serialize global aggregator
values: %w", err)
```

```
        } else if err := f.barrier.NotifyWorkers(&proto.Step{ Type:
proto.Step_POST, AggregatorValues: globalAggrValues }); err != nil {
            return err
        } else if f.origCallbacks.PostStep != nil {
            return f.origCallbacks.PostStep(ctx, g, activeInStep)
        }
        return nil
    }
```

Once again, the master waits for all workers to enter the barrier but this time, it collects the Step messages sent in by each individual worker. Then, the master begins its critical section where it iterates the list of collected Step messages and applies the partial deltas to its own aggregator. Finally, the new global aggregator values are serialized via a call to the serializeAggregatorValues helper and broadcast back to each worker.

As expected, the callback wrapper for the POST_STEP_KEEP_RUNNING step follows exactly the same pattern:

```
    func (f *masterExecutorFactory) postStepKeepRunningCallback(ctx
context.Context, g *bspgraph.Graph, activeInStep int) (bool, error) {
        workerSteps, err :=
f.barrier.WaitForWorkers(proto.Step_POST_KEEP_RUNNING)
        if err != nil {
            return false, err
        }
        for _, workerStep := range workerSteps {
            activeInStep += int(workerStep.ActiveInStep)
        }
        if err := f.barrier.NotifyWorkers(&proto.Step{ Type:
proto.Step_POST_KEEP_RUNNING, ActiveInStep: int64(activeInStep) }); err !=
nil {
            return false, err
        } else if f.origCallbacks.PostStepKeepRunning != nil {
            return f.origCallbacks.PostStepKeepRunning(ctx, g, activeInStep)
        }
        return true, nil
    }
```

Inside the master's critical section, the individual ActiveInStep counts reported by each worker are aggregated and the result is broadcast back to each worker. After exiting the barrier, the master invokes the user-defined callback for the step.

Coordinating the execution of a graph job

So far, we have created the necessary abstractions for reading from and writing to the bi-directional stream established between the workers and the master. What's more, we have implemented a distributed barrier primitive that serves as a rendezvous point for the various graph compute steps that are asynchronously executed by the worker and the master nodes.

Finally, we have defined a set of custom executor factories that enable us to wrap any existing algorithm built with the help of the `bspgraph` package and transparently allow it to use the barrier primitive to ensure that the graph computations are executed in lock-step across all workers.

One thing that we should keep in mind is that running the graph compute algorithm to completion is not a sufficient condition to treat a distributed *compute job* as being complete! We still have to ensure that the results of the computation are persisted to stable storage without an error. The latter task is far from trivial; many things can go wrong while the workers attempt to save their progress as the workers might crash, the store might not be reachable, or a various host of random, network-related failures might occur.

As the old saying goes—building distributed systems is hard! To this end, we need to introduce an **orchestration layer**—in other words, a mechanism that will combine all of the components that we have built so far and include all of the required logic to coordinate the end-to-end execution of a distributed computation job. Should any error occur (at a worker, the master, or both), the coordinator should detect it and signal all workers to abort the job.

Simplifying end user interactions with the dbspgraph package

This chapter explores the various components of the distributed job runner implementation in detail. Nevertheless, we would rather want to keep all of the internal details hidden from the intended user of the dbspgraph package.

Essentially, we need to come up with a simplified API that the end users will use to interact with our package. As it turns out, this is quite easy to do. Assuming that the end users have already created (and tested) their graph algorithm with the help of the bspgraph package, they only need to provide a simple adaptor for interacting with the algorithm implementation. The set of required methods is encapsulated in the Runner interface definition, which is outlined as follows:

```
type Runner interface {
    StartJob(Details, bspgraph.ExecutorFactory) (*bspgraph.Executor, error)
    CompleteJob(Details) error
    AbortJob(Details)
}
```

The first argument to each one of the Runner methods is a structure that contains metadata about the currently executing job. The Details type mirrors the fields of the JobDetails protocol buffer message that the master broadcasts to each worker and is defined as follows:

```
type Details struct {
    JobID string
    CreatedAt time.Time
    PartitionFromID uuid.UUID
    PartitionToID uuid.UUID
}
```

The StartJob method provides a hook for allowing the end users to initialize a bspgraph.Graph instance, load the appropriate set of data (vertices and edges), and use the provided ExecutorFactory argument to create a new Executor instance, which StartJob returns to the caller. As you probably guessed, our code will invoke StartJob with the appropriate custom execution factory depending on whether the code is executing on a worker or master node.

Once both the master and workers have completed the execution of the graph, we will arrange things so that the CompleteJob method is invoked. This is where the end user is expected to extract the computed application-specific results from the graph and persist them to the stable store.

On the other hand, should an error occur either while running the algorithm or while attempting to persist the results, our job coordinator will invoke the AbortJob method to notify the end user and let them properly clean up or take any required action for rolling back any changes already persisted to disk.

The worker job coordinator

We will start by examining the coordinator logic that the worker side executes. Let's take a quick look at the constructor for the `workerJobCoordinator` type:

```
type workerJobCoordinatorConfig struct {
    jobDetails job.Details
    masterStream *remoteMasterStream
    jobRunner job.Runner
    serializer Serializer
}

func newWorkerJobCoordinator(ctx context.Context, cfg
workerJobCoordinatorConfig) *workerJobCoordinator {
    jobCtx, cancelJobCtx := context.WithCancel(ctx)
    return &workerJobCoordinator{
        jobCtx: jobCtx, cancelJobCtx: cancelJobCtx,
        barrier: newWorkerStepBarrier(jobCtx, cfg.masterStream),
        cfg: cfg,
    }
}
```

The constructor expects an external context as an argument as well as a configuration object, which includes the following:

- The job metadata
- A `remoteMasterStream` instance, which we will use to interact with the master
- A user-provided job `Runner` implementation
- A user-provided `Serializer` instance to be used by both the executor factory (marshaling aggregator values) and for marshaling outgoing graph messages that need to be relayed through the master node

Before proceeding, the constructor creates a new *cancelable* context (`jobCtx`), which wraps the caller-provided context. The `jobCtx` instance is then used as an argument for creating a `workerStepBarrier` instance. This approach allows the coordinator to fully control the life cycle of the barrier.

If an error occurs, the coordinator can simply invoke the `cancelJobCtx` function and automatically have the barrier shut down. Of course, the same tear-down semantics also apply if the external context happens to expire.

Running a new job

Once the worker receives a new job assignment from the master, it calls the coordinator's constructor and then invokes its `RunJob` method, which blocks until the job either completes or an error occurs:

```
func (c *workerJobCoordinator) RunJob() error {
    // ...
}
```

Let's break down the `RunJob` implementation into smaller chunks and go through each one:

```
execFactory := newWorkerExecutorFactory(c.cfg.serializer, c.barrier)
executor, err := c.cfg.jobRunner.StartJob(c.cfg.jobDetails, execFactory)
if err != nil {
    c.cancelJobCtx()
    return xerrors.Errorf("unable to start job on worker: %w", err)
}

graph := executor.Graph()
graph.RegisterRelayer(bspgraph.RelayerFunc(c.relayNonLocalMessage))
```

The very first thing that `RunJob` does is to create a `workerExecutor` factory using the configured serializer and the barrier instance that the constructor already set up. Then, the `StartJob` method of the user-provided `job.Runner` is invoked to initialize the graph and return an `Executor` value that we can use. Note that, up to this point, *our code* is totally oblivious to how the user-defined algorithm works!

The next step entails the extraction of the `bspgraph.Graph` instance from the returned `Executor` instance and the registration of a `bspgraph.Relayer` helper, which the graph will automatically invoke when a vertex attempts to send a message with an ID that is not recognized by the local graph instance. We will take a closer look at the `relayNonLocalMessage` method implementation in one of the following sections where we will be discussing the concept of message relaying in more detail. This completes all of the required initialization steps. We are now ready to commence the execution of the graph compute job!

To not only monitor the health of the connection to the master but also asynchronously process any incoming payloads, we will spin up a goroutine:

```
var wg sync.WaitGroup
wg.Add(1)
go func() {
    defer wg.Done()
    c.cfg.masterStream.SetDisconnectCallback(c.handleMasterDisconnect)
```

```
        c.handleMasterPayloads(graph)
    }()
```

While our goroutine is busy processing incoming payloads, RunJob invokes the runJobToCompletion helper method that advances through the various stages of the graph execution's state machine. If an error occurs, we invoke the user's AbortJob method and then proceed to check the cause of the error.

If the job execution failed due to a context cancelation, we replace the error with the more meaningful, typed errJobAborted error. On the other hand, if the handleMasterPayloads method reported a more interesting error, we overwrite the returned error value with the reported error:

```
if err = c.runJobToCompletion(executor); err != nil {
    c.cfg.jobRunner.AbortJob(c.cfg.jobDetails)
    if xerrors.Is(err, context.Canceled) {
        err = errJobAborted
    }
    if c.asyncWorkerErr != nil {
        err = c.asyncWorkerErr
    }
}

c.cancelJobCtx()
wg.Wait() // wait for any spawned goroutines to exit before returning.
return err
```

Before returning, we cancel the job context to trigger a teardown of not only the barrier but also the spawned payload-handling goroutine and Wait on the wait group until the goroutine exits.

Transitioning through the stages of the graph's state machine

The role of the runJobToCompletion method is to execute all stages of the graph's state machine until either the job completes or an error occurs.

As you can see in the following code snippet, we request from the executor instance to run the graph algorithm until its termination condition is met. Then, the worker reports its success to the master by joining the barrier for the EXECUTED_GRAPH step.

Once all other workers reach the barrier, the master unblocks us and we proceed to invoke the CompleteJob method on the user-provided job.Runner instance. Then, we notify the master that the calculations have been stored by joining the barrier for the PERSISTED_RESULTS step.

After the master unblocks us for the last time, we notify the master that we have reached the final stage of the state machine by joining the barrier for the COMPLETED_JOB step:

```
func (c *workerJobCoordinator) runJobToCompletion(executor
*bspgraph.Executor) error {
    if err := executor.RunToCompletion(c.jobCtx); err != nil {
        return err
    } else if _, err := c.barrier.Wait(&proto.Step{Type:
proto.Step_EXECUTED_GRAPH}); err != nil {
        return errJobAborted
    } else if err := c.cfg.jobRunner.CompleteJob(c.cfg.jobDetails); err !=
nil {
        return err
    } else if _, err = c.barrier.Wait(&proto.Step{Type:
proto.Step_PESISTED_RESULTS}); err != nil {
        return errJobAborted
    }

    _, _ = c.barrier.Wait(&proto.Step{Type: proto.Step_COMPLETED_JOB})
    return nil
}
```

When all workers reach the COMPLETED_JOB step, the master will **terminate the connected job stream** with a grpc.OK code. Due to the way that gRPC schedules message transmissions, there is no guarantee that the code will be received by the worker before the stream is actually torn down (in the latter case, we might get back an io.EOF error).

Keep in mind, however, that the master will only disconnect us once all workers reach the last barrier and report that they have successfully persisted their local results. This is the reason why we can safely omit the error check in the last barrier.Wait call.

Handling incoming payloads from the master

As we saw in the previous section, the body of the payload-handling goroutine first registers a disconnect callback with the master stream and then delegates the payload processing to the auxiliary handleMasterPayloads method.

This way, if we suddenly lose the connection to the master, we can simply cancel the job context and cause the job to abort with an error. The following disconnect callback implementation is quite simple:

```
func (c *workerJobCoordinator) handleMasterDisconnect() {
    select {
    case <-c.jobCtx.Done(): // job already aborted or completed
    default:
        c.cancelJobCtx()
    }
}
```

The `handleMasterPayloads` method implements a long-running event processing loop. A `select` block watches for either an incoming payload or the cancelation of the job context.

If the context gets canceled or the `masterStream` closes the channel that we currently read from, the method returns:

```
func (c *workerJobCoordinator) handleMasterPayloads(graph *bspgraph.Graph)
{
    defer c.cancelJobCtx()
    var mPayload *proto.MasterPayload
    for {
        select {
        case mPayload = <-c.cfg.masterStream.RecvFromMasterChan():
        case <-c.jobCtx.Done():
            return
        }
        if mPayload == nil {
            return
        }

        // omitted: process payload depending on its type
    }
}
```

Once a valid payload is received from the master, we examine its content and execute the appropriate action depending on the payload type:

```
if relayMsg := mPayload.GetRelayMessage(); relayMsg != nil {
    if err := c.deliverGraphMessage(graph, relayMsg); err != nil {
        c.mu.Lock()
        c.asyncWorkerErr = err
        c.mu.Unlock()
        c.cancelJobCtx()
        return
    }
```

```
    } else if stepMsg := mPayload.GetStep(); stepMsg != nil {
        if err := c.barrier.Notify(stepMsg); err != nil {
            return
        }
    }
}
```

If the master relayed a message to us, the handler invokes the `deliverGraphMessage` method (see the next section), which attempts to deliver the message to the intended recipient. If the message delivery attempt fails, the error is recorded in the `asyncWorkerErr` variable and the job context is canceled before returning.

The other type of payload that we can receive from the master is a `Step` message, which the master broadcasts to notify workers that they can exit a barrier they are currently waiting on. All we need to do is to invoke the barrier's `Notify` method with the obtained `Step` message as an argument.

Using the master as an outgoing message relay

As we saw in the `RunJob` method's initialization block, once we gain access to an executor instance for the graph, we register a `bspgraph.Replayer` instance which serves as an escape hatch for relaying messages destined for vertices, which are managed by a different graph instance.

This is how the `relayNonLocalMessage` helper method is implemented:

```
func (c *workerJobCoordinator) relayNonLocalMessage(dst string, msg
message.Message) error {
    serializedMsg, err := c.cfg.serializer.Serialize(msg)
    if err != nil {
        return xerrors.Errorf("unable to serialize message: %w", err)
    }
    wMsg := &proto.WorkerPayload{Payload:
&proto.WorkerPayload_RelayMessage{
        RelayMessage: &proto.RelayMessage{
            Destination: dst,
            Message:     serializedMsg,
        },
    }}
    select {
    case c.cfg.masterStream.SendToMasterChan() <- wMsg:
        return nil
    case <-c.jobCtx.Done():
        return errJobAborted
    }
}
```

We invoke the user-defined serializer to marshal the application-specific graph message into an `any.Any` protocol buffer message and attach it to a new `WorkerPayload` instance as `RelayMessage`. The implementation then blocks until the message is successfully enqueued to the `masterStream` outgoing payload channel or the job context gets canceled.

On the other hand, when the master relays an incoming graph message to this worker, the coordinator's `handleMasterPayloads` method will invoke the `deliverGraphMessage` method, the listing of which follows:

```
func (c *workerJobCoordinator) deliverGraphMessage(graph *bspgraph.Graph,
relayMsg *proto.RelayMessage) error {
    payload, err := c.cfg.serializer.Unserialize(relayMsg.Message)
    if err != nil {
        return xerrors.Errorf("unable to decode relayed message: %w", err)
    }

    graphMsg, ok := payload.(message.Message)
    if !ok {
        return xerrors.Errorf("unable to relay message payloads that do not
implement message.Message")
    }

    return graph.SendMessage(relayMsg.Destination, graphMsg)
}
```

This time, the serializer is used to unpack the incoming `any.Any` message back to a type that is compatible with the `message.Message` interface, which is expected by the graph's `SendMessage` method. As the intended recipient is a local vertex, all we need to do is to pretend we are a local graph vertex and simply invoke the graph's `SendMessage` method with the appropriate destination ID and message payload.

The master job coordinator

In this section, we will explore the implementation of the job coordinator component that is responsible for orchestrating the execution of a distributed graph computation job on the master node.

In a similar fashion to how the worker job coordinator was implemented, we will start by defining a configuration struct to hold the necessary details for creating a new coordinator instance and then proceed to define the `masterJobCoordinator` type:

```
type masterJobCoordinatorConfig struct {
    jobDetails job.Details
    workers    []*remoteWorkerStream
```

```
    jobRunner   job.Runner
    serializer  Serializer
    logger      *logrus.Entry
}

type masterJobCoordinator struct {
    jobCtx       context.Context
    cancelJobCtx func()

    barrier    *masterStepBarrier
    partRange  *partition.Range
    cfg        masterJobCoordinatorConfig
}
```

As you can see, the configuration options for the master coordinator are pretty much the same as the worker variant with the only exception being that the master coordinator is additionally provided with a slice of remoteWorkerStream instances. It corresponds to the workers that the master has assigned to this particular job. The same symmetry pattern between the two job coordinators types is also quite evident in the set of fields in the masterJobCoordinator definition.

Once the master node has gathered enough workers for running a new job, it will call the newMasterJobCoordinator constructor, the implementation of which is shown as follows:

```
func newMasterJobCoordinator(ctx context.Context, cfg
masterJobCoordinatorConfig) (*masterJobCoordinator, error) {
    partRange, err := partition.NewRange(cfg.jobDetails.PartitionFromID,
cfg.jobDetails.PartitionToID, len(cfg.workers))
    if err != nil {
        return nil, err
    }

    jobCtx, cancelJobCtx := context.WithCancel(ctx)
    return &masterJobCoordinator{
        jobCtx:       jobCtx,
        cancelJobCtx: cancelJobCtx,
        barrier:      newMasterStepBarrier(jobCtx, len(cfg.workers)),
        partRange:    partRange,
        cfg:          cfg,
    }, nil
}
```

One of the key responsibilities of the master coordinator is to evenly split the UUID space into chunks and assign each chunk to one of the workers. To this end, before allocating a new coordinator instance, the constructor will first create a new partition range (see `Chapter 10`, *Building, Packaging, and Deploying Software*, for details on the `Range` type) using the extents provided by the caller via the `job.Details` parameter.

Given that our proposed cluster configuration uses a single master and multiple workers, the extents from the job details parameter will always cover the **entire** UUID space.

Running a new job

Once the master node creates a new `masterJobCoordinator` instance, it invokes its `RunJob` method to kick off the execution of the job. Since the method is a bit lengthy, we will break it down into a set of smaller blocks:

```
execFactory := newMasterExecutorFactory(c.cfg.serializer, c.barrier)
executor, err := c.cfg.jobRunner.StartJob(c.cfg.jobDetails, execFactory)
if err != nil {
    c.cancelJobCtx()
    return xerrors.Errorf("unable to start job on master: %w", err)
}

for assignedPartition, w := range c.cfg.workers {
    w.SetDisconnectCallback(c.handleWorkerDisconnect)
    if err := c.publishJobDetails(w, assignedPartition); err != nil {
        c.cfg.jobRunner.AbortJob(c.cfg.jobDetails)
        c.cancelJobCtx()
        return err
    }
}
```

The first two lines in the previous block should look a bit familiar. We are following exactly the same initialization pattern as we did with the worker coordinator's implementation, which is we first create our custom executor factory and invoke the user-provided `StartJob` method to obtain an executor for the graph algorithm. Then, we iterate the list of worker streams and invoke the `publishJobDetails` helper to construct and send a `JobDetails` payload to each connected worker.

But how does the `publishJobDetails` method actually figure what UUID range to include in each outgoing `JobDetails` message? If you recall from Chapter 10, *Building, Packaging, and Deploying Software*, the `Range` type provides the `PartitionExtents` convenience method, which gives a partition number in the `[0, numPartitions)` range. It returns the UUID values that correspond to the beginning and end of the requested partition. So, all we need to do here is to treat the worker's index in the worker list as the partition number assigned to the worker!

Once the `JobDetails` payloads are broadcast by the master and received by the workers, each worker will create its own local job coordinator and begin executing the job just as we saw in the previous section.

As the master is dealing with multiple worker streams, we need to spin up a goroutine for handling incoming payloads from each worker. To ensure that all goroutines properly exit before `RunJob` returns, we will make use of `sync.WaitGroup`:

```
var wg sync.WaitGroup
wg.Add(len(c.cfg.workers))
graph := executor.Graph()
for workerIndex, worker := range c.cfg.workers {
    go func(workerIndex int, worker *remoteWorkerStream) {
        defer wg.Done()
        c.handleWorkerPayloads(workerIndex, worker, graph)
    }(workerIndex, worker)
}
```

While our goroutines are busy handling incoming payloads, the master executes the various stages of the graph's state machine:

```
if err = c.runJobToCompletion(executor); err != nil {
    c.cfg.jobRunner.AbortJob(c.cfg.jobDetails)
    if xerrors.Is(err, context.Canceled) {
        err = errJobAborted
    }
}

c.cancelJobCtx()
wg.Wait() // wait for any spawned goroutines to exit before returning.
return err
}
```

Once the job execution completes (with or without an error), the job context is canceled to send a stop signal to any still-running payload processing goroutines. The `RunJob` method then blocks until all goroutines exit and then returns.

Transitioning through the stages for the graph's state machine

The runJobToCompletion implementation for the master job coordinator is nearly identical to the one used by the worker:

```
func (c *masterJobCoordinator) runJobToCompletion(executor
*bspgraph.Executor) error {
    if err := executor.RunToCompletion(c.jobCtx); err != nil {
        return err
    } else if _, err :=
c.barrier.WaitForWorkers(proto.Step_EXECUTED_GRAPH); err != nil {
        return err
    } else if err := c.barrier.NotifyWorkers(&proto.Step{Type:
proto.Step_EXECUTED_GRAPH}); err != nil {
        return err
    } else if err := c.cfg.jobRunner.CompleteJob(c.cfg.jobDetails); err !=
nil {
        return err
    } else if _, err :=
c.barrier.WaitForWorkers(proto.Step_PESISTED_RESULTS); err != nil {
        return err
    } else if err := c.barrier.NotifyWorkers(&proto.Step{Type:
proto.Step_PESISTED_RESULTS}); err != nil {
        return err
    } else if _, err := c.barrier.WaitForWorkers(proto.Step_COMPLETED_JOB);
err != nil {
        return err
    }
    return nil
}
```

Again, the user-defined algorithm is executed until the terminating condition is met. Assuming that no error occurred, the master simply waits for all workers to transition through the remaining steps of the graph execution state machine (EXECUTED_GRAPH, PERSISTED_RESULTS, and COMPLETED_JOB).

Note that, in the preceding implementation, the master does not invoke NotifyWorkers on the barrier for the COMPLETED_JOB step. This is intentional; once all workers reach this stage, there is no further operation that needs to be performed. We can simply go ahead and close each workers' job stream.

Handling incoming worker payloads

The `handleWorkerPayloads` method is responsible for handling incoming payloads from a particular worker. The method blocks waiting for either a new incoming payload to appear or the job context to be canceled:

```
func (c *masterJobCoordinator) handleWorkerPayloads(workerIndex int, worker
*remoteWorkerStream, graph *bspgraph.Graph) {
    var wPayload *proto.WorkerPayload
    for {
        select {
        case wPayload = <-worker.RecvFromWorkerChan():
        case <-c.jobCtx.Done():
            return
        }

        if relayMsg := wPayload.GetRelayMessage(); relayMsg != nil {
            c.relayMessageToWorker(workerIndex, relayMsg)
        } else if stepMsg := wPayload.GetStep(); stepMsg != nil {
            updatedStep, err := c.barrier.Wait(stepMsg)
            if err != nil {
                c.cancelJobCtx()
                return
            }

            c.sendToWorker(worker, &proto.MasterPayload{
                Payload: &proto.MasterPayload_Step{Step: updatedStep},
            })
        }
    }
}
```

Incoming payloads contain either a message relay request or a `Step` message, which the worker sends to request admission to the barrier for a particular type of step.

In the latter case, the `Step` message from the worker is passed as an argument to the master barrier's `Wait` method. As we explained in a previous section, the `Wait` method blocks until the master invokes the `NotifyWorkers` method with its own `Step` message.

Once that occurs, the new step message is wrapped in `MasterPayload` and transmitted to the worker via the stream.

Relaying messages between workers

For the master to be able to relay messages between workers, it needs to be able to *efficiently* answer the following question: *"given a destination ID, which partition does it belong to?"*

This certainly sounds like a query that the `Range` type should be able to answer! To jog your memory, this is what the `Range` type definition from `Chapter 10`, *Building, Packaging, and Deploying Software*, looks like:

```
type Range struct {
    start        uuid.UUID
    rangeSplits []uuid.UUID
}
```

The `start` field keeps track of the range's start UUID while `rangeSplits[p]` tracks the **end** UUID value for the p_{th} partition. Therefore, the UUID range for a partition p can be calculated as follows:

$$UUIDRange(p) = \begin{cases} [start, rangeSplits[0]] & p = 0 \\ [rangeSplits[p-1], rangeSplits[p]] & p > 0 \end{cases}$$

Before we examine how the UUID-to-partition number query is actually implemented, try as a simple thought exercise to think of an algorithm for answering this type of query (no peeking!).

One way to achieve this is to iterate the `rangeSplits` slice and locate a range that includes the specified ID. While this naive approach would yield the correct answer, it will unfortunately not scale in a scenario where you might have hundreds of workers exchanging messages with each other.

Can we do any better? The answer is yes. We can exploit the observation that the values in the `rangeSplits` field are stored in sorted order and use the handy `Search` function from the Go `sort` package to perform a binary search.

Here is a much more efficient implementation of this type of query:

```
func (r *Range) PartitionForID(id uuid.UUID) (int, error) {
    partIndex := sort.Search(len(r.rangeSplits), func(n int) bool {
        return bytes.Compare(id[:], r.rangeSplits[n][:]) < 0
    })

    if bytes.Compare(id[:], r.start[:]) < 0 || partIndex >=
len(r.rangeSplits) {
        return -1, xerrors.Errorf("unable to detect partition for ID %q",
id)
```

```
        }
        return partIndex, nil
    }
```

The `sort.Search` function executes a binary search on a slice and returns the *smallest* index for which a user-defined predicate function returns **true**. Our predicate function checks that the provided ID value is *strictly less* than the end UUID of the partition currently being scanned.

Now that we have the means to efficiently answer UUID-to-partition queries, let's take a look at the implementation of the `relayMessageToWorker` method, which is invoked by the worker payload handler for message relay requests:

```go
func (c *masterJobCoordinator) relayMessageToWorker(srcWorkerIndex int,
relayMsg *proto.RelayMessage) {
    dstUUID, err := uuid.Parse(relayMsg.Destination)
    if err != nil {
        c.cancelJobCtx()
        return
    }

    partIndex, err := c.partRange.PartitionForID(dstUUID)
    if err != nil || partIndex == srcWorkerIndex {
        c.cancelJobCtx()
        return
    }

    c.sendToWorker(c.cfg.workers[partIndex], &proto.MasterPayload{
        Payload: &proto.MasterPayload_RelayMessage{RelayMessage: relayMsg},
    })
}
```

The first thing we need to do is to parse the destination ID and make sure that it actually contains a valid UUID value.

Then, we call the `PartitionForID` helper to look up the index of the partition that the destination ID belongs to and forward the message to the worker assigned to it.

What if it turns out that the worker that asked us to relay the message in the first place is *also* the one we need to relay the message to? In such a scenario, we will treat the destination ID as being invalid and abort the job with an error. The justification for this decision is that if the local graph was aware of that particular destination, it would simply locally enqueue the message for delivery instead of attempting to relay it through the master node.

Defining package-level APIs for working with master and worker nodes

At this point, we have implemented all required internal components for running both the master and the server nodes. All we need to do now is to define the necessary APIs for allowing the end users to create and operate new workers and master instances.

Instantiating and operating worker nodes

To create a new worker, the user of the package invokes the NewWorker constructor, which returns a new Worker instance. The definition of the Worker type looks as follows:

```
type Worker struct {
    masterConn *grpc.ClientConn
    masterCli  proto.JobQueueClient
    cfg WorkerConfig
}
```

The Worker type stores the following:

- The client gRPC connection to the master
- An instance of the JobQueueClient that the protoc compiler has automatically generated for us from the RPC definition for the job queue
- The required components for interfacing with the user's **bspgraph**-based algorithm implementation (that is, a job Runner and Serializer for graph messages and aggregator values)

After obtaining a new Worker instance, the user has to connect to the master by invoking the worker's Dial method:

```
func (w *Worker) Dial(masterEndpoint string, dialTimeout time.Duration)
error {
    var dialCtx context.Context
    if dialTimeout != 0 {
        var cancelFn func()
        dialCtx, cancelFn = context.WithTimeout(context.Background(),
dialTimeout)
        defer cancelFn()
    }
    conn, err := grpc.DialContext(dialCtx, masterEndpoint,
grpc.WithInsecure(), grpc.WithBlock())
    if err != nil {
        return xerrors.Errorf("unable to dial master: %w", err)
```

```
        }

    w.masterConn = conn
    w.masterCli = proto.NewJobQueueClient(conn)
    return nil
}
```

Once a connection to the master has been successfully established, the user can ask the worker to fetch and execute the next job from the master by invoking the worker's `RunJob` method. Let's see what happens within that method:

```
stream, err := w.masterCli.JobStream(ctx)
if err != nil {
    return err
}

w.cfg.Logger.Info("waiting for next job")
jobDetails, err := w.waitForJob(stream)
if err != nil {
    return err
}
```

First of all, the worker makes an RPC call to the job queue and obtains a gRPC stream. Then, the worker invokes the `waitForJob` helper, which performs a blocking `Recv` operation on the stream and waits for the master to publish a job details payload. After the payload is obtained, its contents are validated and unpacked into a `job.Details` instance, which is returned to the `RunJob` method:

```
masterStream := newRemoteMasterStream(stream)
jobLogger := w.cfg.Logger.WithField("job_id", jobDetails.JobID)
coordinator := newWorkerJobCoordinator(ctx, workerJobCoordinatorConfig{
    jobDetails:    jobDetails,
    masterStream:  masterStream,
    jobRunner:     w.cfg.JobRunner,
    serializer:    w.cfg.Serializer,
    logger:        jobLogger,
})
```

Next, the worker initializes the required components for executing the job. As you can see in the previous code, we create a wrapper for the stream and pass it as an argument to the job coordinator constructor.

We are now ready to delegate the job execution to the coordinator! However, before we do that, there is one last thing we need to do, that is, we need to fire up a dedicated goroutine for handling the send and receive ends of the wrapped stream:

```
var wg sync.WaitGroup
wg.Add(1)
go func() {
    defer wg.Done()
    if err := masterStream.HandleSendRecv(); err != nil {
        coordinator.cancelJobCtx()
    }
}()
```

Finally, we invoke the coordinator's `RunJob` method and emit a logline depending on whether the job succeeded or failed:

```
if err = coordinator.RunJob(); err != nil {
    jobLogger.WithField("err", err).Error("job execution failed")
} else {
    jobLogger.Info("job completed successfully")
}
masterStream.Close()
wg.Wait()
return err
```

Just as we did so far with all other blocks of code that spin up goroutines, before returning from the `RunJob` method, we terminate the RPC stream (but leave the client connection intact for the next RPC call) and wait until the stream-handling goroutines cleanly exits.

Let's move on to defining the necessary APIs for creating new master instances.

Instantiating and operating master nodes

As you probably guessed, the `Master` type would encapsulate the implementation details for creating and operating a master node. Let's take a quick look into its constructor:

```
func NewMaster(cfg MasterConfig) (*Master, error) {
    if err := cfg.Validate(); err != nil {
        return nil, xerrors.Errorf("master config validation failed: %w",
err)
    }
    return &Master{
        cfg:        cfg,
        workerPool: newWorkerPool(),
    }, nil
}
```

The constructor expects a `MasterConfig` object as an argument that defines the following:

- It defines the address where the master node will be listening for incoming connections.
- It defines the `job.Runner` instance for interfacing with the user-defined graph algorithm.
- It defines `Serializer` for marshaling and unmarshaling aggregator values. Note that, in contrast to the worker implementation, the master only relays messages between the workers and never needs to peek into the actual message contents. Therefore, masters require a much simpler serializer implementation.

Besides allocating a new `Master` object, the constructor also creates and attaches to it a *worker pool*. We haven't really mentioned the concept of a **worker pool** in this chapter, so right about now, you are probably wondering about its purpose.

A worker pool serves as a waiting area for connected workers until the master is asked by the end user to begin the execution of a new job. New workers may connect to (or disconnect from) the master at any point in time. By design, workers are not allowed to join a job that is *already being executed*. Instead, they will always be added to the pool where they will wait for the next job run.

When the end user requests a new job execution from the master, the required number of workers for the job is extracted from the pool and the job details are broadcast to them.

The implementation of the worker pool contains quite a bit of boilerplate code, which has been omitted in the interest of brevity. However, if you're interested in delving deeper, you can explore its source code by examining the contents of the `worker_pool.go` file, which can be found in the `Chapter12/dbspgraph` package in this book's GitHub repository.

Handling incoming gRPC connections

While the constructor returns a new and configured `Master` instance, it does not automatically start the master's gRPC server. Instead, this task is left to the end user, who must manually invoke the master's `Start` method:

```
func (m *Master) Start() error {
    var err error
    if m.srvListener, err = net.Listen("tcp", m.cfg.ListenAddress); err !=
nil {
        return xerrors.Errorf("cannot start server: %w", err)
    }

    gSrv := grpc.NewServer()
```

```
    proto.RegisterJobQueueServer(gSrv, &masterRPCHandler{
        workerPool: m.workerPool,
        logger:     m.cfg.Logger,
    })
    m.cfg.Logger.WithField("addr",
m.srvListener.Addr().String()).Info("listening for worker connections")
    go func(l net.Listener) { _ = gSrv.Serve(l) }(m.srvListener)

    return nil
}
```

As is customary when launching gRPC servers in Go, we first need to create a new
net.Listener instance, then create the gRPC server instance and serve it on the listener
we just created. Of course, before invoking the Serve method on the server, we need to
register a handler for incoming RPCs that adheres to the interface that protoc generated for
us.

To avoid polluting the public API of the Master type with the RPC method signatures, we
employ a small trick—we define an *un-exported* shim that implements the required interface
and registers it with our gRPC server.

The implementation of the handler for the JobStream RPC is just a handful of lines:

```
func (h *masterRPCHandler) JobStream(stream proto.JobQueue_JobStreamServer)
error {
    extraFields := make(logrus.Fields)
    if peerDetails, ok := peer.FromContext(stream.Context()); ok {
        extraFields["peer_addr"] = peerDetails.Addr.String()
    }

    h.logger.WithFields(extraFields).Info("worker connected")

    workerStream := newRemoteWorkerStream(stream)
    h.workerPool.AddWorker(workerStream)
    return workerStream.HandleSendRecv()
}
```

In the interest of making debugging easier, the RPC handler will check whether it can
access any peer-related information for the connected worker and include them in a log
message. Next, the incoming stream is wrapped in remoteWorkerStream and added to the
pool, where it will wait until a new job is ready to run.

The gRPC semantics for handling streaming RPCs dictate that the stream will be
automatically closed once the RPC handler returns. Therefore, we want our RPC handler to
block until either a job completes or an error occurs. An easy way to achieve this is to make
a synchronous call to the wrapped stream's HandleSendRecv method.

Running a new job

After the end user starts the master's gRPC server, they can request a new job execution by invoking the master's `RunJob` method, the signature of which is as follows:

```
func (m *Master) RunJob(ctx context.Context, minWorkers int,
workerAcquireTimeout time.Duration) error {
    // implementation omitted
}
```

Because the worker requirements generally vary depending on the algorithm to be executed, the end user must specify, in advance, the minimum number of workers required for the job as well as a timeout for acquiring the required workers.

If the number of workers is not important from the user's perspective, they can specify a zero value for the `minWorkers` argument. Doing so serves as a hint to the master to either select all workers currently available in the pool or to block until at least one of the following conditions is satisfied:

- At least one worker joins the pool.
- The specified acquire timeout (if non-zero) expires.

Let's break down the `RunJob` methods into chunks, starting from the code that acquires the required workers from the pool:

```
var acquireCtx = ctx
if workerAcquireTimeout != 0 {
    var cancelFn func()
    acquireCtx, cancelFn = context.WithTimeout(ctx, workerAcquireTimeout)
    defer cancelFn()
}
workers, err := m.workerPool.ReserveWorkers(acquireCtx, minWorkers)
if err != nil {
    return ErrUnableToReserveWorkers
}
```

If `workerAcquireTimeout` is specified, the preceding code snippet will automatically wrap the externally provided context with a context that expires after the specified timeout and pass it to the pool's `ReserveWorkers` method.

With the required number of workers streams in hand, the next step entails the allocation of a UUID for the job and the creation of a new `job.Details` instance with a partition assignment that covers the entire UUID space:

```
jobID := uuid.New().String()
createdAt := time.Now().UTC().Truncate(time.Millisecond)
jobDetails := job.Details{
    JobID:           jobID,
    CreatedAt:       createdAt,
    PartitionFromID: minUUID, // 00000000-00000000-00000000-00000000
    PartitionToID:   maxUUID, // ffffffff-ffffffff-ffffffff-ffffffff
}
```

Before commencing execution of the job, we need to create a new job coordinator instance:

```
coordinator, err := newMasterJobCoordinator(ctx,
masterJobCoordinatorConfig{
    jobDetails: jobDetails,
    workers:    workers,
    jobRunner:  m.cfg.JobRunner,
    serializer: m.cfg.Serializer,
    logger:     logger,
})
if err != nil {
    err = xerrors.Errorf("unable to create job coordinator: %w", err)
    for _, w := range workers {
        w.Close(err)
    }
    return err
}
```

After this initialization step, we can invoke the `RunJob` method and run the job to completion:

```
if err = coordinator.RunJob(); err != nil {
    for _, w := range workers {
        w.Close(err)
    }
    return err
}

for _, w := range workers {
    w.Close(nil)
}
return nil
}
```

If the job execution fails, we invoke the `Close` method on each worker stream passing along the error returned by the coordinator's `RunJob` method. Calling `Close` on `remoteWorkerStream` allows the `HandleSendRecv` call from the RPC handler to return with an error that gRPC will automatically propagate back to the worker.

On the other hand, if the work completes without any error, we invoke `Close` with a `nil` error value. This action has exactly the same effect (that is, it terminates the RPC) but in the latter case, no error is returned to the worker.

Deploying a distributed version of the Links 'R' Us PageRank calculator

The PageRank calculator is the only component of the Links 'R' Us project that we haven't yet been able to horizontally scale on Kubernetes. Back in Chapter 8, *Graph-Based Data Processing*, where we used the `bspgraph` package to implement the PageRank algorithm, I promised you that a few chapters down the road, we would take the PageRank calculator code, and **without any code modifications**, enable it to run in distributed mode.

After completing this chapter, I strongly recommend, as a fun learning exercise, taking a look at using the `dbspgraph` package to build a distributed version of either the graph coloring or the shortest path algorithms from Chapter 8, *Graph-Based Data Processing*.

In this section, we will leverage all of the work we have done so far in this chapter to achieve this goal! I would like to point out that while this section will exclusively focus on the PageRank calculator service, everything we discuss here can also be applied to any of the other graph algorithms that we implemented in Chapter 8, *Graph-Based Data Processing*.

Retrofitting master and worker capabilities to the PageRank calculator service

Logically, we don't want to implement a new PageRank service from scratch, especially given the fact that we already created a standalone (albeit not distributed) version of this service in the previous chapter.

What we will actually be doing is making a copy of the standalone PageRank calculator service from `Chapter 11`, *Splitting Monoliths into Microservices*, and adapt it to use the APIs exposed by the `dbspgraph` package from this chapter. Since our copy will share most of the code with the original service, we will omit all of the shared implementation details and only highlight the bits that need to be changed. As always, the full source for the service is available in the `Chapter12/linksrus/pagerank` package in this book's GitHub repository if you want to take a closer look.

Before we proceed, we need to decide whether we will create a separate binary for the master and the worker. Taking into account that a fairly large chunk of the code is shared between the master and the workers, we are probably better off producing a single binary and introducing a command-line flag (we will call it mode) to select between master or worker mode.

Depending on the selected mode, the service will do the following:

- When in *worker* mode: It creates a `dbspgraph.Worker` object, calls its `Dial` method, and finally calls the `RunJob` method to wait until the master publishes a new job.
- When in *master* mode: It creates a `dbspgraph.Master` object, calls its `Start` method, and periodically invokes the `RunJob` method to trigger a PageRank score refresh job.

Serializing PageRank messages and aggregator values

A prerequisite for creating a new `dbspgraph.Master` instance or a `dbspgraph.Worker` instance is to provide a suitable, **application-specific** serializer for both aggregator values and any message that can potentially be exchanged between the graph nodes. For this particular application, graph vertices distribute their accumulated PageRank scores to their neighbors by exchanging `IncomingScore` messages:

```
type IncomingScoreMessage struct {
    Score float64
}
```

In addition, as you can see from the following snippet, which was taken from the PageRank calculator implementation, our serializer implementation also needs to be able to properly handle `int` and `float64` used by the calculator's aggregator instances:

```
// need to run the PageRank calculation algorithm.
func (c *Calculator) registerAggregators() {
    c.g.RegisterAggregator("page_count", new(aggregator.IntAccumulator))
```

```
    c.g.RegisterAggregator("residual_0",
new(aggregator.Float64Accumulator))
    c.g.RegisterAggregator("residual_1",
new(aggregator.Float64Accumulator))
    c.g.RegisterAggregator("SAD", new(aggregator.Float64Accumulator))
}
```

The main benefit of having full control over the serializer used by both the master and the workers is that we get to choose the appropriate serialization format for our particular use case. Under normal circumstances, protocol buffers would be the most logical candidate.

However, given that we only really need to support serialization of `int` and `float64` values, using protocol buffers would probably be overkill. Instead, we will implement a much simpler serialization protocol.

First, let's take a look at how the `Serialize` method is implemented:

```
func (serializer) Serialize(v interface{}) (*any.Any, error) {
    scratchBuf := make([]byte, binary.MaxVarintLen64)
    switch val := v.(type) {
    case int:
        nBytes := binary.PutVarint(scratchBuf, int64(val))
        return &any.Any{TypeUrl: "i", Value: scratchBuf[:nBytes]}, nil
    case float64:
        nBytes := binary.PutUvarint(scratchBuf, math.Float64bits(val))
        return &any.Any{TypeUrl: "f", Value: scratchBuf[:nBytes]}, nil
    case pr.IncomingScoreMessage:
        nBytes := binary.PutUvarint(scratchBuf,
math.Float64bits(val.Score))
        return &any.Any{TypeUrl: "m", Value: scratchBuf[:nBytes]}, nil
    default:
        return nil, xerrors.Errorf("serialize: unknown type %#+T", val)
    }
}
```

The preceding implementation uses a type switch to detect the type of value that was passed as an argument to `Serialize`. The method sets the `TypeUrl` field to a single-character value, which corresponds to the type of the encoded value:

- `"i"`: This specifies an integer value
- `"f"`: This specifies a float64 value
- `"m"`: This specifies a float64 value from `IncomingScoreMessage`

Values are encoded as variable-length integers with the help of the `PutVarint` and `PutUvarint` functions provided by the `binary` package that ships with the Go standard library.

Note that floating-point values cannot be encoded directly to a `Varint`; we must first convert them into their equivalent `uint64` representation via `math.Float64bits`. The encoded values are stored in a byte buffer and attached as a payload to the `any.Any` message, which is returned to the caller.

The `Unserialize` method, the implementation of which is shown as follows, simply reverses the encoding steps:

```go
func (serializer) Unserialize(v *any.Any) (interface{}, error) {
    switch v.TypeUrl {
    case "i":
        val, _ := binary.Varint(v.Value)
        return int(val), nil
    case "f":
        val, _ := binary.Uvarint(v.Value)
        return math.Float64frombits(val), nil
    case "m":
        val, _ := binary.Uvarint(v.Value)
        return pr.IncomingScoreMessage{
            Score: math.Float64frombits(val),
        }, nil
    default:
        return nil, xerrors.Errorf("unserialize: unknown type %q",
v.TypeUrl)
    }
}
```

To unserialize a value contained within an `any.Any` message, we check the contents of the `TypeUrl` field and, depending on the type of encoded data, decode its variable-length integer representation using either the `Varint` or `Uvarint` method.

For floating-point values, we use the `math.Float64frombits` helper to convert the decoded unsigned `Varint` representation of the float back into a `float64` value. Finally, if the `any.Any` value encodes `IncomingScoreMessage`, we create and return a new message instance that embeds the floating-point score value that we just decoded.

Defining job runners for the master and the worker

The step for completing the distributed version of the Links 'R' Us PageRank calculation service is to provide a `job.Runner` implementation that will allow the `dbspgraph` package to interface with the PageRank calculator component that includes the graph-based algorithm that we want to execute.

As a reminder, this is the interface that we need to implement:

```
type Runner interface {
    StartJob(Details, bspgraph.ExecutorFactory) (*bspgraph.Executor, error)
    CompleteJob(Details) error
    AbortJob(Details)
}
```

The glue logic for masters and workers has a different set of requirements. For example, the master will not perform any graph-related computations apart from processing the aggregator deltas sent in by the workers.

Therefore, the master does not need to load any graph data into memory. On the other hand, workers not only need to load a subset of the graph data, but they also need to persist the computation results once the job execution completes.

Consequently, we need to provide not one but two `job.Runner` implementations—one for the master and one for workers.

Implementing the job runner for master nodes

Let's begin by examining the rather trivial `StartJob` method implementation for the master node:

```
func (n *MasterNode) StartJob(_ job.Details, execFactory
bspgraph.ExecutorFactory) (*bspgraph.Executor, error) {
    if err := n.calculator.Graph().Reset(); err != nil {
        return nil, err
    }

    n.jobStartedAt = n.cfg.Clock.Now()
    n.calculator.SetExecutorFactory(execFactory)
    return n.calculator.Executor(), nil
}
```

The `StartJob` method records the time when the job was started and performs the following three tasks:

1. It resets the graph's internal state. This is important as the calculator component instance is re-used between subsequent job runs.
2. It overrides the calculator component's executor factory with the version provided by the `dbspgraph` package.
3. It invokes the calculator's `Executor` method, which uses the installed factory to create and return a new `bspgraph.Executor` instance.

Next, we will examine the implementation of the `AbortJob` and `CompleteJob` methods:

```
func (n *MasterNode) AbortJob(_ job.Details) {}

func (n *MasterNode) CompleteJob(_ job.Details) error {
    n.cfg.Logger.WithFields(logrus.Fields{
        "total_link_count":
n.calculator.Graph().Aggregator("page_count").Get(),
        "total_pass_time":  n.cfg.Clock.Now().Sub(n.jobStartedAt).String(),
    }).Info("completed PageRank update pass")
    return nil
}
```

As far as the `AbortJob` method is concerned, there isn't really anything special that we need to do when a job fails. Therefore, we just provide an empty stub for it.

The `CompleteJob` method does nothing more than log the run time for the job and the *total* number of processed page links. As you probably noticed, the latter value is obtained by directly querying the value of the global `page_count` aggregator, which is registered by the calculator component when it sets up its internal state.

The worker job runner

The worker's `StartJob` implementation is slightly more complicated as we need to load the vertices and edges that correspond to the UUID range assigned to us by the master node. Fortunately, we have already written all of the required bits of code in Chapter 11, *Splitting Monoliths into Microservices*, so we can just go ahead and invoke the loading functions with the appropriate arguments:

```
func (n *WorkerNode) StartJob(jobDetails job.Details, execFactory
bspgraph.ExecutorFactory) (*bspgraph.Executor, error) {
    n.jobStartedAt = time.Now()
    if err := n.calculator.Graph().Reset(); err != nil {
        return nil, err
```

```
      } else if err := n.loadLinks(jobDetails.PartitionFromID,
jobDetails.PartitionToID, jobDetails.CreatedAt); err != nil {
          return nil, err
      } else if err := n.loadEdges(jobDetails.PartitionFromID,
jobDetails.PartitionToID, jobDetails.CreatedAt); err != nil {
          return nil, err
      }
      n.graphPopulateTime = time.Since(n.jobStartedAt)

      n.scoreCalculationStartedAt = time.Now()
      n.calculator.SetExecutorFactory(execFactory)
      return n.calculator.Executor(), nil
  }
```

The `CompleteJob` method contains the necessary logic for updating the Links 'R' Us document index with the fresh PageRank scores that we just calculated. Let's take a look at its implementation:

```
func (n *WorkerNode) CompleteJob(_ job.Details) error {
    scoreCalculationTime := time.Since(n.scoreCalculationStartedAt)
    tick := time.Now()
    if err := n.calculator.Scores(n.persistScore); err != nil {
        return err
    }
    scorePersistTime := time.Since(tick)
    n.cfg.Logger.WithFields(logrus.Fields{
        "local_link_count":     len(n.calculator.Graph().Vertices()),
        "total_link_count":
n.calculator.Graph().Aggregator("page_count").Get(),
        "graph_populate_time":   n.graphPopulateTime.String(),
        "score_calculation_time": scoreCalculationTime.String(),
        "score_persist_time":    scorePersistTime.String(),
        "total_pass_time":       time.Since(n.jobStartedAt).String(),
    }).Info("completed PageRank update pass")
    return nil
}
```

The preceding block of code for persisting the calculation results should seem familiar to you as it has been copied verbatim from Chapter 11, *Splitting Monoliths into Microservices*. The `Scores` convenience method iterates the graph vertices and invokes the `persistScore` callback with the vertex ID and PageRank score as arguments.

The `persistScore` callback (shown as follows) is a simple wrapper for mapping the vertex ID into a UUID value and calling the `UpdateScore` method of the Links 'R' Us document index component:

```
func (n *WorkerNode) persistScore(vertexID string, score float64) error {
    linkID, err := uuid.Parse(vertexID)
    if err != nil {
        return err
    }
    return n.cfg.IndexAPI.UpdateScore(linkID, score)
}
```

Similar to the master job runner implementation, the worker's `AbortJob` method is also an empty stub. To keep our implementation as lean as possible, we won't bother rolling back any already persisted score changes if any of the other workers fails after the local worker has already completed the job. Since the PageRank scores are periodically re-calculated, we expect them to be *eventually consistent*.

Deploying the final Links 'R' Us version to Kubernetes

We have finally reached and conquered the end-goal for the Links 'R' Us project—we have built a feature-complete, microservice-based system where **all** components can be deployed to Kubernetes and individually scaled up or down.

The last thing we need to do is to update our Kubernetes manifests so we can deploy the distributed version of the PageRank calculator instead of the single-pod version from `Chapter 11`, *Splitting Monoliths into Microservices*.

For this purpose, we will create two separate Kubernetes `Deployment` resources. The first deployment provision a **single** pod, which executes the PageRank service in the master node, while the second deployment will provision **multiple** pods that execute the service in worker mode. To facilitate the discovery of the master node by the workers, we will place the master node behind a Kubernetes service and point the workers at the DNS entry for the service.

After applying the proposed changes, our Kubernetes cluster will look as follows:

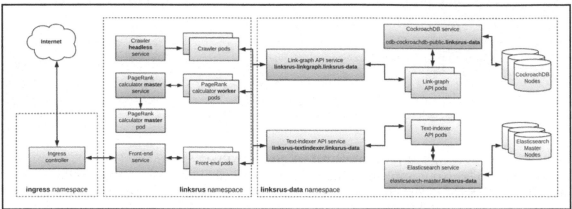

Figure 4: The components of the fully distributed Links 'R' Us version

You can have a look at the full set of Kubernetes manifests for the final version of Links 'R' Us by checking out this book's GitHub repository and examining the contents of the Chapter12/k8s folder.

If you haven't already set up a **Minikube cluster** and white-listed its private registry, you can either take a quick break and manually follow the step-by-step instructions from Chapter 10, *Building, Packaging, and Deploying Software*, or simply run make bootstrap-minikube, which will take care of everything for you.

On the other hand, if you have already deployed any of the Links 'R' Us versions from the previous chapters (either the monolithic or microservice variant), make sure to run kubectl delete namespace linksrus before proceeding. By deleting the linksrus namespace, Kubernetes will get rid of all pods, services, and ingresses for Links 'R' Us but leave the data stores (which live in the linksrus-data namespace) intact.

To deploy all required components for Links 'R' Us, you will need to build and push a handful of Docker images. To save you some time, the Makefile in the Chapter12/k8s folder provides two handy build targets to get you up and running as quickly as possible:

- make dockerize-and-push: This will build all required Docker images and push them to Minikube's private registry.
- make deploy: This will ensure that all required data stores have been provisioned and apply all manifests for deploying the final, microservice-based version of Links 'R' Us in one go.

It's time to give yourself a pat on the back! We have just completed the development of the final version of our Links 'R' Us project. After taking a few minutes to contemplate what we have achieved so far, point your browser to the index page of the frontend and have some fun!

Summary

In this rather long chapter, we performed a deep dive into all of the aspects involved in the creation of a distributed graph-processing system that allows us to take any graph-based algorithm created with the `bspgraph` package from Chapter 8, *Graph-Based Data Processing*, and automatically distribute it to a cluster of worker nodes.

What's more, as a practical application of what we learned in this chapter, we modified the Links 'R' Us PageRank calculator service from the previous chapter so that it can now run in distributed mode. By doing so, we achieved the primary goal for this book—to build and deploy a complex Go project where every component can be independently scaled horizontally.

The next and final chapter focuses on the reliability aspects of the system we just built. We will be exploring approaches for collecting, aggregating, and visualizing metrics that will help us monitor the health and performance of the Links 'R' Us project.

Questions

1. Describe the differences between a leader-follower and a multi-master cluster configuration.
2. Explain how the checkpoint strategy can be used to recover from errors.
3. What is the purpose of the distributed barrier in the out-of-core graph processing system that we built in this chapter?
4. Assume that we are provided with a graph-based algorithm that we want to run in a distributed fashion. Would you consider a computation job as completed once the algorithm terminates?

Further reading

1. **Consul**: *Secure service networking.* https://consul.io

2. **Docker**: *Enterprise container platform.* https://www.docker.com

3. Lamport, Leslie: Paxos Made Simple. In *ACM SIGACT News (Distributed Computing Column) 32, 4 (Whole Number 121, December 2001)* (2001), S. 51–58

4. Malewicz, Grzegorz; Austern, Matthew H.; Bik, Aart J. C; Dehnert, James C.; Horn, Ilan; Leiser, Naty; Czajkowski, Grzegorz: Pregel: *A System for Large-scale Graph Processing.* In *Proceedings of the 2010 ACM SIGMOD International Conference on Management of Data, SIGMOD '10.* New York, NY, USA : ACM, 2010 — ISBN 978-1-4503-0032-2, S. 135–146

5. Ongaro, Diego; Ousterhout, John: *In Search of an Understandable Consensus Algorithm.* In *Proceedings of the 2014 USENIX Conference on USENIX Annual Technical Conference, USENIX ATC'14.* Berkeley, CA, USA : USENIX Association, 2014 — ISBN 978-1-931971-10-2, S. 305–320

13
Metrics Collection and Visualization

"What's measured improves."

- Peter Drucker

In the previous chapters, we converted our initial monolithic application into a set of microservices that are now running distributed inside our Kubernetes cluster. This paradigm shift introduced a new item to our list of project requirements: as system operators, we must be able to monitor the health of each individual service and be notified when problems arise.

We will begin this chapter by comparing the strengths and weaknesses of popular systems for capturing and aggregating metrics. Then we will focus our attention on Prometheus, a popular metrics collection system written entirely in Go. We will explore approaches for instrumenting our code to facilitate the efficient collection and export of metrics. In the last part of this chapter, we will investigate the use of Grafana for visualizing our metrics and the Alertmanager for handling, grouping, deduplicating, and routing incoming alerts to a set of notification system integrations.

The following topics will be covered in this chapter:

- Explaining the differences between essential SRE terms such as SLIs, SLOs, and SLAs
- Comparison of push- and pull-based systems for metrics collection and an analysis of the pros and cons of each approach
- Setting up Prometheus and learning how to instrument your Go applications for collecting and exporting metrics
- Running Grafana as the visualization frontend for our metrics
- Using the Prometheus ecosystem tools to define and handle alerts

Technical requirements

The full code for the topics that will be discussed in this chapter has been published in this book's GitHub repository under the `Chapter13` folder.

 You can access this book's GitHub repository, which contains all the code and required resources for the chapters in this book, by pointing your web browser to the following URL: `https://github.com/PacktPublishing/Hands-On-Software-Engineering-with-Golang`.

To get you up and running as quickly as possible, each example project includes a Makefile that defines the following set of targets:

Makefile target	Description
`deps`	Install any required dependencies
`test`	Run all tests and report coverage
`lint`	Check for lint errors

As with the other chapters in this book, you will need a fairly recent version of Go, which you can download from `https://golang.org/dl`.

To run some of the code in this chapter, you will need to have a working Docker [3] installation on your machine.

Monitoring from the perspective of a site reliability engineer

As we saw in `Chapter 1`, *A Bird's-Eye View of Software Engineering*, monitoring the state and performance of software systems is one of the key responsibilities associated with the role of a **site reliability engineer (SRE)**. Before we delve deeper into the topic of monitoring and alerting, we should probably take a few minutes and clarify some of the SRE-related terms that we will be using in the following sections.

Service-level indicators (SLIs)

An SLI is a type of metric that allows us to quantify the perceived quality of a service from the perspective of the end user. Let's take a look at some common types of SLIs that can be applied to cloud-based services:

- **Availability** is defined as the ratio of two quantities: the time that the service can be used by the end user/customer and the total time that the service is deployed (including any downtime). For example, if we were operating a service that was offline for maintenance for about 53 minutes over the course of the *last year*, we could claim that the service had **99.99%** availability for the same period.
- **Throughput** is defined as the number of requests that a service processes in a given time period (for example, requests per second).
- **Latency** is yet another interesting SLI and is defined as the time it takes for the server to process an incoming request and return a response to the client.

Service-level objectives (SLOs)

Back in Chapter 5, *The Links 'R' Us Project*, where the Links 'R' Us project was first introduced, we briefly discussed the concept of SLOs and even provided some example SLOs for the system we would be working on.

An SLO is defined as the range of values for an SLI that allows us to deliver a particular level of service to an end user or customer.

Depending on the underlying SLI, SLOs can either be specified either as a lower bound (SLI >= target), an upper bound (SLI <= target), or both (lower-bound <= SLI >= upper bound).

SLO definitions generally consist of three parts: a description of the thing that we are measuring (the SLI), the expected service level expressed as a percentage, and the period where the measurement takes place. Let's take a quick look at some SLO examples:

- The system's uptime, when measured in a period of a single month, must be at least 99%
- The response time for 95% of service requests to X, when measured in a period of a year, must not exceed 100 ms
- The CPU utilization for the database, when measured in a period of a day, must be in the range [40%, 70%]

Service-level agreements (SLAs)

An SLA is an implicit or explicit contract between a service provider and one or more service consumers. The SLA outlines a set of SLOs that have to be met and the consequences for both meeting and failing to meet them.

Note that, depending on the type of service being offered, the role of the consumer can be fulfilled either by an external third party or an internal company stakeholder. In the former case, an SLA would typically define a list of financial penalties for failing to meet the agreed SLOs. In the latter case, SLA terms can be less strict but must nevertheless be factored in when authoring SLAs for other downstream services.

Having understood these SRE-related terms, let's move on to metrics.

Exploring options for collecting and aggregating metrics

The sheer complexity and level of customization that is inherent in modern, microservice-based systems has led to the development of specialized tooling to facilitate the collection and aggregation of metrics.

In this section, we will be briefly discussing a few popular pieces of software for achieving this task.

Comparing push versus pull systems

Monitoring and metrics aggregation systems can be classified into two broad categories based on the entity that initiates the data collection:

- In a **push-based** system, the client (for example, the application or a data collection service running on a node) is responsible for transmitting the metrics data to the metrics aggregation system. Examples of such systems include StatsD [11], Graphite [5], and InfluxDB [6].
- In a **pull-based** system, metrics collection is the responsibility of the metrics aggregation system. In an operation commonly referred to as *scraping*, the metrics system initiates a connection to the metrics producers and retrieves the set of available metrics. Examples of such systems include Nagios [7] and Prometheus [10]. We will be exploring Prometheus in more detail in the following section.

Push- and pull-based systems come with their own set of pros and cons. From a software engineer's perspective, push systems are oftentimes considered to be easier to interface with. All of the aforementioned push system implementations support a text-based protocol for submitting metrics. You can simply open a socket (TCP or UDP) connection to the metrics collector and start submitting metric values. As a matter of fact, if we were using either StatsD or Graphite and wanted to increment a counter named `requests`, we could do so using nothing more than the standard Unix command-line tools, like so:

```
# Incrementing a statsd counter
echo "requests:1|c" | nc statsd.local 8125

# Incrementing a graphite counter
echo "requests 1 `date +%s`" | nc graphite.local 2003
```

The lack of a proper flow control mechanism is one of the caveats associated with push-based systems. If the rate of metrics production suddenly spikes beyond the collector's ability to process, roll up, and/or index incoming metrics, it is quite possible that the collector will eventually become unavailable or respond to queries with severe lag.

On the other hand, in a pull-based system, the ingestion rate for metrics is under the control of the collector. Collectors can react to sudden spikes in metric production rates by adjusting their scrape rates to compensate.

Pull-based systems are generally considered to be more scalable than their push-based counterparts.

For some anecdotal evidence on how a system such as Prometheus can be scaled up to support scraping a large number of nodes, I would definitely recommend checking out Mathew Campbell's fascinating talk on some of the strategies that are used by DigitalOcean to collect metrics at scale [1].

Of course, pull-based systems come with their own set of cons. To begin with, in a pull-based system, the collector needs to be provided with a list of endpoints to scrape! This implies either the need for an operator to manually configure these endpoints or alludes to the availability of some kind of discovery mechanism for automating this process.

Secondly, this model assumes that the collector can **always** establish a connection to the various endpoints. However, this may not always be possible! Consider a scenario where we want to scrape a service that has been deployed to a private subnet. That particular subnet is pretty much locked down and does not allow ingress traffic from the subnet that the collector is deployed to. In such a case, our only option would be to use a push-based mechanism to get the metrics out (while ingress traffic is blocked, egress traffic is typically allowed).

Capturing metrics using Prometheus

Prometheus is a pull-based metrics collection system that was created at SoundCloud and subsequently released as open source. The following illustration (extracted from the official Prometheus documentation) describes the basic components that comprise the Prometheus ecosystem:

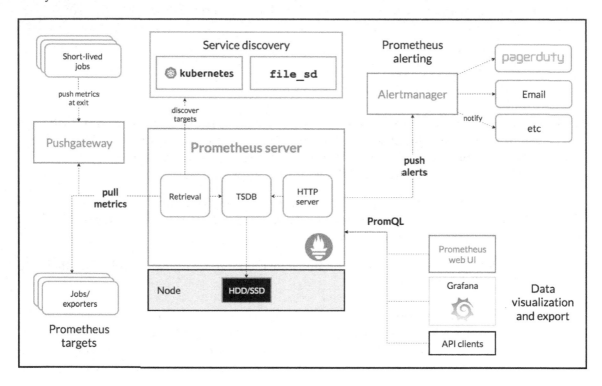

Figure 1: The Prometheus architecture

Let's briefly describe the role of each component shown in the preceding diagram:

- The **Prometheus server** is the core component of Prometheus. Its primary responsibility is to periodically scrape the configured set of targets and persist any collected metrics into a time-series database. As a secondary task, the server evaluates an operator-defined list of alert rules and emits alert events each time any of those rules are satisfied.
- The **Alertmanager** component ingests any alerts emitted by the Prometheus server and sends notifications through one or more communication channels (for example, email, Slack, or a third-party pager service).

- The service discovery layer enables Prometheus to dynamically update the list of endpoints to scrape by querying an external service (for example, Consul [2]) or an API such as the one provided by a container orchestration layer such as Kubernetes.
- The **Pushgateway** component emulates a push-based system for collecting metrics from sources that cannot be scraped. This includes both services that are not directly reachable (for example, due to strict network policies) by Prometheus, as well as short-lived batch jobs. These services can push their metrics stream to a gateway, which acts as an intermediate buffer that Prometheus can then scrape like any other endpoint.
- Clients retrieve data from Prometheus by submitting queries written in a bespoke query language referred to as **PromQL**. An example of such a client is **Grafana** [4], an open source solution for querying and visualizing metrics.

We will explore these components in more detail in the following sections.

Supported metric types

When it comes to a sophisticated metrics collection system such as Prometheus, you would normally expect support for a wide array of metric types. Unless you have prior experience using Prometheus, you will probably be surprised to find out that it only supports four types of metrics. In practice, however, when these metric types are combined with the expressiveness of the PromQL language, these are all we need to model any type of SLI we can think of! Here is the list of metrics supported by Prometheus:

- **Counters**: A counter is a cumulative metric whose value *increases monotonically* over time. Counters can be used to track the number of requests to a service, the number of downloads for an application, and so on.
- **Gauges**: A gauge tracks a single value that can go up or down. A common use case for gauges is to record usage (for example, CPU, memory, and load) stats about a server node and metrics such as the total number of users currently connected to a particular service.
- **Histograms**: A histogram samples observations and assigns them to a preconfigured number of buckets. At the same time, it keeps track of the total number of items across all buckets, thus making it possible to calculate quantiles and/or aggregations for the histogram contents. Histograms can be used to answer queries such as, "what is the response time for serving 90% of requests in the last hour?"

- **Summaries**: Summaries are similar to histograms in that both metric types support bucketing and the calculation of quantiles. However, summaries perform quantile calculations directly on the client and can be used as an alternative for reducing the query load on the server.

Automating the detection of scrape targets

Prometheus's flexibility really shines when it comes to configuring the set of endpoints to be scraped. In this section, we will examine an indicative list of options for statically or dynamically configuring the set of endpoints that Prometheus pulls metrics from. For the full list of supported discovery options, you can refer to the Prometheus documentation [8].

Static and file-based scrape target configuration

A static scrape configuration is considered the canonical way of providing scrape targets to Prometheus. The operator includes one or more static configuration blocks in the Prometheus configuration file that define the list of target hosts to be scraped and the set of labels to apply to the scraped metrics. You can see an example of such a block in the following code:

```
static_configs:
  - targets:
      - "host1"
      - "host2"
    labels:
      service: "my-service"
```

An issue with the static config approach is that after updating the Prometheus configuration files, we need to restart Prometheus so it can pick up the changes.

A better alternative is to extract the static configuration blocks to an external file and then reference that file from within the Prometheus configuration via the `file_sd_config` option:

```
file_sd_configs:
  - files:
      - config.yaml
    refresh_interval: "5m"
```

When file-based discovery is enabled, Prometheus will watch the specified set of files for changes and automatically reload their contents once a change has been detected.

Querying the underlying cloud provider

Out of the box, Prometheus can be configured to leverage the native APIs offered by cloud providers such as AWS, GCE, Azure, and OpenStack to detect provisioned compute node instances and make them available as targets for scraping.

Each node discovered by Prometheus is automatically annotated with a series of *provider-specific* meta labels. These labels can then be referenced by operator-defined match rules to filter out any nodes that the operator is not interested in scraping.

As an example, let's say that we only want to scrape the EC2 instances that contain a tag with the name scrape and the value true. We can use a configuration block such as the following one to achieve this:

```
ec2_sd_configs:
  # omitted: EC2 access keys (see prometheus documentation)
  relabel_configs:
    - source_labels: ["__meta_ec2_tag_scrape"]
      regex: "true"
      action: "keep"
```

When Prometheus discovers a new EC2 instance, it will automatically iterate its set of tags and generate labels whose names follow the pattern __meta_ec2_tag_<tagkey> and set their value to the observed tag value. The filtering rule in the preceding snippet will discard any nodes where the value of the __meta_ec2_tag_scrape label does not match the provided regular expression.

Leveraging the API exposed by Kubernetes

The last scrape target discovery method that we will be discussing in this chapter is highly recommended for workloads running on top of Kubernetes, such as the Links 'R' Us project. Once enabled, Prometheus will invoke the API endpoints exposed by Kubernetes to obtain information about the resource types that the operator is interested in scraping.

Prometheus can be configured to create scrape targets for the following types of Kubernetes resources:

Resource Type	Description
node	Creates a scrape target for each node in the Kubernetes cluster and allows us to collect machine-level metrics that can be exported by running a tool such as node-exporter [9].
service	Scans the Kubernetes Service resources and creates a scrape target for each exposed port. Prometheus will then attempt to pull any metrics exposed by the pods behind the service by performing periodic HTTP GET requests to each exposed port at the service's IP address. This approach relies on the fact that Service resources act as load balancers by delegating each incoming request to a different pod and might be a better-performing alternative compared to pulling metrics from all the pods at the same time.
pod	Discovers all Kubernetes Pod resources and creates a scrape target for each one of their containers. Prometheus will then perform periodic HTTP GET requests to pull the metrics out of each individual container in parallel.
ingress	Creates a target for each path on an Ingress resource.

In a similar fashion to the cloud-aware discovery implementation, Prometheus will annotate the discovered set of targets with a resource-specific set of meta labels. Based on the previous examples, can you guess what the following configuration block does?

```
kubernetes_sd_configs:
  # omitted: credentials and endpoints for accessing k8s (see prometheus
documentation)
  - role: endpoints
    relabel_configs:
      - source_labels:
["__meta_kubernetes_service_annotation_prometheus_scrape"]
        action: "keep"
        regex: "true"
```

Since we specified a role equal to endpoints, Prometheus will obtain the list of pods associated with that service. Prometheus will then create a scrape target for *each pod* if – and only if – their parent **service** contains an annotation with the name prometheus_scrape and the value true. This trick makes it really easy to enable automatic scraping for any service in our cluster simply by editing Kubernetes manifests.

Instrumenting Go code

In order for Prometheus to be able to scrape metrics from our deployed services, we need to perform the following sequence of steps:

1. Define the metrics that we are interested in tracking.
2. Instrument our code base so that it updates the values of the aforementioned metrics at the appropriate locations.
3. Collect the metric data and make it available for scraping over HTTP.

One of the key benefits of microservice-based architectures is that software engineers are no longer constrained by the use of a single programming language for building their services. It is quite common to see microservices written in Go communicating with other services written in Rust or Java. Nevertheless, the need to monitor services across the board still remains ubiquitous.

To make it as easy as possible for software engineers to integrate with Prometheus, its authors provide client libraries for different programming languages. All these clients have one thing in common: they handle all the low-level details involved in registering and exporting Prometheus metrics.

The examples in the following sections have a dependency on the official Go client package for Prometheus. You can install it by executing the following command:

```
go get -u github.com/prometheus/client_golang/prometheus/...
```

Registering metrics with Prometheus

`promauto` is a subpackage of the Prometheus client that defines a set of convenience helpers for creating and registering metrics with the minimum possible amount of code. Each of the constructor functions from the `promauto` package returns a Prometheus metric instance that we can immediately use in our code.

Let's take a quick look at how easy it is to register and populate some of the most common metrics types supported by Prometheus. The first metric type that we will be instantiating is a simple counter:

```
numReqs := promauto.NewCounter(prometheus.CounterOpts{
    Name: "app_reqs_total",
    Help: "The total number of incoming requests",
})

// Increment the counter.
numReqs.Inc()
```

```
// Add a value to the counter.
numReqs.Add(42)
```

Each Prometheus metric must be assigned a unique name. If we attempt to register a metric with the same name twice, we will get an error. What's more, when registering a new metric, we can optionally specify a help message that provides additional information about the metric's purpose.

As shown in the preceding code snippet, once we obtain a counter instance, we can use the `Inc` method to increment its value and the `Add` method to add an arbitrary positive value to the counter.

The next type of metric that we will be instantiating is a gauge. Gauges are quite similar to counters with the exception that their value can go either up or down. In addition to the `Inc` and `Add` methods, gauge instances also provide the `Dec` and `Sub` methods. The following block of code defines a gauge metric for tracking the number of pending items in a queue:

```
queueLen := promauto.NewGauge(prometheus.GaugeOpts{
    Name: "app_queue_len_total",
    Help: "Total number of items in the queue.",
})

// Add items to the queue
queueLen.Inc()
queueLen.Add(42)

// Remove items from the queue
queueLen.Sub(42)
queueLen.Dec()
```

To conclude our experimentation with the different types of Prometheus metrics, we will create a histogram metric. The `NewHistorgram` constructor expects the caller to specify a strictly ascending list of `float64` values that describe the width of each bucket that's used by the histogram.

The following example uses the `LinearBuckets` helper from the `prometheus` package to generate 20 distinct buckets with a width of 100 units. The lower bound of the *left-most* histogram bucket will be set to the value 0:

```
reqTimes := promauto.NewHistogram(prometheus.HistogramOpts{
    Name:    "app_response_times",
    Help:    "Distribution of application response times.",
    Buckets: prometheus.LinearBuckets(0, 100, 20),
})
```

```
// Record a response time of 100ms
reqTimes.Observe(100)
```

Adding values to a histogram instance is quite trivial. All we need to do is simply invoke its `Observe` method and pass the value we wish to track as an argument.

Vector-based metrics

One of the more interesting Prometheus features is its support for partitioning collected samples across one or more dimensions (*labels*, in Prometheus terminology). If we opt to use this feature, instead of having a single metric instance, we can work with a **vector** of metric values.

In the following example, we have just launched an A/B test for a new website layout and we are interested in tracking the number of user registrations for each of the page layouts that we are actively trialing:

```
regCountVec := promauto.NewCounterVec(
    prometheus.CounterOpts{
        Name: "app_registrations_total",
        Help: "Total number of registrations by A/B test layout.",
    },
    []string{"layout"},
)

regCountVec.WithLabelValues("a").Inc()
```

This time, instead of a single counter, we will be creating a vector of counters where every sampled value will be automatically tagged with a label named `layout`.

To increment or add value to this metric, we need to obtain the correct counter by invoking the variadic `WithLabelValues` method on the `regCountVec` variable. This method expects a string value for each defined dimension and returns the counter instance that corresponds to the provided label values.

Exporting metrics for scraping

After registering our metrics with Prometheus and instrumenting our code to update them where needed, the only additional thing that we need to do is expose the collected values over HTTP so that Prometheus can scrape them.

The promhttp subpackage from the Prometheus client package provides a convenience helper function called Handler that returns an http.Handler instance that encapsulates all the required logic for exporting collected metrics in the format expected by Prometheus.

The exported data will not only include the metrics that have been registered by the developer but it will also contain an extensive list of metrics that pertain to the Go runtime. Some examples of such metrics are as follows:

- The number of active goroutines
- Information about stack and heap allocation
- Performance statistics for the Go garbage collector

The following example demonstrates a minimal, self-contained hello-world kind of application that defines a counter metric and exposes two HTTP routes: /ping and /metrics. The handler for the first route increments the counter, while the latter exports the collected Prometheus metrics:

```go
func main() {
    // Create a prometheus counter to keep track of ping requests.
    numPings := promauto.NewCounter(prometheus.CounterOpts{
        Name: "pingapp_pings_total",
        Help: "The total number of incoming ping requests",
    })

    http.Handle("/metrics", promhttp.Handler())
    http.Handle("/ping", http.HandlerFunc(func(w http.ResponseWriter, _
*http.Request) {
        numPings.Inc()
        w.Write([]byte("pong!\n"))
    }))

    log.Fatal(http.ListenAndServe(":8080", nil))
}
```

Try to compile and run the preceding example. You can find its sources in the Chapter13/prom_http folder in this book's GitHub repository. While the example is running, switch to another Terminal and execute a few curl localhost:8080/ping commands to increment the pingapp_pings_total counter.

Then, execute a `curl localhost:8080/metrics` command and examine the list of exported metrics. The following screenshot displays the last few lines of output upon executing the preceding command:

```
●  ● ●                              5. bash (bash)
# HELP go_memstats_stack_sys_bytes Number of bytes obtained from system for stack allocator.
# TYPE go_memstats_stack_sys_bytes gauge
go_memstats_stack_sys_bytes 425984
# HELP go_memstats_sys_bytes Number of bytes obtained from system.
# TYPE go_memstats_sys_bytes gauge
go_memstats_sys_bytes 7.0453248e+07
# HELP go_threads Number of OS threads created.
# TYPE go_threads gauge
go_threads 9
# HELP pingapp_pings_total The total number of incoming ping requests
# TYPE pingapp_pings_total counter
pingapp_pings_total 129
# HELP promhttp_metric_handler_requests_in_flight Current number of scrapes being served.
# TYPE promhttp_metric_handler_requests_in_flight gauge
promhttp_metric_handler_requests_in_flight 1
# HELP promhttp_metric_handler_requests_total Total number of scrapes by HTTP status code.
# TYPE promhttp_metric_handler_requests_total counter
promhttp_metric_handler_requests_total{code="200"} 4
promhttp_metric_handler_requests_total{code="500"} 0
promhttp_metric_handler_requests_total{code="503"} 0
bash-3.2$ █
```

Figure 2: A subset of the metrics that have been exported by our example Go application

As you can see, the output includes not only the current value of the `pingapp_pings_total` counter but also several other important metrics that the Prometheus client automatically captured from the Go runtime for us.

Visualizing collected metrics using Grafana

By this point, you should have already selected a suitable metrics collection solution for your applications and instrumented your code base to emit the metrics that you are interested in tracking. To make sense of the collected data and reason about it, we need to visualize it.

For this task, we will be using Grafana [4] as our tool of choice. Grafana offers a convenient, end-to-end solution that can be used to retrieve metrics from a variety of different data sources and construct dashboards for visualizing them. The supported list of data sources includes Prometheus, InfluxDB, Graphite, Google Stackdriver, AWS CloudWatch, Azure Monitor, SQL databases (MySQL, Postgres, and SQL Server), and Elasticsearch.

If you have already set up one of the preceding data sources and want to evaluate Grafana, the easiest way to do so is to spin up a Docker container using the following command:

```
docker run -d \
    -p 3000:3000 \
    --name=grafana \
    -e "GF_SECURITY_ADMIN_USER=admin" \
    -e "GF_SECURITY_ADMIN_PASSWORD=secret" \
    grafana/grafana
```

You can then point your browser at `http://localhost:3000`, log in with the preceding credentials, and follow one of the several comprehensive guides available at Grafana's website to configure your first dashboard.

In terms of supported visualization widgets, the standard Grafana installation supports the following widget types:

- **Graph**: A flexible visualization component that can plot single- and multi-series line charts or bar charts. Furthermore, graph widgets can be configured to display multiple series in overlapping or stacked mode.
- **Logs panel**: A list of log entries that are obtained by a compatible data source (for example, Elasticsearch) whose contents are correlated with the information displayed by another widget.
- **Singlestat**: A component that condenses a series into a single value by applying an aggregation function (for example, min, max, avg, and so on). This component may optionally be configured to display a sparkline chart or to be rendered as a gauge.
- **Heatmap**: A specialized component that renders the changes in a histogram's set of values over time. As shown in the following screenshot, heatmaps comprise a set of vertical slices where each slice depicts the histogram values at a particular point in time. Contrary to a typical histogram plot, where bar heights represent the count of items in a particular bucket, heatmaps apply a color map to visualize the frequency of items within each vertical slice.
- **Table**: A component that is best suited for rendering series in tabular format.

The following screenshot demonstrates the built-in Grafana widgets as they would appear in an example dashboard:

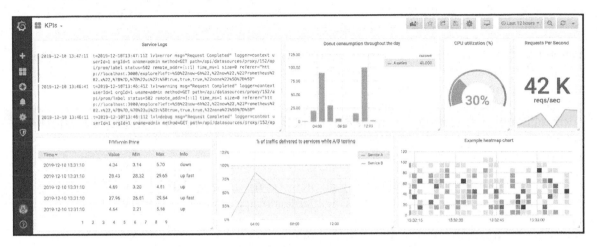

Figure 3: An example dashboard built with Grafana

Apart from the default, built-in widgets, the operator can install additional widget types by leveraging Grafana's plugin mechanism. Examples of such widgets include world map, radar, pie, and bubble charts.

Using Prometheus as an end-to-end solution for alerting

By instrumenting our applications and deploying the necessary infrastructure for scraping metrics, we now have the means for evaluating the SLIs for each of our services. Once we define a suitable set of SLOs for each of the SLIs, the next item on our checklist is to deploy an alert system so that we can be automatically notified every time that our SLOs stop being met.

A typical alert specification looks like this:

*When the value of metric **X** exceeds threshold **Y** for **Z** time units, then execute actions **a1, a2, a_n***

What is the first thought that springs to mind when you hear a fire alarm going off? Most people will probably answer something along the lines of, *there might be a fire nearby*. People are naturally conditioned to assume that alerts are always temporally correlated with an issue that must be addressed immediately.

When it comes to monitoring the health of production systems, having alerts in place that require the immediate intervention of a human operator once they trigger is pretty much a standard operating procedure. However, this is not the only type of alert that an SRE might encounter when working on such a system. Oftentimes, being able to proactively detect and address issues before they get out of hand and become a risk for the stability of production systems is the only thing that stands between a peaceful night's sleep and that dreaded 2 AM page call.

Here is an example of a proactive alert: an SRE sets up an alert that fires once the disk usage on a database node exceeds 80% of the available storage capacity. Note that when the alarm does fire, the database is still working without any issue. However, in this case, the SRE is provided with ample time to plan and execute the required set of steps (for example, schedule a maintenance window to resize the disk assigned to the DB) to rectify the issue with the minimum disruption possible to the database service.

Contrast the preceding case with a different scenario where the SRE is paged because the database did run out of space and, as a result, several services with a downstream dependency on the database are now offline. This is a particularly stressful situation for an SRE to be in as the system is already experiencing downtime.

Using Prometheus as a source for alert events

In order to use Prometheus as an alert-generating source, operators must define a collection of alert rules that Prometheus should monitor. The alert rule definitions live in external YAML files that are imported by the main Prometheus configuration file using a `rule_files` block, as follows:

```
# prometheus.yml

global:
  scrape_interval:      15s

rule_files:
  - 'alerts/*.yml'
```

Prometheus organizes multiple alert rules into **groups**. Rules within a group are always evaluated *sequentially* while each group is evaluated in *parallel*.

Let's take a look at the structure of a simple alert definition. The following snippet defines an alert group with the name `example` that contains a single alert definition:

```
groups:
- name: example
  rules:
  - alert: InstanceDown
    expr: up == 0
    for: 5m
    labels:
      severity: page
    annotations:
      playbook: "https://sre.linkrus.com/playbooks/instance-down"
```

Each alert block must always be assigned a unique name, as well as a **PromQL** (short for **Prometheus query language**) expression that Prometheus will recalculate each time it evaluates the alert rule. In the preceding example, the rule expression is satisfied once the value of the `up` metric becomes equal to zero.

The optional `for` clause can be used to defer the triggering of the alert until a particular time period elapses, during which the alert expression must always be satisfied. In this example, the alert will only fire if the `up` metric remains zero for at least 5 minutes.

The `labels` block allows us to attach one or more labels to the alert. In this case, we tag the alert with a `severity: page` annotation to advise the component that's responsible for handling the alert that it should page the SRE that is currently on call.

Finally, the `annotations` block allows the operator to store additional bits of information, such as detailed descriptions of the alert or a URL pointing to a playbook for dealing with this kind of alert.

A playbook is a succinct document that distills the best practices for resolving a particular problem. These documents are authored in advance and are normally attached to all outgoing notifications that are triggered due to an alert.

When an SRE gets paged, being able to access the playbook associated with a particular alert is an invaluable asset for quickly diagnosing the root cause of the problem and reducing the **mean time to resolution (MTTR)**.

Handling alert events

Prometheus will periodically evaluate the configured set of alert rules and emit alert events when the preconditions for a rule are met. By design, the Prometheus server is only responsible for emitting alert events; it does not include any logic whatsoever for processing alerts.

The actual processing of emitted alert events is handled by the Alertmanager component. The Alertmanager ingests the alert events emitted by Prometheus and is responsible for grouping, deduplicating, and routing each alert to the appropriate notification integrations (referred to as **receivers** in Alertmanager terminology).

We will begin our brief tour of the Alertmanager component by elaborating on how operators can use its built-in grouping and filtering functionality to manage incoming alert events. Next, we will learn about the basics of defining alert receivers and configuring routing rules to ensure that alerts are always delivered to the correct receiver.

Grouping alerts together

Dealing with a large volume of alerts that fire concurrently certainly seems like a daunting task from an SRE's point of view. To cut through the noise, Alertmanager allows operators to specify a set of rules for grouping together alerts based on the content of the labels that have been assigned to each alert event by Prometheus.

To understand how alert grouping works, let's picture a scenario where 100 microservices are all trying to connect to a Kafka queue that is currently unavailable. *Each* of the services fires a high-priority alert, which, in turn, causes a new page notification to be sent to the SRE that is currently on-call. As a result, the SRE will get swamped with hundreds of page notifications about exactly the same issue!

To avoid situations like this, a much better solution would be to edit the Prometheus alert rule definition and ensure that all alert events for the queue service are annotated with a particular label, for example, `component=kafka`. Then, we can instruct the Alertmanager to group alerts based on the value of the `component` label and consolidate all those related to Kafka into a *single page notification*.

Selectively muting alerts

Another handy Alertmanager feature that you should be aware of is **alert inhibition**. This feature allows the operator to *mute* notifications for a set of alerts when a specific alert is currently firing.

When the Alertmanager loads its configuration file, it looks for the list of alert inhibition rules under the top-level `inhibit_rules` key. Each rule entry must adhere to the following schema:

```
source_match:
  [ <labelname>: <labelvalue>, ... ]
source_match_re:
  [ <labelname>: <regex>, ... ]

target_match:
  [ <labelname>: <labelvalue>, ... ]
target_match_re:
  [ <labelname>: <regex>, ... ]

[ equal: '[' <labelname>, ... ']' ]
```

The `source_match` and `source_match_re` blocks work as selectors for the alert that activates the inhibition rule. The difference between the two blocks is that `source_match` attempts an exact match, whereas `source_math_re` matches label values of incoming alerts against a regular expression.

The `target_match` and `target_match_re` blocks are used to select the set of alerts that will be suppressed while the inhibition rule is active.

Finally, the `equal` block prevents the inhibition rule from activating unless the source and target rules have the same value for the specified labels.

> To prevent an alert from inhibiting itself, alerts that match both the source and the target side of a rule are not allowed to be inhibited.

As a proof of concept, let's try to define a rule that suppresses any alert that fires during the weekend. A prerequisite for setting up this rule is to create a Prometheus alert that **only** fires during the weekend. Then, we can add the following block to the Alertmanager's configuration file:

```
inhibit_rules:
  - source_match:
      alertname: Weekend
    target_match_re:
      alertname: '*'
```

When the `Weekend` alert is firing, any other alert (excluding itself) will be automatically muted!

Configuring alert receivers

A receiver is nothing more than a fancy way of referring to a collection of notification integrations that can send out alerts through various channels. Out of the box, the Alertmanager supports the following integrations:

- **Email**: Send out an email with alert details
- **Slack/Hipchat/WeChat**: Post alert details to a chat service
- **PagerDuty/Opsgenie/VictorOps**: Send a page notification to the SRE currently on call
- **WebHooks**: An escape hatch for implementing custom integrations

When the Alertmanager loads its configuration file, it looks for the list of receiver definitions under the top-level `receivers` key. Each receiver block must adhere to the following schema:

```
name: <string>
email_configs:
  [ - <email_config>, ... ]
pagerduty_configs:
  [ - <pagerduty_config>, ... ]
slack_configs:
  [ - <slack_config>, ... ]
opsgenie_configs:
  [ - <opsgenie_config>, ... ]
webhook_configs:
  [ - <webhook_config>, ... ]
# omitted for brevity: configs for additional integrations
```

Each receiver must be assigned a unique name that, as we will see in the following section, can be referenced by one or more routing rules. The operator must then specify a configuration for each notification mechanism that should be activated when an alert reaches the receiver.

However, if the operator does not provide **any** configuration block, the receiver behaves like a black hole: any alert that reaches it simply gets dropped.

Routing alerts to receivers

Now, let's take a closer look at the tree-based mechanism used by the Alertmanager for routing incoming alerts to a particular receiver. The top-level section of the Alertmanager's configuration file must **always** define a `route` block. The block represents the root node of the tree and can contain the following set of fields:

- `match`: Specifies a set of label values that must match the values from the incoming alert to consider the current route node as matched.
- `match_re`: Similar to `match`, with the exception that label values are matched against a regular expression.
- `receiver`: The name of the receiver to deliver the incoming alert to if the alert matches the current route.
- `group_by`: A list of label names to group incoming alerts by.
- `routes`: A set of child `route` blocks. If an alert does not match any of the child routes, it will be handled based on the configuration parameters of the current route.

To understand how tree-based routing works in practice, let's step through a simple example. For the purpose of this example, the Alertmanager configuration file contains the following routing configurations:

```
route:
  receiver: 'default'
  # All alerts that do not match the following child routes
  # will remain at the root node and be dispatched to 'default-receiver'.
  routes:
  - receiver: 'page-SRE-on-call'
    match_re:
      service: cockroachdb|cassandra
  - receiver: 'notify-ops-channel-on-slack'
    group_by: [environment]
    match:
      team: backend

receivers:
  # omitted: receiver definitions
```

Let's see how the Alertmanager figures out the appropriate receiver for various incoming alerts by inspecting their label annotations:

- If an incoming alert includes a `service` label whose value matches either `cockroachdb` or `cassandra`, the Alertmanager will dispatch the alert to the `page-SRE-on-call` receiver.

- On the other hand, if the alert includes a `team` label whose value is equal to `backend`, the Alertmanager will dispatch it to the `notify-ops-channel-on-slack` receiver.
- Any other incoming alert that doesn't match any of the two child routes will be dispatched to the `default` receiver by default.

This completes our tour of the Alertmanager tool. Granted, configuring alert rules for your applications can, at first, seem like a daunting task. Hopefully, the knowledge you've obtained by reading this chapter will allow you to begin experimenting with Prometheus and set up a few rudimentary Alertmanager test rules. With a little bit of practice and once you get the hang of the rule syntax, you will find that writing more sophisticated rules for monitoring your production applications will become a breeze!

Summary

At the start of this chapter, we talked about the pros and cons of using a metrics collection system such as Prometheus to scrape and aggregate metrics data from not only our deployed applications but also from our infrastructure (for example, Kubernetes master/worker nodes).

Then, we learned how to leverage the official Prometheus client package for Go to instrument our code and export the collected metrics over HTTP so that they can be scraped by Prometheus. Next, we extolled the benefits of using Grafana for building dashboards by pulling in metrics from heterogeneous sources. In the final part of this chapter, we learned how to define alert rules in Prometheus and gained a solid understanding of using the Alertmanager tool to group, deduplicate, and route alert events that are emitted by Prometheus.

By exploiting the knowledge gained from this chapter, you will be able to instrument your Go code-base and ensure that important metrics for your applications' state and performance can be collected, aggregated and visualized. Moreover, if your current role also includes SRE responsibilities, you can subsequently feed these metrics into an alerting system and receive real-time notifications when the SLAs and SLOs for your services are not met.

Next up, we will cover a few interesting ideas for extending what we have built in this book so as to further your understanding of the material.

Questions

1. What is the difference between an SLI and an SLO?
2. Explain how SLAs work.
3. What is the difference between a push- and pull-based metrics collection system?
4. Would you use a push- or pull-based system to scrape data from a tightly locked down (that is, no ingress) subnet?
5. What is the difference between a Prometheus counter and a gauge metric?
6. Why is it important for page notifications to be accompanied by a link to a playbook?

Further reading

- Campbell, Matthew: *Scaling to a Million Machines with Prometheus* (PromCon 2016): https://promcon.io/2016-berlin/talks/scaling-to-a-million-machines-with-prometheus
- **Consul**: Secure service networking: https://consul.io
- **Docker**: Enterprise container platform: https://www.docker.com
- **Grafana**: The open observability platform: https://grafana.com/
- **Graphite**: An enterprise-ready monitoring tool that runs equally well on cheap hardware or a cloud infrastructure: https://graphiteapp.org/
- **InfluxDB**: A time-series database designed to handle high write and query loads: https://www.influxdata.com/products/influxdb-overview
- **Nagios**: The industry standard In IT infrastructure monitoring: https://www.nagios.org
- **Prometheus**: Configuration options: https://prometheus.io/docs/prometheus/latest/configuration/configuration
- **Prometheus**: Exporter for machine metrics: https://github.com/prometheus/node_exporter
- **Prometheus**: Monitoring system and time-series database: https://prometheus.io
- **StatsD**: Daemon for easy but powerful stats aggregation: https://github.com/statsd/statsd

14
Epilogue

At this point, I would like to congratulate you on completing this book and extend to you a big thanks for taking the time to read every single chapter up to the very end. I sincerely hope that you had as much pleasure reading this book as I had writing it and that you can take some of the principles and concepts that we discussed through these pages and apply them to your current and future Go projects.

Having said that, I have a small favor to ask of you. Should you locate any errors either in the content of this book or the accompanying code, please don't hesitate to reach out and let me know. What's more, I would certainly love hearing your thoughts on the topics that were addressed in this book! You can contact me either via Packt Publishing or through this book's GitHub repository.

If you are up to the challenge, here is a list with a few interesting ideas that you can try next to further your understanding of both this book's material and its accompanying code:

- Support crawling for dynamic pages that render their content with the help of JavaScript frameworks such as React, Vue, and so on. Add a headless browser to the mix so that the crawler can execute JavaScript code and process the content of the rendered page.
- Reduce the impact of the crawler component on remote servers. Modify the link submission page of the frontend so that webmasters can specify a preferred time window for crawling a particular domain. Then, update the crawler implementation to take this information into account when scheduling the refresh interval for each individual link.
- Update the crawler to recognize and honor the contents of `robots.txt` files when deciding whether to crawl links from a particular domain.

- Leverage the `bspgraph` package from `Chapter 8`, *Graph-Based Data Processing*, to implement other popular graph-based algorithms and then execute them in a distributed fashion by switching your code so that it uses the `dbspgraph` package from `Chapter 12`, *Building Distributed Graph-Processing Systems*. If you are unsure of where to start, try implementing one of the following algorithms:
    - Check whether a graph is bipartite.
    - Determine whether a graph contains a Hamiltonian cycle.
    - Detect whether a directed graph contains cycles.
- Add support for checkpoints to the `dbspgraph` package's implementation. After a configurable number of super-steps, the master node should ask every worker to create a checkpoint of their current state. If a worker crashes, the master should then instruct workers to load their state from the last known checkpoint, redistribute the UUID ranges among the remaining workers, and resume the execution of the computation job.

Assessments

Chapter 1

1. Software engineering is defined as the application of a systematic, disciplined, quantifiable approach to the development, operation, and maintenance of software.

2. Some of the key questions that a software engineer must be able to answer are as follows:

   - What are the business use cases that the software needs to support?
   - What components comprise the system and how do they interact with each other?
   - What technologies will be used to implement the various system components?
   - How will the software be tested to ensure that its behavior matches the customer's expectations?
   - How does load affect the system's performance and what is the plan for scaling the system?

3. An SRE spends approximately half of their time on operations-related tasks such as dealing with support tickets, being on call, automating processes to eliminate human errors, and so on.

4. The waterfall model does not provide a detailed view of the processes that comprise each model step. In addition, it does not seem to support cross-cutting processes such as project management or quality control that run in parallel with the waterfall steps. A significant caveat of the waterfall model is that it operates under the assumption that all customer requirements are known in advance. The iterative enhancement model attempts to rectify these issues by executing small incremental waterfall iterations that allow the development team to adapt to changes in requirements.

4. According to the lean development model, the most common sources of waste are as follows:

    - The introduction of non-essential changes when development is underway
    - Overly complicated decision-making processes for signing off new features
    - Unneeded communication between the various project stakeholders and the development teams

6. The team decides to focus on speedy delivery at the expense of code quality. As a result, the code base becomes more complex and defects start accumulating. Now, the team must dedicate a part of their development time to fixing bugs instead of working on the requested features. Consequently, the implementation stage becomes a bottleneck that reduces the efficiency of the entire development process.

7. The key responsibility of the Product Owner is to manage the backlog for the project. On the other hand, the Scrum Master is responsible for organizing and running the various Scrum events.

8. The retrospective serves as a feedback loop for incrementally improving the team's performance across sprints. The team members should be discussing both the things that went well during the last sprint as well as the things that didn't. The outcome of the retrospective should be a list of corrective actions to address the problems that were encountered during the sprint.

9. Automation is important as it reduces the potential for human error. In addition, it reduces the time that's needed to test and deploy changes to production. Measuring is equally important as it allows DevOps engineers to monitor production services and receive alerts when their behavior diverges from the expected norm.

10. The company is expected to operate in a high-risk environment. For one, the new gaming console depends on a piece of technology that is not available yet and is being developed by a third party. What's more, the market is already saturated: other, much larger competitors could also be working on their own next-gen console systems. The expected competitive advantage for ACME Gaming Systems may be rendered obsolete by the time their new system is released. This is yet another source of risk. Given the high risk that's involved, the spiral model with its risk assessment and prototyping processes would be the most sensible choice for developing the software that will power the new console.

Chapter 2

1. The following is what the SOLID acronym initials stand for:
   - Single responsibility
   - Open/Closed
   - Liskov substitution
   - Interface segregation
   - Dependency inversion

2. The code conflates two responsibilities: retrieving/mutating the state of a document and creating a signature for the document's content. Furthermore, the proposed implementation is inflexible as it forces the use of a specific signing algorithm. To address this problem, we can remove the `Sign` method from the `Document` type and provide an external helper that can sign not only instances of `Document` but also any type that can export its content as a string:

```
type ContentProvider interface {
    Content() string
}

type ECDADocumentSigner struct {//...}

func (s ECDADocumentSigner) Sign(pk *ecdsa.PrivateKey,
contentProvider ContentProvider) (string, error) { //... }
```

3. The idea behind the interface segregation principle is to provide clients with the smallest possible interface that satisfies their needs and thus avoid depending on interfaces that will not actually be used. In the provided example, the write method receives an `*os.File` instance as an argument. However, as the function implementation probably only needs to be able to *write* data to the file, we could achieve the same result by passing an `io.Writer` in the place of the `*os.File` instance. Apart from breaking the dependency to the `*os.File` concrete type, this change will also allow us to reuse the implementation for any type that implements `io.Writer` (for example, sockets, loggers, or others).

4. The use of `util` as a package name is not a recommended practice due to the following reasons:
   - It provides little context as to the package's purpose and contents.
   - It can end up as the home for miscellaneous, possibly unrelated types and/or methods that would undoubtedly violate the single responsibility principle.

5. Import cycles cause the Go compiler to emit compile-time errors when you attempt to compile and/or run your code.

6. Some of the advantages of using zero values when defining new Go types are as follows:

   - An explicit constructor is not required as Go will automatically assign the zero value to the fields of an object when it is allocated.
   - The types can be embedded into other types and used out-of-the-box without any further initialization (for example, embedding a `sync.Mutex` into a struct).

Chapter 3

1. The purpose of software versioning is twofold. First, it allows software engineers to validate whether an external dependency can be safely upgraded without the risk of introducing issues to production systems. Secondly, being able to explicitly reference required software dependencies via their versions is a prerequisite for implementing the concept of repeatable builds.

2. A semantic version is a string that satisfies the following format: `MAJOR.MINOR.PATCH`:

   - The major component is incremented when a breaking change is introduced to the software
   - The minor component is incremented when new functionality is introduced to the software in a backward-compatible way
   - The patch version is incremented when a backward-compatible fix is applied to the code

3. In the first case, we would increment the **minor** version as the new API does not break backward compatibility. In the second case, we would increment the **major** version as the new required parameter breaks compatibility with older versions of the API. Finally, in the third case, we would increment the **patch** version.

4. One approach would be to tag each build with a unique, monotonically increasing number. Alternatively, we could annotate build artifacts with a timestamp that indicates when they were created.

5. The pros of vendoring are as follows:

   - The capability to run reproducible builds for current or older versions of a piece of software
   - Being able to access the required dependencies locally, even if they disappear from the place where they were originally hosted

The cons of vendoring are as follows:

- Engineers should monitor the change logs for their dependencies and manually upgrade them when security fixes become available.
- If the authors of the vendored dependencies do not follow semantic versioning for their packages, upgrading a dependency can introduce breaking changes that must be addressed before it's able to compile our code.

6. Some differences between the dep tool and Go modules are as follows:
    - Go modules fully integrate with the various commands, such as `go get`, `go build`, and `go test`.
    - While the dep tool selects the **highest** common version for a package, Go modules select the **minimum** viable version.
    - Go modules support multi-versioned dependencies.
    - Go modules do away with the *vendor* folder that's used by the dep tool.

Chapter 4

1. A stub satisfies a particular interface and returns **canned** answers for every invocation to the methods it implements. Mocks allow us to specify the following in a declarative way:
    - The order and parameters of the expected set of method invocations
    - The set of values to be returned for each combination of inputs

2. A fake object provides a fully working implementation whose behavior matches the objects that they are meant to substitute. For example, instead of having our tests communicate with a real **key-value (KV)** store, we might inject a fake object that provides a compatible, in-memory implementation of the KV store's API.

3. A table-driven test consists of three main components:
    - A type that encapsulates the parameters for running the test and its expected outcome. In Go programs, this is typically facilitated using an anonymous struct.
    - A slice of test cases to evaluate.
    - The test runner. Here, a for loop that iterates the list of test cases invokes the code under test with the correct set of parameters and verifies that the obtained results match the expectations for each test case.

4. The purpose of unit testing is to ensure that a particular unit of code (a function, method, or package), when exercised in **isolation**, behaves according to a set of specifications. To this end, a unit test will typically use a mechanism such as stubs, mocks, or fake objects to replace any external dependencies of the code under test. On the other hand, integration tests are designed to exercise multiple units together so as to verify that they interoperate correctly.

5. Integration tests are designed to exercise multiple units together so as to verify that they interoperate correctly. In a similar fashion to unit tests, integration tests will oftentimes use a mechanism such as stubs, mocks, or fake objects as a substitute for external components (for example, databases, web servers, and so on). On the other hand, functional tests do not use any sort of mocking mechanism as their primary purpose is to test the behavior of the **complete** system.

6. The ambassador pattern injects a proxy between an application and a service it depends on. The proxy is typically run as a sidecar process alongside the application and exposes APIs to do the following:
    - Divert outgoing service calls to a different version of the service
    - Mock responses to outgoing service calls
    - Inject faults to requests or responses for testing purposes

Chapter 5

1. Functional requirements outline the list of core functionalities that a system will implement, as well as the set of interactions between the system and any external actors. On the other hand, non-functional requirements list the mechanisms and metrics that we can use to ascertain whether a proposed design is a good fit for solving a particular problem.

2. A user story is comprised of the following two key components:
    - A requirement specification must always be expressed from the viewpoint of the actor interacting with the system
    - A set of acceptance criteria (also known as the *definition of done*) for evaluating whether the story goals have been successfully met

3. An attacker could submit a carefully crafted link with a link-local address that would trick the crawler into making a call to the metadata API offered by the cloud provider hosting our project and subsequently caching the response to the search index. Moreover, the attacker could submit a URL file as its protocol type and cause the crawler to read a local file from the machine and leak its contents to the search index.

4. A **service-level objective (SLO)** consists of the following parts:
   - A description of the thing being measured
   - The expected service level, specified as a percentage
   - The time period where the measurement takes place

5. A UML component diagram provides a high-level view of the core components that comprise a system and visualizes their dependencies in terms of implemented and required interfaces.

Chapter 6

1. Relational databases are a better fit for transactional workloads and for performing complex queries. They can scale horizontally using mechanisms such as data sharding but at the cost of requiring additional coordination for executing queries. On the other hand, NoSQL databases are best suited for crunching massive volumes of **denormalized** data. By design, NoSQL databases can efficiently scale horizontally (even across data centers), with many NoSQL offerings promising a linear increase in query performance as more nodes are added to the cluster. The main caveat of NoSQL databases is that they can only satisfy two facets of the **CAP (consistency, availability,** and **partition tolerance)** theorem.

   A relational database would be a great fit for systems that perform a large volume of concurrent transactions, such as the ones you would expect to find in a bank. On the other hand, a system that needs to process a large number of events for analytics purposes would probably benefit more from a NoSQL solution.

2. To scale a DBMS for a read-heavy workload, we would deploy multiple read replicas and update our applications to send read-only queries to the replicas and write queries to the master node. For a write-heavy workload, we would deploy multiple master nodes and enable data sharding so that writes can be efficiently distributed across the master nodes.

3. According to the CAP theorem, distributed systems can only satisfy two of the following properties: consistency, availability, and partition tolerance. When deciding on which NoSQL solution to use, we must identify which two of the CAP terms are the most important for our particular application (CP, AP, or CA) and then limit our search to those NoSQL offerings that satisfy our selected CAP requirements.

4. Having an abstraction layer allows us to decouple the business logic from the underlying database system. This makes it much easier to switch to a different DBMS in the future, without having to update our business logic. Furthermore, testing our business logic code also becomes easier and faster as we can use a mechanism such as stubs, mocks, or fake objects to avoid running our tests against an actual database instance.

5. First, you would need to add the new method to the `Indexer` interface. Then, following a test-driven approach, you would need to add a test for the expected behavior of the new method to the `SuiteBase` type in the `indextest` package. Finally, you would need to visit all the types that adhere to the `Indexer` interface (in this case, the bleve and Elasticsearch indexers) and add an implementation for the new method.

Chapter 7

1. The Go `interface{}` type conveys no useful information about the underlying type. If we use it for representing an argument to a function or a method, we effectively bypass the compiler's ability to statically check the function/method arguments at compile-time and instead have to manually check whether the input can be safely cast into a supported known type.

2. Instead of running the compute-intensive stages locally, we can migrate them to a remote machine with enough computing resources. The respective local stages can then be replaced with a proxy that transmits the local payload data to the remote machine via a **remote procedure call (RPC)**, waits for the results, and pushes them to the next local stage. The following diagram outlines the proposed solution:

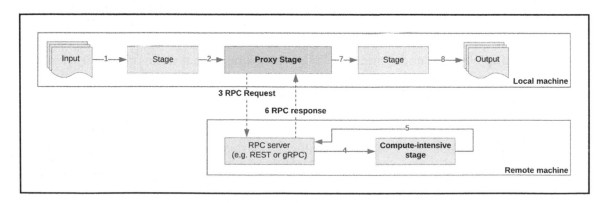

3. Each processor function must satisfy the `Processor` interface, whose definition is as follows:

```
type Processor interface {
    Process(context.Context, Payload) (Payload, error)
}
```

In addition, we also defined the `ProcessorFunc` type, which acts as an adaptor for converting a function with a compatible signature into a type that implements the `Processor` interface.

For this particular use case, we can define a function that receives a `Processor` and a logger (for example, from the `logrus` package) instance and returns a new `Processor` that decorates the call to the `Process` method with additional logic that emits a log entry if an error occurs. The `makeErrorLoggingProcessor` function shows one of the possible ways of implementing this pattern:

```
func makeErrorLoggingProcessor(proc Processor, logger
*logrus.Logger) Processor {
    return ProcessorFunc(func(ctx context.Context, p Payload)
(Payload, error) {
        out, err := proc.Process(ctx, p)
        if err != nil {
            logger.Error(err)
        }
        return out, err
    })
}
```

4. A synchronous pipeline processes one payload at a time in **first-in, first-out (FIFO)** order and waits for it to exit the pipeline before processing the next available payload. As a result, if a single payload takes a long time to be processed, it effectively delays processing the payloads that are queued behind it. In an asynchronous pipeline, each stage operates asynchronously and can immediately begin processing the next payload as soon as the current payload has been sent to the next stage.

5. A dead-letter queue is a mechanism for deferring error handling for pipeline payloads to a later time. When the pipeline encounters an error while processing a payload, it appends the payload to the dead-letter queue, along with the error that occurred. The application can then introspect the contents of the dead-letter queue and decide how it wants to handle each error according to its business logic (for example, retry the failed payload, log or ignore the error, and so on).

6. A fixed-size worker pool contains a predetermined number of workers that are created at the same time as the pool and remain active (even when they are idle) until the pool is destroyed. A dynamic pool is configured with lower and upper worker limits and can automatically grow or shrink on demand to accommodate changes in the rate of incoming payloads.

7. To measure the total time that each payload spent in the pipeline, we will modify the `pipeline.Payload` struct and add a new *private* field of the `time.Time` type called `processStartedAt`. This new field will be used to record the timestamp when the payload entered the pipeline. Next, we will modify the `linkSource` implementation to populate `processStartedAt` when it emits a new `Payload`. Finally, we will update the (currently empty) `Consume` method of `nopSink` to calculate the elapsed time via a call to `time.Since`.

Chapter 8

1. The BSP computer is an abstract computer model made up of a collection of potentially heterogeneous processors that are interconnected via a computer network. Processors can not only access their own local memory, but they can also use the network link to exchange data with other processors. In other words, the BSP computer is effectively a **distributed memory** computer that can perform computations in parallel.

2. The **Single Program Multiple Data (SPMD)** technique models distributed data processing tasks as a self-contained piece of software that runs on a single-core machine. The program receives a set of data as input, applies a processing function to it, and emits some output. Parallelism is then achieved by splitting the dataset into batches, launching multiple instances of the **same** program to process each batch in parallel, and combining the results.

3. A super-step is broken down into two phases, or sub-steps:
   - A compute step, where each processor executes (in parallel) a single iteration of the user's program using the data that was assigned to the processor as input.
   - A communication step that runs after **all** the processors complete the compute step. During this step, processors communicate through the network and compare, exchange, or aggregate the results of their individual computations.

4. The following block of code demonstrates how we can create an aggregator to keep track of the minimum int64 value we've seen so far. The use of an int64 pointer allows us to detect whether *any* value has been seen so far (otherwise, the pointer will be nil) and if so, the minimum value that's been seen by the Aggregate method. Atomic access to the int64 value is enforced via the use of sync.Mutex:

```go
type MinInt64Aggregator struct {
    mu        sync.Mutex
    minValue *int64
}
func (a *MinInt64Aggregator) Aggregate(v interface{}) {
    a.mu.Lock()
    if intV := v.(int64); a.minValue == nil || intV < *a.minValue {
        a.minValue = &intV
    }
    a.mu.Unlock()
}
func (a *MinInt64Aggregator) Set(v interface{}) {
    a.mu.Lock()
    intV := v.(int64)
    a.minValue = &intV
    a.mu.Unlock()
}
func (a *MinInt64Aggregator) Get() interface{} {
    a.mu.Lock()
    defer a.mu.Unlock()
    if a.minValue == nil {
        return nil
    }
    return *a.minValue
}
func (a *MinInt64Aggregator) Delta() interface{} { return a.Get() }
func (a *MinInt64Aggregator) Type() string { return
"MinInt64Aggregator" }
```

5. Under the random surfer model, a user performs an initial search and lands on a page from the link graph. From that point on, users randomly select one of the following two options:
   - They can click any outgoing link from the current page and navigate to a new page
   - Alternatively, they can decide to run a new search query

The preceding steps continue in perpetuity.

6. A PageRank score reflects the probability that a random surfer lands on a particular web page. In other words, the score expresses the importance (ranking) of each web page relative to every other web page on the internet.

7. At each step of the PageRank algorithm, each link distributes its accumulated PageRank score to its outgoing links. Dead-ends receive the PageRank scores from pages that are linked to them but never redistribute them as they have no outgoing links. If we don't take steps to handle these problematic cases, the graph dead-ends will end up with a significantly higher (and incorrect) PageRank score compared to regular pages in the graph.

Chapter 9

1. The following table summarizes the CRUD endpoints for a user entity:

HTTP Verb	Path	Expects (JSON)	Returns (JSON)	HTTP Status	Description
POST	/users	A user entry	The new user entry and its ID	200 (success) or 201 (created)	Create a new user
GET	/users	Nothing	An array with user entries	200 (success)	Get a list of users
GET	/users/:id	Nothing	The user with the specified ID	200 (success) or 404 (not found)	Get user by ID
PUT	/users/:id	A user entry	The updated user entry	200 (success) or 404 (not found)	Update user by ID
PATCH	/users/:id	A *partial* user entry	The updated user entry	200 (success) or 404 (not found)	Update individual fields for a user by ID
DELETE	/users/:id	Nothing	Nothing	200 (success) or 404 (not found)	Delete user by ID

2. Basic authentication headers are transmitted as plaintext. By ensuring this information is transmitted over a TLS-encrypted channel, we prevent malicious actors from intercepting user credentials.

3. If a malicious adversary manages to install their own **certificate authority** (**CA**) on their targets' trusted certificate stores, they can mount a **man-in-the-middle** (**MitM**) attack and snoop on the TLS traffic between the target and any third party.

4. In a three-legged OAuth2 flow, the following occurs:
    1. A user visits service A and attempts to log in via service B.
    2. The backend server for A generates an authorization URL for service B and redirects the user's browser to it. The generated URL includes the set of permissions that were requested by A and a URL that B should redirect the user to once they consent to granting access.
    3. The user is redirected to service B and consents to the permissions that were requested by service A.
    4. The user's browser is redirected to service A with an access code embedded in the URL.
    5. The backend server for service A contacts service B and exchanges the access code with an access token.
    6. Service A uses the token to access some resource (for example, user details) on service B on behalf of the user.

5. Protocol buffers are superior to JSON for request/response payloads for the following reasons:
    - They utilize a much more compact binary format to serialize payloads
    - Protocol buffer messages are strictly typed and support versioning
    - The protoc compiler can be used to generate the required code for working with protocol buffer messages in a variety of programming languages

6. gRPC supports the following RPC modes:
    - **Unary RPC**: The client performs a request and receives a response.
    - **Server-streaming RPC**: The client initiates an RPC connection to the server and receives a stream of responses from the server.
    - **Client-streaming RPC**: The client initiates an RPC connection to the server and sends a stream of requests via the open connection. The server processes the requests and sends a single response.
    - **Bidirectional streaming RPC**: The client and the server share a bidirectional channel where each side can asynchronously send and receive messages.

Chapter 10

1. Some of the benefits of containerization are as follows:
    - The same container image can run on a local development machine or a cloud instance
    - It is trivial to deploy a new version of a piece of software and perform a rollback if something goes wrong
    - It introduces an extra layer of security as applications are isolated from both the host and other applications

2. Master nodes implement the *control plane* of a Kubernetes cluster. Worker nodes pool their resources (CPUs, memory, disks, GPUs, and so on) and execute the workloads that have been assigned to them by the master nodes.

3. A regular Kubernetes service acts as a load balancer for distributing incoming traffic to a collection of pods. Regular services are reachable via the cluster IP address that's assigned to them by Kubernetes. A headless service provides the means for implementing a custom service discovery mechanism. It is not assigned a cluster IP address and DNS queries for it are returned the full list of pods behind the service.

4. Since both the OAuth2 client ID and secret are sensitive pieces of information, the recommended Kubernetes approach for sharing them with the frontend would be to create a secret resource.

5. A Kubernetes deployment creates a pod with non-predictable IDs, whereas a stateful set assigns predictable names that are constructed by concatenating the stateful set name and the pod ordinal (for example, web-0, web-1, and so on). Another difference is that while Kubernetes deployments spin up the required number of pods in parallel, a stateful set spins up pods sequentially.

Chapter 11

1. A microservice-based architecture brings a lot of benefits to the table. However, at the same time, it adds a lot of complexity to a system and requires additional effort to make it resilient against network issues, to monitor its internal state, and to debug issues when something goes wrong. Consequently, selecting this pattern for an MVP or PoC is often considered to be a form of premature optimization that likely introduces more issues than it solves.

2. When the number of errors from a particular downstream service exceeds a particular threshold, the circuit breaker is tripped and all future requests automatically fail with an error. Periodically, the circuit breaker lets some requests go through and after a number of successful responses, the circuit breaker switches back to the open position, thereby allowing all the requests to go through.

3. Being able to trace requests as they travel through a system allows us to do the following:
   - Figure out how much time the request spends in each service and identify potential bottlenecks
   - Understand and map the dependencies between services
   - Pinpoint the root cause of issues that affect production systems

4. Log entries may contain sensitive information such as credit card numbers, security credentials, customer names, addresses, or social security numbers. Unless we actively sanitize these entries, this information will end up in the logs and could be potentially visible to entities (employees or third parties) that are not authorized to access this kind of information.

5. To collect logs from the pods running in a Kubernetes cluster, we can use one of the following strategies:
   - Use a daemon set to run a log collector on each Kubernetes node. The log collector digests the log files from each pod running on the node and ships them to a centralized log storage location.
   - Deploy a sidecar container in the same pod as the application whose logs we want to collect. The sidecar digests the application logs (which could be a single file or multiple files) and ships them to a centralized log storage location.
   - Ship logs directly from within the application.

Chapter 12

1. In a leader-follower configuration, the nodes hold an election and elect a leader for the cluster. All reads and writes go through the cluster leader, while the other nodes monitor the leader and automatically hold a new election if the leader becomes unavailable. As the name implies, in a multi-master configuration, the cluster has several master nodes and each of the master nodes can serve both read and write requests. The master nodes implement some form of distributed consensus algorithm (Raft, Paxos, and so on) to ensure that they always share the same view of the cluster's state.

2. When implementing the checkpoint strategy, workers are periodically asked by the master to persist their current state to durable storage. If this operation succeeds, a new checkpoint is created. If a worker crashes or becomes unavailable, the master will request for the remaining healthy workers to load their state from the last known checkpoint and resume executing the computation job from that point on.

3. The distributed barrier is a synchronization primitive that notifies the master node when all the workers have reached the same exact point of execution. This primitive is a prerequisite for executing compute jobs under the BSP model (see Chapter 8, *Graph-Based Data Processing*), which requires that all the processors execute each super-step in the lockstep.

4. While the algorithm itself has completed without any errors, something might go wrong if one or more workers attempt to persist their results to durable storage. Consequently, a computation job can't really be considered as completed until **all** the workers have persisted the results of the computation.

Chapter 13

1. A **service-level indicator (SLI)** is a type of metric that allows us to quantify the perceived quality of the service from the perspective of the end user (for example, metrics such as availability, throughput, and latency). A **service-level objective (SLO)** is the range of values for some SLIs that allow us to deliver a particular level of service to an end user or customer.

2. A **service-level agreement (SLA)** is an implicit or explicit contract between a service provider and one or more service consumers. The SLA outlines a set of SLOs that have to be met and the consequences (financial or not) for meeting and failing to meet them.

3. In a push-based metrics collection system, the metric-producing clients connect to the metrics collection and aggregation service over a TCP or UDP connection and publish their metrics. In a pull-based system, the metrics collection system, at its own leisure, connects to each client and collects (scrapes) any new metrics.

4. Due to the network security policies in place, the metrics collection service would not be able to establish a connection to any of the metrics producers in the locked-down subnet. However, the applications running on that subnet should still be able to access other subnets, including the one that the metrics collection service runs on. Consequently, the logical choice in such a situation is to use a push-based system.

5. The value of a Prometheus counter can only increase, while the value of a Prometheus gauge can both increase and decrease.

6. A playbook is a short document that distills the best practices for resolving a particular type of problem. Having access to the playbook associated with a particular alert reduces the **mean time to resolution** (**MTTR**) as SREs can follow the playbook instructions to quickly diagnose the root cause of the problem and apply the recommended set of steps to fix it.

Other Books You May Enjoy

If you enjoyed this book, you may be interested in these other books by Packt:

Hands-On System Programming with Go

Alex Guerrieri

ISBN: 978-1-78980-407-2

- Explore concepts of system programming using Go and concurrency
- Gain insights into Golang's internals, memory models and allocation
- Familiarize yourself with the filesystem and IO streams in general
- Handle and control processes and daemons' lifetime via signals and pipes
- Communicate with other applications effectively using a network
- Use various encoding formats to serialize complex data structures
- Become well-versed in concurrency with channels, goroutines, and sync
- Use concurrency patterns to build robust and performant system applications

Go Programming Cookbook - Second Edition
Aaron Torres

ISBN: 978-1-78980-098-2

- Work with third-party Go projects and modify them for your use
- Write Go code using modern best practices
- Manage your dependencies with the new Go module system
- Solve common problems encountered when dealing with backend systems or DevOps
- Explore the Go standard library and its uses
- Test, profile, and fine-tune Go applications

Leave a review - let other readers know what you think

Please share your thoughts on this book with others by leaving a review on the site that you bought it from. If you purchased the book from Amazon, please leave us an honest review on this book's Amazon page. This is vital so that other potential readers can see and use your unbiased opinion to make purchasing decisions, we can understand what our customers think about our products, and our authors can see your feedback on the title that they have worked with Packt to create. It will only take a few minutes of your time, but is valuable to other potential customers, our authors, and Packt. Thank you!

Index

Made in the USA
Columbia, SC
16 August 2020